S0-AOV-813

ANNUAL REVIEW OF POLITICAL SCIENCE

Production Editor: Kim Transier
Bibliographic Quality Control: Mary A. Glass
Online Quality Control: Noël J. Thomas
Subject Indexer: Bruce Tracy

ANNUAL REVIEW OF POLITICAL SCIENCE

VOLUME 4, 2001

NELSON W. POLSBY, *Editor*
University of California, Berkeley

www.AnnualReviews.org   science@AnnualReviews.org   650-493-4400

ANNUAL REVIEWS
4139 El Camino Way • P.O. BOX 10139 • Palo Alto, California 94303-0139

ANNUAL REVIEWS
Palo Alto, California, USA

International Standard Serial Number: 1094-2939
International Standard Book Number: 0-8243-3304-7

∞ The paper used in this publication meets the minimum requirements of American National Standards for Information Sciences—Permanence of Paper for Printed Library Materials, ANSI Z39.48-1992.

TYPESET BY TECHBOOKS, FAIRFAX, VA
PRINTED AND BOUND IN THE UNITED STATES OF AMERICA

PREFACE

I think it is probably a sign of life in a scholarly enterprise when there are complaints that a discipline is being devoured by an encroaching fungus-like fad. Forty years ago, when I began my career as a political scientist, the threat was something called "political behavior" or "behavioralism" or "the behavioral persuasion." Then, some senior and some junior members of the profession flying this banner thought that it would be interesting to see if the study of politics could be made to resemble other branches of the study of human behavior. Their style of work included making more explicit the relations between individual instances and general propositions. They liked to dwell on the justifications for believing what they believed, wrote about "evidence," framed "hypotheses," had frequent recourse to statistics, and so on. The idea was to move "beyond" reporting anecdotes or legalisms or proverbs in order to give a true account of what people in politics were actually doing (how they were "behaving") that might "cumulate" into a compelling body of knowledge worthy of the label "science."

On the whole, it was not programmatic statements recommending this style of work that recruited new practitioners, but rather good examples of work in this mode, of which in time there were more than a few. Political scientists, and readers of political science, learned things we wanted to know by adopting this style of work, and in due course it became a respectable and a familiar way of doing political science. Older, more humanistic approaches to the study of politics had to move over and make room. For a while this alarmed and annoyed some scholars. There were skirmishes. Some departments were inhospitable to new approaches, for a while, and in some the new drove out the old, for a while. In the longer run, humanism made a comeback, and an uneasy truce on the whole prevailed.

So long as scholars take seriously the emotional commitments they make as they discover what interests them, acquire intellectual capital and learn how to do their work, I do not see how border warfare of this sort can be avoided. Nor do I think we would willingly pay the price in the stagnation of our discipline if no such ferment were going on.

We have, thankfully, a new, allegedly hegemonic, fungus. It is called variously "rational choice," "formal theory," or "positive theory," and borrows mostly from economics. The style of work features "models," and attempts to trace the goal-seeking of individuals in a way that critics believe is excessively stylized. Critics say the clarity and parsimony that this style of work encourages frequently highlight what older, less regimented scholars already know. And so forth.

An *Annual Review of Political Science* cannot aspire to adjudicate such claims. Some of them will be justified on the merits, some not. We should be entirely happy to make room for new approaches and also for more familiar work and for complaints about each. We can observe, those of us who are old enough, that we have heard noises like this before, and that they sound to us like the hum—or the ruckus—that arises from the normal activity of a vital community of scholars.

Nelson W. Polsby
Editor

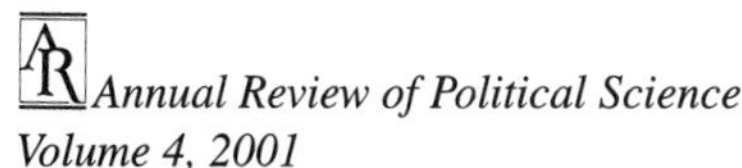

Annual Review of Political Science
Volume 4, 2001

CONTENTS

ERRATA

An online log of corrections to *Annual Review of Political Science* chapters (if any have yet been occasioned, 1997 to the present) may be found at http://polisci.AnnualReviews.org/

Related Articles

From the ***Annual Review of Anthropology***, Volume 30 (2001)

Social Movements: Changing Paradigms and Forms of Politics, Marc Edelman

From the ***Annual Review of Psychology***, Volume 52 (2001)

Decision Technology, Ward Edwards and B. Fasolo

Problems for Judgment and Decision Making, Reid Hastie

Nature and Operation of Attitudes, Icek Ajzen

Disrespect and the Experience of Injustice, Dale T. Miller

From the ***Annual Review of Sociology***, Volume 27 (2001)

Collective Identity and Social Movements, Francesca Polletta and James M. Jasper

The Scale of Justice: Observations on the Transformation of Urban Law Practice, John P. Heinz, Robert L. Nelson, and Edward O. Laumann

Is Globalization Civilizing, Destructive, or Feeble? A Critique of Five Key Debates in Social Science Literature, Mauro F. Guillén

Education and Stratification in Developing Countries, Claudia Buchman and Emily Hannum

Urban Poverty After The Truly Disadvantaged: The Rediscovery of the Family, the Neighborhood, and Culture, Mario Small and Katherine Newman

Hate Crime: An Emergent Research Agenda, Donald P. Green, Laurence H. McFalls, and Jennifer K. Smith

US Social Policy in Comparative and Historical Perspective: Concepts, Images, Arguments and Research Strategies, Edwin Amenta, Chris Bonastia, and Neil Caren

ANNUAL REVIEWS is a nonprofit scientific publisher established to promote the advancement of the sciences. Beginning in 1932 with the *Annual Review of Biochemistry*, the Company has pursued as its principal function the publication of high-quality, reasonably priced *Annual Review* volumes. The volumes are organized by Editors and Editorial Committees who invite qualified authors to contribute critical articles reviewing significant developments within each major discipline. The Editor-in-Chief invites those interested in serving as future Editorial Committee members to communicate directly with him. Annual Reviews is administered by a Board of Directors, whose members serve without compensation.

Annu. Rev. Polit. Sci. 2001. 4:1–20

TRANSNATIONAL POLITICS: Contention and Institutions in International Politics

Sidney Tarrow
Department of Government, Cornell University, Ithaca, New York 14853; e-mail: sgt2@cornell.edu

Key Words social movements, NGOs, transnational advocacy networks, contentious politics, international institutions

■ **Abstract** Recent scholars have broadened the study of transnational relations, once limited to political economy, to include contentious international politics. This is a refreshing trend, but most of them leap directly from globalization or some other such process to transnational social movements and thence to a global civil society. In addition, they have so far failed to distinguish among movements, nongovernmental organizations (NGOs), and transnational networks and do not adequately specify their relations with states and international institutions. In particular, few mechanisms are proposed to link domestic actors to transnational ones and to states and international institutions. This paper argues that mass-based transnational social movements are hard to construct, are difficult to maintain, and have very different relations to states and international institutions than more routinized international NGOs or activist networks. These latter forms may be encouraged both by states and international institutions and by the growth of a cosmopolitan class of transnational activists. Rather than being the antipodes of transnational contention, international institutions offer resources, opportunities, and incentives for the formation of actors in transnational politics. If transnational social movements form, it will be through a second-stage process of domestication of international conflict.

INTRODUCTION

"For two exceptional centuries," declares Tilly (1994:3), "European states and their extensions elsewhere succeeded remarkably in circumscribing and controlling the resources within their perimeters....But in our era...at least in Europe, the era of strong states is now ending." Tilly happily admits that his declaration is informed by a "series of speculations, conjectures, and hypotheses." But let us, at least for the moment, assume that his instinct is right—that the strong, consolidated, Westphalian state really is in decline. The question for students of contentious politics and international relations is whether the resulting gap (*a*) is cyclical and will thus be filled by states' oft-proven capacity for adjustment and renewal; (*b*) is being

1094-2939/01/0623-0001$14.00

filled by forms of nonterritorial institutional governance; (*c*) is providing space for social movements and other nongovernmental forms of collective action to thrust into political space formerly occupied by institutions; or (*d*) some combination of the three.

Although some scholars have predicted greater power for new agencies of international governance (Young 1997), many others see the new world of transnational politics in more contentious, social-movement terms (Guidry et al 2001). Some boldly foresee global social movements reaching across transnational space to contest multilateral economic institutions (O'Brien et al 2000), creating something resembling a "global civil society" (Wapner 1996) or bringing into existence a "world polity" (Boli & Thomas 1999). Others, more cautious but still predicting major challenges to the world of states, see "transnational activist networks" representing the interests of resource-poor actors (Keck & Sikkink 1998). Still others see combinations of governmental and nongovernmental, state and international actors intersecting (Risse 2000).

My view is that these predictions go too directly from globalization or some other such process to transnational social movements and thence to a global civil society. They fail to adequately distinguish social movements, nongovernmental organizations (NGOs), and transnational networks and do not adequately specify their relations with each other or with states and international institutions. In particular, few mechanisms are proposed that link domestic actors to transnational ones and to states and international institutions. I argue that mass-based transnational social movements, which I define in terms of contentious collective action, are hard to construct, are difficult to maintain, and have very different relations to states and international institutions than the less contentious family of international NGOs or activist networks. These latter forms are encouraged both by states and international institutions and by the growth of a cosmopolitan class of transnational activists. If transnational social movements form, it will be through a second-stage process of domestication of international conflict in which international institutions serve as a magnet. I do not see international institutions as the antipode of transnational contention; they offer resources, opportunities, and incentives for actors in transnational politics.

Three Cautions

Before turning to these issues, let us remind ourselves of three lessons from history—too often forgotten by those who see a global civil society appearing in short order.

The first is that states remain dominant in most areas of policy—for example, in maintaining domestic security—even if they have become weaker in their ability to control capital flows (Krasner 1995, Risse 2000, Spruyt 1994:ch. 9). States still control their borders and exercise legal dominion within them. True, citizens can travel more easily than before and can form networks beyond borders (Keck & Sikkink 1998); but they still live in states and, in democratic ones at least, they have the opportunities, the networks, and the well-known repertoires of national polities (Tarrow 1998, Tilly 1995). Those are incentives to operate on native ground that the hypothetical attractions of "global civil society" cannot easily match.

Second, although transnational action is frequently linked causally to the recent wave of globalization (Rosenau 1990, 1999), globalization has been around for at least a century—even longer, if we include the "Atlantic" revolution of the eighteenth century or the Protestant Reformation (Jacobson 1979:11, Keck & Sikkink 1998:ch. 2). These are not mere historical quibbles; since transnational organizations and contention appeared well before globalization, their increase must rely on mechanisms other than today's version of economic interdependence.

My third caution is that social movements, transnational networks, and NGOs are not the only agents operating transnationally. States have always reached beyond their borders and played a key transnational role (Huntington 1973). They are doing so increasingly—e.g. by signing international agreements, interfering in the internal lives of other (usually weaker) states, and building international institutions. These state-led institutions are usually designed to fulfill state purposes, often to respond to transnational activities that states cannot control (Keohane & Nye 1974) or to provide "insurance" that other states will honor their commitments (Keohane 1989). The dominant states in the international system have a profound effect on transnational relations, not only by controlling nonstate actors but often by subsidizing them (Uvin 2000:15), and by providing models of transnational politics from their own domestic templates (Huntington 1973). In both respects the United States plays a key role, at once the target of much transnational organizing and the state most supportive of NGO activity (Uvin 2000:21).

I begin this review with a rapid survey of the changes in the treatment of transnational politics in the international relations literature since the 1970s (for similar efforts see Jacobson 2000 and Risse 2000). The second section outlines the contributions of a new group of scholars—students of contentious politics—to this literature. The third section defines and distinguishes the three main types of transnational actors that appear in the literature: transnational social movements, international nongovernmental organizations (INGOs), and transnational advocacy networks (TANs). In the fourth section, I turn to the hypothetical relations between transnational contention and international institutions. I close with a number of research questions about the study of transnational contention.

FROM THE OLD TO THE NEW TRANSNATIONALISM

The last three decades have seen a paradigm shift in the way political scientists and others have looked at transnational politics. Nye & Keohane, who popularized the term in the early 1970s, were reacting against the "realist" paradigm in international relations (1971b:372–79). In that well-known paradigm, international organizations "are merely instruments of governments, and therefore unimportant in their own right" (1974:39). Nye & Keohane criticized the realist approach and its assumption that states are unitary actors. They proposed an alternative, which they called the world politics paradigm (1971b:379–95). Their work triggered a debate that has gone through many phases in international relations theory since then.

Realism, with its emphasis on states as the only important actors in international politics, has remained the stated or unstated target of much of the field of transnational politics. This fixation has made it difficult for students of transnational politics to assess the role of states without looking over their shoulders at the realists (Risse 2000:2). For example, few analysts since Huntington have made much of the fact that the world's remaining hegemon has a concept of international relations that is fully congruent with its dominant pluralist model of domestic politics (but see Uvin 2000).

The debate on transnational politics has taken several stages. In their 1971 edited book, *Transnational Relations and World Politics*, Keohane & Nye addressed all forms of transnational activity ["contacts, coalitions, and interaction across state boundaries that are not controlled by the central foreign policy organs of governments" (Nye & Keohane 1971a:xi)]; in a 1974 article, they narrowed the concept of transnationalism to the international activities of nongovernmental actors, distinguishing these from "transgovernmental actors"—a term they now used to refer to "sub-units of governments on those occasions when they act relatively autonomously from higher authority in international politics" (1974:41)—and from "international organizations," which they defined as "multilevel linkages, norms, and institutions between governments prescribing behavior in particular situations."

Though it was tighter than their original one, even Keohane & Nye's sharpened 1974 concept of transnational relations covered a lot of ground. It was useful in directing attention to "the tremendous increase in the number and significance of private international interactions in recent decades and the much larger and diverse number of private individuals and groups engaging in such interactions" (Huntington 1973:335). But it had three unfortunately narrowing effects.

First, since their work coincided with the discovery or rediscovery of the field of international political economy, most scholars focused mainly on transnational economic relations and, in particular, on the multinational corporation. Indeed, many of the contributions to *Transnational Relations and World Politics* did exactly that. As late as Keohane & Milner's 1996 reader, interest was limited largely to economic relations. To the extent that students of transnational relations looked at contentious politics, it was usually in the form of resistance to transnational economic penetration (Arrighi & Silver 1984, Walton 1989); to the extent that they studied states' internal politics, it was mainly through foreign economic policy making. This political economy focus distracted scholars from recognizing until recently that much of transnational organizing deals with political and humanitarian issues such as refugees, violence against women and children, and human rights (Keck & Sikkink 1998, Risse et al 1999)—and not economics per se.

Second, Keohane & Nye recognized transnational contention only under the narrow heading of the diffusion of ideas and attitudes, treating them separately from their more sustained discussion of "international pluralism"—by which they meant "the linking of national interest groups in transnational structures, usually involving transnational organizations for purposes of coordination" (Nye & Keohane 1971a:xviii). This disjunction of contention from pluralism has persisted (Jacobson 2000); as a result, there was no integration between the field of transnational politics and the growing field of contentious politics until the 1990s, and some international relations specialists, despite their interest in "global social movements," barely draw on this literature (O'Brien et al 2000).

Third, although they did not explicitly say so, Keohane & Nye's emphasis on free-wheeling transnational interaction left the impression that transnational activity occurs at the cost of states. This implication, vigorously combated in Huntington's critique of their work (1973:342), left several unasked questions about the role of states in transnational politics: When will states stimulate transnational activity in their interests and on behalf of which internal interest groups? When will they create international institutions that provide a forum for nonstate actors? When they will provide models for transnational activity isomorphic with their own way of conceiving the world? And when they will advance the interests of nonstate actors?

It was the waning of the cold war and the enormous diffusion of transnational NGOs in the 1980s and 1990s (Smith et al 1997, Boli & Thomas 1999) that opened up the field of transnational politics beyond political economy and took it in new directions. This was reflected in three streams of work in the 1980s and 1990s: work by sociological institutionalists such as John Meyer and his associates from Stanford; research by political scientists on the domestic structures underpinning transnational relations; and a newer turn toward constructivism that unites international relations specialists with students of contentious politics.

Sociological Institutionalism

We can deal briefly with the Stanford school of institutional sociology (see Boli & Thomas 1999 for a full treatment and bibliography). Early in the 1980s, Meyer observed that institutions and the norms that they embody are frequently observed in widely dispersed parts of the world. World systems theorists had noticed this too but attributed it to the profit-making needs of core capitalism. Meyer found isomorphism in so many sectors of human activity—from educational institutions to welfare systems to state structures—that he detached the phenomenon from capitalism and saw it as part of a global process of rationalization.

The discovery of transnational isomorphism in norms and institutions could lead investigators to examine the role of actors of diffusion, and this could connect directly with the processes of transnational politics. But although some students developed models of diffusion (see Strang & Soule 1998 for a review), this was not the main thrust of the Stanford school. Meyer and his collaborators and students were more interested in mapping isomorphism than in understanding the mechanisms of diffusion—and in fact, in their work the diffusion process is more frequently inferred from the presence of similar structures than traced through the actions of particular actors. Some scholars influenced by Meyer, such as Finnemore (1996), do focus on actors and organizations; others, like Soysal (1994), focus on political norms, e.g. citizenship, with implications for political action; and still others infer intranational causation from transnational/national correlations (Loya 2000). For the most part, however, the Stanford school has contributed more to our knowledge of the commonalities of norms and institutions across space than to our understanding of the social mechanisms and political processes that connect actors transnationally.

Domestic Structures and Transnational Relations

Meanwhile, international relations specialists focusing on domestic structures attempted to open the field of transnational politics beyond the old realist/nonrealist debate (Risse-Kappen 1995). Risse-Kappen and his colleagues revived attention to "transgovernmental politics" (see especially the chapter by Cameron in Risse-Kappen 1995); they included transnational economic relations but also went beyond them; and they related transnational politics to international institutions. Two changes in particular were notable, both in their 1995 book and in the new literature that followed it. First, international relations scholars now attempted to deal with the intersections between transnational relations and domestic structure; second, they advanced a more normatively charged concept of transnational relations.

Nye and Keohane—especially Keohane [see his presidential address to the International Studies Association (Keohane 1989)]—had called for attention to the domestic sources of transnational politics. But the early transnational literature provided little ground on which nonstate political variables might prove important in tracking the domestic scope and directions of transnational politics. Risse-Kappen and his collaborators attacked this problem deliberately. "Under similar international conditions, differences in domestic structures determine the variation in the policy impact of transnational actors" (Risse-Kappen 1995:25). In order to gain impact, transnational actors must, first, gain access to the political system of their target state and, second, generate and/or contribute to winning policy coalitions (1995:25).

Risse-Kappen and his collaborators generated predictions about how variations in domestic structure would affect the impact of transnational actors. For example, Risse-Kappen argued that decentralized political systems and pluralistic societies will be more open to transnational penetration than closed and hierarchical ones. However, as Evangelista showed (1995, 1999), the need for coalition building in such systems can pose formidable obstacles to transnational actors once they gain a purchase; conversely, although the "closed" Soviet system was harder for transnational arms-control advocates to access, once contacts were established they could have great impact.

There were three main weaknesses in the "domestic structure" argument.

1. It was extremely generic, including elements as general as political culture, openness (e.g. openness to whom?), and pluralism.

2. It could not predict why some transnational actors succeed while others fail in the same context [see Keck & Sikkink (1998:202)].
3. It made no clear distinctions between different types of transnational actors; it lumped together INGOs, social movements, and transnational advocacy networks.

Those who followed Risse-Kappen and his colleagues after 1995 offered a partial answer to these problems—a constructivist turn that focused attention on the resonance between transnational goals and domestic norms.

The Normative Turn

The move toward norms in the study of transnational activism was part of a more general discovery of "constructivism" by international relations scholars in the 1990s (Risse 2000:2).[1] In various areas of international relations, norms were defined as "a standard of appropriate behavior for actors with a given identity" (Katzenstein 1996:5). This rekindled the conflict with realism but gave it a new twist. If norms could be shown to have an autonomous role in structuring international debate irrespective of the policies of strong states, and if it could be shown that interests are constituted and reconstituted around learning, norm diffusion, and identity shift, then nonstate factors in transnational space—not only hegemonic states—could be shown to have teeth.

Much creative work has grown out of the concern with norms and identities in the international system.

1. Transnational normative consensus could be shown to result in international agreements that were capable of constraining state behavior (Klotz 1995, Price 1997).
2. International normative agreements could create political opportunities for domestic actors living under governments which would otherwise be reluctant to tolerate dissidence (Thomas 2001, Risse et al 1999).
3. Even where international normative consensus was lacking, strong states could endow international institutions with the authority to enforce behavior consistent with these norms—as in the interventions by the United Nations and NATO in Yugoslavia.
4. Norms could contribute to the construction of new identities, which in some cases could bridge national identities, providing a normative basis for transnational coalitions or principled issue networks.

But the focus on norms could become a problem. Potential drawbacks include the following:

---

[1]For a review and some stimulating hypotheses, see Finnemore & Sikkink (1998). Also see Finnemore (1996), Katzenstein (1996), Klotz (1995), Price (1997), and Thomas (2001).

1. A considerable amount of transnational activity is driven by material interests—labor internationalism, for example (Waterman 1998, Blyton et al 2000).
2. In transnational relations as in the broader constructivist paradigm, it is not always clear where norms are lodged.
3. The assumption of normative consensus underlying much of this work is challenged by the often-contested nature of international norms.
4. If norms are more than the result of contingent coalitions of interest, it will have to be shown that they are actually translated into state policies (Fox 1999, Risse 1999).

Like sociological institutionalism, the normative turn is better at mapping changes in world culture than at tracing the mechanisms through which transnational factors influence domestic politics.

These three developments in the study of transnational politics—sociological institutionalism, domestic structures, and the normative turn—have had an unexpected benefit. They helped to provide a bridge between international relations and a previously distinct tradition—the field of contentious politics. In the 1980s and early 1990s, the latter group of scholars had already absorbed and profited from constructivism (Snow et al 1986; Melucci 1988, 1996). It also had a well-grounded tradition of studying the impact of domestic structures of opportunity and constraint on social movements (McAdam et al 1996, Tarrow 1998); and social movement scholars were becoming increasingly conscious of transnational and international influences on contentious politics (Tilly 1994, McAdam 1998, Tarrow 1998:ch. 11). Let us turn to this tradition's contributions to the new transnational politics.

CONTENTIOUS TRANSNATIONAL POLITICS[2]

The convergence of social movement and international relations scholars was scattered but dramatic. It had four main sources in real-world politics:

1. Grassroots insurgencies (e.g. in Chiapas) that framed their claims globally and sought international support from sympathetic foreign groups and INGOs;
2. International protest events (e.g. the "Battle of Seattle") that brought together coalitions of transnational and national groups against highly visible targets like the World Trade Organization or the International Monetary Fund;
3. The successes of some transnational activist coalitions against some national states, e.g. in aid of the Brazilian rubber tappers (Keck 1995);

[2]This section is based on an online bibliography (see Tarrow & Acostavalle 1999).

4. The activism of INGOs within and around international institutions (Willetts 1996, Fox & Brown 1998, Jacobson 2000, O'Brien et al 2000, Stiles 2000) and internatonal treaty writing (Price 1997).

These are different kinds of evidence at different levels collected through a variety of methods. The first type of evidence relates to fundamentally domestic contention that is framed by activists as transnational and enjoys international support. The second type depends on particular domestic and international opportunities and resources and—as the Washington and Philadelphia follow-ups to the Seattle protests showed—is difficult to sustain. The third type results mainly from elite coalitions using the leverage of either third-party states or international institutions, often with weak domestic support in targeted states. And the fourth type involves transnational activists in cooperative relations with states and international institutions.

Important data came from former activists, who brought energy, real-time information, and commitment to studying contention to the field. They also brought perspectives from comparative politics, cultural anthropology, and sociology to a field formerly restricted to professional international relations specialists. From the early 1990s on, a creative cross-fertilization began to develop between international relations specialists interested in transnational relations and social movement scholars interested in transnational contention.

The new work can be divided roughly into five groups, with some overlap between them.

1. Some investigators examined the development of a wide spectrum of nonstate actors who organized transnationally (Stiles 2000, Smith et al 1997, Boli & Thomas 1999, della Porta et al 1999, Keck & Sikkink 1998, O'Brien et al 2000, Guidry et al 2001).
2. Some focused on particular movement families, such as the peace movement (Rochon 1988), human rights and democratization (Risse et al 1999, Loya 2000), the environment (Young 1997), conflicts over dam construction (Khagram 1999, Khagram et al 2001), immigrant rights (Soysal 1994), or indigenous peoples' movements (Brysk 1998).
3. Some focused on organizations—either particular ones (Finnemore 1996, Wapner 1996), organizations in the aggregate (Boli & Thomas 1999), or transnational networks of organizations (Keck & Sikkink 1998).
4. Some studied international treaties in which nonstate actors were legitimized and supported (Thomas 2001), in which activists played a constitutive role (Price 1997), or against which activists mobilized (Ayres 1998).
5. Some looked at particular binational or regional contention in the context of international agreements or institutions (Ayres 1998; Fox 2000; Imig & Tarrow 1999, 2000, 2001a,b).

The study of transnational politics, once heavily influenced by transnational economic relations and harnessed to an argument against realism, has begun to overlap increasingly with the study of contentious politics. But as in any marriage between partners from different traditions, assumptions are not always the same and the casual adoption of the language or conventions of others led to misunderstandings.

The most general problem was the adoption of the term globalization, with its shifting combination of economic, political, and cultural meanings.[3] The fusion of the various meanings of globalization is an important tool for organizers trying to mobilize scattered followers into social movements, permitting them to access broader frames and target distant enemies. But its adoption by scholars has had two unfortunate effects: (*a*) fostering insensitivity to the regional—and certainly not global—scope of much transnational activity; and (*b*) producing a conceptual confusion between the global framing of an activity and the empirical scope of the activity (see the critique in Tarrow 1998:ch. 11).

A second problem in the field of transnational contentious politics is that many students who came to it with a commitment to the goals of a particular social movement sector (especially those from the peace, environment, feminist, and indigenous rights movements) saw the universe of nonstate actors through the lens of that sector. They also tended to focus on "good" movements, such as the peace and human rights movements, and gave much less attention to the more dangerous sectors of transnational activism—for example, militant fundamentalism. (For an exception, see Rudolf & Piscatori 1997.) Such scholars often saw states as unremittingly hostile to transnational actors, when empirical data show conclusively that states— particularly western states—are deeply implicated in their funding and promotion (Uvin 2000). Finally, scholars shifting their research interest from domestic activism to the transnational level were quick to transfer the ideologically attractive category "social movement" to activities that would be more recognizable as lobbying, communication, and educational and service activity if they were observed at home. Let us turn to these important distinctions and the relations among different actors in transnational space.

FORMS OF TRANSNATIONAL ACTION

Are the actors on the transnational scene social movements, INGOs, or some looser configuration such as transnational advocacy networks (TANs)? Analysts in this burgeoning field have been better at describing activities than at conceptualizing them in clear analytical terms. For example, one group of scholars declares their interest in the impact of "global social movements" on multilateral economic

[3]For reasons of space, I cannot hope to deal fairly with the massive literature on globalization that has appeared over the past few years. For a survey on globalization and politics, see Berger (2000). For a strong claim that global social movements are forming, see O'Brien et al (2000). For a more skeptical view of major works in the globalization tradition, see Yashar (2000).

institutions, yet focuses empirically on INGOs (O'Brien et al 2000). Before scientific progress can be made in any new empirical field, the nature and variety of the units must be carefully defined. As Keck & Sikkink (1998:210) observe, "to understand how change occurs in the world policy we have to understand the quite different logics and process among the different categories of transnational actors."

Transnational Social Movements

Although some investigators define social movements in terms of their "social change goals" (Smith et al 1997), this opens them to the danger of including institutionalized, passive, and service-oriented groups within their definition. The danger can be seen in the case of so-called European social movements that operate in Brussels, which often turn out to be tame, EU-subsidized lobbies (Imig & Tarrow 2001a). There is a solution to this definitional puzzle: to identify social movements not by their goals, which they share with many non–social movements, but by the kind of actions in which they routinely engage—contentious politics, which I define as

> episodic, collective interaction among makers of claims and their objects when a) at least one government is a claimant, an object of claims, or a party to the claims and b) the claims would, if realized, affect the interests of at least one of the claimants. (McAdam et al 2001)

Social movements are a particularly congealed form of contention within this universe which I define as

> socially mobilized groups engaged in sustained contentious interaction with powerholders in which at least one actor is either a target or a participant. (McAdam et al 2001)

To be transnational, an entity ought to have social and political bases outside its target state or society; but to be a social movement, it ought to be clearly rooted within social networks and engaged in contentious, sustained interaction. This produces a definition of transnational social movements as

> socially mobilized groups with constituents in at least two states, engaged in sustained contentious interaction with powerholders in at least one state other than their own, or against an international institution, or a multinational economic actor.

The strategic advantage of this definition is that it points to the behavior of movements interacting with other groups and institutions, and leads us to examine empirically the relations among social movements and other institutional forms, and trace potential transitions between these forms. The major other forms are INGOs and transnational advocacy networks.

International Nongovernmental Organizations

A truism of transnational politics is that the number of INGOs is growing rapidly. Boli & Thomas (1999:20) count nearly 6000 INGOs founded between 1875 and 1988. They find not only a growing founding rate of INGOs after 1945 but a declining rate of dissolution. But although the term has gained great currency in recent debates, it is surprising how little consensus there seems to be on the definition or operationalization of INGOs.[4] Boli & Thomas offer three descriptions. They see INGOs as "the primary organizational field in which world culture takes structural form" (1999:6), as "transnational bodies exercising a special type of authority we call rational voluntarism" (1999:14), and as groups whose "primary concern is enacting, codifying, modifying, and propagating world-cultural structures and principles" (1999:19). Their operational definition is "the entire population of INGOs classified as genuinely international bodies by the Union of International Associations"—that is, all "not-for-profit, non-state organizations" (1999:20).

I propose a definition of INGO that is broad enough to include a wide range of organizations but also distinguish them from social movements. International nongovernmental organizations are organizations that operate independently of governments, are composed of members from two or more countries, and are organized to advance their members' international goals and provide services to citizens of other states through routine transactions with states, private actors, and international institutions.

Starting from this definition, the main distinction between INGOs and social movements becomes primarily behavioral. Although both may have social change goals, transnational social movements engage in sustained contentious interaction with states, multinational actors, or international institutions, whereas INGOs engage in routine transactions with the same kinds of actors and provide services to citizens of other states. This clear analytical distinction between the categories of movements and INGOs will make it easier to examine the relations between them, to ask whether transitions are occurring from one type to the other, and to compare their relationships to grassroots social movements.

This last issue is particularly crucial. Even the briefest examination of INGOs will show that they are largely made up of dedicated, cosmopolitan, well-educated people who can afford to travel around the world, are adept at languages, and have the technical, intellectual, and professional skills to serve and represent the interests of those they support to international institutions and powerful states. Although social movements need leaders as well—and have become more professional in recent decades (Meyer & Tarrow 1998)—they are, by our definition at least, based on "socially mobilized groups engaged in sustained contentious interaction with powerholders." Conflating INGOs with social movements makes it impossible to

[4]Evelyn Bush points out to me that the Union for International Associations, the major source of data on transnational associations, has recently urged that "INGO" be replaced by "transnational associational network," since the former term includes so many mixed organizations including various degrees of governmental involvement. I retain the term because it is in common usage.

examine this key behavioral distinction, as well as the fundamental question of whether a shift is taking place from social movements into INGOs, or if the latter are responsible for changes in the former.

Transnational Activist Networks

Outside their service activities, in which they are normally independent, INGOs frequently operate in temporary or long-term alliances with other actors (state and nonstate, transnational and domestic) to advance their policy goals. This has added a new and dynamic category to the study of transnational politics— transnational activist networks. As Keck & Sikkink define it (1998:2), "A transnational advocacy network includes those relevant actors working internationally on an issue, who are bound together by shared values, a common discourse, and dense exchanges of information and services." Such networks "are most prevalent in issue areas characterized by high value content and informational uncertainty" (Keck & Sikkink 1998:2). These authors thus draw on the normative turn in international relations theory described above, with special relevance to such heavily normative areas as human rights (Risse et al 1999).

Transnational advocacy networks are not alternatives to social movements or INGOs; on the contrary, they can contain them—in the loose way that networks contain anything—as well as containing governmental agents in either their official or unofficial capacities. They are the informal and shifting structures through which NGO members, social movement activists, government officials, and agents of international institutions can interact and help resource-poor domestic actors to gain leverage in their own societies. In Keck & Sikkink's model, resource-rich NGOs—working through their own states, international institutions, or both—try to activate a transnational network to put pressure on a target state. Keck & Sikkink's "boomerang" effect illustrates the potential relationships within these networks (1998:13).

At this stage, Keck & Sikkink's important work suggests the following research problems:

1. It is unclear how they see TANs relating to the existing state system. Do their operations depend—incidentally or fundamentally—on the power of the states they come from? The majority of their member groups come from the wealthy states of the North; does the power of these states lie behind the capacity of network activists to persuade other states to accede to the claims of resource-weak allies within them?
2. Most of the empirical work on TANs has focused on normatively oriented groups. Does the same logic of coalition building and deployment of the power of third-party states and/or international institutions occur when the basis of domestic support is material interest?
3. Are TANs occasional interlopers in the relations between states and their citizens or are they becoming core links in the formation of transnational social movements among citizens of different states?

4. How do TANs relate to international institutions? In Keck & Sikkink's paradigm, they are intermediate links between activist networks and their allies. But if the activists depend on international institutions, how far beyond their policies can their campaigns go? If they do not depend on them, what is the major source of their leverage on the states that they and their local allies challenge? Institutions deserve more specification than they have received so far from students of transnational contention.

TRANSNATIONAL CONTENTION AND INTERNATIONAL INSTITUTIONS

The "global civil society" thesis derived transnational social movements directly from trends in economic interdependence (Wapner 1996, O'Brien et al 2000). That thesis is unspecified, deterministic, and undifferentiated. A more mediated, institutionally routed, and more probabilistic model made up of a chain of hypotheses seems more appropriate.

First, although economic and cultural trends create objective reasons to posit a growth of transnational actors, social movement theory shows that objective interests or conflicts, on their own, do not. There are three obstacles: the weakness or absence of social networks outside people's neighborhoods, towns, cities, social groups, and political allegiances; the weakness or absence of transnational collective identities; and the absence of mechanisms to compete with the political opportunities of national polities (McAdam et al 1996, Tarrow 1998).

Second, states have created international institutions to serve their collective interest and monitor each other's behavior. Once created, these institutions are mandated to intervene in selected sectors of their societies, thus affecting relations among domestic groups and between them and their governments. This creates internal incentives for transnational activism.

Third, once international institutions exist, their officers' desire for legitimation and sources of information induces them to create external incentives for transnational activism (Jacobson 2000:155).

Fourth, these internal and external incentives combine to create a cosmopolitan, transnational, activist elite that staffs INGOs and comes together within and against the policies of international institutions.

Fifth, these elites form alliances with powerful states, elements within international institutions, and domestic social movements to form transnational activist networks. These networks can reach into societies to intervene in their relations with their governments, international institutions, and multinational economic actors.

Sixth, the influence of TANs on these societies encourages domestic groups to adapt their norms, model their behaviors, and frame their own claims around issues that are domesticated from international politics (Jacobson 2000:156).

Seventh, but only as a long-term probabilistic result of these processes, and mediated by the nature and constraints of their national states, domestic social movements from different countries become aware of their common interests and values, encounter one another through common campaigns against international institutions, and thus form transnational social movements.

The argument from international institutions differs from the "global civil society" thesis in three important ways. First, it specifies an increase of transnational contention through the resources, incentives, and opportunities of international institutions—and not directly through globalization. Second, it offers an explanation for the wide variations we see between sectors of transnational activity. As Risse argues (2000:27; see also Risse-Kappen 1995), "the higher the degree of international institutionalization in a given issue-area, the greater the policy impact of transnational actors." Third, it makes the growth of transnational activism problematic and nondeterministic.

An institutional approach to transnational contention suggests several mechanisms through which domestic activists can find one another, gain legitimacy, form collective identities, and go back to their countries empowered with alliances, common programs, and new repertoires of collective action. We can identify at least four such mechanisms, which I define as follows:

1. Brokerage: making connections between otherwise unconnected domestic actors in a way that produces at least a temporary political identity that did not exist before (Smith 2000).
2. Certification: the recognition of the identities and legitimate public activity of either new actors or actors new to a particular cite of activity.
3. Modeling: the adoption of norms, forms of collective action or organization in one venue that have been demonstrated in another.
4. Institutional appropriation: the use of an institution's resources or reputation to serve the purposes of affiliated groups.

No single international institution is going to provide the mechanisms to facilitate all of these steps (indeed, most fall well short of that threshold). But the list can help scholars to specify the ways in which nonstate actors with weak resources and opportunities in their own societies can develop transnational ties that can be "boomeranged" on behalf of their own claims.

CONCLUSIONS

International institutions serve as a kind of "coral reef," helping to form horizontal connections among activists with similar claims across boundaries.[5] This leads to the paradox that international institutions—created by states, and usually powerful ones—can be the arenas in which transnational contention is most likely to

[5]I am grateful Ron Jepperson for suggesting this metaphor.

form against states. I do not maintain that states create international institutions in order to encourage contention; states are more likely to delegate than to fuse sovereignty. But because international institutions seek autonomy as they mediate among the interests of competing states, they can provide political opportunities for weak domestic social actors, encouraging their connections with others like themselves and offering resources that can be used in intranational and transnational conflict. We see a highly developed version of this process in the case of the European Commission, which actively subsidizes citizen lobbies in Brussels and—on some occasions—encourages them to lobby their own governments and legitimize European projects (Imig & Tarrow 2001a,b).

But there are questions. In this model, INGOs broker temporary coalitions with international institutions and third-party states to strengthen their intervention in domestic conflicts. But as everybody knows, brokerage involves compromise, if not dependency. How independent of these institutions and states can INGO activists be in their interventions in national settings is an empirical question that has not yet been addressed.

A second question, or rather a set of questions, follows from the first. To the extent that INGO activists are dependent on powerful external actors, how do they relate to domestic social movements? Are they simply resource providers, partners in the development of domestic claims and identities, or big brothers? When their campaigns wind down, what remains of the domestic links in the TANs they have formed? Do their domestic allies collapse into repressed quiescence, become empowered but wholly national actors, or—as the final stage in the institutional model above hypothesizes—transnationalize their own activities?

Third, what are the analytical stakes in this growing area of research? If researchers can be convinced to define their terms precisely and consistently and relate these actors and agencies to one another over time, we may be able to answer the question that is too often taken as an assumption in the literature: Is there a trend toward nonterritorial governance in the world system, and if so, will that governance be interstate, supranational, or civil-society dominated?[6]

A final provocative thought: If the process of transnationalization described above is robust, then a global civil society will result not from domestic groups moving outward from their societies and replacing government with governance, but from the activities of state-created international institutions, stimulated by transnational activists, reflecting on domestic contention, institutions, and identities. And if that is the case, then the distinction between international relations and domestic politics will really need to be challenged.

[6]Because of space limitations, I do not consider here a hybrid alternative suggested by Murphy (personal communication)—namely that "transnational social actors have an impact...on the creation and reform of intergovernmental organizations which, in turn, end up having a great deal of influence in specific realms." For an example, the International Landmine Treaty, see Price (1997).

ACKNOWLEDGMENTS

I wish to thank Evelyn Bush for thoughtful research assistance and comments on an earlier draft. Extensive comments were also offered by Bruce Bueno de Mesquita, John Boli, Matt Evangelista, Martha Finnemore, Doug Imig, Bob Jervis, Roger Karapin, Peter Katzenstein, Hanspeter Kriesi, Tom Loya, Doug McAdam, Rose McDermott, John Meyer, Craig Murphy, Thomas Risse, Kathryn Sikkink, Jackie Smith, Charles Tilly, Steve Weber, and members of the Villa La Fonte group of the European University Institute.

LITERATURE CITED

Arrighi G, Silver B. 1984. Labor movements and capital migration. In *Labor in the Capitalist World-Economy*, ed. C Bergquist, pp. 183–216. Beverly Hills/London: Sage

Ayres JM. 1998. *Defying Conventional Wisdom: Political Movements and Popular Contention Against North American Free Trade.* Toronto: Univ. Toronto Press

Berger S. 2000. Globalization and politics. *Annu. Rev. Polit. Sci.* 3:43–62

Blyton P, Lucio MM, McGurk J, Turnbull P. 2000. *Globalisation and trade union strategy: industrial restructuring and human resource management in the international civil aviation industry.* Unpubl. pap., Cardiff Univ. Dep. Indust. Relat., Cardiff, UK

Boli J, Thomas J, eds. 1999. *Constructing World Culture: International Nongovernmental Organizations Since 1875.* Stanford, CA: Stanford Univ. Press

Brysk A. 1998. *From tribal village to global village: Indian rights and international relations in Latin America.* Unpubl. pap., Polit. Sci. Dep., Univ. Calif., Irvine, CA

Cameron D. 1995. Transnational relations and the development of the European economic and monetary union. See Risse-Kappen 1995, pp. 37–78

della Porta D, Hanspeter K, Rucht D, eds. 1999. *Social Movements in a Globalizing World.* London: Macmillan

Evangelista M. 1995. Transnational relations, domestic structure, and security policy in the USSR and Russia. See Risse-Kappen 1995, pp. 146–88

Evangelista M. 1999. *Unarmed Forces: Transnational Relations and the Demise of the Soviet Threat.* Ithaca, NY/London: Cornell Univ. Press

Finnemore M. 1996. *National Interests in International Society.* Ithaca, NY/London: Cornell Univ. Press

Finnemore M, Sikkink K. 1998. International norm dynamics and political change. *Int. Org.* 52:887–917

Fox JA. 1999. *The World Bank inspection panel: lessons from the first five years.* Unpubl. pap., Chicano/Latino Res. Cent., Univ. Calif., Santa Cruz, CA

Fox JA. 2000. *Assessing binational civil society coalitions.* Chicano/Latino Res. Cent. Work. Pap. No. 26. Univ. Calif., Santa Cruz, CA

Fox JA, Brown LD. 1998. *The Struggle for Accountability: the World Bank, NGOs, and Grassroots Movements.* Cambridge, MA/London: MIT Press

Guidry JA, Kennedy MD, Zald MN. 2001. *Globalizations and Social Movements: Culture, Power, and the Transnational Public Sphere.* Ann Arbor: Univ. Mich. Press

Huntington SP. 1973. Transnational organizations in world politics. *World Polit.* 25:333–68

Imig D, Tarrow S. 1999. Europeanization of movements? A new approach to transnational contention. In *Social Movements in a Globalising World,* ed. D della Porta, H Kriesi, D Rucht, pp. 144–79. London: Macmillan

Imig D, Tarrow S. 2000. Processing contention in a Europeanising polity. *West Eur. Polit.* 23:

Imig D, Tarrow S, eds. 2001a. *Contentious Europeans: Protest and Politics in an Integrating Europe.* Boulder, CO: Rowman & Littlefield

Imig D, Tarrow S. 2001b. Mapping the Europeanization of contention: evidence from a quantitative data analysis. See Imig & Tarrow 2001a

Jacobson HK. 1979. *Networks of Interdependence: International Organizations and the Global Political System.* New York: Knopf

Jacobson HK. 2000. International institutions and system transformation. *Annu. Rev. Polit. Sci.* 3:149–66

Katzenstein PJ. 1996. Introduction: alternative perspectives on national security. In *The Culture of National Security: Norms and Identity in World Politics,* ed. PJ Katzenstein, pp. 1–23. New York: Columbia Univ. Press

Keck M. 1995. Social equity and environmental politics in Brazil: lessons from the rubber tappers of Acre. *Comp. Polit.* 27:409–24

Keck M, Sikkink K. 1998. *Activists Beyond Borders. Advocacy Networks in International Politics.* Ithaca, NY: Cornell Univ. Press

Keohane RO. 1989. *International Institutions and State Power: Essays in International Relations Theory.* Boulder, CO: Westview

Keohane RO, Milner HV, eds. 1996. *Internationalization and Domestic Politics.* New York/Cambridge: Cambridge Univ. Press

Keohane RO, Nye JS, eds. 1971. *Transnational Relations and World Politics.* Cambridge, MA: Harvard Univ. Press

Keohane RO, Nye JS Jr. 1974. Transgovernmental relations and international organizations. *World Polit.* 27:39–62

Khagram S. 1999. *Transnational struggles for power and water: the political economy of big dam building and development in the Third World.* PhD thesis, Dep. Polit. Sci., Stanford Univ., Stanford, CA

Khagram S, Riker J, Sikkink K, eds. 2001. *Reconstructing World Politics: Transnational Social Movements and Norms.* Minneapolis/St. Paul: Univ. Minn. Press. In press

Klotz A. 1995. *Norms in International Relations: The Struggle Against Apartheid.* Ithaca, NY/ London: Cornell Univ. Press

Krasner S. 1995. Power politics, institutions, and transnational relations. See Risse-Kappen 1995, pp. 257–79

Loya T. 2000. *The international organizations of the prodemocracy movement.* Presented at annu. meet. Am. Sociol. Assoc., Aug. 12–16, Washington, DC

McAdam D. 1998. On the international origins of domestic political opportunities. In *Social Movements and Political Institutions in the United States,* ed. A Costain, AS McFarland, pp. 251–67. Boulder, CO: Rowman & Littlefield

McAdam D, McCarthy J, Zald M, eds. 1996. *Comparative Perspectives on Social Movements.* New York/Cambridge: Cambridge Univ. Press

McAdam D, Tarrow S, Tilly C. 2001. *Dynamics of Contention.* New York/Cambridge: Cambridge Univ. Press

Melucci A. 1988. Getting involved: identity and mobilization in social movements. In *From Structure to Action: Comparing Social Movements Across Cultures, International Social Movement Research I,* ed. B Klandermans, H Kriesi, S Tarrow, pp. 329–48. Greenwich, CT: JAI

Melucci A. 1996. *Challenging Codes: Collective Action in the Information Age.* Cambridge/New York: Cambridge Univ. Press

Meyer DS, Tarrow S, eds. 1998. *Towards a Movement Society? Contentious Politics for a New Century.* Boulder, CO: Rowman & Littlefield

Nye JS Jr, Keohane RO. 1971a. Introduction. See Keohane & Nye 1971, pp. ix–xxix

Nye JS Jr, Keohane RO. 1971b. Conclusion. See Keohane & Nye 1971, pp. 371–98

O'Brien R, Goetz AM, Aart J, Williams M, eds. 2000. *Contesting Global Governance: Multilateral Economic Institutions and Global Social Movements*. London/New York: Cambridge Univ. Press

Price R. 1997. *The Chemical Weapons Taboo*. Ithaca, NY/London: Cornell Univ. Press

Risse T. 1999. International norms and domestic change: arguing and communicative behavior in the human rights area. *Polit. Sociol.* 27:529–59

Risse T. 2001. Transnational actors, networks, and global governance. In *Handbook of International Relations*, ed. W Carlsnaes, T Risse, B Simmons. London: Sage. In press

Risse T, Ropp SC, Sikkink K, eds. 1999. *The Power of Human Rights: International Norms and Domestic Change*. New York/Cambridge: Cambridge Univ. Press

Risse-Kappen T, ed. 1995. *Bringing Transnational Relations Back In: Non-State Actors, Domestic Structures and International Institutions*. Ithaca, NY/London: Cornell Univ. Press

Rochon T. 1988. *Mobilizing for Peace: The Antinuclear Movements in Western Europe*. Princeton, NJ: Princeton Univ. Press

Rosenau J. 1990. *Turbulence in World Politics: A Theory of Change and Continuity*. Princeton, NJ: Princeton Univ. Press

Rosenau J. 1999. Towards an ontology for global governance. In *Approaches to Global Governance Theory*, ed. M Hewson, TJ Sinclair, pp. 287–301. Albany, NY: State Univ. NY Press

Rucht D. 1999. The transnationalization of social movements: trends, causes, problems. See della Porta et al. 1999, pp. 206–22

Rudolf SH, Piscatori J, eds. 1997. *Transnational Religion and Fading States*. Boulder, CO: Westview

Smith J. 2000. *Globalization and political contention: brokering roles of transnational social movement organizations*. Presented at annu. meet. Am. Sociol. Assoc., Aug. 12–16, Washington, DC

Smith J, Chatfield C, Pagnucco R, eds. 1997. *Transnational Social Movements in Global Politics*. Syracuse, NY: Syracuse Univ. Press

Snow D, Rochford EB, Worden S, Benford R. 1986. Frame alignment processes, micromobilization, and movement participation. *Am. Sociol. Rev.* 51:464–81

Soysal V. 1994. *Limits of Citizenship: Migrants and Postnational Membership in Europe*. Chicago: Univ. Chicago Press

Spruyt H. 1994. *The Sovereign State and its Competitors*. Princeton, NJ: Princeton Univ. Press

Stiles K, ed. 2000. *Global Institutions and Local Empowerment: Competing Theoretical Perspectives*. NewYork: St. Martins

Strang D, Soule S. 1998. Diffusion in organizations and social movements: from hybrid corn to poison pills. *Annu. Rev. Sociol.* 24:265–90

Tarrow S. 1998. *Power in Movement: Social Movements and Contentious Politics*. New York/Cambridge: Cambridge Univ. Press. 2nd ed.

Tarrow S, Acostavalle M. 1999. *Transnational politics: a bibliographic guide to recent research on transnational movements and advocacy groups*. Columbia Int. Aff. Online https://wwwc.cc.columbia.edu/sec/dlc/ciao.wpsfrm.html.

Thomas D. 2000. *The Helsinki Effect: International Norms, Human Rights, and the Demise of Communism*. Princeton, NJ: Princeton Univ. Press

Tilly C. 1994. The time of states. *Soc. Res.* 61:269–95

Tilly C. 1995. *Popular Contention in Great Britain, 1758–1834*. Cambridge, MA: Harvard Univ. Press

Uvin P. 2000. From local organizations to global governance: the role of NGOs in international relations. See Stiles 2000, pp. 9–29

Walton J. 1989. Debt, protest and the state in Latin America. In *Power and Popular Protest: Latin American Social Movements*, ed. S Eckstein, pp. 299–324. Berkeley/Los Angeles: Univ. Calif. Press

Wapner P. 1996. *Environmental Activism and World Civic Politics.* Albany: State Univ. NY Press

Waterman P. 1998. *Globalization, Social Movements and the New Internationalisms.* London/Washington, DC: Mansell

Willetts P, ed. 1996. *'The Conscience of the World': The Influence of Non-Governmental Organisations In the UN System.* Washington, DC: Brookings Inst.

Yashar D. 2000. *Globalization and collective action.* Unpubl. pap., Dep. Polit., Princeton Univ., Princeton, NJ

Young O, ed. 1997. *Global Governance: Drawing Insights from the Environmental Experience.* Cambridge, MA: MIT Press

Annu. Rev. Polit. Sci. 2001. 4:21–41

MECHANISMS IN POLITICAL PROCESSES

Charles Tilly
Fayerweather Hall, Columbia University, New York 10027; e-mail: ct135@columbia.edu

Key Words explanation, episodes, democratization, covering law, propensity

■ **Abstract** Ostensibly theoretical disputes in political science often involve competing approaches to explanation, including skepticism, covering law arguments, reconstructions of propensities, system models, and explanations featuring causal mechanisms. Mechanism- and process-based accounts, including cognitive, environmental, and relational effects, deserve more attention than they have received in recent political science. Analyses of democratization illustrate these points.

INTRODUCTION

Early in their careers, political science students commonly learn an exercise resembling the scales and arpeggios every beginning instrumentalist must master—essential for gaining a sense of the discipline, but by no means the heart of virtuoso performance. The exercise consists of identifying a phenomenon—nationalism, revolution, balance of power, or something else—then lining up two or three ostensibly competing explanations of the phenomenon. An effective performer of the exercise proposes to adjudicate among competing positions by means of logical tests, crucial cases, observations of covariation across cases, or perhaps a whole research program whose results the newcomer can report in a doctoral dissertation.

Although scales and arpeggios appear intermittently in concert pieces, no soloist who played nothing but scales and arpeggios, however skillfully, would last long on the concert circuit. Those of us who teach the political science equivalent of these exercises generally recognize their limitations, even if we continue to use them to limber our (and our students') mental sinews. Rarely can (much less does) a single inquiry offer definitive proof or disproof for any particular social-scientific theory of nationalism, revolution, balance of power, or any other political phenomenon. To assemble evidence that one's chosen opponents might recognize as definitive generally requires moving far onto the opponents' preferred epistemological, ontological, and methodological terrain. An opponent worth opposing, furthermore, usually commands a sufficiently rich array of ideas that minor adjustments in a refuted argument rapidly generate new arguments that have not yet suffered falsification. Veteran performers therefore usually learn to make their cases cumulatively, and on stages of their own choosing.

The worst, however, is yet to come. Behind many ostensibly theoretical disputes in political science lurk disagreements about the nature of valid explanations. Confrontations among advocates of realist, constructivist, and institutionalist approaches to international relations, for example, concern explanatory strategies more than directly competing propositions about how nations interact. Similarly, rampant debates about nationalism more often hinge on specifying what analysts must explain, and how, than on the relative validity of competing theories. Recent debates about democratization concern not only the choice of explanatory variables but also the very logic of explanation. Within political science as a whole, wrangles over the value of rational choice models no doubt offer the most vigorous and visible recent examples; despite challenges to specific arguments and empirical claims, the most serious of those disputes pivot on the character of valid explanations.

Rational choice advocates assume that intentional human decision making causes social processes, therefore that explanation consists of pinpointing contexts and rationales of human decisions. Some critics of rational choice accept choice-theoretic criteria of explanation but reject standard characterizations of how choices occur. Many others, however, reject the whole enterprise as irrelevant. The latter are not simply proposing alternative theories; they are reaching for other criteria of explanation. They are at best engaging metatheoretical debates.

COMPETING VIEWS OF EXPLANATION

To clarify the issues and point to possible resolutions, this essay locates mechanism- and process-based accounts within the range of competing approaches to explanation, drawing especially on analyses of democratization. It also urges the significance of environmental and relational mechanisms as they interact with the cognitive mechanisms that have prevailed recently in political scientists' uses of mechanistic explanations.

In political science, as in social science and history at large, five views of explanation compete for attention: skepticism, covering laws, propensity, system, and mechanism.

Skepticism

Skepticism considers political processes to be so complex, contingent, impenetrable, or particular as to defy explanation. In the skeptic's view, investigators can perhaps reconstruct the experiences of actors undergoing what they or others call democratization, but attempts at generalization will inevitably fail. Short of an extreme position, nevertheless, even a skeptic can hope to describe, interpret, or assign meaning to processes that are complex, contingent, particular, and relatively impenetrable. Thus skeptics continue to describe, interpret, and assign meaning to the Soviet Union's collapse without claiming to have explained that momentous process.

Covering Law

In covering law accounts, explanation consists of subjecting robust empirical generalizations to higher- and higher-level generalizations, the most general of all standing as laws. In such accounts, models are invariant—they work the same under all conditions. Investigators search for necessary and sufficient conditions of stipulated outcomes, those outcomes often conceived of as dependent variables. Studies of covariation among presumed causes and presumed effects therefore serve as validity tests for proposed explanations; investigators in this tradition sometimes invoke John Stuart Mill's methods of agreement, differences, residues, and concomitant variation, despite Mill's own doubts of their applicability to human affairs.

The rules of causal inference proposed by the standard text of King et al (1994) do not require general laws, but they belong to this tradition (Ragin 2000:14). In principle, either democratization occurs in similar ways everywhere under specifiable necessary and sufficient conditions or the elements of democratization (e.g. creation of representative institutions) conform to general laws. The covering law analyst's job is to establish empirical uniformities, then to subsume them under such generalizations.

Propensity

In propensity accounts, explanation consists of reconstructing a given actor's state at the threshold of action, with that state variously stipulated as motivation, consciousness, need, organization, or momentum. With the understanding that certain orientations of actors may be universally favorable or even essential to democratization, explaining democratization thus entails reconstructing the internal conditions of efficacious actors immediately preceding and during transitions from nondemocratic to democratic regimes. The actors in question may be individuals, but analysts often construct propensity accounts of organizations or other collective actors. Explanatory methods of choice then range from sympathetic interpretation to reductionism, psychological or otherwise. Thus many students of democratization seek to characterize the attitudes of major actors in democratic transitions, then to verify those characterizations through interviews, content analyses, or biographical reconstructions.

System

Authors of covering law and propensity accounts sometimes talk of systems, but systemic explanations, strictly speaking, consist of specifying a place for some event, structure, or process within a larger self-maintaining set of interdependent elements and showing how the event, structure, or process in question serves and/or results from interactions among the larger set of elements. Functional explanations typically qualify, since they account for the presence or persistence of some element by its positive consequences for some coherent larger set of social relations or processes. Nevertheless, systemic accounts can avoid functionalism by making more straightforward arguments about the effects of certain kinds of relations to larger systems.

Within the realm of democratization, systemic accounts typically argue that only certain kinds of social settings sustain democracy because democratic institutions serve or express powerful values, interests, or structures within those settings. Thus analyses in the mass society tradition, now largely abandoned, treated totalitarianism and democracy as stemming from different degrees and forms of integration between ordinary people and society as a whole.

Mechanism and Process

Mechanism- and process-based accounts explain salient features of episodes, or significant differences among them, by identifying within those episodes robust mechanisms of relatively general scope (Elster 1989, 1999; Coleman 1990; Stinchcombe 1991; Padgett & Ansell 1993; Bunge 1997; Hedström & Swedberg 1998). Similarly, they search for recurrent concatenations of mechanisms into more complex processes. Compared with covering law, propensity, and system approaches, mechanism- and process-based explanations aim at modest ends—selective explanation of salient features by means of partial causal analogies. In the analysis of democratization, for example, such mechanisms as brokerage and cross-class coalition formation compound into crucial recurrent processes, such as enlargement of polities. Later in this essay I propose an array of mechanisms and processes that figure widely in democratization.

Mechanisms, too, entail choices. A rough classification identifies three sorts of mechanism: environmental, cognitive, and relational. Environmental mechanisms are externally generated influences on conditions affecting social life; words such as disappear, enrich, expand, and disintegrate—applied not to actors but their settings—suggest the sorts of cause-effect relations in question. Cognitive mechanisms operate through alterations of individual and collective perception, and are characteristically described through words such as recognize, understand, reinterpret, and classify. Relational mechanisms alter connections among people, groups, and interpersonal networks; words such as ally, attack, subordinate, and appease give a sense of relational mechanisms.

Some advocates of mechanistic explanation (e.g. Hedström & Swedberg 1998) not only privilege cognitive mechanisms but also conceive of explanation as moving to a lower level of aggregation—explaining war, for example, by identifying mechanisms that operate at the level of the individual or the small group but aggregate into larger scale effects. The common distinction between micro foundations and macro effects springs from such a conception of explanation. That intellectual strategy has the advantage of remaining close to the main line of political science explanations and the disadvantage of ignoring a wide range of significant cause-effect connections. In fact, relational mechanisms (e.g. brokerage) and environmental mechanisms (e.g. resource depletion) exert strong effects on political processes without any necessary connection to individual-level cognitive mechanisms.

Causal mechanisms do, to be sure, make appearances outside of mechanism-centered analyses. System theorists have often appealed to equilibrating mechanisms, although those mechanisms have proved notoriously difficult to specify and observe. Propensity explanations often incorporate cognitive mechanisms such as satisficing and rationalizing. Satisfactory covering law accounts require not only broad empirical uniformities but also mechanisms that cause those uniformities. To the extent that mechanisms become uniform and universal, furthermore, their identification starts to resemble a search for covering laws.

But two big differences between covering law and mechanism-based explanations intervene. First, practitioners of mechanistic explanation generally deny that any strong, interesting recurrences of large-scale social structures and processes occur. They therefore question the utility of seeking law-like empirical generalizations—at any level of abstraction—by comparing big chunks of history.

Second, although mechanisms by definition have uniform immediate effects, their aggregate, cumulative, and longer-term effects vary considerably depending on initial conditions and on combinations with other mechanisms. For example, the mechanism of brokerage always connects at least two social sites more directly than they were previously connected, but the activation of brokerage does not in itself guarantee more effective coordination of action at the connected sites; that depends on initial conditions and combinations with other mechanisms.

As represented by manuals, courses, and presidential addresses, approved political science doctrine generally favors some combination of propensity and covering law explanations. To explain political action means to reconstruct accurately the state of an actor—especially, but not exclusively, the intentions of a cogitating individual—at the point of action, but to locate that state as a special case of a general law concerning human behavior. Such a doctrine rests on an implausible claim: that ultimately all political processes result from extremely general uniformities in the propensities of human actors, especially individual actors. Despite more than a century of strenuous effort, political scientists have securely identified no such uniformities. But they have recurrently identified widely operating causal mechanisms and processes. Rather than continuing to search for propensity-governing covering laws, it would therefore make sense to switch whole-heartedly toward specification of mechanisms and processes.

MECHANISMS, PROCESSES, AND EPISODES

Let us adopt a simple distinction among mechanisms, processes, and episodes.

Mechanisms form a delimited class of events that change relations among specified sets of elements in identical or closely similar ways over a variety of situations. For example, brokerage—the joining of two or more previously less connected social sites through the intervention of third parties—constitutes a political mechanism of extremely general scope.

Processes are frequently occurring combinations or sequences of mechanisms. For example, scale shift—an alteration in the range of sites engaging in coordinated action—regularly results from a concatenation of brokerage with the mechanisms of diffusion, emulation, and attribution of similarity.

Episodes are bounded streams of social life. For example, depending on our analytical purposes, we can adopt the Mexican presidential election of 2000, the 1999–2000 campaign leading to that election, or the entire period of opposition mobilization from 1988 to 2000 as the episode under examination.

Episodes sometimes acquire social significance because participants or observers construct names, boundaries, and stories corresponding to them—this revolution, that emigration, and so on. The manner in which episodes acquire shared meanings deserves close study. But we have no a priori warrant to believe that episodes grouped by similar criteria spring from similar causes. Students of episodes therefore face three logically distinct problems: (*a*) delineating episodes so that they provide material for coherent comparisons, (*b*) grouping episodes according to causal similarity and dissimilarity, and (*c*) explaining how some episodes acquire politically significant names and meanings.

Political scientists have invested considerable energy in the delineation of episodes. Analysts often chop continuous streams of social life into episodes according to conventions of their own making, delineating generations, social movements, fads, and the like (Azar & Ben-Dak 1973, Olzak 1989, Cioffi-Revilla 1990, Brockett 1992, Diani & Eyerman 1992, Ragin & Becker 1992, White 1993, Gerner et al 1994, Favre et al 1997, Mohr & Franzosi 1997, Franzosi 1998a,b, Hug & Wisler 1998, Rucht et al 1998, Shapiro & Markoff 1998, Oliver & Myers 1999, Rucht & Koopmans 1999, Mohr 2000). Students of democratization (e.g. Stephens 1989, Inkeles 1991, Rueschemeyer et al 1992, Lafargue 1996, Bratton & van de Walle 1997, Mueller 1997, Ramirez et al 1997, Collier 1999, López-Alves 2000) have frequently lined up ostensibly comparable episodes in different countries and periods in order to establish generalizations concerning preconditions, transitions, or democratic consolidation.

In general, analysts of mechanisms and processes regard the coherence and significance of episodes as something to be proven rather than assumed. They reject the common view that the episodes people call revolutions, social movements, or democratic transitions constitute sui generis phenomena, each conforming to a coherent internal logic. These analysts find that uniformly identified episodes provide convenient frames for comparison as they seek to identify crucial mechanisms and processes within them. Choice of episodes, however, crucially influences the effectiveness of such a search. It makes a large difference, for example, whether students of generational effects distinguish generations by means of arbitrary time periods or presumably critical events.

DEMOCRATIZATION AS A CASE IN POINT

To clarify the stakes of choices among skepticism, covering law accounts, propensity explanations, system ideas, and mechanism/process explanations, it will help to narrow our empirical focus. Instead of reviewing international relations disputes, rational choice controversies, and similar well-defined sites of competing-paradigm exercises across political science, the remainder of this essay concentrates on democratization, a field of energetic inquiry where disputes over explanatory principles have not yet achieved such sophistication. This field invites attention because some of political science's brightest ideas concern democratization, yet specialists in the subject generally proceed as if they were engaged in well-joined comparisons of competing theories. (That happens, I speculate, especially where competing practical proposals lie close at hand; ostensibly competing *explanations of* democratization link to competing *programs for* democratization.) In fact, skepticism, covering law accounts, propensity analyses, system ideas, and mechanism/process explanations all jostle for space within the zone of democratization. Explanatory choices faced by democratization specialists pervade most of political science—indeed social science and history as a whole. Thus, we can observe the whole world in a fairly small pond.

Rather than surveying alternative approaches to democratization, I focus on exemplary recent works by Collier (1999) and Yashar (1997). Reflecting on other political scientists' attempts to explain democratization, Collier writes as if alternative theories were competing. She concludes that recent analyses have concentrated excessively on deliberate elite decisions at the expense of social processes and popular actors. Classical theorists of democracy from Aristotle onward stressed either broad historical processes or necessary structural and cultural conditions for democratization, but those classical traditions have given way to quick specifications of favorable conditions followed by extensive analyses of elite agency:

> The dominant framework used in theoretical and comparative accounts, then, has not only adopted an actor-based perspective rather than a structural one but also tends to privilege certain kinds of actors: individual elites rather than collective actors, strategically defined actors rather than class-defined actors, and state actors over societal actors.
>
> (Collier 1999:8)

More than competing explanations confront each other here. Collier is describing alternative principles of explanation, and therefore alternative specifications of what students of democratization must explain. In the accounts she criticizes (but, ironically, ultimately joins), explanation consists of specifying the motivations and actions of those power holders that proposed and enacted democratizing reforms during moments of relatively rapid and definitive movement into democratic terrain.

The field's current emphasis on strategic elite decision making marks a decided shift from once prevalent analyses of political culture, social structure, and institutional processes. Much earlier work conceived of explanation as identifying durable features of polities that caused democratization to begin, succeed, or fail. Scholars such as Rokkan and Moore once offered long-term political process explanations of democratization and its alternatives [Rokkan 1969, 1970; Moore 1993 (1966); see also Torsvik 1981, Stephens 1989, Immerfall 1992, Skocpol 1998). By self-consciously criticizing, extending, and modifying the Moore-inspired analysis of Rueschemeyer et al (1992, 1993), Collier gestures toward that earlier tradition.

Yet Collier herself implicitly accepts most of the recent shift away from long-term explanation; she pleads mainly for inclusion of workers as sometime advocates and agents of democracy. Her concentration on temporally compact "democratic episodes" during which polities passed from nondemocratic to democratic regimes draws attention away from the long-term processes dear to Rokkan, Moore, and their followers. Collier's systematic comparison of 38 such episodes in 27 countries demonstrates how often organized workers did, indeed, participate directly and consequentially in transitions to more democratic regimes.

Collier concludes that in episodes of democratization occurring between 1848 and 1931 (mainly in Europe), workers played a less central part than previous analyses—especially those of Rueschemeyer et al—have suggested. In episodes from 1974 to 1990 (mainly in Latin America), however, workers figured more centrally than today's transitologists have generally allowed. Thus Collier challenges elite-centered analyses but adopts their conception of explanation: in Collier's book, explanation consists of correctly attributing agency to crucial actors at the point of transition.

Not all challengers to elite-centered explanations travel in the same direction. Yashar (1997) joins Collier in stressing the limits of both necessary-condition and elite-centered analyses. Like Collier, furthermore, she rejects attempts to build one-size-fits-all general theories of democratization.

> Grand theorizing at one time attempted to do so, by focusing on structural patterns of agrarian capitalism, industrialization, levels of development, and international capital. Subsequent middle-range theorizing maintained an emphasis on structural patterns but focused on particular sets of cases. While these grand and middle-range theories delineated general patterns that were particularly inimical to or supportive of democracy, they were less clear about the process and causal mechanisms by which particular democracies were founded. More recently, scholars have attempted to redress these problems by focusing on the particular actors involved in founding and overthrowing democracies. These agency- and process-oriented explanations, however, have assumed a largely descriptive cast and have proven less than successful in explaining the conditions under which newly founded democracies endure.
>
> (Yashar 1997:2)

So saying, however, Yashar begins to break with Collier's analysis of democratization. She constructs a historically grounded comparison of democratization and its failures in Costa Rica and Guatemala from the 1870s to the 1950s. Both countries installed authoritarian regimes in the 1870s, both regimes resisted popular mobilization for reform during the 1930s, both installed left-populist governments in the 1940s, and in both cases, the critical transition to divergent democratic and authoritarian regimes began with concerted, armed opposition to those left-populist governments. Yashar seeks to explain both (*a*) divergent outcomes to similar crises and (*b*) subsequent survival of distinctly different regimes. In doing so she switches away from necessary conditions and elite strategies toward the operation of very general causal mechanisms within historically specific settings.

Yashar (1997) addresses two distinct questions: (*a*) During the period 1941–1954 (more precisely 1941–1948 in Costa Rica, 1944–1954 in Guatemala), why did a democratizing coalition come to power in Costa Rica but not in Guatemala? (*b*) Subsequently, why did Costa Rica continue a process of democratization while Guatemala veered into repressive authoritarianism? Her explanations center on the mechanisms that caused Costa Rica's reform coalition of the 1940s to survive and Guatemala's to splinter, both in the face of determined opposition from armed forces and members of the agrarian elite.

Yashar's answer does not lie in the more peaceful proclivities of Costa Rican elites. Although a military invasion followed by a coup did initiate Guatemala's definitive swing toward authoritarianism in 1954, it was not incremental adjustment but civil war that initiated Costa Rica's definitive swing toward democracy in 1948. The fact that the United States backed Guatemala's 1954 invasion and coup, Yashar shows, by no means explains the different fates of the two countries. Similar domestic political processes, permuted in subtly different organizational contexts, yielded dramatically disparate outcomes.

After the critical period of 1948–1954, Guatemala and Costa Rica struck off in nearly opposite directions. Backed by the United States, the Guatemalan government built up its military strength. It sought to penetrate and subdue the countryside through military and paramilitary force. During the 30 years of civil war that followed, Guatemala suffered some 100,000 deaths and 38,000 disappearances (Stanley 1996:3). Meanwhile, Costa Rica's 1949 constitution abolished the army and established civilian-controlled police forces, thus initiating a transition to relatively nonviolent domestic politics after the civil war of 1948. Government assistance programs and political party mobilization integrated Costa Rican rural dwellers into national politics. After 1954, divergences between authoritarian Guatemala and democratic Costa Rica only sharpened.

Minimizing international demonstration effects, Yashar argues that similar processes produced different outcomes in the two countries.

> First, a publicly expressed division within the elite in the context of rising popular demands for political and economic inclusion precipitated the formation of democratizing reform alliances. Second, the Liberal period

> shaped the reform strategies deployed and the alliances formed. Third, the balance of power within the reform coalition determined the stability of the reform coalition itself.
>
> (Yashar 1997:70)

More concretely, in both countries agrarian elites mobilized against city-based reform governments during the 1940s, but the crucial mechanism of coalition-formation produced different outcomes in Costa Rica and Guatemala.

In Costa Rica, a split in the governing coalition left middle-class opponents of the previous populist-reformist regime in control of the governmental apparatus. Those new governors outflanked both the previous labor-communist-populist coalition and the agrarian opposition by nationalizing Costa Rican banks, imposing an emergency tax, and dismantling the army. Their government then proceeded to solidify its rural support by means of welfare programs, market controls, and party-based political mobilization. Both flanks reluctantly but durably accepted integration into the new regime.

Despite having followed a trajectory parallel to Costa Rica's into the 1940s, Guatemala later pursued a startlingly different path. As in Costa Rica, a left-populist government came to power in Guatemala during the 1940s and generated widespread elite opposition. A 1947 labor code and a 1952 agrarian reform, both liberal in conception, further stimulated antiregime mobilization by the rural oligarchy. Unlike its politically divided Costa Rican counterpart, the Guatemalan Catholic hierarchy generally aligned itself with the opposition to organized labor and to what the Church denounced as communism. Middle-class activists split among labor advocates, moderate reformers, and anticommunists.

Within a deeply fragmented opposition to the regime, the military offered the strongest connections and the greatest capacity for collective action. With US backing, a small "liberation army" invaded from Honduras in June 1954. Although that force remained close to the Honduran border, within 10 days the Guatemalan army—likewise with US support—had assumed power. In telling these two contrasting stories, Yashar makes a strong case that coalition-shaping mechanisms caused crucial differences between authoritarian Guatemala and democratic Costa Rica.

Making the same comparison after the fact, other analysts frequently point to supposedly durable national differences in political economy or political culture as causes of the contrasting outcomes. Pursuing a larger comparison among El Salvador, Nicaragua, Guatemala, and Costa Rica, for example, Paige stresses differences between positions of the Guatemalan and Costa Rican coffee elites.

> The Guatemalan elite was overwhelmingly landed and agrarian, with a relatively weak agro-industrial fraction. Debt servitude, serfdom, and other forms of legal bondage created class relations similar to those of the European feudal manor.... Although these relations began to change with the post-World War II rationalization of coffee, before the 1970s institutions of coerced labor inhibited popular mobilization and created a strong interest in

> authoritarian political structures to control the unfree population.... The most striking contrast with the Guatemalan elite was that of Costa Rica, in which the agrarian fraction was relatively weakly developed because it lost control over substantial amounts of land to a persistent class of family farmers.... The Costa Rican elite was overwhelmingly an elite of processors. Class relations revolved around the relationship between these processors and the small holders, not between the landowners and their laborers.... Politics revolved around the gentlemanly disagreements between large and small property owners, and the elite soon found that such conflicts could be easily managed by the gradual extension of the franchise to rural property owners and the establishment of democratic institutions.
>
> (Paige 1997:87)

Despite his book's later concessions to the recent influence of neoliberal ideologies, Paige generally depends on durable features of class structure for his explanations of democratization or its absence. In his accounts, divergences of the 1940s and 1950s sprang from structural differences established decades earlier.

In contrast, Yashar insists on considerable similarities between the political economies and governmental regimes of Guatemala and Costa Rica up to the 1940s. Although differing political arrangements laid down by previous history strongly affected the postwar political realignments of Guatemala and Costa Rica, Yashar demonstrates dramatically widening divergences between the two polities during and after the struggles of 1941–1954.

Yashar conducts her analysis soberly, leading to the conclusion that in the two cases at hand, the longer-term outcomes of struggles over property distribution and control of the countryside—struggles not fought explicitly between advocates and opponents of democracy as such—fundamentally affected subsequent democratization and its failures. She argues sensibly that both kinds of struggle matter more generally in democratization, and urges deep historical investigations of similar causal processes elsewhere. Her account of democratization stresses a search for robust causal mechanisms rather than for general models, universally applicable necessary and sufficient conditions, or analyses of agency at crucial points of transition.

MECHANISMS OF DEMOCRATIZATION

How might a full-fledged reorientation of explanation to causal mechanisms and processes facilitate the study of democratization? Let me sketch an illustrative mechanism-based argument. Democracy, for present purposes, consists of protected consultation—relations between agents and subjects of a government in which (*a*) different categories of subjects enjoy relatively broad and equal access to agents, (*b*) governmental disposition of persons, activities, and resources within the government's purview responds to binding consultation of subjects, and (*c*) subjects receive protection against arbitrary action by governmental agents.

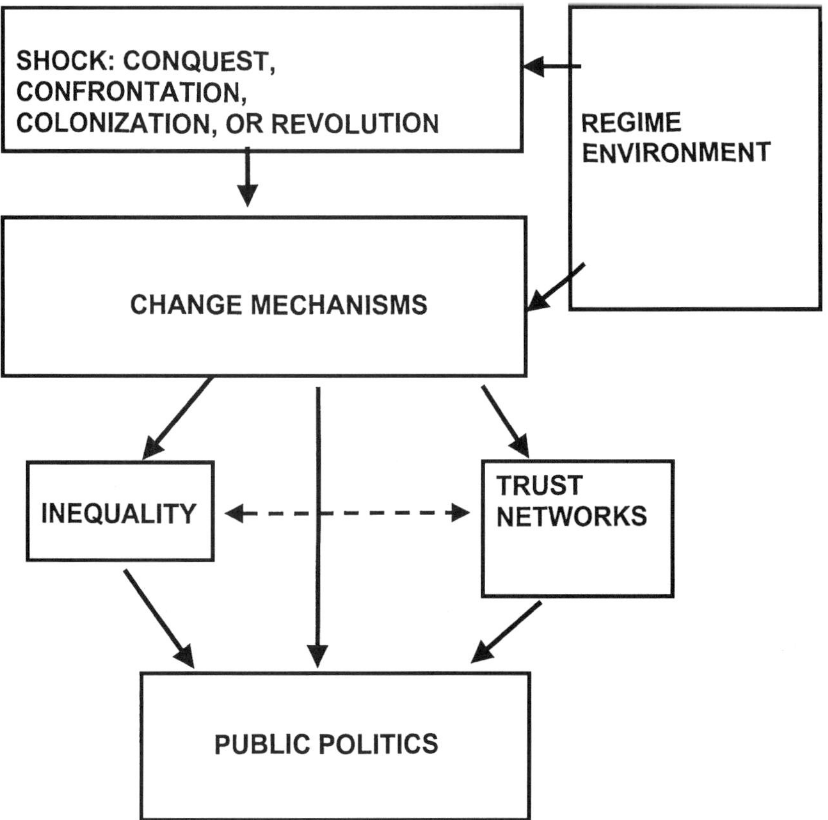

Figure 1 A mechanism-based account of democratization. For clarity, this diagram erases the distinction between transitions to democratic regimes and survival of democratic regimes, on the assumption that the same mechanisms and processes explain transition and survival.

Democratization is any move toward protected consultation, de-democratization any move away from protected consultation.

How and why do such moves occur? Figure 1 summarizes the argument's broadest terms. Democratization, runs the argument, emerges from interacting changes in three analytically separable but interdependent sets of social relations: public politics, inequality, and networks of trust. In the course of democratization, the bulk of a government's subject population acquires binding, protected, relatively equal claims on the government's agents, activities, and resources. In a related process, categorical inequality declines in those areas of social life that either constitute or immediately support participation in public politics. Finally, a significant shift occurs in the locus of interpersonal networks on which people rely when undertaking risky, long-term enterprises such as marriage, long-distance trade, membership in crafts, and investment of savings; such networks move from evasion of governmental detection and control to involvement of government agents and presumption that such agents will meet their long-term commitments. Only where the three sets of changes intersect does effective, durable democracy emerge.

A variety of changes, bundled together as "regime environment" in Figure 1, activate mechanisms that in turn generate incremental alterations in public politics, inequality, and networks of trust. Changes of inequality and of trust networks have independent effects on public politics. Regime environment also produces occasional shocks in the form of conquest, confrontation, colonization, or revolution. Such shocks accelerate the standard change mechanisms, thus causing relatively rapid alterations of public politics, inequality, and networks of trust. Whether incremental or abrupt, those alterations interact. Under rare but specifiable conditions, those interactions lead to democratization. Democratization is not a product but a special condition of public politics. Although these ideas emerged from my effort to explain variations in democratization and its failures across Europe since 1650, they coincide with the arguments Yashar (1997) applies to the experiences of Costa Rica and Guatemala.

What mechanisms produce the changes in question? Table 1 lists likely suspects. It includes both individual mechanisms and robust processes—sequences and combinations of mechanisms that recur over a wide range of circumstances and produce substantially similar immediate effects. Following the idea that democratization consists of changing relations between subjects and governments, the list concentrates on relational mechanisms and processes. A fuller account would include more cognitive and environmental mechanisms, for example (*a*) shifts in beliefs about the likelihood that governmental agents will meet their commitments and (*b*) increases or decreases in the government's resource base. Since previous treatments of democratization have stressed cognitive and/or environmental mechanisms, however, it seems useful to bring out the likely importance of relational mechanisms in this discussion.

Table 1 groups mechanisms and processes in three categories: those affecting relations between categorical inequality and public politics, those affecting relations between trust networks and public politics, and those operating chiefly within public politics. The causal account, therefore, proceeds at three levels. First, any changes that increase insulation between nongovernmental inequalities and public politics, integrate interpersonal trust networks into public politics, and push public politics itself toward protected consultation promote democratization wherever they occur. Second, particular mechanisms and processes favor insulation of inequality, integration of trust networks, and transformation of public politics. Third, when confrontation, colonization, conquest, and revolution promote democratization, they do so by accelerating the same mechanisms and processes that promote incremental democratization.

Parts of this argument are deliberately tautological. To say that transformation of public politics in the direction of protected consultation promotes democratization merely restates the definition of democracy adopted here. The tautologies, however, serve important purposes. They specify what students of democratization must explain. They thereby focus the search for explanations on proximate causes of those explananda—mechanisms that directly alter connections

TABLE 1 Sample mechanisms and processes promoting democratization[a]

Inequality
Dissolution of coercive controls supporting current relations of exploitation and opportunity hoarding
Education and communication that alter adaptations supporting current relations of exploitation and opportunity hoarding
Education and communication that supplant existing models of organization and hence alter emulation of inequality in formation of new organizations
Equalization of assets and/or well-being across categories within the population at large
Insulation of existing categorical inequalities from public politics
Networks of Trust
Creation of external guarantees for government commitments
Incorporation and expansion of existing trust networks into the polity
Governmental absorption or destruction of previously autonomous patron-client networks
Disintegration of existing trust networks
Expansion of the population lacking access to effective trust networks for their major long-term, risky enterprises
Appearance of new long-term, risky opportunities that existing trust networks cannot handle
Substantial increase of government's resources for risk reduction and/or compensation of loss
Visible governmental meeting of commitments to the advantage of substantial new segments of the population
Public Politics
Coalition formation between segments of ruling classes and constituted political actors that are currently excluded from power
Brokerage of coalitions across unequal categories and/or distinct trust networks
Central co-optation or elimination of previously autonomous political intermediaries
Bureaucratic containment of previously autonomous military forces
Dissolution or segregation from government of nongovernmental patron-client networks
Imposition of uniform governmental structures and practices through the government's jurisdiction
Mobilization-repression-bargaining cycles during which currently excluded actors act collectively in ways that threaten survival of the government and/or its ruling classes, governmental repression fails, struggle ensues, and settlements concede political standing and/or rights to mobilized actors
Extraction-resistance-bargaining cycles during which governmental agents demand resources that are under control of nongovernmental networks and committed to nongovernmental ends, holders of those resources resist, struggle ensues, and settlements emerge in which people yield resources but receive credible guarantees with respect to constraints on future extraction

[a]For clarity, the table excludes negative complements of these mechanisms and processes, e.g. fortification (rather than dissolution) of coercive controls supporting current relations of exploitation and opportunity hoarding.

between trust networks and public politics, for example, and other mechanisms that shift the intersection between governmental and nongovernmental inequalities. As Collier's (1999) analysis encourages us to believe, proximate causes certainly include cognitive mechanisms and processes—but they also emphatically include relational and environmental mechanisms.

France Versus Britain

A quick comparison of France and the British Isles from 1650 to 2000 will concretize the program of theory and research that follows. First we must decide on the units of observation. Neither polity had constant boundaries over the entire period. Even disregarding the fact that in 1650 the Fronde deprived young Louis XIV and his government of control over much of their nominal territory, the France of that time lacked Roussillon, much of Provence, Corsica, Savoy, Franche-Comté, most of Alsace-Lorraine, and significant sections of the North. Even after 1800, France's territory expanded and contracted several times.

Nor did the British polity remain constant. A traveler through the British Isles in 1650 would have seen a Scotland rebelling openly against English hegemony and a Scottish military force in northern England backing Charles Stuart's claim to succeed his father Charles I; just the previous year, England's contentious revolutionaries had united temporarily to decapitate King Charles. In Ireland, Catholic leaders were battling not only each other but also the English invading force of Oliver Cromwell. Nor—as current struggles in Ulster make clear—did territorial uncertainty cease with the Glorious Revolution of 1688–1689. To trace democratization and its failures in "France" and the "British Isles" over the 350-year period requires frequent readjustment of the governments, territories, and populations at risk.

These specifications made, some important puzzles arise. Why did the French create some of the world's most widely emulated democratic institutions, yet fluctuate rapidly between relatively democratic and undemocratic regimes in 1789–1793, 1829–1832, 1847–1851, 1868–1875, and 1936–1946? Why were the same British who struggled their way to fairly stable democracy in Great Britain after 1815 never able to perform the trick in Ireland? Why did some French and British colonies end up fairly democratic and others quite authoritarian? Such questions make it clear that confrontation, conquest, colonization, and revolution all affected the prospects for democracy in France and the British Isles multiple times since 1650.

The mechanism-based program laid out above suggests answering such questions by tracing alterations in trust networks, categorical inequality, and their intersections with public politics year by year over the entire period. That procedure will not explain anything, but it will specify what must be explained. In nineteenth-century France, for example, connections between public politics and workers' trust networks as represented by mutual aid societies, trade networks, and migration systems clearly waxed and waned in rhythm with the rise and fall of protected consultation; how and why those connections changed deserve close attention from anyone who seeks to explain French democratization.

Table 1's roster of mechanisms suggests looking closely at disintegration of existing trust networks as well as governmental absorption and destruction of previously autonomous patron-client networks. France's tumultuous movement into less undemocratic institutions between the later Second Empire and World War I, for example, resulted in part from the decay of vast, clandestine networks of artisans and their replacement by legal workers' organizations integrated into public politics by means of political parties, recognized labor unions, and such institutions as Bourses du Travail.

On the British side of the Channel, the equally tumultuous 1830s provide a splendid opportunity for examination of democratizing mechanisms at work. In surprising parallels to the democratizing processes described by Yashar (1997), the British government twice quelled insurrection by engineering compromises that produced democratic consequences. First, after repeated earlier failures of campaigns for Catholic political rights, Wellington's government forced through Catholic Emancipation (1829) in response to an enormous Irish mobilization despite strong anti-Catholic organization within Great Britain itself. Then Grey's government responded to vast agitation within Great Britain—agitation inspired by and built in part on the organizational webs of Catholic Emancipation—by passing the Reform Act (1832) over the initially fierce opposition of the king, the House of Lords, and substantial portions of the national power structure. That the 1832 act excluded most of the workers who had participated in mobilization for parliamentary reform and thereby contributed to the subsequent rise of worker-based democracy-demanding Chartism only confirms the importance of examining the actual mechanisms by which democratization occurs.

AGENDA

Adoption of mechanistic explanations has strong implications for research and analysis in political science. Let me single out four of them: (*a*) simultaneous downgrading and upgrading of contentious episodes as objects of study, (*b*) reorientation of explanations from episodes to processes, (*c*) comparative examination of mechanisms and processes as such, and (*d*) integration of cognitive, relational, and environmental mechanisms.

Simultaneous Downgrading and Upgrading of Contentious Episodes as Objects of Study

The downgrading consists of denying sui generis reality to contentious episodes. As conventional or arbitrary entities, events we call revolutions, nationalist mobilizations, wars, and episodes of democratization take shape as retrospective constructions by observers, participants, and analysts. They do not have essences, natural histories, or self-motivating logics. Moreover, they intersect with more routine processes, which is all the more reason to avoid segmenting their study.

Episodes also require upgrading, however. Once we recognize that we have snipped them from their historical and social contexts, we must make explicit the procedures and criteria that mark their beginnings, ends, boundaries, and participants. That calls for the development of expertise in delineating comparable events. The process by which a given episode acquires the standing of revolution, social movement, war, strike, or something else has political weight and content; such designations affect not only how subsequent analysts explain them but also how participants behave and how third parties react to them. Thus the social processes that label and bound episodes belong on our agenda.

We must also notice that choices of scale—for example, the choice among particular elections, electoral campaigns, and whole transitions from nondemocratic to democratic regimes as the unit of observation—significantly affect both the nature of comparisons among episodes and the likely relative prominence of various mechanisms and processes. Many mechanisms and processes operate at multiple scales; disintegration of trust networks often produces changes in small groups as well as in whole countries. But others occur much more frequently at one scale than another; commitment occurs at the scale of the individual and produces collective action at an interpersonal scale. Tactical innovation happens mainly at a local scale, followed by diffusion (a cognitive-relational process) to broader scales.

Democratization, in contrast, depends by definition on the presence of government and polity, and thus it occurs at scales from community to world region. A major challenge is to examine how the mechanisms and processes that characterize contention at one scale affect it at another—for example, between the local and the global in democratic transitions (Markoff 1996, 1999).

Reorientation of Explanations from Episodes to Processes

Although recent analyses support retention of comparable episodes as units of observation, they also recommend abandonment of efforts to explain all salient features of whole episodes. They thereby rule out the common procedure of matching episodes to general models in order to demonstrate that the model does not fit some salient feature of the episode, then modifying the general model to improve the fit. Recent studies of democratization do not offer much hope of gaining explanatory leverage by matching whole episodes with invariant general models of mobilization, transition, or consolidation, much less with invariant general models of democratization in all its varieties.

Instead, political scientists should concentrate their explanations on selected features of episodes (for example, why rapid shifts in identity occurred) or on recurrent processes in families of episodes (for example, how and why cross-class alliances frequently create or expand revolutionary situations). In either mode, explanation consists of identifying crucial mechanisms and their combination into transforming processes.

Comparative Examination of Mechanisms and Processes as Such

Far beyond the zone of democratization, the mechanisms and processes enumerated in Table 1 deserve comparative analysis for their own sake. Bureaucratic containment of previously autonomous military forces, for example, seems almost a necessary condition for democratization, but it also has significant effects on the capacity of government, the likelihood of civil war, the level of domestic violence, and even the prospect that a given state will engage in international war. It would advance political inquiry to encourage comparative research into the mechanisms of bureaucratic containment while continuing close examination of historical episodes. Similarly, political science could only gain from superior comparative knowledge concerning mechanisms and processes that connect or disconnect inequalities within and outside public politics.

Integration of Cognitive, Relational, and Environmental Mechanisms

Proceeding from the view that recent theorists of political phenomena, including democratization, have slighted relational processes, this essay deliberately emphasizes relational mechanisms. Nevertheless, my concrete analyses have repeatedly invoked combinations of relational with cognitive and/or environmental mechanisms. The mechanism called "insulation of existing categorical inequalities from public politics," for example, inevitably includes a cognitive component defining boundaries among categories. Changing conceptions of racial, ethnic, gender, religious, or class differences therefore affect that insulation or its failure. Such shifts, furthermore, often result partly from changing balances of resources among people on opposite sides of categorical boundaries—for example, disproportionate increase of numbers or wealth on one side of the line

Under such circumstances, it is not clear in principle whether we are observing (*a*) two or three distinct mechanisms that frequently conjoin or (*b*) a combination of cognitive, relational, and environmental changes that is sufficiently invariant to justify treating it as a single robust process. Nor can we decide in general and in advance how the elements interact—whether, for example, cognitive shifts always precede relational changes or vice versa. Interaction among cognitive, relational, and environmental mechanisms presents urgent problems for theory and research on political processes.

BACK TO FAMILIAR GROUND

Political scientists should not find the analysis of mechanisms and processes alien. Aristotle's treatment of democracy and its ills, after all, specified mechanisms and processes by which transitions from one sort of regime to another occurred. Aristotle recognized distinctions within his major regime types, for example five types of democracy, of which the fifth

> is that in which not the law, but the multitude, have the supreme power, and supersede the law by their decrees. This is a state of affairs brought about by the demagogues. For in democracies which are subject to the law the best citizens hold the first place, and there are no demagogues; but where

> the laws are not supreme, there demagogues spring up. For the people becomes a monarch, and is many in one; and the many have the power in their hand, not as individuals, but collectively...this sort of democracy is to other democracies what tyranny is to other forms of monarchy.
>
> (Barnes 1984:II, 2050–51)

Under these circumstances, furthermore, demagogues often stir up the rabble to attack the rich and thereby seize power for themselves. In this way, democracy turns into tyranny. Aristotle proceeded repeatedly from ostensibly static categories to dynamic causal processes. In thinking through the effects of different military formats, for example, he offered a shrewd causal account:

> As there are four chief divisions of the common people, farmers, artisans, traders, labourers; so also there are four kinds of military forces—the cavalry, the heavy infantry, the light-armed troops, the navy. When the country is adapted for cavalry, then a strong oligarchy is likely to be established. For the security of the inhabitants depends upon a force of this sort, and only rich men can afford to keep horses. The second form of oligarchy prevails when a country is adapted to heavy infantry; for this service is better suited to the rich than to the poor. But the light-armed and the naval element are wholly democratic; and nowadays, where they are numerous, if the two parties quarrel, the oligarchy are often worsted by them in the struggle.
>
> (Barnes 1984:II, 2096–97)

Amid the specification of favorable conditions for different sorts of regime, we find Aristotle identifying struggle-centered mechanisms by which transitions from regime to regime actually occur. A short version of my sermon therefore reads as follows: Emulate Aristotle.

ACKNOWLEDGMENTS

I am grudgingly grateful to Sidney Tarrow, Deborah Yashar, and Viviana Zelizer for proving that an earlier version of this article was unfit for publication. I have adapted a few paragraphs from McAdam et al (2001).

LITERATURE CITED

Azar E, Ben-Dak J, eds. 1973. *Theory and Practice of Events Research*. New York: Gordon, Breach

Barnes J, ed. 1984. *The Complete Works of Aristotle*. Princeton, NJ: Princeton Univ. Press. 2 vols.

Bratton M, van de Walle N. 1997. *Democratic Experiments in Africa. Regime Transitions in Comparative Perspective*. Cambridge, UK: Cambridge Univ. Press

Brockett C. 1992. Measuring political violence and land inequality in Central

America. *Am. Polit. Sci. Rev.* 86:169–76

Bunge M. 1997. Mechanism and explanation. *Philos. Soc. M. Sci.* 27:410–65

Cioffi-Revilla C. 1990. *The Scientific Measurement of International Conflict. Handbook of Datasets on Crises and Wars, 1495–1988 A.D.* Boulder, CO: Lynne Rienner

Coleman J. 1990. *Foundations of Social Theory.* Cambridge, MA: Harvard Univ. Press

Collier R. 1999. *Paths Toward Democracy. The Working Class and Elites in Western Europe and South America.* Cambridge: Cambridge Univ. Press

Diani M, Eyerman R, eds. 1992. *Studying Collective Action.* Newbury Park, CA: Sage

Elster J. 1989. *Nuts and Bolts for the Social Sciences.* Cambridge: Cambridge Univ. Press

Elster J. 1999. *Alchemies of the Mind. Rationality and the Emotions.* Cambridge: Cambridge Univ. Press

Favre P, Fillieule O, Mayer N. 1997. La fin d'une étrange lacune de la sociologie des mobilisations. L'étude par sondage des manifestants. Fondements théoriques et solutions techniques. *Rev. Fr. Sci. Polit.* 47:3–28

Franzosi R. 1998a. Narrative analysis, or why (and how) sociologists should be interested in narrative. *Annu. Rev. Sociol.* 24:517–54

Franzosi R. 1998b. Narrative as data: linguistic and statistical tools for the quantitative study of historical events. New methods for social history. *Int. Rev. Soc. Hist.* 43(Suppl. 6):81–104

Gerner D et al. 1994. Machine coding of event data using regional and international sources. *Int. Stud. Q.* 38:91–119

Hedström P, Swedberg R, eds. 1998. *Social Mechanisms. An Analytical Approach to Social Theory.* Cambridge: Cambridge Univ. Press

Hug S, Wisler D. 1998. Correcting for selection bias in social movement research. *Mobilization* 3:141–62

Immerfall S. 1992. Macrohistorical models in historical-electoral research: fresh look at the Stein-Rokkan tradition. *Hist. Soc. Res.* 17:103–16

King G, Keohane R, Verba S. 1994. *Designing Social Inquiry. Scientific Inference in Qualitative Research.* Princeton, NJ: Princeton Univ. Press

Korzeniewicz R, Awbrey K. 1992. Democratic transitions and the semiperiphery of the world-economy. *Sociol. For.* 7:609–40

Lafargue J. 1996. *Contestations démocratiques en Afrique.* Paris: Karthala, IFRA

López-Alves F. 2000. *State Formation and Democracy in Latin America, 1810–1900.* Durham, NC: Duke Univ. Press

Markoff J. 1996. *Waves of Democracy. Social Movements and Political Change.* Thousand Oaks, CA: Pine Grove Press

Markoff J. 1999. Where and when was democracy invented? *Comp. Stud. Soc. Hist.* 41: 660–90

Mohr J, ed. 2000. Relational analysis and institutional meanings: formal models for the study of culture. *Poetics* 27(2,3) (Spec. issue)

Mohr J, Franzosi R, eds. 1997. Special double issue on new directions in formalization and historical analysis. *Theory Soc.* 28(2,3) (Spec. issue)

Moore B. 1993 [1966]. *Social Origins of Dictatorship and Democracy.* Boston: Beacon

Mueller C. 1997. International press coverage of East German protest events, 1989. *Am. Sociol. Rev.* 62:820–32

Mueller C. 1999. Escape from the GDR, 1961–1989: hybrid exit repertoires in a disintegrating Leninist regime. *Am. J. Sociol.* 105:697–735

Oliver P, Myers D. 1999. How events enter the public sphere: conflict, location, and sponsorship in local newspaper coverage of public events. *Am. J. Sociol.* 105:38–87

Olzak S. 1989. Analysis of events in the study of collective action. *Annu. Rev. Sociol.* 15:119–41

Padgett J, Ansell C. 1993. Robust action and the rise of the Medici, 1400–1434. *Am. J. Sociol.* 98:1259–1319

Paige J. 1997. *Coffee and Power. Revolution and the Rise of Democracy in Central America*. Cambridge, MA: Harvard Univ. Press

Ragin C. 2000. *Fuzzy-Set Social Science*. Chicago: Univ. Chicago Press

Ragin C, Becker H, eds. 1992. *What is a Case? Exploring the Foundations of Social Inquiry*. Cambridge: Cambridge Univ. Press

Ramirez F, Soysal Y, Shanahan S. 1997. The changing logic of political citizenship: cross-national acquisition of women's suffrage rights, 1890 to 1990. *Am. Sociol. Rev.* 62:735–45

Rokkan S. 1969. Models and methods in the comparative study of nation building. *Acta Sociol.* 12:52–73

Rokkan S. 1970. *Citizens, Elections, Parties*. Oslo: Universitetsforlaget

Rucht D, Koopmans R, eds. 1999. Protest event analysis. *Mobilization* 4(2) (Spec. issue)

Rucht D, Koopmans R, Neidhardt F, eds. 1998. *Acts of Dissent. New Developments in the Study of Protest*. Berlin: Sigma Rainer Bohn

Rueschemeyer D, Stephens E, Stephens J. 1992. *Capitalist Development and Democracy*. Chicago: Univ. Chicago Press

Rueschemeyer D, Stephens E, Stephens J. 1993. The impact of economic development on democracy. *J. Econ. Persp.* 7:71–85

Shapiro G, Markoff J. 1998. *Revolutionary Demands. A Content Analysis of the Cahiers de Doléances of 1789*. Stanford, CA: Stanford Univ. Press

Skocpol T, ed. 1998. *Democracy, Revolution, and History*. Ithaca, NY: Cornell Univ. Press

Stephens J. 1989. Democratic transition and breakdown in Western Europe, 1870–1939: a test of the Moore thesis. *Am. J. Sociol.* 94:1019–77

Stinchcombe A. 1991. The conditions of fruitfulness of theorizing about mechanisms in social science. *Philos. Soc. Sci.* 21:367–88

Torsvik P, ed. 1981. *Mobilization, Center-Periphery Structures and Nation-Building*. Bergen: Universitetsforlaget

White R. 1993. On measuring political violence: Northern Ireland, 1969 to 1980. *Am. Sociol. Rev.* 58:575–85

Yashar D. 1997. *Demanding Democracy. Reform and Reaction in Costa Rica and Guatemala, 1870s–1950s*. Stanford, CA: Stanford Univ. Press

Annu. Rev. Polit. Sci. 2001. 4:43–65

DEMOCRATIZATION AND ECONOMIC REFORM

V. Bunce
Department of Government, Cornell University, 208 Kline Road, Ithaca, New York 14850; e-mail: vjb2@cornell.edu

Key Words democracy, capitalism, new democracies, economic recession, governing mandates

■ **Abstract** Are democratization and economic reform in tension with each other, or are they mutually supportive processes? A survey of new democracies in Latin America, Southern Europe, and the postsocialist world suggests that the answer varies by region. In the postsocialist cases, the relationship is positive and robust; in the other two regions, the relationship is negligible. Region, however, cannot serve as the explanation. Instead, what emerge as critical—and what happen to vary by region—are three factors that shape the relationship between democratization and economic reform: the timing of democratization, the agenda of transformation, and variations in governing mandates.

GLOBAL TRENDS

The last several decades of the twentieth century witnessed two global trends. The first was the decline of authoritarian politics and the subsequent rise of new democratic regimes (for reviews, see Remmer 1995, Geddes 1999, Bunce 2000a). This process began in Southern Europe with the collapse of the Salazar dictatorship in 1974 and the death of Franco a year later. Both Portugal and Spain thereupon began a transition to democracy—albeit through contrasting approaches. In short order, one country after another in South and Central America followed suit; Mexico officially joined her neighbors in 2000, completing arguably one of the longest transitions on record with the first victory of an opposition party in the presidential elections—which leaves Cuba the only holdout against the regional trend. Similar developments took place in Southeast Asia and East Asia, though the largest country spanning the two regions—China—managed to maintain rule by its Communist Party. Perhaps the most surprising entry into the democratic column was Eastern Europe and the Soviet Union. In 1989–1991, the hegemony of the Communist Party ended throughout the region. In many cases, what followed was the rapid introduction of democratic politics—or, at least, liberalized orders. Indeed, of the 27 countries that now make up this region as a consequence of the dissolution of the Soviet, Yugoslav, and Czechoslovak states, only two have

1094-2939/01/0623-0043$14.00

failed to hold multiple competitive elections during the first postsocialist decade (Dawisha & Deets 1999).

Many of these new democracies are fragile and may well prove fleeting. Moreover, evidence has accumulated that a sizeable number of these new democracies are seriously flawed in their design and especially their functioning (O'Donnell 1994, Karl 1995, Bunce 1999a). However, this does not detract from one inescapable conclusion. Mass publics today have a greater chance than they have ever had of living in a democratic order. The third wave of democratization, therefore, has demonstrated unprecedented geographical reach (Huntington 1991).

The other global trend has been the spread of capitalism. As Marx argued, capitalism is by nature restless. Moreover, it has always had a voracious geographical appetite. However, the contemporary era is distinguished by two developments. First, although scholars have asserted for a century that capitalism is a global phenomenon, it is only in the past decade that capitalism has achieved genuine global hegemony. This is largely because the alternative to capitalism, state socialism, has withered away—either because of sustained market reforms, as in China, or because of the collapse of communist party hegemony, as in east-central Europe and significant portions of the former Soviet Union. Second, debates continue about whether the forms and practices of capitalism are converging (Garrett 1998, Soskice 1999, Iversen & Pontusson 2000). However, what is not debatable is that the 1980s and the 1990s witnessed a growing consensus (now beginning to unravel) around two arguments: that there is one path to sustained economic growth and that certain policies are always preferable, irrespective of economic context. The policies in question have been termed the Washington consensus (Williamson 1990), which Grzegorz Kolodko, the former Finance Minister of Poland, has succinctly summarized as "liberalize as much as you can, privatize as fast as you can, and be tough in fiscal and monetary measures" (quoted in Interview 1998:2; also see Przeworski 1992, Kahler 1990, Stiglitz 2000).

That democratization and neoliberal economic reforms are global trends is a noncontroversial claim. Also indisputable is the argument that these two developments seem to be related (Centeno 1994). Indeed, how could they be otherwise, given the economic consequences of these reforms, the importance of the economy to the public, and the importance of public support to elected officials? What is in considerable contention is *how* they relate to each other. In particular, are democratization and economic reform in tension with each other or are they compatible? This article reviews the literature that bears on this question. First, I briefly discuss the terrain of this study, core concepts, and key considerations in the analysis of democratization and economic reform. I then lay out the case for conflict between these two processes, followed by the opposite case suggesting their complimentarity. The paper closes by arguing that the cross-national evidence in support of conflict is limited. However, there is some support for the argument that democratization and economic reform are compatible and mutually supportive. Even more interesting is that both the form and the strength of this relationship seem to vary by region, reflecting cross-regional variations in the authoritarian past, the agenda of reform, and the payoffs attached to different approaches to democratization and economic reform.

CASES AND CONCEPTS

The focus of the discussion that follows is democratization, not democracy. Thus, of interest are those cases where democracy is relatively new, that is, under construction with its future uncertain (O'Donnell et al 1986, Dahl 1998). I ignore established democracies and their economic reforms—for example, Thatcherism in the United Kingdom.

Because of both the high correlation between economic development and democratic sustainability (Londregan & Poole 1996, Przeworski et al 1996, Przeworski & Limongi 1997) and global patterns in the rise of new democracies, the concern with democratization means that this review concentrates on a large group of middle- and lower-income countries. Precisely because this group is so large and relevant analyses of it are so numerous, I limit the discussion to studies of three regions: Latin America, Southern Europe, and the postsocialist world. This gives us more than 50 cases; good cross-regional reach; and considerable variance in the forms, speed, and consequences of economic reforms, as well as the origins, the design, and the practices of democratic governance. To provide one example, in the Freedom House measures of democracy (scores ranging from one to four, with one being full provision of civil liberties and political rights), the average score for Latin America is 2.5 and the average score for the postsocialist region is 3.7 (Comparative Survey 1997).

Democracy

Before discussing democratization, it is necessary to clarify what is meant by democracy. There are nearly as many definitions as there are democracies (for a sampling, see Lipset 1959; Dahl 1971, 1998; Przeworski 1991, 1995; Schmitter & Karl 1991). The experiences of democratization over the past 25 years suggest that a precise definition providing analytical leverage is one that treats democracy as a regime combining three characteristics: freedom, uncertain results, and certain procedures (Bunce 1991, 2000a). This definition, by the way, works as well for capitalism, especially given recent recognition of the role of the state in capitalist economies—a role that was forgotten in the emphasis on state "subtraction" but that received due recognition in studies of capitalism that predate the consensus around neoliberal policies (see Popov 1999, Schamis 2000; earlier, Polanyi 1957, North 1990).

Each of these three aspects of democracy implies certain preconditions. They need to be spelled out, primarily because, in the West, they are easy to take for granted since they have been long in place and produce, as a result, predictable and largely desirable outcomes—whereas they are only partially in evidence in many new democracies, with the consequence of producing unexpected and often suboptimal dynamics (see especially Moser 1999). Put simply, having the basic forms of democracy does not necessarily mean having the foundations, and the quality of democracy—and perhaps its sustainability—is often short-changed.

Let us turn, first, to freedom, or whether members of the political community have the full array of civil liberties and political rights. The key questions here include not only the provision of rights and liberties but also how the political community is defined; that is, whether liberties and rights are available, irrespective of social status, national identification, gender, and the like. Next, we must examine whether political results are in fact uncertain. This outcome rests on many prior considerations—most obviously whether politics is competitive, but also whether competition is institutionalized through political parties that offer ideological choice and have the incentives and capacity to connect government and governed; whether elections are regularly held, free and fair, and select those elites who actually shape public policy; and whether governing mandates are provisional. When combined, all these factors determine whether politicians operating within an order called democracy actually have the incentives and the capacity to be fully accountable to the electorate. The final aspect of our definition of democracy, procedural certainty, refers to rule of law; the control of elected officials over the bureaucracy; and a legal and administrative order that is hegemonic and transparent, commmands compliance, and is consistent in its operation across time, circumstances, and space (see O'Donnell 1993, Holmes 1997). Stepan put it succinctly: "No usable state, no democracy" (*Russia on the Brink* 1998:17).

This definition of democracy has several important implications concerning the relationship between democratization and economic reform. One is that competition is a necessary, but by no means sufficient, condition for democracy. Another is that the three-part definition—freedom, uncertainty of results, and certainty of procedure—presents these characteristics in descending order of frequency and ease of attainment among new democracies. Finally, this definition highlights some problems common to new democracies: poorly institutionalized party systems, unaccountable political leaders who have concentrated their powers, and legal systems that fail to extract compliance and to be fair, consistent, and binding.

For these reasons, most analysts agree that new democracies are both thin and fragile. This is understood to be particularly the case in the postsocialist world, given the unparalleled penetration and despotism of state socialism [to borrow from Mann (1993)] and the fact that democracy there is entirely new, not recycled from the past (as it is in Latin America and Southern Europe).

Economic Reform

The other part of the equation is economic reform. At the very minimum, the term economic reform—more precisely, market reforms or neoliberal reforms—refers to all policies that promote marketization, privatization, and free trade. This usually includes the following: macroeconomic stabilization (primarily to deal with inflation and budgetary imbalances), microeconomic liberalization (facilitation of private firms, elimination of price controls, withdrawal of subsidies, expansion of foreign trade, and changes in currency convertibility), and institutional reforms, most notably privatization of state-owned firms and changes in the tax, banking, and capital market systems and their legal foundations. Not surprisingly, economic reforms, as a result, usually decrease growth in the short term (Blanchard et al 1991, Clague et al 1997). This is because "stabilization entails a reduction in demand, structural reforms engender closings of inefficient firms, and privatization temporarily disorganizes the economy" (Pereira et al 1993:2).

It is essential to recognize the limitations of "economic reform" as the umbrella term for ongoing policy changes in diverse regions. In Latin America and Southern Europe, we observe the liberalization of an existing capitalist economy; in the postsocialist setting, we observe a capitalist economy being constructed, not just from scratch (which gives the misleading impression of a tabula rasa), but with state socialism—capitalism's opposite in principles and operation—as the point of departure. The obvious contrast here is between reform, as we usually understand the term, and revolution—as three Eastern European finance ministers have taken great pains to point out (Balcerowicz 1995, Blejer & Coricelli 1995, Kolodko 1999). Although there are some rough similarities between import-substitution industrialization in Latin America and state socialism, most notably with respect to protectionism, rentseeking, authoritarian politics, and poor economic performance (especially during the 1980s), they should not detract from key differences between these two sets of economies—for example, state intervention versus state ownership, markets (albeit imperfect) versus state planning, money as the indicator of purchasing power versus political power as the currency of favor, unemployment versus the labor hunger of enterprises, considerable social inequalities versus limited inequalities, and, finally, economies based on consumer sovereignty versus economies based on "shortage" (Hirschman 1968, 1987; Winiecki 1990; Kornai 1992).

If the point of departure is different, then so necessarily is the process of economic reform. Put simply, revising existing economic institutions, though complicated no doubt by coalitions formed around import substitution (but see Schamis 1999), is a far less daunting task than inventing—quickly—the institutions of a market economy (Poznanski 1996, Kolodko 1999). Just as important is the contrast between a capitalist economy that evolved over time through trial and error, and capitalism imposed as a doctrine—indeed, even in the absence of its principal agent, the bourgeoisie (Murrell 1992, Przeworski 1995:viii, Poznanski 1996, Eyal et al 1998). These contrasts account for one important contrast between the "south" and the "east," namely the far more dramatic recessionary effects of economic reform (whether measured in terms of size or duration) in the postsocialist world (Bunce 1999b, Popov 1999; for comparison, Remmer 1991). Indeed, these economic downturns are without historical precedent (Greskovits 1998). For example, the Russian economy today is half the size it was at the beginning of the transition, and Russia's economic performance is not, by any means, the worst in the region (Popov 2000).

There is an ongoing debate in political science about what constitutes the most successful reform strategy, i.e. one that returns the economy, after a brief recessionary period, to sustained growth. Although everyone agrees that macroeconomic stabilization is critical and that liberalization of trade and prices is essential, economists now disagree on five issues. One is whether reforms should proceed slowly or quickly (Murrell 1993, Roland 1994, Balcerowicz 1995, Aslund et al 1996). This assumes, of course, the political capacity to choose—an assumption that political scientists and some economists find hard to swallow (Appel 1999, Shlaifer & Treisman 2000). Another is how reforms should be sequenced. A third is the emphasis that should be placed on institutional reforms, the appropriate timing of those reforms, and which ones are judged optimal (Sachs 1993, Murrell 1996, Poznanski 1996, Gray & Hendley 1997, Sachs & Pistor 1997, Kolodko 1999; on privatization in particular, see Appel 1997).

Sometimes overlooked in these discussions are the ways in which economic reforms necessarily re-form the state as well—for example, with respect to the "hardening" of both budgets and property rights, changes in the banking system and in institutions governing foreign trade, and, more generally, the provision of a stable business environment (Gaidar 1995, Schamis 2000). One result is that "neither 'state retreat' nor 'state shrinking' capture the deeper institutional effects of marketization" (Schamis 2000:193). The state, in short, does not only withdraw; it also facilitates. Market-oriented incentives complement market-oriented laws and institutions (Gray & Hendley 1997:143).

Economists, as well as political scientists, also disagree about whether and to what extent policy makers should soften the distributional consequences of these reforms, given considerations of equity and the very practical matters of demand suppression, political stability, and maintenance of the reform coalition (Milanovic 1992, Pereira et al 1993, Przeworski 1993, Kolodko 1998, Pinto et al 1999). A key issue here is whether reforms should be modified in their consequences by providing some shelter for those groups most adversely affected. Although such policies violate the goals of eliminating subsidies and reducing the noise that obscures market signals, such policies are desirable for reasons of both justice and political feasibility. The problem, however, is that many economies undergoing market reforms lack the institutional capacity to target appropriate sectors of the population—in the Latin American cases, because of limited development in social policy institutions, and in the postsocialist setting, because social policy institutions were not designed to deal with such issues as poverty and unemployment. What these systems often do have, however, is the capacity to curry to well-positioned rentseekers, who support these reforms because of their political privileges in the past and calculations about expected gains in the future (Schamis 2000). But even these considerations may fall under the category of political feasibility, or choices between one set of opportunity costs and another (Shlaifer & Treisman 2000).

The final, more fundamental issue is whether in fact policies matter all that much, or whether the key determinant of economic responses to reform is the point of departure, including such factors as state capacity and trade distortions

(Popov 2000). This leads to yet another fundamental question. Is the particular setting of economic reform—or what could be called the legacies of the past—so critical that reform must be tailor-made to specific conditions and not treated as a ready-to-wear proposition (Hendley 1997, Ledeneva 1998, Woodruff 2000)? This argument has received considerable support in recent years in analyses of both the Russian disaster and policy responses to the August 1998 economic crisis in that country and elsewhere (Sapir 1999, Stiglitz 2000, Thornhill 2000).

TENSIONS BETWEEN DEMOCRATIZATION AND ECONOMIC REFORM

Those who believe democratization and economic reform are essentially in tension base their case on two sets of arguments. The first emphasizes the inherent tensions between the logic of democracy and the logic of economic reform. As has long been argued, there are conflicts between markets—which, unfettered, produce sizeable socioeconomic inequalities—and democracy, which rests on political equality (Lindblom 1977, Dahl 1992). This conflict can also be formulated as the domain of rights versus the domain of dollars (Okun 1982). To put it a third way, democracy can empower distributive coalitions, which in turn undermine economic growth (Olson 1981; but see the mixed evidence for this proposition in Remmer 1990, Putnam 1993). In the setting of democracy and economic reform, the tensions flow from one source in particular: the politics of accountability versus the kind of politics presumed necessary for economic reform. Accountable politics implies that politicians need to win votes; that publics reward politicians who produce benefits and punish those who do not; that mass political preferences vary, as do the preferences of politicians; and that policy making is sensitive to the diverse interests of the electorate and the diverse interests of politicians, and is therefore a matter of repeated rounds of compromises at the margins of the status quo. Also implied are short-term horizons on the part of publics and their representatives.

As analysts have noted, economic reform has a very different set of preconditions. Economic reforms undermine economic performance in the short term (at best), and are, as a result, unpopular—whether individuals respond simply to their own economic situations or take a sociotropic perspective and react to the performance of the economy as a whole. For this reason and because the future success of economic reforms is merely an article of faith, politicians' consideration of such reforms is fraught with conflict. Indeed, nothing is more conflictual in democratic politics than debates about redistributive policies. What economic reform requires, therefore, seems to be precisely what democracy cannot deliver—on the one hand, publics either unconcerned about short-term economic outcomes or content to anticipate long-term, but as yet unknown, benefits; and, on the other, politicians insulated from voters, consensual in their ideologies, and capable of adopting long-term perspectives (see Kaufman 1986, Haggard & Kaufman 1992a–c, Pereira et al 1993, Haggard & Kaufman 1995).

Even if we assume for the moment that economic reform is introduced, we still see tensions. Publics can rebel in reaction to economic stress (Walton & Seddon 1994). This, in turn, can lead elites to either defect from democratic politics or, if they stay the democratic course, compromise the economic reforms midstream, often resulting in unusually poor economic performance—which then generates, not surprisingly, even more political conflict. At the same time, economic reforms can undermine the state and produce considerable corruption, while more generally mortgaging rule of law (Holmes 1997, EBRD 1999; Orenstein 1998, Rose-Ackerman 1999). This, in turn, increases the costs of doing business, deters foreign investment, and undermines both the efficiency of economic reform and the quality of democracy. Under a corrupt order, a gap grows between public and elite gains from the so-called reforms—accompanied, not surprisingly, by falling public support of these reforms (Kullberg & Zimmerman 1999). The stage is then set for the politics of partial reform, wherein rentseekers join their economic gains with enhanced political privileges and use them to block both a return to the past and further progress on either democratization or economic reform (Hellman 1998). They reap benefits from the political and economic gap between a fully expressed and well-functioning order and the reality of a rentseeker's paradise, and they want that gap to remain.

All these scenarios seem particularly relevant to conditions prevalent in new democracies (Stallings 1989, Pereira et al 1993, Haggard & Kaufman 1995). Two premises (both debatable) are crucial: that these democracies are fragile and that economic reforms are costly, especially in the short term. In new democracies, publics are unusually fickle, and political parties are both fickle and limited in their institutional development and their capacity to structure public opinion (but see Tworzecki 1996, Kitschelt et al 1999 on east-central Europe, and Przeworski et al 1999). This means, for example, that publics may be unusually sensitive to their economic experiences and less constrained by party attachments in reacting to those experiences. It also means that politicians have strong incentives to play to these sentiments, particularly given the unusually low barriers to the entry of new parties and new political candidates, if not the formation of new or nostalgic social movements. Indeed, in the face of economic decline and the uncertainties of regime transition, deficits in civil society and social capital provide a fertile environment for the rise of populist movements—as specialists on Latin America, east-central Europe, and Russia have noted (Roberts 1995, Knight 1998, Tismaneanu 1998, Weyland 1998, Shenfield 2000). All these arguments appear in accounts of democratic breakdown during, say, the interwar period—though the impact of either economics or variations in social capital on democratic breakdown is far from settled (see Berman 1997, 1998; Bermeo 1998; Hanson & Kopstein 1997).

At the same time, many authoritarian regimes had registered poor economic performance prior to their departure—though the role of the economy in causing transitions to democracy is in some question (Remmer 1990, 1991; Bunce 1999c; O'Donnell et al 1996). The legacy of economic problems is either the failure to adopt economic reforms, or, if they are adopted, the onset of substantial political instability in their wake. Political instability does not only jeoparidize nascent democracies (as we saw with shock therapy in Bolivia, Peru, and Argentina); it also has economic effects counter to the practices and goals of economic reform. As Haggard & Kaufman (1992c:277) have suggested, "Political instability shortens the time horizon of politicians and can provide recurrent incentives to inflate, overvalue the currency, and borrow." Capital flight is also encouraged (Frieden 1991).

Other conditions present in new democracies point in the same direction. One is the cultural legacy of the authoritarian past, which means in practice that elites are easily tempted to suspend democratic rules and publics are poorly situated to stop them. Another is the overall weakness of democratic institutions, which makes coalitions in support of economic reform hard to establish and, if forming, hard to sustain. Weak institutions also make implementation very difficult.

These considerations could lead to any of three conclusions. First, democratization and economic reform are incompatible (also see Bienen & Herbst 1996 for the African case). Second, for economic reforms to be successful, at least the early stages require insulation of decision makers from external pressures (Haggard & Kaufman 1992a, 1995; Sachs 1993). A third possibility is that successful reform requires sequencing, i.e. democratic governance should be consolidated first and economic reforms introduced thereafter (Maravall 1993; but see Yashar 1997). In that way, democracy is secure and the political and institutional capacity for economic reforms is in place. This is, of course, not always possible—for example, when the economy is in serious macroeconomic imbalance or when international institutions lack the resources and the commitment to "float" new democracies with serious economic problems. In Spain, the desirability of sequencing was joined by unusual capacity to pursue that strategy. However, it must be noted that Spain was in many respects singular. Most new democracies have far more severe economic problems; they cannot rely on, say, the European Union or the German Social Democrats to provide support, and each is one of many standing in line for it (Story & Pollack 1991).

COMPATIBILITY OF DEMOCRATIZATION AND ECONOMIC REFORM

The case for complementarity between democratization and economic reform proceeds from one observation. Just as all socialist economies (defined as central planning and state ownership of the means of production) have been combined with authoritarian regimes (Nove 1980), so all democracies today, as in the past, feature capitalist economies—though capitalism has, admittedly, been flexible in its choices of political regime partners, as we know from the history of Latin America and contemporary China since the introduction of the Deng reforms in 1978. However, even these examples highlight one larger point. The more liberalized the economy, the more probable democratic governance and, in less politically open settings, the greater the political pressures pushing for competition and civil liberties.

The explanation for this follows from several arguments. First, capitalism disperses resources that undermine authoritarian governance. Second, capitalism generates competition among descending and ascending political groups, which can then unravel the coalitions supporting authoritarian politics—except where collusion between new and old dominant groups is facilitated by the agrarian structure or where control over the agrarian order collapses and revolution results (Moore 1966). A third argument focuses on dynamics within state socialist systems in particular. When these systems introduced economic reforms, they were usually in response to declining economic performance, growing ideological disputes within the elite stratum, and/or public protests. Because these systems were fused and centralized political economies and because their problems indicated a weakening of control at the top within the party-state and between the party-state and society, economic reforms tended to both reflect and contribute to liberalization of politics. For that reason, there was a high correlation between economic reform and more open politics during the communist era in both the Soviet Union and Eastern Europe (as they were then termed). Indeed, this was even the case for China during the 1980s.

Perhaps the most persuasive explanation, however, lies with underlying principles rather than political struggles. I refer not simply to the notions of individual liberty and autonomy from the state that figure so prominently in conservative inquiries into political economy. Rather, I refer to two dimensions of politics and economics. One is whether outcomes are certain or uncertain (i.e. monopoly versus competition). The other is less familiar, but just as critical: whether procedures are certain or uncertain (i.e. capricious rule of individuals versus rule of law). If we array these characteristics on a two-by-two table and focus on both political and economic regimes, we find that capitalism and democracy occupy the same quadrant (Bunce 1991). Both combine uncertain outcomes with certain procedures. Indeed, what makes competition produce efficient outcomes is precisely secure property rights and (more generally) well-specified, transparent, and consistent rules of the economic game—just as what makes democracy effective is secure votes, free, fair, and regular elections, and (more generally) well-specified, transparent, and consistent rules of the political game. Another way to think about this relationship is to recognize that, in the absence of certain procedures, the incentives to play the game decline, as do the benefits derived from competition. Yet another way to put this is that capitalism and democracy each strike a balance between order and disorder, and each reaps benefits from the balance the other establishes.

Central to this comparison is the role of the state in both democratization and economic reform. The state is crucial to both projects, and it is precisely because of that fact that economic reform and democratization can be judged complementary processes. As Schamis concluded in his comparative study of economic reform and the state in Latin America, Great Britain, and east-central Europe:

> the market and democracy are, in fact, mutually reinforcing, not so much because economic freedom and political freedom go together, or because there are no command economies.... Marketization contributes to democracy because, by strengthening property rights, reorganizing revenue collection

> systems, and centralizing administrative and coercive resources, market reform experiments are potentially conducive to significant increases in stateness. Even if the concentration of power in the executive may make democracy sub-optimal in the short run, in the long run, however, it generates the conditions under which a democratic political order can thrive. (Schamis 2000:208)

These arguments for a positive relationship between democratization and economic reform are supported by other considerations that target some specifics of the relationship. Przeworski (1993) has argued that, although there are necessarily potential tensions between the two, there are also more subtle ways in which they can support one another. In particular, if publics are included in the reform process, there will be dual saluatory effects. New democracies will function as real democracies (an investment in both their quality and sustainability), and the likelihood of sustained reforms will increase, given enhanced legitimacy and prospects for implementation. Both consequences flow from the fact that such reforms, shaped in a more democratic context, will be more sensitive to public concerns and therefore more likely to elicit the cooperation of the public.

A second supportive argument questions the evidence for polarization among parties and publics in response to economic downturns and/or the imposition of economic reforms—in Latin America, interwar Europe, and even in postsocialist Europe (Remmer 1990, Berman 1998, Bermeo 1998, Weyland 1998, Dmitriev 1999). Indeed, in the postsocialist context, one can note a positive relationship between commitment to sustained economic reforms and a narrowing of the political spectrum.

The case for the linkage between economic reforms and political instability in new democracies has also come into question. Economic performance does not relate well to political protest (Ekiert & Kubik 2000); the very provision of the right to vote in competitive elections can function as a mechanism for venting frustration and thereby stabilizing democracy (Greskovits 1998); and economic concerns do not figure as prominently as we might assume in the determination of voting preferences (Colton 1995, Powers & Cox 1997). This final point implies that at least some new democracies may benefit from their very newness, in the sense that publics value their newly won freedoms and vote, at least initially, on the basis of values more than interests (Rychard 1991). In this sense, the frailty of new democracies, so emphasized in the literature, may be questioned (Remmer 1990, Bunce 2000b).

Let us conclude by providing several other pieces to this puzzle. One is the positive relationship between dispersion of executive powers and progress on economic reforms in the postsocialist world (Hellman 1996, Stark & Bruszt 1998). The other asks us to rethink our understanding of public responses to dissatisfaction with the economy. As the Latin American and postsocialist cases suggest, governments that introduce economic reforms often lose political support (see Remmer 1990; Bunce 1999a,c). As a result, both the number of elections held and the rate of governmental turnover tend to be very high. However, we must remember that (*a*) one measure of democratic consolidation is peaceful turnover in governing parties, and (*b*) governmental turnover is not the same thing as political instability, particularly when ideological differences among parties are limited and when the design of electoral systems and other institutions, along with patterns in electoral results, encourage the formation of capable governments.

Several conclusions, diametrically opposed to those offered in the earlier section, follow from these arguments. Democratization and economic reform are compatible processes. Indeed, one can argue from the above evidence that each may further the agenda of the other; that is, that their combination contributes to both the introduction and continuation of market reforms, on the one hand, and the consolidation of democracy, on the other. In this way, the widely recognized coincidence between democracy and capitalism in the West may very well apply to situations where democracy is new and the capitalist economy is either being introduced or liberalized.

WHO IS RIGHT?

There are compelling reasons—theoretical and empirical, contemporary and historical—to argue that democratization and economic reform are compatible processes, and yet to argue with equal vigor that these two dynamics of change are in considerable tension with each other. The question then becomes, which interpretation is right? The evidence points to a surprising answer. In Latin America and Southern Europe, the relationship is mixed, tending toward the positive direction, in the postsocialist context, it is robust and positive (DeMelo et al 1996; Bunce 2000a; Fish 1998; H Kwon, unpublished paper). These conclusions seem to hold, moreover, when a variety of controls are introduced [though some concerns have been raised with respect to geographical-cultural considerations and patterns exhibited in time-series versus cross-sectional data (see Kopstein & Reilly 1999, Barnes & Kurtz 2000)]. Thus, we can conclude, at least on the basis of studies dealing directly with the relationship between democratization and economic reform, that there is little support for the notion of tradeoffs; that these two arenas of change are not necessarily interactive, at least in a patterned way (though this conclusion may change when additional mediating factors are introduced); that democratization and economic reform can be mutually supportive; and, finally, that this variant on the relationship is most evident in the postsocialist setting.

These conclusions are surprising for several reasons, as already noted. One is that the arguments suggesting incompatibility between democratization and economic reform were quite persuasive. Moreover, for Latin America and Southern Europe in particular, they were backed up by references to specific cases. The other is that several characteristics of the postsocialist region would seem to make its regimes less, not more, likely to demonstrate a positive correlation between democratization and economic reform. I refer to the supposed precariousness of new democracies, on the one hand, and, on the other, the necessarily radical character of economic reforms in that context and their dramatic recessionary effects. One would expect politicians to be unusually resistent to reforms, especially where democratization provides accountability; they should resist reforms that can only come about through the suspension of democratic procedures and those that generate conflicts too great for nascent democratic institutions to manage.

How, then, can we interpret the regional effects in these data? We can begin by noting that geographical location cannot constitute an explanation. Region, after all, is merely a summary term for other variables (see King 1996). Equally unsatisfactory would be substituting differences in the authoritarian past for "place" and leaving the matter at that.

The problem is twofold. First, although state socialism and Latin American/ Southern European forms of authoritarianism differed from each other, as already noted in the discussion of economic revolution versus reform, there were also considerable variations within these two versions of authoritarian politics. For example, while state socialism did have certain homogenizing effects as a result of its common origins in the Soviet experience (which even extended to socialist Yugoslavia, despite the early rebellion against the Soviet model), state socialism nonetheless produced quite variable economic and political trends in its last several decades. At the same time, few specialists would be comfortable with an argument that treated bureaucratic authoritarianism, for example, as applicable to all of Latin America and Southern Europe. Indeed, these differences, plus a desire to return to the past as a causal agent and to gain analytical leverage, particularly with respect to issues surrounding the consolidation of democracy, have led some specialists in these regions to explore variations in authoritarian rule in order to account for variations in democratic politics (see Geddes 1999). This leads to a straightforward conclusion. The impact of the authoritarian past can serve only as the beginning, not the end, of the discussion (Greskovits & Schamis 1999, Bunce 2000a). Finally, there is a methodological consideration. As Przeworski & Teune (1970) argued, the goal of comparative inquiry should be to substitute place names with variables.

The trick, therefore, is to translate what appears to be a regional effect into mediating variables. I see three as crucial. The first is the size of the electoral mandate in the first democratic election; the second is whether the government is liberal; and the third is whether the policy agenda joins democratization and economic reform. In the postsocialist world, three combinations materialized: large victories by the opposition forces, with strong commitment to both democratization and economic reform (as in, say, the Czech Republic, Slovenia, and the Baltic states); large mandates, but for the communists, with no commitment to either democratization or economic reform (Belarus and virtually all of Central Asia, minus the Kyrgyz Republic); and, finally, limited mandates, with communists either winning or sharing power with the opposition forces and a government divided in its commitments to both democratization and economic reform (e.g. Russia, Ukraine, Bulgaria, and Romania). In the first instance, democratization and economic reform were highly compatible; in the second, both were rejected; and in the third, both were compromised.

In Latin America and Southern Europe, however, these contrasts were not clear. Mandates tended to be small; winners tended to combine opposition forces with the old guard (who were rightest); and commitment to democratization and economic reform was quite variable, reflecting in part the first two considerations. In these contexts, as a result, a patterned relationship between democratization and economic reform failed to materialize. There were tradeoffs in some cases and complementarities in others.

These generalizations require us to take a step backward and compare the transitional context in the "south" (Latin America and Southern Europe) versus the "east" (the postsocialist region). One key difference was in the timing of transition. Because the south was at the beginning of the third wave and because its states had experienced fragile and transitory democratic governance, there was considerable uncertainty surrounding the most recent movement from authoritarian to democratic rule. Indeed, this is a theme in virtually all studies of these transitions (O'Donnell et al 1986, Hamann 1997). This is also why pact making between authoritarian and opposition elites is viewed with such favor (Karl 1990, Higley & Gunther 1992). Pacting reduces uncertainty by limiting the speed of change, demobilizing publics, and giving authoritarian elites a stake in the new order. Pacting is viewed, in short, as a mechanism for establishing a rough consensus through compromise and thereby enhancing both intra-elite cooperation and popular compliance. For these reasons, moreover, pacting is also seen as advantageous for economic reform.

> Not only have they created the political space necessary to adopt drastic policy measures, pacts have also inhibited popular participation in policy formation processes, thereby offering guarantees of economic policy continuity and limited socialist redistribution to propertied elites who have historically mounted the major challenges to democracy in the region.
> (Remmer 1991:794; see also Zimmerman & Saalfeld 1988)

The more general point, however, is the importance of what I term bridging—blurring the line between the old and the new order. By using this term, we can include a second characteristic common to most successful cases of democratization in the south: continuity in bureaucratic personnel (with the state off the reform agenda), and even in governing officials, as a consequence of the victory of rightest parties in founding elections (see Fishman 1990). Because of pacting and continuity in personnel, however, bridging has a dual face. It secures democracy and makes economic reform possible, but at the same time it limits reforms in both politics and economics. Thus, the search for consensus and stability in the context of these regime transitions both expanded and constrained political and economic choices. This was especially true given the context of continuing uncertainty and often fragmented party systems (Haggard & Kaufman 1995).

The postsocialist world presents a different context for transformation, largely because of when these transitions began and their specific legacies of the past. By 1989, democratization had become a global process, having spread even to Africa and Asia. Many of the earliest cases, moreover, had demonstrated that new democracies could survive and prosper. At the same time, state socialism had created in some countries a popular consensus around democratization, if only because democracy represented the polar opposite of the authoritarian regime—that is, to use my earlier language, uncertain outcomes and certain procedures. This can be seen, for example, in variations during the socialist era in episodes of popular protest and reform socialism. Also important for some of these countries during the socialist era was a marriage between liberalism and nationalism—a fusion between opposition to communism, national identities, and liberal political ideologies. This was most obvious in the case of Poland, the leader of the events of 1989 (see Bunce 1999c). Two other factors further reduced uncertainty in some of these countries where this consensus was in place: the existence of international institutions suporting human rights, democratization, and economic reform (which were particularly influential in east-central Europe, the eastward boundary of the European Union); and the outcome of the founding elections. It is important to rcognize that the best predictor of both democratization and economic reform in the postsocialist region seems to be whether the opposition forces registered a decisive victory in the first competitive election (Bunce 1994, Fish 1998). This occured when national, indeed nationalist, fronts emerged from the wreckage of communism, commanded widespread popular support, and embraced liberal ideology.

What I am suggesting, therefore, is that breakage, not bridging, was the strategy that proved more successful in the east. In judging success, I refer to indicators of both (*a*) the vitality and durability of democracy and (*b*) commitment to sustained economic reforms. Success through breakage occurred largely because conditions in the timing and content of transformation made the extreme situation possible: more certainty, considerable intra-elite and public consensus, and less authoritarian "drag" on policy making, all of which reflected large governing mandates enjoyed by liberal opposition parties. In certain ways, then, the end of state socialism created for some countries the optimal conditions for democratization and economic reform—what Balcerowicz (1995) terms "extraordinary politics"—and what is recognized more generally as the power of large mandates to translate, if ideology is willing, into innovative policies, economic and otherwise. It is also interesting to note in this regard the familiar argument, applied primarily to East Asia, regarding the importance of elite consensus for robust economic performance (Sapir 1999).

However, this leaves one question—why economic reform and not just democratization was central to regime priorities when mandates were large in the post-socialist context. This introduces a final contrast: the content of the government's policy agenda. In the south, many economies had already undergone some reforms prior to democratization (this was the case for Hungary as well). Moreover, the economic pressures to pursue market reforms, though present in the south, were less compelling than in the east, given contrasts in both macroeconomic imbalances at the time of transition and the more fundamental contrast, noted above, between economic reforms and an economic revolution. Finally, if economic necessity was variable, so was political feasibility. The existence of a capitalist economy and prior episodes of democratization had left well-defined and diverse interests in place. As a result, the management of economic reform as a political process was difficult and rested on a variety of considerations specific to each case. The diversity of interests, joined with thin mandates, the uncertain nature of these transitions, and the inclusiveness of pacting, coupled with heightened fears where pacting did not materialize, muddied the relationship between democratization and economic reform.

In the postsocialist context, however, the ideological spectrum of the government ranged from fully liberal to fully illiberal. If we focus on the first variant, we can see why democratization and economic reform were joined. This was not just a matter of belief or the empowerment derived from mandate. It was also judged a political necessity. State socialism had fused politics and economics and created, in the process, a conjoined economic and political monopoly. To end that system and to build a new one required a single tactic: fullscale and rapid deregulation of both the polity and the economy. Without a two-front war, both battles would be lost. The empirical evidence has borne out this assumption.

Before we leave this question of mandates and policy agenda and their impact on the relationship between democratization and economic reform, we need to recognize two further points. First, much has been made of the destructive consequences of nationalism, especially for democratization but also for economic reforms. This argument has been applied, in particular, to the postsocialist world. However, this interpretation ignores conditions—in a minority of cases, to be sure—where national identities are well-formed and congruent with state boundaries; where nationalism is closely tied to a liberal project; and where nationalism played a key role in ending authoritarian rule. Under these conditions, nationalism is an asset, not only for democracy but also for economic reform. This is because nationalism lengthens the time horizons of publics as well as leaders (see Abdelal 1999). This was precisely what happened, for example, in Poland, an old state, and in the new states of Slovenia, Lithuania, Estonia, and Latvia.

The second point is that this discussion of governing mandates and ideological commitments implies the explanatory power of the authoritarian past. In many studies, particularly of postsocialist transitions, the power of the past is often treated as a general condition, shaping every aspect of the transformation; it is often assumed to mean obstacles to democratization and economic reform; and it is often used to support arguments about the considerable difficulties of comparing postsocialist countries with other countries having a different authoritarian lineage. The claim made here, however, is different. All I am suggesting is that the authoritarian past seems to affect the relationship between democratization and economic reform, and, depending on developments during state socialism, the past can enable or constrain the new political and economic order. Finally, differences between state socialism and authoritarianism in Latin America do not call into question either the logic or the benefits of comparing these two regions (Bunce 2000b, Greskovits 2000).

CONCLUSIONS

The rapid expansion of democratic regimes around the world has produced a lively debate concerning their prospects for survival and consolidation. This issue assumes particular importance in the face of another global trend, the introduction of market reforms. The question then becomes whether the two processes are complementary. Is there, in brief, a positive or a negative correlation between democratization and economic reform?

Three conclusions follow from this survey of theoretical arguments and empirical studies of democratization and economic reform in three regions, namely Latin America, Southern Europe, and the postsocialist area. First, both interpretations have considerable merit, given their theoretical foundations and supportive studies that target elements of this relationship. One can argue with some confidence that democratization and economic reform will be highly interactive, and that the form of this interaction will suggest either compatibility or tradeoffs between the two. Second, empirical studies that directly address this question leave us with two answers, depending upon the region considered. In Latin America and Southern Europe, the relationship between democratization and economic reform is weak. There is no clear pattern suggesting a predictable interaction, either positive or negative. However, in the postsocialist region, the relationship is both positive and robust. Thus, the more democratic the regime, the greater its propensity to introduce and sustain economic reforms. Conversely, less democracy combines with less economic reform; at the extreme, continuation of authoritarian rule is associated with the absence of economic reform. Region has powerful effects; democratization can coexist quite happily with economic reforms; and the case for a clear tradeoff between the two, though no doubt relevant to individual cases (as we see, for instance, in Argentina or Peru), has little support once we expand the number of cases—within or across regions.

The regional effect should be understood not as a question of geography but rather as indicative of intervening factors. Three were highlighted above: whether democratically elected governments have sizeable mandates, whether the government is liberal, and whether the policy agenda is committed to deepening democracy and reforming the economy. Capacity, commitment, and policy content, therefore, are critical. Together, they help account for variations between the east and the south. This, in turn, gives greater precision to the argument that the authoritarian past is important in shaping the politics and economics that follow.

LITERATURE CITED

Abdelal R. 1999. *Economic nationalism after empire: a comparative perspective on nation, economy and security in post-soviet Eurasia.* PhD thesis. Cornell Univ., Ithaca, NY. 296 pp.

Appel H. 1997. Voucher privatisation in Russia:

structural consequences and mass response in the second period of reform. *Eur.-Asia Stud.* 49:1433–49

Appel H. 1999. *Reconsidering the determinants of economic policy-making: lessons from privatization in transition countries.* Presented at Annu. Meet. Am. Polit. Sci. Assoc., 94th, Atlanta

Aslund L, Boone P, Johnson S. 1996. How to stabilize: lessons from post-communist countries. *Brookings Pap. Econ. Activity* 1: 217–313

Balcerowicz L. 1995. *Socialism, Capitalism, Transformation.* Budapest: Centr. Eur. Univ. Press

Barnes S, Kurtz M. 2000. *Ten years of post-communist transitions: Does economic liberalization lead to democratization?* Presented at Annu. Meet. Midwest Polit. Sci. Assoc., 45th, Chicago

Berman S. 1997. Civil society and the collapse of the Weimar Republic. *World Polit.* 49:401–29

Berman S. 1998. Path dependency and political action: reexamining responses to the depression. *Comp. Polit.* 30:379–400

Bermeo N. 1998. *Getting mad or going mad: citizens, scarcity and the breakdown of democracy in interwar Europe.* Monogr. 10, Cent. Stud. Democr., Univ. Calif., Irvine, CA

Bienen H, Herbst J. 1996. The relationship between political and economic reform in Africa. *Comp. Polit.* 29:23–42

Blanchard O, Dornbusch R, Krugman P, Layard R, Summers L. 1991. *Economic Reforms in the East.* Cambridge, MA: MIT Press

Blejer M, Coricelli F. 1995. *A Dialogue with Reformers in Eastern Europe.* London: Elgar

Bunce V. 1991. Stalinism and the management of uncertainty. In *The Transition to Democracy in Hungary*, ed. G Szoboszlai, pp. 138–64. Budapest: Inst. Polit. Sci.

Bunce V. 1994. Sequencing political and economic reforms. In *East-Central European Economies in Transition*, ed. J Hardt, R Kaufman, pp. 46–63. Washington, DC: Joint Econ. Comm./US Congr.

Bunce V. 1999a. The political economy of post-socialism. *Slavic Rev.* 58:756–93

Bunce V. 1999b. The return of the left and the future of democracy in eastern and central Europe. In *Political Parties: Essays in Honor of Samuel Eldersveld*, ed. B Yesilada, pp. 151–76. Ann Arbor: Univ. Mich. Press

Bunce V. 1999c. *Subversive Institutions: The Design and the Destruction of Socialism and the State.* Cambridge: Cambridge Univ. Press

Bunce V. 2000a. Comparative democratization: big and bounded generalizations. *Comp. Polit. Stud.* 333:703–34

Bunce V. 2000b. *The lessons of postcommunism for recent democratization.* Presented at Annu. Meet. Am. Polit. Sci. Assoc., 96th, Washington, DC

Centeno MA. 1994. Between rocky democracies and hard markets: dilemmas of the double transition. *Annu. Rev. Sociol.* 20:125–41

Clague C, Keefer P, Knack S, Olson M. 1997. Democracy, autocracy, and the institutions supportive of economic development. In *Institutions and Economic Development: Growth and Governance in Less Developed and Postsocialist Countries*, ed. J Clague, pp. 91–120. Baltimore, MD: Johns Hopkins Univ. Press

Colton T. 1995. Economics and voting in Russia. *Post-Sov. Aff.* 12:122–47

1997. The comparative survey of freedom. *Freedom Rev.* 28:16–19

Dahl R. 1971. *Polyarchy.* New Haven, CT: Yale Univ. Press

Dahl R. 1992. Why free markets are not enough. *J. Democr.* 3:82–89

Dahl R. 1998. *On Democracy.* New Haven, CT: Yale Univ. Press

Dawisha K, Deets S. 1999. *The divine comedy of postcommunist elections.* Work. pap., Dep. Gov./Cent. Postcommunist Soc., Univ. Maryland

DeMelo M, Denizer C, Gelb A. 1996. From plan to market: patterns of transition. *Transit. Newsl. Reforming Econ.* 6:4–6

Dmitriev M. 1999. Party economic programs and implications. In *Primer on Russia's 1999 Duma Elections*, ed. M McFaul, N Petrov, A Ryabov, with E Reisch, pp. 37–58. Moscow: Carnegie Moscow Cent.

European Bank for Reconstruction and Development (EBRD). 1999. EBRD and World Bank survey reveals intimate state enterprise relationship. *Transit. Newsl. Reforming Econ.* 10:6–10

Ekiert G, Kubik J. 2000. *Rebellious Civil Society*. Ann Arbor: Univ. Michigan Press

Esping-Anderson G. 1990. *The Three Worlds of Welfare Capitalism*. Cambridge, UK: Polity

Eyal G, Szelenyi I, Townsley E. 1998. *Making Capitalism without Capitalists: Class Formation and Elite Struggles in Post-Communist Europe*. London: Verso

Fish S. 1998. The determinants of economic reform in the post-communist world. *East Eur. Polit. Soc.* 12:31–78

Fishman R. 1990. Rethinking state and regime: southern Europe's transition to democracy. *World Polit.* 42:422–40

Frieden J. 1991. *Debt, Development and Democracy*. Princeton, NJ: Princeton Univ. Press

Gaidar E. 1995. *Gosudarstvo i evoliutsiia*. Moscow: Evratsiia

Garrett G. 1998. *Partisan Politics in the Global Economy*. Cambridge: Cambridge Univ. Press

Geddes B. 1999. What do we know about democratization after twenty years? *Annu. Rev. Polit. Sci.* 2:129–48

Gourevitch P. 1986. *Politics in Hard Times: Comparative Responses to International Crisis*. Ithaca, NY: Cornell Univ. Press

Gray CW, Hendley K. 1997. Developing commercial law in transition economies: examples from Hungary and Russia. In *The Rule of Law: Economic Reform in Russia*, ed. J Sachs, K Pistor, pp. 139–68. Boulder, CO: Westview

Greskovits B. 1998. *The Political Economy of Protest and Patience*. Budapest: Centr. Eur. Univ. Press

Greskovits B. 2000. Rival views of postcommunist market society: on the path dependency of transitology. In *Democratic and Capitalist Transitions in Eastern Europe*, ed. M Dobry, pp. 19–48. Dordrecht: Kluwer

Greskovits B, Schamis H. 1999. *Democratic capitalism and the state in Eastern Europe and Latin America*. Presented at Annu. Meet. Am. Polit. Sci. Assoc., 95th, Atlanta

Haggard S, Kaufman R. 1992a. Economic adjustments and the prospects for democracy. See Haggard & Kaufman 1992d, pp. 319–50

Haggard S, Kaufman R. 1992b. Institutions and economic adjustment. See Haggard & Kaufman 1992d, pp. 3–40

Haggard S, Kaufman R. 1992c. The political economy of inflation in middle income countries. See Haggard & Kaufman 1992d, pp. 270–318

Haggard S, Kaufman R. 1992d. *The Politics of Economic Adjustment*. Princeton, NJ: Princeton Univ. Press

Haggard S, Kaufman R. 1995. *The Political Economy of Democratic Transitions*. Princeton, NJ: Princeton Univ. Press

Hamann K. 1997. The pacted transition to democracy and labour politics in Spain. *S. Eur. Soc. Polit.* 2:110–38

Hanson S, Kopstein J. 1997. The Weimar/Russia comparison. *Post-Sov. Aff.* 13:252–83

Hellman J. 1998. Winners take all: the politics of partial reform in postcommunist transitions. *World Polit.* 50:203–34

Hellman J. 1996. Constitutions and economic reform in the postcommunist transition. *E. Eur. Const. Rev.* 5:46–56

Hendley K. 1997. Legal development in Post-Soviet Russia. *Post-Sov. Aff.* 13:228–51

Higley J, Gunther R. 1992. Spain: the very model of a modern elite settlement. In *Elites and Democratic Consolidation*, ed. J Higley, R Gunther, pp. 3–27. Baltimore, MD: Johns Hopkins Univ. Press

Hirschman AO. 1968. The political economy of import-substituting industrialization in Latin America. *Q. J. Econ.* 82:2–32

Hirschman AO. 1987. On the political

economy of Latin American development. *Latin Am. Res. Rev.* 22:7–36

Holmes S. 1997. What Russia teaches us now. *Am. Prospect* 33:30–39

Huntington S. 1991. *The Third Wave: Democratization in the Late Twentieth Century*. Norman: Univ. Okla. Press

1998. Interview with Grzegorz Kolodko: economic neoliberalism almost became irrelevant. *Transit. Newsl. Transforming Econ.* 9:1–6

Kahler M. 1990. Orthodoxy and its alternatives: explaining approaches to stabilization and adjustment. In *Economic Crisis and Policy Choice*, ed. J Nelson, pp. 33–61. Princeton, NJ: Princeton Univ. Press

Iversen T, Pontusson J. 2000. Comparative political economy: a northern European perspective. In *Unions, Employers and Central Banks: Macroeconomic Coordination and Institutional Change in Social Market Economies*, ed. T Iverson, J Pontusson, D Soskice, pp. 1–37. Cambridge: Cambridge Univ. Press

Karl T. 1990. Dilemmas of democratization in Latin America. *Comp. Polit.* 23:1–22

Karl T. 1995. The hybrid regimes of Central America. *J. Democr.* 6:134–50

Kaufman R. 1986. Liberalization and democratization in South America: perspectives from the 1970s. In *Transitions from Authoritarian Rule*, ed. G O'Donnell, P Schmitter, L Whitehead, pp. 85–107. Baltimore, MD: Johns Hopkins Univ. Press

King G. 1996. Why context should not count. *Polit. Geogr.* 15:159–64

Kitschelt H, Mansfeldova Z, Markowski R, Toka G. 1999. *Post-Communist Party Systems: Competition, Representation, and Inter-Party Cooperation*. Cambridge: Cambridge Univ. Press

Knight A. 1998. Populism and neo-populism in Latin America, especially Mexico. *J. Latin Am. Stud.* 30:223–48

Kolodko G. 1998. *Equity issues in policymaking in transition economies*. Presented at Conf. Econ. Policy and Equity, Washington, DC

Kolodko G. 1999. *Ten years of post-socialist transition: lessons for policy reform*. Washington, DC: World Bank/Dev. Res. Group

Kopstein J, Reilly D. 1999. Explaining the why of the why: a comment on Fish's determinants of economic reforms in the post-communist world. *E. Eur. Polit. Soc.* 13:613–26

Kornai J. 1992. *The Socialist System: The Political Economy of Communism*. Princeton, NJ: Princeton Univ. Press

Kullberg J, Zimmerman W. 1999. Liberal elites and socialist masses and problems of Russian democratization. *World Polit.* 51:323–58

Kwon H. 1999. *The Impact of Regional Context on Democratization: An Empirical Test*. Unpubl. manuscript, Cornell Univ.

Ledeneva AV. 1998. *Russia's Economy of Favors: Blat, Networking, and Informal Exchange*. Cambridge: Cambridge Univ. Press

Lindblom C. 1977. *Politics and Markets*. New York: Basic

Lipset S. 1959. Some social requisites of democracy: economic development and political legitimacy. *Am. Polit. Sci. Rev.* 53:245–59

Mann M. 1993. *The Sources of Social Power*. Vol. II. *The Rise of Classes and Nation-States*, 1760–1914. Cambridge: Cambridge Univ. Press

Londregan J, Poole K. 1996. Does high income promote democracy? *World Polit.* 49:56–91

Maravall JM. 1993. Politics and policy: economic reforms in southern Europe. In *Economic Reforms in New Democracies: A Social Democratic Approach*, ed. LCB Pereira, JM Maravall, A Przeworski, pp. 77–131. Cambridge: Cambridge Univ. Press

Milanovic B. 1992. The world of welfare socialism and the transition to capitalism. *Transit. Newsl. Reforming Econ.* 3:1–3

Moore B. 1966. *Social Origins of Dictatorship and Democracy*. Boston: Beacon

Moser R. 1999. Independents and party formation: elite partisanship as an intervening variable in Russian politics. *Comp. Polit.* 31:740–71

Murrell P. 1992. Conservative political philosophy and the strategy of economic transition. *E. Eur. Polit. Soc.* 6:3–16

Murrell P. 1993. What is shock therapy? What did it do in Poland and Russia? *Post-Sov. Aff.* 9:111–40

Murrell P. 1996. How far has the transition progressed? *J. Econ. Persp.* 10:25–44

North D. 1990. *Institutions, Institutional Change, and Economic Performance*. Cambridge: Cambridge Univ. Press

Nove A. 1980. Socialism, centralised planning and the one-party state. In *Authority, Politics and Policy in the USSR*, ed. TH Rigby, A Brown, P Reddaway, pp. 77–97. New York: St. Martin's

O'Donnell G, Schmitter P, Whitehead L. 1986. *Transitions from Authoritarian Rule*, Vols. 1–4. Baltimore: Johns Hopkins Univ. Press

O'Donnell G. 1993. On the state, democratization and some conceptual problems: a Latin American view with glances at some postcommunist countries. *World Dev.* 21:1355–69

O'Donnell G. 1994. Delegative democracy. *J. Democr.* 5:55–69

O'Donnell G. 1996. Illusions about consolidation. *J. Democr.* 7:34–51

Okun A. 1982. *Equality and Efficiency: The Big Trade-off.* Washington, DC: Brookings Inst.

Olson M. 1981. *The Rise and Decline of Nations*. New Haven, CT: Yale Univ. Press

Orenstein M. 1998. Lawless from above and below: economic radicalism and political institutions. *SAIS Rev.* 18:35–50

Pereira LCB, Maravall JM, Przeworski A. 1993. *Economic Reforms in New Democracies: A Social Democratic Approach*. Cambridge: Cambridge Univ. Press

Pereira LCB, Maravall JM, Przeworski A. 1993. Introduction. See Pereira et al 1993, pp. 3–47

Pinto B, Drebenstov V, Morozov A. 1999. Nonpayments cycle in Russia suffocates economic growth: proposal of World Bank economists. *Transit. Newsl. Reforming Econ.* 10:1–5

Polanyi K. 1957. *The Great Transformation*. Boston: Beacon

Popov V. 1999. *Explaining the magnitude of the transformational recession*. Moscow: Grad. School Int. Bus.

Popov V. 2000. *The political economy of growth in Russia*. Program on New Approaches to Russian Security, No. 17. Davis Cent., Harvard Univ.

Powers D, Cox JH. 1997. Echoes from the past: the relationship between satisfaction with economic reforms and voting behavior in Poland. *Am. Polit. Sci. Rev.* 91:617–33

Poznanski K. 1996. *Poland's Protracted Transit. Institutional Change and Economic Growth, 1970–1994*. Cambridge: Cambridge Univ. Press

Przeworski A. 1991. *Democracy and the Market*. Cambridge: Cambridge Univ. Press

Przeworski A. 1992. The neoliberal fallacy. *J. Democr.* 3:45–59

Przeworski A. 1993. Economic reform, public opinion and political institutions. See Pereira et al 1993, pp. 122–48

Przeworski A. 1995. *The Sustainability of Democracy*. Cambridge: Cambridge Univ. Press

Przeworski A, Alvarez M, Cheibub J, Limongi F. 1996. What makes democracies endure? *J. Democr.* 7:39–55

Przeworski A, Limongi F. 1997. Modernization: facts and theories. *World Polit.* 49:155–84

Przeworski A, Stokes SC, Manin B. 1999. *Democracy, Accountability and Representation*. Cambridge: Cambridge Univ. Press

Przeworski A, Teune H. 1970. *The Logic of Comparative Inquiry*. New York: Wiley-Interscience

Putnam R. 1993. *Making Democracy Work: Civic Traditions in Modern Italy*. Princeton, NJ: Princeton Univ. Press

Remmer K. 1990. Democracy and economic crisis: the Latin American experience. *World Polit.* 42:315–35

Remmer K. 1991. The political impact of

the economic crisis in Latin America in the 1980s. *Am. Polit. Sci. Rev.* 85:777–800

Remmer K. 1995. New theoretical perspectives on democratization. *Comp. Polit.* 28:105–19

Roberts A. 1998. Neoliberalism and the transformation of populism in Latin America. *World Polit.* 48:2–116

Roland G. 1994. The role of political constraints in transition economies. *Econ. Transit.* 2:59–78

Rose-Ackerman S. 1999. *Corruption and Government: Causes, Consequences and Reform.* Cambridge: Cambridge Univ. Press

Russia on the Brink. 1998. Helen Kellogg Inst. Int. Stud. No. 31. Univ. Notre Dame

Rychard A. 1991. Stare and nowe instytucje zycia publicznego. In *Polacy 90*, ed. L Kolinska-Bobarska, A Rychard, E Wnuk-Lipinski, pp. 201–23. Warsaw: Polish Acad. Sci.

Sachs J. 1993. *Poland's Jump to a Market Economy.* Cambridge, MA: MIT Press

Sachs J, Pistor K. 1997. Introduction: progress, pitfalls, scenarios and lost opportunities. In *The Rule of Law and Economic Reform in Russia*, ed. J Sachs, K Pistor, pp. 10–22. Boulder, CO: Westview

Sapir J. 1999. Russia's crash in August 1998: diagnosis and prescription. *Post-Sov. Aff.* 15:10–36

Schamis H. 1999. Distributional coalitions and the politics of economic reform in Latin America. *World Polit.* 50:235–65

Schamis H. 2000. *Re-forming the State: the Politics of Privatization in Latin America and Europe.* Unpublished book manuscript

Schmitter P, Karl T. 1991. What democracy is...and is not. *J. Democr.* 2:75–88

Shenfield S. 2001. Foreign assistance as genocide: the crisis in Russia, the IMF, and interethnic relations. In *International Institutions and Ethnic Conflict*, ed. M Esman, R Herring. Ann Arbor: Univ. Michigan Press. In press

Shlaifer A, Treisman D. 2000. *Without a Map: Political Tactics and Economic Reform in Russia.* Cambridge, MA: MIT Press

Soskice D. 1999. Divergent production regimes: coordinated and uncoordinated market economies in the 1980s and 1990s. In *Continuity and Change in Contemporary Capitalism*, ed. H Kitschelt, P Lange, G Marks, J Stephens, pp. 101–34. Cambridge: Cambridge Univ. UK/USA

Stallings B. 1992. International influences on economic policy: debt, stabilization, and structural reform. In *The Politics of Economic Adjustment: International Constraints, Distributive Conflicts, and the State*, ed. S Haggard, R Kaufman, pp. 127–49. Princeton, NJ: Princeton Univ. Press

Stallings B, Kaufman R. 1989. Debt and democracy in the 1980s: the Latin American experience. In *Debt and Democracy in Latin America*, ed. B Stallings, R Kaufman, pp. 3–38. Boulder, CO: Westview

Stark D, Bruszt L. 1998. *Postsocialist Pathways: Transforming Politics and Property in East Central Europe.* Cambridge: Cambridge Univ. Press

Stiglitz J. 2000. What I learned at the world economic crisis. *New Republic* 88:1–3

Story J, Pollack B. 1991. Spain's transit. Domestic and external linkages. In *Encouraging Democracy: The International Context of Regime Transitions in Southern Europe*, ed. G Pridham, pp. 125–55. New York: St. Martin's

Thornhill J. 2000. Russia's unique economy may have led to 1998 crisis. *Finan. Times,* Feb. 22, p. 3

Tismaneanu V. 1998. *Fantasies of Salvation: Democracy, Nationalism and Myth in Postcommunist Europe.* Princeton, NJ: Princeton Univ. Press

Walton J, Seddon D. 1984. *Free Markets and Food Riots: The Politics of Global Adjustment.* Oxford, UK: Blackwell

Weyland K. 1998. Swallowing the bitter pill: sources of popular support for neoliberal reform in Latin America. *Comp. Polit. Stud.* 31:539–68

Winiecki J. 1990. Why economic reforms fail in the socialist system—a property rights–based approach. *Econ. Inquiry* 28:195–221

Woodruff D. 2000. *Money Unmade: Barter and the Fate of Russian Capitalism*. Ithaca, NY: Cornell Univ. Press

Yashar D. 1997. *Demanding Democracy: Reform and Reaction in Costa Rica and Guatemala, 1870s–1950s*. Stanford, CA: Stanford Univ. Press

Zimmerman E, Saalfeld T. 1988. Economic and political reactions to the world economic crisis in the 1930s in six European countries. *Int. Stud. Q.* 32:305–34

Annu. Rev. Polit. Sci. 2001. 4:67–92

PSYCHOLOGY AND INTERNATIONAL RELATIONS THEORY

J. M. Goldgeier[1] and P. E. Tetlock[2]

[1]*Department of Political Science, George Washington University, 2201 G. Street NW, Washington, DC 20052; e-mail: jimg@gwu.edu;*

[2]*Departments of Psychology and Political Science, Ohio State University, 142 Townshend Hall, 1885 Neil Avenue, Columbus, Ohio 43210; e-mail: tetlock.1@osu.edu*

Key Words error and bias, tradeoff reasoning, prospect theory, accountability pressures, internalization

■ **Abstract** Organized around several major theoretical traditions in international relations, this essay suggests which literature in psychology should be of greatest interest to different kinds of international relations scholars. New work in cognitive social psychology and behavioral decision theory simultaneously expands on and qualifies earlier error-and-bias portraits of the foreign policy maker, thereby enriching our understanding of internal divisions within the realist camp. Work on bounded rationality in competitive markets and mixed-motive games, as well as the literature on the power of human emotions to shape judgments of what represents an equitable allocation of scarce resources or a just resolution of conflicts of interest, can inform neo-institutionalist and constructivist theories. Developments in cross-cultural social psychology shed light on constructivist arguments about the creation and maintenance of international social order that typically rest on assumptions about decision making that are qualitatively different from realist and institutionalist approaches to world politics.

INTRODUCTION

At first glance, the central macro-level theories of international politics appear to rely on minimal assumptions about human cognition and motivation. For realists, states are power or security maximizers; for liberals and neoliberal institutionalists, they are wealth or utility maximizers. For constructivists, human nature is itself a social construction and the appropriate focus is on the intricate webs of normative understanding that shape and are shaped by international actors. Although most scholars in these traditions believe that their models have little or no need to rely on psychological models of individual and group behavior, we argue in this review that they are wrong for a host of interrelated reasons.

They are wrong partly because when we scrutinize what these traditions trumpet as their most distinctive explanatory achievements, we discover that their capacity to explain relevant trends or events hinges on a wider range of implicit psychological assumptions that it is useful to make explicit. In this sense, these macro theorists are already more psychological than they think. And when we shift attention to each tradition's explanatory shortcomings, we believe these can be at least partly corrected by incorporating other psychological assumptions into the conceptual frameworks. In this sense, these macro theories are not as psychological as they should be. We also argue that one of the major benefits of weaving psychological analysis into the fabric of international relations theorizing will be the gradual unveiling of boundary conditions on the applicability of competing frameworks.

The goal of this essay is to demonstrate how developments in psychology can inform what international relations (IR) theorists generally refer to as second-level and third-level arguments about interstate politics (Waltz 1959). We are not arguing that all important regularities in world politics are reducible to psychological laws. Indeed, we suspect that, strictly speaking, none are so reducible. Our guiding philosophy of social science is contextualist, not reductionist. Psychological arguments acquire explanatory force only when they are systematically assimilated into political frameworks that take into account the structural, economic, and cultural conditions within which policy makers work.

This essay considers several major theoretical traditions in IR and suggests which literature in psychology should be of greatest interest to different kinds of IR scholars. Because of space constraints, we focus chiefly on neorealism, neoliberal institutionalism, and constructivism, and within each, we emphasize those aspects of the frameworks that link up in particularly compelling ways with the social psychological literature.

Following the path-breaking work of Jervis (1976) on cognitive constraints on rational decision making within a realist framework, we identify work in cognitive social psychology and behavioral decision theory that simultaneously expands on and qualifies Jervis's error-and-bias portrait of the foreign policy maker and thereby enriches our understanding of internal divisions within the realist camp.

Following developments in behavioral economics, we argue that neoliberal institutionalist and constructivist theories could draw much more effectively than they do from work on bounded rationality in competitive markets and mixed-motive games (Simon 1957, 1982; Kahneman & Tversky 1979, 1984). Also important is the literature on the power of human emotions—often tightly coupled to ideology as well as conceptions of fairness and procedural justice—to shape judgments of what represents an equitable allocation of scarce resources or a just resolution of conflicts of interest.

Following developments in cross-cultural social psychology, we contend that constructivist arguments about the creation and maintenance of international social order typically rest on assumptions about decision making that are qualitatively different from realist and institutionalist approaches to world politics. Experimental work on tradeoff reasoning sheds light on why some decision makers may view a choice as immoral whereas others are comfortable rationally weighing costs and benefits (e.g. considering the use of taboo biological, chemical, or nuclear weapons systems) or why some decision makers perceive a choice to be moral that others would find irrational (e.g. refusing to enter into a profitable trading or beneficial security relationship with a country that violates human rights internally or fails to protect its environment).

There is no single school of psychological thought from which we draw. Different facets of psychology shed light on the diverse problems addressed by IR theories: identifying and responding to threats to security, recognizing opportunities to achieve more effective economic coordination, and building transnational communities that are not readily reducible to a security or economic calculus. The psychological formulations on which we draw most extensively include the following:

1. the well-known work on cognitive bias and error and the less well-known work on how robust those biases are when decision makers are accountable to skeptical constituencies and/or face the prospect of intellectually sharper adversaries taking advantage of their cognitive foibles;
2. prospect theory and related formulations regarding risk-taking propensities that highlight the importance of the status quo and that specify how risk tolerance varies as a function of whether decision makers frame problems as potential losses or potential gains;
3. theories of procedural and distributive justice that remind us that most people, policy makers included, have strong moral intuitions about how institutions should make decisions and the types of decisions institutions should make (moral intuitions that are often in conflict with the purely instrumental prescriptions of *homo economicus*);
4. theories of cross-cultural psychology that go beyond specifying how people think to advance testable propositions specifying how they relate to one another. In particular, we discuss normative taxonomies of relational schemata that can help constructivists to classify the different kinds of transnational communities that have arisen or might arise and to understand how normative logics change as transformations of these communities occur.

REALISM

Ironically, given the emphatic rejection of psychology by leading structural realists (Waltz 1959, 1979), it turns out that the incorporation of explicit psychological assumptions is more advanced in the realist—and particularly the neorealist—framework. This is partly because of the seminal influence of Jervis's work on the sources of misperception and partly because misperceptions in the domain of war and peace are so visibly costly to states and their societies, triggering great interest in the failure of some states to play the international power game well.

Those who believe they have the least need to take account of psychological processes are the strict structural realists (Waltz 1979, Mearsheimer 1990, Layne 1993). Within this orthodox camp, some treat states as security maximizers in an anarchic state system that requires them to practice balance-of-power politics (Waltz 1979, Grieco 1990, Layne 1993); others attribute more grandiose objectives to states and depict them as power maximizers pursuing hegemonic aspirations (Mearsheimer 1994/1995, 2001). Waltz's framework predicts a general tendency for states to make rational, security-maximizing decisions as they are socialized into the international system (and states that are slow to learn the rules disappear). For Mearsheimer, states are under even greater pressure to form accurate representations of the world and respond to the actions of other powers in a timely manner. Either way, states tend to be deeply suspicious and deem it prudent to make worst-case assumptions about the actions of other states in the system, since the penalties for being wrong in a self-help environment are so severe.

Even these pure versions of neorealism implicitly reflect psychological assumptions. The security-maximizing defensive positionalist argument allows for the possibility that states can become satisfied with their position in the system. These status quo powers will tend to be loss averse and disinclined to pursue expansionist policies that could trigger counterbalancing by other states. The power-maximizing offensive variant views states as more gain seeking and assumes they are never satisfied short of hegemony.

Prospect theory—arguably the most influential alternative to subjective expected-utility maximization—can play a role within realism in helping to distinguish conditions under which the Waltz or Mearsheimer model of state motivation applies. Prospect theory posits that under certain conditions, decision makers should be especially willing to take riskier courses of action than would be justified based on calculations of their expected final asset position, and these conditions are as follows: First, they have not made psychological peace with their losses; second, they underweight subjective probabilities of failure by treating small probabilities as functionally equivalent to zero; and third, they overweight subjective probabilities of success by treating large probabilities as equivalent to 1.0 (certainty). By contrast, decision makers should be especially reluctant to take courses of action as risky as those stipulated by expected-value calculations when they have renormalized perceptions of what is rightfully theirs in response to recent gains, when they overweight small probabilities of failure by dwelling on them, and when they underweight large probabilities of success by ruminating over how things could go wrong.

Prospect theory has received extensive support in the experimental literature on choice, and although critical information is often missing (Boettcher 1995), it has been widely applied in the IR field (Levy 1992; Farnham 1994, 1997; McDermott 1998). When states are in the domain of losses (or, like Serbia, have not psychologically adjusted to ancient losses), they are more likely to take the irredentist approach that Mearsheimer posits (e.g. Germany in 1939, Japan in 1941). When states are in the domain of gain, they are more likely to accept the status quo, as Waltz would predict (examples, arguably, are the US reluctance to incur any casualties in interventions abroad in the 1990s—Haiti, Somalia, Bosnia, and Kosovo—as well as NATO's hesitation about expanding into parts of Eastern Europe more sensitive to Russia, notwithstanding Russia's palpable weakness).

Prospect theory also sheds light on the oft-noted differences between deterrence and compellence. It is far more difficult to induce a state to give up something that it already possesses than to prevent it from taking something that it does not possess (Schelling 1967). Indeed, prospect theory—and associated work on the endowment effect, which is the increase in value one places on something once one possesses it (Kahneman et al 1991)—suggests crude quantitative estimates of how much more difficult it is: Prospective gains often need to be roughly twice as large as prospective losses to be of commensurate value.

The Number of "Poles"

Structural realists argue that errors in statecraft are more likely as the number of great powers increases. With more great powers, uncertainty grows about who will ally with whom. In this view, a bipolar world—one with only two great powers (as existed during the Cold War)—is most stable. For other realists, the focus is not on the static distribution of power at any given moment but rather on the dynamic ebb and flow of military, economic, and technological capabilities of declining and rising powers (Blainey 1973; Gilpin 1981; Wohlforth 1993, 1999; Schweller 1996, 1998), an ebb and flow that inevitably increases uncertainty about the proper course of action for hegemons and challengers alike.

Regardless of the source of the difficulty—the complexity created by multipolarity or the ambiguities created by chance—even these psychologically minimalist variants of realism open the door to considerations of error and bias. The greater complexity of multipolarity increases the difficulty of timely and accurate information processing regarding the distribution of capabilities. The finite information-processing capacity of states (and implicitly the decision makers within them) can be overwhelmed by environments with unfavorable signal-to-noise ratios. Miscalculation becomes more likely either when the balance is harder to measure or when there is increasing uncertainty about one's future position in the system. This greater likelihood of miscalculation, in turn, increases the prospects for war.

The psychological literature suggests that decision makers are susceptible to dilution effects. They often lose confidence in the diagnosticity of predictively useful cues when those cues are embedded in arrays of utterly nondiagnostic cues (Nisbett et al 1981, Tetlock & Boettger 1989). From this standpoint, the more unfavorable the signal-to-noise ratio, the greater the risk that decision makers will be distracted by irrelevancies, which may have been intentionally introduced by adversaries to confuse the real issues at stake.

The dilution literature and the broader body of work on information overload mean that sometimes decision makers are distracted because there are too many balls in the air (multipolarity), sometimes because the ball is moving too fast (periods of hegemonic transition), at other times because, although there is only one ball, there are lots of other things in the air (complex pluralistic polities that send out contradictory cues), and finally because the air is so hazy and the illumination so poor that the ball may be difficult to see (gauging the intentions and capabilities of closed states). Thus, at least four key properties of the information environment interact with cognitive constraints on decision makers in ways that can produce misperception and miscalculation.

Misperceptions

Some realists have gone much further than the strict structuralists in building psychological constructs into their frameworks. They posit that misperceptions—slippages between reality and decision makers' representations of reality—are not random (the proverbial trembling hand of game theorists) but rather can take systematic forms. Random errors can be explained away easily by strict structuralists and game theorists, but more systematic errors should be a difficult psychological pill to swallow because they call into question the efficiency and thoroughness of the process by which states are socialized into a ruthlessly competitive system in which ultimately only the fittest survive.

One class of misperceptions concerns one's would-be allies. For example, Waltz (1979) has identified two errors that occur in multipolar international environments—states may do too much or they may do too little. First, states can couple themselves too tightly to allies and get dragged into war (World War I model); second, states can free-ride and mistakenly count on others to take care of the balancing against potential aggressors (World War II model). Work seeking to explain these patterns has focused on misperceptions of the offense/defense balance and of the balance of power as a key determinant of which error occurs (Christensen & Snyder 1990, Christensen 1997). When offensive dominance is wrongly thought to prevail—as in 1914—excessive coupling is to be expected; when defensive dominance is wrongly thought to prevail—as in the mid-1930s—free-riding should be common.

This pattern can be amplified by simplistic analogical reasoning that leads states to draw on the wrong historical precedents (states are prone to fighting the last war). The failure to engage in timely Bayesian updating of assessments of changes in military technology and/or intra-alliance behavior leads to systematic lags between perceptions and reality. Despite arguments to the contrary (Gerber & Green 1999), the psychological literature on judgment and choice suggests that most decision makers are not natural Bayesians (Edwards 1962; Tetlock 1998, 1999). People, even experts, are often too slow to change their minds in response to unexpected events, especially in environments in which causality can be indefinitely contested because no one knows for sure what would have happened in the counterfactual worlds in which alternative policies were pursued.

A second class of misperceptions concerns potential adversaries (Jervis 1976). Again, states must balance the risk of two conflicting perceptual errors. Type I errors involve incorrectly labeling status quo powers (Waltz's and Grieco's defensive positionalists) as expansionist, precipitating a conflict spiral; type II errors involve incorrectly labeling expansionist powers (Mearsheimer's hegemony seekers) as status quo, leading to failures of deterrence. During the Cold War, this debate was central to ideological arguments between liberals and conservatives in both Washington and Moscow over how to deal with the other superpower (Osgood 1981, Garthoff 1994). One implication of Jervis's argument (which relies heavily on experimental social psychology of the 1960s and 1970s) is that type I errors are more common than type II errors as a result of the fundamental attribution error (in which observers are too quick to draw strong dispositional inferences of hostile intent from situationally motivated defensive preparations) and belief perseverance (in which observers are too slow to revise their initial causal inferences in response to unexpected events). Other work on cognitive factors in IR demonstrates that misperceptions occur in a variety of types of international relationships, not just those regarding allies and adversaries (Herrmann & Fischerkeller 1995).

Realists might challenge this argument on one of the following grounds, each compatible with a major line of psychological research on judgment and choice:

1. The state system is overwhelmingly populated by expansionist actors, so the base rate favors an across-the-board inference of expansionist intent.
2. The costs of making a type II error are typically so much more severe than those of making a type I error that making many fundamental attribution errors is a cost worth paying.

One example of this type of adaptive error is the Bush administration's response to Gorbachev's cooperative initiatives. Outsiders criticized both the "strategic pause" announced in 1989 and the general White House attitude that Gorbachev was simply tricking the West into letting its guard down. Many American officials were slow to accept that Soviet policies represented a fundamental redefinition of Soviet interests. Realists would argue, however, that rather than succumbing to error, these officials could not adjust more rapidly because the penalties for being wrong would have been so severe, and in some cases their prior experiences (particularly their involvement in the failed détente of the 1970s) added to their concerns (Tetlock & Goldgeier 2000).

Evolution

The common misconception that realist and psychological theory are inevitably in tension with each other—formally advanced in Waltz's influential 1959 book—should be called into question here (see also Mercer 1995). On the one hand, certain strands of evolutionary psychology reinforce the realist emphasis on the benefits of being suspicious. On the other hand, realist arguments, far from precluding cognitive bias and error, reinforce psychological analyses that highlight the benefits of making snap judgments of intentionality, especially for potentially threatening conduct, as well as the perils of changing one's mind too soon. For instance, Skyrms (1996) documents that evolutionary theory guarantees only that organisms are in a continual process of maximizing their genetic fit to their ever-changing local environments, not that organisms are perfect Bayesians (truth seekers) or utility maximizers, as normative theories actually require. Indeed, nature might even select for the kind of cognitive biases that US National Security Adviser Brent Scowcroft and others exhibited in 1989. As Stich (1990:25) comments, "A very cautious, risk-averse inferential strategy—one that leaps to the conclusion that danger is present on very slight evidence—will typically lead to false beliefs more often, and true ones less often, than a less hair-trigger one that waits for more evidence before rendering a judgment. Nonetheless, the unreliable, error-prone, risk-averse strategy may well be favored by natural selection. For natural selection does not care about truth; it cares only about reproductive success [read national survival]. And from the point of view of reproductive success, it is often better to be safe and wrong than sorry." Of course, this argument assumes that false positives are evolutionarily inconsequential, an assumption that the spiral theorists, worried about the World War I model, would challenge.

The key point here is that it is possible to grant evolutionary processes of natural selection—whether they have operated on human beings since the Pleistocene or they have operated on nation-states since Westphalia—a central role in shaping mental or organizational mechanisms of decision making (Cosmides & Tooby 1994, Pinker 1997) and still have plenty of room for a psychological research program that demonstrates deviations from rationality defined by perceptual-accuracy criteria.

Revisionist structural realists have begun to explore these attribution errors as they seek to understand how states try to balance against threats rather than power (Walt 1987, 1996). At times, these analyses resemble arguments underlying theories about the democratic peace from a social psychology point of view. For example, Walt (1996) has shown how states undergoing revolutionary transformations change threat perceptions in the international environment and produce systematic errors as others react to the rise of these revolutionary states and exaggerate the threat. Revolutions increase uncertainty for other actors in world politics, since there is a tendency to assume that ideologically alien domestic systems foreshadow threatening international conduct. Walt demonstrates that miscalculations abound owing to reliance on biased information, self-defeating spirals of suspicion occur in numerous cases, and ideology is an impediment to accurate assessments of other states. As psychologists would expect, once a regime is assigned to an ideological outgroup, observers exaggerate and there is reduced ability and motivation to empathize (Brewer & Brown 1998). We feel justified in making nasty inferences about these alien regimes for which we might have weak evidence, and it may prove difficult to reassess regimes that move away from revolutionary aspirations because of our preference for confirmatory strategies of hypothesis testing (Dawes 1998).

Other realists have attributed self-defeating expansionism to a leader's need to satisfy diverse coalitions in order to stay in power (Snyder 1991). Different groups within the elite place contradictory accountability demands on policy makers, thereby making the overall policy less coherent. For example, Soviet leaders Nikita Khrushchev and Leonid Brezhnev needed to placate, on the one hand, the ideologues and military who wanted to expand into the Third World, and, on the other, the technocrats who wanted the benefits of detente (Anderson 1993, Richter 1994, Snyder 1987/1988). The expansionist behavior was not only costly in itself but also impaired the ability of the Soviet Union to gain economic rewards from the United States. In such cases, the payoff to each specific elite group is rational, but the sum total of payoffs produces irrational, contradictory behavior. Domestic rationality may produce international irrationality (Lebow 1981, Fearon 1998). External observers, however, often underestimate the internal complexity of interactions among factions that produce policy outputs. This underestimation may be the product of cognitive biases toward overcentralization (Jervis 1976, Vertzberger 1990) and entitativity—seeing a collective entity as a single unit (Brewer & Brown 1998)—or a more strategic decision to hold other states tightly accountable for their conduct.

Moderating Variables

Since Jervis wrote in the mid-1970s, we have learned a lot in experimental social psychology and behavioral economics about the social and market forces that can either amplify or attenuate deviations from rationality. Let us assume, as many experimental researchers do (although not all—see Gigerenzer & Goldstein 1996), that a root cause of error and bias is the tendency of both individual and collective actors to over-rely on simple, easy-to-execute heuristics that often give people unjustifiable confidence in their judgments and decisions. Insofar as this diagnosis is correct, it follows that social, political, and economic systems that encourage actors to engage in more self-critical and reflective forms of information processing should often have the net effect of attenuating bias. Conversely, social, political, and economic systems that encourage mindless conformity, defensiveness, and the perpetuation of shared misconceptions should have the net effect of amplifying bias.

Two important sets of social-institutional moderators of rationality merit mention. First are organizational and domestic accountability pressures. Decision makers virtually never work in social isolation, with the occasional bizarre exceptions of leaders such as Adolf Hitler, Josef Stalin, Kim Il Sung, and Saddam Hussein, who centralized enormous authority in themselves. Decision making more typically unfolds in complex social and political networks of accountability. There are several possible ways of structuring these accountability networks or systems so as to promote more flexible, complex, rigorous, and systematic forms of thinking.

Experimental work indicates that, ideally, decision makers should feel accountable prior to making irrevocable commitments, and they should feel accountable to audiences whose judgment they respect and whose continuing esteem they value. In addition, the simple conformity option—telling people what they want to hear—should be short circuited either by creating normative ambiguity (decision makers should not know what others want to hear) or by creating normative conflict (decision makers know what others want to hear but the others represent diverse interests that want contradictory things). (See Tetlock 1992, Tetlock & Lerner 1999, Lerner & Tetlock 1999.) These are exactly the types of accountability preconditions that characterize multiple-advocacy policy groups (George 1980), many organizational prescriptions for averting groupthink (Janis 1982, Tetlock et al 1992), and arguments in political science about the underlying institutional-political mediators of the democratic-peace effects (Doyle 1983, Russett 1995, Owen 1997, Elman 1997).

Second are competitive market pressures. Skeptics have long suspected that judgmental biases hold up only in single-play situations in which respondents rarely receive feedback concerning the appropriateness or effectiveness of their decisions and respondents have little material incentive to get the answer right anyway. The skeptics overstated their case but there is some truth to this objection. Certain classes of errors and biases—especially breakdowns in consistency and transitivity produced by reliance on simple (lexicographic) decision rules—can be corrected when we move the choice process into open and transparent market settings that provide for repeated play, interaction with attentive competitors, and rapid, unequivocal feedback on the consequences of one's choices (Kagel & Roth 1995, Camerer & Hogarth 1999).

Combining these two lines of argument, it is possible to identify an ideal set of conditions under which the error-and-bias portrait of the decision maker should be of minimal predictive usefulness. Ideally, the inner advisory group deliberates under the norms of multiple advocacy, is accountable to the institutions of a self-correcting democratic polity, and is making decisions in a policy domain in which critical information is readily available; and mistakes are quickly and publicly punished. These conditions arc most likely to be satisfied in what is commonly called the zone of peace and prosperity (Goldgeier & McFaul 1992, Russett 1995, Singer & Wildavsky 1996). To be sure, decision makers will still make mistakes in this privileged zone, but the mistakes will be fewer, less systematic, and less serious than elsewhere, and when mistakes do occur, decision makers will correct them more rapidly. An example is the swift response of leaders to what Friedman (1999) calls the electronic herd and its imposition of a "golden straitjacket." The research agenda becomes one of identifying the relative resistance of biases to de-biasing pressures. Holding properties of the environment constant, we suspect the most tenacious biases will prove to be those that are widely shared and relatively subtle, and therefore difficult to identify and exploit. And even if the environment is more conducive to better cognitive performance, emotions associated with stress—such as fear and anxiety—may alter the impact of de-biasing pressures (Crawford 2000).

The Dangers of Being Too Smart

Psychology can illuminate a long-standing problem identified by prominent realists during the Cold War, namely, the reluctance of thoughtful decision makers to accept the radical strategic implications of the nuclear revolution (Waltz 1979; Jervis 1984, 1989). In this case, the problem was not the typical shortcomings caused by cognitive bias; rather, the error was being "too smart" or hyper-rational. An insightful illustration from behavioral game theory, the "guess-the-number" game first studied by Nagel (1995), illuminates the problem. Contestants guess a number between 0 and 100, with the goal of guessing as close as possible to two thirds of the average number chosen. In a world where all the players are known to be rational, in the sense that they will form expectations about the guesses of others who themselves are carrying out as many levels of deduction as necessary, the equilibrium in this game is 0. In a contest run at Thaler's (2000) urging by the *Financial Times*, the most popular guesses were 33 (the right guess if everyone else chooses a number at random) and 22 (the right guess if everyone picks 33). The average guess turned out to be 18.91 and the winning guess was 13.

To model how people play this game, we must allow for two kinds of individual differences in sophistication: logical and psychological. First, agents differ in the number of logical levels of processing they work through. A guess of 33 reflects one level (I guess that the average guess will be 50 and 2/3 of 50 is 33), 22 is two levels (I infer that you will work through the preceding argument so I will guess 2/3 of 33 or 22), and so on. Second, agents differ in their psychological assumptions about other actors and the likelihood of those actors working through the necessary inferences to reach the logically correct answer. Agents who guess 0 are logically sophisticated but psychologically naive. The intriguing implication here is that good judgment requires a game-theoretic appreciation for what the technically correct answer is as well as psychological savvy in appreciating how close people can come to approximating that solution. The lesson for IR is that games can have both logical and psychological equilibria (see Green & Shapiro 1994).

The implication for debates over nuclear doctrine emerges from Jervis's critique of the so-called countervailing strategy. With perfect logic from a conventional perspective, influential American strategists argued the following: The United States' current policy posture rests on the threat that if the other side attacks somewhere in a limited fashion, we would launch all-out nuclear war. But this threat is not credible, so we are not deterring a limited attack. We need options at each level of escalation, and we need dominance at each level, so that the other side will know that our potential response is credible and thus they will be deterred from starting even a small-scale attack.

For Jervis, the countervailers were "too rational." They recognized that the threat of all-out war was incredible, so they worried that it would not be taken seriously and thus would not deter. Stability at the top level of nuclear war led to less stability at lower levels (the stability-instability paradox). Jervis and others, such as Brodie, Waltz, and Bundy, argued that the nature of nuclear weapons meant that uncertainty was enough. The threat was effective not because the Soviets were certain that the United States would carry it out, but because in war it was a possibility, and the costs of nuclear war were so great that this possibility was sufficient to deter Soviet attack. Given the peculiar psychology of nuclear weapons and the feelings of ultimate dread they inspire, efforts to create limited-war-fighting options were at best unnecessary (wasted resources) and at worst counterproductive by sending the message that it may be permissible to escalate to "low" levels of conflict previously regarded as unthinkable.

INSTITUTIONALISM

Although realists disagree about many things, there is one matter on which they concur: In the absence of a common threat, sustained interstate cooperation is extremely difficult because (*a*) states are more concerned about relative than absolute gains, (*b*) states are always tempted to defect (and there is no higher authority to stop them or others from doing so), and (*c*) the penalties for being too sanguine about the intentions of others are so severe.

The institutionalist challenge arose in response to this pessimistic appraisal of the prospects for cooperation in the international system. The microeconomic variant of institutionalism articulated by Keohane [building on the earlier work of Coase (1960) and Williamson (1965) in economics and of neofunctionalists such as Haas (1958, 1964)] accepted that the international system is anarchic and populated by unitary, egoistic actors but nonetheless insisted that it is possible for such actors—in principle and in practice—to create institutional frameworks that permit them to secure the gains of cooperation by lowering their fear of being exploited to a tolerable level. Theoretically, transnational institutions should arise whenever it is economically rational to create them (although they might need a hegemon to get them started).

Psychologists are likely to be skeptical and to view such a claim as simultaneously too restrictive and too expansive. The claim is too restrictive because regimes can arise via mechanisms other than transaction-cost calculations—for example, shared norms of fairness or the desire to punish free-riders. The claim is too expansive because actors may fail to form regimes even if all of the economic institutionalists' preconditions are met; shared mindsets may blind actors to the feasibility or benefits of coordination. [See Thompson (1998) for experimental evidence on the fixed-pie fallacy; see Herrmann et al (2001) for survey evidence of mindset impediments in mass public opinion to movements toward the Pareto frontier in international trade.]

In the neoliberal institutionalist model, actors who recognize that they confront a repeated play situation and that the transaction costs for continuing to improvise ad hoc solutions are high rationally enter into binding compacts that can persist despite changes in the balance of power among the member states. Contrary to many realist views that institutions largely serve the interests of the powerful states and have minimal independent effect on state interests (Gilpin 1981, Mearsheimer 1994/1995), neoliberal institutionalists believe that international institutions can alter state interests over time as domestic political actors learn the value of continued participation in the international regime (Keohane 1984, Keohane & Martin 1995).

The key issues on which we believe psychology can inform these types of institutional analyses are when and why states seek to create institutions in the first place; when and why states live up to institutional norms and principles; and whether and when, over time, institutions transform the conceptions of state interests held by decision makers.

Creating Institutions

There are many policy domains in which institutionalists have sought to demonstrate the process by which states, theoretically locked in "prisoner's dilemma" relationships, successfully escape from the suboptimal mutual defection cell of the payoff matrix and land in the Pareto-optimal mutual cooperation cell. These include the postwar arrangements to facilitate trade by restricting the sovereign authority of states unilaterally to set tariffs and other barriers blocking entry to domestic markets, the rise of the European community to manage a range of economic, environmental, and social issues, and the creation of transnational environmental regimes to cope with perceived externalities of commercial and industrial development (e.g. CFC production, Mediterranean pollution control, restrictions on fishing and whaling, the law of the sea restrictions on resource development).

It should go without saying that ideas—policy makers' individual or shared mental representations of the problem—shape judgments about whether institutional solutions are feasible and desirable and what forms those institutional solutions should take. Goldstein & Keohane (1993:3) formally recognize this point when they declare, "Ideas influence policy when the principled or causal beliefs they embody provide road maps that increase actors' clarity about goals or ends-means relationships, when they affect outcomes of strategic situations in which there is no unique equilibrium, and when they become embedded in political institutions." In our view, the usefulness of adopting a cognitive psychological approach to the role of ideas hinges on the potential for systematic slippage between policy-guiding mental representations of reality and reality itself. Here we invoke the transparency of the environment as a fundamental moderator of the value of resorting to psychological levels of explanation for institution formation. The greater the transparency, the less latitude there is for slippage between reality and mental representations of reality.

"Transparency" has many meanings but two are especially important in this connection. First is the observer's ability to discern basic facts. Second is the ability to draw sound causal inferences, which can include, for example, the clarity of reward-punishment contingencies in the environment.

Epistemic communities (Haas 1997) can both advance and reflect causal transparency. At one end of the transparency continuum are policies shaped by epistemic communities possessing great authority and prestige by virtue of their technical and scientific achievements in teasing apart cause-effect relationships. This is especially likely in domains where investigators can test theoretical hypotheses in controlled and replicable experiments [and there is minimal reliance on what Tetlock & Belkin (1996) call counterfactual control groups]. Here we have in mind the near consensus among biomedical specialists on the appropriate strategies (or methods of developing strategies) for coping with transnational epidemics, the near consensus among climatologists on the effect of CFCs on the ozone layer of the atmosphere, or the near consensus among physicists and engineers on the prerequisites for nuclear proliferation. Virtually no one in the mainstream of the political elite in the advanced countries is prepared to question advice emanating from these communities on their issues of expertise.

At the other end of the transparency continuum are those policy domains in which the epistemic communities are either deeply divided or relatively undeveloped. Although there is substantial consensus among economists regarding the virtues of free trade, there are still pockets of sharp disagreement on details (strategic trade and infant industry arguments), as well as deeper professional rifts over the advisability of encouraging free flow of capital across national borders. Similarly, scientists differ on the sources, scope, pace, and effects of global warming.

We recognize that all inductive knowledge is tentative, and even well-established epistemic communities can fall prey to belief perseverance and groupthink. Nonetheless, the potential explanatory role of psychological constructs expands rapidly as we move from domains where the design of institutions is guided by "well-known facts" and "solid science" to those where the expert community is deeply divided and there is ample opportunity for cognitive and emotional biases to taint evaluations of evidence and options.

Compliance and Transformation

IR theorists are deeply divided over the issues of why states comply with the demands of international institutions and whether over time those institutions can change state conceptions of their interests (Simmons 1998). Imagine a social influence continuum. At one end is compliance, where decision makers accede to the rules of international institutions as a result of exclusively utilitarian calculations of the material rewards and punishments of participating in those institutions. Historical prototypes would be military alliances formed to counter direct threats, and the World Trade Organization, which lowers trade barriers for members and provides sanctioning mechanisms to punish norm violators.

Toward the middle of the continuum are decision makers who do what is expected of them because they seek to establish particular social identities in the eyes of certain domestic or international audiences whose opinion they value, and because they may be unwilling to bear the reputation costs of defecting. This form of social influence—sometimes called identification by social and organizational psychologists—should be less context-specific than mere compliance (which should shift on or off as a function of the cost-benefit calculus). Identification should persist even when it is materially inconvenient, but it still does not represent full-fledged internalization (Kelman 1958).

The self-presentational goals that drive identification do not always lead to "benign" outcomes. Although historical examples include states with dubious civil liberties practices or suspect records on respecting ecosystems signing on to human rights or environmental agreements in order to be part of the community of "modern" and "civilized" states, examples also include moderate Arab states in the 1960s and 1970s paying lip service to pan-Arabism and the destruction of Israel, as well as India's and Pakistan's efforts to join the nuclear club in order to achieve the status thought to accompany membership.

The calculations at the identification point of the spectrum are still largely utilitarian, but the benefits are measured not so much in economic and security terms as in social and reputational categories. As we continue toward the internalization end of the continuum, we find states not only doing the right thing but doing so for what they perceive to be the right reasons. The calculation is no longer utilitarian [in March & Olsen's (1998) terms, following the logic of consequential action] but rather is guided by moral, religious, or ideological ideals (March & Olsen's rule-bound logic of appropriate action). Historical prototypes might include Scandinavian and Canadian approaches to foreign aid, in which there are minimal assumptions of economic or security quid pro quos, and the attitudes of certain revolutionary states seeking to export their ideology to their neighbors.

A contribution of psychologists is to delineate the conditions under which decision makers are especially likely to change their underlying attitudes to bring them into line with initially counterattitudinal behavior. Cognitive dissonance and self-perception research using forced-compliance paradigms suggests, for example, that decision makers are especially likely to internalize attitudes consistent with their behavior when they believe they had some elements of free choice (see Bem 1967, Larson 1985). It is critical here that the external pressure for compliance not be too heavy-handed; otherwise, people will attribute their behavior to external demands and not internal values or attitudes. As good diplomats have long known, heavy-handed pressure tactics often backfire, and even when they do work, the effects are often fleeting.

Most psychologists would probably agree that most political actors (psychopaths excluded) will gradually internalize the norms of fair play implicit in international institutions. These norms can become functionally autonomous from the interests that may once have inspired them. This internalization process should be especially reliable in democracies, in which leaders must justify departures from widely held norms of fair play to a variety of constituencies (Tetlock & Goldgeier 2000).

This does not mean that procedural justice issues are easy to solve. Leading institutionalists have argued that a poorly understood issue is the extent to which the effectiveness of institutions hinges on whether they are dependent on political decision making or on relatively independent experts or judicial processes (Martin & Simmons 1998, Simmons 1998). The cognitivists have something to say here. Institutions will typically have a hard time establishing that they possess minimal prerequisites of procedural justice (neutrality, equal respect, fairness) in the eyes of participating nation-states. Experimental work reveals that even scrupulous attempts on the part of mediators to achieve neutrality are often misperceived as partisan by both of the contending parties (Ross & Griffin 1991). Domestic political opponents of international institutions can then play on these cognitive biases and mobilize substantial resistance to continued participation in the institution.

Rational choice approaches to norm enforcement stress the danger of free-riding. In the absence of a sovereign, no single party wants to incur the costs of punishing norm violators, so defectors escape sanction (see Coleman 1990). A rapidly growing body of work in experimental social psychology and microeconomics has revealed, however, that people are often willing to make substantial sacrifices to punish cheaters in implicit or explicit social contracts (Fehr & Schmidt 1999). The more deeply internalized the norms and the more egregious the transgression, the sharper the emotional reaction and the more willing people are to go out of their way to punish transgressors and even to punish those who fail to punish transgressors (Axelrod 1984, Crawford 2000). This analysis suggests that international institutions built on shared conceptions of distributive and procedural justice may be able to perpetuate themselves even in the absence of strong central authority.

Finally, just as prospect theory sheds light on the causes of the asymmetry between deterrence and compellence, it also helps us to understand the differential reactions observers often have to the distribution versus the redistribution of scarce resources in both domestic and international economic debates. Because the loss function falls much more rapidly than the gain function rises, prospect theory leads us to expect that even observers trying to be scrupulously neutral will display a preference for upholding the claims of the status quo. It will also be easier to build up psychological momentum to defend the status quo (and avoid imposing painful losses) than it will be to create momentum to overturn the status quo (bestow gains on the have-nots).

CONSTRUCTIVISM

Whereas realists and institutionalists posit a choice process organized around March & Olsen's logic of consequential action (explicitly utilitarian weighing of costs and benefits), many constructivists posit a choice process heavily informed by the logic of obligatory action, in which people make up their minds in part by matching their conceptions of who they are (social identities) with their assessments of the normative context (what does this situation call for actors of my type to do?).

Insofar as explicit assumptions are made about the motivations of individual actors, these assumptions stress norm-following logics that provide guidelines for legitimate and illegitimate behavior as the actors (*Homo sociologicus*) construct an identity as part of a given social order, itself constructed by the interaction of the actors in the system (Wendt 1999). Examples include the demise of dueling and slave trading (Mueller 1989); the rise of human rights norms, especially the sensitivity to racism (Risse et al 1999); environmentalism (Haas et al 1993); the nonuse of weapons of mass destruction and other constraints on the conduct of war (Legro 1995, Price 1997, Tannenwald 1999); and the changing purpose of military intervention (Finnemore 1996).

At a foundational level, a cognitive psychological analysis of world politics is compatible with the constructivist program. A natural starting point for a cognitive analysis is to consider (*a*) the nature of the information-processing task that observers confront when they try to draw causal inferences or policy lessons from world politics and (*b*) the capacity limitations of the human mind. Cognitivists are impressed by the complexity of world politics (the number and variety of alternative explanations that competing schools of thought can typically advance) and the inherently ambiguous feedback that policy makers receive in a path-dependent system that runs once and only once (no one has empirical access to the counterfactual worlds in which alternative policies were pursued). From a cognitivist point of view, all causal inferences and policy lessons are the product of mental constructions of what would, could, or might have happened had a different set of antecedent conditions held or policies been tried. There is, in principle, an infinite number of possible background factors that one could enter as antecedents in one's counterfactual constructions of alternative worlds. In practice, of course, observers must rely on draconian simplifying rules that reduce the number of scenarios to be entertained to a humanly manageable number. These simplifying rules are generally drawn from the shared understandings of epistemic communities.

Notwithstanding this fundamental point of agreement, the efforts to incorporate insights from cognitive science into the constructivist program are only beginning (Finnemore & Sikkink 1998, Wendt 1999). One obvious candidate is the nature of tradeoff reasoning, where a profound disjuncture emerges between rationalists and constructivists (Katzenstein et al 1998, Ruggie 1998). For example, realists expect states rationally to measure the costs and benefits of entering or leaving a military alliance or of taking preemptive military action; institutionalists expect states to examine the costs and benefits of entering or exiting a trading or arms control or environmental regime. By contrast, there are large classes of issues for which constructivists would expect tradeoff reasoning to be extremely difficult. For example, realists may have no trouble believing states will engage in a cost/benefit analysis to determine whether to use a weapon of mass destruction to further their military aims (Sagan 2000), whereas constructivists believe that norms and practices lead decision makers to place boundaries on the thinkable. The constructivists are more open to the possibilities of categorical exclusionary logic than the rationalists, and constructivists have argued that detailed case studies demonstrate that the way decision makers approach subjects such as the use of weapons of mass destruction supports their way of thinking (Price 1997, Tannenwald 1999).

Tetlock et al (2000) distinguish three types of tradeoffs: routine, taboo (secular versus sacred), and tragic (sacred versus sacred). A routine tradeoff is the type of reasoning one deploys whenever one goes shopping and must compare the relative importance of secular values, which are subject to legal market-pricing in one's social world. (Would I rather have a larger stock portfolio or a Mercedes-Benz?) A tradeoff is taboo if it pits a secular value such as money against a sacred value such as protection of human rights or ecosystems. Taboo tradeoffs are not just cognitively demanding (the familiar incommensurability problem: How much of one value am I willing to give up to achieve an increment on another value?); they are also morally corrosive (the less familiar "constitutive incommensurability" problem, in which merely to think certain thoughts or to make certain comparisons undercuts one's claim to embody shared moral values). Finally, a tradeoff is tragic if it pits two sacred values against each other, e.g. protection of endangered species against protection of indigenous cultures.

These distinctions are psychologically and politically consequential. Decision makers caught making taboo tradeoffs are often ostracized by the moral communities within which they once held leadership roles. Indeed, they may be condemned even if the actual decision they rendered would have been perfectly acceptable had it been semantically framed as a routine or tragic tradeoff. Not surprisingly, decision makers go to great efforts to portray their decision process as free of any taint of taboo tradeoffs, and their adversaries struggle equally tenaciously to convince key constituencies that the boundaries of the unthinkable have been breached.

Should tradeoff reasoning be treated as a defining property of rationality, good judgment, and maturity? For realists, institutionalists, and economic liberals, who argue that decision makers are utilitarians, the answer is yes. Leaders think in terms of how much of x they are willing to give up for a given increment of y. For Kantian liberals and constructivists, it is possible to identify large classes of important issues for which decision makers should find compensatory tradeoff reasoning illegitimate. Tragic, but not taboo, tradeoffs are permissible.

For example, regarding weapons systems, constructivists might expect leaders to believe that it is preferable to kill more people with conventional arms than to break a taboo by dropping one small atomic bomb (putting precedent-setting to the side). Realists believe states view actions as mandatory if they promote self-interest (improve one's position in the system). For constructivists, leaders may find actions mandatory in order to preserve international norms, actions that might be unthinkable for a decision maker in a realist mode. Metternich and Kissinger would not think of using military force to serve humanitarian purposes (particularly if these harm self-interest in other areas, e.g. damaging relations with Russia and China by acting in Kosovo), whereas many constructivists posit a world in which upholding norms against genocide is not only thinkable but mandatory.

A second way in which psychological analyses can insinuate themselves into constructivist approaches to world politics derives directly from prospect theory and work on endowment effects. A major focus of debates that constructivists attempt to explain is fairness: Who owes what to whom? What counts as a just claim on this or that territory or resource? Prospect theory leads us to expect that competing social conceptions of fairness ultimately rest on competing perceptual encodings of the appropriate endowment reference point. Those who challenge the status quo deny the legitimacy of the current allocation of resources and hence downplay the moral seriousness of the pain inflicted on the haves and play up the moral seriousness of the gains that should have gone (in an ideal counterfactual world) to the have-nots. Whether the issue is the forgiveness of loans or the arbitrariness of postcolonial borders in Africa or the Middle East, activists' cognitive constructions of what should be done reflect their perceptual framing of the problem.

Those who take the status quo as their analytical starting point are predisposed to be unsympathetic to redistributive claims advanced by the have-nots. Although the G-7 leaders backed debt forgiveness in 1999 for the poorest of the poor, it is taking them a long time to act, perhaps because many in the G-7 societies ask why international banks or the taxpayers of wealthy countries should subsidize loan defaults by bankrupt and corrupt sub-Saharan countries. Conversely, those who are less fixated on the world that is—and prone to give more weight to counterfactual worlds that could or should have been—are predisposed to be more sympathetic to redistributive claims on behalf of have-nots. Rather than viewing such claims as illegitimate, greedy, and self-serving bids for gain, they see them as just attempts to undo losses imposed by exploitative classes or nations. It should be relatively easy for these activists to imagine worlds that could have been, and might yet be, in which the capricious allocation of resources in this world is rendered more equitable.

Work on emotions in bargaining games reinforces this possibility (Rabin 1993). Economists have traditionally treated human beings as exclusively self-interested and have assumed that when self-interest collides with ethical values, self-interest will generally prevail. But this is not necessarily so—as experimental economists have themselves discovered. The ultimatum game offers a simple demonstration that emotions, coupled with strong, deeply internalized intuitions about fairness, can shape strategic interaction.

In the ultimatum game, one player (the Proposer) is given a sum of money, often \$10, and offers some portion x to the other player (the Responder). The Responder can either accept the offer, in which case the Responder gets x and the Proposer gets $\$10 - x$, or reject the offer, in which case both players get nothing. Experimental results consistently reveal that very low offers (less than 20% of the total sum) are often rejected. The Responders appear to react emotionally, indeed indignantly, to the low offers. They do not try to maximize their own payoffs; even in single-play, anonymous games, they turn down low offers and receive zero instead. There is also evidence that, when the veil of anonymity is lifted, players and third-party observers censure those who fail to censure "exhorbitant greed."

For better or for worse, such conduct is far more common than neoclassical economic theorizing would lead us to expect. The emotions activated in the ultimatum game, insofar as they are linked to envy, may sabotage mutually beneficial trade agreements in which the benefits are shared asymmetrically. But, on the positive side, the same emotions, insofar as they are linked to a deep-rooted justice motive (Welch 1993), may help to deter would-be exploiters from taking what is perceived to be unfair advantage of other parties.

Finally, constructivist analysts can usefully draw on psychology to address what we view as one of the more compelling criticisms of the constructivist program, namely, its inability to specify the conditions under which different groups view different norms as applicable (Checkel 1998). Two lines of research may be especially helpful. First, at the most abstract or process level, experimental work on "natural categories" warns us that such categories are organized not on the principles of classical logic (which are supposed to specify well-defined necessary and sufficient conditions for placing a given instance inside the category) but rather on the principles of fuzzy logic (which stipulate that people often judge whether a given instance falls into a category's orbit based on the instance's family resemblance to other category members or to idealized prototypes). Looking for the essential defining features of key normative concepts such as sovereignty or human rights is, from this standpoint, rather futile.

Second, at a more concrete or content level of analysis, recent theoretical advances in cross-cultural psychology suggest taxonomies of norms that can regulate relationships among individuals or groups. These taxonomies, in turn, can serve as platforms for generating hypotheses about when decision makers are more or less likely to rely on various normative rules as guides to action. Coupling neorealism with Fiske's (1991) model of relational schemata yields five possibilities. The first possibility is the familiar neorealist presocial, anarchic mode of relating, in which no one owes anyone anything, invocations of higher authorities are viewed as meaningless rhetorical flourishes, and there is the omnipresent danger that one's security will be challenged by other actors. The other four possibilities identify a mutually exclusive and exhaustive set of the forms that normative coordination can take. Starting with the most cognitively complex form of organization—market pricing—actors agree to coordinate their actions by assuming the roles of buyers and sellers in competitive markets, to respect property rights and contractual obligations (the reputation costs of failing to do so are prohibitive), and to maximize expected utility by engaging in compensatory tradeoff reasoning that requires ratio comparisons of competing values. This market-pricing relational template, with supplementary assumptions about transaction costs and monitoring, captures the spirit of neoinstitutionalist approaches to world politics, in which the state system is undergoing a gradual transformation from a presocial Hobbesian anarchy into rule-regulated networks of commerce.

The other three relational schemata within the Fiskean scheme in theory define the constructivist agenda. Norms can take the form of equality matching (e.g. tit-for-tat reciprocity, in which a state calibrates positive or negative responses to the direction and magnitude of other states' latest moves), authority ranking (e.g. the patron-client or hegemon-satellite relationship, in which the low-status party owes obedience to the high-status party within a certain range of activity), and communal sharing (e.g. the decision of nation-states to abolish boundaries and merge into a common political entity).

The relational model followed by a given institution or community will lead to different kinds of norm-following logics and thus different implementation rules. The Warsaw Treaty Organization, for example, was an authority ranking system in which the Soviet Union allowed latitude in some highly constrained areas but ruthlessly used force to squelch attempts by local elites to stray from Moscow's norm of one-party control. This logic leads to very different understandings and expectations than the equality-matching norms of the World Trade Organization, which allows states to engage in precisely calibrated tit-for-tat behavior if it deems them the object of unfair trade practices. The Warsaw Treaty Organization was also organized quite differently from its main rival, the North Atlantic Treaty Organization, and thus norms of behavior were different despite the presence of a hegemon in each institution (Ruggie 1993). If constructivism is to explain how actors' identities are mutually constituted with structures, then we need to know which relational schema structures interaction at any given moment in time and how normative logics differ depending on which of the three is dominant.

Interesting cases for the constructivists to explore have been those communities that started with one type of logic and over time developed something quite different. When Haas (1958) began writing about the uniting of Europe in the 1950s, the dominant schema within that nascent community was equality matching. Over time, an institution has developed that increasingly, although still very imperfectly, affirms the norms of communal sharing (all for one and one for all). Enthusiasts consider the abolition of border controls and local currencies only the first steps to a full-scale European entity. By this light, constructivists can compare the development of norm-following logics as relational schemata change within a given set of international relationships that are becoming marked by greater communal sharing, such as the European Union (Moravcsik 1998), or within a security community such as NATO (Adler & Barnett 1998). Developing in a different direction is the relationship between Russia and its former satellites in Europe. The Soviet Union built a bloc in Eastern Europe that was ostensibly based on the ideals of communal sharing but instead followed an authority ranking pattern. Since the collapse of the empire in 1989, the relationship has evolved to one of equality matching, which is what Central and Eastern Europeans want and what some Russians have had a hard time accepting. Shifting relational gears can be painful. Standard assertions of sovereignty can look like deliberate disrespect.

CONCLUSION

Many IR theorists dismiss psychological arguments, claiming either that they are too reductionist to explain the big patterns we find in world politics or that they are too flimsy or messy to explain anything at all. As this essay suggests, however, psychology's role in identifying boundary conditions is extremely useful in refining arguments within a given theoretical tradition. Prospect theory's identification of the conditions under which we expect more risk-averse or risk-taking behavior than in an expected-utility model can help explain when a more defensive or offensive realist argument should prevail or when redistributive schemes are likely to have greater or less appeal. Understanding the role of transparency or of domestic/organizational accountability pressures in ameliorating typical errors and biases helps us understand variation in decision-making abilities across types of political systems and might shed light on debates such as those regarding the democratic peace. Work in cross-cultural psychology suggests that there may be a surprisingly small number of basic normative templates from which international organizations can be constituted.

Macrolevel theorists, rather than dismissing psychological theories for presenting obstacles to explaining the broad contours of international behavior, should welcome psychology's help in refining ideas in key debates regarding power, institutions, and norms. Ironically, the buzzwords that dominate recent macrolevel approaches to refine or advance theories are perceptions, ideas, and identity (see Goldstein & Keohane 1993, Katzenstein 1996, Walt 1996). Now is the time for IR theorists to take advantage of systematic arguments about psychological factors to address more explicitly the psychological dimensions of these variables (Goldgeier 1997, Tetlock & Goldgeier 2000). The effort should not be to reduce explanations of behavior to psychological factors but rather to consider how environment and cognition interact in systematic and identifiable patterns to produce the variation we find in world politics.

ACKNOWLEDGMENTS

We would like to thank Paul Brewer, Dalia Dassa Kaye, Martha Finnemore, Donald Green, Ernst Haas, Richard Herrmann, Robert Jervis, Peter Katzenstein, and Randall Schweller for their comments.

LITERATURE CITED

Adler E, Barnett MN, eds. 1998. *Security Communities*. New York: Cambridge Univ. Press

Anderson RD Jr. 1993. *Public Politics in an Authoritarian State: Making Foreign Policy During the Brezhnev Years*. Ithaca, NY: Cornell Univ. Press

Axelrod RM. 1984. *The Evolution of Cooperation*. New York: Basic Books

Bem D. 1967. Self-perception: an alternative interpretation of cognitive dissonance phenomenon. *Psychol. Rev.* 74:183–200

Blainey G. 1973. *The Causes of War*. New York: Free

Boettcher W. 1995. Context, methods, numbers, and words: prospect theory in international relations. *J. Confl. Resol.* 39:561–83

Brewer MB, Brown RJ. 1998. Intergroup relations. See Gilbert et al 1998, 2:554–94

Camerer CF, Hogarth RM. 1999. The effects of financial incentives in experiments: a review and capital-labor-production framework. *J. Risk Uncer.* 19:1–3, 7–42

Checkel JT. 1998. The constructivist turn in international relations theory. *World Polit.* 50:324–48

Christensen TJ. 1997. Perceptions and alliances in Europe, 1865–1940. *Int. Organ.* 51:65–97

Christensen TJ, Snyder J. 1990. Chain gangs and passed bucks: predicting alliance patterns in multipolarity. *Int. Organ.* 44:137–68

Coase R. 1960. The problem of social cost. *J. Law Econ.* 3:1–44

Coleman JS. 1990. *Foundations of Social Theory*. Cambridge, MA: Belknap Press of Harvard Univ. Press

Cosmides L, Tooby J. 1994. Origins of domain specificity: the evolution of functional organization. In *Mapping the Mind: Domain Specificity in Cognition and Culture*, ed. LA Hirschfeld, S Gelman, pp. 85–116. New York: Cambridge Univ. Press

Crawford NC. 2000. The passion of world politics: propositions on emotion and emotional relationships. *Int. Secur.* 24:116–56

Dawes RM. 1998. Behavioral decision making and judgment. See Gilbert et al 1998, 2:497–548

Doyle MW. 1983. Kant, liberal legacies, and foreign affairs. Parts 1 and 2. *Phil. Pub. Aff.* 12:205–54, 323–53

Edwards W. 1962. Dynamic decision theory and probabilistic information processing. *Human Factors* 4:59–73

Elman MF, ed. 1997. *Paths to Peace: Is Democracy the Answer?* Cambridge, MA: MIT Press

Farnham BR, ed. 1994. *Avoiding Losses/Taking Risks: Prospect Theory and International Conflict*. Ann Arbor: Univ. Mich. Press

Farnham BR. 1997. *Roosevelt and the Munich Crisis: A Study of Political Decision-making*. Princeton, NJ: Princeton Univ. Press

Fearon JD. 1998. Domestic politics, foreign policy, and theories of international relations. *Annu. Rev. Polit. Sci.* 1:289–313

Fehr E, Schmidt K. 1999. A theory of fairness, competition, and cooperation. *Q. J. Econ.* 114:817–68

Finnemore M. 1996. Constructing norms of humanitarian intervention. See Katzenstein 1996, pp. 153–85

Finnemore M, Sikkink K. 1998. International norm dynamics and political change. *Int. Organ.* 52:887–917

Fiske AP. 1991. *Structures of Social Life: The Four Elementary Forms of Human Relations*. New York: Free (Macmillan)

Friedman T. 1999. *The Lexus and the Olive Tree*. New York: Farrar Straus & Giroux

Garthoff R. 1994. *Détente and Confrontation: American-Soviet Relations from Nixon to Reagan*. Washington, DC: Brookings. Rev. ed.

George AL. 1980. *Presidential Decisionmaking in Foreign Policy: The Effective Use of Information and Advice*. Boulder, CO: Westview

Gerber A, Green D. 1999. Misperceptions about perceptual bias. *Annu. Rev. Polit. Sci.* 2:189–210

Gigerenzer G, Goldstein DG. 1996. Reasoning the fast and frugal way: models of bounded rationality. *Psychol. Rev.* 103:650–69

Gilbert DT, Fiske ST, Lindzey G, eds. 1998. *The Handbook of Social Psychology*. New York: McGraw Hill. 4th ed.

Gilpin R. 1981. *War and Change in World Politics*. Cambridge: Cambridge Univ. Press

Goldgeier JM. 1997. Psychology and security. *Secur. Stud.* 6:137–66

Goldgeier JM, McFaul M. 1992. A tale of two worlds: core and periphery in the post–cold war era. *Int. Organ.* 46:467–91

Goldstein J, Keohane RO, eds. 1993. *Ideas and Foreign Policy: Beliefs, Institutions and Political Change*. Ithaca, NY: Cornell Univ. Press

Green DP, Shapiro I. 1994. *Pathologies of Rational Choice Theory: A Critique of Applications in Political Science*. New Haven, CT: Yale Univ. Press

Grieco JM. 1990. *Cooperation among Nations: Europe, America, and Non-Tariff Barriers to Trade*. Ithaca, NY: Cornell Univ. Press

Haas EB. 1958. *The Uniting of Europe*. Stanford, CA: Stanford Univ. Press

Haas EB. 1964. *Beyond the Nation-State: Functionalism and International Organization*. Stanford, CA: Stanford Univ. Press

Haas PM, ed. 1997. *Knowledge, Power and International Policy Coordination*. Columbia: Univ. So. Carol. Press

Haas PM, Keohane RO, Levy MA, eds. 1993. *Institutions for the Earth: Sources of Effective International Environmental Protection*. Cambridge, MA: MIT Press

Herrmann RK, Fischerkeller MD. 1995. Beyond the enemy image and spiral model: cognitive-strategic research after the cold war. *Int. Organ.* 49:415–50

Herrmann R, Tetlock PE, Diascro M. 2001. How Americans think about trade: resolving conflicts among power, money, and principles. *Int. Stud. Q.* In press

Janis IL. 1982. *Groupthink: Psychological Studies of Policy Decisions and Fiascoes*. New York: Houghton Mifflin. 2nd ed.

Jervis R. 1976. *Perception and Misperception in International Politics*. Princeton, NJ: Princeton Univ. Press

Jervis R. 1984. *The Illogic of American Nuclear Strategy*. Ithaca, NY: Cornell Univ. Press

Jervis R. 1989. *The Meaning of the Nuclear Revolution: Statecraft and the Prospect of Armageddon*. Ithaca, NY: Cornell Univ. Press

Kagel JH, Roth AE. 1995. *The Handbook of Experimental Economics. Princeton*, NJ: Princeton Univ. Press

Kahneman D, Knetsch JL, Thaler RH. 1991. Anomalies: the endowment effect, loss aversion, and status quo bias. *J. Econ. Persp.* 5:193–206

Kahneman D, Tversky A. 1979. Prospect theory: an analysis of decision under risk. *Econometrica* 47:263–91

Kahneman D, Tversky A. 1984. Choices, values and frames. *Am. Psychol.* 39:341–50

Katzenstein PJ, ed. 1996. *The Culture of National Security: Norms and Identity in World Politics*. New York: Columbia Univ. Press

Katzenstein PJ, Keohane RO, Krasner SD. 1998. International organization and the study of world politics. *Int. Organ.* 52:645–85

Kelman HC. 1958. Compliance, identification, and internalization: three processes of attitude change. *J. Confl. Resol.* 2:51–60

Keohane RO. 1984. *After Hegemony*. New York: Columbia Univ. Press

Keohane RO, Martin LL. 1995. The promise of institutionalist theory. *Int. Secur.* 20:39–51

Larson DW. 1985. *Origins of Containment*. Princeton, NJ: Princeton Univ. Press

Layne C. 1993. The unipolar illusion: why new great powers will rise. *Int. Secur.* 17:5–51

Lebow RN. 1981. *Between Peace and War: The Nature of International Crisis*. Baltimore, MD: Johns Hopkins Univ. Press

Legro JW. 1995. *Cooperation under Fire: Anglo-German Restraint during World War II*. Ithaca, NY: Cornell Univ. Press

Lerner J, Tetlock PE. 1999. Accounting for the effects of accountability. *Psychol. Bull.* 125:255–75

Levy J. 1992. Prospect theory and international relations: theoretical applications and analytical problems. *Polit. Psychol.* 13:283–310

March JG, Olsen JP. 1998. The institutional dynamics of international political orders. *Int. Organ.* 52:943–70

Martin LL, Simmons BA. 1998. Theories and empirical studies of international institutions. *Int. Organ.* 52:729–58

McDermott R. 1998. *Risk-taking in International Politics: Prospect Theory in American Foreign Policy*. Ann Arbor: Univ. Mich. Press

Mearsheimer JJ. 1990. Back to the future: instability in Europe after the cold war. *Int. Secur.* 15:5–56

Mearsheimer JJ. 1994/1995. The false promise of international institutions. *Int. Secur.* 19:5–49

Mearsheimer JJ. 2001. *The Tragedy of Great Power Politics*. New York: Norton. In press

Mercer J. 1995. Anarchy and identity. *Int. Org.* 49:229–52

Moravcsik A. 1998. *The Choice for Europe: Social Purpose and State Power from*

Messina to Maastricht. Ithaca, NY: Cornell Univ. Press

Mueller J. 1989. *Retreat from Doomsday: The Obsolescence of Major War*. New York: Basic Books

Nagel R. 1995. Unraveling in guessing games: an experimental study. *Am. Econ. Rev.* 85(5): 1313–26

Nisbett RE, Zukier H, Lemley RE. 1981. The dilution effect: nondiagnostic information weakens the implications of diagnostic information. *Cogn. Psychol.* 13:248–77

Osgood RE. 1981. *Containment, Soviet Behavior and Grand Strategy*. Berkeley, CA: Inst. Int. Stud.

Owen JM. 1997. *Liberal Peace, Liberal War: American Politics and International Security*. Ithaca, NY: Cornell Univ. Press

Pinker S. 1997. *How the Mind Works*. New York: Norton

Price R. 1997. *The Chemical Weapons Taboo*. Ithaca, NY: Cornell Univ. Press

Rabin M. 1993. Incorporating fairness into game theory and economics. *Am. Econ. Rev.* 83:1281–302

Richter JG. 1994. *Khrushchev's Double Bind: International Pressures and Domestic Coalition Politics*. Baltimore, MD: Johns Hopkins Univ. Press

Risse T, Ropp SC, Sikkink K, eds. 1999. *The Power of Human Rights: International Norms and Domestic Change*. New York: Cambridge Univ. Press

Ross L, Griffin D. 1991. Subjective construal, social inference, and human misunderstanding. See Zanna 1992, 24:319–59

Ruggie JG, ed. 1993. *Multilateralism Matters: The Theory and Praxis of an Institutional Form*. New York: Columbia Univ. Press

Ruggie JG. 1998. *Constructing the World Polity: Essays on International Institutionalization*. London: Routledge

Russett B, with W Antholis, CR Ember, M Ember, Z Maoz. 1995. *Grasping the Democratic Peace: Principles for a Post–Cold War World*. Princeton, NJ: Princeton Univ. Press

Sagan SD. 2000. The commitment trap: why the United States should not use nuclear threats to deter biological and chemical weapons attacks. *Int. Secur.* 24(4):85–115

Schelling TC. 1967. *Arms and Influence*. New Haven, CT: Yale Univ. Press

Schweller R. 1996. Neorealism's status-quo bias: what security dilemma? *Sec. Stud.* 5: 90–121

Schweller R. 1998. *Deadly Imbalances: Tripolarity and Hitler's Strategy of World Conquest*. New York: Columbia Univ. Press

Simmons BA. 1998. Compliance with international agreements. *Annu. Rev. Polit. Sci.* 1:75–93

Simon HA. 1957. *Models of Man*. New York: Wiley

Simon HA. 1982. *Models of Bounded Rationality*. Cambridge, MA: MIT Press

Singer M, Wildavsky AB. 1996. *The Real World Order: Zones of Peace, Zones of Turmoil*. London: Chatham House. Rev. ed.

Skyrms B. 1996. *Evolution of the Social Contract*. New York: Cambridge Univ. Press

Snyder J. 1987/1988. The Gorbachev revolution: a waning of Soviet expansionism? *Int. Secur.* 12:93–131

Snyder J. 1991. *Myths of Empire: Domestic Politics and International Ambition*. Ithaca, NY: Cornell Univ. Press

Stich S. 1990. *The Fragmentation of Reason: Preface to a Pragmatic Theory of Cognitive Evaluation*. Cambridge, MA: MIT Press

Tannenwald N. 1999. The nuclear taboo: the United States and the normative basis of nuclear non-use. *Int. Organ.* 53:433–68

Tetlock PE. 1992. The impact of accountability on judgment and choice: toward a social contingency model. See Zanna 1992, 25:331–76

Tetlock PE. 1998. Close-call counterfactuals and belief system defenses: I was not almost wrong but I was almost right. *J. Pers. Soc. Psychol.* 75:639–52

Tetlock PE. 1999. Theory-driven reasoning about possible pasts and probable futures: Are we prisoners of our preconceptions? *Am. J. Polit. Sci.* 43:335–66

Tetlock PE, Belkin A. 1996. *Counterfactual Thought Experiments in World Politics: Logical, Methodological, and Psychological Perspectives*. Princeton, NJ: Princeton Univ. Press

Tetlock PE, Boettger R. 1989. Accountability: a social magnifier of the dilution effect. *J. Pers. Soc. Psychol.* 57:388–98

Tetlock PE, Goldgeier J. 2000. Human nature and world politics: cognition, influence, and identity. *Int. J. Psychol.* 35:87–96

Tetlock PE, Kristel OV, Elson SB, Green MC, Lerner JS. 2000. The psychology of the unthinkable: taboo trade-offs, forbidden base rates, and heretical counterfactuals. *J. Pers. Soc. Psychol.* 78:853–70

Tetlock PE, Lerner J. 1999. The social contingency model: identifying empirical and normative boundary conditions on the error-and-bias portrait of human nature. In *Dual Process Models in Social Psychology*, ed. S Chaiken, Y Trope, pp. 571–85. New York: Guilford

Tetlock PE, McGuire C, Peterson R, Feld P, Chang S. 1992. Assessing political group dynamics: a test of the groupthink model. *J. Pers. Soc. Psychol.* 63:402–23

Thaler RH. 2000. From homo economicus to homo sapiens. *J. Econ. Pers.* 14:133–41

Thompson L. 1998. *The Mind and Heart of the Negotiator*. Upper Saddle River, NJ: Prentice Hall

Vertzberger Y. 1990. *The World in Their Minds*. Stanford, CA: Stanford Univ. Press

Walt SM. 1987. *The Origins of Alliances*. Ithaca, NY: Cornell Univ. Press

Walt SM. 1996. *Revolution and War*. Ithaca, NY: Cornell Univ. Press

Waltz KN. 1959. *Man, The State and War*. New York: Columbia Univ. Press

Waltz KN. 1979. *Theory of International Politics*. Reading, MA: Addison-Wesley

Welch D. 1993. *Justice and the Genesis of War*. New York: Cambridge Univ. Press

Wendt A. 1999. *Social Theory of International Politics*. New York: Cambridge Univ. Press

Williamson O. 1965. A dynamic theory of interfirm behavior. *Q. J. Econ.* 79:579–607

Wohlforth WC. 1993. *The Elusive Balance: Power and Perceptions During the Cold War*. Ithaca, NY: Cornell Univ. Press

Wohlforth WC. 1999. The stability of a unipolar world. *Int. Secur.* 24:3–41

Zanna M, ed. 1992. *Advances in Experimental Social Psychology*. New York: Academic

Annu. Rev. Polit. Sci. 2001. 4:93–115

Political Traditions and Political Change: The Significance of Postwar Japanese Politics for Political Science

Bradley Richardson[1] and Dennis Patterson[2]

[1]*Department of Political Science, Ohio State University, Columbus, Ohio 43210; e-mail: brichar@columbus.rr.com;* [2]*Department of Political Science, Michigan State University, East Lansing, Michigan 48824; e-mail: patter95@msu.edu*

Key Words electoral mobilization, informal structure, fragmentation dynamic, negotiated parliamentarism, contingent institutionalism

■ **Abstract** The extensive literature on postwar Japanese politics often stresses unique phenomena representative of Japanese exceptionalism, even though both Japanists and specialists on other areas of the world would profit from integrating Japanese political studies with broader comparative themes. This review seeks to correct a tendency toward scholarly isolation by addressing four themes in Japanese postwar experience and relating them to comparative political science research on other countries and regions. The four themes are styles of electoral mobilization, informalism and process as factors in party organization, power and performance in postwar policy making, and post-1993 electoral institution change.

INTRODUCTION

Some of the literature on Japanese postwar politics has made Japan's political experience less attractive than it should be to political scientists studying other countries. Many Japan watchers have attributed to Japan's postwar politics a level of exclusivity that renders the country utterly unlike other electoral democracies. Even though we do not believe all democracies operate in exactly the same way, we feel that overemphasizing Japan's exceptionalism has isolated Japanese studies from the mainstream of political science. This review suggests specifically how Japanese experience relates to research on other political systems, making Japanese studies more meaningful to persons researching other political milieux as well as suggesting a more cosmopolitan outlook to Japanists.

In this essay, we attempt to demonstrate that the study of Japan's postwar political patterns offers insights into larger questions pursued by political scientists. We begin by comparing several long-established political patterns in what the Japanese have called the 1995 system—which was in place from 1955 to 1993—with

1094-2939/01/0623-0093$14.00

observations about other, mainly European, countries. We then address recent institutional changes in Japan and note that their significance derives from sorting out the elements of change from those of continuity. We have chosen to focus on four areas that we judge will best accomplish the aims set out above. These areas are (*a*) the parochial nature of electoral mobilization, (*b*) political party organization and its tendency toward both institutionalization and deinstitutionalization, (*c*) the policy process, including debates over the role of the bureaucracy, a dominant party, and parliament, and (*d*) electoral system change.

THE 1955 SYSTEM: Parochial Electoral Mobilization in a "Matrix" Society

Elections inevitably involve an interaction between what politicians do to gain popular support and the reactions of democratic publics to the politicians' efforts. Although the individual act of voting has received extensive systematic attention from political scientists, how parties and candidates mobilize electoral support has not. Studies of elections and electoral behavior have taken either a macro societal approach (Lipset & Rokkan 1967, Lipset 1981, Lane & Ersson 1991), which emphasized broad social cleavages as the roots of electoral behavior or a micro-psychological approach, which focused on people's political attitudes as reflected in answers to surveys (Campbell et al 1960, Butler & Stokes 1969). How parties, candidates, and groups actually run election campaigns has received relatively little research attention despite the potentially critical role such behavior plays in linking society with politics and candidacies with the vote.

Japanese-Style Campaigns and Organization

Despite its neglect elsewhere, electoral mobilization has been a frequent theme in descriptions of Japan's political arrangements between 1955 and 1993. Curtis' (1971) investigation of the vote-gathering tactics of a member of parliament from Japan's southern island of Kyushu was the first major work in English on this topic. Curtis found that his informant negotiated with local social and political elites and organizations to mobilize the rural vote. Rural society at the time was so organizationally and relationally redundant that developing positive support from local leaders was the key to influencing ordinary people. In contrast, in a small city, the same candidate established a support association (*koenkai*), an organization or club that enlisted both ordinary voters and local elites as members. Support associations held regular meetings and subsidized entertainment and vacation trips for members. *Koenkai* also served as a vehicle for citizen contacts with the world of politicians and politics in the articulation of demands for representation of local and occupational interests and personal favors, not unlike politicians' political networks in Gans' (1962) Boston. Support associations also kept records of important events in their members' lives, such as weddings and funerals, and arranged for a congratulatory gift or expression of condolence at the appropriate time.

Flanagan (1968) was developing a theory of Japanese voting support mobilization at about the same time as Curtis' field study. Works by other authors in this same period rounded out the picture of a highly mobilized electorate. Richardson (1967a) described different mobilization styles in local elections depending on whether candidates sought votes from concentrated flatland hamlets, hamlets shaped like strings in hilly or mountainous areas, or social networks made up of former schoolmates and work colleagues. In addition, new candidates tended to place a higher weight on individual favors to gain support, whereas later in their careers they stressed their accomplishments as representatives of local interests.

Parochial electoral mobilization styles prevailed in most kinds of elections in postwar Japan. This was true even for secondary organizations in most cases. Secondary organizations were often cited as significant in the mobilization efforts of individual candidates at both the national (House of Representatives) and local levels. However, in the House of Councillors nationwide district, large organizations with a national base, such as trade unions, had advantages in gathering votes over most individual candidacies (Richardson 1967b). Many upper house members were elected from the ranks of organizations' leadership as a result.

Watanuki (1991) has addressed the issue of Japan's parochial styles of political mobilization by calling attention to the resemblance of Japanese patterns of political support to a matrix, i.e. a structure with myriads of individual pockets having their own special character and tradition. Moreover, even though it is often assumed that parochial candidate mobilization was mainly a rural and small-town phenomenon, studies of neighborhoods in large cities (Dore 1958, Bestor 1989) have shown that parochially focused campaigns and support networks are found in most kinds of residential situations, except large apartment complexes and the middle- to upper-middle–salaried class suburbs. Surveys of voters [Watanuki 1986, Akarui Senkyo Suishin Kyokai (League for the Advancement of Clean Elections) 1997] confirm their case-based results.

Contributing to the phenomenon of parochial campaigns and representation is the large number of persons in micro-community–style neighborhoods who are connected with Japan's many small and medium-sized businesses. These occupational categories involve 70% of Japan's work force (Patterson 1994, Miyake 1995, Richardson 1997). Small retailers are especially numerous and, since they usually live and conduct their business in the same building and depend on their neighbors for custom, they are usually involved in local affairs. Even many small manufacturers live and work in the same house or a few minutes away. Both shopkeepers and small manufacturers tend to be more engaged in community life than persons who commute to work at some distance, such as government bureaucrats and employees of large firms. Small-business owners and employees also frequently live in the same district for long periods. The result is an active micro-community life based on redundant social networks and organizational memberships that can be turned into channels for political mobilization and representation of local interests. Widespread community-based electoral mobilization and representation of local interests, in turn, have led politicians to provide a large subsidy and loan system for farmers and small businesses plus regulation of large businesses in ways that favor small enterprise (Calder 1988, Upham 1993). Although hardly unique to Japan, an enormous emphasis on local area assistance is one of the special characteristics of Japanese public finance (Patterson 1994).

Japan Versus Other Systems

Electoral mobilization in Japan and elsewhere has national as well as regional and local components. Parties parade on the national media stage, organize state and provincial support, and, depending on the country and election system, may gather votes in local communities. The Japanese electoral mobilization literature complements research in Western European industrialized countries and the United States by calling attention to the importance of community social structure and its relationship to the personal vote—including community-constituency service, organization, and leadership—as portrayed by Cain et al (1987) in Britain and the United States. Although election campaigns may be more decentralized in Japan than in most modern countries, the findings of the Japanese mobilization literature are certainly comparable to those on Europe by Dogan (1967), Powell (1970), Rose (1968), and Stephens (1981), all of which refer to the importance of local and regional electoral bases in the formation and sustenance of traditional social cleavages. There are also parallels with the Japanese studies in the early American voting literature (e.g. Key 1950, Berelson et al 1954). Indeed, both the Japanese and foreign literatures repeatedly emphasize the importance of some of the same micro-context variables: constituency service and leadership, concentrated populations, local organization mobilization, local grievances and traditions, and the importance of local personalities.

Japanese candidates' emphasis on personal campaigns has been said to have cultural roots because such campaigns use existing social organizations and networks for political purposes (Richardson 1974). Others, however, have argued that candidate-centered campaigns and the electorate's resulting emphasis on candidate over party (according to surveys) were the consequence of competition among multiple candidates from the same party in Japan's old multimember district election system (Rochon 1981). Despite its lack of the ascriptive social cleavages found in Europe and, in a lesser sense, North America (Flanagan & Richardson 1977), Japan's tradition of the mobilization of local electorates nonetheless serves as a reminder of the importance of micro-level patterns of political support and the ways in which this support is derived in systems often described in solely aggregated versions of electoral phenomena.

The individual candidates' mobilization styles described above were established under the 1955 system. However, even under this system, the electoral context in Japan changed substantially as the postwar period progressed and, as a result, so did political parties' manner of mobilizing voters. The Liberal Democratic Party (LDP) was slowly losing electoral support throughout much of the postwar period, especially during the late 1960s and 1970s. As the party's dependable level of mobilized support became less and less adequate to assure its retention of a majority of lower house seats, the LDP began to seek additional support outside its traditional core support groups. The target electors were members of Japan's growing "middle mass" (Murakami 1982), who could not always be mobilized in the same ways as traditional party supporters in Japan had been, thus conforming to Duverger's (1963) dictum that the middle class is hard to organize. Consequently, the LDP was forced to rely more on the use of public goods in the 1970s and 1980s (Calder 1988, Ramseyer & Rosenbluth 1993). However, even during this era, much public largesse ended up in peripheral rather than urban constituencies (Schlesinger 1997).

Although Japan's recent election system reforms (see below) have changed the ground rules, research in progress (Richardson 2000; Richardson & Patterson 1998) indicates that electoral mobilization styles have yet to change dramatically. In a 1997 fax survey addressed to 300 House of Representatives members from the new small election districts, nearly all of the 123 successful Dietmembers who responded said that they mobilized votes through local organizations and social networks. Respondents to voter surveys conducted at the time of the 1996 election (e.g. Akarui Senkyo Suishin Kyokai 1997) likewise indicated that (*a*) they voted on the basis of candidate qualities in large proportions—actually more than under the "1995 system" in the 1980s—although (*b*) they were contacted by candidates less frequently than respondents to surveys in earlier elections (a plausible effect of institutional change, as we discuss below). It is still unclear how much competition under a series of new party systems (three since 1993) will affect traditional styles of political mobilization and how these effects will influence configurations of party electoral power over the long term. Generational change within the parliamentary parties and an underlying trend toward greater electorate mobility and detachment from local organizations (Richardson 2000) may over time erode traditional mobilizational styles more than institutional change, but this remains to be seen. Either way, voting in Japanese elections may be more volatile as time goes on than it was under the 1995 system.

THE 1995 SYSTEM: Informalism and Contingent Institutionalization in Japanese Political Parties

The same political party, the LDP, dominated Japanese politics for the entire 38-year duration of the 1955 system. The LDP was an unusually complex set of organizations, and comprehending how it functioned adds to political science's understanding of political parties and their internal dynamics. Especially important for political science is the LDP's ability to manage a broad range of internal disagreements that derived from the clamoring demands of a large number of semi-institutionalized informal factions and other groups within the party. There was also considerable diversity of opinion reflective of its "catch-all" status

(Kirchheimer 1966) and the broad range of private interests to which the party was beholden.

The Importance of Informal Organization

Much of the research conducted on political parties has emphasized their formal structures and various internal structural relationships. Whether parties were centralized or decentralized and relationships between party executives and parliamentary groups are long-established concerns in the party-organization literature (Michels 1959, Duverger 1963). These same concerns are also reflected in pioneering studies of the LDP (Thayer 1969, Fukui 1970). However, what was different about the LDP, as is reflected in virtually all research on the party, was the size, importance, and institutionalized nature of its informal organizations. Whereas academic research on European parties always cited the presence of internal informal organization at some point—Michels' elites and Duverger's cadres are examples—an extensive description of informal structures, their imputed origins, and their consequences for the party was the leitmotif in most accounts of party politics in Japan.

The most conspicuous of the informal organizations within the LDP were the factions led by senior politicians in the parliamentary party. Ranging in number from 5 to 12, and in size from a mere handful of Dietmembers to nearly 150 in one case, the factions served mainly as mechanisms for career advancement. Senior politicians used their factions as a political base to form coalitions with other factions backing a slate of top government and party appointments. In the 1950s and 1960s, there was ordinarily a kind of two-party system within the party's leadership, composed of a dominant mainstream factional coalition opposed by a minority cluster of anti-mainstream groups. In the 1970s (when the LDP's majority in the Diet was razor thin) and later, all-party coalitions were the rule (Krauss 1984).

By joining a faction, or being sponsored as a new candidate for parliament by a faction, rank-and-file members of parliament were ensured of steady advancement through party and government positions as they accumulated tenure within the faction and Diet. The entire factional system was governed by a set of institutionalized informal norms (see below). The factions over time developed into almost formal organizations as their functions and procedures became more institutionalized. The institutionalization of informal norms and expectations in turn became important to party and faction longevity, as did other inducements to faction members, such as election campaign support, subsidies for ordinary support organization expenses, frequent faction meetings, and social gatherings designed to ensure intrafaction and intrasubfaction loyalty and integrity (Richardson 1997).

Although the intraparty factions dominated the party's recruitment processes, other informal or semiformal groups were more prominent in policy making. Occasionally, faction leadership took policy positions to try to unseat a party president, but policy groups, Dietmembers' groups linked with specific interests, and captive committees in the LDP's large internal policy-making organ—the Policy

Affairs Research Council (PARC)—more commonly took the lead on particular ideological or private interest issues. Policy leagues composed of "hawks" and "doves" on security issues and pro-PRC (People's Republic of China) versus pro-ROC (Taiwan) Dietmembers dominated party debates on Japan's military defense and China relations in the 1960s and 1970s. Other policy groupings, centering on LDP Dietmembers' specialization in the concerns of small business, agriculture, foreign policy, education, and other topical or pressure group issues, were prominent in the 1980s. These groupings were called *zoku*, roughly translated as "policy families."

The informal groups in the LDP behaved much like political parties in a complex multiparty system. Multiple groups contested top appointments and lesser promotions almost perennially, a concern which spilled over into leadership strategies on major issues. [Tax reform, agricultural market liberalization, and small-business policy are examples from the 1980s—other issues were prominent earlier (Donnelly 1977, Richardson 1997).] But in most instances, policy channels were more the domain of policy leagues and policy "families," since intrafaction ideological views and constituency allegiances were themselves so diverse that finding consensus within any faction was almost impossible.

To round out the portrait of informal organization in the LDP, it must be recognized that there were factions in prefectural parties as well as in some cities and constituencies. There were also strong local interests represented in the aforementioned Dietmember support organizations. Because of the multitude of pressures from outside the party and the complexity of interests within it, the LDP was as much a political system—a cluster of multiple, ongoing political processes—as a simple, definable structural arrangement. Although its formal and informal organization were and are widely described as centralized (Fukui 1970, Johnson 1986), in reality there are upward and downward pressures, and internal consensus or pluralism predominates depending on specific issues and times (Richardson 1997). Although power and interests were far more complexly dispersed in the LDP than in Kitschelt's elegant model of European Socialist parties (1994), the Japanese party showed the same tendency to manifest highly visible process-dependent characteristics. Simple structural portraits of parties viewed as unitary organizations are highly misleading.

Internal Pluralism

At times, the LDP's internal tensions and pluralism led almost to party breakdown. A conflict-fragmentation dynamic (Richardson 1997) took hold, in which frustrated elements of the party criticized leadership for policy failures or involvement in corruption and speculated about the need for a new political party involving links with opposition groups. Often there was a flurry of intraparty reform group activity, especially among "young" Dietmembers, whose electoral bases were fragile because of their short tenure. The dynamic was observable in 1972, at the end of Eisaku Sato's long tenure as prime minister; in 1974, when Kakuei Tanaka was accused of corruption involving Japanese purchase of Lockheed aircraft, and on several other occasions before and during the party's dramatic implosion in 1993. Throughout these incidents, Panebianco's (1988) insistence that parties are inherently and ultimately coalitions was demonstrated. The intermittent frailty of the LDP in the face of internal conflicts and external pressures serves as a reminder of the inadequacy of looking solely at parties' structural profiles or viewing them as unitary organizational actors whose changes come primarily from external challenges or party ideology (Duverger 1963, Wilson 1980).

Contingent Institutionalization

Polsby (1968) described the American Congress as institutionalized because it contained long-surviving structures, posed barriers to entry, and had a complex internal organization. Historical sociology (Steinmo et al 1992) and political economy (Hall 1986, North 1990) have somewhat similarly described long-lasting patterns of behavior as reflective of formally or informally derived institutionalization. The LDP, like other large Japanese parties, had highly visible institutionalized elements during the heyday of the 1955 system. These elements included the following:

1. A formal organizational structure framed policy-making procedures and provided a hierarchy of regularly functioning executive, representational bodies and units dedicated to development and operationalization of legislative and electoral strategies, including coordinated selection of election candidates (Fukui 1980, 1987; Richardson 1997).
2. An array of informal structures and social networks existed, which included factions, subfactions, policy leagues, and policy families. (The factions were the most durable because their membership rarely changed except through retirement, death, or intentional recruitment of new members.) There were also barriers to entry, and despite their informal origins, the factions had internal hierarchies of positions and regularly active membership units, including groups of Dietmembers with similar levels of electoral success. Some subgroups within the factions also had a similar hierarchy of offices (Richardson 1997).
3. An elaborate array of informal norms defined the amount of seniority necessary for MPs to be eligible for selection at each level of appointed office in the party or government, and there were expectations regarding the legitimate duration of one person's service as prime minister, what political successes or failures justified longer or shorter terms, and what "generation" of intraparty faction leaders offered likely candidates for the party presidency and prime ministership.

Nevertheless, despite the seeming strength of the above and other institutionalized elements, including coordination groups such as a party-cabinet liaison group and the Supreme Advisors (made up of former prime ministers and heads of the

House of Councillors), the LDP partially disintegrated in 1993 with the departure of part of its largest faction and quite a few individual members. The fragmentation of the party was accompanied by a proliferation of internal reform groups (Richardson 1997, Hrebnar & Nakamura 2000) and an intraparty generational cleavage pitting "young" MPs with less certain electoral futures against older, more secure party members. In addition, the factions themselves retreated to the status of "study groups" for several months, and although they were called factions again after the party returned to power in mid-1994 in a coalition with part of the Social Democratic Party, journalistic evidence does not indicate a full-scale return to the previous degree of institutionalized behavior. Rather, journalists suggest that the factions are weaker than before, especially in regard to internal hierarchical control. The LDP, in short, has been in a state of uncertain flux matching and contributing to the many uncertainties in post-1993 Japanese politics.

The partial collapse of Japan's dominant political party and its internal institutions was accompanied by the formation through defections and mergers of seven significant new parties in 1993–1996. There was also significant generational turnover in the Diet in 1993, as new parties fielded new candidates and the LDP endeavored to replace departed members. All of these events suggest that there has been a period of de-institutionalization in the LDP as well as in the Japanese party system in general. De-institutionalization in turn reflects the response of individuals and intraparty groups to electoral and career uncertainty. Affiliation with a party sufficiently credible to win power and to serve as both a channel for representation of local and group interests and as a mechanism for personal advancement was the glue that held the LDP together. Institutionalization of structures and practices in the LDP was contingent on the party's ability to serve its members' needs. The LDP was first and foremost a coalition [as Panebianco (1988) argues all parties are], and its institutionalization depended on this basic fact.

THE 1955 SYSTEM POLICY PROCESS: Negotiated Parliamentarism Versus Dominant Ministries

Debates abound over how Japan was ruled under the 1955 system and the direction and impact of national economic policy during that period. Some have argued that the center of power and policy making in Japan is the administrative bureaucracy. Ministries such as Finance and International Trade and Industry were seen as Japan's dominant political institutions, making policy through the influence of their expertise and role in drafting legislation. Proponents of the dominant-bureaucracy point of view have cited the recency of authoritarian government in Japan, the fact that early postwar conditions favored the power of the bureaucracy while impeding that of the National Diet, and the role of government in Japan's self-conscious growth (Johnson 1982a, 1986). Others have argued that power and policy rest with the actions of the dominant LDP. Proponents of this view tend to proceed from the perspective of principal-agent theory. Some argue that what has varied over time has been the LDP's propensity to involve itself directly in the governing process (Ramsayer & Rosenbluth 1993).

A host of other studies emphasize different aspects of the governing process in postwar Japan. Some researchers, for instance, characterized the Japanese parliament as a puppet body in which the opposition parties were powerless while the LDP dictated parliamentary schedules and outcomes (Baerwald 1974, Pempel 1977b, Dore 1986). Others argued that the LDP rank and file became more powerful as the postwar period progressed and elected officials gained more knowledge and experience in the governing process (Sato & Matsuzaki 1986). A few researchers see the interactions between the bureaucracy, political parties, interest groups, individual politicians, and parliament as a complex process encompassing many interdependent relationships (Masumi 1985). There is much to sort out in the policy-making literature on Japan.

The Dominant-Bureaucracy Hypothesis and Alternative Interpretations

Although all Japan scholars have viewed Japan's bureaucracy as among the most powerful and capable in the world, it was only after the publication of Johnson's (1982a) study of the Ministry of International Trade and Industry (MITI) and related works (Johnson 1982b) that a view of bureaucrats as ruling and politicians as reigning became prevalent. Johnson and other proponents offer many reasons why bureaucrats are dominant in Japan. All begin with the idea that history endowed Japan's bureaucrats with more power than other government institutions, an asymmetrical power distribution that postwar developments did not quickly change. It is true that Japan's democratic development followed a path similar to Western Europe's up until the 1930s. Elections for the lower house of Japan's national parliament began in 1890 under a limited suffrage system that granted the vote to mainly landowners. The franchise was gradually expanded apace with economic, social, and political change to the point that, by 1925, virtually all males could vote. This phase of Japan's development was characterized by an ascendant parliament and the development of an assertive party system. On the other hand, prewar development took place within a constitutional system that gave bureaucratic ministers unusually strong powers in the belief that these were consistent with Japan's need for central leadership to promote economic development and respond to other early modernization needs. The constitution, plus the ascendancy of the military during the 1930s depression and a strong postwar commitment to economic rehabilitation and growth, may have provided opportunities for various ministries to demonstrate leadership at certain points in Japan's recent history. These experiences and the recruitment of many top bureaucrats in the Finance, Foreign Affairs, and International Trade and Industry ministries from two or three national universities (Koh 1989) led many analysts to believe that Japan is led by a powerful bureaucratic elite akin to that of France (Suleiman 1974).

In various writings on the growth policies of Japan's MITI and related topics, Johnson (e.g. 1982a) concluded that Japan was a ministry-led "developmental state." Johnson has referred to Japanese politics as "softly authoritarian" rather than democratic because he believes that officials who are not elected make policy decisions and write the nation's laws. Supporters of these interpretations or derivative arguments include Pempel (1977a), Anchordoguy (1989), Okimoto (1989), and a host of Japanese and American journalists and policy analysts.

Johnson's principal assertions have frequently been qualified or even challenged by academic research. Calder (1988), in his general treatment of governing in postwar Japan, saw the LDP's policy interventions as examples of compensating economically deprived constituencies and other interests, for political reasons, more than as examples of deference to the will of powerful bureaucrats. Ramseyer & Rosenbluth (1993) similarly advanced the idea that bureaucrats play the role of agent in the political process, either carrying out party politicians' wishes directly or acting in anticipation of their desires. Trezise & Suzuki (1976) and Garon & Mochizuki (1993) have reported involvement by politicians and interest groups in policy making from early in the postwar period. More recently, Katz (1999) has argued that elected officials have been central all along and that it is politicians who, in policy areas of mutual concern, share common interests with the government's various ministries and agencies.

Evidence confronting the dominant-bureaucracy idea is also found in work that examines specific policy areas or government ministries. This group includes Campbell's (1977) analysis of the Finance Ministry and budget process and his more recent work on changes in health care policy (1992). Both books show various scenarios in which members of Japan's LDP were involved in policy making and others in which bureaucrats dominated. Other extensive treatments include Kato's (1994) evaluation of the tax reform process, which shows that bureaucrats must continually revise tax reform proposals to please the nation's elected officials. Kohno & Nishizawa (1990) have similarly shown that elections were at the center of construction spending in Japan's election districts between 1955 and 1985. Others, such as Park (1986) and Campbell (1989), have reported that bureaucratic officials look to supportive constituencies in pressure groups and the LDP for help in promoting their policy preferences. Donnelly (1977) similarly described bidirectional political influence characteristic of agricultural policy making, especially in the government's annual ritual of setting of the price of rice. In some years, bureaucrats dominated outcomes; in other times, the LDP farm bloc won; and occasionally, Japan's prime minister had to play the role of arbiter between the various power centers.

Other studies have focused on the area of policy making that proponents of the dominant-bureaucracy view (e.g. Okimoto 1989) consider beyond the reach of the parochial political interests of elected officials, namely industrial policy. In a pioneering study, Beason & Weinstein (1996) developed a methodology to calibrate the impact of specific policy efforts on the various sectors of Japan's economy and found not only that government efforts had no positive impact on productivity growth but also that government assistance was inversely linked to growth in particular industries. Richardson (1997) documented the same patterns by comparing value-added data for specific industries in growth and recession periods with government aid levels. Patterson (1994) likewise called attention to the government's use of large portions of Fiscal Investment Loan Plan (FILP) money, long considered the government's principal industrial policy tool, for loans to small and medium-sized enterprises to maintain the LDP's political support in that sector. Richardson (1997) characterized these politically motivated programs as examples of Japan's "Welfare Inc." and "Clientelism Inc." as opposed to the better known "Japan Inc." image of collusion between powerful ministries, corporate interests, and acquiescent politicians (Kaplan 1972).

One of the arguments of of dominant-bureaucracy proponents has been that the shape of political power in postwar Japan was influenced by the prevalence of former bureaucrats in the Diet. This view implies that former bureaucrats who became members of the LDP and got elected to the House of Representatives essentially colonized the LDP and the top echelons of the party and government (cabinets were in fact dominated by ex-bureaucrats before the mid-1980s) for the purpose of keeping politicians focused on bureaucratic wishes. However, such an interpretation ignores research demonstrating that bureaucrats do not view themselves as the dominant players in the policy-making process (Muramatsu & Krauss 1984). Changes in political recruitment over time also altered the balance of influence within the LDP and Diet between former bureaucrats, whose numbers have decreased, and Dietmembers from alternative backgrounds, who have become more numerous. In addition, many of Japan's Dietmembers today are second-generation politicians whose fathers were former local politicians who had worked their way up to national status through the party, not "descended from bureaucratic heaven," as the Japanese expression goes.

By themselves, these trends over time in recruitment of the LDP's leadership and parliamentary party are important. At the same time, Japan's pattern of recruitment of ex-bureaucrat Diet members is not unique. France, for example, displays as much or greater dominance of top positions by persons from bureaucratic backgrounds (Wright 1989), and many bureaucrats (including quite a few who have yet to retire) can be found in German parliamentary parties (Loewenberg 1967, Paterson & Southern 1992). The second-generation-politician phenomenon can also be found in other countries.

The dominant-bureaucracy hypothesis rests in part on the high level of technocratic skills attributed to ministry bureaucrats. Yet, interestingly, studies have shown that the technocratic skills that allegedly enable Japan's bureaucrats to pick economic winners or predict the future were not consistently visible in concrete policy predictions and applications. For example, Friedman (1988) found that MITI's predictions were inaccurate for both output targets and product mixes in the machine tool industry, partly because MITI had too few officials supervising an industry with literally thousands of small firms and no single industry organization. Samuels (1987) noted similar errors in prediction of business cycles that affected the demand for domestic coal, as well as industry noncompliance with various MITI measures. Komiya et al (1988) and Richardson (1997) reported various other examples of industry noncompliance and frequent support for weak rather than strong industries. Finally, Fong (1990) cited MITI's lack of success in assuring corporate cooperation and compliance in the ministry's famous fifth-generation computer project.

The disjuncture between Johnson's work and other studies partly reflects that Johnson mainly described MITI's policies and policy debates—obviously a valuable contribution—but did not explore their implementation. Despite his claim that postwar Japan is a developmental state, his evidence did not reach far enough to unequivocally support such an interpretation. Few would deny that Japan's bureaucratic ministries are powerful and led by graduates of schools with highly competitive admissions, but the ministries' outputs fall short of the miracles formerly attributed to them.

Dominant-Party Influence

Between the dominant-bureaucracy view and its opposition is an understanding of power and policy making that focuses on Japan's dominant party, the LDP and its Diet membership, and the interest groups to which it has been most beholden. Campbell (1977) pondered whether Rose's (1969) concern that British MPs find it difficult to run ministries applied to postwar Japan. However, research shows that Japanese cabinet appointees appear to be freer from intraparty affairs and parliamentary duties than their British counterparts were in Rose's view (Richardson 1997). They also confront the problem of the brief tenures of ministry appointments by exercising greater policy expertise than they did earlier (Richardson 1997), which reflects the LDP's long stay in power and accumulated experience based on ties with particular interests (Sato & Matsuzaki 1986). Campbell noted several important instances in which politicians were the main source of policy leadership in earlier times. Masumi (1995) likewise has weighed in on the side of LDP policy influence, noting many cases in which the LDP overcame ministry preferences or even initiated ideas that the bureaucracy had to put into legislative proposals. Indeed, in the 1980s, the LDP went so far as to create a coordination council to reconcile party and cabinet minister views even though both ministers and party leaders were from the same party (Richardson 1997).

Perhaps the most striking example of LDP influence on policy was the development over time of a "second legislature," the Policy Affairs Research Council, within the dominant party [Fukui 1987, Nihon Keizai Shimbunsha (Japan Economic Newspaper Inc.) 1983]. The PARC was organized in divisions that paralleled cabinet ministry jurisdictions; under each division there were also special committees/councils, and attached to these were subcommittees and specialized committees. Like the US Congress, the PARC holds hearings on prominent controversial issues, especially those affecting multiple LDP client constituencies.

There are also captive subcommittees and specialized committees that lobby for particular causes within the PARC (Richardson 1997). The PARC's existence and extensive institutionalization obviously resulted from the LDP's long tenure and catch-all status.

Japanese-Style Corporatism

The PARC also symbolized the LDP's deep dependence on a select number of interests, mainly, according to the "corporatism without labor" school (Pempel & Tsunekawa 1979), big business and agriculture. The corporatist view postulated an intimacy based on mutual dependence that constrained both LDP power and interest group influence, depending on the times and the issue. [This was not a corporatism based on economic pacts between big business and labor like those reported in small European countries (Katzenstein 1984).] Whatever the case for Japanese-style corporatism, which Pempel (1987) states became less restrictive over time, recent research (Garon & Mochizuki 1993) points out that Japanese-style corporatism did not actually exclude labor to the extent argued earlier. Nor did the initial Japanese-style corporatism thesis acknowledge the importance of small-business interests and their difference from big-business concerns, nor consider the demands of numerous social policy groups that were addressed starting in the 1970s (Muramatsu & Krauss 1987, Calder 1988, Richardson 1997).

Negotiated Parliamentarism

The assumptions of the "corporatism without labor" thesis are part of a broadly accepted view that Japan's opposition parties had little or no influence within the Diet and, relatedly, that the parliamentary process was a sham cloaking virtually total control by the LDP. This was the view of various works by Baerwald (e.g. 1974), Dore (1986), and most writings on Japanese politics before Mochizuki's (1982) pathbreaking analysis of Diet procedures and processes. Among other things, Mochizuki showed how consensus rules were used by Diet committee directors to delay or effectively veto LDP legislation. The dominant party in this case negotiated quid pro quo agreements to give up something in exchange for opposition party concessions on the same or other legislative issues. Mochizuki's treatise was preceded by less completely documented but still telling analyses of cross-party negotiations and agreements between dominant party and opposition on various issues (Kobayashi 1973, Misawa 1973). Finally, in a systematic analysis of Diet procedures over almost all of the 1955–1993 period, Richardson (1997) showed that Japan's parliament was like legislatures in most other parliamentary democracies on several dimensions. Consensual issues dominated legislative agendas just as they do in Britain and elsewhere (Loewenberg & Patterson 1988, Norton 1990). Moreover, concessions—including delays, termination, and negotiated amendments—took place between the dominant party and opposition on up to 47% of controversial bills; the figure for amendments alone was higher than has been reported for Britain's House of Commons in recent years.

The 1955 system operated under limits on ministry influence; upward pressures from small business, farmers, and other groups in the LDP's PARC; contradictions in the economic dirigiste experience; and integration of labor, small business, and opposition parties into parliamentary and other political processes. As a result, it was far from totally one-sided and irresponsible. This strong tendency toward policy-making pluralism and negotiated parliamentarism has continued with only minor modifications since 1993's partial collapse of the LDP. To be sure, journalistic sources indicate that several ministries have been weakened by scandals involving leading personnel or policy flops. Some decline in the government's influence may also have been caused by its failure to end an eight-year recession. Several examples of strenuous intraparty negotiations over parliamentary bills have also been featured in the press and other mass media. But as yet there is no indication that dramatic change in the policy-making process has taken place to the degree reported in the Western press.

POST–1955 SYSTEM ELECTORAL LAW CHANGE: Manipulated Institutionalism

The final area we examine in this essay concerns the Japanese government's decision to change its House of Representatives election system. The old system, which had consisted of 130 multimember districts averaging 3 to 5 seats, was replaced by a mixed system that combined 300 single-member districts with 11 proportional representation districts containing 200 (since then reduced to 180) seats. (Electors cast a single, nontransferable vote under the old system and a single vote in each of the two kinds of districts under the new system.) The reform legislation was enacted on the final day of an extended Diet session in January 1994 after five years of debate in an environment of increasing public dissatisfaction with the state of Japanese politics. The recent debate was preceded by earlier discussions of electoral reform dating back to the 1970s (Reed 1993, Christensen 1994).

Before returning to the question of what institutional change has produced, we should mention the long series of studies of the old multimember district system, which addressed (*a*) the effects of the former system on competition between candidates versus parties (Rochon 1981; Taagepera & Shugart 1989; Cox 1991, 1994) and (*b*) the LDP's success in making rational nomination decisions under the multimember district system (Cox & Niou 1994; Cox 1997, 1999; Cox & Rosenbluth 1996; Browne & Patterson 1999a,b; Browne & Patterson 2000; Reed 2000). Like quite a few works in the institutionalist tradition, some studies assumed that institutions influence behavior in a simple, direct, causal fashion. Rationality under the old system was seen as simply mechanically defined seat maximization without attention to the concerns and processes that generate nomination decisions. Although this position undoubtedly contains some truth at times, it also leaves much out. For example, Gunther (1989) has shown that institutions alone do not shape behavior but influence both parties and electorates in combination with other factors. In Japan, such factors could include the Japanese preference for deep constituency mobilization, which creates candidates who are very hard to dissuade from running. In addition, candidate selection is often a collective decision involving local factions and vested interests as well as national party organs, so that assumptions of unitary actor control are not appropriate. The extent to which institutions are actually designed to produce specific political results is also left out of many studies. Yet the introduction in Europe of proportional representation systems, which political sociologists would later claim dictated behavior, actually reflected efforts by parties to institutionalize the status quo in the late 1800s (Lorwin 1966). Accounts of the history of electoral institutions in Japan (Christensen 1994, Kohno 1997, Patterson 1998) and the United States (Rae 1971) likewise point to parties' efforts to institutionalize the contemporary status quo. The contribution of Japanese research to the institutionalist tradition is, in our opinion, to confirm that institutions (*a*) are contingent on other factors in their effects and (*b*) are often consciously designed to preserve a particular set of political outcomes that are already in place.

According to some sources, many observers of Japanese politics were surprised that the weak governments that ruled Japan during the five years of debate over a new system were actually able to scrap the old system and replace it with a new set of rules in 1994 (Christensen 1994). Political conditions in the late 1980s favored the alteration of Japan's old lower-house electoral system. The old system symbolized everything that was wrong with Japanese politics, and as the process of designing a new set of electoral rules for Japan began in earnest, the message to the Japanese public was that a new system would place parties and policy—not individuals and the pork barrel—at the center of politics. Still, disagreements proliferated over the exact form the new system should take, reflecting anxiety over the potential effects of a new set of electoral rules on individual MPs' electoral fortunes and those of the respective political parties. Nothing influences the electoral fortunes of politicians more directly than the rules under which they stand as candidates.

Since the creation of the new set of House of Representatives election rules, two elections have been held, one in October 1996 and a second in June 2000. Election results in both instances suggest that perhaps changes in the voting system in Japan were not so remarkable as was widely thought at the time of their enactment. In the first two lower-house elections held under the new system, virtually no change occurred in the vote shares of parties that had appeared in at least two elections. In the 1993 election held under the old rules, the LDP obtained 36.6% of the vote. When we aggregate the vote from all of the new system's districts, we note that the LDP received 35.1% of the vote in 1996 and 36.1% of the vote in 2000. Changes in the seat shares obtained by some other parties were equally unremarkable. Between 1993 and 1996, the change in the percentage of seats held by the LDP was 5.0%, and the figures for the Socialists and the Communists were 3.1% and 2.2%, respectively. These percentages are comparable to the average interelection seat change under the old system for the LDP—4.9% between 1958 and 1993—while the averages for the Socialists and Communists in the same period were 3.51% and 1.68%. Even though the LDP's base had declined over time relative to the opposition parties, short-term change still followed old patterns. Equally important, the proliferation of new parties begun in 1993 had not in any sense been reduced to the bipolar configuration sought by many reformers in either 1996 or 2000.

As we have said, history (Cain 1985, Lorwin 1966, Kohno 1997) shows that changes in a nation's electoral rules often take place with some implicit guarantee that the status quo will be protected or at least that the electoral uncertainty attending such a change will be reduced significantly. Elections held under new rules should thus produce behavior and outcomes that approximate conditions prior to the election. Even though short-term forces defined by election-specific issues and candidacy effects can produce deviations, elected officials have a strong incentive to agree to new electoral rules if the system is designed in a way that does not manifestly reduce their chance of surviving electorally.

For parties that did not change their identities, electoral reform seems not to have altered the outcomes of the 1996 and 2000 elections. We can also show highly suggestive evidence that the new system's district boundaries were drawn in a way to protect incumbents, or, in other words, that the candidate component of the 1993–2000 electoral experience was fairly stable. To make this determination, we used data provided by Japan's Seiji Koho Senta (Political Public Relations Center) (1996). The Center ranked each incumbent in the country based on the total number of votes that he or she obtained in the 1993 election in the areas defined by the new election-district boundaries, which were in most instances derived by cutting up the old constituencies. This produced an initial ranking for each incumbent in each new district based on her or his performance in the last election under the old system, which could then be compared with that person's behavior and performance in 1996.

If candidate incumbency was a priority in new constituency design, there should be a close fit between incumbents' areas of greatest strength under the former system, the shape of new constituencies negotiated by representatives of the different parties, and candidates' success under the new system. If incumbents stand for reelection and win in those districts where they had done the best in the past, this is the best evidence available to suggest that the boundaries were drawn with that specific candidate's reelection in mind. We therefore expect to see all incumbents standing for reelection in 1996 under the new system in the district in which they ranked highest in 1993's election based on the old districts. We also expect many of them to win. An analysis of incumbent candidacies in all post-1994 single-member election districts showed that in fact 85% of all incumbent candidates ran in new districts where they had been ranked number one in 1993's old-system election (Patterson 1998). Of those candidates, all but 2.5% won in the new district. The persistence of old patterns was obviously designed into the new election system.

Although it seems clear that election districts were redrawn to accommodate strong local incumbents' interests, a second provision of reform virtually guaranteed that "surplus" incumbents—those not given party endorsements in redrawn districts taken from their former constituencies because of perceived weakness or factional opposition—would still find their way into the Diet. These kinds of incumbents were typically assigned to their party's PR list in the relevant regional constituency, thus further reducing the chances for their failure under the new system, and, in fact, 12% of the incumbent candidates standing for reelection in 1996 entered the Diet through this mechanism. These practices, plus placing party "stars" at the top of regional lists, further blurred the extent to which the new system can be said to have truly changed Japan's electoral mechanisms. Finally, 3% of the incumbents who ran in single-seat districts were not ranked number one under the old system in the constituency in which they chose to run in 1996, yet they refused to seek the safety net of a PR list position. Some were successful, some were not.

Despite evidence of continuity in many areas, the electoral process still changed somewhat under the new 1994 rules. Successful incumbent single-member district candidates in most constituencies had to mobilize many more votes—typically up to three times as many as they had received as candidates under the old system. Even though the new system was designed to fit candidates' strengths, candidates' vote-gathering needs were considerably greater than before. Existing candidate electoral machines also lost substantial numbers of former supporters in areas no longer included in the relevant new constituency. Some adjustment was still necessary, despite the way in which the new election boundaries were drawn. There was also a large increase in successful new candidacies in both the 1993 and 1996 elections relative to the pre-1993 average, as newly formed parties added candidates and/or the LDP replaced Dietmembers who had defected to other parties in 1993. This increase added to the ranks of so-called young MPs, who were more reform-minded and restive than their seniors owing to their feelings of electoral vulnerability. That there was change is obvious, although it occurred in more complicated ways than were reported by the popular media.

CONCLUSION

Japanese politics shares many features with political systems in other industrialized countries. There are also inevitably some differences. Acknowledging this, however, does not mean that our attempts to explain Japan's postwar political trajectory should be outside the types of explanations used in mainstream political science for American, European, and other contexts.

LITERATURE CITED

Akarui Senkyo Suishin Kyokai. 1997. *Dai 41kai Shugiin Giin Sosenkyo no Jittai* [The Results of the 41st House of Representatives Election]. Tokyo: Akarui Senkyo Suishin Kyokai

Allinson GD. 1993. Citizenship, fragmentation and the negotiated polity. In *Political Dynamics in Contemporary Japan*, ed. GD Allinson, Y Sone, pp. 17–49. Ithaca, NY: Cornell Univ. Press

Anchordoguy M. 1989. *Computers Inc.: Japan's Challenge to IBM*. Cambridge, MA: Harvard Univ. Counc. East Asian Stud.

Baerwald H. 1974. *Japan's Parliament: An Introduction*. Cambridge: Cambridge Univ. Press

Beason R, Weinstein D. 1996. Growth, economies of scale, and targeting in Japan, 1955–1990. *Rev. Econ. Stat.* 78:286–95

Berelson B, Lazarsfeld P, McPhee W. 1954. *Voting: A Study of Opinion Formation in a Presidential Election Campaign*. Chicago: Univ. Chicago Press

Bestor T. 1989. *Neighborhood Tokyo*. Stanford, CA: Stanford Univ. Press

Browne EC, Patterson D. 1999a. An empirical theory of rational nominating behavior applied to Japanese district elections. *Br. J. Polit. Sci.* 29:259–89

Browne EC, Patterson D. 1999b. Rejoinder to Cox's comment on 'an empirical theory of rational nominating behavior applied to Japanese district elections.' *Br. J. Polit. Sci.* 29:569–75

Browne EC, Patterson D. 2000. Rejoinder to Reed's comment on 'an empirical theory of rational nominating behavior applied to Japanese district elections.' *Br. J. Polit. Sci.* In press

Butler D, Stokes D. 1969. *Political Change in Britain: Forces Affecting Political Choice*. New York: St. Martin's

Cain B. 1985. Assessing the partisan effects of redistricting. *Am. Polit. Sci. Rev.* 79:320–33

Cain B, Ferejohn J, Fiorina M. 1987. *The Personal Vote: Constituency Service and Electoral Independence*. Cambridge, MA: Harvard Univ. Press

Calder K. 1988. *Crisis and Compensation: Public Policy and Political Stability in Japan*. Princeton, NJ: Princeton Univ. Press

Campbell A, Converse P, Miller W, Stokes D. 1960. *The American Voter*. New York: Wiley

Campbell JC. 1977. *Contemporary Japanese Budget Politics*. Berkeley: Univ. Calif. Press

Campbell JC. 1989. Bureaucratic primacy: Japanese policy communities in an American perspective. *Governance* 2:5–22

Campbell JC. 1992. *How Policies Change: The Japanese Government and the Aging Society*. Princeton, NJ: Princeton Univ. Press

Christensen RV. 1994. Electoral reform in Japan: how it was enacted and changes it may bring. *Asian Surv.* 35:589–605

Cox GW. 1991. SNTV and d'Hondt are equivalent. *Elec. Stud.* 10:118–32

Cox GW. 1994. Strategic voting equilibria under the single nontransferable vote. *Am. J. Polit. Sci.* 88:608–21

Cox GW. 1997. *Making Votes Count: Strategic Coordination in the World's Electoral Systems*. New York: Cambridge Univ. Press

Cox GW. 1999. A comment on Browne and Patterson's 'an empirical theory of rational nominating behavior applied to Japanese district elections.' *Br. J. Polit. Sci.* 29:565–69

Cox GW, Niou E. 1994. Seat bonuses under the single nontransferable vote system: evidence from Japan and Taiwan. *Comp. Politics* 26:221–36

Cox GW, Rosenbluth F. 1996. Factional competition for the party endorsement. *Br. J. Polit. Sci.* 26:259–69

Curtis GL. 1971. *Electioneering Japanese Style*. New York: Columbia Univ. Press

Dogan M. 1967. Political cleavage and social stratification in France and Italy. See Lipset & Rokkan 1967, pp. 129–98

Donnelly MW. 1977. Setting the price of rice: a study in political decisionmaking. See Pempel 1977, pp. 143–200

Dore R. 1958. *City Life in Japan: A Study of a Tokyo Ward*. Berkeley: Univ. Calif. Press

Dore R. 1986. *Flexible Rigidities: Industrial Policy and Structural Adjustment in the Japanese Economy 1970–80*. Stanford, CA: Stanford Univ. Press

Duverger M. 1963. *Political Parties*. New York: Wiley

Flanagan SF. 1968. Voting behavior in Japan: the persistence of traditional patterns. *Comp. Polit. Stud.* 1:391–412

Flanagan SF, Richardson BM. 1977. *Japanese*

Electoral Behavior: Social Cleavages, Social Networks and Partisanship. No. 2-6-024, Sage Contemp. Polit. Sociol. Ser., ed. R Rose. London: Sage

Flanagan SF, Kohei S, Miyake I, Richardson BM, Watanuki J. 1991. *The Japanese Voter*. New Haven, CT: Yale Univ. Press

Fong GR. 1990. State strength, industry structure and industrial policy. *Comp. Polit.* 22:273–99

Friedman D. 1988. *The Misunderstood Miracle: Industrial Development and Political Change in Japan*. Ithaca, NY: Cornell Univ. Press

Fukui H. 1970. *Party in Power: The Japanese Liberal Democrats and Policymaking*. Berkeley: Univ. Calif. Press

Fukui H. 1980. Japan: factionalism in a dominant party system. In *Political Parties and Factionalism in Comparative Perspective*, ed. F Belloni, D Bellor, pp. 43–72. Santa Barbara, CA: ABC-Clio

Fukui H. 1987. The policy research council of Japan's Liberal Democratic Party: policy making role and practice. *Asian Thought Soc.* 11:3–30

Gans HJ. 1962. *The Urban Villagers*. New York: Free Press of Glencoe

Garon S, Mochizuki M. 1993. Negotiating social contracts. In *Postwar Japan as History*, ed. A Gordon, pp. 145–66. Berkeley: Univ. California Press

Gunther R. 1989. Electoral laws, party systems, and elites: the case of Spain. *Am. Polit. Sci. Rev.* 83:835–58

Hall PA. 1986. *Governing the Economy: The Politics of State Intervention in Britain and France*. Cambridge, UK: Polity

Hrebnar RJ, Nakamura A. 2000. The Liberal Democratic Party. In *The Japanese Party System: From One-Party Rule to Coalition Government*, ed. RJ Hrebnar, pp. 85–147. Boulder, CO: Westview

Johnson C. 1982a. *MITI and the Japanese Miracle: The Growth of Industrial Policy, 1925–75*. Stanford, CA: Stanford Univ. Press

Johnson C. 1982b. Political institutions and economic performance: the government business relationship in Japan, South Korea and Taiwan. In *The Political Economy of New Asian Industrialism*, ed. FC Deyo, pp. 136–64. Ithaca, NY: Cornell Univ. Press

Johnson C. 1986. Tanaka kakuei, structural corruption and the advent of machine politics in Japan. *J. Jpn. Stud.* 12:1–28

Kaplan EJ. 1972. *Japan—The Government Business Relationship: A Guide for the American Businessman*. Washington, DC: US Dep. Commerce

Kato J. 1994. *The Probem of Bureaucratic Rationality: Tax Politics in Japan*. Princeton, NJ: Princeton Univ. Press

Katz R. 1999. *Japan: The System that Soured*. New York: ME Sharpe

Katzenstein PJ. 1984. *Corporatism and Change: Austria, Switzerland and the Politics of Industry*. Ithaca, NY: Cornell Univ. Press

Key V. 1950. *Southern Politics in State and Nation*. New York: Knopf

Kirchheimer O. 1966. The transformation of the Western European party systems. In *Political Parties and Political Development*, ed. J La Palombara, M Weiner, pp. 177–200. Princeton, NJ: Princeton Univ. Press

Kitschelt H. 1994. *The Transformation of European Social Democracy*. New York: Cambridge Univ. Press

Kobayashi N. 1973. The small and medium enterprises organization law. In *Japanese Politics: An Inside View*, ed. H Itoh, 2:49–67. Ithaca, NY: Cornell Univ. Press

Koh BC. 1989. *Japan's Administrative Elite*. Berkeley: Univ. Calif. Press

Kohno M. 1997. *Japan's Postwar Party Politics*. Princeton, NJ: Princeton Univ. Press

Kohno M, Nishizawa Y. 1990. A study of the electoral business cycle in Japan. *Comp. Polit.* 22:151–66

Komiya R, Okuno M, Suzumura K. 1988. *Industrial Policy of Japan*. San Diego, CA: Acad. Press

Krauss ES. 1984. Conflict in the Diet: toward conflict management in Diet politics. In

Conflict in Japan, ed. ES Krauss, TP Rohlen, PG Steinhoff, pp. 243–93. Honolulu: Univ. Hawaii Press

Lane JE, Ersson SO. 1991. *Politics and Society in Western Europe*. London: Sage

Lipset SM. 1981. *Political Man: The Social Bases of Politics*. Baltimore, MD: Johns Hopkins Univ. Press

Lipset SM, Rokkan S, eds. 1967. *Party Systems and Voter Alignments: Cross National Perspectives*. New York: Free

Loewenberg G. 1967. *Parliament in the German Political System*. Ithaca, NY: Cornell Univ. Press

Loewenberg G, Patterson S. 1988. *Comparing Legislatures*. Lanham, MD: Univ. Press America

Lorwin VR. 1966. Belgium: religion, class and language in national politics. *Political Opposition in Western Democracies*, ed. R Dahl, 5:147–87. New Haven, CT: Yale Univ. Press

Masumi J. 1985. *Postwar Politics in Japan, 1945–55*. Berkeley, CA: Cent. Jpn. Stud. Jpn. Res. Monogr. 6

Masumi J. 1995. *Contemporary Politics in Japan*. Berkeley: Univ. Calif. Press

Michels R. 1959. *Political Parties*. New York: Dover

Misawa S. 1973. An outline of the policymaking process in Japan. In *Japanese Politics: An Inside View*, ed. H Itoh, pp. 12–48. Ithaca, NY: Cornell Univ. Press

Miyake I. 1995. Jimoto rieki shiko to hoshuka [feelings of local self-interest and conservatism]. *Leviathan* 7:31–46

Mochizuki M. 1982. Managing and influencing the Japanese legislative process: the role of parties and the national Diet. PhD thesis. Harvard Univ., Cambridge, MA. 539 pp.

Murakami Y. 1982. The age of new middle mass politics: the case of Japan. *J. Jpn. Stud.* 1:29–72

Muramatsu M, Krauss ES. 1984. Bureaucrats and politicians in policymaking. *Am. Polit. Sci. Rev.* 78:126–46

Muramatsu M, Krauss ES. 1987. The conservative policy line and the development of patterned pluralism. In *The Political Economy of Japan. Vol 1. The Domestic Transformation*, ed. K Yamamura, Y Yasuba, pp. 516–54. Stanford, CA: Stanford Univ. Press

Muramatsu M, Krauss ES. 1990. The dominant party and social coalitions in Japan. In *Uncommon Democracies: The One-Party Dominant Regimes*, ed. TJ Pempel, pp. 282–95. Ithaca, NY: Cornell Univ. Press

Muramatsu M. 1993. Patterned pluralism under challenge. In *Political Dynamics in Contemporary Japan*, ed. GD Allinson, Y Sone, pp. 50–71. Ithaca, NY: Cornell Univ. Press

Nihon Keizai Shimbunsha. 1983. *Jiminto Seichokai* [The Liberal Democratic Party Policy Affairs Research Council]. Tokyo: Nihon Keizai Shimbunsha

North DC. 1990. *Institutions, Institutional Change and Economic Performance*. Cambridge: Cambridge Univ. Press

Norton P, ed. 1990. *Parliaments in Western Europe*. London: Frank Cass

Okimoto DI. 1989. *Between MITI and the Market: Japanese Industrial Policy for High Technology*. Stanford, CA: Stanford Univ. Press

Panebianco A. 1988. *Political Parties: Organization and Power*. Cambridge: Cambridge Univ. Press

Park Y. 1986. *Bureaucrats and Ministers in Japanese Government*. Berkeley: Ctr. Jpn. Stud., Univ. Calif.

Paterson WE, Southern D. 1992. *Governing Germany*. Oxford, UK: Blackwell

Patterson D. 1994. Electoral interest and economic policy: the political origins of financial aid to small business in Japan. *Comp. Polit. Stud.* 27:425–47

Patterson D. 1998. New rules and old outcomes: understanding the impact of Japan's new electoral system. In *Confidence and Uncertainty in Japan, Proc. Ann. Conf. Jpn. Stud. Assoc. Can.*, ed. M Donnelly, pp. 81–92. Toronto: Univ. Toronto–York Univ. Joint Cent. for Asia-Pacific Stud.

Pempel TJ, ed. 1977a. *Policymaking in*

Contemporary Japan. Ithaca, NY: Cornell Univ. Press

Pempel TJ. 1977b. The bureaucratization of policymaking in postwar Japan. *Am. J. Polit. Sci.* 18:647–64

Pempel TJ. 1987. The unbundling of "Japan, Inc.": the changing dynamics of Japanese policy formation. *J. Jpn. Stud.* 13:271–306

Pempel TJ, Tsunekawa K. 1979. Corporatism without labor? The Japanese anomaly. In *Trends Toward Corporatist Intermediation*, ed. P Schmitter, G Lembruch, pp. 231–70. London/Beverly Hills, CA: Sage

Polsby N. 1968. The institutionalization of the U.S. House of Representatives. *Am. Polit. Sci. Rev.* 62:144–68

Powell B. 1970. *Social Fragmentation and Political Hostility: An Austrian Case Study*. Stanford, CA: Stanford Univ. Press

Rae DW. 1971. *The Political Consequences of Electoral Laws*. New Haven, CT: Yale Univ. Press. Rev. ed.

Ramsayer JM, Rosenbluth FM. 1993. *Japan's Political Marketplace*. Cambridge, MA: Harvard Univ. Press

Reed SR. 1993. *Making Common Sense of Japan*. Pittsburgh, PA: Univ. Pittsburgh Press

Reed SR. 2000. What is rationality and why should we care: a comment on Browne and Patterson. *Br. J. Polit. Sci.* In press

Richardson BM. 1967a. Japanese local politics: support mobilization and leadership styles. *Asian Surv.* 8:860–75

Richardson BM. 1967b. A Japanese house of councillors election: support mobilization and political recruitment. *Mod. Asian Stud.* 1:385–402

Richardson BM. 1974. *The Political Culture of Japan*. Berkeley: Univ. Calif. Press

Richardson BM. 1988. Constituency candidates vs. parties in Japanese voting behavior. *Am. Polit. Sci. Rev.* 82:695–718

Richardson BM. 1997. *Japanese Democracy: Power Coordination and Performance*. New Haven, CT: Yale Univ. Press

Richardson BM. 2000. *Is Japan losing faith? If so, how and why?* Presented at Faith in Polit. in Jpn. and US Conf., Quebec City, Quebec, Aug. 5–8

Richardson B, Patterson D. 1998. *The personal vote and institutional change in Japan*. Presented at Annu. Meet. Am. Polit. Sci. Assoc., 94th, Sept. 3–6, Boston

Richardson BM. 1998. Society and voting in Japan. Presented for US-Japan Program, Harvard Univ., Oct. 1

Rochon TR. 1981. Electoral systems and the basis for the vote: the case of Japan. In *Parties, Candidates and Voters in Japan: Six Quantitative Studies*, Mich. Quant. Stud. Jpn. Stud., No. 2, ed. JC Campbell, pp. 1–28. Ann Arbor: Ctr. Jpn. Stud.

Rose R. 1968. Class and party divisions: Britain as a test case. *Sociology* 2:129–62

Rose R. 1969. The variability of party government: a theoretical and empirical critique. *Polit. Stud.* 17:413–45

Samuels RJ. 1987. *The Business of the Japanese State*. Ithaca, NY: Cornell Univ. Press

Sato S, Matsuzaki T. 1986. *Jiminto Seiken* [The Liberal-Democratic Party Regime]. Tokyo: Chuo Koronsha

Schlesinger JM. 1997. *Shadow Shogun: The Rise and Fall of Japan's Postwar Political Machine*. New York: Simon & Schuster

Seiji Koho Senta. 1996. *Shosenkyoku Handobukku* [Small District Handbook]. Tokyo: Seiji Koho Senta

Steinmo S, Thelen K, Longstreth F. 1992. *Structuring Politics: Historical Institutionalism in Comparative Analysis*. Cambridge: Cambridge Univ. Press

Stephens D. 1981. The changing Swedish electorate: class voting, contextual effects and voter volatility. *Comp. Polit. Stud.* 13:163–204

Suleiman E. 1974. *Politics, Power and Bureaucracy in France: The Administrative Elite*. Princeton, NJ: Princeton Univ. Press

Taagepera R, Shugart MS. 1989. *Seats and Votes: The Effects and Determinants and Electoral Systems*. New Haven, CT: Yale Univ. Press

Thayer N. 1969. *How the Conservatives Rule Japan*. Princeton, NJ: Princeton Univ. Press

Trezise PH, Suzuki Y. 1976. Politics, government and economic growth in Japan. In *Asia's New Giant: How the Japanese Economy Works*, ed. H Patrick, H Rosovsky, pp. 753–811. Washington, DC: Brookings

Upham FK. 1993. *Legal regulation of the Japanese retail industry: the large scale retail stores law and prospects for reform. USJP Occas. Pap. 89-102*. Harvard Univ. Program US-Jpn. Relat./Reischauer Inst. Jpn. Stud.

Watanuki J. 1986. Candidates and voters in Japan's 1983 general election. In *Electoral Behavior in the 1983 Japanese General Election*, ed. J Watanuki, T Inoguchi, I Miyake, I Kabashima, pp. 1–25. Tokyo: Sophia Univ. Inst. Int. Relat.

Watanuki J. 1991. Social structure and voting behavior. See Flanagan et al 1991, pp. 49–83

Wilson F. 1980. Sources of party transformation: the case of France. In *Western European Party Systems: Trends and Prospects*, ed. PH Merkl, pp. 526–51. New York: Free

Wright V. 1989. *The Government and Politics of France*. London: Allen & Unwin

Annu. Rev. Polit. Sci. 2001. 4:117–38

RELIGION AND COMPARATIVE POLITICS

Anthony Gill
Department of Political Science, University of Washington, Seattle, Washington 98195; e-mail: tgill@u.washington.edu

Key Words secularization, fundamentalism, church and state, religious economy

■ **Abstract** Although scholars tend to downplay the role of religion in political life, the vast majority of people in the world profess a strong allegiance to some spiritual faith. Secularization theory has long held that religion would become irrelevant, leading many comparative scholars to ignore this potentially significant variable. A recent resurgence in religious fundamentalism and "new religious politics" has led more scholars to consider religious actors as important. However, research in this area befalls many of the same problems inherent in earlier secularization theories. A new body of scholarship, known as the "religious economy" school, seeks to address these problems by developing theories built on solid microlevel foundations of human behavior. This line of research holds great promise for the study of religion in comparative politics.

INTRODUCTION

God is dead. Or so thought Nietzsche. For nearly a century and a half, one of the most firmly held beliefs in the social sciences was that religion and religious organizations inevitably would fade from social (and perhaps even private) life. Modernization, in the form of scientific progress and bureaucratic specialization, would cleanse society of superstition and the need to rely on churches for social welfare. Yet despite such prognostications, the World Values Survey revealed that more than three quarters of the respondents in 43 countries continue to profess a belief in some supernatural deity, 63% consider themselves religious, and 70% claim to belong to a religious denomination (Inglehart et al 1998).[1]

Many empirical indicators suggest that religious belief and practice are as prevalent as in times past, if not more so (Finke & Stark 1992, Stark 1999). New religious groups are emerging far more quickly than secularization theorists would predict, and established faiths (e.g. Catholicism, Islam) continually demonstrate the ability

[1]No page numbers are given for this book, as data are listed in tables. For references, see Tables V143, V151, and V166. The data come from national surveys administered between 1990 and 1993. These figures are all the more remarkable because they include communist (or formerly communist) countries where religious practice is curtailed severely if not outright illegal.

to win converts in many parts of the world. Even in communist and formerly communist countries, spiritual groups refuse to die and are making an impressive comeback after decades of government-sanctioned repression (Greeley 1994).

Unfortunately, most comparative political scientists (and political scientists generally) consider religion to be a peripheral subject matter, perhaps because most researchers in this field still cling subconsciously to the secularization thesis. This is a serious oversight for two reasons. First, given the degree to which religious beliefs and organizations are deeply ingrained in almost every nation, ignoring religion means overlooking a potentially important variable in explaining politics. Observers of the 1979 Iranian Revolution were taken by surprise by the mobilizing potential of Islam in a nation seemingly moving through rapid modernization (read secularization). Likewise, few expected the Catholic Church would be a key player in the demise of Polish communism. The electoral mobilization of Protestant minorities in Peru allowed Alberto Fujimori to win a surprise victory in the first round of balloting in 1992 and eventually become president. And in countries such as Algeria, India, the Philippines, and Yugoslavia, religious motivations overlay political conflicts with violent ramifications. Without doubt, religion continues to make its presence felt in the realm of politics across the globe.

The study of religion is also important for a second reason. The insights drawn from research on religious beliefs and organizations have a direct bearing on questions of major importance to comparative political scientists. The broad topics of collective action, institutional design and survival, and the connection between ideas and institutions come immediately to mind. Religious movements have shown a remarkable ability to mobilize collective action, including political protest (Stark & Bainbridge 1985:506–30, Smith 1996). The mere fact that Judaism, Christianity, Islam, Buddhism, and Hinduism continue to attract adherents after several millennia speaks volumes about the mobilizing power of these ideational movements. All these spiritual traditions have served as a locus for political mobilization in recent decades, indicating that they are far from becoming politically or socially obsolete.

Lessons about institutional organization can be drawn as well. The Roman Catholic Church exists as the world's longest-standing hierarchical organization, far outlasting any secular governing institution. At times, the Church even served as a quasi-governing institution for Europe when secular governments were weak or in short supply (Ekelund et al 1996). What is even more amazing is that the Vatican commands the loyalty and obedience of hundreds of millions of geographically dispersed people without maintaining a standing army or police force. Understanding the mechanisms of this control and how such a governing hierarchy operates would be of intrinsic interest for political scientists. Yet, the literature on the rise and decline of states usually overlooks this interesting case. This may be because of its small size (although the Vatican claims over a third of the world's population as adherents) or because it is seen as the center of an ideational movement rather than a governing hierarchy. Granted, the Holy See does base its legitimacy more on theology than other governments base theirs on ideology. But this should be taken as an unparalleled opportunity for political scientists to explore the nexus between ideas and institutions.

Although religion is still a marginal topic in comparative politics, the past two decades witnessed a renewed interest in the study of religion among a small but growing number of scholars. Fueled by the "explosive" and surprising growth of fundamentalist movements in the some of the world's largest faiths—Judaism, Christianity, Islam, and Hinduism—this revived interest comes with a downside, however. As with most academic fads concerning dramatic, global phenomena, research on religious fundamentalism tends to produce studies emphasizing "big" processes with very little microlevel foundational basis. The broad concepts employed (e.g. globalization, modernization) present problems in developing testable hypotheses. Nonetheless, this problem is easily rectified. Several political scientists, sociologists, and even economists are recasting the study of religion and politics in ways that will benefit the study of politics as a whole. What is surprising is that much of this work roots itself in rational choice theory (Warner 1993), a school of thought seemingly incapable of dealing with the "irrational" world of spirituality. The "religious economy school," as it is known, helps provide the microlevel foundations for building a general theoretical understanding of religion. Marrying this approach to the ideational work that has been done on religion offers the exciting possibility of understanding how ideas and institutions interact on a regular basis.

This chapter surveys recent work in both the sociology of religion and the subfield of religion and comparative politics with the intent of showing political scientists that the study of religion is a worthwhile pursuit. This is not to say that all researchers must include religious variables in their analyses. Instead, I merely want to shed light on the general theoretical and empirical findings that scholars studying religion can bring to comparative politics at large. I begin by examining the secularization thesis and its general weakness as an explanatory framework. The intent here is to expose a number of widely held misconceptions about religion's role in society and politics. I then examine ideational explanations for the recent resurgence in fundamentalism and new religiopolitical movements. It is ironic that many of the hypotheses used to explain the resurgence of religion rely on the exact same variables used to explain the supposed decline of religion. Finally, I introduce the "religious economy" school as a corrective (albeit incomplete) for the flaws of earlier research. Although most rational choice theorizing about religion has been done by sociologists and economists, a small group of political scientists are building upon their research to construct what could be called a political economy of religion.

SECULARIZATION AND ITS CRITICS

If there ever were an award for the most durable, yet outdated, theoretical perspective in the social sciences, secularization theory would be the winner, or at least a close runner-up. The notion that religion would eventually become an irrelevant player in both social and private life dates back to the nineteenth century. Despite strong empirical evidence to the contrary (cf Stark & Bainbridge 1985), and notwithstanding the reconsideration among sociologists of religion (Warner 1993), this view persists among many political scientists. In order to understand why the secularization thesis has had such a strong hold on social scientists, it is worthwhile to first understand what religion is before examining explanations for its alleged obsolescence (and resurgence).

Defining Religion

Defining religion is a slippery enterprise. Given the broad panoply of what are often seen as religious movements—from Judaism to yoga, Buddhism to UFO cults—a single definition that encompasses all these entities has yet to be devised (Hamilton 1995:1–21). Nevertheless, the most commonly assumed definition is summarized by Smith (1996:5): "religion is a system of beliefs and practices oriented toward the sacred or supernatural, through which the life experiences of groups of people are given meaning and direction." In an often-confusing world, religions are belief systems that provide ordered meaning and prescribe actions. The supernatural component is key to the definition, as it allows us to differentiate religions from secular ideologies, although it presents a problem in classifying something like Confucianism. This definition, however, does cover the "big three" Western faiths (Judaism, Christianity, and Islam) and the bulk of Eastern religions (e.g. Hinduism, Taoism, and most variants of Buddhism). As such, this definition encompasses the spiritual beliefs and practices of the vast majority of the world's population.

Religion frequently takes on an institutional form. (For rhetorical simplicity, the institutionalized form of religion can be called a "church," although this is a mostly Christian term.) Almost all religious traditions have some form of rules dictating who is a member of the spiritual community and which members can make official pronouncements regarding doctrinal content. Thus, religion involves authoritative relationships. Recognizing this fact is an essential part of the broader definition of religion, specifically as it pertains to the study of politics; it raises the issue of church-state relations. Persons in authority generally seek the means of preserving their power. For religious authority, this may often mean reaching out for the assistance of the state, as religious groups typically lack the backing of coercive power. Overlapping authority between state and religious leaders may also cause conflict (e.g. on matters of obligatory military service). Religious leaders may use their institutional position to challenge unpopular governments as a means of preserving their authority or credibility among parishioners. In essence, by acknowledging that religion commonly takes on institutional forms, the role of interests becomes as critical to the analysis of religion and politics as are beliefs and values. I return to this important point below. For now, suffice it to say that identifying both the ideational and institutional aspects of religion is important to understanding secularization and its consequences for politics.

Modernization, Secularization, and Politics

The concept of secularization is a simple notion premised on the prediction that the all-encompassing process of modernization will replace religion. Lechner (1991:1104), an ardent defender of the secularization thesis, states,

> [I]n certain societies transcendently anchored worldviews and institutions lose social and cultural influence as a result of the dynamics of rationalization (the process in which various social spheres come to operate according to their own standards).... Rationalization produces a pattern of cultural pluralization, social differentiation, and organizational specialization in societies with originally influential, if not dominant, religious cultures and institutions, such as Western societies prior to the Great Transformation.... Specifically, where official churches used to control substantial economic resources, the relative wealth and capital of these churches has declined; where authority was once legitimated mainly in religious terms and major political conflicts crucially involved religious motives, bureaucratized states now exercise rational-legal authority and separate civil and ecclesiastical spheres; where full membership in the societal community used to depend on one's religious identity and religiously motivated exclusiveness was common, inclusion on the basis of citizenship has transformed the meaning of membership.

Three interrelated trends occur as modernity washes away religion, affecting both ideas and institutions. First, a greater reliance on scientific explanation to understand life erodes the supernatural explanations needed in the past. Hence, we would expect that steady progress of science would be correlated with a decline in religious belief among the population, and the most scientifically sophisticated countries should be the least religious. Second, as the population loses faith in spiritual explanations, the institutions (churches) championing such explanations lose their social clout. It is ironic that the schismatic nature of Christianity reinforces this trend. As more distinct denominations arise claiming to have the ultimate truth, and because there can be only one ultimate truth, people begin doubting the veracity of all religions (Berger 1967).[2]

Religious pluralism thus destroys religion itself. Over time, then, religious organizations and their leaders should be in gradual retreat from the public square. This tendency reinforces the first trend; without public exposure to religious institutions, individual religiosity declines. Finally, religious groups find themselves becoming irrelevant socially because increasingly bureaucratized states take over the many welfare functions that churches performed in the past (e.g. assistance to the poor). All three of these trends supposedly proceed in unilinear fashion, with no reversal.

[2]To be fair, Berger (1997) has since recanted his position, though his earlier work stands as one of the hallmarks of secularization theory.

Politically, secularization theory has two important predicted consequences. First, religious values and beliefs should play a decreasing role in political decision making and should serve less as a basis for mobilizing collective action today than in the past. Many of the new social movements that arise will be more secular in nature (cf Inglehart 1990). Social movements should have little in the way of spiritual content, and religious leaders should not be prominent among such movements. Religious cleavages in electoral politics should also disappear. Second, at the institutional level, secularization predicates the eventual separation of church and state. As the state takes over the social welfare functions of churches, little reason remains to support churches with public funds or official policy. This is not to say that church-state separation will be a smooth process, free of conflict. In fact, state leaders may very well go on the offensive against religious organizations because "government competes with religious ritual by introducing ritual of its own" (Wallace 1966:261). Thus, the secularization process will at times appear as a pitched battle between forces of progress and those longing for a more traditional time. This insight, as we see below, will prove critical in explaining anomalies in the secularization thesis.

Secularization Reconsidered

Although secularization theory was being critiqued as far back as the 1960s (see Martin 1965), political events in the late 1970s and 1980s brought the paradigm crashing down. In 1979, Islamic clerics overthrew a supposedly modernized Iranian regime with widespread popular support. That same year saw Catholics, rallying around a new "liberation theology," toss a Nicaraguan dictator from power. Nascent revolutionary groups across Latin America began courting progressive Catholics for their movements. Conservative evangelicals in the United States founded the Moral Majority and played an important role in the presidential election of Ronald Reagan. And clashes between Hindus and Muslims in India began having serious political overtones in the world's most populous democracy. Secularization theorists predicted none of this. Once thought to be near extinction, religion came roaring back with a vengeance. It is not surprising that scholarship on spiritual movements and religion and politics witnessed a renaissance.

Although a number of scholars viewed the renewed political energy of religion as a backlash against the secularization/modernization process, thereby resuscitating what seemed to be an outdated theory (see below), others began arguing that secularization was never a good theory to begin with. Empirically, it did not fit the facts. Most survey evidence showed that various measures of religiosity in the United States and Europe were not trending downward but were essentially flat or increasing slightly (Hadden 1987, Greeley 1989, Stark & Iannaccone 1994). The United States—arguably the most modern country in the world—continues to show exceptionally high levels of religiosity compared with many other parts of the world. Moreover, "new" religious movements (e.g. Mormons, Jehovah's Witnesses) are expanding at historically rapid rates around the world (Iannaccone

& Stark 1997, Stark 1996:4–21), even in Russia, where a secular state attempted to stamp out religious belief for over 70 years (Greeley 1994).

Finally, the theory of the long, gradual decline of religiosity presumes that some "golden age" of religiosity existed in the past from which to decline from. Even that contention is coming under considerable scrutiny now. Medieval Europe was rife with nonpious individuals, especially among the lower classes, who were not served by priests (Duffy 1987, Brooke & Brooke 1984). The myth that the British colonies in America spilled over with spirituality overlooks the fact that most settlers were drifters who had little connection to church, family, or community (Finke & Stark 1992). And even in Latin America, supposedly a bulwark of Catholicism for five centuries, attendance at Mass has always been abysmally low, largely because of a lack of priests to administer the sacraments (Poblete 1965). Although survey evidence is scant, most scholars do assume that people in all these situations—medieval Europe, the colonial United States, and Latin America throughout much of its history—believed in some supernatural deity or power. The real problem was that the institutional outreach of churches was weaker back then than it is today. Over time, the social penetration of churches has increased, not declined as secularization theorists would predict (Finke & Stark 1992). These findings should give pause to comparative political scientists. That religion influenced politics more in earlier eras should not be casually assumed (cf Juergensmeyer 1995:382). Too often, religion is used as a secondary means of explaining residuals in predicted models.

Although all the above observations chiseled away at the foundation of secularization theory, the wrecking ball was the sudden emergence of religious fundamentalism and its aggressive political agenda during the latter half of the twentieth century. The current research agenda in the area of religion and comparative politics is dominated by attempts to explain the origins of new religiopolitical movements.

FUNDAMENTALISM AND THE NEW RELIGIOUS POLITICS

In 1991, the first of a massive four-volume set examining religious fundamentalism was published under the auspices of The Fundamentalism Project (Marty & Appleby 1991), reflecting a renewed interest in studying new religious movements in every part of the world. The third volume in the series was devoted entirely to looking at the political impact of such movements (Marty & Appleby 1993). Nonetheless, all four volumes directed attention to the political ramifications of religious fundamentalisms, as it appeared as if all the movements under observation were tightly connected to some "subversive" political action (Marty & Appleby 1991:ix). Indeed, the dominant feature of most new religious movements arising in the past 30 years has been their confrontational, and frequently conservative, stance against existing secular authorities. As such, these movements have also been referred to as religiopolitical groups, or as part of a "new religious politics" (Keddie 1998). Islamic revolutionary groups bent on toppling secular rulers appeared with force in Iran, Egypt, and Algeria. Ultra-orthodox and messianic Jewish groups have frustrated attempts to broker peace agreements in Israel. The New Christian Right in the United States sought to overturn a variety of laws that they considered damaging to a moral lifestyle. The Bharatiya Janata Party and Vishwa Hindu Parishad movement in India reacted to the perceived excesses of pluralist democracy. Liberation theologians and Christian base communities in Latin America, unique among the subjects of comparative religious studies in being progressive, became vocal opponents of dictatorial regimes.[3]

Given that religion has long been viewed as a pillar of the status quo, these developments were all the more surprising to scholars.

Origins of Fundamentalism

Explaining the origins of these new religiopolitical, fundamentalist movements dominates the literature on religion in comparative politics. Marty & Appleby (1991:22–23, emphasis in original) summarize the most widely accepted thesis related to this puzzle.

> *Fundamentalisms arise or come to prominence in times of crisis, actual or perceived.* The sense of danger may be keyed to oppressive and threatening social, economic, or political conditions, but the ensuing crisis is perceived as a *crisis of identity* by those who fear extinction as a people or absorption into an overarching syncretistic culture to such a degree that their distinctiveness is undermined in the rush to homogeneity.

The exact nature of these crises is diverse (Keddie 1998), but the primary driving force behind all of them is a factor common to previous theories of religion—modernization. "Modernity tends to undermine the taken-for-granted certainties by which people lived through most of history. This is an uncomfortable state of affairs, for many an intolerable one, and religious movements that claim to give certainty have great appeal" (Berger 1999:11).

The causal linkage between modernization and fundamentalist revivals may be triggered by material conditions. As Davis (1991:784) explains,

> [S]ociety and culture do not always develop in tandem. On the contrary, social and cultural differentiation may get "out of sync." Take, for example, the social and existential suffering caused by rapid, unbalanced economic growth, or by catastrophic bouts of inflation or deflation. Society sometimes deals with such crises by deliberately imposing upon itself a simpler cultural system, represented in symbols harking back to earlier or more "primitive"

[3]Religiously based civil rights activists in the 1960s could also be considered part of the new religious politics, given their activism against the status quo, but most studies of the "new religious politics" overlook this movement, as its goals were largely secular.

> levels of development, or by values believed to be better or more authentic because they originated "in the beginning". . . .

The adverse psychological impact of urbanization—which in turn is the result of industrialization and capitalization of agriculture—frequently appears as an explanation for the rise in religious fundamentalism (Martin 1990, Beyer 1994, Haynes 1998, Keddie 1998). Stated simply, material hardship prompts a general social anomie, prompting people to join new religious groups that promise to end the cause of those hardships.

Material conditions are not the only source of new religiopolitical groups. It is frequently argued that the modernization project not only is associated with increased economic progress but also contains important ideological and cultural components. The ideas emanating from Europe and the United States about what modernity should look like are coming under increasing fire by new religious movements.

Democracy and the political culture of pluralism, human rights, and liberal tolerance are basic products of cultural modernity. As early as the Renaissance, we find Machiavelli departing from the concept of divine order in establishing the idea that man can govern himself. The notion of government of the people by the people (that is, popular sovereignty) later served as a basis for the legitimacy of the secular nation-state, and some believe that scientific advancements have contributed to a global civilization that will unite all of humanity.

> [R]eligious fundamentalists are challenging these assumptions. Modernity has fostered the idea of man/woman as an individual; fundamentalism is returning the individuals to the collectivity. . . . Thus, the organic bonding to a civilization, not the free will to be a participating member of a democratic body politic, is the alternative view of man presented by fundamentalism.
>
> (Tibi 1998:24)

Secular nationalisms in the Third World, a political remnant of colonialism, are now being challenged by political actors with a vision of an alternate form of social governance—the "new religious state" (Juergensmeyer 1995, 1996).

It is interesting that the primary explanatory variable proposed to account for decreasing levels of religion in society is the same variable being posited for the increase in religious activism: modernization. This presents a theoretical conundrum. Where religion is said to be anemic or in decline (e.g. Europe), modernization is the culprit. Where religion is on the rise (e.g. in the United States or the Third World), again it is modernization at work. The same independent variable supposedly explains two diametrically opposed outcomes. Of course, this problem could be resolved by clearly specifying the mechanisms by which different aspects of modernization lead to different outcomes in different contexts. Keddie (1998) comes the closest to achieving this by arguing that where a strong religious tradition ("religiosity and communalism") already exists and is shared by a widespread part of the population, the various manifestations of modernization will provoke the creation of new religious movements. Secular nationalism is the alternative result "in countries where religiosity and communalism are weak" (Keddie 1998:723). Although this is a worthy attempt to untangle the thorny theoretical problem posed above, Keddie unfortunately does not operationalize her contextual variables to a degree sufficient for testing, although her general definitions leave open this possibility (1998:702).

Still, Keddie's proposal is a clear advance over the vast majority of the literature on fundamentalist movements, which fails to move beyond broad generalizations that are difficult to test empirically. Operationalizing cultural mindsets is an inherently difficult task. Whether a cultural community reacts to modernization by secularizing or adopting religious fundamentalism can only be inferred by the presence of secularization or a fundamentalist revival. Theoretically, the dependent variable is linked to the definition of the independent variable and the argument becomes tautological. Moreover, there is a problem with the unit of analysis. Modernization supposedly affects entire cultures, or at least certain subcultures (e.g. urban migrants). Yet, there is scant evidence that entire cultures convert to new religiopolitical movements. In fact, casual observation suggests that active participants in religious fundamentalist movements represent only a small minority of the target population affected by the ills of modernization. What is missing from current theories of fundamentalism (at least within the political science literature) is a methodological emphasis on the individual. In other words, these theories lack solid microlevel foundations. Until these theoretical and methodological problems can be resolved, explanations of new religiopolitical movements will remain nonfalsifiable "grand theorizing" to the same extent that the secularization thesis was before.

Politics of Fundamentalism

Regardless of the theoretical and methodological difficulties in explaining the origins of fundamentalism, scholars have now begun debating the political ramifications of new religiopolitical movements. Given the theoretical literature on the origins of fundamentalism, it should come as no surprise that political conflict is the most likely outcome of fundamentalist revival. Not only is the conflict posed in terms of church versus (secular) state, but it is also viewed as a "clash of civilizations" (Huntington 1996). Political battles in the post–Cold War world will be fought over two dramatically different conceptions of governmental organization—one based on the notion of popular sovereignty (democracy) and the other rooted in "divine right" (religious nationalism) (Juergensmeyer 1995). The conflict is inherently international, as the sovereign boundaries of these two worldviews do not coincide perfectly. Secular states, it is argued, construct ideologies (or "imagined communities") based primarily on allegiance to geographical territory. The new religious movements view national membership as adherence to a set of doctrinal strictures.[4]

[4]This is not true of doctrines that restrict membership based on ethnicity or other characteristics that would prohibit conversion into the group.

The criteria for membership and participation in these two realms often are incompatible, leading not only to civil war in religiously pluralistic nations but also to international conflict. As Tibi (1998:25–26) notes in discussing Islamic fundamentalism,

> Democracies are secular nation-states based on popular sovereignty. This Western model has come to serve as a basis for the unity of humanity, despite manifold differences of religion and ethnicity. On the contrary, the idea of the "Government of God," as a divine order. . ., which is presented by Islamic fundamentalists as a global alternative to the secular state, exacerbates the division of humanity into civilizations. Fundamentalist politics also tear at the populations of existing multireligious and multiethnic states. . .into gerrymandered agglomerations. . . . The sundering of the population of Bosnia-Herzogovina into three collectivities, each belonging to a distinct civilization, is another topical case in point. No prudent observer can preclude such a destiny for India or other such states, if fundamentalists continue to draw the fault lines of conflict that they have publicly announced. . . . The global character of religious fundamentalism heralds an age of disorder and open strife, on both the state level and the level of global international system.

Unlike traditional international wars that were pitched along geographic lines, the "inevitable" clash of civilizations will be fought in much less conventional ways, namely through terrorism (Juergensmeyer 2000).

At the heart of this argument is the notion that religion, and particularly religious fundamentalism, is incompatible with democratic governance (Kepel 1994). Democracy relies on the will of the people, which can be fickle and relativistic. Compromise and tolerance constitute essential values in functioning democracies. Religion, on the other hand, deals in absolute truths. When laws are given by the will of God, there can be no room for compromise. Tolerance for alternative views becomes akin to acceptance of heresy. Sprinzak (1993:484), in his discussion of Jewish fundamentalism in Israel, observes that fundamentalism erodes the basis for democracy.

> It is important to note that no democracy on earth is devoid of tensions, conflicts, corruption, and some degree of violence. But if the majority of the conflicting parties respect a certain set of democratic ideals and cultural tenets, these tensions do not become pathological and the system can cope. If, on the other hand, the conflicts evolve without an overall respect for these values, the system is in trouble. For a democracy to survive decently, it is not enough that all the partners to the regime formally respect its institutions. A respect for its values and a positive orientation toward its legal order are necessary. This is today the Achilles' heel of Israel's democracy and the problem with the new religious radicalism. Even those ultranationalists and fundamentalists who say they are committed to democracy in their own way

> are a serious danger because their commitment is instrumental and their allegiance is conditional.

Taking into account the rapid global expansion of fundamentalist movements, Sprinzak's conclusion bodes ill for the prospect of consolidating the most recent wave of democracy.

Not all scholars share this pessimistic prognosis. First, it has been noted that fundamentalist movements and their political activism are not all that new. Messianic movements have come and gone for several millennia (Stark & Bainbridge 1985:506–30, Cohn 1961). Second, it has been argued that members of the most extreme fundamentalist groups are only a tiny minority of the faiths they represent. Although even small bands of fanatics can wreak havoc with the proper weapons, this hardly constitutes a global movement approaching a clash of civilizations. This argument has been applied largely to cases of Islamic fundamentalism, "shattering the myth" that all Muslims are extremists (Lawrence 1998). Both Robinson (1997) and Esposito & Voll (1996) argue that Islamic fundamentalism need not be incompatible with democracy and that the outcome hinges less on doctrine and metaphysical values than on strategic calculations of interests in various contexts. Likewise, Nasr (1995) discovered that effective participation in democratic governance tames the more extremist tendencies in Islamic fundamentalist movements. Gerges (1999) has found that in diplomatic circles, the "clash of civilizations" theory is not a guiding policy force, as most policy makers do not consider there to be an ongoing global culture war. Examining a slightly different problem related to potential culture clashes, Laitin (1986) demonstrated that religious traditions—even when potentially in conflict—need not be the most salient cleavage in politics.

Perhaps the most novel argument dealing with the political roles of religious extremists comes from Kalyvas (2000), who compared an Islamic fundamentalist movement in contemporary Algeria with a fundamentalist (ultramontanist) Catholic movement in nineteenth-century Belgium. Both movements were ideologically opposed to political liberalization, but whereas the Algerian case resulted in a breakdown of democracy via (secular) military coup in the face of Islamic militancy, the Catholic Church acquiesced in Belgium. The divergent outcomes were attributable not to theology (both groups were outwardly hostile toward democracy) but rather to institutional design. In both instances, it became apparent to several religious leaders that a fierce resistance to the democratization process would harm the long-term interests of their institutions. But whereas the hierarchical nature of the Catholic Church allowed the Vatican to impose its will over extremist bishops and communicate a credible commitment to Belgian politicians, the decentralized nature of Islam made such a commitment impossible for moderate Algerian Muslims. What such scholars as Kalyvas, Robinson, Laitin, and Nasr introduce in their analysis that is missing in the majority of work on religious fundamentalism is attention to the microlevel foundational interests driving religious actors. Such attention to detail has been a major corrective to highly abstract discussions of religion employing diffuse concepts and theories that are difficult to operationalize and test.

Beyond Fundamentalism: Ideational Models of Religious Politics

Not all research on the resurgence of religion and the "new religious politics" deals with conservative fundamentalist movements. The primary exception to this rule has been the case of liberation theology and progressive Catholicism in Latin America. Here is an example of a resurgent religious movement that does not look back to more traditional times in an effort to stave off the effects of secularization and modernization. Instead, while offering critiques of the modernization process, it has embraced a progressive outlook, incorporating many of the secular arguments that more conservative religiopolitical groups have attacked (e.g. secular socialism, Marxism, liberal democracy). In doing so, progressive Catholics became a champion for democracy in several parts of Latin America. The political battles waged by liberation theologians and their compatriots were less about clashing civilizations than about class conflict.

However, similar to the analyses of conservative religiopolitics, studies of progressive Catholicism have emphasized ideational factors in explaining how an institution that ardently supported the status quo in the past could change so rapidly. As Mainwaring (1986:7) argues, "the starting point for understanding the [Catholic] Church's politics must be its conception of its mission. The way the Church intervenes in politics depends fundamentally on the way it perceives its religious mission." Changes in the worldview of the international Catholic Church during the Second Vatican Council (1962–1965) are widely cited as the principal cause for Latin American Catholicism taking on a more activist political role (Sigmund 1990, Shepherd 1995). Although external socioeconomic factors (e.g. growing poverty) played a role in prompting this rethinking of the Church's role, the principal variable explaining religious change was the rise of a new "insurgent consciousness" (Smith 1991).[5]

A recent conservative retrenchment within the Catholic Church, away from liberation theology and the more progressive policies of Vatican Council II, has been widely attributed to an ideological shift in Rome, which was then imposed on lower levels of the Church. And as progressive Catholicism has faded, the rise of evangelical Protestantism in the region has caught the attention of scholars (Martin 1990, Stoll 1990). Although Latin American Protestantism has not shown the political activism of other fundamentalisms around the world, its conservative nature has prompted numerous scholars to hypothesize that it, too, is a reaction to secularization and social anomie (cf Sexton 1978).

What these studies of progressive Catholicism share with the writings on more conservative fundamentalist groups is the emphasis on ideational factors in the realm of religion and politics. In many ways, this emphasis seems reasonable, given that religion is essentially about beliefs and values. Given that these ideas,

[5]To their credit, both Smith (1991) and Mainwaring (1986) present nuanced ideational models that incorporate the role of institutions and other socioeconomic factors in a sophisticated manner.

beliefs, and values are what differentiate religions from most other social actors (save secular ideological movements), it makes sense to assume ideational factors would be at the center of any religious political action. However, an overemphasis on ideational variables risks ignoring the facts that almost all religions take on some strict institutional form and that these institutions impose certain interests and constraints on actors. Rounding out an analysis of religion and politics requires taking institutional and interest-based factors more seriously.

RELIGIOUS ECONOMY: The Role of Interests and Institutions

Within the past two decades, a handful of sociologists and economists have been proposing controversial new theories to explain a variety of religious behavior. Their work has caused a major stir within the religious studies community (see Warner 1993) and is now beginning to influence the study of religion and politics. The work of these scholars is based on microeconomic (or rational choice) theories of human behavior, long thought to be an inappropriate lens for viewing religious behavior.[6]

Although the religious economy literature is not as focused on one central theme as the work on the issues of secularization or fundamentalism, its goal is to explain religion's historical resilience, i.e. to understand why strict religions tend to have the greatest success in expanding. In this regard, the religious economy school speaks directly to secularization theorists and scholars examining fundamentalism (as fundamentalists tend to have "strict" religions). The benefit of this new approach, however, is that it starts with a firm basis in microlevel analysis, beginning with individuals and working upward to larger social systems.

Individuals, Institutions, and Markets

Contrary to what one might expect, recent economic theories of religion do not reduce religion to materialistic causes. The initial assumption is that religious people find some intrinsic value in believing in a religious creed, whether for peace of mind or for salvation (Stark 2000). Given that, the question becomes how consumers (parishioners) and producers (clerics) strive to satisfy their religious desires. Explanations proceed from the level of the individual consumer to the institutional level of producers (clerics and churches) and finally to the market (i.e. the interaction of various churches with each other and the government).

At the individual level, religious economy models begin with the assumption that people maximize benefits net of costs. When trying to obtain as much spiritual

[6]Actually, the use of economics to study religion can be traced back to Adam Smith. However, most abridged versions of Smith's lengthy *Wealth of Nations* exclude his profound insights on religion.

satisfaction as they can, they allocate various resources (e.g. time, money) to religious activities. Building on Becker's (1964) theory of human capital, Iannaccone (1990) presents a unified model of religious capital that helps explain religious conversion, allocation of time versus financial resources in religious participation, and the effects of religious intermarriage. Although the findings of this specific study do not have a direct bearing on comparative political research, it does provide important indirect implications for politics. First, in pluralistic religious markets, denominational mobility (i.e. conversion to other faiths) is not uncommon, which suggests that religious tradition is not an immutable feature of culture. In other words, religious preferences can vary across a "culturally homogenous" population and no single religion will likely satisfy all people (see also Stark 1992). This helps provide a microlevel foundational basis for the question of governmental regulation of religion (see below). It is this attention to methodological individualism that provides the second important implication of Iannaccone's model. By starting his theoretical inquiries with individuals, Iannaccone is able to construct more complete theories of macrobehavior that are connected directly to individual action. In doing so, he avoids diffuse statements about higher levels of analysis (communities, cultures) common to the literature on secularization and fundamentalism, which typically start and end their political analysis at the level of society.

Iannaccone and his colleagues have extended the religious economy approach to help explain institutional behavior. Perhaps one of the most vexing questions facing the study of religion at this level of analysis is why strict religions grow so rapidly. Previous theories, including explanations within the fundamentalist literature, assume it is due to some mass psychological or cultural dislocation. Iannaccone (1992, 1994) argues instead that strict religions are able to overcome free-rider problems more effectively than "low-cost" religions. By imposing strict codes of behavior on adherents (e.g. dress codes, dietary restrictions), religious groups are able to dissuade free riders from joining the organization and diluting its resources. Moreover, because strict religions tend to dissuade participants from partaking in activities outside the religious organization, more time and monetary resources from those individuals can be directed to the group goal. In the end, although strict religions may cost members more, they end up providing more benefits per member. As such religious movements grow, however, it becomes more difficult to monitor and punish free-riding behavior, leading to a drain on organizational resources and a decline in growth rates (see also Stark & Bainbridge 1985, Finke & Stark 1992). Institutions that are able to promote continual strictness tend to be the most effective and enduring religions in history. These findings are instructive for theories of political and social movements and add to the already burgeoning literature on collective-action problems (cf Lichbach 1995).

Finally, of perhaps greatest relevance to comparative politics, the religious economy school has introduced new explanations for the vitality (or anemia) of religion at the society level. Noting that religious preferences tend to be pluralistic in society, the theory holds that no single denomination can adequately supply the entire demand for religious goods (answers to questions about salvation, etc). Societies that allow religious pluralism to flourish tend to see high levels of religiosity in terms of both belief and practice (Iannaccone 1991). Although Islamic countries seem to be the exception to this rule (religious monopolization and vitality coexisting), the unique decentralized structure of this religion provides incentives for maintaining evangelical vigor. In Islam, each cleric (*alim*) is responsible for his own income via the contributions he can gather from followers. No overarching authority provides salaries (except in institutions of higher learning). Thus, keeping oneself well fed means aggressively attracting paying believers, thus promoting religious vitality. This incentive structure is similar to those of many Pentecostal churches in the United States and Latin America.

Given that religious goods are easy to produce and, thus, production has low barriers to entry (Gill 1999a), the only means of enforcing a religious monopoly is by government fiat (Stark 1992). In effect, secularization is not an effect of culture or the battle of ideas as much as it is a function of government regulation of the religious market. Where government restrictions on religion impose high costs on consumers and producers, religious activity diminishes. Stark & Iannaccone (1994) have demonstrated that Europe is highly secular not because of its Enlightenment culture but because religion is highly regulated in these economies, often favoring one or two specific denominations (see also Chaves & Cann 1992, Monsma & Soper 1997). Governments that have deregulated religion—i.e. increased the level of religious liberty—have seen increases in religious participation (Finke 1990, Finke & Iannaccone 1993, Gill 2000a), contrary to the predictions of secularization theory (Berger 1967).

Realizing that government regulation can have a dramatic effect on the overall level of religiosity in society opens the door to a new realm of church-state studies. Rather than seeing the separation of church and state as a natural process of secularization and modernization (Casanova 1994:40, Helmstadter 1997:7), one must pay careful attention to the political negotiations surrounding a broad array of regulatory laws affecting religion (Gill 1999b, 2000b). Zoning regulations, levels of taxation, media restrictions, and government subsidies all impose differential costs on religious evangelization. This calls, then, for a political economy of religion, which incorporates the interests of political actors into the study of religious markets. To date, the religious economy school has noted the importance of government regulation in determining religious market outcomes, but scholars have yet to explain the variation in levels of religious regulation across nations. Based on the economic concept of opportunity costs, Gill (2000b) is attempting to construct such a theory, taking into account the interests politicians have in maintaining power. He argues that the form of religious regulation in a nation is a function of the relative bargaining power of religious and political actors. Religious liberty is enhanced under conditions of growing de facto religious pluralism coinciding with increased political competition.

Interest-Based Theories of Religion and Politics

In the past decade, comparative political scientists have begun to realize the benefits of examining religion from an interest-based and institutional perspective. The empirical agenda of this research is less cohesive than either the secularization and fundamentalist literatures, given that scholars in this developing tradition prefer to focus on specific historical questions rather than broad global phenomena. Nonetheless, the theoretical methods they use are helping to introduce the importance of incorporating microlevel analysis into the study of religion and comparative politics.

Kalyvas (1996) was among the first to champion this approach in comparative politics. He sets out to explain why Christian Democratic parties arose in Europe against the desires of the Catholic Church and proclerical Conservative parties during the nineteenth century. The answer lies in the unintended consequences of pursuing short-term institutional interests. In an effort to combat liberal attempts at restricting Church prerogatives, bishops in several countries promoted the development of lay organizations to rally Catholic support. However, once these organizations were formed, they began competing with the Church itself to represent Catholics in the political arena. Moreover, in order to win political office, they downplayed "the salience of religion in politics to appeal to broader categories of voters and strike alliances with other political forces" (Kalyvas 1996:18), precisely the outcome Church leaders wanted to avoid. Recently, Gould (1999) has extended Kalyvas' analysis to explain how liberal politicians were able to overcome stiff religious opposition to the policies of economic, political, and religious liberalization. It is ironic that defeating religious opponents meant coopting clergy (particularly Protestant ministers) by enhancing their religious authority. Liberals also found it strategically wise to rally a peasant base around religious issues, thereby providing an electoral buffer against any possible clerical attacks.

In the same vein as the other two studies, Warner (2000) looks at the relationship between the Catholic Church and political parties in post–World War II Europe. Modeling the Church as an interest group seeking to reassert its institutional prominence in society, she explains how relations with previous wartime governments imposed constraints on the postwar political strategies of the Catholic bishops. In doing so, Warner applies economic research on credible commitments and asset specificity to show how decisions concerning political alliances early on reduce the ability to switch allies in the future, depending on the institutional makeup of the Church and party structure. In Italy, the Church distanced itself from the fascist regime and was able to credibly commit to a partnership with the Christian Democrats. However, once this alliance was forged, it was difficult for bishops to back away. The French Church's connection with the Vichy government severely limited the political options available to bishops in the Fourth Republic and thus became only a weak ally to the French Popular Republican Movement. However, this gave French bishops greater bargaining leverage in their ability to threaten to withdraw votes, although the highly decentralized nature of the French Church limited this threat.

Although Kalyvas, Gould, and Warner each examine different questions and choose different cases, these three studies are an important step forward in detailing how institutional religious interests influence politics. Prior to this, most work on religion and politics in Europe considered only the theological and moral roles of religious actors.

In a different part of the world, Gill (1998) contributes to this interest-based analysis of religion by developing an economic model for religious opposition in Latin America. Asking why only some national Catholic episcopacies opposed authoritarian dictators during the 1970s while others remained neutral or supportive, Gill found previous ideational explanations to be inadequate. Explaining opposition as a shift in episcopal preferences for the poor served only to redefine the question rather than explain why the shift came about in the first place. He argues that the nature of the religious market—either monopolistic or competitive—had a major impact in shifting the Church's pastoral, and ultimately political, strategy. Positing that religious groups attempt to maximize market share, national Catholic Churches that were guaranteed a monopoly position by government fiat were able to retain alliances with unpopular dictators. But where Protestant competitors made inroads among the poor, bishops were forced to take a preferential option for the poor. Making a credible commitment to the poor (following centuries of neglect) meant vocally opposing right-wing dictators. Like the three aforementioned studies on Europe, this work considers institutional interests an important factor in determining how religious actors behave.

Perhaps the most innovative and interesting argument for adopting a neo-institutionalist approach to religion comes from a group of five economists. In a series of articles collected in one book (Ekelund et al 1996), these scholars analyze the behavior of the medieval Catholic Church as if it were an economic firm. Their work is expansive in scope. They address how the Church organized itself to maintain market share and collect revenue in an environment where monitoring and enforcement capabilities were weak. The Church's doctrine on usury is also examined to show how the Church "shadow priced" loans so as to maximize rent. And the secrecy behind confessions and the sale of indulgences is seen as a way of taxing a population with varying price elasticities for salvation; those who feared hell were charged more than those who had less to dread. If the shroud of secrecy surrounding the price of indulgences had been broken, those with highly inelastic demand for salvation would have bid down their prices. Perhaps their most interesting claim counters Weber's famous "Protestant ethic" thesis. Instead of the Church hindering European economic development, it actually enhanced it. The Church's desire to enhance its monopoly power and extract revenue efficiently meant that it created the basic financial and governing infrastructure needed for investors to feel secure. This fascinating work is a must-read for any political scientist interested in the question of state formation.

The religious economy school provides an important corrective to models of religious behavior that rely solely on ideational variables. This is not to say that ideas are unimportant. However, institutional concerns often trump theological prescripts in many political situations. Moreover, starting analysis with the individual helps to provide a needed dose of microlevel analysis to a field of inquiry dominated by metaphysical theorizing. Nonetheless, the economic school ignores the importance of how culture can affect the preferences of actors. Building theories that integrate interests with ideas is the next frontier in the study of religion and politics.

CONCLUSION

World events make it increasingly clear that religion is, and will continue to be, a major player in politics. The serious study of religion and politics is relatively new because the dominant thinking in sociology and political science has long considered religion increasingly irrelevant in social life. As with the discovery of most major global trends (e.g. economic globalization, democratization), the initial stages of research on the role of religion and politics has relied on ill-defined concepts and grand theorizing. This has been typical of the literature on fundamentalism. However, as the research agenda has matured, a greater sensitivity to methodological rigor has become the norm. Scholars are now developing the microlevel foundations that will make it possible to test empirically a variety of hypotheses related to religious political behavior. Given the unique organizational features of religious movements and the central role that theology plays, the investigation of this topic promises to yield substantial benefits to political science.

LITERATURE CITED

Becker GS. 1964. *Human Capital: A Theoretical and Empirical Analysis with Special Reference to Education*. Chicago: Univ. Chicago Press

Berger PL. 1967. *The Sacred Canopy*. New York: Anchor

Berger PL. 1997. Epistemological modesty: an interview with Peter Berger. *Christ. Century* 114:972–75, 978

Berger PL. 1999. *The Desecularization of the World: Resurgent Religion and World Politics*. Grand Rapids, MI: Eerdmans

Beyer P. 1994. *Religion and Globalization*. London: Sage

Brooke R, Brooke C. 1984. *Popular Religion in the Middle Ages*. London: Thames & Hudson

Casanova J. 1994. *Public Religions in the Modern World*. Chicago: Univ. Chicago Press

Chaves M, Cann DE. 1992. Regulation, pluralism and religious market structure: explaining religion's vitality. *Ration. Soc.* 4(3):272–90

Cohn N. 1961. *The Pursuit of the Millenium*. New York: Harper & Row

Davis W. 1991. Fundamentalism in Japan: religious and political. See Marty & Appleby 1991, pp. 782–813

Duffy E. 1987. The late middle ages: vitality of decline? In *Atlas of the Christian Church*, ed. M Douglas, SM Tipton, pp. 86–95. New York: Facts on File

Ekelund RB, Hebert RF, Tollison RD, Anderson GM, Davidson AB. 1996. *Sacred Trust: The Medieval Church as an Economic Firm*. Oxford, UK: Oxford Univ. Press

Esposito JL, Voll JO. 1996. *Islam and Democracy*. Oxford, UK: Oxford Univ. Press

Finke R. 1990. Religious deregulation: origins and consequences. *J. Church State* 32(3):609–26

Finke R, Iannaccone LR. 1993. Supply-side explanations for religious change. *Annals* 527:27–39

Finke R, Stark R. 1992. *The Churching of America: Winners and Losers in Our Religious Economy*. New Brunswick, NJ: Rutgers Univ. Press

Gerges FA. 1999. *American and Political Islam: Clash of Cultures or Clash of Interests*? Cambridge, UK: Cambridge Univ. Press

Gill A. 1998. *Rendering unto Caesar: The Catholic Church and the State in Latin America*. Chicago: Univ. Chicago Press

Gill A. 1999a. The economics of evangelization. In *Evangelization and Religious Freedom in Latin America*, ed. PE Sigmund, pp. 70–84. Maryknoll, NY: Orbis

Gill A. 1999b. The politics of regulating religion in Mexico: the 1992 constitutional reforms in historical context. *J. Church State* 41(4):761–98

Gill A. 2000a. Government regulation, social anomie and Protestant growth in Latin America: a cross-national analysis. *Ration. Soc.* 11(3):287–316

Gill A. 2000b. *The political origins of religious liberty: initial sketch of a general theory*. Presented at Annu. Meet. Am. Pol. Sci. Assoc., 96th, Washington DC

Gould AC. 1999. *Origins of Liberal Dominance: State, Church and Party in Nineteenth-Century Europe*. Ann Arbor: Univ. Mich. Press

Greeley A. 1989. *Religious Change in America*. Cambridge, MA: Harvard Univ. Press

Greeley A. 1994. A religious revival in Russia? *J. Sci. Stud. Relig.* 33(4):253–72

Hadden JK. 1987. Toward desacralizing secularization theory. *Soc. Forces* 65(3):587–611

Hamilton MB. 1995. *The Sociology of Religion: Theoretical and Comparative Perspectives*. London: Routledge

Haynes J. 1998. *Religion in Global Politics*. London: Longman

Helmstadter R. 1997. *Freedom and Religion in the Nineteenth Century*. Stanford, CA: Stanford Univ. Press

Huntington SP. 1996. *The Clash of Civilizations and the Remaking of World Order*. New York: Simon & Schuster

Iannaccone LR. 1990. Religious participation: a human capital approach. *J. Sci. Stud. Relig.* 29(3):297–314

Iannaccone LR. 1991. The consequences of religious market structure: Adam Smith and the economics of religion. *Ration. Soc.* 3(2):156–77

Iannaccone LR. 1992. Sacrifice and stigma: reducing free-riding in cults, communes, and other collectives. *J. Polit. Econ.* 100(2):271–91

Iannaccone LR. 1994. Why strict churches are strong. *Am. J. Soc.* 99(5):1180–211

Iannaccone LR, Stark R. 1997. Why the Jehovah's Witnesses grow so rapidly: a theoretical application. *J. Contemp. Relig.* 12(2):133–57

Inglehart R. 1990. *Culture Shift in Advanced Industrial Society*. Princeton, NJ: Princeton Univ. Press

Inglehart R, Basañez M, Moreno A. 1998. *Human Values and Beliefs: A Cross-Cultural Sourcebook*. Ann Arbor: Univ. Mich. Press

Juergensmeyer M. 1995. The new religious state. *Comp. Polit.* 27(4):379–91

Juergensmeyer M. 1996. The worldwide rise of religious nationalism. *J. Int. Aff.* 50(1):1–20

Juergensmeyer M. 2000. *Terror in the Mind of God: The Global Rise of Religious Violence*. Berkeley: Univ. Calif. Press

Kalyvas SN. 1996. *The Rise of Christian Democracy in Europe*. Cornell, NY: Cornell Univ. Press

Kalyvas SN. 2000. Commitment problems in emerging democracies: the case of religious parties. *Comp. Polit.* In press

Keddie NR. 1998. The new religious politics: where, when, and why do "fundamentalisms" appear? *Comp. Stud. Soc. Hist.* 40(4):696–723

Kepel G. 1994. *The Revenge of God: The Resurgence of Islam, Christianity and Judaism in the Modern World*. Transl. Alan Braley. University Park: Penn. St. Univ. Press (From German)

Laitin DD. 1986. *Hegemony and Culture: Politics and Religious Change among the Yoruba*. Chicago: Univ. Chicago Press

Lawrence BB. 1998. *Shattering the Myth: Islam Beyond Violence*. Princeton, NJ: Princeton Univ. Press

Lechner FJ. 1991. The case against secularization: a rebuttal. *Soc. Forces* 69(4):1103–19

Lichbach MI. 1995. *The Rebel's Dilemma*. Ann Arbor: Univ. Mich. Press

Mainwaring S. 1986. *The Catholic Church and Politics in Brazil, 1916–1985*. Stanford, CA: Stanford Univ. Press

Martin D. 1965. *The Religious and the Secular*. London: Routledge

Martin D. 1990. *Tongues of Fire: The Explosion of Protestantism in Latin America*. Cambridge, UK: Blackwell

Marty ME, Appleby RS. 1991. *Fundamentalisms Observed*. Chicago: Univ. Chicago Press

Marty ME, Appleby RS. 1993. *Fundamentalisms and the State*. Chicago: Univ. Chicago Press

Monsma SV, Soper JC. 1997. *The Challenge of Pluralism: Church and State in Five Democracies*. Lanham, MD: Rowman & Littlefield

Nasr SVR. 1995. Democracy and Islamic revivalism. *Polit. Sci. Q.* 110(2):261–85

Poblete R. 1965. *Crisis Sacerdotal*. Santiago, Chile: Pacífico

Robinson GE. 1997. Can Islamists be democrats? The case of Jordan. *Middle East J.* 51(3):373–87

Sexton JD. 1978. Protestantism and modernization in two Guatemalan towns. *Am. Ethnol.* 5(2):280–302

Shepherd FM. 1995. Church and state in Honduras and Nicaragua prior to 1979. In *Religion and Democracy in Latin America*, ed. WH Swatos, Jr, pp. 117–34. New Brunswick, NJ: Transaction

Sigmund PE. 1990. *Liberation Theology at the Crossroads: Democracy of Revolution*? New York: Oxford Univ. Press

Smith C. 1991. *The Emergence of Liberation Theology: Radical Religion and Social Movement Theory*. Chicago: Univ. Chicago Press

Smith C, ed. 1996. *Disruptive Religion: The Force of Faith in Social Movement Activism*. New York: Routledge

Sprinzak E. 1993. Three models of religious violence: the case of Jewish fundamentalism in Israel. See Marty & Appleby 1993, pp. 462–91

Stark R. 1992. Do Catholic societies really exist? *Ration. Soc.* 4(2):261–71

Stark R. 1996. *The Rise of Christianity: A Sociologist Reconsiders History*. Princeton, NJ: Princeton Univ. Press

Stark R. 1999. Secularization, R.I.P. *Soc. Relig.* 60(3):249–65

Stark R. 2000. Religions effects: in praise of the "idealistic humbug." *Rev. Relig. Res.* 41(3):289–310

Stark R, Bainbridge WS. 1985. *The Future of Religion*. Berkeley: Univ. Calif. Press

Stark R, Iannaccone LR. 1994. A supply-side reinterpretation of the "secularization" of Europe. *J. Sci. Stud. Relig.* 33(3):230–52

Stoll D. 1990. *Is Latin America Turning Protestant*? Berkeley: Univ. Calif. Press

Tibi B. 1998. *The Challenge of Fundamentalism: Political Islam and the New World Disorder*. Berkeley: Univ. Calif. Press

Wallace AFC. 1966. *Religion: An Anthropological View*. New York: Random House

Warner CM. 2000. *Confessions of an Interest Group: The Catholic Church and Political Parties in Europe*. Princeton, NJ: Princeton Univ. Press

Warner RS. 1993. Work in progress toward a new paradigm for the sociological study of religion in the United States. *Am. J. Sociol.* 98(5):1044–93

Annu. Rev. Polit. Sci. 2001. 4:139–87

Toward A Fourth Generation of Revolutionary Theory

Jack A. Goldstone
Department of Sociology, University of California, Davis, One Shields Avenue, Davis, California 95616; e-mail: jagoldstone@ucdavis.edu

Key Words revolutions, social change, state crises, ideology, leadership, mobilization

■ **Abstract** Third-generation theories of revolution pointed to the structural vulnerabilities of regimes as the basic causes of revolutions. In the last decade, critics of structural theories have argued for the need to incorporate leadership, ideology, and processes of identification with revolutionary movements as key elements in the production of revolution. Analyses of revolutions in developing countries and in communist regimes have further argued for incorporating these factors and for the inadequacy of structural theories to account for these events. Rather than try to develop a list of the "causes" of revolutions, it may be more fruitful for the fourth generation of revolutionary theory to treat revolutions as emergent phenomena, and to start by focusing on factors that cement regime stability. Weakness in those factors then opens the way for revolutionary leadership, ideology, and identification, along with structural factors such as international pressure and elite conflicts, to create revolutions.

INTRODUCTION

In recent years, scholarship on the causes, processes, and outcomes of revolutions has sprawled across topics and disciplines like an amoeba, stretching in various directions in response to diverse stimuli. What was once a fairly structured subfield, focusing primarily on a handful of "great revolutions" in Europe and Asia, now grapples with collapsed states in Africa (Migdal 1988, Migdal et al 1994, Zartman 1995), transitions to democracy in Eastern Europe and elsewhere (Banac 1992, Linz & Stepan 1996), movements of Islamic fundamentalism in the Middle East (Keddie 1995b), and guerrilla warfare in Latin America (Wickham-Crowley 1992). Moreover, in addition to identifying key causal factors and outcomes, scholars now seek to explain the micro processes of revolutionary mobilization and leadership, using approaches ranging from rational choice analysis (Opp et al 1995) to sociological and anthropological studies of social movements (Selbin 1993, Aminzade et al 2001a). The study of revolutions has thus blossomed into a multifaceted exploration of a panoply of diverse events.

A short review cannot encompass this range of literature, much less the explosion of historical literature analyzing particular revolutions. I thus aim to present a brief overview of the development of the comparative and theoretical analysis of revolutions in the past decade and to lay out the main concepts and findings that now govern our understanding of how and why revolutions occur. However, the study of revolutions may be reaching an impasse at which it is simply overwhelmed by the variety of cases and concepts it seeks to encompass. I therefore close with some suggestions for shifting the approach, and improving the generalizability, of theories of revolution.

THE NATURE OF THE BEAST

Definitions of Revolution

Definitions of revolution have changed as new events have come forth on the stage of world history. Through the 1980s, most writers on revolution focused on the "great revolutions" of England (1640), France (1789), Russia (1917), and China (1949). Although scholars admitted that other events, such as the Mexican and Cuban revolutions (Womack 1968, Dominguez 1978, Eckstein 1986, Knight 1986), had valid claims to be great revolutions, the most influential comparative studies of revolution from Brinton (1938) to Skocpol (1979) dealt mainly with a handful of European and Asian cases. Skocpol's (1979:4) definition of great social revolutions—"rapid, basic transformations of a society's state and class structures . . . accompanied and in part carried through by class-based revolts from below"—was taken as standard.

Yet Skocpol's definition ignored such matters as revolutionary ideologies, ethnic and religious bases for revolutionary mobilization, intra-elite conflicts, and the possibility of multiclass coalitions. This was intentional, for none of these were seen as central features of revolutions. Through the 1970s and 1980s, the dominant approach to revolutions was structural analysis, rooted in Marxist historical perspectives in which the action of capitalist competition on class and state structures produced class-based conflicts that transformed society.

Skocpol's work capped what I have called the third generation of revolutionary analysis (Goldstone 1980). In that work, a series of scholars including Moore (1966), Paige (1975), Eisenstadt (1978), and many others expanded on the old Marxist class-conflict approach to revolutions by turning attention to rural agrarian-class conflict, state conflicts with autonomous elites, and the impact of interstate military and economic competition on domestic political change. This work, in which revolution was attributed to a conjunction of multiple conflicts involving states, elites, and the lower classes, was a major improvement on simple descriptive generalizations, such as those of Brinton (1938), or of analyses that rested on such broad single factors as "modernization" (Huntington 1968) or "relative deprivation" (Davies 1962, Gurr 1970).

From the 1970s through the 1990s, however, the world saw a host of revolutions that challenged the class-based understanding of revolutions. In Iran and Nicaragua in 1979 and in the Philippines in 1986, multiclass coalitions toppled dictators who had long enjoyed strong support from the world's leading superpower, the United States (Dix 1984, Liu 1988, Goodwin 1989, Farhi 1990, Parsa 2000). In Eastern Europe and the Soviet Union in 1989–1991, socialist and totalitarian societies that were supposed to be impervious to class conflict collapsed amid popular demonstrations and mass strikes (Banac 1992, Dunlop 1993, Oberschall 1994a, Urban et al 1997, Beissinger 1998). The Iranian Revolution and the Afghan Revolution of 1979 proudly proclaimed themselves as religious struggles, not based primarily on class issues (Keddie 1981; Arjomand 1988; Moghadam 1989; Ahady 1991; Moaddel 1993; Foran 1993a). And the host of anticolonial and antidictatorial revolutions in the Third World, ranging from Angola to Zaire, became so numerous and affected so many people that the parochial practice of defining revolutions in terms of a few cases in European history plus China became untenable (Boswell 1989, Foran 1997b). In addition, whereas the "great revolutions" had all led fairly directly to populist dictatorship and civil wars, a number of the more recent revolutions—including that of the Philippines, the revolutionary struggle in South Africa, and several of the anticommunist revolutions of the Soviet Union and Eastern Europe—seemed to offer a new model in which the revolutionary collapse of the old regime was coupled with a relatively nonviolent transition to democracy (Goldfarb 1992, Diamond & Plattner 1993).

In response to these events, theories of revolution evolved in three directions. First, researchers sought to apply the structural theory of revolution to an increasingly diverse set of cases, well beyond the small number of "great" social revolutions. These included studies of guerrilla wars and popular mobilization in Latin America (Eckstein 1989b, Midlarsky & Roberts 1991, Wickham-Crowley 1992, McClintock 1998); studies of anticolonial and antidictatorial revolutions in developing nations (Dix 1984; Dunn 1989; Shugart 1989; Goodwin & Skocpol 1989; Farhi 1990; Kim 1991, 1996; Goldstone et al 1991; Foran 1992, 1997b; Foran & Goodwin 1993; Johnson 1993; Goldstone 1994a, Snyder 1998); studies of revolutions and rebellions in Eurasia from 1500 to 1850 (Barkey 1991, 1994; Goldstone 1991; Tilly 1993); studies of the Islamic revolution against the Shah in Iran (Skocpol 1982, Parsa 1989, McDaniel 1991); and studies of the collapse of communism in the Soviet Union and Eastern Europe (Bunce 1989; Chirot 1991; Goodwin 1994b, 2001; Lupher 1996; Goldstone 1998a).

Second, in part propelled by the above-noted works, which found in these new cases a powerful role for ideologies and diverse multiclass revolutionary coalitions, there emerged direct attacks on the "third generation" approach. Scholars called for greater attention to conscious agency, to the role of ideology and culture in shaping revolutionary mobilization and objectives, and to contingency in the course and outcome of revolutions (Sewell 1985; Rule 1988, 1989; Baker 1990; Kimmel 1990; Foran 1993b, 1995, 1997a; Emirbayer & Goodwin 1994, 1996; Goodwin 1994a, 1997; Selbin 1997). Important new comparative studies of revolutions demonstrated the importance of these additional factors in recent events (Eisenstadt 1992, 1999; Johnson 1993; Selbin 1993; Colburn 1994; Sohrabi 1995; Katz 1997; Foran 1997b; Paige 1997).

Third, analysts of both revolutions and social movements realized that many of the processes underlying revolutions—e.g. mass mobilization, ideological conflicts, confrontation with authorities—have been well studied in the analysis of social movements. Indeed, some of the more extensive and radical social movements that involved major changes to the distribution of power, such as the international movement for women's rights, the labor movement, and the US civil rights movement, were revolutionary in the risks taken by activists and the institutional restructurings produced by their efforts. Thus, a new literature on "contentious politics" has developed that attempts to combine insights from the literature on social movements and revolutions to better understand both phenomena (McAdam et al 1997; Goldstone 1998b; Hanagan et al 1998; Tarrow 1998; Aminzade et al 2001a; McAdam et al, in preparation).

As a result of these critiques, the simple state- and class-based conception of revolutions advanced by Skocpol no longer seems adequate. A huge range of events now claim our attention as examples of revolution, ranging from the fascist, Nazi, and communist transformations of nations in the first part of this century to the collapses of communist regimes at its end; from the idealistic revolutions of America and France at the end of the eighteenth century to the chaotic revolutionary wars in Africa at the end of the twentieth. Two recent surveys of revolution (Tilly 1993, Goldstone 1998c) list literally hundreds of events as "revolutionary" in character. Nonetheless, these events still have a common set of elements at their core: (*a*) efforts to change the political regime that draw on a competing vision (or visions) of a just order, (*b*) a notable degree of informal or formal mass mobilization, and (*c*) efforts to force change through noninstitutionalized actions such as mass demonstrations, protests, strikes, or violence.

These elements can be combined to provide a broader and more contemporary definition of revolution: an effort to transform the political institutions and the justifications for political authority in a society, accompanied by formal or informal mass mobilization and noninstitutionalized actions that undermine existing authorities.

This definition is broad enough to encompass events ranging from the relatively peaceful revolutions that overthrew communist regimes to the violent Islamic revolution in Afghanistan. At the same time, this definition is strong enough to exclude coups, revolts, civil wars, and rebellions that make no effort to transform institutions or the justification for authority. It also excludes peaceful transitions to democracy through institutional arrangements such as plebiscites and free elections, as in Spain after Franco.

Types of Revolutions

Revolutions are distinguished sometimes by outcomes, sometimes by actors. Revolutions that transform economic and social structures as well as political institutions, such as the French Revolution of 1789, are called great revolutions; those that change only state institutions are called political revolutions. Revolutions that involve autonomous lower-class revolts are labeled social revolutions (Skocpol 1979), whereas sweeping reforms carried out by elites who directly control mass mobilization are sometimes called elite revolutions or revolutions from above (Trimberger 1978). Revolutions that fail to secure power after temporary victories or large-scale mobilization are often called failed or abortive revolutions; oppositional movements that either do not aim to take power (such as peasant or worker protests) or focus on a particular region or subpopulation are usually called rebellions (if violent) or protests (if predominantly peaceful). Despite these differences, all of these revolutionary events have similar dynamics and characteristics (McAdam et al, in preparation).

Revolutions do not always feature the same set of key actors, nor do they all unfold in the same way. Popular mobilization may be primarily urban (as in Iran and Eastern Europe), feature extensive peasant revolts (Wolf 1969), or involve organized guerrilla war. Huntington (1968) pointed out that major revolutions show at least two distinct patterns of mobilization and development. If military and most civilian elites initially are actively supportive of the government, popular mobilization must take place from a secure, often remote, base. In the course of a guerrilla or civil war in which revolutionary leaders gradually extend their control of the countryside, they need to build popular support while waiting for the regime to be weakened by events—such as military defeats, affronts to national pride and identity, or its own ill-directed repression or acts of corruption—that cost it domestic elite and foreign support. Eventually, if the regime suffers elite or military defections, the revolutionary movement can advance or begin urban insurrections and seize the national capital. Revolutions of this type, which we may call peripheral revolutions, occurred in Cuba, Vietnam, Nicaragua, Zaire, Afghanistan, and Mozambique.

In contrast, revolutions may start with the dramatic collapse of the regime at the center (Huntington 1968). If domestic elites are seeking to reform or replace the regime, they may encourage or tolerate large popular demonstrations in the capital and other cities, and then withdraw their support from the government, leading to a sudden collapse of the old regime's authority. In such cases, although the revolutionaries take power quickly, they then need to spread their revolution to the rest of the country, often through a reign of terror or civil war against new regional and national rivals or remnants of the old regime. Revolutions of this type, which we may call central revolutions, occurred in France, Russia, Iran, the Philippines, and Indonesia.

A variant of elite/popular mobilization dynamics is that some revolutions combine these types in different stages. In the Mexican and Chinese Revolutions, the old regimes initially fell in a central-type collapse; the Huerta and Nationalist regimes that first consolidated power were themselves overthrown by a peripheral mobilization.

Recent events suggest yet a third pattern of revolution, a general collapse of the government, as occurred in the totalitarian states of Eastern Europe and the

Soviet Union. In these countries, the state socialist regimes maintained firm control of rural and urban society through the party apparatus. When a combination of elite-led reform efforts, changing international alignments (the economic advance of capitalist countries, the Soviet Union's peace talks with the United States, and Hungary's open borders allowing mass German emigration), and popular strikes and demonstrations undermined the resolve of communist leaders, the entire national state apparatus rapidly degenerated (Karklins 1994, Hough 1997, Lane & Ross 1999). Although there were sometimes major confrontations in the capital cities (as in Moscow and Bucharest), the critical popular actions in several cases were taken by workers far from the capital—such as coal miners in the Soviet Union and Yugoslavia and shipyard workers in Gdansk in Poland—or by urban protestors in other cities, such as Leipzig in East Germany. There was thus no need for the revolutionary leaders taking power in the capital to spread their revolution by force throughout the country; the very breadth of the prior totalitarian regimes ensured that when they collapsed there were few or no competing power centers, except for the centrifugal forces lurking in autonomous and ethnically distinctive provincial governments (Bunce 1999). The main problem facing the new postsocialist regimes was not spreading the revolution but rather building new national institutions that could cope with the emergent private, criminal, and bureaucratic entrepreneurs rushing to fill the vacuum of power (McFaul 1995, Stark & Bruszt 1998).

Another typology rests on the guiding ideology of revolutionary movements. It distinguishes "liberal" or constitutional revolutions, which dominated the eighteenth and nineteenth centuries and seem to be reappearing with the revolutions in the Philippines and Eastern Europe; communist revolutions, which became prominent in the twentieth century; and Islamic revolutions, which appeared in the last quarter of the twentieth century.

As this brief survey makes clear, a full understanding of revolutions must take account of the plasticity of elite and popular alignments, of the processes of revolutionary mobilization and leadership, and of the variable goals and outcomes of revolutionary actors and events. If a fourth-generation theory of revolutions is to emerge, it must embrace these factors. The sections below examine what we know (or think we know) about the causes, processes, and outcomes of revolution and bring together the contributions of often disparate approaches, such as comparative case studies, rational choice models, and quantitative/statistical analysis.

CAUSES OF REVOLUTIONS

The International System

Skocpol (1979) was crucial in pointing out the effects that international military and economic competition can have on domestic state stability. The costs of war or economic shifts can undermine elite and popular loyalty to a government and put state finances in disarray. Yet this only begins to suggest how international influences can trigger and shape revolutions.

Ideological influences can spread across boundaries, with both the example and the content of revolutionary movements in one nation influencing others (Arjomand 1992, Colburn 1994, Katz 1997, Halliday 1999). One can thus point to several waves of revolutions in history, including the Atlantic revolutions of the United States (1776), Holland (1787), and France (1789), propelled by antimonarchical sentiment; the European Revolutions of 1848, propelled by liberalism; the anticolonial revolutions of the 1950s through 1970s, propelled by nationalism; the communist revolutions of 1945–1979 in Eastern Europe, China, Cuba, Vietnam, and other developing countries; the Arab Nationalist revolutions in the Middle East and North Africa in 1952–1969; the Islamic revolutions in Iran, Sudan, and Afghanistan; and the anticommunist revolutions in the Soviet Union and Eastern Europe. In each of these waves, international influences powerfully shaped outcomes and the direction of the revolutionary movements (Johnson 1993, Katz 1997, Boswell & Chase-Dunn 2000).

Direct military and diplomatic intervention by other countries can also shape revolutions, although often not as the interveners might have wished. Intervention by the Soviet Union could not defeat the Islamic Afghan Revolution, and interventions by the United States not only failed to prevent, but probably helped radicalize, the revolutions in Cuba, Nicaragua, Vietnam, and Iran by supporting the prerevolutionary regimes (Wickham-Crowley 1992, Halliday 1999, Snyder 1999, Pastor 2001). On the other hand, US intervention did reverse the abortive Mossadeq revolution in Iran in 1953, and Soviet support did encourage Marxist revolutions around the globe.

Halliday's (1999) general rule is "don't invade a revolution." Because of their great ability to mobilize populations for conflict (Skocpol 1994), revolutions are highly resistant to external intervention once they have already mobilized a national population. If intervention is to be effective in averting a revolution, it must generally occur prior to mass mobilization by the revolutionary movement. However, if a revolutionary movement and a regime are in stalemate, international diplomatic intervention can play a critical role in achieving a peaceful resolution, as occurred in Nicaragua in 1990 and in Zimbabwe in 1979 (Shugart 2001).

In some cases, it is the absence of intervention or the withdrawal (or threatened withdrawal) of ongoing support for a regime that allows a revolutionary movement to grow. Goldfrank (1979) and other scholars (Goodwin & Skopol 1989, Wickham-Crowley 1992) have labeled this a permissive or favorable world context. US preoccupation with World War I helped create an interval for Mexican revolutionary movements to spread; the exhaustion of European states and the defeat of Japan provided openings for multiple anticolonial revolutions after World War II; US concern for global human rights under President Carter spread the perception that support of the Shah of Iran and the Somoza regime in Nicaragua was diminishing; and the reduction of cold war tensions between the United States and the Soviet Union under Gorbachev provided an opening for dissidents, workers, and urban protestors to test the resolve of communist regimes.

A further conduit of international influence on the prospects for revolution is through international trade networks and the actions of transnational agencies and alliances. Scholars have found that under certain domestic conditions, countries with an unfavorable trading position in the world economy have a high risk of rebellions (Boswell & Dixon 1990, Jenkins & Schock 1992). In addition, currency crises and policies imposed by the International Monetary Fund can hobble governments and result in unpopular price movements, sometimes provoking violent protests (Walton 1989, Walton & Ragin 1990, Boswell & Dixon 1993, Walton & Seddon 1994). The Helsinki agreement on international human rights clearly invigorated the dissident movements in European communist regimes (Stokes 1993). At the same time, however, all other things equal, higher overall levels of participation in international trade and participation in international regional alliances are associated with a reduced risk of state collapse in countries around the world since World War II (Goldstone et al 2001). Evidently, high levels of economic and diplomatic engagement with the world provide some constraint on domestic competition and conflict. Conversely, it tends to be smaller, more isolated nations such as Rwanda and Cambodia that have been the site of the most severe and genocidal competitions for state power (Harff 1991, 1995).

Relationships Among States, Elites, and Popular Groups

Although the international environment can affect the risks of revolution in manifold ways, the precise impact of those effects, as well as the overall likelihood of revolution, is determined primarily by the internal relationships among state authorities, various elites, and various popular groups (peasants, workers, and regional or ethnic or religious minorities). It is now a truism, but worth restating, that fiscally and militarily sound states that enjoy the support of united elites are largely invulnerable to revolution from below. Popular misery and widespread grievances tend to produce pessimism, passive resistance, and depression, unless the circumstances of states and elites encourage actors to envision a realistic possibility of change (Scott 1985, 1990).

Skocpol (1979) specified a compact set of structural conditions that make a state vulnerable to social revolution: autonomous elites able to hamper state actions and peasant communities capable of autonomous resistance to landlord rule. However, close analyses of Skocpol's work have shown that these conditions are not wholly applicable even in her own cases (Nichols 1986, Sewell 1996, Goldstone 1997a, Mahoney 1999). Russia's elites in 1917 were clearly incapable of blocking actions by the Tsar and were able to act only because of the overwhelming defeat of the Tsar's forces by Germany in World War I. China's peasants had been under tight rural control by landed gentry since suppression of the Taiping rebellion in the mid-nineteenth century and played little role in the Republican or Nationalist revolutions of the early twentieth century. It was only when organized and mobilized by the Chinese Communist Party that the peasantry was able to play a revolutionary role. In addition, Skocpol underestimated the role of workers in the Russian Revolution of 1917 (Bonnell 1983); her scheme thus misses the overwhelming impact of urban protests by workers and students in shaping such events as the Iranian Revolution, the Nicaraguan Revolution, the Philippines Revolution and the Great Cultural Revolution and Tiananmen revolts in China (Farhi 1990, Wasserstrom & Perry 1994, Calhoun 1994b, Perry & Li 1997, Parsa 2000). Although these problems indicate the weakness of Skocpol's simplified structuralism, her approach, and indeed the richness of her overall analysis, has spurred a deeper understanding of how shifting state/elite/popular relationships lead to state breakdown and upheavals.

First, it appears clear from many studies that it is not merely state/elite conflicts, nor even necessarily the autonomous position of elites, that govern political stability and change. Rather, the key issues are (*a*) whether states have the financial and cultural resources to carry out the tasks they set for themselves and are expected to carry out by elites and popular groups, (*b*) whether elites are largely united or deeply divided or polarized, and (*c*) whether opposition elites link up with protest by popular groups.

The tasks that rulers set for themselves vary enormously from state to state. Large states may have imperial ambitions, whereas small states may seek merely to survive in peace. Personalist rulers need to maintain flexible resources to support extensive patronage; democratic states need to manage party competition while still maintaining an effective bureaucratic and judicial government. Traditional monarchies faced few expectations from elites and popular groups—to respect custom in raising revenues and to provide opportunities for elites and their families to maintain their rank. States in modern developing nations, however, are expected to promote economic growth and to mediate ethnic and regional claims on resources. Almost all states are also expected to uphold national pride and traditions; modern states are expected to realize the nationalist ambitions of dominant ethnic groups for a state that will embody and defend their distinctive character (Goodwin & Skocpol 1989, Tilly 1993).

States also have a wide range of resources on which to draw to meet these goals and expectations. Domestic revenues in the form of taxation and exploitation of natural resources may be complemented by revenues from foreign aid and direct foreign investment. Funds may be borrowed and resources sold or mortgaged against future expectations of increased tax or other revenues. Some governments may also gain revenue from nationalized enterprises—although these often fail to return projected profits.

Trouble arises when revenues no longer meet state expenses, whether because of an enlargement of state goals or a reduction in income. The ways in which trouble can arise are so many as to defy brief listing. Overambitious military and/or development adventures can strain state finances; so can a failure to adjust revenues to keep pace with inflation and growing national populations. Overestimates of future revenues can lead to reckless borrowing; corruption can drain funds away from useful purposes and leave state coffers bare. Small but growing deficits can gradually eat away at state fiscal strength; military debacles or deadlocks with elites over fiscal matters can precipitate loss of fiscal control and either runaway inflation or sudden state bankruptcies. In some cases, price shifts in key commodities in the economy can adversely affect economic growth and state revenues. Symptoms of fiscal illness can thus range from a slow depletion of state credit to ballooning debts to rapid price inflation to military incapacity to unanticipated shortfalls and bankruptcies.

Still, states are rarely so wholly in control of a society's resources that they cannot adjust to adversity if elites will contribute their efforts and resources to state reorganization. The threat of revolution appears when fiscal weakness arises while elites are reluctant to support the regime or are severely divided over whether and how to do so.

Such reluctance may reflect the financial difficulties of elites themselves. Elites who are struggling to maintain their wealth, or who see themselves being arbitrarily or unfairly fleeced by their rulers, will not readily support a weak and needy regime. Elites may also be alienated by exclusion from power or by assaults on their privileges or control of elite positions. But just as often elite (and popular) allegiance is lost through squandering or neglect of cultural resources.

State rulers operate within a cultural framework involving religious beliefs, nationalist aspirations, and notions of justice and status. Rulers violate these at their peril. Rulers who sell offices or appoint favorites to high positions may win their loyalty but incur the resentment of those left out. Rulers who seek to overturn traditional religious and cultural habits had better be sure of strong military and bureaucratic support to withstand the popular and elite protests that will ensue (Oberschall & Kim 1996). Rulers who lose face in military or diplomatic contests, or who appear too dependent on the whims of foreign powers, may lose the faith and support of their own peoples. The Puritan/Catholic contests in seventeenth-century England, the Jansenist controversies in prerevolutionary France, the devastating military defeats suffered by Tsarist Russia, and the controversies over Westernizing practices in Iran all involved rulers who violated cultural or nationalist beliefs and thereby forfeited elite and popular support (Skocpol 1979, Hunt 1983, Arjomand 1988, Van Kley 1996). In Russia, where cultural norms tolerated authoritarian regimes but required in return the state's paternal protection of the people, the blatant disregard for ordinary people shown in the Black Sunday massacres undermined support for the Tsar. The same cultural norms helped to support the Soviet Union, until the Communist Party's wooden response to the Chernobyl nuclear disaster and other health and welfare issues similarly alienated its population.

The joint need to manage state tasks and cultural standing can be summed up in two words: effectiveness and justice. States and rulers that are perceived as ineffective may still gain elite support for reform and restructuring if they are perceived as just. States that are considered unjust may be tolerated as long as they are perceived to be effective in pursuing economic or nationalist goals, or just too effective to challenge. However, states that appear both ineffective and unjust will forfeit the elite and popular support they need to survive.

Three social changes or conditions, though neither necessary nor sufficient to bring about revolution, nevertheless so commonly undermine both effectiveness and justice that they deserve special mention. First is defeat in war—or even overextension, when a state attempts military tasks beyond its fiscal and logistic capacity. Military defeat can bring financial and bureaucratic disorder because of the losses of men and resources expended or taken by the enemy, or because of reparations. Defeat can also bring about loss of national pride, and the increased taxes and resources taken from the population for the war effort may exceed norms of what is reasonable and fair. Particularly galling is the waste of lives and resources for a losing cause. Bueno de Mesquita et al (1992) found a weak association between war and ensuing revolution but found this relationship much stronger among countries that initiated wars and then lost them. It is this combination that produces the greatest joint loss of both effectiveness and cultural standing for the state.

Second, sustained population growth in excess of economic growth frequently alters the relationships among states, elites, and popular groups in ways that undermine stability. If increased demand produces inflation, real revenues to the government will fall unless taxes are raised; but that may be seen as highly unreasonable if peasants have less land, and workers are finding jobs scarce and their pay declining due to increased competition for jobs and resources. Urban population may increase disproportionately—and faster than urban administrations can increase housing, health, and police services—if the agricultural sector cannot absorb the population increase. Moreover, as the price of land or other scarce resources rises, those elites or aspiring elites who control those resources will benefit disproportionately to other elite groups, upsetting the normal processes of elite recruitment and social mobility. If the state demands higher taxes while popular living conditions are declining, and if elite patterns of hierarchy and mobility are being upset while the state is demanding more resources or more authority, then perceptions of both effectiveness and justice may be severely damaged. Although some states may find the means, through economic growth or making favorable elite alliances, to cope with rapid population increase, it is not surprising that rebellions and revolutions have been exceptionally widespread during periods when population has grown exceptionally fast—e.g. in the late sixteenth and early seventeenth century, the late eighteenth and early nineteenth century, and in parts of the developing world in the twentieth century (Goldstone 1991, 1997b).

Third, colonial regimes and personalist dictatorships are particularly prone to the dual faults that lead to revolution. Colonial regimes, by their nature, are an affront to the nationalist aspirations and power aspirations of native elites. While effective, they may be able to coopt local elites; however, should the balance of power shift between the colonial regime and the domestic elites with their potential popular support, colonial regimes will degenerate into revolutionary confrontations. Similarly, personalist dictatorships, because they exclude all but a tiny proportion of the elites from sharing in the fruits of power, have far less "justice" in the eyes of elites than more broadly based authoritarian regimes, such as military juntas, or regimes with a clear ethnic, regional, or class base. Personalist regimes may support themselves by claiming to offer exceptional nationalist achievements or by being ruthless and effective in managing domestic affairs. However, economic reverses, loss of foreign support, or loss of nationalist credentials through corruption or excessive subordination to foreign powers can fatally undermine their effectiveness and spur a multiclass coalition against their narrow base (Goodwin & Skocpol 1989, Wickham-Crowley 1992, Goldstone 1994a, Goodwin 1994b, Foran 1997b, Snyder 1998).

Levi (1997), using rational choice models to analyze political behavior, has shown how state violations of norms of fairness lead to "the withdrawal of compliance," and that this undermines governance. More than 60 years earlier, historian Crane Brinton (1938) noticed elites withdrawing their support from regimes prior to the outbreak of revolution, denouncing them as immoral and ineffective, and labeled this "the desertion of the intellectuals." By whatever name, any set of circumstances that leads to a state's loss of both perceived effectiveness and perceived justice leads to the defection of elites and loss of popular support; this is a crucial element in the causal pattern of revolutions.

Elite theory and comparative historical analyses have produced numerous case studies in which state breakdown was due to elite divisions and defections from the regime (Kileff & Robinson 1986, Arjomand 1988, Higley & Burton 1989, Wickham-Crowley 1989, Bunce 1989, Paige 1989, Goldstone 1991, Goldstone et al 1991, Bearman 1993, Haggard & Kaufman 1995, DeFronzo 1996, Hough 1997, Lachmann 1997, Dogan & Higley 1998, Snyder 1998, Parsa 2000). Conversely, in many cases state stability emerged from violence through the forging of elite pacts (O'Donnell et al 1986, Burton & Higley 1987, Higley & Gunther 1992, Shugart 2001).

However, division among elites is not sufficient to create instability. If they are highly factionalized and fragmented, elites can be reduced to incapacity when faced with a strong authoritarian leader. What is crucial for political crises to emerge is for elites to be not only divided but polarized—that is, to form two or three coherent groupings with sharp differences in their visions of how social order should be structured (Green 1984, Eisenstadt 1999).

Of course, even if elites are divided and sharply opposed to the state, the result may merely be coups d'etat (Jenkins & Kposowa 1990) or reforms. In order for a revolutionary situation to develop, there must also be mass mobilization. This may be traditional, informal, elite-directed, or some combination of these types.

Traditional mobilization occurs within the context of local communities to which individuals have long-standing commitments, such as peasant villages or urban craft guilds (Magagna 1991). Usually triggered by some news of political change, such as plans for state reforms, elections, or news or even rumors of war or local attacks [as Markoff (1996) has shown in the case of the French Revolution of 1789], much peasant mobilization is defensive, even reactionary, aimed at calling attention to economic distress or high levels of taxation. Direct attacks on landlords are less common and are usually prompted by news that the state's authority has been challenged or broken down. Traditional mobilization may also take place in cities through traditional workers' guilds, or through religious communities, and it too is often defensive and conservative in intent (Calhoun 1983).

Informal mobilization occurs when individuals' decisions to engage in protest actions are made not through communal organizations to which they have long-standing formal ties but instead through loosely connected networks based on personal friendship, shared workplace, or neighborhood. Such informal organization generally occurs in response to a crisis; neighborhoods or friends then mobilize themselves to take unconventional actions. Gould (1995) demonstrated the role of neighborhood ties in popular mobilization during the French commune of 1870; Opp et al (1995) and Pfaff (1996) have shown that informal organization lay behind the "spontaneous" Leipzig protests that brought down the East German communist regime; Denoeux (1993) detailed the role played by informal networks in urban protest in the Middle East. Proximity and friendships among students helped mobilize protest in the Tiananmen revolt in China (Zhao 2001) and in the revolutions of 1979 in Iran and of 1986 in the Philippines (Parsa 2000).

Traditional and informal organization are not inherently revolutionary in themselves and usually lead only to abortive rural rebellions and urban protest. They become effective in creating revolutionary change when they link up with elite opposition to the regime. In some cases, as in the rural revolts of the French and Russian Revolutions and the Irish revolts of 1640, their impact is to frighten authorities into taking radical steps, shattering efforts by elites to move slowly or wrangle indefinitely. In other cases, dissident elites place themselves at the head of popular revolts, linking up varied local movements and giving them direction and coherence, as the Bolsheviks did with workers' revolts in 1917, or as the radical clerical leader Ayatollah Khomeini did with protests based in the *medresas* and bazaars of Iran.

A third way for elites to link up with popular mobilization is to create and direct the organizations through which mobilization takes place. Although it would be too much to say that the Communist Party fully controlled rural revolt in China in the 1940s, the Chinese Communist Party nonetheless played a key role in organizing peasants to redistribute land, curb landlord influence, and undertake armed struggle against the Nationalist regime (Friedman et al 1991, Selden 1995). In Latin America in the 1970s, most effectively in Nicaragua, priests established Christian base communities to mobilize opposition to the existing economic and political regimes (Levine & Manwaring 1989, Van Vugt 1991). At the same time, radical students and politicians, following the model of Fidel Castro in Cuba, sought to mobilize Latin American peasantries through communist guerrilla movements (Wickham-Crowley 1992). In the 1980s, church leaders in Poland, the Philippines, and East Germany played a critical role in creating formal and informal linkages between workers, intellectuals, and professionals in opposition to the regime (Osa 1997, Parsa 2000, Stokes 1993).

Of course, elites can countermobilize as well. Traugott (1985) has demonstrated that there was little difference in occupation or income between the revolutionary

Parisian workers who fought on the barricades in 1848 and the Parisian workers in National Guard units fighting against them. The difference lay almost entirely in their mobilization experiences; the rebels had mobilized through neighborhood and workplace, whereas the National Guard members had been mobilized by the bourgeoisie of Paris to defend their rather more middle-class revolution against the King. Indeed, mobilization is usually competitive, with varied revolutionary and counterrevolutionary organizations seeking to rally supporters at the same time, often in chaotic circumstances. Although in hindsight we may identify one successful mobilizing group with its constituency to such a degree that the direction and magnitude of mobilization appear inevitable, in fact that is rarely the case. More likely, a triumphant revolutionary mobilization emerged from a contest for supporters engaging multiple allies and competitors (Meyer & Staggenborg 1996, Glenn 1999).

Given this enormous range of modes of popular organization, there is no easy way to predict the form or direction that popular mobilization will take simply from structural factors. Although there is a substantial literature on peasants in revolutions (Wolf 1969, Migdal 1974, Paige 1975, Scott 1976, Popkin 1979, Wickham-Crowley 1991, Skocpol 1994), and an ongoing debate about the degree to which inequality leads to revolutionary unrest (Muller 1985, Midlarsky 1986, Muller & Seligson 1987, Weede 1987, Lichbach 1989, Midlarsky 1999), none of these literatures has produced consensus. As Zamosc (1989) argues, it appears that peasants are not inherently conservative or revolutionary; rather, their aspirations take different forms depending on the state and elite responses and alliances they encounter. The single constant that one can derive from experience is that successful revolutions occur only where there is some linkage or coalition between popular mobilization and elite antiregime movements (Liu 1984, Dix 1983, Goodwin & Skocpol 1989, Eckstein 1989a, Aya 1990, Farhi 1990, Goldstone et al 1991, Wickham-Crowley 1992, Foran 1997b, Paige 1997).

PROCESSES OF REVOLUTIONS: Networks, Ideology, Leadership, Gender

Networks, Organizations, and Identities

The varied, competitive, and contingent nature of revolutionary mobilization has led scholars to place far more emphasis on the processes by which revolutions develop. Structural conditions may set the stage for conflict, but the shape and outcome of that struggle is often determined only in the course of the revolutionary conflict itself. How do elites link up with popular protest movements? How do individuals come together to act collectively, often in the face of great risk of repression or even death? How are diverse groups with distinct interests brought together to form wide-ranging coalitions? And how do particular leaders and groups emerge to dominate and set the course of a revolution? These questions can only be addressed by attention to the organizational, ideological, and strategic elements of revolutionary action.

One key finding is that revolutionary actors do not act, or even think of themselves as acting, alone. They are recruited through preexisting networks of residence, occupation, community, and friendship. They are set in motion by organizations that range from small and informal bands of activists, such as the Charter 77 group in the Czechoslovak Revolution, to the highly disciplined, centralized, and bureaucratic revolutionary parties of China and the Soviet Union. They identify themselves with broader causes and groups and make sacrifices in their name (Cohen 1985; Calhoun 1994a,c; Somers & Gibson 1994).

In this respect, they are much like actors in more routine movements of social protest. Analysts of social movements in democratic societies have found that people are recruited to movements along the lines of membership in groups and friendship with people already tied to the movement (Snow et al 1980, McPherson et al 1992, McAdam 1995). Whether in the student movement, feminist movements, or the civil rights movement, the common denominator for successful activism is that actors become invested in the identities of the protest group, that they shape their actions by identification with the costs and benefits for a larger whole (Morris 1984, Hirsch 1990, Taylor & Whittier 1992).

Identities, however, are not inherent—particularly protest identities (Abrams & Hogg 1990). In order to create and maintain identities relevant to revolutionary action, elites and states must produce and cement novel identifications for people who normally just think of themselves as workers or peasants, friends or neighbors. Making certain identities more salient, indeed creating protest identities—that is, a sense of being part of a group with shared and justified grievances, with the ability to remedy those grievances by collective action—is a considerable project (Snow et al 1986, Snow & Benford 1988).

For many years, resource mobilization theorists argued that mobilizing people for collective action revolved around building organizations, such as unions, revolutionary parties, and grass-roots movement organizations such as the National Organization for Women or the Southern Christian Leadership Conference (McCarthy & Zald 1977, Tilly 1978). Such "social movement organizations" were held to be at the heart of sustained collective actions. However, recent studies of recruitment and of the experience of movement participants has shown that formal organization is neither necessary nor sufficient to create the sense of commitment and energy needed for risky collective action to occur (McAdam 1988, Calhoun 1994b, Gould 1995, Pfaff 1996). Instead, the formation of protest identities seems to be critical. Although formal organizations can often help choose tactics for protest and sustain a movement through reverses and lean times, informal organization—as shown in the 1989–1991 revolutions in Eastern Europe—can also bring people together for large-scale, risky, and effective challenges to state authority.

Protest identities—feelings of attachment and affection for a protest group—appear to have three sources. First, the group helps to justify and validate the individual's grievances and anger against the status quo. Second, the group—if it provides concrete benefits or takes actions that seem effective in defending its members and pursuing change—gives a sense of empowerment, autonomy, and efficacy to its members, earning their affective allegiance (Knoke 1988, Lawler 1992). Third, the state itself may create or reinforce a sense of oppositional identity by labeling a group as its enemies or by acting against the group, thus demonstrating that the group is now outside the protection and justice of the state. Members then are forced to look to the group for justice and protection. The protest group, in other words, gains commitment through manifesting the same qualities that are expected from the state, namely justice and effectiveness.

Indeed, it is precisely because the protest group fulfils these functions in way that the state has failed to do, or in a way deemed superior to that of the state, that individuals are willing to transfer their allegiance from the state to the protest or revolutionary group (Finkel et al 1989). In some cases, the revolutionary movement literally becomes the state in the areas under its control, as did the Communist Party in the 1940s in rural China and many guerrilla movements in Latin America, taking over functions of law enforcement, justice, and even taxation (Wickham-Crowley 1991, Selden 1995, McClintock 1998). In other cases, the revolutionary movement gains allegiance by validating the grievances and aspirations of its members through solidarity rituals and by taking actions against the state that may be largely symbolic (Melucci 1989).

In either case, however, the creation and maintenance of protest identities is a substantial task that draws on cultural frameworks, ideologies, and talented leadership.

Ideology and Cultural Frameworks

The perception that the state is ineffective and unjust whereas revolutionary movements of opposition are virtuous and efficacious is rarely a direct outcome of structural conditions (Gamson 1988, Gamson & Meyer 1996). Material deprivations and threats need to be seen not merely as miserable conditions but as a direct result of the injustice and the moral and political failings of the state, in sharp contrast to the virtue and justice of the opposition (Martin et al 1990). Even defeat in war, famine, or fiscal collapse may be seen as natural or unavoidable catastrophes rather than as the handiwork of incompetent or morally bankrupt regimes. Similarly, acts of state repression against protesters may be seen as necessary peacekeeping or conversely as unjustified repression; kidnappings, arson, and bombings may be painted as reprehensible and cowardly terrorist acts or as patriotic measures for liberation of the oppressed. Which interpretation prevails depends on the ability of states and revolutionary leaders to manipulate perceptions by relating their actions and current conditions to existing cultural frameworks and to carefully constructed ideologies (DeNardo 1985, Chong 1991, Berejikian 1992).

Analysts of revolution use the term cultural frameworks to denote the long-standing background assumptions, values, myths, stories, and symbols that are widespread in the population. Naturally, the frameworks of elites and popular groups may differ, and those of different regional, ethnic, and occupational groups may vary. Thus we find a set of roughly overlapping frameworks rather than a homogenous set of beliefs. Ideologies, in contrast, are consciously constructed, perhaps eclectic but more coherent beliefs, arguments, and value judgments that are promulgated by those advocating a particular course of action. In the early twentieth century, Christianity, German patriotism, and a belief in the virtues of the Frankish tribes and pioneers who conquered the forests of central Europe were part of the cultural framework of Germany; Nazism in contrast was an ideology (Skocpol 1994).

As this example shows, those ideologies that are most effective are those that strike roots in prevailing cultural frameworks, appropriating older stories and images and retooling them to resonate with the issues of the present day (Nash 1989, Shin 1996). The Chinese Communists initially linked their justification for ruling China to restoring the patriarchal order of the traditional Chinese family, which had been undone by the economic chaos and military defeats suffered under the Nationalist regime (Stacey 1983). Similarly, Communist organizers in Vietnam had no success until they incorporated ethnic Vietnamese content and cultural themes into their appeals (Popkin 1988).

Foran (1997b) has argued that revolution is impossible without drawing on a "culture of rebellion" from widely remembered prior conflicts. For example, the 1970s Sandinista revolt in Nicaragua drew its name and its claim to virtue from the peasant leader Sandino, who fought against US domination of Nicaragua at the beginning of the century. Similarly, the Zapatista rebellion in Chiapas, Mexico in the 1990s drew its name and identified its ideals with the peasant leader Zapata of the Mexican Revolution of 1910. However, these examples do not imply that only countries that have actively recalled rebellions in their recent past have the cultural foundation for later uprisings. Revolutionary entrepreneurs have proved quite nimble at appropriating cultural foundations for revolt from the distant past, or even the imagined past or future. Millennial beliefs dating back to Native American legends were appropriated and reconfigured to draw popular support for the Mexican Revolution; similarly, the millennial beliefs of Chinese Buddhist sects undergirded some of the revolutionary imagery of the Chinese Communists (Rinehart 1997). In the English Revolution of 1640, regicides drew on the myth of the Norman yoke (though they were of ancient Norman lineage themselves), in which the English royal line planted in 1066 by the invasion of William of Normandy was decried as a foreign oppressor that enslaved free Anglo-Saxon Englishmen. In their revolt against Spain in the sixteenth and seventeenth centuries, the Dutch presented themselves as descendants of the ancient Helvetian tribes who had fought Roman imperial rule; in the French Revolution, in an ironic turnaround, the French revolutionaries liked to identify with the Roman founders of the Republic and their struggle against the Tarquin kings.

Any cultural framework may provide the basis for revolutionary or antirevolutionary ideologies. Christianity and Islam have long been the bastion of conservative established church organizations; but in recent years Islamic fundamentalists and Christian base communities seem as radical as the English Puritans of the seventeenth century. Communism has been both a revolutionary ideology and the cloak for a conservative and privileged elite that was overthrown by liberal intellectuals and nationalist workers. Whether or not a revolutionary ideology emerges from a given cultural framework seems to depend entirely on how elements of that framework are adapted to particular circumstances or combined with new elements and adopted by particular groups.

Ideologies, in addition to providing value judgments and clothing of virtue for revolutionaries, may accelerate revolutionary momentum in two other, reinforcing ways. First, revolutionary ideologies usually present their struggle as destined to succeed; having history or God on their side will ensure the triumph of their followers (Martin et al 1990). Second, revolutionary ideologies aim to bridge the varied cultural frameworks of different groups and provide a basis for the multigroup and cross-class coalitions so important for challenging state power (Chong 1993). These functions reinforce each other. As a revolutionary group attracts a broader range of followers, it begins to seem destined to succeed; at the same time, the more likely a movement's success appears, the more followers it will attract.

Constructing an ideology that will (*a*) inspire a broad range of followers by resonating with existing cultural guideposts, (*b*) provide a sense of inevitability and destiny about its followers' success, and (*c*) persuade people that the existing authorities are unjust and weak is no simple task. Neither is planning a strategic and tactical campaign of opposition or skillfully taking advantage of spontaneous uprisings and chance events. Thus, the course and outcomes of revolutions depend to a considerable degree on the skills and actions of state and revolutionary leaders.

Leadership

Popular histories of revolutions are filled with accounts of larger-than-life personalities: Cromwell, Washington, Robespierre, Napoleon, Lenin, Stalin, Mao, Castro, Guevarra, Cabral, Mandela, Aquino. Sometimes it seems that the origins and outcome of the revolutions are inseparable from the will and fate of these revolutionary leaders. Yet collective biographies of revolutionary leaders have shown that although many are exceptionally charismatic, many are not, and indeed as a whole the background and personality profiles of revolutionary leaders do not markedly differ from those of conventional political leaders (Rejai & Phillips 1988). Moreover, in structural theories of revolution, these leaders hardly ever appear, or if mentioned, they seem to be unwitting dupes of history whose best intentions are always frustrated by deeper social, political, or economic forces.

This disconnect can be understood by focusing on the skills of revolutionary leaders themselves. Successful leaders excel at taking advantage of favorable political and economic circumstances. Poor leaders generally act when circumstances are highly unfavorable to success. The resulting pattern—leaders appear to succeed only when conditions favor them and to fail otherwise—makes revolutionary success appear to be strictly a matter of background conditions and obscures the role of leadership in actually making a revolution out of merely potentially favorable circumstances. The importance of leadership is clearest in fairly extreme cases such as the "New Jewel" Revolution in Grenada, where poor leadership led an apparently successful revolution to self-destruct (Selbin 1993), or cases such as the Chinese Communist Revolution, where outstanding leadership was able to sustain a revolutionary movement through apparently crushing defeat and to plan for circumstances that would allow victory (Selden 1995).

The failure of revolutionary leaders to achieve their proclaimed aims—liberty, equality, prosperity—is also taken as evidence of the minor impact of leadership. Yet it is not that simple; after a revolution, its supporters often divide and fall out among themselves, military confrontations test and reshape revolutionary regimes, and once they attain absolute power, many leaders are blinded by it and indulge in megalomaniac fantasies. Thus it is no surprise that revolutions often fail to achieve their prerevolutionary aims. However, this does not mean leadership is insignificant, only that its impact is complex. It requires varied kinds of leadership not only to build a revolutionary movement that can help topple an old regime, but also to win the internecine struggles that follow the collapse of the old order, and to withstand the military blows that often rain down on a new regime. And if a revolutionary leadership survives all this and falls into megalomaniac excess, the resultant suffering only demonstrates the impact of revolutionary leaders on the fate of ordinary people and of nations (Friedman et al 1991, Chirot 1994).

Studies of leadership have found that there are two distinct types and that they usually must be combined—either in one person or through the cooperation of two or more—for an enterprise to succeed. Interestingly, these two types of leadership, "people-oriented" and "task-oriented" (Aminzade et al 2001b, Selbin 1993), mirror the two dimensions of successful governance or mobilization, namely justice and effectiveness. People-oriented leaders are those who inspire people, give them a sense of identity and power, and provide a vision of a new and just order around which their followers unite their energies and their purposes. Task-oriented leaders are those who can plot a strategy suitable to resources and circumstances, set the timetables for people and supplies to reach specific ends, manage money effectively, and respond to shifting circumstances with appropriate strategies and tactics. The purely people-oriented leader is personified by the religious prophet; the purely task-oriented leader is figured by the brilliant military general. Movements with only strong people-oriented leadership may end up as devoted but tiny cults (Hall et al 2000); movements that have strong task-oriented leadership but no vision often fail to consolidate themselves in popular consciousness, and their revolutionary character will soon fade away (Selbin 1993).

It generally seems to require two or more people or groups to fulfill the roles of visionaries and organizers of a revolution, even though the division of tasks is not always clear-cut. Puritan preachers and Oliver Cromwell's generalship combined to inspire and effect the Puritan Revolution in Britain; Jefferson and Adams were firebrands of the American Revolution, but it would have failed without Washington's generalship and power brokering at the Constitutional Convention; the Jacobins' vision for France might have failed sooner if not for Napoleon's military victories; Lenin had Trotsky to lead the uprising of the workers and to build the Red Army; Fidel Castro had Ché Guevarra and his brother Raul to fuel and organize the Cuban Revolution; the Ortega brothers had complementary ideological and military roles in leading the Nicaraguan Revolution; and Ayatollah Khomeini relied on the liberal professional Bani-Sadr to help institutionalize the Iranian Revolution and ward off the military attack from Iraq.

In many cases, the visionary and practical leaders clash in the course of the revolution, and one side takes over. In China, Mao and his initial successors, the Gang of Four, clearly leaned toward the visionary side regardless of the practical costs; in Russia, the dull and practical party-builders under Brezhnev won out shortly after Stalin's death. Interestingly, in both these cases, the result was a counterthrust—in China the ultrapragmatic Deng regime, in the Soviet Union the attempt to reinspire the nation with an infusion of liberal ideas under Gorbachev. In Iran, the more extreme ideological clerical groups initially won out over liberal pragmatists, as did the communist-leaning Sandinistas in Nicaragua over their more liberal allies. In the Iranian case, US pressure actually reinforced the extreme visionaries, and the current counterthrust of moderates remains weak; in Nicaragua, US pressure weakened the visionaries and allowed a pragmatic coalition under Violetta Chamorro to rise to power. Thus, there is no guarantee the "right" balance of people-oriented and task-oriented leadership will be sustained, and the course of a revolution can veer in different directions accordingly.

In addition to visionary and pragmatic leadership, Robnett (1997) has identified the dimension of "bridge" leadership, which carries both the ideology and the organizational tasks of mobilizing down to the grass-roots level. Bridge leaders are those neighborhood and community organizers who mediate between top leadership and the vast bulk of followers, turning dreams and grand plans into on-the-ground realities.

Interestingly, Robnett, who focused on the US civil rights movement, identified a strong gender component to this dimension of leadership. She found that whereas the main ideological and strategic leaders of the movement were black (and some white) males, the bridge leaders were largely female. Thus the civil rights movement, as has been shown elsewhere (McAdam 1988), despite its radicalism regarding race relations, mapped in its own leadership organization the prevailing patriarchal gender bias of the racist society it was fighting.

Gender Relations and Revolutionary Movements

Numerous studies have now documented the extensive role played by women in revolutions, from the English and French Revolutions (Davies 1998, Hufton 1992) to recent Third World revolutions (Tétreault 1994, Wasserstrom 1994, Diamond 1998). Women have been active in street demonstrations, guerrilla warfare, provision of food and supplies, and bridge leadership. However, despite this massive participation, there is often less connection than one would expect between female participation in revolutions and the gender character of the movement or the emergence of women as autonomous leaders.

Moghadam (1997) and Taylor (1999) have pointed out that protest and revolutionary movements always, whether implicitly or explicitly, have a gender agenda in their own organization and goals. Since almost all societies in history have been patriarchal, protest movements and revolutions generally oppose patriarchal regimes and institutions. They therefore must make a choice. While opposing the existing political institutions, do they nonetheless adopt and reproduce the patriarchal character dominant in society in their own movement? Or do they seek to overturn that character in their movement and in their vision of a new society?

Often, there is a significant divergence between rhetoric and practice. The Russian and Cuban revolutions consciously aimed to create a gender-equal society, and they did succeed in bringing many more women into the workplace and the professions (Goldman 1993, Smith & Padula 1996). However, they recruited few women to major leadership roles and did not alter the basically male-biased values of their societies. The English, French, and American Revolutions inspired many women to play critical grass-roots roles and even included female ideals in their revolutionary iconography (Hunt 1992). However, they took no action to change the traditional role of women in society. The Iranian Revolution involved many westernized, educated women who consciously adopted traditional Islamic female dress as a symbol of their opposition to Western cultural imperialism and their support for the revolution. Yet these women were surprised to find that they were excluded from further efforts to shape the revolution, and that the very antiwestern Islamist modes of self-representation they adopted to help make the revolution became part of their enhanced repression afterward (Moghadam 1994, Fantasia & Hirsch 1995).

Even feminist movements have been torn over issues of how to engender their movements. Early feminists were concerned that embracing antisexual or prohomosexual attitudes would undermine their struggle for political emancipation and voting rights within mainstream society; modern feminists would prefer to undermine all traditional gender relations as part of the struggle against patriarchy and welcome gay and lesbian rights activists as partners in their cause (Taylor & Whittier 1992, Rupp 1997).

The key question about engendering revolutionary movements is whether in patriarchal societies women can ever be sufficiently persuasive and powerful to become visionary or effective leaders in their own right. The major female revolutionary leaders—Aquino in the Philippines, Chamorro in Nicaragua, Aung San Suu Ki in Burma—all acquired a leadership mantle from martyred husbands or fathers. This pattern also appears among democratic female leaders in Asia, such as India's Indira Ghandi, Pakistan's Benazir Bhutto, and Sri Lanka's Sirimavo Bandaranaike. To date, despite the widespread participation of women in revolutionary movements and their crucial contributions as bridge leaders, they have yet to play an independently dominant leadership role (except in the movement for women's political equality, if one treats it as revolutionary). Nor have revolutions, even where they have brought women full participation in voting and workplace opportunities, brought rapid transformations in the household and leadership status of women in their societies.

A PARADOX OF REVOLUTIONARY PROCESSES: Is Repression a Barrier or Spur to Revolutions?

The perception that structural conditions are the main, if not the sole, determinant of revolutions is strengthened by the fact that revolutions sometimes seem to come about despite all efforts of the state to appease or repress them. Often, paradoxically, fierce repression is unable to daunt, or even inflames, revolutionary opposition (Lichbach 1987, Weede 1987, Olivier 1991, Khawaja 1993, Kurzman 1996, Rasler 1996, Moore 1998). In many cases, state reforms only encourage revolutionaries to demand more. Yet in other cases, most recently in the democracy movements in Burma and in China, apparently highly favorable conditions and considerable mass mobilization were crushed by state repression (Walder 1989, Carey 1997, Brook 1998). And in Prussia in 1848, in Britain in 1830, and in South Africa in 1994, reforms combined with repression effectively defused and ended revolutionary movements. When do repression and reform work to halt the progress of revolution, and when do they fail or even backfire and provoke or inflame revolutionary action?

While perceptions of state injustice and ineffectiveness may lead to opposition, the development of such conflicts has a contingent and metamorphic character. The actions and reactions of regimes, regime opponents, counter-movements, and the broader public all reshape the processes of group identification, perceptions of the efficacy and justice of the regime and its opponents, and estimates of what changes are possible (Gartner & Regan 1996, Kurzman 1996, Rasler 1996, Zhao 2001). Movements of reform may become radicalized and revolutionary, initially small confrontations may spiral into mass uprisings, or large popular movements may be crushed.

It is well known that many revolutions and rebellions, from the English and French Revolutions to the Mau-Mau revolt in Kenya and *La Violencia* in Colombia, grew out of efforts to reform, not overthrow, the ruling regimes (Walton 1984, Speck 1990). A combination of unexpected popular pressures from below, conflicts between conservative and radical factions of the reform movement, reactions to international interventions, and temporizing or provocative actions by the regime, gave precedence to both more radical leadership and more revolutionary policies (Furet 1981). In fact, the structural conditions that give rise to social protest movements, unsuccessful rebellions, and revolutions are generally quite similar. The transformation of social movements into rebellions or revolutions depends on how regimes, elites, and publics respond to the conflict situation (Goldstone 1998b).

When facing demands for change, ruling regimes may employ any combination of concessions and repression to defuse the opposition (Davenport 1995). Choosing the right combination is not an easy task. If a regime that has already lost its perceived effectiveness and justice offers concessions, these may be seen as "too little, too late," and simply increase the popular demands for large-scale change. This is why Machiavelli advised rulers to undertake reforms only from a position of strength; if undertaken from a position of weakness, they will further undermine support for the regime. The efforts of the Dowager Empress in late Imperial China, and of Gorbachev in the waning days of the Soviet Union, to encourage westernizing reforms led to escalating criticism of the old regimes and ultimately to their complete rejection and overthrow (Teitzel & Weber 1994).

Repression is also a matter of degree and of context. Repression that is powerful, or that is focused on a small "deviant" group, may be seen as evidence of state effectiveness and cow the opposition. However, repression that is not strong enough to suppress opponents, or that is so diffuse and erratic that innocents are persecuted, or that is aimed at groups that the public considers representative and justified in their protest, can quickly undermine perceptions of the regime's effectiveness and justice (White 1989, Goldstone & Tilly 2001). Thus the deaths of Pedro Chamorro in Nicaragua and of Benigno Aquino in the Philippines, the diffuse persecution of ordinary citizens by Batista in Cuba, and the deaths inflicted on protestors in Iran by the forces of the Shah in 1978 spurred accelerations of popular protest. In contrast, the overwhelming force used against the Tiananmen Square protestors, who were publicly labeled as counterrevolutionary traitors, broke public resistance to communist rule in China for at least a decade (Zhao 2001).

Perceptions of the vulnerability of rulers also make a difference to the effect of repression. When the regime is judged to be losing support and capable of being overthrown, protestors may bear great risks, and great regime violence may simply further persuade people that the regime has got to go; yet when a regime is seen as unshakeable, indiscriminate violence and terror may simply reduce the opposition to silence (Mason & Krane 1989, Opp & Roehl 1990, Opp 1994, Brockett 1995).

Rulers, however, have few guideposts to help them determine in advance whether a given level of concession or repression is sufficient. Lack of information and overconfidence further conspire to produce inappropriate responses. Worse yet, rulers often veer back and forth between concessions and repression, appearing inconsistent and therefore both ineffective and unjust (Goldstone & Tilly 2001). For example, both Marcos in the Philippines and Milosevic in Serbia believed they could rig victory in elections, and therefore they made the apparent concession of calling elections to justify their authoritarian rule. When, despite their efforts, it was widely perceived that they lost the elections, they then had to fall back on repression to maintain their rule. But because of the perceived electoral losses, military and police resolve to defend the regime was weakened, and repression of popular protests failed, leading to the collapse of the regime.

Foreign intervention can also lead to switches from repression to concessions and vice versa. The more active human rights policies of Jimmy Carter led Somoza in Nicaragua and the Shah of Iran to reduce repression, giving a space for opponents to undertake more active public resistance. In the ensuing dance of repression, concessions, and protest, the regimes were not repressive enough to crush their opponents but were repressive enough to increase perceptions of their injustice and swing elites and publics to support the opposition, strengthening the revolution. In contrast, in 1956 in Hungary and 1968 in Czechoslovakia, the regimes were vacillating enough to encourage reformers to demand radical change in socialist rule; yet massive external repression from the Soviet Union quashed the widespread public uprisings.

In general, a strong regime facing a weak opposition can readily maintain itself by concessions or repression; however, a regime with major financial or military weakness facing widespread elite and popular opposition has a hard time surviving. In these cases, structural conditions largely determine outcomes. However, in many cases a regime's strength or weakness and the degree of public support or opposition are either intermediate or simply unclear at the beginning of a conflict (Kuran 1989, 1995b). In such cases, structural conditions offer no secure guide to what will ensue, and it is the interaction of the regime and its opponents that determines what will follow. An apparently strong regime that represses weakly or inconsistently, or that offers concessions deemed inadequate, can quickly undermine its own position (Kurzman 1996). Moreover, a regime that makes reform appear unlikely can undercut the moderates among its opponents and give more radical elements the upper hand in recruiting public support (Walton 1984, McDaniel 1991, Seidman 1994).

Because authoritarian regimes are often so distant from understanding their own subjects, or so overconfident in their estimation of their own power, errors by such regimes are common, and often an apparently secure regime that has lasted many years suddenly unravels in the face of a rapidly expanding opposition that in prior years no one had anticipated—Iran in 1979, the Philippines in 1986, and the Eastern European and Soviet communist regimes in 1989–1991. In contrast, regimes that appear structurally weak, such as the personal rule of Mobutu in Zaire, can persist for many years if the use of concessions and repression is skillful in dividing and neutralizing, rather than uniting and inflaming, the opposition (Snyder 1998).

MICRO-LEVEL FOUNDATIONS AND QUANTITATIVE ANALYSIS

The study of revolutions (and of peaceful democratic transitions) has been dominated in the past two decades by scholars using the case-study approach with national trajectories as cases. Scholars have therefore emphasized systemic macro-level factors in their analysis, such as the relations among states, elites, popular groups, and foreign nations; the ideologies or cultural frameworks of nations or large groups; and trends in national-level conditions such as social mobility, state debt, or population increase. This approach, relying on system-level analysis of a small number of cases, has been the subject of considerable controversy (Lieberson 1991, Collier 1993, King et al 1994, Goldthorpe 1997, Goldstone 1997a, Katznelson 1997, Ragin 1997, Rueschemeyer & Stephens 1997, Mahoney 2000). Although most scholars still believe the case-study approach has merit, two other approaches have also attracted major research efforts: micro-level analysis of the motivations of individuals involved in revolutionary actions (including social psychological and rational choice modeling approaches) and quantitative analysis of factors associated with the incidence of revolutions (both Boolean and large-*N* statistical analyses).

Micro-Level Foundations: The Rationality of Revolution

We have already alluded to the findings of social psychological analysis in our discussion of networks and leadership. Scholars have pointed out that individuals who participate in rebellious and risky protest activity are generally motivated, recruited, and sanctioned through preexisting communities to which they belong, but that activation of a specifically oppositional group identity depends on the actions of revolutionary entrepreneurs and states (Klandermans 1984, Klandermans & Oegema 1987). Commitment to an oppositional identity depends on believing in the efficacy of protest, which is reinforced by small-scale victories and benefits conferred by revolutionary groups; in addition, unjust actions or evidence of state weakness can push individuals to withdraw from identification with the state and to fall back on communities, informal networks, and opposition movements as alternative foci of political loyalty.

Rational choice models have further reinforced these findings. At one time, rational choice theorists argued that macro, case-based studies of revolution lacked micro foundations (Friedman & Hechter 1988, Kiser & Hechter 1991). They even argued that since individuals faced risks and costs if they participated in protest behavior, but reaped the same benefits if protest succeeded whether they participated or not, revolutionary action was irrational for individuals (Olson 1965, Tullock 1971). However, scholars have now demonstrated that in practice, this collective action problem for individuals can be resolved in many ways, and that revolutionary action can indeed have solid micro-level foundations in rational behavior.

Lichbach (1995, 1996) has shown that there are four main families of solutions to the collective action problem, each offering a way to motivate individuals to join in protest—changing incentives, using community obligations, arranging contracts, and using authority. In practice, they appear in various combinations and provide a plethora of ways to create collective action. Thus the research agenda of rational choice theory in regard to revolutions is no longer one of posing obstacles to collective action; instead, rational choice analysis has joined with other approaches in seeking to identify the processes by which collective action solutions are achieved, and the general characteristics of those solutions.

All these solutions rest on sanctioning and group identification. Although this can be considered problematic in itself (Hechter 1987), empirical studies in anthropology, survey research, and psychological experiments all demonstrate a widespread tendency of people to practice norms of fairness and group orientation (Oliver 1984, Klosko 1987, Knoke 1988, Finkel et al 1989, Fiske 1990, Hirsch 1990, Piliavin & Charng 1990). People who strongly identify with a group generally feel an obligation to act if the group acts, and believe that other group members will act with them. The main check on protest activity then is not the collective action problem but whether people believe that the group will be efficacious if action is taken (Opp 1989, Macy 1990, Macy 1991, Oberschall 1994b). Once it is realized that groups, and not individuals, are the foundational unit for decisions regarding protest actions, then rational choice models predict patterns of revolutionary mobilization consistent with experience in a wide variety of cases across time and across different cultural settings (Taylor 1988a, Chong 1991, Tong 1991, Goldstone 1994b, Hardin 1995, Moore 1995, White 1995).

Now that it is clear that group identification allows the individual collective action problem to be overcome, rational choice analysis has focused on clarifying the kinds of group structure that favor protest action and the patterns by which mobilization is likely to occur. Such studies have shown that neither a simple homogeneous group with strong ties (such as a traditional peasant village) nor a highly heterogeneous group (such as a diverse urban population) is ideal for mobilization. Rather, mobilization flows most readily in groups where there is a tightly integrated vanguard of activists who initiate action, with loose but centralized ties to a broader group of followers (Heckathorn 1990, Heckathorn 1993, Marwell & Oliver 1993, Kim & Bearman 1997, Chwe 1999, Yamaguchi 2000). This helps account for the observations that peasants with more resources and more at stake often play a key role in leading peasant villages to rebel (Wolf 1969) and that urban revolts are rooted in smaller neighborhood, occupational, or religious communities (Gould 1995).

Rational choice models also demonstrate why revolutionary mobilization is prone to rapid and often surprising spirals of escalation. If the key to protest mobilization is convincing groups that their actions will be effective against the regime, then two bits of information are crucial: the relative weakness or resolve of the regime and the number of other groups that support the action. Shifts in perception or information can suddenly make groups that long harbored concerns about regime injustice or effectiveness believe that now their action can make a difference. Single events or crises that provide new information can thus precipitate sudden mobilization based on previously concealed preferences and beliefs, producing a "bandwagon" effect as more groups add their actions to what appears to be an increasingly favorable juncture for action (Kuran 1989, Carley 1991, Chong 1991, Macy 1991, Karklins & Peterson 1993, Koopmans 1993, Lohmann 1993, Lichbach 1995). These models provide a framework for understanding the explosive mobilization seen in events such as the sudden collapse of communist control in the Soviet Union and Eastern Europe (Kuran 1991).

The past decade of rational choice research on revolutions has thus underlined the same topics—leadership, group identity, network ties—emphasized in recent comparative historical studies. Instead of posing paradoxes, rational choice analysts have now moved toward providing a firm micro-level foundation for understanding the causes and dynamics of revolutionary action.

Quantitative Analyses

Though many case-study analyses used quantitative techniques to analyze particular relationships, they remained focused on a small number of cases. In order to overcome this limitation, scholars have undertaken analysis of global data sets to search for general correlates of revolutionary activity.

An early wave of quantitative analysis of revolutions in the 1960s, based mainly on linear regression using global country-year data sets, focused on issues in modernization and deprivation theory (Feierabend et al 1969, Gurr 1968). Evaluations of such models found them lacking in consensus (Gurr 1980), and they gave way to structural and case-comparative analyses in the 1970s and 1980s (Skocpol 1979). However, in recent years a new wave of quantitative analysis has arisen that seeks to combine the virtues of large-*N* statistical analysis and sensitivity to case-based research and that focuses more on the character of the state.

The major new method used is Boolean analysis (Ragin 1987), which assigns binary "absent" or "present" values to variables for each of a large number of specific cases. It thus retains the specifics of each case and allows for multiple configurations of independent variables. Algorithms are then used to deduce the minimum set, or sets, of variables that characterize particular outcomes.

Foran (1997b) and Wickham-Crowley (1992) have used Boolean analysis to good effect in analyzing several dozen cases of Third World revolutions. They find that full-scale social revolutions are rare and are associated with the most distinctive set of variables. Other kinds of revolutions—failed revolutions, political revolutions, rural rebellions—are associated with other, more varied combinations. However, their analyses do not produce a clear theory of the causes of revolution because they use different sets of variables and different sets of cases. The Boolean method is very sensitive to the specific cases used and the variables tested. In Foran's analysis, every successful social revolution had a "culture of rebellion"; in Wickham-Crowley's analysis, this variable was not included and appears unnecessary to distinguish the successful social revolutions from other events. What the Boolean analyses do demonstrate is that there is no single set of factors whose absence or presence always leads to revolution or nonrevolution. Rather, different factors combine in a variety of ways to produce different types and outcomes of revolutionary conflict.

More conventional regression analyses have also moved away from simply using country-years as data points, with all the problems of multiple and complex autocorrelation that involves. Analyses of insurgency and civil war by Collier et al (2000) use regionally aggregated data to ask why civil conflict is more common in Africa than elsewhere; the analysis of Fearon & Laitin (2000) uses data aggregated over decades to create a panel format for analyzing succeeding events. Olzak (1992) uses event-history analysis to explore the development of ethnic conflict in several well-defined cases. Interestingly, the Collier, Fearon & Laitin, and Olzak studies all aimed to test the same hypothesis—whether violent ethnic conflict (often a cause or accompaniment in revolutions) can be traced to the ethnic composition of a population. In all these studies, quantitative analysis of competing hypotheses rejected the view that ethnic composition itself is the prime cause of violence; instead, such factors as economic competition and lack of economic growth lead to political strife.

Yet another approach to blending case and quantitative analysis has been taken by the State Failure Task Force (Esty et al 1998, Goldstone et al 2001), a collaborative effort by academics and US government agencies to build a massive data base on major domestic political conflicts. The task force first identified over 100 discrete cases of civil war, rebellion, and revolution in the world from 1955 to 1995. For every year in which a "problem" case started, the task force then selected three other countries at random from among all those countries in the world that had no such internal conflicts for the decade centered on that year ("stable" cases). In this way, every problem case was matched with three randomly chosen control cases. Data on the problem countries were then pooled and compared with data on the control countries to seek factors associated with major political conflicts. This method produced over 400 cases for the pooled data analysis; nonetheless, each case of conflict was treated as a whole and was the basis for comparisons.

The task force repeated this analysis for global and regional data sets and produced fairly consistent findings. The three variables most often associated with political upheavals were regime type, international trade, and infant mortality. Regime type had a surprising, U-shaped relationship to political unrest: Democracies and autocracies were both fairly stable; however, partial democracies were at extremely high risk. Countries with a larger portion of their gross national product (GNP) tied to international trade, and with lower infant mortality, were generally more stable. These factors may seem sharply different from those evoked by Foran (1997c), Goodwin (2001), and other recent case studies of revolution. However, they can be reconciled. Partial democracies are precisely those states in which elites and rulers have begun the process of conflict, reform, and concessions; states have thus shown some weakness and are at a highly unstable juncture. Having a large portion of GNP involved in international trade requires adherence to rule of law and manageable levels of corruption; it may also restrain elite competition. Conversely, countries that have below-expected involvement in international trade for the size of their economy are likely to have elite factions that are distorting trade or economic activity for their benefit, heightening intra-elite conflicts. Infant mortality is known to be an excellent summary measure for standard of living; it thus addresses popular perceptions of the effectiveness of the regime in providing for the popular welfare and nationalist programs of economic development. That all three measures must be relatively high to pose high risks of revolution confirms the conjunctural approach of case studies.

These new quantitative approaches are still being developed. Nonetheless, it is striking that, with regard to the causes of political upheaval, all of them point in the same general direction as the case-study analyses of revolutions. In all the major studies, regardless of methods, it is those factors that affect the strength of the state, competition among elites, and popular living standards that determine the stability or instability of the ruling regime. It may be hoped that this new generation of quantitative studies will reinforce and enrich, rather than rail against, comparative case studies.

OUTCOMES OF REVOLUTIONS

The outcomes of revolutions have generated far less scholarly inquiry than the causes, with the possible exception of outcomes regarding gender. This may be because the outcomes of revolutions are assumed to follow straightforwardly if the revolutionaries succeed. However, such research as we have on outcomes contradicts this assumption; revolutionary outcomes often take unexpected twists and turns.

Stinchcombe (1999) offered the reasonable argument that a revolution is over when the stability and survival of the institutions imposed by the new regime are no longer in doubt. Yet even this definition is ambiguous, as it can take weak and strong forms. By the weak definition, a revolution is over when the basic institutions of the new regime are no longer being actively challenged by revolutionary or counterrevolutionary forces. By this standard, the French Revolution ended in Thermidor 1799 when Napoleon took power, the Russian Revolution of 1917 ended in 1921 with the Bolshevik victory over the White armies, and the Mexican Revolution of 1910 ended in 1920 with Obregon's presidency. Yet a strong definition, by which a revolution has ended only when key political and economic institutions have settled down into forms that will remain basically intact for a substantial period, say 20 years, gives far different results. By this definition, as Furet (1981) has argued, the French Revolution ended only with the start of the French Third Republic in 1871. The Russian Revolution of 1917 would not be considered over until after Stalin's purges of the 1930s; and the Mexican Revolution of 1910 would be dated as lasting through the Cárdenas reforms, to 1940. For that matter, the Chinese Revolution that began in 1910 has yet to end, as none of the Republican, Nationalist, Communist, or Great Proletarian Cultural Revolutions produced a lasting socioeconomic order.

Sadly, there is no scholarly consensus, and different analysts use weak, strong, or idiosyncratic definitions to determine when a revolution has ended. Yet although it is difficult to say precisely when a revolution is over, it is nonetheless possible to discuss the consequences that most commonly unfold after the fall of the old regime.

Domestic Outcomes

Revolutionaries frequently claim that they will reduce inequality, establish democracy, and provide economic prosperity. In fact, the record of actual revolutions is rather poor in regard to all of these claims (Weede & Muller 1997).

Although many revolutions engage in some initial redistribution of assets (particularly land), no revolutionary regime has been able to maintain more than a symbolic equality. Rewards to administrators and top economic producers quickly lead to differentiation of incomes (Kelley & Klein 1977). This has been true in both capitalist and communist revolutionary regimes. In addition, many regimes that begin with radical and populist economic schemes eventually revert to "bourgeois" and capitalist economic organization, such as Mexico, Egypt, and most recently China (Katz 1999).

Until very recently, revolutions have invariably failed to produce democracy. The need to consolidate a new regime in the face of struggles with domestic and foreign foes has instead produced authoritarian regimes, often in the guise of populist dictatorships such as those of Napoleon, Castro, and Mao, or of one-party states such as the PRI state in Mexico or the Communist Party-led states of the Soviet Union and Eastern Europe. Indeed, the struggle required to take and hold power in revolutions generally leaves its mark in the militarized and coercive character of new revolutionary regimes (Gurr 1988). It is therefore striking that in several recent revolutions—in the Philippines in 1986, in South Africa in 1990, in Eastern European nations in 1989–1991—the sudden collapse of the old regime has led directly to new democracies, often against strong expectations of reversion to dictatorship (Foran & Goodwin 1993, Weitman 1992, Pastor 2001). The factors that allowed democracy to emerge in these cases appear to be several: a lack of external military threat, a strong personal commitment to democracy by revolutionary leaders, and consistent external support of the new democratic regimes by foreign powers.

Economic performance is more puzzling. One might expect revolutions to unleash great energy for rebuilding economic systems, just as they lead to rebuilding of political institutions. Yet in fact this rarely if ever takes place. For the most part, long-term economic performance in revolutionary regimes lags that of comparable countries that have not experienced revolutions (Eckstein 1982, 1986). This may be in part because the elite divisions and conflicts that both precede and often follow revolution are inimical to economic progress (Haggard & Kaufman 1995).

It appears that the very effort that goes into rebuilding political institutions throttles economic growth (Zimmermann 1990). Revolutionary regimes are generally more centralized and more bureaucratic than the ones they replace (Skocpol 1979). In addition, to secure their authority, revolutionary leaders are often quite restrictive in regard to entrepreneurial activity; five-year plans and state supervision or ownership of major economic enterprises place economic activity in narrow channels.

Revolutionary regimes can often focus resources and create hothouse growth in selected industries. The Soviet Union and China were fairly successful in creating nineteenth-century-style heavy industrial complexes. Yet neither of them, nor Iran, nor Nicaragua, nor any other revolutionary regime, has succeeded in generating the broad-based economic innovation and entrepreneurship required to generate sustained rapid economic advance (Chirot 1991).

It may be, however, that the new democratizing revolutions will prove an exception. They appear to be less economically restrictive and less heavily bureaucratic than the regimes they replaced. Poland, the Czech Republic, and the former East Germany have all shown strong economic gains. Nonetheless, most revolutionary states even recently have either been so rigid as to continue to restrain economic activity (e.g. Belarus and the Central Asian postsoviet republics), or so weak and disorganized as to be unable to promote and secure a broad economic advance (e.g. Russia, Georgia, South Africa). The general tendency of revolutions to produce poor economic performance thus seems intact, although with a few hopeful exceptions.

As noted above, another area in which revolutionary outcomes usually fall short of expectations is the social emancipation of women and their elevation to leadership roles. Although modern socialist revolutions have generally brought women into the professions and the labor force, they have not changed their essentially secondary status (Lapidus 1978, Cole 1994). Despite women's extensive participation and grass-roots leadership in most of the revolutions in history, gender equality has remained absent, or if articulated, still illusory, in the outcome of revolutionary struggles (Lobao 1990, Randall 1993, Foran et al 1997).

Religious and ethnic minorities often do worse, rather than better, under revolutionary regimes. While revolutions often promise equality in the abstract to all followers, when counterrevolution or external interventions threaten the revolutionary regime, any groups not bound by ethnic and religious solidarity to the new government become suspect in their loyalties and may be singled out for persecution. Such has been the fate of the Ba'hai under the Islamic revolution in Iran, the Miskito Indians in Nicaragua, and those Croats, Muslims, and Serbs who found themselves on the wrong sides of borders in the revolutionary breakup of Yugoslavia (Gurr 1994).

With so many disappointments in the outcomes of revolutions, why have they nonetheless been so vigorously pursued? To answer that question, we need to recall one causal factor—the role of leadership—and one area in which revolutionary outcomes have met or even exceeded expectations, namely the augmentation of state power.

The major objectives of revolutionary leaders are to restructure the bases of political power, to leave their mark on the political and/or economic and social organization of society, and to alter the status of their nation in the international system. Whatever their other failings, revolutions have been remarkably successful in mobilizing populations and utilizing that mobilization for political and military power (Skocpol 1994). Although the eventual goals of democratization or equality or prosperity have often been elusive, the immediate leadership aims of seizing and expanding state authority, changing the rules for access to political power, and restructuring beliefs and institutions have been wildly successful for leaders from Napoleon to Hitler to Lenin to Castro.

The ability of successful revolutionary leaders to reshape their societies (if not always with the expected ultimate results) thus continues to inspire revolutionary entrepreneurs. As we have seen, a major feature of revolutionary mobilization is the effort of a committed core or vanguard to mobilize a mass following based on ideological depictions of the present regime as fundamentally ineffective and unjust. Under such conditions, especially when prodded by concessions or repression and when the old regime seems vulnerable, popular mobilization against the regime is possible. The continued appeal of revolution, despite a lengthy history of frustration of mass aspirations, must be understood in the context of leadership dynamics and mobilization processes that focus attention on present injustices rather than future results (Martin et al 1990).

In addition, revolutions have a significant impact on the position of countries in the international arena. These outcomes provide the basis for potent nationalist appeals to both elites and popular groups (Hall 1993, Calhoun 1998).

Outcomes in the International System

Walt (1996) has demonstrated why one of the first results of revolutions is often external war. The sudden appearance of a new regime upsets old alliances and creates new uncertainties. Foreign powers may judge the new regime as either vulnerable or dangerous; either judgment can lead to war. New revolutionary regimes, inexperienced in foreign affairs, may make similar errors of judgment regarding their neighbors. Still, regimes conscious of extreme weakness, such as Russia after the Bolshevik revolution and the United States in the aftermath of the War of Independence, may go out of their way to avoid international conflicts (Conge 1996).

Aside from these miscalculations, revolutionary regimes may take actions that precipitate or exacerbate military strife. Many revolutions, from the Puritan Revolution in England and the liberal French Revolution to the communist revolutions in Russia, China, and Cuba and the Islamic revolution in Iran, explicitly made changing the world part of their revolutionary program. Armstrong (1993) has shown how these efforts upset the existing international balance of power. However, the degree to which war is sought or welcomed to pursue these goals is a product of actions and reactions among revolutionary factions and external powers. We have noted that revolutions are made by coalitions and involve both visionary and pragmatic wings of leadership. Foreign threats may give leverage to the more visionary and radical elements in the revolutionary coalitions, who deliberately seek combat and missionary adventures (Blanning 1986, Sadri 1997). In contrast, where more moderate and pragmatic leaders remain in charge, and foreign powers support rather than threaten the new regime, internal impetus for war is likely to be weak, as was the case following the revolutions in the United States, Bolivia, and Zimbabwe (Snyder 1999).

Eventually, even revolutionary regimes must accommodate to the reality of the international states system and assume a position in the constellation of international powers (Armstrong 1993). Revolutions can produce long-lasting shifts in national standing and alignments in the international system. Some revolutions provide new aggressive energy to older nations, leading them to become regional or global threats to older powers. Thus Japan after the Meiji Restoration, Germany after the Nazi revolution, and Russia after Stalin's consolidation of the communist revolution became expansionary states. The outcome of World War II, arguably a product of both the communist revolution in Russia and the Nazi revolution, brought Russian expansionism into Eastern Europe and split the German nation, shaping the major cleavages in the international system for 50 years. Anticolonial revolutions, of course, add new states to the international system and reduce the influence of colonial powers in the regions they formerly ruled. Many other revolutions occur in defiance of foreign patrons who supported the old regime; in Afghanistan, Vietnam, Nicaragua, Cuba, and Iran, such revolutions led to extended hostilities between the old patron power and the new regime. Both kinds of revolution satisfy revolutionary elites' strong yearnings for nationalist assertiveness and autonomy while reinforcing the general population's sense of power. Even in Mexico and the Philippines, where the revolutionaries did not assume a strongly hostile stance toward the United States (which had supported their prevolutionary regimes), the eruption of nationalist sentiment accompanying the revolutions led to nationalizing of assets in Mexico and expulsion of the United States from its Philippine military bases. Thus, in ways subtle as well as dramatic, the outcomes of revolutions reshape international relations for many decades, often giving new initiative and autonomy to states in which revolutions took place (Siverson & Starr 1994).

RECONCEPTUALIZING REVOLUTION

Over 20 years ago, Skocpol (1979) laid down what has become the dominant paradigm for analysis of revolutions. In her view, although marginal elites play a key role in guiding revolutions, and world historical possibilities such as the availability of communist templates affect outcomes, the major forces making revolutions and their outcomes are structural features of states and the international system.

In this approach, the stability of regimes is normal and unproblematic; the task of theory is to isolate a short and consistent list of conditions or factors that undercut that stability and facilitate popular mobilization. Once those factors arise, and regime crisis ensues, the actions of the opposition to overthrow and transform the regime are treated as unproblematic and normal consequences, with the ultimate outcome of the revolution being set by the structural constraints and opportunities provided by the domestic economy and the international political and economic system. Agency, leadership, and specific actions of the old regime, revolutionary factions, or foreign powers are considered either inconsequential or driven by prevailing structural conditions.

Twenty years and some two dozen revolutions later, this view is ready to be stood on its head. Stability is clearly not unproblematic; all across central sub-Saharan Africa, in the Balkans, in the Kurdish regions of Turkey and Iran, in Georgia, Chechnya, Tajikistan, and East Timor and other parts of Indonesia, stability remains elusive. The collapse of autocratic regimes in Iran, Nicaragua, the Philippines, and Yugoslavia, and the collapse of one-party states in Eastern Europe and the Soviet Union, have shown how pervasive and sudden the loss of stability can be.

In addition, a short and consistent list of the factors leading to revolution appears to be a chimera. In addition to the international military pressures and elite conflicts over taxation pointed to by Skocpol, analysts of revolution have demonstrated that economic downturns, cultures of rebellion, dependent development, population pressures, colonial or personalistic regime structures, cross-class coalitions, loss of nationalist credentials, military defection, the spread of revolutionary ideology and exemplars, and effective leadership are all plausibly linked with multiple cases of revolution, albeit in different ways in different cases (Goldstone et al 1991, Goodwin 1994b, Foran 1997b). Moreover, conditions conducive to mobilization include traditional village and workplace communities, informal urban networks, repressive and/or concessionary responses of states to opposition actions, guerrilla organizations, revolutionary parties, and effective ideological framing and organization by visionary and pragmatic leadership (Wickham-Crowley 1992, Selbin 1993, Gould 1995, Goldstone & Tilly 2001).

The preceding list includes not only structural factors but also conditions linked to leadership, ideology, culture, and coalitions. Regime characteristics alone seem to provide no help in ascertaining when and where revolution will strike; colonial regimes, communist regimes, and personalist dictatorships have all fallen to revolution. Democracies in Europe have fallen to fascist and Nazi revolutions, while democracies in Latin America—such as Peru and Colombia—have struggled to secure their territories against armed revolutionary movements (McClintock 1998). Conversely, many personalist regimes have persisted for decades (Snyder 1998). Nor can the outcomes of revolutions plausibly be read off of structural conditions. The emergence of democracy or dictatorship, war or peace, gender agendas, and Islamic, communist, or liberal regimes appears to be a contingent result of decisions by revolutionary leaders, foreign powers, and popular supporters, and of interactions among them (Karl & Schmitter 1991, Selbin 1993, Linz & Stepan 1996, Aminzade et al 2001b). Those scholars who have argued for a need to combine structural and agency approaches to regime change thus appear strongly vindicated (Karl 1990, Kitschelt 1992, Emirbayer and Goodwin 1994, Foran 1997c, Selbin 1997, Snyder 1998, Mahoney & Snyder 1999).

A fourth generation of revolution theory therefore needs to reverse all of Skocpol's key stipulations. It would treat stability as problematic, see a wide range of factors and conditions as producing departures from stability, and recognize that the processes and outcomes of revolutions are mediated by group identification, networks, and coalitions; leadership and competing ideologies; and the interplay among rulers, elites, popular groups, and foreign powers in response to ongoing conflicts.

Problematic Stability

"All happy families resemble one another; every unhappy family is unhappy in its own way." What Tolstoy wrote of families may well apply to states and nations. Stable regimes enjoy a short and consistent list of conditions: The rulers appear effective and just in their actions; the majority of military, business, religious, intellectual, and professional elites are loyal to the regime; and most popular groups face steady or improving and fair conditions regarding work, income, and relationships with rulers and elites. Dictatorship or democracy, one-party state or military regime, traditional empire or constitutional regime, states that meet these conditions are "happy" states.

When these conditions begin to degenerate, stability declines. The laundry list of factors that may produce degeneration is long, ranging from global transformations of the economy or political system to localized corruption or unsatisfactory reforms by the ruling clique. Any factors that overstrain the military or financial capacity of the regime can lead to ineffectiveness; any actions that traduce traditional or legal norms or inflict unexpected harms can undercut perceptions of justice. Changing macro-level conditions, such as deteriorating access to jobs, falling real incomes, or heightened elite competition for positions, can produce accusations of both injustice and ineffectiveness. Changing micro-level conditions, such as spreading perceptions of regime vulnerability and of solidarity within and across networks, can persuade people to act against a regime. The precise combination of factors by which a particular state becomes "unhappy" may be highly specific to that regime—in fact, even Skocpol's cardinal cases of Russia, China, and France showed different combinations of factors with varying magnitudes (Goldstone 1997a, Mahoney 1999).

In this view, stability is not an inertial state but implies an ongoing, successful process of reproducing social institutions and cultural expectations across time (Thelen 1999). Failure to sustain that process, not any particular combination of incident factors or conditions, is what leads to state crises.

A Process-Centered View: Revolution as an Emergent Phenomenon

Once a regime loses its grip on the essential conditions of stability, a process of opposition mobilization and struggle begins, which in turn affects perceptions and relationships among actors. In this struggle, opposition actors, rulers, and countermovements deploy ideologies, seek to link up with different groups and networks, and build a sense of the justice and inevitable triumph of their cause. In some cases, a long struggle is required for the opposition to build support and for the state to lose it; in other cases, perceptions and actions shift so quickly that the state collapses with startling rapidity. Which actors, and how many, cease to support the regime; which leaders and factions come to dominate the revolutionary coalition; which foreign powers seek to intervene, on whose side, and with what effort—all will determine the contours of the revolutionary struggle and its outcome.

If these considerations are valid, future theories of revolution will have to feature separate models for the conditions of state failure, the conditions of particular kinds and magnitudes of mobilization, and the determinants of various ranges of revolutionary outcomes, each of which may be the result of contingent outcomes of prior stages in the revolution's unfolding.

Fortunately, rational choice and network analyses have provided some guide to these dynamics. Vanguard groups, interpersonal networks, and cross-class coalitions are clearly pivotal in these processes; without them, revolutions are unlikely to develop. In addition, the ideology and organizational position of key actors can help account for the variety of outcomes. A negotiated transfer of power to Nelson Mandela and the pragmatic African National Congress leadership in South Africa was always more likely to yield a democratic regime than a violent transfer of power dominated by more radical black-power movements such as the Azanian People's Organization. Similarly, US support for the pragmatic moderates in the Philippines, and the popular support for Corazon Aquino, made a democratic outcome more likely than it would have been if the communist New People's Army had taken power through assault on an increasingly ineffective and unpopular United States–backed Marcos regime.

Predictions and Extensions of Theories of Revolution

Given the important role of leadership, action/response patterns, and emergent perceptions and coalitions, many authors have argued that predicting revolutions is impossible (Keddie 1995a, Kuran 1995a, Tilly 1995). Others have argued that if we know what conditions are crucial to stability, then prediction in a probabilistic sense, if not a strictly determinate one, is possible (Collins 1995, Goldstone 1995). It is too soon to determine whose claims are correct.

Goldstone (1991, 1998a) has argued that a three-factor model, with proxies to track state financial health, elite competition for positions, and population well-being, can be used to longitudinally assess the risks of revolutionary crises in cases ranging from early modern monarchies to the collapse of the Soviet Union. More strikingly, a family of quantitative models developed by the State Failure Task Force, using various combinations of factors to denote the effectiveness of state institutions, population well-being, and elite conflicts, would have accurately predicted over 85% of major state crises events occurring in 1990–1997, using models based on 1955–1990 data (Goldstone et al 2001). However, further emphasizing the divergence between state crisis and the unfolding pattern of revolutionary conflict noted above, the State Failure Task Force, despite its high success in predicting the onset of state crises, has had no success in using prior conditions to predict the magnitude and eventual outcome of such events.

These findings suggest that despite the multiplicity of causes of state crises, models that focus on measures of regime stability may yet provide probabilistic estimates of whether state crisis is becoming more or less likely over time. However, future revolutions may continue to surprise us.

A further advantage of focusing on conditions that maintain stability, rather than the myriad of factors that can lead to its decline, is that such models have a fractal quality that is germane to social structure, which is self-similar on various scales. That is, society can be conceived of as having rulers, elites, and popular elements, but so can provinces, cities, and various formal organizations. A model of social stability (as opposed to causes of national revolutions) may be applicable across a wide variety of social scales (Goldstone, in preparation). Goldstone & Useem (1999) demonstrated that the incidence of prison riots in maximum-security institutions can be predicted using a version of the state-stability model. A model of prison stability using measures of prison administration effectiveness, of disaffection by prison guards (who play the role of elites), and of prisoners' perceptions of prison regime fairness provides a far better account of why prisons have revolts than explanations focusing on the characteristics of prisoners or on different patterns of prison authority.

Fractal analyses may prove a useful extension of theories of revolution in two respects. First, Goldstone (1991) has suggested that the reason why revolutions are so massively transformative is that in major social revolutions, social order breaks down on multiple scales simultaneously. That is, administrative effectiveness, elite loyalty, popular well-being, and perceptions of fairness are in decline at the national, regional, and local levels of organization. Comparing the conditions for stability across scales may give information on the magnitude of social upheaval and help bridge the micro-macro divide in studies of state crisis. Second, because a large variety of hierarchical organizations exist in societies (e.g. states, business organizations, military organizations, school systems, health systems, private corporations, prison systems), theories on conditions of stability may also have explanatory value for the stability of a host of nonstate organizations.

CONCLUSION

The reign of third-generation theories of revolution appears to be over. No equally dominant fourth-generation theory has yet emerged, but the lineaments of such a theory are clear. It will treat stability as problematic and focus on conditions that sustain regimes over time; it will feature a prominent role for issues of identity and ideology, gender, networks, and leadership; and it will treat revolutionary processes and outcomes as emergent from the interplay of multiple actors. Even more importantly, fourth-generation theories may unify the results of case studies, rational choice models, and quantitative data analyses, and provide extensions and generalization to cases and events not even conceived of in earlier generations of revolutionary theories.

Visit the Annual Reviews home page at www.AnnualReviews.org

LITERATURE CITED

Abrams D, Hogg M, eds. 1990. *Social Identity Theory*. New York: Springer-Verlag

Ahady A. 1991. Afghanistan: state breakdown. See Goldstone et al 1991, pp. 162–93

Aminzade R, Goldstone JA, McAdam D, Perry EJ, Sewell W Jr, et al. 2001a. *Voice and Silence in Contentious Politics*. Cambridge, UK: Cambridge Univ. Press. In press

Aminzade R, Goldstone JA, Perry EJ. 2001b. Leadership dynamics and dynamics of contention. See Aminzade et al 2001a, in press

Arjomand SA. 1988. *The Turban for the Crown: The Islamic Revolution in Iran*. New York: Oxford Univ. Press

Arjomand SA. 1992. Constitutions and the struggle for political order. *Eur. J. Sociol.* 33:39–82

Armstrong D. 1993. *Revolution and World Order: The Revolutionary State in International Society*. Oxford: Oxford Univ. Press

Aya R. 1990. *Rethinking Revolutions and Collective Violence*. Amsterdam: Het Spinhuis

Baker KM. 1990. *Inventing the French Revolution*. Cambridge, UK: Cambridge Univ. Press

Banac I, ed. 1992. *Eastern Europe in Revolution*. Ithaca, NY: Cornell Univ. Press

Barkey K. 1991. Rebellious alliances: the state and peasant unrest in early seventeenth century France and the Ottoman Empire. *Am. Sociol. Rev.* 56:699–715

Barkey K. 1994. *Bandits and Bureaucrats: The Ottoman Route to State Centralization*. Ithaca, NY: Cornell Univ. Press

Bearman PS. 1993. *Relations into Rhetorics: Local Elite Social Structure in Norfolk, England 1540–1640*. New Brunswick, NJ: Rutgers Univ. Press

Beissinger M. 1998. Nationalist violence and the state: political authority and contentious repertoires in the former USSR. *Comp. Polit.* 30:401–33

Berejikian J. 1992. Revolutionary collective action and the agent-structure problem. *Am. Polit. Sci. Rev.* 86:647–57

Blanning TCW. 1986. *The Origins of the French Revolutionary Wars*. London: Longman

Bonnell VE. 1983. *Roots of Rebellion: Workers' Politics and Organizations in St. Petersburg and Moscow, 1900–1914*. Berkeley: Univ. Calif. Press

Boswell T, ed. 1989. *Revolution in the World-System*. New York: Greenwood

Boswell T, Chase-Dunn C. 2000. *The Spiral of Capitalism and Socialism*. Boulder, CO: Lynne Rienner

Boswell T, Dixon WJ. 1993. Marx's theory of rebellion: a cross-national analysis of class exploitation, economic development, and violent revolt. *Am. Sociol. Rev.* 58:681–702

Brinton C. 1938. *The Anatomy of Revolution*. New York: Norton

Brockett C. 1995. A protest-cycle resolution of the repression/popular protest paradox. In *Repertoires and Cycles of Collective Action*, ed. M Traugott, pp. 117–44. Durham, NC: Duke Univ. Press

Brook T. 1998. *Quelling the People*. Stanford, CA: Stanford Univ. Press

Bueno de Mesquita B, Siverson RM, Woller G. 1992. War and the fate of regimes: a comparative analysis. *Am. Polit. Sci. Rev.* 86:638–45

Bunce V. 1989. The Polish crisis of 1980–1981 and theories of revolution. See Boswell 1989, pp. 167–88

Bunce V. 1999. *Subversive Institutions: the Design and the Destruction of Socialism and the State*. Cambridge, UK: Cambridge Univ. Press

Burton M, Higley J. 1987. Elite settlements. *Am. Sociol. Rev.* 52:295–307

Calhoun C. 1983. The radicalism of tradition. *Am. J. Sociol.* 88:886–914

Calhoun C. 1994a. The problem of identity in collective action. In *Macro-Micro Linkages in Sociology*, ed. J Huber, pp. 51–75. Newbury Park, CA: Sage

Calhoun C. 1994b. *Neither Gods nor Emperors: Students and the Struggle for Democracy in China*. Berkeley: Univ. Calif. Press

Calhoun C, ed. 1994c. *Social Theory and the Politics of Identity*. Oxford, UK: Blackwell

Calhoun C. 1998. *Nationalism*. Minneapolis: Univ. Minn. Press

Carley K. 1991. A theory of group stability. *Am. Sociol. Rev.* 56:331–54

Carey P. 1997. *From Burma to Myanmar: Military Rule and the Struggle for Democracy*. London: Res. Inst. Stud. Confl. and Terrorism

Chirot D. 1994. *Modern Tyrants*. New York: Free

Chirot D, ed. 1991. *The Crisis of Leninism and the Decline of the Left: the Revolutions of 1989*. Seattle: Univ. Wash. Press

Chong D. 1991. *Collective Action and the Civil Rights Movement*. Chicago: Univ. Chicago Press

Chong D. 1993. Coordinating demands for social change. *Ann. Am. Acad. Polit. Soc. Sci.* 2:126–41

Chwe MS-Y. 1999. Structure and strategy in collective action. *Am. J. Sociol.* 105:128–56

Cohen J. 1985. Strategy or identity: new theoretical paradigms and contemporary social movements. *Sociol. Res.* 52:663–716

Colburn FD. 1994. *The Vogue of Revolution in Poor Countries*. Princeton, NJ: Princeton Univ. Press

Cole J. 1994. Women in Cuba: the revolution within the revolution. See Goldstone 1994c, pp. 299–307

Collier D. 1993. The comparative method. In *Political Science: The State of the Discipline II*, ed. A Finifter, pp. 105–19. Washington, DC: Am. Polit. Sci. Assoc.

Collier P, Elbadawi I, Sambanis N. 2000. *Why are there so many civil wars in Africa? Prevention of future conflicts and promotion of inter-group cooperation*. Presented at UNCA Ad Hoc Expert Group Meet. Econ. Civil Confl. in Africa, Addis Ababa, Ethiopia, Apr. 7–8

Collins R. 1995. Prediction in macrosociology: the case of the Soviet collapse. *Am. J. Sociol.* 100:1552–93

Conge PJ. 1996. *From Revolution to War: State Relations in a World of Change*. Ann Arbor: Univ. Mich. Press

Davenport C. 1995. Multi-dimensional threat perception and state repression: an inquiry into why states apply negative sanctions. *Am. J. Polit. Sci.* 3:683–713

Davies JC. 1962. Toward a theory of revolution. *Am. Sociol. Rev.* 27:5–19

Davies S. 1998. *Unbridled Spirits: Women of the English Revolution, 1640–1660*. London: Women's

DeFronzo J. 1996. *Revolutions and Revolutionary Movements*. Boulder, CO: Westview. 2nd ed.

DeNardo J. 1985. *Power in Numbers*. Princeton, NJ: Princeton Univ. Press

Denoeux G. 1993. *Urban Unrest in the Middle East : A Comparative Study of Informal Networks in Egypt, Iran, and Lebanon*. Albany, NY: SUNY Press

Diamond L, Plattner M, eds. 1993. *Capitalism, Socialism, and Democracy Revisited*. Baltimore, MD: Johns Hopkins Univ. Press

Diamond MJ, ed. 1998. *Women and Revolution: Global Expressions*. Dordrecht and Boston: Kluwer

Dix R. 1983. The varieties of revolution. *Comp. Polit.* 15:281–95

Dix R. 1984. Why revolutions succeed and fail. *Polity* 16:423–46

Dogan M, Higley J. 1998. *Elites, Crises, and the Origins of Regimes*. Boulder, CO: Rowman & Littlefield

Dominguez J. 1978. *Cuba: Order and Revolution*. Cambridge, MA: Harvard Univ. Press

Dunlop JB. 1993. *The Rise of Russia and the*

Fall of the Soviet Empire. Princeton, NJ. Princeton Univ. Press

Dunn J. 1989. *Modern Revolutions: An Introduction to the Analysis of a Political Phenomenon*. Cambridge, UK: Cambridge Univ. Press. 2nd ed.

Eckstein S. 1982. The impact of revolution on social welfare in Latin America. *Theory Soc.* 11:43–94

Eckstein S. 1986. The impact of the Cuban Revolution: a comparative perspective. *Comp. Stud. Soc. Hist.* 28:503–34

Eckstein S. 1989a. Power and popular protests in Latin America. See Eckstein 1989b, pp. 1–60

Eckstein S, ed. 1989b. *Power and Popular Protest: Latin American Social Movements*. Berkeley: Univ. Calif. Press

Eisenstadt SN. 1978. *Revolution and the Transformation of Societies*. New York: Free

Eisenstadt SN. 1992. Frameworks of the great revolutions: culture, social structure, history, and human agency. *Int. Soc. Sci. J.* 133:385–401

Eisenstadt SN. 1999. *Fundamentalism, Sectarianism, and Revolution: the Jacobin Dimension of Modernity*. New York : Cambridge Univ. Press

Emirbayer ME, Goodwin J. 1994. Network analysis, culture and the problem of agency. *Am. J. Sociol.* 99:1411–54

Emirbayer ME, Goodwin J. 1996. Symbols, positions, objects: toward a new theory of revolutions and collective action. *Hist. Theory* 35:358–74

Esty D, Goldstone JA, Gurr TR, Harff B, Levy M, Dabelko GD, Surko P, Unger AN. 1998. *State Failure Task Force Report: Phase II Findings*. McLean, VA: Sci. Appl. Int. Corp.

Fantasia R, Hirsch EL. 1995. Culture in rebellion: the appropriation and transformation of the veil in the Algerian Revolution. In *Social Movements and Culture*, ed. H Johnston, B Klandermans, pp. 144–59. Minneapolis: Univ. Minn. Press

Farhi F. 1990. *States and Urban-based Revolution. Iran and Nicaragua*. Urbana and Chicago: Univ. Ill. Press

Fearon JD, Laitin DD. 2000. *Ethnicity, insurgency, and civil war*. Presented at LiCEP Meet., Duke Univ., Durham, NC, Apr. 21–23

Feierabend IK, Feierabend RL, Nesvold BA. 1969. Social change and political violence: cross-national patterns. In *Violence in America: Historical and Comparative Perspectives*, ed. HD Graham, TR Gurr, pp. 606–68. New York: Praeger

Finkel SE, Muller EN, Opp K-D. 1989. Personal Influence, collective rationality, and mass political action. *Am. Polit. Sci. Rev.* 83:885–903

Fiske AP. 1990. The cultural relativity of selfish individualism: anthropological evidence that humans are inherently sociable. *Rev. Pers. Soc. Psychol.* 12:176–214

Foran J. 1992. A theory of Third World social revolutions: Iran, Nicaragua, and El Salvador compared. *Crit. Sociol.* 19:3–27

Foran J. 1993a. *Fragile Resistance: Social Transformation in Iran from 1500 to the Revolution*. Boulder, CO: Westview

Foran J. 1993b. Theories of revolution revisited: toward a fourth generation? *Sociol. Theory* 11:1–20

Foran J. 1995. Revolutionizing theory/revising revolution: state, culture, and society in recent works on revolution. See Keddie 1995a, pp. 112–35

Foran J. 1997a. Discourses and social forces: the role of culture and cultural studies in understanding revolutions. See Foran 1997c, pp. 203–226

Foran J. 1997b. The comparative-historical sociology of Third World social revolutions: why a few succeed, why most fail. See Foran 1997c, pp. 227–267

Foran J, ed. 1997c. *Theorizing Revolutions*. London: Routledge

Foran J, Goodwin J. 1993. Revolutionary outcomes in Iran and Nicaragua: coalition fragmentation, war, and the limits of social transformation. *Theory Soc.* 22:209–47

Foran J, Klouzal L, Rivera J-P. 1997. Who

makes revolutions? Class, gender and race in the Mexican, Cuban, and Nicaraguan Revolutions. *Res. Soc. Mov. Confl. Change.* 20:1–60

Friedman D, Hechter M. 1988. The contribution of rational choice theory to macrosociological research. *Sociol. Theory* 6:210–18

Friedman E, Pickowicz PG, Selden M, Johnson KA. 1991. *Chinese Village, Socialist State.* New Haven, CT: Yale Univ. Press

Furet F. 1981. *Interpreting the French Revolution.* Cambridge, UK: Cambridge Univ. Press

Gamson WA. 1988. Political discourse and collective action. In *From Structure to Action: Social Movement Participation Across Cultures*, ed. B Klandermans, H Kriesi, S Tarrow, pp. 219–44. Greenwich, CT: JAI

Gamson WA, Meyer DS. 1996. Framing political opportunity. In *Comparative Perspectives on Social Movements*, ed. D McAdam, JD McCarthy, MN Zald, pp. 275–90. Cambridge, UK: Cambridge Univ. Press

Gartner SS, Regan PM. 1996. Threat and repression: the non-linear relationship between government and opposition violence. *J. Peace Res.* 33:273–88

Glenn JK. 1999. Competing challengers and contested outcomes to state breakdown: the Velvet Revolution in Czechoslovakia. *Soc. Forces* 78:187–212

Goldfarb JC. 1992. *After the Fall: the Pursuit of Democracy in Central Europe.* New York: Basic Books

Goldfrank WL. 1979. Theories of revolution and revolution without theory: the case of Mexico. *Theory Soc.* 7:135–65

Goldman WZ. 1993. *Women, the State, and Revolution: Soviet Family Policy and Social Life, 1917–1936.* Cambridge, UK: Cambridge Univ. Press

Goldstone JA. 1980. Theories of revolution: the third generation. *World Polit.* 32:425–53

Goldstone JA. 1991. *Revolution and Rebellion in the Early Modern World.* Berkeley: Univ. Calif. Press

Goldstone JA. 1994a. Revolution in modern dictatorships. See Goldstone 1994c, pp. 70–77

Goldstone JA. 1994b. Is revolution individually rational? *Ration. Soc.* 6:139–66

Goldstone JA, ed. 1994c. *Revolutions: Theoretical, Comparative, and Historical Studies.* Fort Worth, TX: Harcourt Brace. 2nd ed.

Goldstone JA. 1995. Predicting revolutions and rebellions: why we could (and should) have forseen the revolutions of 1989–91 in the U.S.S.R. and Eastern Europe. See Keddie 1995a, pp. 39–64

Goldstone JA. 1997a. Methodological issues in comparative macrosociology. *Comp. Soc. Res.* 16:121–32

Goldstone JA. 1997b. Population growth and revolutionary crises. See Foran 1997c, pp. 102–20

Goldstone JA. 1998a. The Soviet Union: revolution and transformation. See Dogan & Higley 1998, pp. 95–123

Goldstone JA. 1998b. Social movements or revolutions? On the evolution and outcomes of collective action. In *Democracy and Contention*, ed. M Guigni, D McAdam, C Tilly, pp. 125–45. Boulder, CO: Rowman & Littlefield

Goldstone JA, ed. 1998c. *The Encyclopedia of Political Revolutions.* Washington, DC: Congr. Q.

Goldstone JA. *Revolutions, Social Movements, and Social Change: Structures and Processes in Contentious Politics.* Cambridge, MA: Harvard Univ. Press. In preparation

Goldstone JA, Gurr T, Harff B, Levy M, Marshall M, Surko P, Unger A, et al. 2001. *State Failure Task Force Phase III Report.* McLean, VA: Sci. Appl. Int. Corp.

Goldstone JA, Useem B. 1999. Prison riots as micro-revolutions: an extension of state-centered theories of revolution. *Am. J. Sociol.* 104:985–1029

Goldstone JA, Gurr TR, Moshiri F, eds. 1991. *Revolutions of the Late Twentieth Century.* Boulder, CO: Westview

Goldstone JA, Tilly C. 2001. Threat (and opportunity): popular action and state response in the dynamics of contentious action. See Aminzade et al 2001a, in press

Goldthorpe JH. 1997. Current issues in comparative macro-sociology: a debate on methodological issues. *Comp. Soc. Res.* 16:1–26

Goodwin J. 1989. Colonialism and revolution in Southeast Asia: a comparative analysis. See Boswell 1989, pp. 59–78

Goodwin J. 1994a. Toward a new sociology of revolutions. *Theory Soc.* 23:731–66

Goodwin J. 1994b. Old regimes and revolutions in the Second and Third Worlds: a comparative perspective. *Soc. Sci. Hist.* 18:575–604

Goodwin J. 1997. State-centered approaches to social revolutions: strengths and limitations of a theoretical tradition. See Foran 1997c, pp. 11–37

Goodwin J. 2001. *No Other Way Out: States and Revolutionary Movements 1945–1991*. Cambridge, UK: Cambridge Univ. Press

Goodwin J, Skocpol T. 1989. Explaining revolutions in the contemporary Third World. *Polit. Soc.* 17:489–507

Gould RV. 1995. *Insurgent Identities: Class, Community, and Protest in Paris from 1848 to the Commune*. Chicago: Univ. Chicago Press

Green JD. 1984. Countermobilization as a revolutionary form. *Comp. Polit.* 16:153–69

Gurr TR. 1968. A causal model of civil strife: a comparative analysis using new indices. *Am. Polit. Sci. Rev.* 62:1104–24

Gurr TR. 1970. *Why Men Rebel*. Princeton, NJ: Princeton Univ. Press

Gurr TR, ed. 1980. *Handbook of Political Conflict*. New York: Free

Gurr TR. 1988. War, revolution, and the growth of the coercive state. *Comp. Polit. Stud.* 21:45–65

Gurr TR. 1994. Minorities in revolution. See Goldstone 1994c, pp. 308–14

Haggard S, Kaufman RR. 1995. *The Political Economy of Democratic Transitions*. Princeton, NJ: Princeton Univ. Press

Hall JA. 1993. Nationalisms: classified and explained. *Daedalus* 122:1–26

Hall JR, Schuyler PD, Trinh S. 2000. *Apocalypse Observed: Religious Movements and Violence in North America, Europe, and Japan*. New York: Routledge

Halliday F. 1999. *Revolution and World Politics*. London: Macmillan

Hanagan MP, Moch LP, Te Brake W, eds. 1998. *Challenging Authority: The Historical Study of Contentious Politics*. Minneapolis: Univ. Minn. Press

Hardin R. 1995. *One for All*. Princeton, NJ: Princeton Univ. Press

Harff B. 1991. Cambodia: revolution, genocide, intervention. See Goldstone et al 1991, pp. 218–234

Harff B. 1995. Rescuing endangered peoples: missed opportunities. *Soc. Res.* 62:23–40

Hechter M. 1987. *Principles of Group Solidarity*. Berkeley: Univ. Calif. Press

Heckathorn DD. 1990. Collective sanctions and compliance norms: a formal theory of group-mediated social control. *Am. Sociol. Rev.* 55:366–84

Heckathorn DD. 1993. Collective action and group heterogeneity: voluntary provision versus selective incentives. *Am. Sociol. Rev.* 58:329–50

Higley J, Burton M. 1989. The elite variable in democratic transitions and breakdowns. *Am. Sociol. Rev.* 54:17–32

Higley J, Gunther R, eds. 1992. *Elites and Democratic Consolidation in Latin America and Europe*. Cambridge, UK: Cambridge Univ. Press

Hirsch EL. 1990. Sacrifice for the cause: group processes, recruitment and commitment in a student social movement. *Am. Sociol. Rev.* 55:243–54

Hough J. 1997. *Democratization and Revolution in the USSR 1985–1991*. Washington, DC: Brookings Inst.

Hufton OH. 1992. *Women and the Limits of Citizenship in the French Revolution*. Toronto: Univ. Toronto Press

Hunt W. 1983. *The Puritan Moment: the Coming of Revolution in an English County*. Cambridge, MA: Harvard Univ. Press

Hunt LA. 1992. *The Family Romance of the*

French Revolution. Berkeley: Univ. Calif. Press
Huntington SP. 1968. *Political Order in Changing Societies*. New Haven, CT: Yale Univ. Press
Jenkins JC, Kposowa AJ. 1990. Explaining military coups d'etat: black Africa, 1957–1984. *Am. Sociol. Rev.* 55:861–75
Jenkins JC, Schock K. 1992. Global structures and political processes in the study of domestic conflict. *Annu. Rev. Sociol.* 18:161–85
Johnson V. 1993. The structural causes of anticolonial revolutions in Africa. *Alternatives* 18:201–27
Karklins R. 1994. Explaining regime change in the Soviet Union. *Europe-Asia Studies* 46:29–45
Karklins R, Petersen R. 1993. Decision calculus of protesters and regimes: Eastern Europe 1989 *J. Polit.* 55:588–614
Karl TL. 1990. Dilemmas of democratization in Latin America. *Comp. Polit.* 23:1–21
Karl TL, Schmitter PC. 1991. Modes of transition in Latin America, Southern and Eastern Europe. *Int. Soc. Sci. J.* 128:269–84
Katz M. 1997. *Revolutions and Revolutionary Waves*. New York: St. Martin's
Katz M. 1999. *Reflections on Revolutions*. New York: St. Martin's
Katz M, ed. 2001. *Revolution: International Dimensions*. Washington, DC: Congr. Q.
Katznelson I. 1997. Structure and configuration in comparative politics. See Lichbach & Zuckerman 1997, pp. 81–112
Keddie N. 1981. *Roots of Revolution: An Interpretive History of Modern Iran*. New Haven, CT: Yale Univ. Press
Keddie NR, ed. 1995a. *Debating Revolutions*. New York: NY Univ. Press
Keddie NR. 1995b. *Iran and the Muslim World: Resistance and Revolution*. New York: NY Univ. Press
Kelley J, Klein HS. 1977. Revolution and the rebirth of inequality: a theory of stratification in post-revolutionary society. *Am. J. Sociol.* 83:78–99
Khawaja M. 1993. Repression and popular collective action: evidence from the West Bank. *Sociol. Forum* 8:47–71
Kileff C, Robinson LW. 1986. The elitist thesis and the Rhodesian Revolution: implications for South Africa. See Midlarsky 1986, pp. 111–23
Kim H, Bearman PS. 1997. The structure and dynamics of movement participation. *Am. Sociol. Rev.* 62:70–93
Kim Q-Y. 1996. From protest to change of regime: the 4–19 Revolt and the fall of the Rhee regime in South Korea. *Soc. Forces* 74:1179
Kim Q-Y, ed. 1991. *Revolutions in the Third World*. Leiden, the Netherlands: Brill
Kimmel MS. 1990. *Revolution: A Sociological Interpretation*. Cambridge, UK: Polity
King G, Keohane RO, Verba S. 1994. *Designing Social Inquiry: Scientific Inference in Qualitative Research*. Princeton, NJ: Princeton Univ. Press
Kiser E, Hechter M. 1991. The role of general theory in comparative-historical sociology. *Am. J. Sociol.* 97:1–30
Kitschelt H. 1992. Political regime change: structure and process-driven explanation? *Am. Polit. Sci. Rev.* 86:1028–34
Klandermans B. 1984. Mobilization and participation: social-psychological expansions of resource-mobilization theory. *Am. Sociol. Rev.* 49:583–600
Klandermans B, Oegema D. 1987. Potentials, networks, motivations and barriers: steps toward participation in social movements. *Am. Sociol. Rev.* 52:519–31
Klosko G. 1987. Rebellious collective action revisited. *Am. Polit. Sci. Rev.* 81:557–61
Knight A. 1986. *The Mexican Revolution*, 2 vols. Cambridge, UK: Cambridge Univ. Press
Knoke D. 1988. Incentives in collective action organizations. *Am. Sociol. Rev.* 53:311–29
Koopmans R. 1993. The dynamics of protest waves: West Germany, 1965 to 1989. *Am. Sociol. Rev.* 58:637–58
Kuran T. 1989. Sparks and prairie fires: a theory

of unanticipated political revolution. *Public Choice* 61:41–74

Kuran T. 1991. Now out of never: the element of surprise in the Eastern European Revolution of 1989. *World Polit.* 44:7–48

Kuran T. 1995a. The inevitability of future revolutionary surprises. *Am. J. Sociol.* 100:1528–51

Kuran T. 1995b. *Private Truths, Public Lies: the Social Consequences of Preference Falsification.* Cambridge, MA: Harvard Univ. Press

Kurzman C. 1996. Structural opportunity and perceived opportunity in social-movement theory. *Am. Sociol. Rev.* 61:153–70

Lachmann R. 1997. Agents of revolution: elite conflicts and mass mobilization from the Medici to Yeltsin. See Foran 1997c, pp. 73–101

Lane D, Ross C. 1999. *The Transition from Communism to Capitalism.* New York: St. Martin's

Lapidus GW. 1978. *Women in Soviet Society: Equality, Development, and Social Change.* Berkeley: Univ. Calif. Press

Lawler EJ. 1992. Affective attachments to nested groups: a choice-process theory. *Am. Sociol. Rev.* 57:327–39

Levi M. 1997. *Consent, Dissent, and Patriotism.* Cambridge, UK: Cambridge Univ. Press

Levine DH, Manwaring S. 1989. Religion and popular protest in Latin America: contrasting experiences. See Eckstein 1989b, pp. 203–34

Lichbach MI. 1987. Deterrence or escalation? The puzzle of aggregate studies of repression and dissent. *J. Confl. Resolut.* 31:266–97

Lichbach MI. 1989. An evaluation of "does economic inequality breed political conflict?" studies. *World Polit.* 41:431–70

Lichbach MI. 1995. *The Rebels' Dilemma.* Ann Arbor: Univ. Mich. Press

Lichbach MI. 1996. *The Cooperators' Dilemma.* Ann Arbor: Univ. Mich. Press

Lichbach MI, Zuckerman AS, eds. 1997. *Comparative Politics: Rationality, Culture, and Structure.* Cambridge, UK: Cambridge Univ. Press

Lieberson S. 1991. Small N's and big conclusions: an examination of the reasoning in comparative studies based on a small number of cases. *Soc. Forces* 70:307–20

Linz JJ, Stepan A. 1996. *Problems of Democratic Transition and Consolidation: Southern Europe, South America, and Post-Communist Europe.* Baltimore, MD: Johns Hopkins Univ. Press

Liu MT. 1988. States and urban revolutions: explaining the revolutionary outcomes in Iran and Poland. *Theory Soc.* 17:179–210

Lobao L. 1990. Women in revolutionary movements: changing patterns of Latin American guerrilla struggles. In *Women and Social Protest*, ed. G West, RL Blumberg, pp. 180–204. Oxford, UK: Oxford Univ. Press

Lohmann S. 1993. A signaling model of information and manipulative political action. *Am. Polit. Sci. Rev.* 8:319–33

Lupher M. 1996. *Power Restructuring in China and Russia.* Boulder, CO: Westview

McAdam D. 1988. *Freedom Summer.* New York: Oxford Univ. Press

McAdam D. 1995. Recruitment to high-risk activism: the case of Freedom Summer. *Am. J. Sociol.* 92:64–90

McAdam D, Tarrow S, Tilly C. 1997. Toward a comparative perspective on social movements and revolution. See Lichbach & Zuckerman 1997, pp. ??

McAdam D, Tarrow S, Tilly C. *Dynamics of Contention.* Cambridge, UK: Cambridge Univ. Press. In preparation

McCarthy JD, Zald MN. 1977. Resource mobilization and social movements. *Am. J. Sociol.* 82:1112–41

McClintock C. 1998. *Revolutionary Movements in Latin America: El Salvador's FMLN and Peru's Shining Path.* Washington, DC: US Inst. Peace

McDaniel T. 1991. *Autocracy, Modernization, and Revolution in Russia and Iran.* Princeton, NJ: Princeton Univ. Press

McFaul M. 1995. State power, institutional change, and the politics of privatization in Russia. *World Polit.* 47:210–44

McPherson JM, Popielarz PA, Drobnic S. 1992. Social networks and organizational dynamics. *Am. Sociol. Rev.* 57:153–70

Macy M. 1990. Learning theory and the logic of the critical mass. *Am. Sociol. Rev.* 55:809–26

Macy M. 1991. Chains of cooperation: threshold effects in collective action. *Am. Sociol. Rev.* 56:730–47

Magagna VV. 1991. *Communities of Grain: Rural Rebellion in Comparative Perspective*. Ithaca, NY: Cornell Univ. Press

Mahoney J. 1999. Nominal, ordinal, and narrative appraisal in macrocausal analysis. *Am. J. Sociol.* 104:1154–96

Mahoney J. 2000. Strategies of causal inference in small-N analysis. *Sociol. Methods Res.* 28:387–424

Mahoney J, Snyder R. 1999. Rethinking agency and structure in the study of regime change. *Stud. Comp. Int. Dev.* 34:3–32

Markoff J. 1996. *The Abolition of Feudalism: Peasants, Lords, and Legislators in the French Revolution*. University Park, PA: Penn. State Univ. Press

Martin J, Scully M, Levitt B. 1990. Injustice and the legitimation of revolution: damning the past, excusing the present, and neglecting the future. *J. Pers. Soc. Psychol.* 59:281–90

Marwell G, Oliver P. 1993. *The Critical Mass in Collective Action: A Micro-social Theory*. Cambridge, UK: Cambridge Univ. Press

Mason TD, Krane DA. 1989. The political economy of death squads: toward a theory of the impact of state-sanctioned terror. *Int. Stud. Q.* 33:175–98

Melucci A. 1989. *Nomads of the Present: Social Movements and Individual Needs in Contemporary Society*. Philadelphia: Temple Univ. Press

Meyer DS, Staggenborg S. 1996. Movements, countermovements, and the structure of political opportunity. *Am. J. Sociol.* 101:1628–93

Midlarsky MI, ed. 1986. *Inequality and Contemporary Revolutions*. Denver, CO: Univ. Denver Press

Midlarsky MI. 1999. *The Evolution of Inequality*. Stanford, CA: Stanford Univ. Press

Midlarsky MI, Roberts K. 1991. Class, state, and revolution in Central America: Nicaragua and El Salvador compared. *J. Confl. Resolut.* 29:489–509

Migdal JS. 1974. *Peasant Politics, and Revolution*. Princeton, NJ: Princeton Univ. Press

Migdal JS. 1988. *Strong Societies and Weak States: State-Society Relations and State Capabilities in the Third World*. Princeton, NJ: Princeton Univ. Press

Migdal JS, Kohli A, Shue V, eds. 1994. *State Power and Social Forces: Domination and Transformation in the Third World*. New York: Cambridge Univ. Press

Moaddel M. 1993. *Class, Politics, and Ideology in the Iranian Revolution*. New York: Columbia Univ. Press

Moghadam VM. 1989. Populist revolution and the Islamic states in Iran. See Boswell 1989, pp. 147–63

Moghadam VM. 1994. Islamic populism, class, and gender in post-revolutionary Iran. In *A Century of Revolution: Social Movements in Iran*, ed. J Foran, pp. 189–222. Minneapolis: Univ. Minn. Press

Moghadam VM. 1997. Gender and revolutions. See Foran 1997c, pp. 137–67

Moore B Jr. 1966. *Social Origins of Dictatorship and Democracy*. Boston: Beacon

Moore WH. 1995. Rational rebels: overcoming the free-rider problem. *Polit. Res. Q.* 48:417–54

Moore WH. 1998. Repression and dissent: substitution, context, and timing. *Am. J. Polit. Sci.* 42:851–73

Morris AD. 1984. *The Origins of the Civil Rights Movement*. New York: Free

Muller EN. 1985. Income inequality, regime repressiveness, and political violence. *Am. Sociol. Rev.* 50:47–61

Muller EN, Seligson MS. 1987. Inequality and insurgency. *Am. Polit. Sci. Rev.* 81:425–51

Nash J. 1989. Cultural resistance and class consciousness in Bolivian tin-mining communities. See Eckstein 1989b, pp. 182–202

Nichols E. 1986. Skocpol on revolution: comparative analysis vs. historical conjuncture. *Comp. Soc. Res.* 9:163–86

Oberschall A. 1994a. Protest demonstrations and the end of communist regimes in 1989. *Res. Soc. Mov. Confl. Change* 17:1–24

Oberschall A. 1994b. Rational choice in collective protests. *Ration. Soc.* 6:79–100

Oberschall A, Kim H-J. 1996. Identity and action. *Mobilization* 1:63–86

O'Donnell G, Schmitter P, Whitehead L, eds. 1986. *Transitions from Authoritarian Rule: Prospects for Democracy*, 4 vols. Baltimore, MD: Johns Hopkins Univ. Press

Oliver P. 1984. If you don't do it, nobody will. *Am. Sociol. Rev.* 49:601–10

Olivier J. 1991. State repression and collective action in South Africa, 1970–84. *S. Afr. J. Sociol.* 22:109–17

Olson M Jr. 1965. *The Logic of Collective Action: Public Goods and the Theory of Groups*. Cambridge, MA: Harvard Univ. Press

Olzak S. 1992. *The Dynamics of Ethnic Competition and Conflict*. Stanford, CA: Stanford Univ. Press

Opp K-D. 1989. *The Rationality of Political Protest*. Boulder, CO: Westview

Opp K-D. 1994. Repression and revolutionary action: East Germany in 1989. *Ration. Soc.* 6:101–38

Opp K-D, Voss P, Gern C 1995. *Origins of a Spontaneous Revolution: East Germany, 1989*. Ann Arbor: Univ. Mich. Press

Opp K-D, Roehl W. 1990. Repression, micromobilization, and political protest. *Soc. Forces* 69:521–47

Osa M. 1997. Creating solidarity: the religious foundations of the Polish social movement. *E. Eur. Polit. Soc.* 11:339–65

Paige JM. 1975. *Agrarian Revolution*. New York: Free

Paige JM. 1989. Revolution and the agrarian bourgeoisie in Nicaragua. See Boswell 1989, pp. 99–128

Paige JM. 1997. *Coffee and Power: Revolution and the Rise of Democracy in Central America*. Cambridge, MA: Harvard Univ. Press

Parsa M. 1989. *The Social Origins of the Iranian Revolution*. New Brunswick, NJ: Rutgers Univ. Press

Parsa M. 2000. *States, Ideologies, and Social Revolutions: A Comparative Analysis of Iran, Nicaragua, and the Philippines*. Cambridge, UK: Cambridge Univ. Press

Pastor R. 2001. Preempting revolutions: the boundaries of U.S. influence. See Katz 2001, pp. 169–97

Perry EJ, Li X. 1997. *Proletarian Power: Shanghai in the Cultural Revolution*. Boulder, CO: Westview

Pfaff S. 1996. Collective identity and informal groups in revolutionary mobilization: East Germany in 1989. *Soc. Forces* 75:91–10

Piliavin JA, Charng H-W. 1990. Altruism: a review of recent theory and research. *Annu. Rev. Sociol.* 16:27–65

Popkin S. 1979. *The Rational Peasant: The Political Economy of Rural Society in Vietnam*. Berkeley: Univ. Calif. Press

Popkin S. 1988. Political entrepreneurs and peasant movements in Vietnam. See Taylor 1988b, pp. ??

Ragin CC. 1987. *The Comparative Method: Moving Beyond Qualitative and Quantitative Strategies*. Berkeley: Univ. Calif. Press

Ragin CC. 1997. Turning the tables: how case-oriented research challenges variable-oriented research. *Comp. Soc. Res.* 16:27–42

Randall M. 1993. *Gathering Rage: The Failure of Twentieth Century Revolutions to Develop a Feminist Agenda*. New York: Monthly Rev.

Rasler K. 1996. Concessions, repression, and political protest in the Iranian Revolution. *Am. Sociol. Rev.* 61:132–52

Rejai M, Phillips K. 1988. Loyalists and revolutionaries. *Int. Polit. Sci. Rev.* 9:107–18

Rinehart J. 1997. *Revolution and the Millennium: China, Mexico, and Iran*. Westport, CT: Praeger

Robnett B. 1997. *How long? How long? African-American Women in the Struggle for Civil Rights*. New York: Oxford Univ. Press

Rueschemeyer D, Stephens J. 1997. Comparing historical sequences: a powerful tool for causal analysis. *Comp. Soc. Res.* 16:55–72

Rule J. 1988. *Theories of Civil Violence*. Berkeley: Univ. Calif. Press

Rule J. 1989. Rationality and non-rationality in militant collective action. *Sociol. Theory* 7:145–60

Rupp LJ. 1997. *Worlds of Women: the Making of an International Women's Movement*. Princeton, NJ: Princeton Univ. Press

Sadri HA. 1997. *Revolutionary States, Leaders, and Foreign Relations: A Comparative Study of China, Cuba, and Iran*. Westport, CT: Praeger

Scott JC. 1976. *The Moral Economy of the Peasant: Rebellion and Subsistence in South East Asia*. New Haven, CT: Yale Univ. Press

Scott JC. 1985. *Weapons of the Weak: Everyday Forms of Peasant Resistance*. New Haven, CT: Yale Univ. Press

Scott JC. 1990. *Domination and the Arts of Resistance: Hidden Transcripts*. New Haven, CT: Yale Univ. Press

Seidman GW. 1994. *Manufacturing Militance: Workers Movements in Brazil and South Africa, 1970–1985*. Berkeley: Univ. Calif. Press

Selbin E. 1993. *Modern Latin American Revolutions*. Boulder, CO: Westview

Selbin E. 1997. Revolution in the real world: bringing agency back in. See Foran 1997c, pp. 123–36

Selden M. 1995. *China in Revolution: the Yenan Way Revisited*. Armonk, NY: Sharpe

Sewell W Jr. 1985. Ideologies and social revolutions: reflections on the French case. *J. Mod. Hist.* 57:57–85

Sewell W Jr. 1996. Three temporalities: toward an eventful sociology. In *The Historic Turn in the Human Sciences*, ed. TJ McDonald, pp. 245–80. Ann Arbor: Univ. Mich. Press

Shin G-W. 1996. *Peasant Protest and Social Change in Colonial Korea*. Seattle: Univ. Wash. Press

Shugart MS. 1989. Patterns of revolution. *Theory Soc.* 18:249–71

Shugart MS. 2001. Guerrillas and elections: an institutionalist perspective on the costs of conflict and competition. See Katz 2001, pp. 198–238

Siverson RM, Starr H. 1994. Regime change and the restructuring of alliances. *Am. J. Polit. Sci.* 38:145–61

Skocpol T. 1979. *States and Social Revolutions*. Cambridge, UK: Cambridge Univ. Press

Skocpol T. 1982. Rentier state and Shi'a Islam in the Iranian Revolution. *Theory Soc.* 11:265–303

Skocpol T. 1994. *Social Revolutions in the Modern World*. Cambridge, UK: Cambridge Univ. Press

Smith LM, Padula A. 1996. *Sex and Revolution: Women in Socialist Cuba*. New York: Oxford Univ. Press

Snow DA, Benford RD. 1988. Ideology, frame resonance, and participant mobilization. *Int. Soc. Mov. Res.* 1:197–217

Snow DA, Rochford Jr EB, Worden SK, Benford RD. 1986. Frame alignment processes, micromobilization, and movement participation. *Am. Sociol. Rev.* 51:464–81

Snow DA, Zurcher LA, Ikland-Olson S. 1980. Social networks and social movements: a microstructural approach to differential recruitment. *Am. Sociol. Rev.* 45:787–801

Snyder R. 1998. Paths out of sultanistic regimes: combining structural and voluntarist perspectives. In *Sultanistic Regimes*, ed. HE Chehabi, JJ Linz, pp. 49–81. Baltimore, MD: Johns Hopkins Univ. Press

Snyder RS. 1999. The U.S. and Third World revolutionary states: understanding the breakdown in relations. *Int. Stud. Q.* 43:265–90

Sohrabi J. 1995. Historicizing revolutions: constitutional revolutions in the Ottoman Empire, Iran, and Russia 1905–1908. *Am. J. Sociol.* 100:1383–447

Somers M, Gibson G. 1994. Reclaiming the epistemological "other": narrative and the social constitution of identity. See Calhoun 1994c, pp. 37–99

Speck WA. 1990. *Reluctant Revolutionaries: Englishmen and the Revolution of 1688*. New York: Oxford Univ. Press

Stacey J. 1983. *Patriarchy and Socialist Revolution in China*. Berkeley: Univ. Calif. Press

Stark DC, Bruszt L. 1998. *Postsocialist Pathways: Transforming Politics and Property in East Central Europe*. New York: Cambridge Univ. Press

Stinchcombe AL. 1999. Ending revolutions and building new governments. *Ann. Rev. Polit. Sci.* 2:49–73

Stokes G. 1993. *The Walls Came Tumbling Down: The Collapse of Communism in Eastern Europe*. New York: Oxford Univ. Press

Tarrow S. 1998. *Power in Movement: Social Movements and Contentious Politics*. Cambridge, UK: Cambridge Univ. Press. 2nd ed.

Taylor M. 1988a. Rationality and revolutionary collective action. See Taylor 1988b, pp. 63–97

Taylor M, ed. 1988b. *Rationality and Revolution*. Cambridge, UK: Cambridge Univ. Press

Taylor V. 1999. Gender and social movements. *Gender Soc.* 13:8–33

Taylor V, Whittier N. 1992. Collective identity in social movements: lesbian feminist mobilization. In *Frontiers in Social Movement Theory*, ed. AD Morris, CM Mueller, pp. 104–30. New Haven, CT: Yale Univ. Press

Teitzel M, Weber M. 1994. The economics of the Iron Curtain and the Berlin Wall. *Ration. Soc.* 6:58–78

Tétreault MA, ed. 1994. *Women and Revolution in Africa, Asia, and the New World*. Columbia: Univ. S. Carolina Press

Thelen K. 1999. Historical institutionalism in comparative politics. *Annu. Rev. Polit. Sci.* 2:369–404

Tilly C. 1978. *From Mobilization to Revolution*. Reading, MA: Addison-Wesley

Tilly C. 1993. *European Revolutions 1492–1992*. Oxford: Blackwell

Tilly C. 1995. To explain political processes. *Am. J. Sociol.* 100:1594–610

Tong J. 1991. *Disorder under Heaven: Collective Violence in the Ming Dynasty*. Stanford, CA: Stanford Univ. Press

Traugott M. 1985. *Armies of the Poor: Determinants of Working-Class Participation in the Parisian Insurrection of June 1848*. Princeton, NJ: Princeton Univ. Press

Trimberger EK. 1978. *Revolution from Above: Military Bureaucrats and Development in Japan, Turkey, Egypt, and Peru*. New Brunswick, NJ: Transaction Books

Tullock G. 1971. The paradox of revolution. *Public Choice* 1:89–99

Urban M, Igrunov V, Mitrokhin S. 1997. *The Rebirth of Politics in Russia*. Cambridge, UK: Cambridge Univ. Press

Van Kley DK. 1996. *The Religious Origins of the French Revolution: from Calvin to the Civil Constitution, 1560–1791*. New Haven, CT: Yale Univ. Press

Van Vugt JP. 1991. *Democratic Organization for Social Change: Latin American Christian Base Communities and Literary Campaigns*. New York: Bergin & Garvey

Walder AG. 1989. The political sociology of the Beijing Upheaval of 1989. *Probl. Communism* (Sep.–Oct.):41–48

Walt SM. 1996. *Revolution and War*. Ithaca, NY: Cornell Univ. Press

Walton J. 1984. *Reluctant Rebels*. New York: Columbia Univ. Press

Walton J. 1989. Debt, protest, and the state in Latin America. See Eckstein 1989b, pp. 299–328

Walton J, Ragin C. 1990. Global and national sources of political protest: Third World responses to the debt crisis. *Am. Sociol. Rev.* 55:876–90

Walton J, Seddon D. 1994. *Free Markets & Food Riots: the Politics of Global Adjustment*. Oxford, UK: Blackwell

Wasserstrom JN. 1994. Gender and revolution in Europe and Asia. *J. Women's Hist.* 5170–83,6:109–20

Wasserstrom JN, Perry EJ, eds. 1994. *Popular Protest and Political Culture in Modern China*. Boulder, CO: Westview. 2nd ed.

Weitman S. 1992. Thinking the revolutions of 1989. *Br. J. Sociol.* 43:13–24

Weede E. 1987. Some new evidence on correlates of political violence: income inequality, regime repressiveness, and economic development. *Eur. Sociol. Rev.* 3:97–108

Weede E, Muller EN. 1997. Consequences of revolutions. *Ration. Soc.* 9:327–50

White JW. 1995. *Ikki: Social Conflict and Political Protest in Early Modern Japan*. Ithaca, NY: Cornell Univ. Press

White R. 1989. From peaceful protest to guerrilla war: micromobilization of the Provisional Irish Republican Army. *Am. J. Sociol.* 94:1277–302

Wickham-Crowley T. 1989. Winners, losers, and also-rans: toward a comparative sociology of Latin American guerrilla movements. See Eckstein 1989b, pp. 132–81

Wickham-Crowley T. 1991. *Exploring Revolution: Essays on Latin American Insurgency and Revolutionary Theory*. Armonk, NY: Sharpe

Wickham-Crowley T. 1992. *Guerrillas and Revolution in Latin America*. Princeton, NJ: Princeton Univ. Press

Wolf ER. 1969. *Peasant Wars of the Twentieth Century*. New York: Harper & Row

Womack J. 1968. *Zapata and the Mexican Revolution*. New York: Knopf

Yamaguchi K. 2000. Subjective rationality of initiators and of threshold-theoretical behavior of followers in collective action. *Ration. Soc.* 12:185–225

Zamosc L. 1989. Peasant struggles of the 1970s in Colombia. See Eckstein 1989b, pp. 102–31

Zartman WI. 1995. *Collapsed States: the Disintegration and Restoration of Legitimate Authority*. Boulder, CO: Lynne Rienner

Zhao D. 2001 *The Power of Tiananmen: State-Society Relations and the 1989 Beijing Student Movement*. Chicago: Univ. Chicago Press

Zimmermann E. 1990. On the outcomes of revolutions: some preliminary considerations. *Sociol. Theory* 8:33–47

Annu. Rev. Polit. Sci. 2001. 4:189–215

POLITICAL CONSEQUENCES OF MINORITY GROUP FORMATION

M. Hechter[1] and D. Okamoto[2]

[1]*Department of Sociology, University of Washington, Box 353340, Seattle, Washington 98195-3340; e-mail: hechter@u.washington.edu*

[2]*Department of Sociology, University of Arizona, Tucson, Arizona 85721; e-mail: dina@u.arizona.edu*

Key Words minority groups, ethnicity, nationalism, conflict, social identity, collective action

■ **Abstract** Given the global trend of increasing ethnocultural diversity and the outbreak of nationalist movements based on cultural, linguistic, and territorial identities, this review focuses on social and political mechanisms that lead to the emergence of minority group collective action. This kind of collective action is seen as a function of three necessary conditions: the formation of distinctive social identities, the overcoming of free riding, and the development of institutional structures promoting the demand for greater autonomy. The article examines the debates, theories, and empirical evidence concerning these three conditions. We conclude by noting that the most important impediment to progress in this field is the relative paucity of historical and cross-national databases that are required to test many of the theories in the literature.

INTRODUCTION

The boundaries of states rarely coincide with those of national or ethnic groups (Ra'anan 1990). Most states contain several culturally distinct groups whose language, religion, tradition, and historical experiences are not shared and often are at odds with one another. In 1972, Connor (1972) noted that only 12 of the 132 states then extant were culturally homogeneous. Since then, the disjuncture between state and ethnonational boundaries has grown larger. Moreover, the United Nations estimated that in 1993, as many as 100 million individuals lived outside their country of birth or citizenship, and that at least 18 million were refugees (Williams 1994). Migration, fragmentation, and annexation have been contributing to ethnocultural diversity on a global scale. These trends are of interest to political scientists because multiethnic states are at some risk of experiencing violent ethnic conflict, secessionist movements, and government-sponsored ethnic cleansing.

The current prevalence of secessionist and nationalist movements raises deep questions about how states foster unity among people with diverse cultures and historical experiences, how individuals construct social identities, and how minority groups manage to engage in collective action. In this essay, we review the principal social and political factors that lead to the emergence of nationalist identities and movements among minorities—that is, groups whose members share a distinctive social identity based on their culture, language, territory, or individual ascriptive traits.

Readers are urged to consult prior reviews on closely related topics: ethnicity (Yinger 1985), ethnic conflict in comparative perspective (Williams 1994), ethnic mobilization (Olzak 1983), and ethnic and nationalist violence (Brubaker & Laitin 1998). This review, by contrast, is organized on the premise that minorities affect statewide political outcomes only under three conditions: when (*a*) they have distinctive social identities, (*b*) they have the potential to engage in collective action, and (*c*) their political demands are not likely to be met by the existing institutional arrangements. We discuss each of these conditions for the mobilization of minority groups by examining the debates and theories in the literature and corresponding empirical evidence.

A word about this evidence. The bulk of the literature on minorities focuses on particular movements and on the unique historical, economic, political, and cultural circumstances that led to them. These case studies provide a rich narrative that can clarify concepts, apply—and sometimes test—theoretical perspectives, and suggest new hypotheses. Comparative case studies, in particular, seek to extract patterns from sets of broadly comparable cases. Fruitful typologies and conceptual schemes have also developed out of this methodological tradition. For example, typologies of nationalism (Mughan 1979, Meadwell 1983, Rogowski 1985) and a taxonomy of macropolitical forms of ethnic conflict regulation (McGarry & O'Leary 1993) have been useful in describing different movements.

Large data sets permit more rigorous testing of rival theoretical propositions both within and across polities. These data sets typically consist of survey data gathered from individual respondents (Sekulic et al 1994, Diez Medrano 1994, Bollen & Diez Medrano 1998) or are compiled from official statistics about the sociodemographic characteristics of minority groups and reports of collective-action events, generally derived from samples of newspapers (Olzak 1992, Gurr 1993). Case studies provide the historical background from which statistical models can be sensibly interpreted and understood (see Ganguly 1996). Most analyses, whether qualitative or quantitative, focus on culturally distinct groups with strong nationalist movements (Belanger & Pinard 1991, Hechter 1999, Leifer 1981). However, some analyses focus on entire states (Bollen & Diez Medrano 1998).

CONDITIONS PROMOTING THE FORMATION OF MINORITY SOCIAL IDENTITY

The Micro Foundations of Minority Social Identity

Although there are a number of alternative microscopic approaches to social identity [including those based on evolutionary biology (van den Berghe 1981,

Whitmeyer 1997)], social psychological theories have received the greatest empirical validation. The first prominent social psychological theory of identity formation is known as realistic group conflict theory. Borrowing its inspiration from Marx and Simmel, early social psychologists (Lewin 1948, Sherif 1966) argued that the principal cause of identification with groups is mutual dependence (see Brown 1986:Ch. 6). This mutual dependence, in turn, arises from peoples' experience of a common situation or predicament (Rabbie & Horwitz 1988). Experimental research confirms that people arbitrarily selected into groups and subjected to differential treatment on that account indeed develop strong identification with their groups. However, the effect of differential treatment goes beyond mere identification: Given decisions about the allocation of resources, individuals tend to provide more of the resources at their disposal to in-group rather than out-group members. The key implication of realistic group conflict theory is that social identities are likely to be a by-product of intergroup stratification.

More recent research, however, challenges the idea that dependence and conflict over resources are necessary conditions for the development of group identity. Currently, the most popular explanation for the formation and salience of group identification is social identity theory (Tajfel 1974, 1981; Tajfel & Turner 1979; Abrams & Hogg 1990; Hogg et al 1995). According to this theory, individuals have a fundamental desire to attain positive self-esteem. This desire, in turn, motivates two kinds of sociocognitive processes: categorization, in which individuals are led to distinguish between social groups; and self-enhancement, in which people come to emphasize norms and stereotypes that favor the in-group.

The novel finding in this research is that in order to produce group identification and in-group bias in a given population, all a third party has to do is categorize individuals (studies of this sort are part of the "minimal group" research paradigm). In one well-known experiment, for example, Tajfel (1970) arbitrarily divided in two a group of British university students based on their preference for an abstract image painted by either Klee or Kandinsky. Once categorized, the members of each group began to develop a social identity and made biased allocations of resources favoring the in-group. There is some evidence that given categorization, such discrimination in favor of one's group leads to an increase in members' self-esteem (Oakes & Turner 1980, Lemyre & Smith 1985).

At the same time, social identity theory also implies that identification patterns vary with the stratification of groups. According to the theory, individuals identify with high-prestige groups because doing so contributes positively to their self-esteem. By the same token, individuals avoid identifying with low-prestige groups because doing so lowers their self-esteem. This hypothesis too has largely been supported by the empirical literature. However, some research on the link between self-esteem and a negative social identity is inconsistent with social identity theory. Sachdev & Bourhis (1984) found that group members engaged in comparable levels of discrimination whether they were in high- or low-prestige groups. Other experimental research indicates that social identification with a group may actually be increased when the group is threatened or stigmatized. For example, Turner and his colleagues (1984) reported that in-group defeat produces even higher levels of in-group preference than does success among committed group members. Many studies also indicate that identification with disadvantaged or stigmatized groups is associated with high rather than low individual self-esteem (Rosenberg 1979, Cross 1985, Crocker & Major 1989). There is more evidence that in-group favoritism enhances self-esteem than that low self-esteem motivates intergroup discrimination (Hogg & Abrams 1990, Crocker et al 1993).

If everyone desires positive self-esteem, then how do people come to terms with membership in low-prestige groups? They may (*a*) attempt to gain entry into the dominant group (social mobility), (*b*) interpret their group's traits as a badge of pride rather than disparagement (social creativity), or (*c*) engage in collective action designed to raise their group's status (social change) (Tajfel & Turner 1979). These strategies have been explored at some length (van Kippenberg 1984, van Kippenberg & van Oers 1984, Taylor et al 1987, Jackson et al 1996). For example, Ellemers and her colleagues (1988) found that group members engaged in collective strategies when intergroup boundaries were highly impermeable. However, the evidence is mixed: Jackson et al (1996) found that permeability of group boundaries had the predicted effects on social creativity strategies but not on social mobility strategies.

The evidence lends partial support to social identity theory. As predicted, categorization does lead to in-group identification, and identification, in turn, leads to higher self-esteem among group members. However, a negative social identity does not always lead to low self-esteem, and—a finding at variance with the theory—the strategies designed to combat such an identity are not necessarily carried out. In laboratory-created groups, experiments suggest that group members engage in social mobility and social creativity strategies to combat a negative social identity, but the results are mixed for real social groups (Ellemers et al 1988, Jackson et al 1996). Moreover, social identity theory does not predict which coping strategy will be selected in a given condition.

If members perceive that their group has shared interests, the salience of their social identity independent of third-party categorization is raised. Because social identity theory assumes that there is no mutual dependence between group members (Turner 1987), this finding is important. Flippen et al (1996:883) argue that "people form social categories on the basis of similarity/dissimilarity with others, but these categories do not become in-groups/out-groups until some kind of perceived mutual dependence creates the belief that members of different categories will act for or against self-interest." When subjects perceive that they have interest interdependence with other group members in minimal group experimental settings, they will favor these members, but categorization is not sufficient to produce in-group bias in the absence of mutual dependence (Locksley et al 1980; Rabbie et al 1987, 1989; Flippen at al 1996). All told, then, social psychological research highlights the effects of two independent mechanisms for the formation of all types of social identities—interest interdependence and categorization.

Each of these mechanisms is implicated in two important macrosocial processes associated with the formation of durable and distinct group identities: state building, which often results in the categorization of minority groups, and the development of labor markets, which often produces mutual dependence.

The Macro Foundations of Minority Social Identity

Distinctive social identities are nurtured by a collective sense of a common ancestry, a common religion, and, in the most general sense, a common history. Early theorists of ethnicity and nationalism claimed ethnic communities were natural, primordial, and given (Shils 1957, Geertz 1963, Isaacs 1975). These theorists focused on the content of culture to explain the intensity and meaning of ethnic attachments and viewed racial and ethnic boundaries as fundamental, ascriptive, and immutable. Many contemporary scholars agree that ethnicity is not rigidly ascribed but is socially constructed (Barth 1969, Horowitz 1975, Anderson 1983, Gellner 1983, Calhoun 1998, Hechter 1999). For example, several studies have documented movement across racial and ethnic boundaries, where new groups were created from previously diverse cultural groups: Cornell (1988) on pan-Indian consciousness; Padilla (1985) on Latino identity; Espiritu (1992) on Asian-American panethnicity; Young (1976) and Nnoli (1989) on pan-Igbo ethnicity in Nigeria; and Young (1976) and Nagata (1981) on pan-Malay ethnicity in Malaysia. Some scholars even emphasize the notion that ethnic communities are created by the interests of ethnic entrepreneurs and state elites (Wallerstein 1980, Gellner 1983, Brown 1998, Hechter 1999). Brass (1991) is a forceful proponent of this position: "Ethnicity and nationalism are . . . political constructions. They are creations of elites who draw upon, distort, and sometimes fabricate material from the cultures of the groups they wish to represent in order to protect their well-being or existence or to gain political and economic advantage for their groups as well as for themselves." The claim that ethnic group boundaries are not primordial, but socially constructed, is now the dominant view.

That said, there remain dissenters who argue that the content of culture cannot be discounted as a condition for the construction of ethnic boundaries. Conversi (1995:82) argues that the construction of ethnic identities relies on the "pre-existing diffusion of shared symbols and cultural elements as well as on memories of a shared past and myths of a common destiny." Likewise, Smith (1996) suggests that economic and political circumstances are important in explaining why nationalisms emerge, but just as vital are "deep" ethnosymbolic resources (Armstrong 1982, Hastings 1997). In particular, the durability and character of a given nationalism can be largely explained by analyzing the ethnohistorical, religious, and territorial heritages that its proponents draw on. These ethnoheritages set the limits and provide the pattern within which modern elites must operate if they are to be successful in mobilizing their conationals. Likewise, Ollapally & Cooley (1996) argue that in order to understand why certain identity affiliations associated with identity movements are ultimately selected over other competing identities within the same space, the content of the identities must be examined.

Whereas some writers see the roots of national identity as extending far into premodern history, others (Anderson 1983, Hobsbawm & Ranger 1983) view them as invented traditions emanating from the rise of market society ("print capitalism") or state-building activities (Hobsbawm 1992). Smith (1998) offers a useful summary of the controversy about the modernity of nationalism. Perhaps the most judicious conclusion is that national identity is a (relatively) modern construction that is sometimes built on prior cultural foundations.

Direct Rule, State Building, and National Mobilization Prior to industrialization, central rulers were unable to exert direct control over geographically distant territories, many of which were culturally distinct from the core areas of their states (Hechter 2000). As a result, they were compelled to employ some form of indirect rule to govern these peripheries (Tilly 1990). Under indirect rule, central rulers designated either local authorities or their own nominees as their agents. In return for guaranteeing the security of their territories and revenue for the center, these agents were given sweeping governance powers. They were responsible for maintaining the peace and protecting against invaders, they adjudicated disputes, and they provided the bulk of the public goods enjoyed by their subjects.

Industrialization and modern communications technology made it possible for central rulers to govern geographically remote territories directly. In attempting to seize a greater proportion of governance and public goods provision, central rulers were thwarted at every turn by indirect rulers—those local political and ecclesiastical authorities whose powers they sought to usurp (de Swaan 1988). In their struggles to maintain power, local elites sometimes mobilized nationalist movements based on the cultural distinctiveness of their populations. These movements challenged the political stability as well as the legitimacy of the modernizing state. Prior to direct rule, local leaders demanded, and tended to receive, the loyalty of their subjects. With the growth of direct rule, central rulers demanded an increasingly great share of that loyalty, and to win it they engaged in a variety of state-building activities designed to promote the ideology of the national state (Hobsbawm 1992, Breuilly 1993). State building invariably led to a categorization of populations into two classes: those who adhered to the dominant (and legitimate) culture, and those who did not. As a result, central rulers made strenuous efforts to stamp out peripheral languages, religions, and social mores (Weber 1976). As social identity theory implies, these typically heavy-handed state-building policies—which constitute a blunt form of categorization—tend to produce a reactive nationalism in peripheral areas. State-building efforts often erupt in conflict against the state in order to gain or restore control over a homeland, or to change the balance of rights and resources in a particular region (Esman 1985, Horowitz 1985). Thus, the timing of state-building activities in the Ottoman Empire is closely correlated with the timing of nationalist resistance movements among its culturally distinct subject territories (Hechter 2000).

Labor Markets and Intergroup Stratification Once it was widely believed that the rise of market society would slowly but surely reduce the political salience of cultural differences. According to this view, cultural differences would cease to matter because market forces would ensure that people from different cultures (and ethnicities) would live, go to school, and work together. Because of these forces, places in educational institutions and jobs in the economy would be awarded on the basis of individual skills rather than cultural (or ascriptive) characteristics (Parsons 1951). Because there was no reason to expect that culture had any implications for one's skills, in a market society one's cultural background should have little influence on one's earning power. In consequence, there should be little residential or occupational segregation. As neighborhoods, schools, and firms became increasingly culturally heterogeneous, cultural intermarriage naturally would follow and the social basis of cultural distinctions would melt away.

Based as it is on neoclassical economic principles, the logic of this diffusionist expectation is crystal clear. However, it is inconsistent with much empirical reality. It is a truism that cultural distinctions have important political implications in nearly every society in the world—not least in the most advanced societies. Intergroup conflict persists because development, and migration, tend to have differential effects on cultural groups (Gellner 1964). One of the principal sources of these effects emanates from labor market processes.

Two different labor market mechanisms have been proposed in the literature. The first suggests that distinct social identities emerge as a by-product of mutual interaction and shared experience. In particular, a market society tends to create a cultural division of labor in which individuals with distinctive cultural markers cluster hierarchically or segmentally. In a hierarchical cultural division of labor, high-status occupations tend to be reserved for individuals of the dominant culture while jobs at the bottom of the stratification system are for others (Hughes 1943, Hughes & Hughes 1952, Bonacich 1972, Hechter 1999, Boswell & Brueggemann 2000). The Indian caste system offers an extreme example. Cultural markers that confine individuals to separate social classes take on high salience. In a segmental cultural division of labor (Hechter 1978), distinctive cultural groups are clustered into highly specialized occupations. In the 1970 census, Greek immigrants to the United States, for example, were disproportionately found in restaurant employment. Dutch immigrants, however, had no comparable occupational specialization. Because of their similar work experience and propinquity, individuals who are concentrated in the same occupations tend to develop distinctive identities. On this account, Greek immigrants had a stronger social identity (as indicated by rates of endogamy, for instance) than their Dutch counterparts.

The second mechanism suggests that distinctive social identities tend to be triggered only when out-group members begin to compete for jobs effectively controlled by insiders. Competition theorists (Deutsch 1953; van den Berghe 1967; Barth 1969; Hannan 1979; Ragin 1979; Nielsen 1980; Olzak 1982, 1992; Banton 1983) argue that economic and political modernization erode the social bases for smaller-scale ethnic identities (such as villages, tribes, or dialects) while encouraging collective action based upon larger-scale ethnic boundaries (such as regional or party lines). According to this view, urbanization, the expansion of industrial and service sectors, the increasing scale and complexity of production organization, the development of peripheral regions, and state building create the potential for ethnonational movements and political parties because these factors initiate contact and competition between culturally distinct populations. At the heart of competition theory lies a biological metaphor: Social boundaries are formed when an out-group invades an in-group's established ecological niche. For competition theorists, therefore, national and ethnic boundaries are activated when socioeconomic development decreases the barriers between different ethnic populations, spurring intergroup competition over scarce resources.

Cultural division of labor and competition mechanisms have often been framed as alternatives. As a consequence of this framing, a large literature has attempted to assess their relative merits. In his study on the Celtic fringe in Britain, Hechter (1999) provides historical evidence that a cultural division of labor existed in preindustrial Ireland and Wales. Using electoral and census data from British counties, he found that variations in conservative voting patterns from 1885 to 1966 were explained more by cultural variables than by class-related variables, which supports predictions from the cultural division of labor theory over those of the developmental model. Using the same data as Hechter (1999), Leifer (1981) also tested the cultural division of labor and developmental perspectives to further isolate the effect of ethnic ties on mobilization. Using regression analyses, he found that dual subordination (interaction of economic disadvantage and ethnic subordination) and economic disadvantage had no significant effect on voting patterns, which supports neither perspective. However, Leifer's results do reveal that ethnic subordinate status is significant, which indicates that ethnic ties are important in explaining mobilization, but not in ways anticipated by the cultural division of labor model.

Ragin (1979) and Nielsen (1980) analyzed ethnic separatist voting patterns by examining the sources of support for the Welsh nationalist party in Britain and the Flemish nationalist party in Belgium. Both researchers claim that the highest levels of support for the ethnic nationalist party came from economically advanced areas. Employment in the tertiary and advanced sectors increased nationalist support, which suggests that competition within these sectors due to recent incorporation of the peripheral population increased ethnic solidarity. Similarly, Olzak (1982) found that participation in more advanced sectors of the Quebec economy was not associated with ethnic separatism, but that the proportion of bilinguals—which she takes as an indicator of language competition—increased ethnic separatism. Olzak concluded that collective behavior and separatist voting patterns in Quebec supported the ethnic competition perspective. Diez Medrano (1994) tested these mechanisms by analyzing the voting patterns in the Basque country in northern Spain. He found that the concentration of immigrants in blue-collar jobs was positively associated with immigrants voting for Spanish parties. In addition, ethnic segmentation in the labor market was not associated with the voting behaviors of immigrants or natives. He concluded that the cultural division of labor mechanism better explained the ethnic voting patterns in Basque country. Data from Mettam & Williams (1998) on employment patterns in Estonia indicate that at the end of the Soviet era, the segmental cultural divisions of labor that operated in Estonia contributed to Estonian nationalist identity. Finally, cultural division of labor has been used to account for political conflicts between Israeli Jews (Peled 1990, 1998).

All told, both mechanisms are likely to come into play. Each seems to account for nationalist behavior in different countries during different periods of time. For example, Hechter (1999) shows that during one time period, the cultural division of labor is most useful in explaining nationalism in Britain's Celtic fringe, whereas Ragin (1979) suggests that during a subsequent period, the competition model is more effective. Similarly, Nielsen (1980) found that the rise of the Flemish movement, prior to World War II, supports the cultural division of labor analysis, but after 1945 ethnic competition seems to dominate.

Although these two mechanisms have often been treated as mutually incompatible, this conclusion is probably hasty. Nielsen (1985:147) argues that "... it is even possible that one [mechanism] is more correct in the case of one country as compared with another, or even for one country in the case of one historical period and not another, depending on which trends have major causal effects in the situation." Moreover, the two mechanisms may be responsible for explaining related but distinct phenomena (Hechter 1994). It may be that the cultural division of labor explains how and why ethnic and racial identities become salient relative to other social identities, whereas the competition mechanism explains how ethnic collective action is triggered once these salient identities are formed.

Institutional Factors in the Formation of Group Boundaries

Recent scholarship has emphasized a number of institutional factors that lead to the construction of group boundaries. Nagel (1994) claims that political policies and institutions can affect the strength and even the existence of ethnic group boundaries. For example, immigration policies can influence the composition, location, and class position of immigrants, which ultimately affects their process of group formation and assimilation in the host country (Horowitz 1985, Pedraza-Bailey 1985, Light & Bonacich 1988, Espiritu 1996, Reitz 1998). Ethnically linked resource policies can also activate ethnic boundaries. For example, in 1960, the division of the Nigerian state into three regions resulted in the formation of three regionally based, ethnically linked political parties (Nagel 1986). The competition between these political parties led not only to a heightening of ethnic boundaries but also to the eventual disintegration of the Nigerian political system and the secession of the Eastern Region (Biafra). Additionally, official categories, such as census racial classifications, can create a sense of group membership and help to constitute groups (Starr 1978, Brubaker 1996). Political recognition of a particular ethnic group, whether positive or negative, can raise the group's self-awareness and encourage organization. For example, ethnic and cultural identities are often heightened by "racial profiling," purposeful action taken by the state to associate certain crimes and characteristics with an ethnic or cultural group. Political recognition of an ethnic group can also increase identification and mobilization between officially unrecognized groups facing the prospect of exclusion from an ethnically defined political arena (Nagel 1986). Darroch (1981) argues that a variety of Canadian federal programs implemented in the 1980s, including those recommended by the Royal Commission on Bilingualism and Biculturalism, may have encouraged Quebeckers to engage in a more vocal separatist movement. In Nigeria, the ethnic boundary that designated Yoruba peoples from non-Yoruba peoples expanded only after colonization and contact with groups who did not share the same descent myth and language (Nnoli 1989). Similarly, a politicized pan-Malay ethnicity began to emerge only after British colonization (Young 1976, Nagata 1981, Ongkili 1985).

Determinants of Assimilation in Countries of Immigration

Assimilation is a process in which the boundaries of culturally distinct groups gradually become attenuated. Assimilation has been intensively studied in countries of immigration, particularly in the United States (Park 1950, Gordon 1964, Hirschman 1983, Yinger 1985). In these countries, the government has actively pursued policies promoting assimilation. Researchers in the United States have attempted to gauge the extent to which certain racial and ethnic groups have assimilated into the host society by using such indicators as educational and occupational attainment, wage inequality, language maintenance, neighborhood segregation, and interethnic and interracial friendships and marriages. Assimilation has been relatively rapid in countries of immigration because the cultural minorities in these countries tend to be spatially dispersed. Even so, research on ethnic and racial groups in the United States helps us to understand some of the conditions that promote assimilation in the multicultural context.

Educational and occupational assimilation clearly is affected by generation and cohort status. Using census data, Lieberson & Waters (1988) observed that American men of European ancestry increased their educational and occupational attainment with each new generation. Niedert & Farley (1985) found that the occupational returns for educational attainment improved when comparing first and third generations for European groups, Asians, and Mexicans. In addition, Alba's (1988) evidence suggests that there is convergence across birth cohorts of European

Americans: Rates of college attendance and graduation among European men and women in later cohorts increased to match the rates of their American-born British counterparts. However, several studies have documented the low levels of achievement among certain groups, such as African-Americans, which may increase with each new generation but which do not converge with the core Anglo group with respect to education, income, and occupation (Chiswick 1978, Featherman & Hauser 1978, Niedert & Farley 1985).

The mode of incorporation also influences the subsequent development of immigrant communities (Portes & Rumbaut 1990, Reitz 1998). In their analysis of the educational progress of second generations, Portes & MacLeod (1996) found that the relative advantages or disadvantages associated with Cuban and Vietnamese immigrant communities, due to different modes of incorporation, remained significant even after controlling for family socioeconomic status. In a comparative study of the United States, Canada, and Australia, Reitz (1998) found that social institutions, such as education, labor markets, and social welfare, shaped the extent to which immigrants will assimilate in terms of socioeconomic status. For example, in the United States, the laissez faire immigration policy, less-regulated labor markets, and weak welfare state combine to produce lower entry-level earnings for immigrants, which retards the assimilation process. More generally, immigrants who are granted legal status, the prospect of citizenship, and resettlement assistance by the host community will assimilate more rapidly, both economically and in their social and psychological integration (Light 1984, Bailey & Waldinger 1991, Zhou 1992, Portes & Stepick 1993).

Studies of spatial assimilation (Massey 1985)—the integration of ethnic minorities into neighborhoods where the dominant group resides—indicate that for Asians and Latinos, the most powerful determinant of the racial and ethnic composition of their neighborhoods is their own socioeconomic status. The more income and education one has, the larger the percentage of Caucasians in the neighborhood (Massey & Denton 1987, Alba & Logan 1993, Logan et al 1996, Alba et al 1997). For African-Americans, this relationship does not hold. Even when African-Americans do move to the suburbs, they experience relatively high levels of segregation compared with Asians and Latinos (Massey & Denton 1988). Overall, African-Americans still face a spatial assimilation process hampered by racial stereotypes (Massey & Denton 1988, 1993).

For Latinos but not Asians, linguistic assimilation is another predictor of moving into suburban neighborhoods largely populated by Caucasians (Alba & Logan 1991, Alba et al 1997). Alba and his colleagues (1999) compared the determinants of suburbanization in 1980 and 1990. In the 1990s, the effect of linguistic assimilation in addition to recent immigrant status for Asians, Afro-Caribbeans, and Cubans was much weaker. Such findings indicate that the achievement of spatial assimilation is not necessarily associated with other forms of assimiliation.

More than any other intergroup indicator, intermarriage represents the final outcome of assimilation (Gordon 1964). Intermarriage rates are also affected by generation: With each new generation of Asian-Americans (Montero 1980, Wong

1989, Lee & Yamanaka 1990, Hwang et al 1994) and Latinos (Murguia & Frisbie 1977, Schoen et al 1978, Fitzpatrick & Gurak 1979, Gurak & Fitzpatrick 1982), the rates increase. In addition, research indicates that members of ethnic or racial minority groups with higher levels of education tend to marry outside their groups more often than do their less-educated counterparts (Sandefur & McKinnell 1986, Lieberson & Waters 1988, Schoen & Wooldredge 1989, Kalmijn 1993).

Intermarriage is also affected by the relative size and distribution of racial and ethnic populations. Several studies indicate that group size is negatively related to intermarriage rates because members of small populations have less chance of meeting potential spouses from within their group than from other groups (Blau et al 1982, 1984; Blau & Schwartz 1984; Alba & Golden 1986; Schoen 1986; Gilbertson et al 1996). The geographic concentration of an ethnic population also affects intermarriage. For example, Asian-Americans living in California, where they are concentrated, tend to marry outside their group less often than do those living elsewhere in the United States (Wong 1989). Similarly, the rate of endogamy for African-Americans is higher in states where the proportion of African-Americans in the population is higher (Kalmijn 1993). Members of geographically concentrated ethnic groups have a greater probability of meeting potential spouses from within their own groups. In addition, community sanctions against intermarriage are likely to be greater in geographically concentrated groups (Spickard 1989). By the same token, spatial dispersion favors intergroup contact and sociability, and this increases intermarriage rates. There is some empirical support for a positive relationship between heterogeneity and intergroup association (Blau et al 1982, 1984). Although some recent studies produced inconsistent results (South & Messner 1986, Anderson & Saenz 1994, Hwang et al 1994), these may be due to differences in the measurement of group heterogeneity. Other studies found that income inequality, opportunity for contact, status diversity within the ethnic group, and ethnic language maintenance are also significant predictors of intermarriage (South & Messner 1986, Anderson & Saenz 1994). All told, the empirical literature suggests that the size and distribution of the group shape the rate of intermarriage, the final stage of assimilation.

Determinants of Assimilation Elsewhere

There is less research on assimilation in countries with spatially concentrated minority groups. Several studies show that high levels of education and income, residence in an urban area, and youthfulness promote identification with the dominant culture. In his study of the determinants of nationalistic identification with Spain, Herranz de Rafael (1998) found that those who reside in urban areas and perceive themselves to be in higher class positions were more likely to identify with the nation-state. Other variables, such as religious participation, blue-collar occupation, white-collar occupation, political identification, and education, had significant effects, but not consistently. Similarly, Bollen & Diez Medrano (1998), using a national representative survey, found that a high level of education was the most important individual-level variable for explaining attachment to Spain, as measured by feelings of morale and sense of belonging. In the context of the former Yugoslavia, using survey data from Croatia, Bosnia, and Serbia, Sekulic et al (1994) examined the factors that influenced people to identify themselves as members of a multinational state rather than as members of a specific nationality. Their statistical analyses indicate that urban residence, political participation in the Communist Party, having parents of different nationalities, being young, and being Croat led to Yugoslav identification. Similarly, Laitin's (1998) study of Russians in the newly independent republics of the former Soviet Union indicates that education and the number of years a respondent has resided in the republic are both positively and significantly related to assimilation. Thus, the research on the formation of an assimilated national identity indicates that other forms of assimilation—education, socioeconomic status—tend to lead to an assimilated identity within a multinational state.

Laitin (1998) found that the most significant predictor of linguistic and cultural assimilation among Russian-speaking peoples in Kazakhstan, Estonia, Latvia, and the Ukraine was the size of the titular population—nationality groups for which the republics were named—in the respondents' city of residence. Russians in these republics are likely to assimilate when they reside in cities where the percentage of the titular population is high. However, Laitin also found strong interrepublic differences in assimilation. He claims that the different modes of incorporation of elites from peripheral republics resulted in different incentives for assimilation and, therefore, varied outcomes for each republic. To complement the macrostructural elite-incorporation model, he also used a microlevel tipping model to explain the mechanisms behind assimilation. Russians assimilated faster in the Baltic states than in Ukraine or Kazakhstan because of high expected economic returns for linguistic assimilation and acceptance of language by in- and out-group members.

Different forms of assimilation—socioeconomic, spatial, marital, identity—are facilitated by common individual-level factors, such as generation, age, socioeconomic status, and urban residence. However, new studies indicate that some types of assimilation are not necessarily associated with others for all immigrant groups, which suggests that assimilation may not be a unitary process. The evidence reviewed here suggests that structural factors, such as the mode of incorporation and the size and concentration of the ethnic group, contribute to whether ethnic group members integrate into the host society and, if so, how fast. Most of the literature focuses on outcomes; too often, discussions and tests of the causal mechanisms responsible for assimilation are missing (Laitin's research is exceptional in this regard).

CONDITIONS PROMOTING THE COLLECTIVE-ACTION POTENTIAL OF MINORITY GROUPS

The mere existence of distinctive social identities among minorities has no necessary consequences for political mobilization. Nationalist collective action is unlikely to occur in the absence of (*a*) preexisting social groups formed to provide members with insurance, welfare, and other kinds of private goods, (*b*) a widespread demand for autonomy or outright independence, and (*c*) the opportunity to act collectively on behalf of one's ethnic group.

The Capacity to Overcome Free Riding

Scholars have long recognized the importance of mutual dependence as a condition of group formation (Hechter 1987, Rabbie & Horowitz 1988, Belanger & Pinard 1991). Individual group members will be dependent on the group to the degree that they do not have other alternatives by which to pursue their goals. Several other factors, such as altruism, proximity, shared territory, similar preferences, and shared labels (Rabbie & Wilkens 1971, Chai 1996), all contribute to lowering the costs of organizing a group and encourage the formation of minority groups. But even where shared interests and dependence exist, collective action will not occur if group members free ride on the cooperative behavior of other members. Coercing participation or offering selective rewards to those who participate in collective action were originally identified as the only solutions to the free-rider problem (Olson 1965). Because selective incentive solutions are themselves subject to the second-order free-rider problem (Frolich & Oppenheimer 1970), the popularity of this solution has waned in recent years. Theorists recognize that other kinds of incentives and case-specific conditions are likely to be important in promoting mobilization (Lichbach 1995). These include the group's monitoring capacity (Hechter 1987), the magnitude and character of its social rewards (Chong 1991), members' fear of incurring social penalties (Hardin 1995), conformity to internalized norms of political action (Muller et al 1991), and self-conscious cooperation to promote collective rationality [for documentation of the increasing influence of strategic views of collective action, see Hardin (1982), Moore (1995)].

These conditions are likely to flourish in groups once organized to provide their members with private goods (Hechter 2000). For example, the origins of many Western European nationalist movements lay in groups established by interested parties, such as teachers and clergy, to promote or protect peripheral cultures and religions in which they had a significant personal stake (Hroch 1985). Likewise, the American civil rights movement depended heavily on African-American churches to overcome free riding (Morris 1984:807). Two studies employing the Minorities at Risk data set suggest that a group's prior mobilization for political action has a strong effect on its current political behavior (Gurr 1993, Olzak & Tsutsui 1998). A handful of studies find that a group's organizational capacity for mobilization also leads to communal protest and rebellion (Gurr 1993, Lindstrom & Moore 1995, Gurr & Moore 1997). Additionally, the historical loss of group autonomy, grievances, and group coherence have a positive effect on the organizational capacity for rebellion, whereas the loss of group autonomy and institutionalization of democracy increase the ability of an ethnic group to get its members to engage in, or at least condone, protest behavior (Gurr 1993, Gurr & Moore 1997).

If, as these findings suggest, support for nationalist movements is primarily instrumental, then an important conclusion follows. Nationalist dynamics ought to be related to the central state's actual treatment of minorities. The more responsive the state is to the political demands of its minorities, the less support there should be for antistate—and especially violent—forms of nationalism. This instrumental view, however, implies nothing about the content of minority political demands. There is no reason to believe that the minority's direct material interests (e.g. in jobs or economic growth) must trump its cultural interests (e.g. in a given language or religion). The ultimate rationale of any state is the provision of public goods. The key political question is this: To what extent does the state provide an optimal bundle of the public goods demanded by the minority? For example, if Corsicans want their children to be able to speak the vernacular in school, will Paris accommodate their demand? To the degree that Paris can accommodate the Corsicans, support for Corsican separatism ought to decline.

In turn, the state's response to challenging political activity is important in shaping the extent to which an outbreak of violence will occur. If nationalist political parties are not recognized by the state, and if their activities are repressed, violent collective action is likely to occur. Low levels of repression tend to increase political protest and violence, but high levels of repression decrease the likelihood of these outcomes (Muller 1985, Muller & Seligson 1987, London & Robinson 1989, Boswell & Dixon 1990, Muller & Weede 1990, Gurr & Harff 1994). A semirepressive regime, which may exact sanctions and punishment at a middle level, tends to increase political violence. More studies are needed to better understand the dynamic interactions between states and political dissidents. Current research indicates that dissidents respond to state repression by substituting nonviolent behavior for violent behavior and vice versa (Lichbach 1987, Moore 1998). An important advance in the literature is the finding that there are short- and long-term effects of repression on actors (Opp & Ruehl 1990, Rasler 1996).

Although the instrumental logic that undergirds much of this literature may seem to be unassailable, its implications are far from clear. In fact, there is little consensus about the kinds of political institutions that are most likely to contain nationalism.

Institutional Factors Affecting the Demand for Minority Collective Action

Electoral arrangements have long been implicated in the rise of nationalism. As John Stuart Mill recognized, majoritarian democratic regimes with single-member districts may result in a tyranny of the majority. For this reason, a variety of alternative institutions have been proposed—from proportional representation (Grofman & Lijphart 1986, Lijphart & Aitkin 1994, Sartori 1997), to consociationalism (Lijphart 1984), to various forms of federation (Riker 1964).

Whereas vast literatures are devoted to each of these institutions, it is the role federation plays in nationalism that has garnered the lion's share of recent attention. There are three different views of the matter. One is that federation undercuts nationalist conflict by providing minorities with a more optimal mix of government-provided goods (Brass 1991, Gurr 2000, Hechter 2000). A second view is that federation exacerbates nationalism by providing minority elites with resources (principally patronage and tax revenues) they can use for mobilizing nationalist movements against central authorities (Roeder 1991, Bunce 1999). The third view is that federation has no determinate effects on nationalism because it is subject to a host of noninstitutional contingencies, such as "reputational cascades" (Kuran 1998). Because these rival arguments are based on the same instrumental premises, their merits can only be assessed against the empirical record.

The empirical record, however, is remarkably murky. In fact, the literature lends credence to all three propositions. Although propositions of this kind are best tested with quantitative data, these data tend to be in short supply. Even so, it is possible to make one interesting generalization. Scholars who have attempted quantitative cross-national analyses tend to support the first view (Gurr 2000, Hechter 2000). By contrast, students of the former Soviet empire and its former dependencies (Roeder 1991, Brubaker 1996, Treisman 1997, Laitin 1998, Bunce 1999, Hale 2000, Snyder 2000) seem convinced of the second. Most historians, we suspect, are convinced of the third proposition.

One possible interpretation of the conflicting evidence comes to mind. This interpretation rests on Riker's (1964) view of federation as an exchange relation, or bargain, between relevant agents in the center and in the periphery. The utility of any such bargain depends on the resources each party brings to the relationship. If the center in a federation loses resources—or is perceived as having lost them because of failures in war and an inability to maintain social order—peripheral leaders are likely to be emboldened to strike out on their own (Hechter 2000). Because federation grants them more resources than their counterparts in centralized regimes, nationalism is likely to arise. Moreover, according to this logic, nationalism should arise first in those parts of a federation that have the greatest resources (Hale 2000). In centralized regimes, however, nationalist or secessionist movements may be more likely to break out in less developed, rather than more developed, regions (Horowitz 1985, Hechter 1992). Resolving this issue is an important task for future research. Studies aiming to disentangle the relationship between regime structure and nationalist movements must be not be limited to one particular political context but should be broadly cross-national.

Political Opportunity Structures

The most expansive view of nationalist movements suggests that they depend on the structure of political opportunities (Jenkins & Perrow 1977, Tilly 1978, McAdam 1982, Tarrow 1983, McAdam et al 1996). The concept of political opportunity encompasses far more than regime structure. McAdam (1996) specifies four dimensions of political opportunity: the relative openness or closure of the political system (presumably, federation would figure here), the stability of elite alignments, the presence or absence of elite allies, and the state's capacity for repression.

Political mobilization of all kinds is facilitated when the central state is perceived to be in crisis. When economic and social institutions collapsed in Iran, Algeria, Kazakhstan, Uzbekistan, and Kyrgyztan, Islamic movements offered goods that were previously provided by the state (Ollapally & Cooley 1996). In each case, the collapse of the central state encouraged challenging movements. This account dovetails neatly with our discussion of the importance of prior organization for collective action. The increasingly perceptible weakness of the Soviet state, which could not manage to defeat an Afghan insurgency, led to its fragmentation (Hechter 2000) and to a welter of nationalist movements in the titular republics. Students of revolution likewise point to the importance of national crises that render the powerful vulnerable (Skocpol 1979, Arjomand 1988, Goldstone 1991). In his study of 227 communal groups—"cultural groups that do not have recognized states or institutionalized political status"—in 90 countries, Gurr (1993:160) found that democratization provided opportunities that spurred the mobilization of these groups. Gurr's results show that expansion of state power during the 1960s and 1970s intensified communal rebellion in the 1980s but diminished protest. These effects were especially pronounced in the Third World among ethnonationalists and indigenous peoples, groups who faced the greatest losses of resources and autonomy due to the expansion of direct rule.

Despite its intuitive appeal, the concept of political opportunity is often criticized for its lack of specificity. For example, Gamson & Meyer (1996:275) state that political opportunity is "in danger of becoming a sponge that soaks up virtually every aspect of the social movement environment...it threatens to become an all-encompassing fudge factor for all the conditions and circumstances that form the context for collective action." Political opportunity may be heuristically useful for interpreting the emergence of social movements and political activities, but measurement and specification of the concept need to be improved (see Kriesi et al 1995, Soule et al 1999).

The International Context

To this point in the review we have concentrated on causes of minority collective action that are endogenous to existing state borders. Yet it is evident that the international context has important effects on political outcomes in states. In their study of ethnic mobilization at the world system level, Olzak & Tsutsui (1998) found that during the 1970s, a state's membership in international organizations decreased ethnic violence, whereas during the 1980s, ethnic diversity and membership in international organizations increased ethnic protest. The authors argue that these findings support the claim that the diffusion of global norms about human rights via ties to international organizations constrains violent ethnic activity while encouraging ethnic mobilization and nationalism in dependent, peripheral states.

But how does the political behavior of groups in other countries affect political mobilization and conflict in general? Kuran (1998) claims that the international context affects the process of "ethnic dissimilation" via three distinct mechanisms that work together: (*a*) a demonstration effect, where the ethnic discrimination that is a dominant part of the political discourse in one country heightens ethnic categories among the citizens of another country; (*b*) an expectation effect, where news about the rising ethnic activity in another country alerts people to the possibility that dissimilation can occur in their own countries; and (*c*) a reputation effect, where global norms affect whether dissimilation is a project to be undertaken. However, most studies, including Kuran's (1998), do not actually test causal mechanisms but instead focus on outcomes. Lindstrom & Moore (1995) found that protest and rebellion in neighboring countries influenced mobilization and rebellion by ethnic groups (contagion) but did not find that ethnic groups were influenced by kinship groups in other countries (diffusion). Research suggests that links to kinship in other countries affect conflict occurring between states. Davis et al (1997) and Moore & Davis (1998) examined the effect of transnational ethnic ties on the conflict and cooperation behavior of states in the international system and found that the level of conflict between two states was higher if both states contain members from the same ethnic group and if ethnic group members are politically privileged in one state but not in the other state.

There is also empirical support for the diffusion of tactics across group and state boundaries. In a study examining patterns of peaceful protest in 17 Western industrialized nations (1950–1982), Hill and his colleagues (1998) found that after 1960, when a state had substantial ethnic divisions and widely available access to television, and when the people had seen nonviolent tactics used effectively in the United States, a greater number of peaceful protests occurred. The authors suggest that diffusion of tactics occurs when groups are experiencing the same political conditions. Halperin (1998) argues that prior to 1945, social, economic, and political conditions in Europe did diffuse ethnic conflicts to other states, but that because after World War II minorities and lower classes were integrated into the political process, circumstances today do not encourage such trends.

However, other researchers locate the sources of ethnic conflicts primarily within states and question whether the effects of demonstration and contagion facilitate the outbreak of violence and secession. Saideman (1998) argues that after the fall of communism, the Yugoslav, Czech, and Soviet federations faced similar problems; these nation-states had to rebuild politics and maintain power. Such changing conditions led to insecurity on the part of minorities in the region. Fearon (1998) calls this the commitment problem, where ethnic minorities find themselves without a third party to guarantee that majority leaders will not exploit them in the new state. In this circumstance, secession is seen as a superior alternative. Both Saideman and Fearon criticize the logic of contagion via demonstration effects; proponents of demonstration effects assume that followers will engage in further political action when there is the distinct possibility that secessionist movements or political conflict might actually discourage such behaviors in other nation states. Saideman (1998) points out that the secessionist efforts of Croatia and Bosnia were costly in terms of lives lost and damage done—a situation unlikely to inspire similar activities elsewhere.

Overall, the empirical evidence indicates that links to kinship in other countries do not necessarily affect protest or rebellion activity by ethnic groups unless both groups face similar political circumstances, but that such links affect the level of conflict or cooperation between two neighboring states. There is some evidence that political action in neighboring countries positively affects mobilization and rebellion. However, there is more evidence that political and social circumstances (i.e. disruptive social change, such as the fall of communism) affect whether minorities will engage in secessionist movements. In addition, links to international organizations tend to increase the level of mobilization in the name of sovereignty. Once again, there is a need for identifying and testing the mechanisms behind processes of diffusion and contagion in an international context as the world continues to globalize.

CONCLUSION

Given the variety of minority groups and the different social and political circumstances they face, constructing an overarching theory of minority group collective action is a daunting challenge. As this review has attempted to show, there is much to gain by focusing on causal mechanisms responsible for the political mobilization of minority groups. To enrich our knowledge about these processes and mechanisms, however, it is necessary to explicitly define the "nationalist movements" so often taken to be hallmarks of minority groups' political mobilization. In most of the accounts of nationalist movements in the literature, there is an alarming lack of specificity about what forms this kind of behavior entails. Such accounts could be describing the formation of ethnic political parties or nationalist organizations, protest or rebellion, military activities carried out by nationalist organizations, or secessionist votes. Of course, these categories can be disaggregated ad infinitum. Progress will be slow until some consensus on the types of nationalist movements found in the historical record can be realized. Several scholars have attempted to construct more effective categories of ethnic conflict (Heraclides 1990, Chazan 1991, Carment 1993) and of types of participants in political protest and rebellion (Horowitz 1985, Gurr 1993). We urge others to follow their lead. The most important impediment in this field remains the paucity of historical and cross-national databases adequate to test the many theories that have been advanced to account for the fate of minority groups in an increasingly interdependent world.

LITERATURE CITED

Abrams D, Hogg MA. 1990. *Social Identity Theory: Constructive and Critical Advances.* London: Harvester Wheatsheaf. 224 pp.

Alba RD. 1988. Cohorts and the dynamics of ethnic change. In *Social Structure and the Life Course*, ed. MW Riley, BJ Huber, BB Hess, pp. 211–28. Newbury Park, CA: Sage. 368 pp.

Alba RD, Golden RM. 1986. Patterns of ethnic marriage in the United States. *Soc. Forces* 65:202–23

Alba RD, Logan JR. 1991. Variations on two themes: racial and ethnic patterns in the attainment of suburban residence. *Demography* 28:431–53

Alba RD, Logan JR. 1993. Minority proximity to whites in suburbs: an individual-level analysis of segregation. *Am. J. Sociol.* 98: 1388–427

Alba RD, Logan JR, Crowder K. 1997. White ethnic neighborhoods and assimilation: the greater New York region, 1980–1990. *Soc. Forces* 75:883–912

Alba RD, Logan JR, Stults BJ, Marzan G, Zhang W. 1999. Immigrant groups in the suburbs: a reexamination of suburbanization and spatial assimilation. *Am. Soc. Rev.* 64:446–60

Anderson B. 1983. *Imagined Communities: Reflections on the Origin and Spread of Nationalism.* London: Verso. 160 pp.

Anderson RN, Saenz R. 1994. Structural determinants of Mexican American intermarriage, 1975–1980. *Soc. Sci. Q.* 75:414–30

Arjomand SA. 1988. *The Turban for the Crown: The Islamic Revolution in Iran.* New York: Oxford Univ. Press. 283 pp.

Armstrong JA. 1982. *Nations Before Nationalism.* Chapel Hill: Univ. NC Press. 411 pp.

Bailey T, Waldinger R. 1991. Primary, secondary, and enclave labor markets: a training system approach. *Am. Soc. Rev.* 56:432–45

Banton M. 1983. *Racial and Ethnic Competition.* Cambridge, UK: Cambridge Univ. Press. 434 pp.

Barth F. 1969. *Ethnic Groups and Boundaries: The Social Organization of Cultural Difference.* London: Allen & Unwin. 153 pp.

Belanger S, Pinard M. 1991. Ethnic movements and the competition model: some missing links. *Am. Sociol. Rev.* 56:446–57

Blau PM, Beeker C, Fitzpatrick KM. 1984. Intersecting social affiliations and intermarriage. *Soc. Forces* 62:585–606

Blau PM, Blum TC, Schwartz JE. 1982. Heterogeneity and intermarriage. *Am. Sociol. Rev.* 47:45–62

Blau PM, Schwartz JE. 1984. *Crosscutting Social Circles.* London: Academic. 257 pp.

Bollen C, Diez Medrano J. 1998. Who are the Spaniards? Nationalism and identification in Spain. *Soc. Forces* 77:587–622

Bonacich E. 1972. A theory of ethnic antagonism: the split-labor market. *Am. Sociol. Rev.* 37:533–47

Boswell T, Brueggemann J. 2000. Labor market segmentation and the cultural division of labor in the copper mining industry, 1880–1920. *Res. Soc. Mov. Confl. Change* 22:193–217

Boswell T, Dixon WJ. 1990. Dependency and rebellion: a cross-national analysis. *Am. Sociol. Rev.* 55:540–59

Brass PR. 1991. *Ethnicity and Nationalism.* New Delhi: Sage

Breuilly J. 1993. *Nationalism and the State.* Chicago: Univ. Chicago Press. 474 pp. 2nd ed.

Brown D. 1998. Why is the nation-state so vulnerable to ethnic nationalism? *Nations Nationalism* 4(1):1–15

Brown R. 1986. *Social Psychology: The Second Edition.* New York: Free. 704 pp.

Brubaker R. 1996. *Nationalism Reframed: Nationhood and the National Question in the*

New Europe. Cambridge, UK: Cambridge Univ. Press. 202 pp.

Brubaker R, Laitin DD. 1998. Ethnic and nationalist violence. *Annu. Rev. Sociol.* 24:423–52

Bunce V. 1999. *Subversive Institutions: The Design and the Destruction of Socialism and the State*. New York: Cambridge Univ. Press. 206 pp.

Calhoun C. 1998. *Nationalism*. Minneapolis: Univ. Minn. Press. 164 pp.

Carment D. 1993. The international dimensions of ethnic conflict: concepts, indicators, and theory. *J. Peace Res.* 30:137–50

Chai S. 1996. A theory of ethnic group boundaries. *Nations Nationalism* 2:281–307

Chazan N. 1991. *Irredentism and International Politics*. Boulder, CO: Rienner. 161 pp.

Chiswick BR. 1978. The effect of Americanization on the earnings of foreign-born men. *J. Pop. Econ.* 86:891–921

Chong D. 1991. *Collective Action and the Civil Rights Movement*. Chicago: Univ. Chicago Press. 261 pp.

Connor W. 1972. Nation-building or nation-destroying? *World Polit.* 24:319–55

Conversi D. 1995. Reassessing current theories of nationalism: nationalism as boundary maintenance and creation. *Nationalism Ethn. Polit.* 1:73–85

Cornell S. 1988. *The Return of the Native: American Indian Political Resurgence*. New York: Oxford Univ. Press. 278 pp.

Crocker J, Blaine B, Luhtanen R. 1993. Prejudice, intergroup behaviour and self-esteem: enhancement and protection motives. In *Group Motivation: Social Psychological Perspectives*, ed. M Hogg, D Abrams, pp. 52–67. London: Harvester Wheatsheaf. 240 pp.

Crocker J, Major B. 1989. Social stigma and self-esteem: the self-protective properties of stigma. *Psychol. Rev.* 96:608–30

Cross WE. 1985. Black identity: rediscovering the distinction between personal identity and reference group orientation. In *Beginnings: The Social and Affective Development of Black Children*, ed. M Spencer, G Brookins, W Allen, pp. 155–71. Hillsdale, NJ: Erlbaum. 275 pp.

Darroch GA. 1981. Urban ethnicity in Canada: personal assimilation and political communities. *Can. Rev. Soc. Anthropol.* 11:1–29

Davis DR, Jaggars K, Moore WH. 1997. Ethnicity, minorities, and international conflict patterns. In *Wars in the Midst of Peace: The International Politics of Ethnic Conflict*, ed. J Carment, P James, pp. 148–63. Pittsburgh, PA: Univ. Pittsburgh Press. 302 pp.

de Swaan A. 1988. *In Care of the State: Health Care, Education, and Welfare in Europe and the USA in the Modern Era*. Cambridge, UK: Polity. 339 pp.

Deutsch KW. 1953. *Nationalism and Social Communication*. Cambridge, MA: MIT Press. 292 pp.

Diez Medrano J. 1994. The effects of ethnic segregation and ethnic competition on political mobilization in the Basque country, 1988. *Am. Sociol. Rev.* 59:873–89

Ellemers N, van Knippenberg A, de Vries N, Wilke H. 1988. Social identification and permeability of group boundaries. *Eur. J. Soc. Psychol.* 18:497–513

Esman MJ. 1985. Two dimensions of ethnic politics: defense of homelands, immigrant rights. *Ethn. Racial Stud.* 8:438–40

Espiritu YL. 1992. *Asian American Panethnicity: Bridging Individuals and Institutions*. Philadelphia, PA: Temple Univ. Press. 222 pp.

Espiritu YL. 1996. Colonial oppression, labour importation, and group formation: Filipinos in the United States. *Ethn. Racial Stud.* 19:29–47

Fearon JD. 1998. Commitment problems and the spread of ethnic conflict. See Lake & Rothchild 1998, pp. 107–26

Featherman DL, Hauser RM. 1978. *Opportunity and Change*. New York: Academic. 572 pp.

Fitzpatrick JP, Gurak DT. 1979. *Hispanic Intermarriage in New York City: 1975. Monogr.*

No. 2. New York: Hispanic Res. Cent., Fordham Univ. 100 pp.

Flippen AR, Hornstein HA, Siegal WE, Weitzman EA. 1996. A comparison of similarity and interdependence triggers for in-group formation. *Pers. Soc. Psychol. Bull.* 22:882–93

Frolich N, Oppenheimer JA. 1970. I get by with a little help from my friends. *World Polit.* 23:104–20

Gamson WA, Meyer DS. 1996. Framing political opportunity. See McAdam et al 1996, pp. 291–311

Ganguly S. 1996. Explaining the Kashmir insurgency: political mobilization and institutional decay. *Int. Secur.* 21(2):76–107

Geertz C. 1963. The integrative revolution: primordial sentiments and civil politics in the new states. In *Old Societies and New States: The Quest for Modernity in Asia and Africa*, ed. C Geertz, pp. 105–57. New York: Free. 310 pp.

Gellner E. 1964. *Thought and Change*. London: Weidenfeld & Nicolson. 224 pp.

Gellner E. 1983. *Nations and Nationalism*. Oxford, UK: Blackwell. 150 pp.

Gilbertson GA, Fitzpatrick JP, Lijun Y. 1996. Hispanic intermarriage in New York City: new evidence from 1991. *Int. Migr. Rev.* 30: 445–59

Goldstone J. 1991. *Revolution and Rebellion in the Early Modern World*. Berkeley: Univ. Calif. Press. 608 pp.

Gordon M. 1964. *Assimilation in American Life*. New York: Oxford Univ. Press. 276 pp.

Grofman B, Lijphart A, eds. 1986. *Electoral Laws and Their Political Consequences*. New York: Agathon

Gurak DT, Fitzpatrick JP. 1982. Intermarriage among Hispanic ethnic groups in New York City. *Am. J. Soc.* 87:921–34

Gurr TR. 1993. Why minorities rebel: a global analysis of communal mobilization and conflict since 1945. *Int. Polit. Sci. Rev.* 14(2): 161–201

Gurr TR. 2000. Ethnic warfare on the wane. *Foreign Aff.* 79:52–64

Gurr TR, Harff B. 1994. *Ethnic Conflict in World Politics*. Boulder, CO: Westview. 206 pp.

Gurr TR, Moore WH. 1997. Ethnopolitical rebellion: a cross-sectional analysis of the 1980s with risk assessments for the 1990s. *Am. J. Polit. Sci.* 41(4):1079–103

Hale HE. 2000. The parade of sovereignties: testing theories of secession in the Soviet setting. *Br. J. Polit. Sci.* 30:31–56

Halperin S. 1998. The spread of ethnic conflict in Europe: some comparative-historical reflections. See Lake & Rothchild 1998, pp. 151–84

Hannan MT. 1979. The dynamics of ethnic boundaries in modern states. In *National Development and the World System*, ed. JW Meyer, MT Hannan, pp. 253–75. Chicago: Univ. Chicago Press. 334 pp.

Hardin R. 1982. *Collective Action*. Baltimore, MD: Johns Hopkins Univ. Press. 248 pp.

Hardin R. 1995. *One For All: The Logic of Group Conflict*. Princeton, NJ: Princeton Univ. Press. 288 pp.

Hastings A. 1997. *The Construction of Nationhood: Ethnicity, Religion, and Nationalism*. New York: Cambridge Univ. Press. 235 pp.

Hechter M. 1978. Group formation and the cultural division of labor. *Am. J. Sociol.* 84:293–318

Hechter M. 1987. *Principles of Group Solidarity*. Berkeley: Univ. Calif. Press. 219 pp.

Hechter M. 1992. The dynamics of secession. *Acta Sociol.* 35:267–83

Hechter M. 1994. Review of Olzak, *Dynamics of Ethnic Competition and Conflict*. *Eur. Sociol. Rev.* 10(1):96–98

Hechter M. 1999 (1975). *Internal Colonialism: The Celtic Fringe in British National Development*. New Brunswick, NJ: Transaction. 390 pp.

Hechter M. 2000. *Containing Nationalism*. Oxford/New York: Oxford Univ. Press. 256 pp.

Heraclides A. 1990. Secessionist minorities and external involvement. *Int. Org.* 44:341–78

Herranz de Rafael G. 1998. An empirical survey

of social structure and nationalistic identification in Spain in the 1990s. *Nations Nationalism* 35–59

Hill S, Rothchild D, Cameron C. 1998. Tactical information and the diffusion of peaceful protests. See Lake & Rothchild 1998, pp. 61–88

Hirschman C. 1983. America's melting pot reconsidered. *Annu. Rev. Sociol.* 9:397–423

Hobsbawm E, Ranger T, eds. 1983. *The Invention of Tradition*. Cambridge, UK: Cambridge Univ. Press. 320 pp.

Hobsbawm EJ. 1992. *Nations and Nationalism Since 1780: Programme, Myth, Reality*. Cambridge, UK: Cambridge Univ. Press. 206 pp. 2nd ed.

Hogg MA, Abrams D. 1990. Social motivation, self esteem and social identity. In *Social Identity Theory: Constructive and Critical Advances*, ed. D Abrams, MA Hogg, pp. 28–47. London: Harvester Wheatsheaf

Hogg MA, Terry DJ, White KM. 1995. A tale of two theories: a critical comparison of identity theory with social identity theory. *Soc. Psychol. Q.* 58:255–69

Horowitz DL. 1975. Ethnic identity. In *Ethnicity: Theory and Experience*, ed. N Glazer, DP Moynihan, pp. 111–40. Cambridge, MA: Harvard Univ. Press. 531 pp.

Horowitz DL. 1985. *Ethnic Groups in Conflict*. Berkeley: Univ. Calif. Press. 697 pp.

Hroch M. 1985. *Social Preconditions of National Revival in Europe: A Comparative Analysis of the Social Composition of Patriotic Groups Among the Smaller European Nations*. Cambridge, UK: Cambridge Univ. Press. 220 pp.

Hughes EC. 1943. *French Canada in Transition*. Chicago: Univ. Chicago Press. 227 pp.

Hughes EC, Hughes HM. 1952. *Where Peoples Meet: Ethnic and Racial Frontiers*. Glencoe, IL: Free. 204 pp.

Hwang S, Saenz R, Aguirre BE. 1994. Structural and individual determinants of outmarriage among Chinese-, Filipino-, and Japanese-Americans in California. *Sociol. Inq.* 64:396–414

Isaacs HR. 1975. *Idols of the Tribe: Group Identity and Political Change*. Cambridge, MA: Cambridge Univ. Press. 242 pp.

Jackson LA, Sullivan LA, Harnish R, Hodge CN. 1996. Achieving positive social identity: social mobility, social creativity, and permeability of group boundaries. *J. Pers. Soc. Psychol.* 70:241–54

Jenkins JC, Perrow C. 1977. Insurgency of the powerless: farm worker movements 1946–1972. *Am. Sociol. Rev.* 42:249–68

Kalmijn M. 1993. Trends in black/white intermarriage. *Soc. Forces* 72:119–46

Kriesi H, Koopmans R, Duyvendak JW, Guigni MG. 1995. *The Politics of New Social Movements in Western Europe: A Comparative Analysis*. Minneapolis: Univ. Minn. Press

Kuran T. 1998. Ethnic norms and their transformation through reputational cascades. *J. Legal Stud.* 27:623–60

Laitin DD. 1998. *Identity in Formation: The Russian-Speaking Populations in the Near Abroad*. Ithaca, NY: Cornell Univ. Press. 417 pp.

Lake DA, Rothchild RS, eds. 1998. *The International Spread of Ethnic Conflict*. Princeton, NJ: Princeton Univ. Press. 392 pp.

Lee SM, Yamanaka K. 1990. Patterns of Asian American intermarriage and marital assimilation. *J. Comp. Fam. Stud.* 21:287–305

Leifer EM. 1981. Competing models of political mobilization: the role of ethnic ties. *Am. J. Sociol.* 87:23–47

Lemyre L, Smith PM. 1985. Intergroup discrimination and self-esteem in the minimal group paradigm. *J. Pers. Soc. Psychol.* 42:193–211

Lewin K. 1948. *Resolving Social Conflicts*. New York: Harper & Row. 422 pp.

Lichbach MI. 1987. Deterrence or escalation? *J. Confl. Res.* 31:266–97

Lichbach MI. 1995. *The Rebel's Dilemma*. Ann Arbor: Univ. Mich. Press

Lieberson S, Waters M. 1988. *From Many Strands: Ethnic and Racial Groups in Contemporary America*. New York: Sage. 289 pp.

Light I. 1984. Immigrant and ethnic enterprise in North America. *Ethn. Racial Stud.* 7:195–216

Light I, Bonacich E. 1988. *Immigrant Entrepreneurs: Koreans in Los Angeles, 1965–1982*. Berkeley: Univ. Calif. Press. 495 pp.

Lijphart A. 1984. *Democracies: Patterns of Majoritarian and Consensus Government in Twenty-One Countries*. New Haven, CT: Yale Univ. Press. 229 pp.

Lijphart A, Aitkin D. 1994. *Electoral Systems and Party Systems: A Study of Twenty-Seven Democracies, 1945–1990*. Oxford, UK: Oxford Univ. Press

Lindstrom R, Moore WH. 1995. Deprived, rational or both? "Why minorities rebel" revisited. *J. Polit. Mil. Sociol.* 23:167–90

Locksley A, Ortiz V, Hepburn C. 1980. Social categorization and discriminatory behavior: extinguishing the minimal intergroup discrimination effect. *J. Pers. Soc. Psychol.* 39: 773–83

Logan JR, Alba RD, Leung SY. 1996. Minority access to white suburbs: a multiregion comparison. *Soc. Forces* 74:851–81

London B, Robinson TD. 1989. The effect of international dependence on income inequality and political violence. *Am. Sociol. Rev.* 50:47–31

Massey DS. 1988. Suburbanization and segregation in U.S. metropolitan areas. *Am. J. Soc.* 94:592–626

Massey DS, Denton NA. 1985. Ethnic residential segregation: a theoretical synthesis and empirical review. *Soc. Social Res.* 69:315–50

Massey DS, Denton NA. 1987. Trends in the residential segregation of blacks, Hispanics, and Asians: 1970–1980. *Am. Sociol. Rev.* 52: 802–25

Massey DS, Denton NA. 1993. *American Apartheid: Segregation and the Making of the Underclass*. Cambridge, MA: Harvard Univ. Press

McAdam D. 1982. *Political Process and the Development of Black Insurgency, 1930–1970*. Chicago: Univ. Chicago Press. 304 pp.

McAdam D. 1996. Conceptual origins, current problems, future directions. See McAdam et al, 1996, pp. 23–40

McAdam D, McCarthy J, Zald M, eds. 1996. *Comparative Perspectives on Social Movements: Political Opportunities, Mobilizing Structures, and Cultural Framings*. Cambridge, UK: Cambridge Univ. Press. 426 pp.

McGarry J, O'Leary B. 1993. The macropolitical regulation of ethnic conflict. In *The Politics of Ethnic Conflict Regulation: Case Studies of Protracted Ethnic Conflicts*, ed. J McGarry, B O'Leary, pp. 1–40. New York: Routledge. 321 pp.

Meadwell H. 1983. Forms of cultural mobilization in Quebec and Brittany, 1870–1914. *Comp. Polit.* 15:410–17

Mettam CW, Williams SW. 1998. Internal colonialism and cultural divisions of labour in the Soviet Republic of Estonia. *Nations Nationalism* 4(3):363–88

Montero D. 1980. *Japanese Americans: Changing Patterns of Ethnic Affiliation Over Three Generations*. Boulder, CO: Westview. 171 pp.

Moore WH. 1995. Rational rebels: overcoming the free rider problem. *Polit. Res. Q.* 48:417–54

Moore WH. 1998. Repression and dissent: substitution, context, and timing. *Am. J. Polit. Sci.* 42(3):851–73

Moore WH, Davis DR. 1998. Transnational ethnic ties and foreign policy. See Lake & Rothchild 1998, pp. 89–104

Morris AD. 1984. *The Origins of the Civil Rights Movement*. New York: Free. 354 pp.

Mughan A. 1979. Modernization and ethnic conflict in Belgium. *Polit. Stud.* 27:21–37

Muller EN. 1985. Income inequality, regime repressiveness, and political violence. *Am. Sociol. Rev.* 54:305–8

Muller EN, Dietz HA, Finkel SE. 1991. Discontent and the expected utility of rebellion: the case of Peru. *Am. Polit. Sci. Rev.* 85:1261–82

Muller EN, Seligson MA. 1987. Inequality and insurgency. *Am. Polit. Sci. Rev.* 81:425–51

Muller EN, Weede E. 1990. Cross-national variation in political violence. *J. Confl. Res.* 34: 851–73

Murguia E, Frisbie WP. 1977. Trends in Mexican-American intermarriage: recent findings in perspective. *Soc. Sci. Q.* 58:374–89

Nagata J. 1981. In defense of ethnic boundaries: the changing myths and charters of Malay identity. In *Ethnic Change*, ed. CF Keyes, pp. 87–118. Seattle: Univ. Wash. Press. 331 pp.

Nagel J. 1986. The political construction of ethnicity. In *Competitive Ethnic Relations*, ed. S Olzak, J Nagel, pp. 39–112. New York: Academic. 252 pp.

Nagel J. 1994. Constructing ethnicity: creating and recreating ethnic identity and culture. *Soc. Probl.* 41:152–76

Niedert LJ, Farley R. 1985. Assimilation in the United States: an analysis of ethnic and generational differences in status and achievement. *Am. Sociol. Rev.* 50:840–50

Nielsen F. 1980. The Flemish movement in Belgium after World War II: a dynamic analysis. *Am. Sociol. Rev.* 45:76–94

Nielsen F. 1985. Toward a theory of ethnic solidarity in modern societies. *Am. Sociol. Rev.* 50:133–49

Nnoli O. 1989. *Ethnic Politics in Africa*. Ibadan: Vantage

Oakes PJ, Turner JC. 1980. Social categorization and intergroup behavior: Does minimal intergroup discrimination make social identity more positive? *Eur. J. Soc. Psychol.* 10: 295–301

Ollapally DM, Cooley A. 1996. Identity politics and the international system. *Nationalism Ethn. Polit.* 2(4):479–99

Olson M. 1965. *The Logic of Collective Action*. Cambridge, MA: Harvard Univ. Press. 176 pp.

Olzak S. 1982. Ethnic mobilization in Quebec. *Ethn. Racial Stud.* 5:254–75

Olzak S. 1983. Contemporary ethnic mobilization. *Annu. Rev. Sociol.* 9:355–74

Olzak S. 1992. *The Dynamics of Ethnic Competition and Conflict*. Stanford, CA: Stanford Univ. Press. 271 pp.

Olzak S, Tsutsui K. 1998. Status in the world system and ethnic mobilization. *J. Conf. Res.* 42:691–720

Ongkili JP. 1985. *Nation-Building in Malaysia: 1946–1974*. Singapore: Oxford Univ. Press. 275 pp.

Opp KD, Ruehl W. 1990. Repression, micromobilization and political protest. *Soc. Forces* 69:521–47

Padilla FM. 1985. *Latino Ethnic Consciousness: The Case of Mexican Americans and Puerto Ricans in Chicago*. Notre Dame, IN: Univ. Notre Dame Press. 187 pp.

Park RE. 1950. *Race and Culture*. Glencoe, IL: Free. 403 pp.

Parsons T. 1951. *The Social System*. Glencoe, IL: Free. 575 pp.

Pedraza-Bailey S. 1985. *Political and Economic Migrants in America: Cubans and Mexicans*. Austin: Univ. Texas Press. 242 pp.

Peled Y. 1990. Ethnic exclusionism in the periphery: the case of oriental Jews in Israel's development towns. *Ethn. Racial Stud.* 13: 345–67

Peled Y. 1998. Towards a redefinition of Jewish nationalism in Israel? The enigma of Shas. *Ethn. Racial Stud.* 21:703–27

Portes A, MacLeod D. 1996. Educational progress of children of immigrants: the roles of class, ethnicity, and school context. *Soc. Educ.* 69:255–75

Portes A, Rumbaut RG. 1990. *Immigrant America: A Portrait*. Berkeley: Univ. Calif. Press. 300 pp.

Portes A, Septick A. 1993. *City on the Edge: The Transformation of Miami*. Berkeley: Univ. Calif. Press. 281 pp.

Ra'anan U. 1990. The nation-state fallacy. In *Conflict and Peacemaking in Multiethnic Societies*, ed. JV Montville, pp. 5–20. Lexington, KY: Heath. 558 pp.

Rabbie JM, Horwitz M. 1988. Categories versus groups as explanatory concepts in intergroup relations. *Eur. J. Soc. Psychol.* 18:117–23

Rabbie JM, Schot JC, Visser L. 1987. *Instrumental intragroup cooperation and intergroup competition in the minimal group paradigm*. Presented at Soc. Ident. Conf., Univ. Exeter, Exeter, UK, July 1987

Rabbie JM, Schot JC, Visser L. 1989. Social identity theory: a conceptual and empirical critique from the perspective of a behavioural interaction model. *Eur. J. Soc. Psychol.* 19:171–202

Rabbie JM, Wilkens G. 1971. Intergroup competition and its effects on intragroup and intergroup relations. *Eur. J. Soc. Psychol.* 1:215–34

Ragin CC. 1979. Ethnic political mobilization: the Welsh case. *Am. Sociol. Rev.* 44:619–35

Rasler K. 1996. Concessions, repression, and political protest in the Iranian revolution. *Am. Sociol. Rev.* 61:132–52

Reitz JG. 1998. *Warmth of the Welcome: The Social Causes of Economic Success for Immigrants in Different Nations and Cities*. Boulder, CO: Westview. 298 pp.

Riker WH. 1964. *Federalism: Origin, Operation, Significance*. Boston: Little-Brown. 169 pp.

Roeder PG. 1991. Soviet federalism and ethnic mobilization. *World Polit.* 43:196–233

Rogowski R. 1985. Causes and varieties of nationalism: a rationalist account. In *New Nationalisms of the Developed West: Toward Explanation*, ed. EA Tiryakian, R Rogowski, pp. 87–108. Boston: Allen & Unwin. 394 pp.

Rosenberg M. 1979. *Conceiving the Self*. New York: Basic Books. 319 pp.

Sachdev I, Bourhis RY. 1984. Minimal majorities and minorities. *Eur. J. Soc. Psychol.* 14:35–52

Saideman SM. 1998. Is Pandora's box half empty or half full? The limited virulence of secessionism and the domestic sources of disintegration. See Lake & Rothchild 1998, pp. 127–50

Sandefur GD, McKinnell T. 1986. American Indian intermarriage. *Soc. Sci. Res.* 15:347–71

Schoen R. 1986. A methodological analysis of intergroup marriage. *Sociol. Methods* 16:49–78

Schoen R, Nelson VE, Collins M. 1978. Intermarriage among Spanish surnamed Californians, 1962–1974. *Int. Migr. Rev.* 12:359–69

Schoen R, Wooldredge J. 1989. Marriage choices in North Carolina and Virginia, 1969/71 and 1979/81. *J. Marriage Fam.* 51:465–81

Sekulic D, Massey G, Hodson R. 1994. Who were the Yugoslavs? Failed sources of a common identity in the former Yugoslavia. *Am. Sociol. Rev.* 59:83–97

Sherif M. 1966. In *Common Predicament: Social Psychology of Intergroup Conflict and Cooperation*. New York: Octagon Books. 192 pp.

Shils E. 1957. Primordial, personal, sacred, and civil ties: some particular observations on the relationship of sociological research and theory. *Br. J. Sociol.* 8:130–45

Skocpol T. 1979. *States and Social Revolutions*. Cambridge, UK: Cambridge Univ. Press. 407 pp.

Smith AD. 1996. The resurgence of nationalism? Myth and memory in the renewal of nations. *Br. J. Sociol.* 47:575–98

Smith AD. 1998. *Nationalism and Modernism: A Critical Survey of Recent Theories of Nations and Nationalism*. London: Routledge. 270 pp.

Snyder JL. 2000. *From Voting to Violence: Democratization and Nationalist Conflict*. New York: Norton. 382 pp.

Soule SA, McAdam D, McCarthy J, Su Y. 1999. Protest events: cause or consequence of state action? The U.S. women's movement and federal congressional activites, 1956–1979. *Mobilization* 4(2):239–55

South SJ, Messner SF. 1986. Structural determinants of intergroup association: interracial marriage and crime. *Am. J. Soc.* 91:1409–30

Spickard PR. 1989. *Mixed Blood: Intermarriage and Ethnic Identity in Twentieth-Century America*. Madison: Univ. Wisc. Press. 532 pp.

Starr P. 1978. The sociology of official statistics.

In *The Politics of Numbers*, ed. W Alonso, P Starr, pp. 7–57. New York: Russell Sage Found. 474 pp.

Tajfel H. 1970. Experiments in intergroup discrimination. *Sci. Am.* 223:96–102

Tajfel H. 1974. Social identity and intergroup behavior. *Soc. Sci. Inf.* 13:65–93

Tajfel H. 1981. *Human Groups and Social Categories: Studies in Social Psychology*. Cambridge, UK: Cambridge Univ. Press. 369 pp.

Tajfel H, Turner JC. 1979. An integrative theory of intergroup conflict. In *The Social Psychology of Intergroup Relations*, ed. WG Austin, S Worchel, pp. 33–47. Monterey, CA: Brooks/Cole. 369 pp.

Tarrow S. 1983. *Struggling to Reform: Social Movements and Policy Change During Cycles of Protest. Western Soc. Pap., No. 15.* Ithaca, NY: Cornell Univ.

Taylor DM, Moghaddam FM, Gamble I, Zellerer E. 1987. Disadvantaged group responses to perceived inequality: from passive acceptance to collective action. *J. Soc. Psychol.* 127:259–72

Tilly C. 1978. *From Mobilization to Revolution*. Reading, MA: Random House. 349 pp.

Tilly C. 1990. *Coercion, Capital, and European States, AD 990–1990*. Cambridge, MA: Blackwell. 269 pp.

Treisman DS. 1997. Russia's "ethnic revival": the separatist activism of regional leaders in a postcommunist order. *World Polit.* 49:212–49

Turner JC. 1987. *Rediscovering the Social Group: A Self-Categorization Theory*. Oxford, UK: Blackwell

Turner JC, Hogg M, Turner P, Smith P. 1984. Failure and defeat as determinant of group cohesiveness. *Br. J. Soc. Psychol.* 28:135–47

van den Berghe PL. 1967. *Race and Racism: A Comparative Perspective*. New York: Wiley. 169 pp.

van den Berghe PL. 1981. *The Ethnic Phenomenon*. New York: Elsevier. 301 pp.

van Knippenberg A. 1984. Intergroup differences in group perceptions. In *The Social Dimension*, ed. H Tajfel, pp. 560–78. Cambridge, UK: Cambridge Univ. Press. 751 pp.

van Knippenberg A, van Oers D. 1984. Social identity and equity concerns in intergroup perceptions. *Br. J. Soc. Psychol.* 23:351–61

Wallerstein I. 1980. *The Modern World System: Mercantilism and the Consolidation of the European World-Economy, 1600–1750*. New York: Academic. 370 pp.

Weber E. 1976. *The Making of Modern France*. Stanford, CA: Stanford Univ. Press

Whitmeyer JM. 1997. Endogamy as a basis for ethnic behavior. *Sociol. Theory* 15:162–78

Williams RM. 1994. The sociology of ethnic conflicts: comparative international perspectives. *Annu. Rev. Sociol.* 20:49–80

Wong M. 1989. A look at intermarriage among the Chinese in the United States in 1980. *Sociol. Perspect.* 32:87–107

Yinger JM. 1985. Ethnicity. *Annu. Rev. Sociol.* 11:151–80

Young C. 1976. *The Politics of Cultural Pluralism*. Madison: Univ. Wisc. Press. 560 pp.

Zhou M. 1992. *Chinatown: The Socioeconomic Potential of an Urban Enclave*. Philadelphia, PA: Temple Univ. Press. 275 pp.

Annu. Rev. Polit. Sci. 2001. 4:217–34

Political Knowledge, Political Engagement, and Civic Education

William A. Galston
School of Public Affairs, University of Maryland, College Park, Maryland 20742; e-mail: wg14@umail.umd.edu

Key Words political socialization, participation, democracy, service learning, higher education

■ **Abstract** After decades of neglect, civic education is back on the agenda of political science in the United States. Despite huge increases in the formal educational attainment of the US population during the past 50 years, levels of political knowledge have barely budged. Today's college graduates know no more about politics than did high school graduates in 1950. Recent research indicates that levels of political knowledge affect the acceptance of democratic principles, attitudes toward specific issues, and political participation. There is evidence that political participation is in part a positional good and is shaped by relative as well as absolute levels of educational attainment. Contrary to findings from 30 years ago, recent research suggests that traditional classroom-based civic education can significantly raise political knowledge. Service learning—a combination of community-based civic experience and systematic classroom reflection on that experience—is a promising innovation, but program evaluations have yielded mixed results. Longstanding fears that private schools will not shape democratic citizens are not supported by the evidence.

INTRODUCTION

One of the oldest topics in political theory, civic education is once more on the radar screen of contemporary political science. Compared with previous generations, scholars today are more likely to agree that well-designed institutions are not enough, that a well-ordered polity requires citizens with the appropriate knowledge, skills, and traits of character (Galston 1991:Ch. 10). And it is reasonably clear that good citizens are made, not born. The question is how, by whom, to what end?

Since Plato and Aristotle first discussed the matter, it has been clear that civic education is relative to regime type. Democracies require democratic citizens, whose specific knowledge, competences, and character would not be as well suited to nondemocratic politics. There is an additional level of complexity: How we think about the formation of democratic citizens depends on the specific conception of democracy we embrace (see March & Olsen 2000:148), and this is a matter of considerable debate. What balance is to be struck between representation and direct participation; between self-interest and public spirit; between rights and responsibilities; between liberty and equality; between reasoned deliberation and passionate mobilization; between secular and faith-based foundations of civic discourse and action; between unity and diversity; between civic loyalty and civic dissent? In turn, these theoretical debates have implications for the content and conduct of democratic civic education—the relationship to be established between classroom instruction and community-based experience, for example. Practitioners guided by Barber's conception of "strong democracy" will measure the performance of civic education along dimensions that include, but go beyond, the skills required of average citizens in representative systems (Barber et al n.d.).

Despite these differences, the contours of a rough-and-ready overlapping consensus are now coming into view. This consensus typically replaces either/or choices with both/and propositions. The skills needed to judge the deeds of representatives and to initiate action oneself are both important; civil discourse need not lack passion; the emphasis on the ability to make reasoned public judgment does not give secular reason pride of place over faith; classroom study and community practice both play a role in forming citizens; and so forth. The burgeoning "service-learning" movement discussed below is one indication of this emerging synthesis.

Another key question raises both normative and empirical issues. What degree of civic and political knowledge is required to be a competent democratic citizen? The traditional normative view was that knowledge requirements are high for democratic citizens. The discovery earlier in this century that most Americans have a low level of public knowledge created shock waves among social scientists and sparked a range of revisionist responses. Some argued for elite or expert-centered conceptions of democratic governance; others claimed that even if individual citizens have not mastered the details of public policies and institutions, citizens in the aggregate display well-grounded and stable judgments; still others offered accounts in which citizens with low levels of information are able to use shortcuts, heuristic devices, and cues to make reasonable judgments. More recently, these responses have themselves evoked sharp criticism (e.g. Hoffman 1998, Somin 1998), and many of the revisionists have responded by clarifying their views. Shapiro (1998:524–25), one of the chief proponents of the aggregate rationality thesis states explicitly that the stability of public opinion over time is no guarantee of the quality of those attitudes. Popkin & Dimock (1999), architects of the low-information rationality thesis, show that citizens with low levels of information cannot follow public discussion of issues, are less accepting of the give and take of democratic policy debates, make judgments on the basis of character rather than issues, and are significantly less inclined to participate in politics at all.

Here again, there are signs of an emerging consensus. Competent democratic citizens need not be policy experts, but there is a level of basic knowledge below which the ability to make a full range of reasoned civic judgments is impaired. Moreover, a broad-based discussion during the 1990s has yielded substantial agreement on the content of this knowledge, which in turn has served as the basis for constructing the Civics Assessment of the National Assessment of Educational Progress (Cent. Civic Educ. 1994, Natl. Assess. Gov. Board 1996).

A final introductory issue concerns the role of formal civic education in the political socialization of young people. Although citizens are made rather than born, it does not follow that civic education is the key formative mechanism. To begin with, all education is civic education in the sense that individuals' level of general educational attainment significantly affects their level of political knowledge as well as the quantity and character of their political participation. In addition, noneducational institutions and processes—families, ethnic groups, voluntary associations, and concrete political events, among others—are crucial influences on civic formation. Indeed, the conventional wisdom for the past three decades has been that formal civic education plays an insignificant role in the overall process of civic formation. It is only in the past few years that the pendulum has begun to swing back.

The renewed attention to civic education is more than an academic trend. It reflects as well broader concerns about the condition of US civic culture, especially among the young. To be sure, anxiety about the civic engagement of young adults is nothing new, and its persistence is easy to understand. As far back as solid evidence can be found, at any given historical moment, young adults have tended to be less attached to civic life than are their parents and grandparents. It is not difficult to explain this gap. Civic attachment is linked to factors such as professional interests (and self-interests), stable residential location, home ownership, marriage, and parenthood, all of which are statistically less characteristic of younger adults. In every generation, the simple passage of time has brought maturing adults more fully into the circle of civic life.

If the only significant differences were cross-sectional, today's heightened concern would be myopic. But there are also disturbing trends over time. If we compare generations rather than cohorts—that is, if we compare today's young adults not with today's older adults but with the young adults of the past—we find evidence of diminished civic attachment.

Some of the basic facts are well known. In the early 1970s, about half of the 18–29-year-olds in the United States voted in presidential elections. By 1996, fewer than one third did. The same pattern holds for congressional elections—about one third voted in the 1970s compared with fewer than one fifth in 1998. Less familiar are the trends charted by the annual survey from the University of California, Los Angeles, conducted since the mid-1960s and involving roughly 250,000 matriculating college freshmen each year. Over the more than three decades since the initiation of this survey, every significant indicator of political engagement has fallen by at least half. Only 26% of freshmen think that keeping up with politics is important, down from 58% in 1966. Only 14% say they frequently discuss politics, down from 30%. Acquisition of political knowledge from traditional news sources is way down, and relatively few young people are using the new media to replace newspapers and network TV news as sources of political information (Bennett 1997; Sax et al 1998, 1999; Natl. Assoc. Secr. State 1999; Rahn 1999).

There are signs that these trends have continued unabated throughout the 1990s. For example, a Pew Research Center poll of voters in their late teens and twenties found that fewer than half were thinking "a great deal" about the 2000 election, versus two thirds at the comparable point in 1992. Four in ten said it does not matter who is elected president, twice as high a percentage as in 1992 (Mason & Nelson 2000).

It would be wrong to infer that young adults are retreating into pure privatism. Today's entering freshmen are reporting significantly increased levels of volunteering in their senior year of high school, a trend that seems to be carrying over to their early college years (Sax et al 1998, 1999). But only a fraction of today's young volunteers believe that they will continue this practice through their college years and into the paid workforce. And even if they did, there is no evidence that it would lead to wider political engagement. On the contrary, most young people characterize their volunteering as an alternative to official politics, which they see as corrupt, ineffective, and unrelated to their deeper ideals. They have confidence in personalized acts with consequences they can see for themselves; they have no confidence in collective acts, especially those undertaken through public institutions whose operations they regard as remote, opaque, and virtually impossible to control (Hart-Teeter 1997, Natl. Assoc. Secr. State 1999, Medill News Serv. 2000). In a recent survey conducted for the Kennedy School's Institute of Politics, 60% of students polled said they were actively involved in community service, versus only 7% who had been involved, or planned to get involved, in a political campaign (Mason & Nelson 2000).

To be sure, the interpretation of these trends is contested. Libertarians may well regard the retreat from the public sphere as healthy. Many determined partisans of civil society welcome volunteering as a substitute for government programs. But from political stances ranging from traditional liberal to compassionate conservative, and from a range of normative/theoretical perspectives as well, the attenuation of political knowledge and engagement is worrisome. Even if one rejects the philosophical proposition that active citizenship is essential to human flourishing, or the civic-republican view that public-spirited action is intrinsically superior to self-regarding pursuits, it is hard to avoid the hypothesis that at some point the withdrawal from public engagement endangers the healthy functioning of democratic polities. At the very least, if the tendency to withdraw is asymmetrically distributed among population groups, then the outputs of the political system are likely to become increasingly unbalanced. And if those who withdraw the most are those who have the least, the system will become even less responsive to their needs. Political engagement is not a sufficient condition for political effectiveness, but it is certainly necessary.

The principal purpose of this review, however, is not to expand on these classic themes of normative democratic theory. It is rather to explore the recent scholarship that has renewed interest in the impact of citizen knowledge on the exercise of citizenship and in formal civic education as a component of political socialization. I focus especially on three major academic contributions (Delli Carpini & Keeter

1996, Nie et al 1996, Niemi & Junn 1998), as well as evaluations of specific programs and strategies of civic education. I examine what this literature shows about the power and the limits of political knowledge; about civic education as a way of acquiring politically relevant knowledge, skills, and attitudes; and about the most effective ways of organizing and conducting this education.

THE LEVEL AND DISTRIBUTION OF CIVIC KNOWLEDGE

The most comprehensive recent study of US citizens' attainment of civic knowledge is *What Americans Know about Politics and Why It Matters* (Delli Carpini & Keeter 1996). The authors assemble more than 50 years of survey data drawn principally from the Roper Center, American National Election Studies (ANES), and their own surveys—in sum, more than 2000 factual knowledge questions concerning political institutions and processes, leaders and parties, and public policies. The public's knowledge of institutions and processes is significantly higher than its knowledge of people and policies, perhaps because the former are more stable over time and require less regular monitoring. Along no dimension does the median score of correct answers top 50% (Delli Carpini & Keeter 1996:68). In the aggregate, political knowledge describes a normal distribution around the median, with a large "middle class" and smaller knowledge-rich and knowledge-poor groups (Delli Carpini & Keeter 1996:153–54).

As the authors recognize, these raw statistics do not permit normative conclusions about the their adequacy or inadequacy for informed citizenship; the glass of knowledge can be regarded as half empty or half full (Delli Carpini & Keeter 1996:133). They suggest plausibly that "all things being equal, the more informed people are, the better able they are to perform as citizens" (Delli Carpini & Keeter 1996:219). But how much knowledge is enough? What are reasonable expectations for the majority of citizens?

The National Assessment of Educational Progress (NAEP) Civics Assessment helps clarify this issue. Each NAEP subject-matter assessment is divided into four achievement levels: "below basic," which means little or no demonstrated knowledge of the subject; "basic," which indicates partial mastery; "proficient," the level representing a standard of adequate knowledge; and "advanced." These achievement levels represent absolute thresholds, not percentiles. In principle, every student could reach the level of proficiency.

Within this framework, the recently released results of the 1998 Civics Assessment are not encouraging. Thirty five percent of high school seniors tested below basic, indicating near-total civic ignorance. Another 39% were only at the basic level, less than the working knowledge that citizens are deemed to need (Lutkus et al 1999:23). To be sure, the specification of the four achievement levels can be challenged as not grounded in evidence linking them to specific acts and skills of citizens. Still, the 1998 NAEP Civics Assessment is the fruit of nearly a decade of intellectual spade work and nationwide consensus building (Cent. Civic Educ. 1994, Natl. Assess. Gov. Board 1996). It represents the most plausible judgment we have concerning the knowledge required for civic competence. Moreover, about one quarter of all students meet or exceed the standard of proficiency and, as Delli Carpini & Keeter (1996:219) rightly remark, "the top quartile . . . is not composed of superhumans."

There is no evidence that overall levels of civic knowledge have altered much over time. A recent study comparing the responses to questions that were asked in both the 1988 and 1998 NAEP Civics Assessment found that percentages of correct answers had hardly changed over the decade between the two assessments. Fourth graders did slightly better, eighth graders did slightly worse, and twelfth graders showed no significant change (Weiss et al 2000). More broadly, Delli Carpini & Keeter (1996) find that overall levels of political knowledge have hardly budged over the past half century. This is a remarkable finding in light of the fact that political knowledge is highly correlated with levels of formal education. For example, an analysis of 1992 ANES data shows that on a seven-point scale of political knowledge, almost 40% of all college graduates were in the top two categories, compared with less than 10% of high school graduates. Conversely, 25% of high school graduates were in the bottom two categories, compared with only 4% for college graduates (Popkin & Dimock 1999:128). Yet the percentage of Americans with college degrees is vastly higher than it was 50 years ago. How can it be that political knowledge has failed to increase?

Closer analysis shows that for many (though not all) categories of political knowledge, today's high school graduates are roughly equivalent to the high school dropouts of the late 1940s, and today's college graduates are roughly equivalent to the high school graduates of that earlier epoch (Delli Carpini & Keeter 1996: 197–98). Over the past half century, decreased civic achievement at each level of formal education has been counterbalanced by the changed distribution of students among the levels. One interpretation of these data is that school-based civic instruction is less effective than it once was; another is that formative processes outside of school have weakened (Delli Carpini & Keeter 1996:110, 199).

Delli Carpini & Keeter (1996) also document large differences in political knowledge between subgroups. Not only education but also race, gender, and self-reported levels of political interest are strongly correlated with all dimensions of political knowledge. The regular use of newspapers and radio is correlated with several dimensions, as is the regular discussion of politics with friends and family. Controlling for other measures of media use, watching TV news is negatively correlated with all types of political information (Delli Carpini & Keeter 1996:144–45). As Delli Carpini & Keeter interpret their multidimensional data, most citizens are political generalists rather than specialists; "people who know a lot about one aspect of national politics also know a lot about others" (Delli Carpini & Keeter 1996:151). [This conclusion has been challenged on methodological grounds (Krosnick 1998:188).]

THE SIGNIFICANCE OF CIVIC KNOWLEDGE

Intuitively, it may seem implausible that civic knowledge is central to democratic citizenship. Why does it matter whether young people can identify their senators or name the branches of government? Surprisingly, recent research suggests important links between basic civic information and civic attributes we have reason to care about. The major findings may be summarized as follows:

1. Civic knowledge helps citizens understand their interests as individuals and as members of groups. The more knowledge we have, the better we can understand the impact of public policies on our interests, and the more effectively we can promote our interests in the political process. Delli Carpini & Keeter (1996:238–64) offer a wealth of evidence that political knowledge fosters citizens' "enlightened self-interest"—the ability to connect personal/group interests with specific public issues and to connect those issues with candidates who are more likely to share their views and promote their interests. Political knowledge, then, is a key determinant of instrumental rationality (see also Zaller 1992).
2. Civic knowledge increases the consistency of views across issues and across time. Utilizing panel surveys from ANES, Delli Carpini & Keeter (1996:232–34) find a strong linear relation between political knowledge and the stability of political attitudes. They also find that more knowledgeable voters display much higher levels of ideological consistency (as measured along a unidimensional liberal-conservative axis) between issues than do the less well informed (Delli Carpini & Keeter 1996:236–38).
3. Unless citizens possess a basic level of civic knowledge—especially concerning political institutions and processes—it is difficult for them to understand political events or to integrate new information into an existing framework. (By analogy, imagine trying to make sense of the flow of events in a sports competition for which one does not know the rules of the game.) Popkin & Dimock (1999) distinguish between "personal character" and "political character" (conduct judged in the specific context of political roles, institutions, issues, and responsibilities). They show that low-information citizens are much more likely to judge officials according to their perception of noncontextual personal character. "Without knowledge of how government works, it is difficult to assess the true priorities of a legislator in the American system.... Voters less able to use these political cues will rely on estimates of personal character instead of attitudes about parties and issues.... [R]eliance on personal character as a proxy for political character is related to uncertainty, and uncertainty is related to a lack of understanding about politics" (Popkin & Dimock 1999:125, 127).

4. General civic knowledge can alter our views on specific public issues. For example, the more knowledge citizens have about civic matters, the less likely they are to fear new immigrants and their impact on our country (Popkin & Dimock 2000).
5. The more knowledge citizens have of civic affairs, the less likely they are to experience a generalized mistrust of, or alienation from, public life. Ignorance is the father of fear, and knowledge is the mother of trust. One possible explanation for this relationship is the phenomenon of attribution error. More knowledgeable citizens tend to judge the behavior of public officials as they judge their own—in the context of circumstances and incentives, with due regard for innocent oversights and errors as well as sheer chance. By contrast, less knowledgeable citizens are more likely to view public officials' blunders as signs of bad character (Popkin & Dimock 1999:127–29). Moreover, low-information citizens encountering vigorous political debate with its inevitable charges and countercharges are more likely to conclude that there are no white knights and adopt a "plague on both your houses" stance. For those who understand politics, debate can be as clear as a tennis match; for those who do not, it more closely resembles a food fight (Popkin & Dimock 1999:134).
6. Civic knowledge promotes support for democratic values. For example, the more knowledge citizens have of political principles and institutions, the more likely they are to support core democratic principles, starting with tolerance. Delli Carpini & Keeter (1996:221–24) explore three possible explanations for this linkage and find substantial support for the "social learning" hypothesis that specific knowledge of civil rights and civil liberties increases tolerance for unpopular minorities. Nie et al (1996:71–72) find direct paths from education to both knowledge of democratic principles and tolerance.
7. Civic knowledge promotes political participation. All other things being equal, the more knowledge citizens have, the more likely they are to participate in public matters. For example, the regression analysis of Delli Carpini & Keeter (1996:226–27) shows a highly significant independent effect of political knowledge on the probability of voting. Popkin & Dimock (1996) agree: "The results of our model highlight the strong and independent influence of contextual knowledge on turnout. Controlling for correlated measures of sophistication, knowledge about politics stands out as a consistently strong factor shaping the decision to vote." Their multivariate analysis leads them to conclude, "The dominant feature of nonvoting in America is lack of knowledge about government; not distrust of government, lack of interest in politics, lack of media exposure to politics, or feelings of inefficacy" (Popkin & Dimock 1999:142).

Political knowledge affects participation, not only quantitatively but also qualitatively. Holding socioeconomic status constant, Delli Carpini & Keeter (1996:

259–60) find that more knowledgeable voters are more likely to vote on the basis of national economic conditions than personal economic circumstances. In this important issue area (which may well be generalizable to others), political knowledge makes it more likely that citizens will ask not only "How am I doing?" but also "How are we doing?"

Like other analysts, Nie et al (1996) emphasize the link between absolute years of formal education and the development of prodemocratic principles and attitudes, such as tolerance for unpopular groups. But they also try to demonstrate, with some success, that because key dimensions of political engagement are an inherently scarce "positional good," engagement is linked to relative rather than absolute levels of educational attainment. Education serves as a sorting mechanism; whatever educational attainment may be median at a given time, individuals significantly above the median will tend to be members of social networks that can connect their views more effectively to political leaders and institutions. This matters because the capacity of the political system to pay attention to inputs is inherently limited. (For example, as information technology permits more and more citizens to communicate with their representatives, the impact of each message will decrease.) If the people as a whole are the principal, their elected and appointed agents will always need mechanisms for allocating their time and attention, and position in social networks is one such mechanism. As education levels rise across society, the positive effects of absolute increases in knowledge and understanding are counterbalanced by the negative effects of increased competition for scarce positions of social centrality. These countervailing forces explain the apparent paradox that rising education levels over the past generation have not yielded commensurate—indeed, any—gain in political engagement (Nie et al 1996:Ch. 7, 8). This finding is of particular importance today. Since a generation ago, education has become a more significant sorting mechanism while others have weakened.

This is not an argument against the overall civic rationale for public investment in education. In addition to promoting support for democratic principles, education increases verbal cognitive proficiency and related intellectual skills, which improves an individual's ability to understand political events and act in an instrumentally rational manner (Nie et al 1996:194). Still, if the argument of Nie et al (1996) is correct, some of the traditional expectations for civic education cannot be fulfilled. In particular, there is no reason to predict (or hope) that rising levels of education will translate into increased civic engagement or diminished inequalities of engagement among different groups (Nie et al 1996:190–92).

But is their case compelling? Delli Carpini (1997) notes that although Nie et al conceptualize voting as an attribute of both civic enlightenment (affected by absolute education) and civic engagement (affected by relative education), their analysis of voting trends over the past two decades finds that voting is a function of relative rather than absolute education levels. This result is troubling because voting does not "clearly fit the logic of social network centrality, which assumes limited access to those in power and politics as a zero-sum game" (Delli Carpini

1997:972). Although the content of my vote may cancel out yours, my act of voting does not compete with yours; my ballot does not make it more difficult for your ballot to be counted nor for its effects to be felt by those in power. More broadly, the vision of politics as zero-sum overlooks its more collective, consensual dimensions. And within the competitive arena, there is reason to wonder whether leaders and institutions are always overloaded with voices struggling against one another for scarce attention (Delli Carpini 1997:972). Especially at the local level, public officials complain that citizens often fail to participate in key events—public hearings, town hall meetings, candidate forums, and others—that give them opportunities to hear and be heard directly. If citizens in fact underutilize rather than overwhelm public institutions, then there may be hope that education, properly conducted, could increase political engagement—especially if (as we have seen) the number of years of formal education is a poor predictor of absolute levels of political knowledge and if there is reason to question the measure of political knowledge that Nie et al (1996) employ (for a discussion of these doubts, see Torney-Purta 1997:451, 453). Indeed, a recent study (NH Nie, DS Hillygus, unpublished data) demonstrates a remarkable correlation between verbal ability and political participation among college graduates of the same age, which suggests that the distinction between years of formal education and actual educational attainment is of considerable civic significance.

THE ROLE OF CIVIC EDUCATION IN POLITICAL SOCIALIZATION

In the end, we do not have a compelling reason to doubt that civic knowledge affects civic competence, character, and conduct. But what affects knowledge?

Classroom-Based Civic Education

In a generally admiring review, Torney-Purta (1997:447, 453, 456) notes that the books by both Delli Carpini & Keeter (1996) and Nie et al (1996) suffer from a "missing link." Neither really unpacks the mechanism by which formal education affects political knowledge and understanding. For three decades, the scholarly consensus has been that formal, classroom-based civic education has no significant effect on civic knowledge (Langton & Jennings 1968). Recent findings challenge this consensus and begin to provide insight into both the overall effects of civic education on political knowledge and the specific pedagogical strategies that effectively foster political understanding.

Some of these findings reflect evaluations of individual civic education programs. For example, several research studies conclude that "We the People... The Citizen and the Constitution," a nationwide program of civic education administered by the Center for Civic Education, is especially effective in improving the civic knowledge of elementary, middle, and high school students relative to students in comparison groups. In addition, participants develop a stronger attachment to democratic attitudes and principles and an enhanced sense of political interest and effectiveness (Leming 1996).

Other research is broader based. In a study of political socialization of young people in four communities, Conover & Searing (2000) explore the role of high schools in fostering civic understanding and practice. They focus on four elements of the school experience: the sense of the school as a community; the students' level of civic engagement in school and extracurricular activities; the level of political discussion in school; and the formal academic curriculum. They find that all four elements significantly affect young people's civic consciousness and practice, albeit in different ways. Remarkably, the informal civic education that occurs in such non-civics courses as English literature may be more effective than civic education as currently taught (Conover & Searing 2000:111–13). Conover & Searing (2000:108) regard the overall result of these formative processes as inadequate, even disturbing: "While most students identify themselves as citizens, their grasp of what it means to act as citizens is rudimentary and dominated by a focus on rights, thus creating a privately oriented, passive understanding."

In a major study based on data from the 1988 NAEP Civics Assessment, Niemi & Junn (1998) find significant effects from the amount and recency of civic course work, the variety of topics studied, and the frequency with which current events were discussed in class. These course effects are independent of such background variables as gender, ethnicity, and home environment, as well as interest in government and academic aspirations. Classroom effects are smaller for Hispanics than for Caucasian students, and smaller for African-Americans than for Hispanics. (Class discussion is the only classroom variable that yields significant results for African-Americans.) Differences between girls and boys are small, although boys are more strongly affected by their classroom experiences and home background. Although formal classes are significant for all dimensions of civic knowledge, not surprisingly they have somewhat smaller effects in areas, such as citizens' rights, in which non-school sources are likely to provide relevant information. (Young people's familiarity with the details of criminal suspects' Miranda rights is stunningly high.) Niemi & Junn (1998) find far less significant effects of classroom experience on key dimensions of trust in government, and the overall explanatory power of their multivariate model for trust is small (adjusted $R^2 = 0.05$ compared with 0.31 for civic knowledge). Finally, they conduct a parallel analysis, based on NAEP data, of the civic knowledge effects of American history courses, with results they rightly describe as "strikingly parallel" to civics courses (Niemi & Junn 1998:142).

Niemi & Junn (1998) offer an explanation for the divergence of their findings from those of scholars a generation ago, best exemplified by the work of Langton & Jennings (1968). First, Langton & Jennings did find some effects of civic education on knowledge, which they downplayed in an analysis heavily weighted toward attitudinal items. Second, Langton & Jennings did not take into account the grade in which students took civic education classes; Niemi & Junn show that twelfth-grade classes have more impact than those taken earlier. Third, Langton & Jennings did not include discussion of current events in their analysis, and there are good reasons to believe that these discussions are more likely to provide nonduplicative civic knowledge than are other classroom activities. Finally, the Langton & Jennings measure of political knowledge was technically flawed, including items unlikely to be emphasized in standard civics courses as well as common-knowledge items for which the range of variation between students (hence the effects of formal courses) were bound to be limited.

To be sure, questions of methodology and interpretation can be raised about the analysis of Niemi & Junn (1998). For example, Torney-Purta (1999:258–59) points out that their model leaves about 70% of the variance in knowledge among students unexplained, and 95% of the variance in trust; that nonclassroom variables such as college attendance plans are more significant; and that possible correlations between individual predictors are left unexplored. In a reanalysis of the Niemi & Junn data set, Greene (2000) challenges their specification and interpretation of two of the three classroom variables. He finds that the only significant timing effect is whether a student was enrolled in a civics course at the time the NAEP test was taken, which raises doubts about whether the civic knowledge gained will persist over time. He suggests that, as implemented, the "range of topics" variable may itself test for civic knowledge, rendering it endogenous to what it seeks to predict. He finds the third classroom variable—class discussion—impervious to methodological objection, however (Greene 2000:696–97). In the end, neither he nor Torney-Purta rejects the broad thrust of Niemi & Junn's challenge to conventional wisdom on the effects of civic education.

Niemi & Junn (1998) emphasize the real-world, not merely statistical, significance of their findings. By itself, civic course work raises overall political knowledge by 4%; when combined with the study of a wide range of topics and regular discussion of current events in the classroom, this figure rises to 11%. [Niemi & Junn's conclusions are bolstered by NH Nie & DS Hillygus (unpublished chapter), who show that the content of the college curriculum—in particular, the number of social science courses taken—has a statistically significant impact on political participation among college graduates.] Niemi & Junn's findings suggest the need for improved instruction in such academic areas as basic democratic theory and knowledge of non-American political structures and in such practical skills as the ability to decode simple charts and tables. Finally, although fully recognizing the pedagogical and political obstacles, they recommend a shift away from a national-level emphasis toward local issues, and away from anodine institutional and historical rote work toward discussions of contemporary political controversies (Niemi & Junn 1998:Ch. 7). [The growing evidence against the efficacy of rote and memorization-based civic pedagogy is stressed by Torney-Purta (1997:53–54, 1999:258).] The alternative, although less likely to create community pressures on teachers and school administrators, is more likely to increase cynicism and alienation by painting a picture of conflict-free politics at odds with everyday experience (Frazer 2000:124–25).

Service Learning

Thus far, the analysis has focused on traditional classroom-based civic education. But over the past decade, the most rapid growth has occurred in a different form of civic education, called service learning. The National Center for Educational Statistics defines service learning as "curriculum-based community service that integrates classroom instruction with community service activities." The service must be organized in relation to an academic course or curriculum, must have clear learning objectives, and must address real community needs over a sustained period of time; the learning occurs through both community-based practice and regularly scheduled critical reflection on that practice (Skinner & Chapman 1999:3). As of academic year 1998–1999, 32% of all public schools had incorporated service learning into their curricula, including a remarkable 46% of high schools (versus just 9% of high schools in 1984). Encouraging students to participate more actively in their communities and encouraging them to improve their knowledge of those communities are the most frequently cited goals for service learning (Skinner & Chapman 1999:17). Parallel developments have occurred at the college level, as such organizations as Campus Compact and such scholar-activists as Benjamin Barber, Richard Battistoni, and Harry Boyte have worked to revive the long-neglected civic mission of higher education (see Battistoni 2000). The Corporation for National and Community Service has supported roughly 100 service learning programs each year since 1995 (Gray et al 1999).

As might be expected, this dramatic expansion has sparked a flurry of program evaluations of widely varying quality. Billig (2000), in the most recent survey of the evaluation literature, remarks, "Research in the field of service-learning has not caught up with the passion that educators feel for it." She goes on to catalogue the deficiencies of this research. Few of the studies used control groups; few tracked whether short-term impacts were sustained over time; many relied on self reports; few specified theoretical models or tested hypotheses clearly linked to these models (Billig 2000:660). A wealth of evidence supports the proposition that students participating in community-based service activities are far more likely than others to participate and lead later in life (Youniss et al 1997), but relatively few studies are structured to distinguish the effects of youth participation from the effects of preexisting civic behaviors and attitudes. The ones that do tend to find that service learning has an additional independent effect (Giles & Eyler 1998:67). One of the methodologically strongest studies finds that even if key background variables are held constant, patterns of service activity during college have a substantial effect on the amount of service performed five years later. Indeed, after controlling for the amount of service performed during college, the amount performed during high school has an independent effect on the activities of young adults a decade later (Astin et al 1999:195–96). A massive study of more than 22,000 college students by Astin et al (2000) finds that the positive effects of service by individual students are amplified by discussion of service experiences among students. Service learning is especially effective in generating procivic attitudes and activities because, compared with community service, service learning is "much more likely to generate such student-to-student discussions" (Astin et al 2000:2).

Overall, the literature reveals mixed but encouraging results. One study of 369 middle and high schools students from 10 different service-learning programs found negligible effects on the development of a sense of civic responsibility and engagement (Blyth et al 1997:47–49). A rigorous evaluation of 17 middle and high schools with programs supported by the Corporation for National and Community Service found that a year after the end of the initial experience, most of the positive impacts had disappeared (Melchior et al 1999:15). A RAND evaluation of college-level service learning programs noted the strong influence of self selection on student outcomes and found that the increased civic responsibility manifested by participants was restricted to service activities and did not extend to wider political involvement (Gray et al 1999:55). On the other hand, a study of 3450 undergraduates conducted by Astin & Sax (1998:255–56) found a significant impact of service on 12 civic responsibility measures, including the disposition to participate in politics and bring about social change—results that were confirmed and strengthened by students' responses to seven items pretested when students entered cllege as freshmen. A comprehensive review of service learning evaluations from kindergarten through twelfth-grade students found "inconsistency in virtually all outcome areas." On balance, however, the evidence suggests that students who participate in high-quality programs that integrate community service with systematic reflection on their experience are more likely to develop an understanding of political context and governing institutions, to think of themselves as politically efficacious, and to become civically and politically engaged (Billig 2000:661, Melchior et al 1999:11). One study finds that as high school students' voice in the selection and definition of community engagement increases, so does the effectiveness of service learning in improving students' sense of efficacy, political participation, and tolerance for "out-groups" (W Morgan, M Streb, unpublished paper; see also Hildreth 2000). Another study, in which college students were randomly assigned to either service learning or traditional sections of introductory government courses, found significant effects of service learning in the self-reported importance students attached to "working toward equal opportunity for all U.S. citizens," "volunteering my time helping people in need," and "finding a career that provides the opportunity to be helpful to others or useful to society" (Markus et al 1993:413). Studies conducted by the Walt Whitman Center employing an innovative measure of civic skills found that college-level service learning significantly increases civic and political leadership skills (Barber et al 1997, n.d.). A comprehensive evaluation of California programs for kindergarten through twelfth-grade suggests "cautious optimism" about service learning and emphasizes the importance of program quality (Weiler et al 1999:ix). This emphasis is consistent with other studies (Wade & Saxe 1996:343).

A range of evidence suggests that service learning is significantly more effective in the late high school years than earlier (see especially Melchior et al 1999:11, 17), a result that parallels findings for traditional classroom-based civic education.

Niemi & Junn (1998:144, 156) suggest the plausible interpretation that by twelfth grade, students have a better general understanding of politics and society as a matrix into which new information and concepts can be integrated and that they are "close enough to formal adulthood that civics lessons have a degree of meaningfulness lacking in earlier years." A recent survey of college-level service learning reinforces this finding: Courses for this age group can be effective, but only when the service is clearly related to the academic course work and lasts long enough for students to develop a sense of ownership of the project, and when substantial classroom time is devoted to reflection on community-based experiences (Hepburn et al 2000).

Public Versus Private Schools as Civic Educators

Education for citizenship was one of the major motives for the creation of US public schools, which began a century and a half ago. Ever since, public schools have been regarded as the most appropriate sites for forming citizens, whereas private schools have been regarded with suspicion as sources of separatism, elitism, and antidemocratic principles. Recent research casts doubt on this long-held view, however. Niemi & Junn (1998:84) find only small and inconsistent differences in civic instruction across public and private schools. A study by Campbell (2000) finds that even after correcting for differences of family background among students, private schools were at least as effective as public schools in conveying democratic civic knowledge and principles, with Catholic schools leading the pack. After correcting for a wide range of demographic variables, Wolf et al (2000:21) report, "College students who received most of their prior education in private [elementary and secondary] schools exhibit higher levels of political tolerance than comparable publicly educated students.... [I]t seems unlikely that the private school tolerance advantage is merely a selection effect." If future research confirms these results, we will be compelled to rethink some long-held beliefs about sources of civic unity in the United States, and to reflect anew on the relationship between the ethos of individual schools and the civic purposes of education.

CONCLUSION

Niemi & Junn (1998:157) speak of the "near-abandonment" of work on political socialization, and Conover & Searing (2000:91) characterize political socialization as a field in a "state of disarray" (see also Campbell 2000:5). Niemi & Junn trace this situation to the failure of research during the 1960s and 1970s to establish significant links between what young children think about politics and their views as mature adults (see also Owen 2000). But they point out that what is true of children may not apply to older youth (Niemi & Junn 1998:157–58). Journalists and pundits have long observed what they take to be distinct political generations. Now, research-based evidence is emerging that political stances shaped during the mid-to-late teen years persist throughout adult life (Nie et al 1996:138). Summarizing the results of a three-wave survey of American twelfth graders begun in 1965 and continued through two decades, Jennings (1996:249) states, "What each cohort brings into political maturity has a good deal of continuity and provides a certain degree of stability in terms of what that cohort is likely to draw on as it moves through the rest of the life cycle." Putnam (2000) offers evidence depicting a "long civic generation," born roughly between 1910 and 1940, whose young-adult patterns of exceptional civic interest and engagement have persisted up to the present. By contrast, generations born after 1940 have demonstrated persistent patterns of deepening disengagement (Putnam 2000:Ch. 14). If so, it becomes a matter of more than academic interest to understand better the forces that shape the political outlook of young adults.

It is imperative to renew the long-interrupted tradition of research into political socialization. But this time around, unlike a generation ago, researchers cannot afford to overlook the impact of formal civic education and related school-based experiences on the formation of the civic outlook of young adults.

LITERATURE CITED

Astin AW, Sax LJ. 1998. How undergraduates are affected by service participation. *J. Coll. Stud. Dev.* 39:251–63

Astin AW, Sax LJ, Avalos J. 1999. Long-term effects of volunteerism during the undergraduate years. *Rev. High. Educ.* 22:187–202

Astin AW, Vogelgesang LJ, Ikeda EK, Yee JA. 2000. *Executive Summary: How Service Learning Affects Students.* Los Angeles: High. Educ. Res. Inst., Univ. Calif.

Barber BR, Higgins RR, Smith JK, Ballou J, Dedrick J. n.d. *Civic Skills and Service Learning: Research in Democratic Theory and Practice.* New Brunswick, NJ: Walt Whitman Cent. Cult. Polit. Democr., Rutgers Univ.

Barber BR, Smith JK, Ballou J, Higgins RR, Dedrick J, Downing K. 1997. *Measuring Citizenship Project Final Report.* New Brunswick, NJ: Walt Whitman Cent. Cult. Polit. Democr., Rutgers Univ.

Battistoni RM. 2000. Service learning in political science: an introduction. *Polit. Sci. Polit.* 33:615–16

Bennett SE. 1997. Why young Americans hate politics, and what we should do about it. *Polit. Sci. Polit.* 30:47–53

Billig SH. 2000. Research on K-12 school-based service-learning: the evidence builds. *Phi Delta Kappan* 81:658–64

Blyth DA, Saito R, Beikas T. 1997. A quantitative study of the impact of service-larning programs. See Waterman 1997, pp. 39–56

Campbell DE. 2000. *Making Democratic Education Work: Schools, Social Capital, and Civic Education.* Presented at Conf. Charter Sch., Vouchers, Public Educ., Progr. Educ. Policy Governance, Harvard Univ.

Cent. Civic Educ. 1994. *National Standards for Civics and Government.* Calabasas, CA: Cent. Civic Educ.

Conover PJ, Searing DD. 2000. A political socialization perspective. See McDonnell et al 2000, pp. 91–124

Delli Carpini MX. 1997. Review of NH Nie, J Junn, and K Stehlik-Barry, *Education and Democratic Citizenship in America. Am. Polit. Sci. Rev.* 91:971–72

Delli Carpini MX, Keeter S. 1996. *What Americans Know About Politics and Why It Matters.* New Haven, CT: Yale Univ. Press. 397 pp.

Elkin SK, Soltan KE, eds. 1999. *Citizen*

Competence and Democratic Institutions. University Park: Penn. State Univ. Press. 424 pp.

Frazer E. 2000. Review of RG Niemi and J Junn, *Civic Education*. *Gov. Oppos.* 35:122–25

Galston WA. 1991. *Liberal Purposes: Goods, Virtues, and Diversity in the Liberal State*. Cambridge, UK: Cambridge Univ. Press. 343 pp.

Giles Jr DE, Eyler J. 1998. A service learning research agenda for the next five years. In *Academic Service-Learning: A Pedagogy of Action and Reflection*, ed. RA Rhoads, JPF Howard, pp. 65–72. San Francisco: Jossey-Bass

Gray MJ, Ondaatje EH, Fricker R, Geschwind S, Goldman CA, et al. 1999. *Combining Service and Learning in Higher Education: Evaluation of the Learn and Service America, Higher Education Program*. Santa Monica, CA: RAND Educ.

Greene JP. 2000. Review of RG Niemi and J Junn, *Civic Education*. *Soc. Sci. Q.* 81:696–97

Hart-Teeter 1997. *Public Service and Government Effectiveness: The View of Young Americans*. Presented to Partnership for Trust in Government, Washington, DC

Hepburn MA, Niemi RG, Chapman C. 2000. Service learning in college political science: queries and commentary. *Polit. Sci. Polit.* 33:617–22

Hildreth RW. 2000. Theorizing citizenship and evaluating public achievement. *Polit. Sci. Polit.* 33:627–32

Hoffman T. 1998. Rationality reconceived: the mass electorate and democratic theory. *Crit. Rev.* 12:459–80

Krosnick JA. 1998. Review of MX Delli Carpini and S Keeter, *What Americans Know about Politics and Why It Matters*. *Ann. Am. Acad. Polit. Soc. Sci.* 559:188–89

Langton K, Jennings MK. 1968. Political socialization and the high school civics curriculum in the United States. *Am. Polit. Sci. Rev.* 62:862–67

Leming RS. 1996. *We the People ... The Citizen and the Constitution. ERIC Digest EDO-SO-96-4*. Bloomington, IN: ERIC Digest

Lutkus AD, Weiss AR, Campbell JR, Mazzeo J, Lazer S, et al. 1999. *NAEP 1999: Civics Report Card for the Nation, NCES 2000–457*. Washington, DC: Natl. Cent. Educ. Stat.

March JG, Olsen JP. 2000. Democracy and schooling: an institutional perspective. See McDonnell et al 2000, pp. 148–73

Markus GB, Howard JPF, King DC. 1993. Integrating community service and classroom instruction enhances learning: results from an experiment. *Educ. Eval. Policy Anal.* 15:410–19

Mason JL, Nelson M. 2000. Selling students on the elections of 2000. *Chron. High. Educ.* Sept. 22, p. B16

McDonnell LM, Timpane PM, Benjamin R, eds. 2000. *Rediscovering the Democratic Purposes of Education*. Lawrence: Univ. Press Kansas. 280 pp.

Medill News Serv. 2000. *National Survey, yvote 2000*. Washington, DC: Youth Vote 2000

Melchior A, Frees J, LaCava L, Kingsley C, Nahas J, et al. 1999. *Summary Report: National Evaluation of Learn and Serve America*. Waltham, MA: Cent. Hum. Resourc., Brandeis Univ.

Natl. Assess. Gov. Board. 1996. *Civics Framework for the 1998 National Assessment of Educational Progress. NAEP Civics Consensus Project*. Washington, DC: Natl. Assess. Gov. Board

Natl. Assoc. Secr. State. 1999. *New Millenium Project—Phase I: A Nationwide Study of 15–24 Year Old Youth*. Washington, DC: Natl. Assoc. Secr. State

Nie NH, Junn J, Stehlik-Barry K. 1996. *Education and Democratic Citizenship in America*. Chicago: Univ. Chicago Press. 268 pp.

Niemi RG, Junn J. 1998. *Civic Education: What Makes Students Learn*. New Haven, CT: Yale Univ. Press. 204 pp.

Owen D. 2000. Service learning and political socialization. *Polit. Sci. Polit.* 33:639–40

Popkin SL, Dimock MA. 1999. Political

knowledge and citizen competence. See Elkin & Soltan 1999, pp. 117–46

Popkin SL, Dimock MA. 2000. Knowledge, trust, and international reasoning. In *Elements of Reason: Cognition, Choice, and the Bounds of Rationality*, ed. A Lupia, M McCubbins, SL Popkin, pp. 214–38. New York: Cambridge Univ. Press. 330 pp.

Putnam RD. 2000. *Bowling Alone: The Collapse and Revival of American Community*. New York: Simon & Schuster. 541 pp.

Rahn WM. 1999. *Americans' engagement with and commitment to the political system: a generational portrait*. Presented at Congressional Briefing, Washington, DC

Sax LJ, Astin AW, Korn WS, Mahoney KM. 1998. *The American Freshman: National Norms for Fall 1998*. Los Angeles, CA: High. Educ. Res. Inst., UCLA Grad. Sch. Educ. Inform. Stud.

Sax LJ, Astin AW, Korn WS, Mahoney KM. 1999. *The American Freshman: National Norms for Fall 1999*. Los Angeles, CA: High. Educ. Res. Inst., UCLA Grad. Sch. Educ. Inform. Stud.

Shapiro RY. 1998. Public opinion, elites, and democracy. *Crit. Rev.* 12:501–28

Skinner R, Chapman C. 1999. *Service-Learning and Community Service in K-12 Public Schools, NCES 1999–043*. Washington, DC: Natl. Cent. Educ. Stat.

Somin I. 1998. Voter ignorance and democracy. *Crit. Rev.* 12:413–58

Torney-Purta JV. 1997. Review essay: links and missing links between education, political knowledge, and citizenship. *Am. J. Educ.* 105:446–57

Torney-Purta JV. 1999. Review of RG Niemi and J Junn, *Civic Education*. *Am. J. Educ.* 107:256–60

Wade RC, Saxe DW. 1996. Community service-learning in the social studies: historical roots, empirical evidence, critical issues. *Theory Res. Soc. Educ.* 24:331–59

Waterman AS, ed. 1997. *Service-Learning: Applications from the Research*. Mahwah, NJ: Erlbaum. 184 pp.

Weiler D, Lagoy A, Crane E, Rovner A. 1998. *An Evaluation of K-12 Service-Learning in California: Phase II Final Report. RPP Int.* Sacramento, CA: CalServe Off., Calif. Dep. Educ.

Weiss AR, Lutkus AD, Grigg WS, Niemi RG. 2000. *The Next Generation of Citizens: NAEP Trends in Civics—1988 and 1998. NCES 2000–494*. Washington, DC: Natl. Cent. Educ. Stat.

Wolf PJ, Greene JP, Kleitz B, Thalhammer K. 2000. *Private schooling and political tolerance: evidence from college students in Texas*. Presented at Conf. Chart. Sch., Vouchers, Public Educ., Progr. Educ. Policy Gov., Harvard Univ.

Youniss J, McLellan JA, Yates M. 1997. What we know about engendering civic identity. *Am. Behav. Sci.* 5:620–31

Zaller JR. 1992. *The Nature and Origins of Mass Opinion*. Cambridge, UK: Cambridge Univ. Press. 367 pp.

Annu. Rev. Polit. Sci. 2001. 4:235–69

THEORIES OF DELEGATION

J. Bendor[1], A. Glazer[2], and T. Hammond[3]
[1]*Graduate School of Business, Stanford University, Stanford, California 94305-5015, e-mail: bendor_jonathan@gsb.stanford.edu*
[2]*Department of Economics, University of California, Irvine, California 92697; e-mail: aglazer@uci.edu*
[3]*Department of Political Science, Michigan State University, East Lansing, Michigan 48824; e-mail: thammond@msu.edu*

Key Words information, ally principle, hierarchy, credible commitment, noncooperative game theory

■ **Abstract** We survey modern models of delegation that assume a boss and a subordinate pursue their own goals. Among the major themes covered are the following: the conditions under which the boss will prefer to delegate versus those in which she will prefer to retain authority; how a boss can induce a subordinate to truthfully reveal information; when rational principals will use the ally principle (i.e. delegate to agents with similar goals); delegation in repeated interactions; and how delegation can overcome commitment problems. These themes are relevant to a wide variety of institutions, affecting intralegislative organization, executive-legislative relations, and central banks.

INTRODUCTION

Even God delegates, having told the Israelites after they left Egypt: "Behold, I send an Angel before thee, to keep thee in the way, and to bring thee into the place which I have prepared. Beware of him, and obey his voice, provoke him not; for he will not pardon your transgressions: for my name is in him" (*Exodus* 23:20–21). Delegation, then, may be done even by an all-powerful and an all-knowing entity. Yet the limitations of leaders have long been recognized as a reason for delegation. When Moses complained, "O my Lord, I am not eloquent, neither heretofore, nor since thou hast spoken unto thy servant: but I am slow of speech, and of a slow tongue" (*Exodus* 4:100), God's solution was that Aaron should be Moses's spokesman.

Recent years have seen heightened academic interest in the problem of delegation, as well as the development of sophisticated and insightful theories and models that explain various aspects of delegation. This essay surveys theories that have appeared since the last review of this topic (Aranson et al 1982). It also provides a framework for thinking about delegation, both for legislative-executive and for intra-institutional relations.

Many of the most influential works surveyed here use formal models, particularly noncooperative game theory, as a central method of analysis. That too is a focus of our survey. We hope our survey will help the reader organize the literature and serve as an informal tutorial for political scientists who study delegation but who are not steeped in game theory. And although we consider mostly formal models of delegation, we do consider informal theories. Several of the best-known works are purely verbal, although most are inspired by rational choice theory. Further, the substantive differences between informal theories and formal models are rather small. Hence we treat them together, separating by content rather than form. In discussing results, we emphasize the ally principle. When will rational principals delegate to agents whose preferences are like theirs? That rational bosses prefer agents who are allies is part of an ancient wisdom about political hierarchies; the principle was old before Rome. But as we shall see, in some empirically significant situations, smart superiors will not use it.

The paper is organized as follows. The next section introduces the game-theoretic framework. It analyzes how problematic a delegation situation is by examining the decision makers' choices and payoffs (i.e. the normal form of delegation games). The third section analyzes the extensive form of delegation games (who does what when). The framework is then used to categorize the literature and serves as a springboard for examining it. The fourth section covers delegation in repeated interactions. Theories of delegation as credible commitment are discussed in the fifth section.

A TYPOLOGY OF DELEGATION SITUATIONS

Some elementary noncooperative game theory is useful in constructing a typology of delegation situations. Our typology is deliberately spare; it is constructed out of the minimal set of elements required for an analysis of delegation. Hence, we consider only two decision makers: a boss (or principal) and a subordinate (or agent). Any fewer than two makes delegation impossible; any more is excess baggage. Similarly, each player has two options: The boss can either delegate or not; the subordinate can either work or shirk. (There are many different interpretations of the work-or-shirk choice: specialize or remain uninformed, etc. Essentially, the subordinate can either act in a way that is good for the boss or not do so; see assumption 1, below.) So there are four possible outcomes, and we assume that each person has a strict preference ordering over the four. (Indifference—a knife-edge condition—is an unnecessary complication.) Figure 1 shows the normal form of the game. We assume that each player knows what game he or she is playing (i.e. the feasible actions and payoffs), each knows the other knows, and so on.

Different preference orderings identify different kinds of delegation situations, thus creating a typology. We do not discuss all possible orderings; there are too

		Agent: Work	Agent: Shirk
Boss	Delegate	a, w	b, x
	Control	c, y	d, z

Assumption 1: Agent's effort is valuable for the boss: $a > b$ and $c > d$.

Assumption 2: Both players prefer (delegate, work) to (control, shirk): $a > d$ and $w > z$.

Figure 1 A typology of delegation situations.

many,[1] and some are irrelevant for theories of delegation. Instead, we examine a subset that represents a spectrum of delegation situations, ranging from difficult (delegation is valuable but problematic) to easy. We create this subset by restricting the preference orderings in two ways.

Assumption 1 (A1): The subordinate's effort is valuable for the boss.

We assume that, all else being equal, the boss prefers that her subordinate work rather than shirk. Thus, she is better off, for a given move of hers, if the agent works: $a > b$ and $c > d$. For example, in many of the delegation models analyzed here, the subordinate "works" by acquiring information about a random variable that is unobserved by the boss. Since the boss is typically assumed to be risk averse, she prefers an informed, autonomous subordinate to an ignorant, autonomous one; similarly, she does not prefer an ignorant, controlled agent to an informed, controlled one.

A parallel assumption that we do not make is that the subordinate must prefer having discretion rather than being controlled (holding fixed his move). We are agnostic about this property; there probably are important situations in which it does not hold, e.g. because the subordinate wants the boss held responsible for the outcome, which is more likely if she controlled the reins.

Assumption 2 (A2): Deals between the boss and the subordinate are possible because both prefer the outcome of (delegate, work) to that of (control, shirk).

[1]Each player has 4! preference orderings, creating $(24)^2 = 576$ possible games.

This assumption is at the heart of the normative theory of institutions embraced, explicitly or implicitly, by most of the delegation literature. Although the two actors might conflict over effort—the boss wants the subordinate to work hard whereas the latter might prefer to take it easy—complete conflict does not prevail because there is at least one thing that both can agree on: (control, shirk) is collectively—i.e. Pareto—suboptimal. Thus, there is room for a compromise that would prevent the Pareto-inferior outcome. Simultaneously, A2 creates the possibility that the institution might be caught in a bad equilibrium.[2]

Given A1 and A2, the boss has 5 possible orderings; the subordinate, 12. This leaves a much more manageable subset of 60 games, which fall into 5 major categories. We start with the one in which the delegation "problem" is least pressing and move on to tougher cases.[3]

Category 1: The game has a unique, Pareto-optimal Nash equilibrium.

Consider a busy boss facing many important issues. The task at hand, however, is relatively minor. Given her crowded agenda, the opportunity costs of giving detailed instructions to her subordinate are high. So she has a dominant strategy of delegating: $a > c$ and $b > d$. If the subordinate works hard, great; if not, so be it. Now suppose that the subordinate has no dominant strategy. Instead, his best move depends on what the boss does. If she exerts control, then he optimizes by shirking; if she delegates, then he should exert himself. Since the boss will inevitably delegate, the predicted outcome is (delegate, work).[4] This is benign; one can easily show (given A1 and A2 and the particular assumptions defining this case) that this outcome is efficient. This must often occur in organizations, but students of delegation have mostly ignored it, and for good reason—it is totally unproblematic Being busy, the boss delegates and takes the consequences. The outcome is both stable and efficient. End of story.

Alternatively, suppose that the agent has a dominant strategy of working hard, possibly because the project at hand is personally significant, whereas the boss has a dominant strategy of exerting control. Hence the outcome is (control, work). Here delegation does not occur, but the important point is that this situation is just as unproblematic as the first example. This is an efficient Nash equilibrium, just as (delegate, work) was. And because it is supported by two dominant strategies, it is very stable.

---

[2]Given games with exclusively Pareto-optimal outcomes, one could not address the issue of stable yet inefficient outcomes.

[3]One should note, however, that some delegation games are easy only because another game—e.g. of personnel selection—has been played, and played well. For example, if the subordinate has a dominant strategy of working hard, that says something about the organization's personnel policies.

[4]Because the boss has a strictly dominant strategy, this is the predicted outcome regardless of the timing of moves. So a normal form analysis suffices here. Timing matters in other delegation games, as we will see shortly.

Category 2: There are multiple equilibria, but they are Pareto-ranked.

In all category 1 games, at least one player has a dominant strategy. So these games are strategically simple (given the informational assumptions); for example, the sequence of moves does not matter.

But now consider what happens if the boss's best move depends on what her subordinate does and vice versa. For example, suppose that both have "deal-making" preferences, i.e. if the boss is willing to delegate then the subordinate will work hard and vice versa, but if the boss wants to exert control then the subordinate wants to shirk, and if the subordinate shirks then the boss wants to run things. Then there are two Nash equilibria, which by A2 are Pareto-ranked. (The better equilibrium is not only Pareto-superior to the bad one, it must also be Pareto-optimal.) Thus, delegation here amounts to a coordination problem, handled easily by ordinary communication or signaling via moves. Suppose, for instance, the boss moves first. If she delegates, the subordinate will work hard; if she controls, he will shirk. Anticipating this and preferring the former to the latter, she delegates.

Category 3: There are multiple equilibria that are not Pareto-ranked.

Out of the 60 games we are studying, only 2 have multiple equilibria that involve conflict. The boss prefers to play one equilibrium and the subordinate the other. In one of these, the boss prefers an outcome in which good work is done to one in which it is not ($c > b$), but if the subordinate shirks, then the boss would rather not be closely associated with the unsatisfactory outcome ($b > d$). The subordinate, however, prefers the laid-back equilibrium of (delegate, shirk) to the intense one of (control, work). Hence, conflict over equilibria.

Here the sequence of moves is important, as it is in Chicken and other games with multiple, conflict-laden equilibria. There is a first-mover advantage. If the boss moves first and takes charge by issuing detailed orders, then the subordinate is compelled to work hard. But if the latter can preempt the former by a passive form of worker sabotage, then the boss will distance herself from the issue by delegating. Hence, delegation in this situation is genuinely problematic.

Category 4: The game has a unique, Pareto-inferior Nash equilibrium.

This class of situations is studied intensively in the literature. In almost all of these games, the deficient equilibrium is (control, shirk). Whenever this holds, the culprit is a "bad" dominant strategy of either or both players. For example, suppose in an intralegislative game (e.g. Gilligan & Krehbiel 1987, Diermeier 1995) the floor has a dominant strategy of asserting control over the bill in the last stage. The committee lacks a dominant strategy; instead, it has the conventional "deal-making" conditional best responses (specialize if the floor delegates, otherwise remain uninformed). Given that the floor will control the process no matter what the committee does, the latter will not specialize. The result is a collectively bad equilibrium—the very stuff of much of the delegation literature.

All category 4 games resemble the Prisoner's Dilemma in that collective optimality and individual rationality diverge: Whatever is Pareto-optimal is not Nash.

The sequence of moves is irrelevant in these games, since one or both sides have dominant strategies.

Category 5: No pure Nash equilibria exist.

In almost all of the literature's models of delegation, the games have pure Nash equilibria. However, category 5 shows that this is not inevitable. Suppose that the boss and the subordinate are struggling over the allocation of credit (should the project go well) or blame (if things go badly). The boss can distance herself from the process and avoid some blame if she delegates. But if things work out well, then she would like to claim credit by putting her stamp on the process, i.e. by controlling the subordinate. For the subordinate, however, working hard is not worthwhile if the boss steals the credit, so in this event the subordinate shirks—whence the boss prefers to delegate. But then the credit is there for the taking, so the subordinate wants to work hard. And around they go. Thus, the only Nash equilibrium involves both sides randomizing. Although we have not shown that this outcome is Pareto-inferior, most real-world decision makers would probably consider it a delegation problem. If this pattern persists, then the institution is floundering, unable to settle on a stable arrangement.

WHO DOES WHAT WHEN? THE EXTENSIVE FORMS OF DELEGATION GAMES

Although a delegation game's normal form helps us to categorize delegation problems by their degree of difficulty, it does not represent the timing of moves—who does what when—which helps us understand a game's dynamics. Nor does the normal form tell us who knows what pieces of information when different actions are taken. In contrast, the extensive form shows both who knows what when and who does what when. This feature of delegation games is obviously important when there are informational asymmetries between principal and agent, and scholars in this field tend to regard such asymmetries as central to delegation. Hence, game-theoretic models increasingly use the extensive form. Indeed, one can use this type of analysis to categorize much of the literature by describing assumptions about who does what when and who knows what when. First, we briefly describe two major types of models in these terms; later we add details.

In one class of models, the boss has a choice of either delegating to an agent or not. If she delegates, then the agent makes the choice; if she does not delegate, then she makes the choice herself. Typically what drives these models is that the agent can become more informed than the boss. If the agent is delegated authority, then he has an opportunity to acquire information before he chooses an action, whereas the boss must decide in the face of uncertainty (Figure 2*a*).

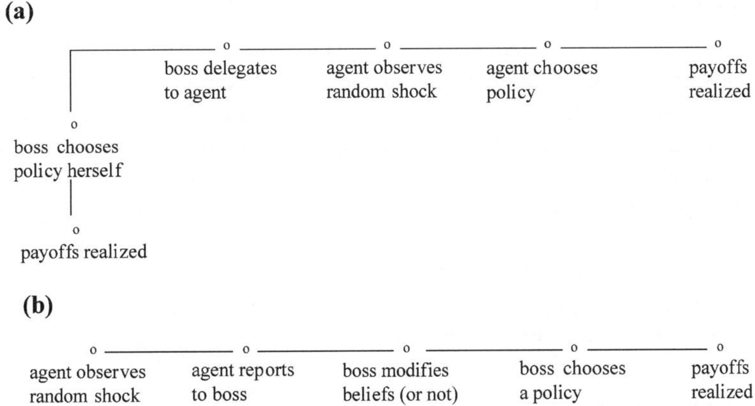

Figure 2 Two types of delegations games: (*a*) Delegation-of-authority game, (*b*) signaling game.

The other main class of models typically reverses the sequence; the agent moves before the boss (for an exception, see Gilligan & Krehbiel 1987). Again the agent may choose to become informed. If he acquires private information, he then reports to the boss. The report may either describe (all or some of) the information gathered by the agent, or it may recommend an action.[5] The boss then decodes the message or the information embedded in the recommended action, and given this information, she chooses an action (Figure 2*b*). These are called signaling models. Models in which the agent can send a message to the boss for free are called cheap-talk models (as in "talk is cheap").

These two types of models represent substantively different kinds of delegation. In the first type, the boss explicitly decides whether or not to give a subordinate the authority to take actions, without requiring that the agent first report back to the boss (e.g. about the information that the agent has gleaned). Presumably time matters here. In the second type, the agent has been given different kinds of authority: either to gather certain kinds of information or to make proposals to the boss.[6] Here the agent lacks the authority to take actions; only the boss has that right.

We now take a closer look at these two major types of models.

---

[5]In some variants, there is little formal difference between reporting information and recommending an action, since the boss may be able to infer the agent's private information from his recommended action. In other variants, however, there is a substantive difference between reporting information and recommending an option; the latter may include constraints on the boss's choice set (e.g. she can choose only between the recommended alternative and the status quo; see Gilligan & Krehbiel 1987). We return to this distinction shortly.

[6]These models typically presume—sensibly—that agents authorized to make proposals are also authorized to gather information.

Delegating the Authority to Act

In the first type of model, the boss moves first by deciding whether or not to delegate the authority to pick policy to one of several possible agents. If the boss controls the issue, then she picks a policy, a random shock is realized, and the outcome and the payoffs are generated by the combination of the selected policy and the shock. If she chooses to delegate, she picks an agent from the feasible set and authorizes him to select a policy. After being picked, the agent learns the value of the disturbance and then chooses a policy. Consequently, he makes a more informed choice than the boss would.[7]

Probably no paper in the literature has used only this stripped-down model, but even this simple formulation illustrates what is generally regarded as the major trade-off facing the boss: Is the gain produced by delegating the decision to a more informed party worth the loss produced by having someone with different preferences make the choice? So before we turn to the inevitably more complicated variants, let us see what this unadorned model can tell us about the fundamental trade-off between expertise and control.

Consider a boss and a set of agents. Each has single-peaked preferences over outcomes in a unidimensional space. Preferences are quadratic, so agent i's utility equals $-(x - x_i)^2$, where x_i is i's ideal point. Quadratic preferences imply that agents are risk-averse; for every feasible outcome, they prefer that outcome (for sure) to any lottery whose mean is that outcome.

Actors choose policies rather than outcomes directly. Policies are perturbed by random shocks (ϵ) to yield outcomes. The conventional assumption is that outcomes equal policies plus the random error: $X = P + \epsilon$. Most of the models assume, for the sake of tractability, that the shock is distributed uniformly (for more general formulations, see Bawn 1995 and Bendor et al 2000). It is convenient to assume that ϵ is centered around zero.

The basic model uses a substantively important (though common) assumption about the relation between extreme values of shocks and policies: If someone chooses a policy after he observes the disturbance, then he can always find a policy that, when added to the shock, yields his ideal point in the outcome space. Thus, the agent is a perfect shock absorber.

All of the above is common knowledge. Given that the agent moves last—there is no ex post auditing in the basic model—it does not matter whether the boss observes the random disturbance or not. It is natural, however, to assume that asymmetric information prevails; the agent knows both the shock and his chosen policy, but the boss observes only the outcome.

Unlike signaling models, which typically have multiple equilibria (see footnote 10 below), this kind of delegation game has a unique equilibrium (setting aside knife-edge possibilities, e.g. two agents who are equidistant from the boss's ideal point). The equilibrium has the following properties:

[7]In many of the models, the agent learns the exact value of the shock; for exceptions, see Bawn (1995) and Bendor et al (2000).

1. The ally principle holds here. If the boss delegates, then she picks the agent whose ideal point is the closest to hers. The reason is simple. Since the agent knows the value of the shock before he chooses a policy and can exploit compensatory flexibility to the hilt, he picks his induced ideal point in policy space, i.e. the one that yields his ideal point in outcome space. The boss naturally wants this outcome to be as close as possible to her own ideal.
2. If the boss does not delegate, then she chooses the policy that maximizes her expected utility, given her knowledge of the shock's distribution and the policy "technology" (outcomes = policy + noise). If ϵ is distributed uniformly around zero, then the expected outcome is her ideal point.
3. The boss has a pair of certainty equivalents in outcome space: She is indifferent between getting such an outcome (for sure) and choosing not to delegate. Hence, these two certainty equivalents define a delegation cutoff rule for the boss: If there is an agent who is ideologically closer to the boss than this threshold, then she delegates; if not, she does not. Everything inside this boundary we call the boss's delegation set.
4. The equilibrium outcome is efficient if and only if the boss delegates. Delegation must be efficient because the agent who has been granted authority gets his ideal outcome, which he strictly prefers to anything else. If the boss controls the policy, then the outcome must be inefficient because everyone is risk-averse and so would prefer that the boss get her ideal outcome for sure (instead of in expectation). This could be achieved if the boss delegated to an agent who promised to implement that outcome and delivered on the promise. That arrangement is technically feasible, but such promises are not credible and so the boss disregards them. Thus, the inability of agents to credibly commit, plus risk aversion, leads to inefficient outcomes (when no agent is in the delegation set).

Comparative Statics of the Basic Model

Let us now see how variations in several of the model's key parameters affect the equilibrium. [All these results are proven for the general N-dimensional setting in Bendor et al (2000).]

Increased Conflict Suppose conflict increases; the ideal points of all agents move away from the boss's. What happens? There are three possibilities. First, if previously no agent was in the delegation set, then nothing changes; the boss continues to exert control. Second, if previously the best agent had been in the delegation set but the shift makes him unacceptable, then the boss switches from delegating to controlling, and the expected outcome shifts toward the boss's ideal point. Third, if the change in preferences is small enough and the delegation set had not been empty, then the boss would still want to delegate. In this case, the expected outcome moves away from her ideal point.

As the best agent's ideal point moves further from the boss's, the latter's expected utility falls or stays constant. Thus, the intuition that the boss is better off with more like-minded agents is upheld in this setting.

Increased Policy Uncertainty Suppose there is an increase in policy uncertainty. Because the boss is risk-averse, this change reduces her expected utility of not delegating. But the value of delegating is unchanged, since the best agent will still be picked and he will attain his ideal outcome. Hence, the boss becomes less choosy; her delegation cutoff moves away from her ideal point. Thus, the value of delegating, relative to not delegating, increases in policy uncertainty.

Increased Aversion to Risk Now hold policy uncertainty constant and make the players more averse to risk. Then the expected utility of controlling the issue falls for the boss, since the (unchanged) uncertainty hurts more. Thus, the boss's tolerance for delegating increases; the delegation set grows larger.

Variants of the Basic Model

We now consider some important variants of the basic delegation-of-action model.

Personnel Uncertainty Suppose the boss can make an educated guess about subordinates' ideal points but does not know them precisely. Consequently, she does not know precisely what a subordinate would do if given authority over the issue. It is fairly straightforward to show that this reduces the value of delegating, if the boss is risk-averse (e.g. Bawn 1995, Bendor et al 2000).

Multiple Principals For most democratic political systems, grants of delegation are made by multiple principals. Even in unicameral parliamentary systems, as in England, grants of delegation are made by the entire Parliament, perhaps by some subset of the Parliament (such as the majority party), and perhaps even by some subset of the majority party (such as the Cabinet), but only rarely by the Prime Minister alone. Similarly, grants of delegation in the United States are made not by some unicameral "Congress" but by the House and Senate, each relying extensively on its own set of committees, and by a President with a veto (which of course may be overridden).

We know of only a few models of delegation in which multiple principals with vetoes play a major role (Calvert et al 1989, Volden 2000; we take up Volden's contribution below). Calvert et al model the appointment of the agent—a bureau chief—as a Nash bargaining game,[8] set in an N-dimensional policy space, between

[8]The appendix discusses the choice of modeling appointments by cooperative game theory (the Nash bargaining solution) or noncooperative theory (the Rubinstein alternating offer game). Today's intellectual fashions favor the latter.

Congress (a unitary actor) and the President. They show (1989:595) that if the ideal point of either principal changes, then the ideal point of the selected bureau chief will move in the same direction. (However, this result presumes that the set of feasible agents corresponds to the entire set of feasible policies.) Their model of appointments also suggests an interesting reconceptualization of agency discretion. That an agency sets policy without direct interference from politicians "does not constitute agency discretion. Rather, agency discretion occurs when the agency succeeds in choosing a policy in line with agency goals, when these goals *differ* from what the executive and legislature expected *at the appointment stage*" (Calvert et al 1989:605, original emphasis).

Hammond & Knott (1996) explicitly discuss problems that multiple principals (e.g. House, Senate, and President) might have in controlling an agency. Their model also has implications for a theory of delegation. In particular, if principals with conflicting objectives have difficulty agreeing on a policy for the agency to adopt (e.g. because of coordination costs), they could at least agree on limiting the agency's discretion so that it cannot adopt a policy that is worse for any principal than the initial status quo. However, because these coordination costs are not explicitly represented, the model can only characterize the upper bound of acceptable discretion. An explicit model of coordination costs might well show that the agency's actual range of discretion would fall inside this upper limit.

Multiple Agents Although as a modeling strategy it makes sense to start off with dyadic theories—a boss delegating authority to just one agent—few interesting cases in the real world of politics involve only a single agent. Most of the time, authority is delegated to a substantial group of people. This leads to two types of interesting and important problems.

One type pertains to shirking and free-riding. When just one person is given authority, that individual can certainly shirk. But when authority is delegated to several people, they can not only shirk but also free-ride on each other's efforts. This can greatly reduce the total effort supplied by the subordinates. There is a substantial literature in economics on the design of incentive systems for motivating groups of individuals [see Miller (1992) for an excellent and accessible introduction to this literature]. However, a problem can plague these systems: The boss has her own kind of shirking, which entails manipulating the subordinates' incentive system for her own benefit (Miller 1992:Ch. 7, Miller & Hammond 1994). Thus, even if problems of the subordinates shirking and free-riding can be overcome, properly motivating the boss herself remains a serious problem. Miller (1992:Ch. 20–21) argues that this problem can be ameliorated if the boss can credibly commit to leaving the subordinates' incentive system alone. The topic of credible commitment is of major importance in the study of delegation, and we return to it below.

The second class of problems arises from a common mode of delegation, wherein a large problem is broken down into several pieces that are doled out to different subunits of the organization (as in, e.g., Shepsle 1979). Each subunit makes what it perceives as the best choice on its own part of the problem, and then the subunits' decisions are aggregated by higher officials into an overall choice. Because each piece of the problem is assigned to just one subunit, shirking and free-riding may be avoided. However, this aggregation process has other undesirable properties. For example, Hammond & Miller (1985), reinterpreting a social choice theorem by Sen (1970), show that this delegation-and-aggregation can produce a Pareto-suboptimal outcome. This possibility seems to be virtually inherent in this kind of multi-person, multi-jurisdiction delegation.

Ex Ante Controls on Agents McCubbins et al (1987, 1989; see Bawn 1995 for a formalization) argue that ex ante controls on agencies sometimes work better than ex post controls. The latter, they assert, can be hindered because a bureau's policy deviation may benefit some of the many principals (e.g. the President, senators, representatives) who passed the legislation in question, and those coalition leaders will block efforts to bring the agency back into line. [This is the explanation for bureaucratic autonomy in Hammond & Knott (1996).] Thus, any one principal's threat to impose sanctions ex post would not work, and the agency's policy choice would stand. McCubbins et al suggest that Congress and the President respond to this weakness of ex post controls by imposing administrative procedures as ex ante controls. [Bawn (1997) and Huber & Shipan (1999) present formal models of delegation in which ex ante and ex post controls can be either complements or substitutes.]

McCubbins et al (1987, 1989) argue that two classes of administrative procedures are important. One class mandates information revelation by the agency. For example, the agency may be required to follow notice-and-comment procedures and provide reasons for its regulatory proposals. These procedures ensure that the agency's political environment mirrors that faced by the principals; the principals' constituents can then challenge a new agency policy before it is adopted. The other class of procedures "stacks the deck" on behalf of the principals' constituents by requiring the agency to heed the demands of particular actors and rely on particular kinds of decision-making standards. For example, statutes can specify that only certain actors have legal standing in agency proceedings, and burden-of-proof requirements can protect the economic and legal positions of favored constituents. These procedures together serve as an autopilot for the agency; as the principals' political environment changes in a particular way, so will the agency's. Overall, McCubbins et al suggest, these procedural tools allow principals to get what they want from the agency, even in a changing environment, without having to pass new legislation (which might be impossible, given disagreements among the multiple principals).

Arnold (1987), Robinson (1989), Horn & Shepsle (1989), Hill & Brazier (1991), and Mashaw (1994) argue that such procedures will be less effective than McCubbins et al suggest. For example, information revelation cannot overcome the impact of multiple principals. Even if an agency must announce its intended decision before final adoption, objections by some principals may be negated by support from others. In such cases, the agency could proceed with its decision without fear of ex post retribution. Moreover, information-revelation procedures can cut two ways: Sometimes the publicity forced by the procedures can help the old coalition maintain its policies, but they might impede these efforts by alerting a broader public. And even if the agency's new political environment mirrors that of the original coalition, enmeshing agency decision making in a complex web of procedures might hinder agency adaptation to this new environment. Most generally, the critics argue that precisely because administrative procedures have political consequences, conflicting principals may find it hard to agree on procedures that will induce the agency to select a particular policy. The less the principals can agree on specific policies in the first place, the less they will be able to agree on administrative procedures that would later lead to a specific policy.

Choosing Institutions Fiorina (1986; see also 1982) presumed that delegation will occur; the question he studied was, to what kind of institution will authority be delegated? Substantively, he focused on the debate in the late 1800s over controlling the railroads' pricing practices. Proponents of regulation had to choose how regulatory authority would be delegated. Should it be delegated by creating a regulatory commission with broad powers? Or should Congress pass a law creating legal standards for railroad behavior, which plaintiffs could then use in court? Congress chose the former course when it created the Interstate Commerce Commission. Why was this choice made?

To answer this question, Fiorina sketched a simple decision-theoretic model. Each legislator compared the expected utility of agency (commission) enforcement of railroad regulation with that of court enforcement, preferring the enforcement method with the higher expected utility. More specifically, each legislator had beliefs, represented by a subjective probability distribution, about the level of regulation that either institution would actually enforce. Regarding preferences, Fiorina assumed that legislators had single-peaked and concave utility functions and so were risk-averse. However, he dropped the conventional assumption of symmetric utility functions. (Indeed, he gave reasons for believing that in this domain they would usually be asymmetric.) The preferences of the median legislator would then determine the legislature's choice. (Presidents played little role in Fiorina's model.)

Because Fiorina was interested in the congressional concerns in the late 1800s about the long-run behavior of the agencies and the courts, he sketched how time would affect the thinking of legislators. In his model, however, time periods entered only via the probability distributions of anticipated effects; short-run versus long-run concerns were not explicitly analyzed. Nonetheless, his model—one of the first formal models of delegation in political science—was an important precursor of the many models that followed over the next 15 years.

Delegation, Information, and Risk Aversion

Almost all of the preceding models (and most of the signaling models as well) assume a risk-averse boss. They either presume or explicitly argue that delegation and risk aversion are tightly connected. The idea is straightforward; delegating to an informed agent can reduce risk, which must benefit a risk-averse principal.

The connection certainly exists, but the literature overstates it. More precisely, an uninformed principal can benefit from delegating to an informed agent even if the boss is risk-seeking or risk-neutral. A simple example will show how. To sharpen the point, we consider a case with nonspatial preferences, so that the principal can in a natural way be risk-neutral over all possible outcomes. Suppose that in an urban machine a (real) boss is thinking about accepting a bribe for a large public works contract. If he takes the bribe he gets $b > 0$; otherwise he gets nothing. However, there is a chance ($p > 0$) that a federal prosecutor will pay attention to the contract; if he does, then he will catch the boss, recover the bribe, and fine him an amount $c > 0$. So the expected amount of money from taking the bribe equals $(1 - p)b - pc$. Suppose this exceeds zero, and the boss is risk-neutral in money. Then he will take the bribe (and the consequences).

But now suppose that he has someone in the district attorney's office to whom he can delegate the matter, for a fee. As an insider, the agent will know for sure whether the DA is watching the public works contract. If the DA is monitoring it, then the agent turns down the bribe, on the boss's behalf. But if not, then the agent is authorized to go through with the deal. (We ignore the possibility that the agent might doublecross the boss.) The expected payoff to the boss is $(1 - p)b + p \cdot 0$, minus the agent's fee. Clearly, if the fee is less than pc, then the boss is better off delegating to the informed agent than he is making the choice by himself, ignorant of the prosecutor's actions.

What drives this example is that the optimal strategy is state-contingent: Accept the bribe if the law isn't looking; otherwise, don't. The optimality of state-contingent plans does not depend on risk aversion. Thus, the value of delegating to an informed agent can turn on the value of information alone; risk aversion is unnecessary.

It is true that the more risk-averse the boss is the more valuable the agent's information is, and the more the boss would be willing to pay him.[9] But this comparative static effect does not undermine the general point. Delegating to an informed agent is optimal for an uninformed principal, but this does not imply that the principal must be risk-averse. Hence we conclude that although uncertainty (or risk) may be central to delegation, risk aversion is not.

[9]In this simple example, we can even quantify the two different benefits from delegation. A risk-neutral boss will pay the agent up to pc, so this is the value of getting the optimal state-contingent plan. Now suppose the boss is risk-averse, so that he is willing to pay up to a fee of f, which exceeds pc. The difference, $f - pc$, is the amount attributable to risk aversion.

Signaling Models of Delegation

Signaling models tend to be complex, but much of their logic can be explained rather simply. The signaling model presented here is stripped down in order to convey key properties as clearly as possible.

Consider a legislature that is deciding how much money to spend on defense. There are three possible levels: low, medium, and high, denoted $\{L, M, H\}$. The issue is one-dimensional, so the floor median (FM) is effectively the boss. The legislature has delegated information-gathering authority to an agent, which may be a legislative committee or an executive agency. Here we consider the agent to be a committee (C). (This model could also be used to analyze delegation between a president and an agency.) The agent is authorized to find out the true level of foreign threat and to report this to the legislature. The foreign threat can also be low, medium, or high ($\{l, m, h\}$).

The FM prefers to match spending to threat level, and it has single-peaked preferences. Thus, if we use $F_{J,k}$ to denote the payoff to the floor, given a spending level of J and a threat of k, we assume that (1) $F_{L,l} > F_{M,l} > F_{H,l}$, (2) $F_{L,m} < F_{M,m} > F_{H,m}$, and (3) $F_{L,h} < F_{M,h} < F_{H,h}$.

The game unfolds as follows. First the agent learns the level of threat and sends a message to the boss. Although the boss can require that the agent submit a report, she cannot enforce either truth-telling or precision. Thus, the agent may misreport his private information, e.g. report that the threat is high when it is medium, or he may send a true but imprecise message, e.g. that the threat is not low (when it is in fact medium). If the boss believes that the agent's message contains useful information, she will modify her beliefs about the threat. (For simplicity, assume that initially she believed that each state could occur with probability one third.)

Whether and how she modifies her beliefs is at the heart of the matter, and so we must analyze this step in detail. Because this is a game-theoretic analysis, revision of beliefs must satisfy several rationality-and-equilibrium requirements. First, her beliefs must be realized in equilibrium; she cannot be systematically fooled by the agent's report. (If the agent sends an imprecise message, then the boss may rationally guess wrong about the threat.) Thus, in equilibrium she must extract all that can be inferred from the message, by using her knowledge about the agent's preferences and the structure of the situation. (Suppose, for example, that the agent has a dominant strategy of saying that the threat is high, regardless of the real state of the world. Then in equilibrium the boss realizes that the report contains no information.) Furthermore, a fully rational boss must revise beliefs according to Bayes' law. Finally, since the agent knows that the boss is rational and hence can anticipate how she changes her beliefs (and ultimately uses them), it must be optimal for him to send the postulated report.

Let us see how all this works out by considering three possible types of agents, identified by how close their preferences are to the FM's.

1. Ally. An agent that is an ally of the FM shares preference properties 1–3. Note that this does not mean that the two have identical preferences.

For example, the FM may have no defense bases in her district (and so $F_{L,l} > F_{M,m} > F_{H,h}$), whereas the committee does (so $C_{M,m} > C_{L,l} > C_{H,h}$). What is crucial is that both want to match spending to threat level.

2. Moderate outlier. A moderate outlier prefers medium spending if the threat is medium or low, so $C_{M,l} > C_{L,l}$. Otherwise, he shares the rest of 1–3 with the FM.
3. Extreme outlier. This agent is a "high demander" for defense spending and prefers H over M and M over L, in all states of the world.

What will happen if the agent is an ally? Clearly, there is an equilibrium in which (*a*) he reports exactly what he observed, (*b*) the FM modifies her beliefs by taking the report at face value, and then (*c*) she picks the spending level that matches the reported threat. Given the boss's response, it is clearly optimal for the agent to tell the precise truth. He too wants the spending to match the threat, and (given the boss's strategy) he can ensure this by reporting accurately.[10] [This is called a (fully) separating equilibrium, because different messages correspond to different states of nature.]

What if the agent is a moderate outlier? The fully separating outcome cannot be sustained as an equilibrium with this type of agent. Here's why. Suppose that the boss responded, as postulated, by completely believing the agent's report. Anticipating this, the agent would never report a low threat; instead, he would say "medium" if the true threat was either medium or low. But then the boss would not rationally take a report of "medium threat" at face value; instead, she would infer from such a message only that the threat is not high. Thus, if the agent is a moderate outlier, then reports cannot be completely informative; hence, information can be lost if an agent who is an ally is replaced by a moderate outlier.

However, there is also a partially separating equilibrium, in which (*a*) the agent tells part of the truth, reporting high threats accurately and in the other situations saying that the threat is "not high," (*b*) the boss revises her beliefs in accord with the message,[11] and (*c*) chooses H if she believes that the threat is h and picks the budget that maximizes her expected utility if she believes that the threat is either medium or low, with equal likelihood. Each player's strategy is optimal given the other's, so this outcome is an equilibrium. Hence, with a moderately outlying agent, some information can be transmitted.

But it is pointless to delegate information gathering to an agent who is an extreme high demander for defense spending. Such a subordinate will never send

[10]Careful readers will note that we said that there is *an* equilibrium in which these good things happen. Signaling games always have multiple equilibria, and in particular always have "uninformative" equilibria in which the agent sends a message that contains no information and the boss ignores the report. Our exposition follows the literature's (underjustified) convention of focusing on the best—most informative—equilibria.

[11]If the report says "not high," then she believes that the chance of a low threat is one half, as is the chance of a medium threat, while the chance of a high threat is zero.

a meaningful message. Realizing this, the FM ignores the report. (If she did not disregard it fully, then the agent would exploit that gullibility by invariably reporting "high." But then the message would, in fact, contain no information, and a rational decision maker does not change beliefs in response to worthless signals.) Thus, the only outcomes involve "pooling equilibria," so-called because in equilibrium the report collapses (pools) all possible states of the world into one signal.

Thus, in this simple signaling model, a rational boss would always prefer allies over moderate outliers and moderate outliers over extreme ones. With allies she can (in some equilibria) obtain the whole truth. With moderate outliers she can (in some equilibria) get some of the facts. But from extreme outliers she learns nothing. (This is a common finding in signaling models. Roughly speaking, the closer the preferences of agent and principal, the more information communicated in the "best" equilibrium.)

Extensions of the Basic Model

This basic model (or more precisely, its already more complicated counterpart in the literature) has been extended in several directions. We consider these extensions serially, as one-at-a-time modifications of the basic model.

Selecting Agents Models of cheap talk suggest that principals do better with agents whose preferences are similar to their own. This naturally led scholars to think about models that endogenized the agent. In a first stage, the boss faced a set of feasible agents and selected one who would be delegated authority to gather information. If principals can select agents, then we get the following prediction about legislative organization: "Legislative committees will *not*, as a matter of practice, be composed predominantly of high demanders or preference outliers" (Krehbiel 1991:95; original emphasis). See, however, Krishna & Morgan (2001) for a modification of that conclusion.

Costly Information Gathering Another natural extension of the basic model is to assume that the agent must pay a cost $c \geq 0$ in order to acquire information. In the simplest versions of this extension, the boss knows whether the agent pays the cost (and so becomes informed) or remains ignorant. In the latter case, the agent is as uninformed as the boss, and so she knows that the report is worthless and therefore ignores it. Hence, in these simple models, the boss listens only to agents who have paid "the price of admission" by incurring the cost of becoming specialists.

One can also turn this point around. Suppose the agent is an extreme outlier. (This could happen in the executive branch if civil service laws protected career officials, even ones with unusual preferences.) Because such an agent will be ignored, it is pointless for him to pay the information-gathering cost. Only allies and moderate outliers will do so (provided, of course, that c is not too high).

Multiple (and Heterogeneous) Agents It is obvious from the defense spending example that having multiple agents will not help the boss if they have similar preferences which differ greatly from hers. A group of extreme outliers will all report that the threat is high, whatever they have observed. Thus, signaling models direct us to consider the wisdom of delegating to multiple agents with heterogeneous preferences (Gilligan & Krehbiel 1989a, Krishna & Morgan 2001). This comports with informal conventional wisdom—it is generally considered prudent to get information from diverse sources—but the signaling models explain in detail how and why this works.

Krishna & Morgan (2001) show that if the committee members' ideal points bracket the FM's (in the one-dimensional policy space), then the FM can devise a clever scheme for playing the two agents off against each other so that all information is revealed in equilibrium under the open rule. (This is desirable for the floor because the open rule gives the committee no proposal power; the floor can pass any bill it pleases.) Thus, they show that employing multiple diverse agents can get the boss just what she wants in a signaling game.

Proposing Options Thus far, the signaling models have concerned situations in which the agent was delegated only a limited authority, to gather information and to report the findings.[12] Proposal power was off-limits. However, as long as the boss's choice set remains unconstrained, adding proposal power to the list of what can be delegated changes little in the formal models. For instance, in several of the Gilligan-Krehbiel models, if the committee proposes a bill and the open rule obtains, this is equivalent to the committee sending the floor a report on its private information, since the bill allows the FM to infer what the committee's underlying private information must be.

However, once there are constraints on the FM's choice set, matters change. The literature has examined two types of constraints, both motivated by legislative procedures. In the closed rule, the boss must choose between the subordinate's proposal and the status quo. In the modified open rule, she gets proposals from two agents and can pick either.

Why would the FM voluntarily constrain her choice set? In an important series of papers, Gilligan & Krehbiel (1987, 1989a,b, 1990) give an intriguing answer: By limiting her options, she cedes influence over the final decision to her subordinate. This seems bizarre—why would a principal give up power to an agent?—but Gilligan & Krehbiel explain why it makes sense. Giving the subordinate a stake in the outcome gives him incentives to improve that outcome. Thus, committees that operate under restrictive rules have more incentive to uncover policy-relevant information. The ensuing reduction of the outcome's variance benefits everyone, since all actors are risk-averse. Formal analysis of homogeneous committees bears out these claims. [See Krishna & Morgan (2001) for some qualifications about heterogeneous committees.]

---

[12]Students of political institutions will recognize, however, that such authority is not trivial. For example, environmental analysts in the Corps of Engineers often had to lobby hard to obtain the authority to investigate suspected environmental impacts of proposed Army Corps projects (Taylor 1984).

From Signaling to Screening

Baron has criticized the assumption of signaling models that the principal will passively await the agent's message. "To the extent [the legislature] has instruments at its disposal to structure the work of the committee, the legislature gains by moving first rather than waiting for the committee to act" (2000:485). He constructs a model in which the floor precommits to providing resources to the committee; the level of resources depends on the nature of the report the agent will send to the legislature. Thus, the boss is committing to a schedule of rewards that depends on the agent's subsequent behavior. Because this incentive system screens the information the agent subsequently transmits, these are called screening models in game theory.

Although many of the results of signaling models stand up in Baron's screening model—for example, the more divergent the players' preferences, the less information transmitted by the agent—there are also many implications that differ (for a clear summary of the overlap and the differences, see Baron 2000:502). Perhaps most importantly, the parent body is strictly better off screening the agent's reports. This conclusion poses a problem for the signaling approach: Given this potential benefit, why would the parent body let the committee move first (Baron 2000:503)?

Screening by Requiring Lengthy Justifications

A natural way to segue from a signaling model into a screening one is to assume that the boss selectively imposes different costs on different signals (e.g. the higher the subordinate's budget request, the longer the required justification). Reconsider the defense spending example. Suppose that the boss is stuck with a moderate outlier for an agent, as defined above. She knows that if she responds appropriately then the agent will truthfully report a high threat, but his message will not distinguish between low and medium threats. What can she do? Under certain circumstances, she can selectively impose signaling costs on the subordinate so that it will be optimal for him to signal m if and only if the threat truly is medium. [The requirement is that the agent is more interested in getting medium appropriations when the threat really is medium than when the threat is low: $V(M,m) - V(L,m) > V(M,l) - V(L,l)$.] When this condition holds, the boss requires the agent to send a lengthy justification for a signal of m. (If the boss gets a message of l, without justification, she believes it.) Preparing such a report takes time, which is costly, and the boss's requirement is sufficiently laborious so as to drive a wedge between sending that message under the two possible states of the world: $V(M,m) - V(L,m) - c > 0$ but $V(M,l) - V(L,l) - c < 0$, where c is the time cost. Then it is optimal for the agent to write a lengthy document if and only if he observes a medium threat. Hence, by screening different types of agents (i.e. agents who observe low threats versus those who observe medium ones), the boss has ensured that delegating information gathering and communication to an agent can result in a fully informative equilibrium, despite the players' (moderate) difference in preferences.

Combining Signaling and the Delegation of Authority

Almost all the work on delegation is one of the above two types. But in a path-breaking work, Epstein & O'Halloran (1999) analyze the behavior of a boss who first receives a report from one agent and then decides whether to delegate authority to another agent—an empirically plausible sequence. (Epstein & O'Halloran's empirical setting is legislative-executive relations, so they interpret the boss as the FM, the reporting agent as a congressional committee, and the implementing agent as a bureau, but this setup applies to intra-executive structures as well. Imagine a boss, a staffer writing a report, and a "line" subordinate responsible for implementation.)

As usual, of course, realism comes at a price—analyzing the model is rather complicated—but Epstein & O'Halloran (1999) show that the presence of multiple agents with different responsibilities leads to interesting new conclusions. Their most interesting results, relative to what one can find using the simpler, dyadic principal-agent models, all have a coalitional flavor. They arise from how (for example) the presence of the committee affects the boss's stance toward the agency, or how the agency's presence affects the committee's posture toward the FM. Let us look at two of these results. First, the ally principle suggests that, in general, the further the agency is from the boss, the less likely the latter is to delegate. Epstein & O'Halloran derive a significant variant of this principle: The closer the committee is to the boss, the less likely the latter is to delegate authority to the agency[1999:68 (Figure 4.3)]. (Students of bureaucracy will recognize this as a source of conflict between staff and line.) Why? Recall that the value of delegating to an informed subordinate is that he can condition his action on information unavailable to the boss. But in the context of signaling games, the ally principle says that in general, the closer are principal and agent, the more information is communicated in the latter's report, in equilibrium. Hence, the boss becomes more informed via the signaling game, whence the value of delegating discretion to the agency falls (or remains constant).

Second, consider what can happen when the committee and the agency are ideologically close, as happens in some "iron triangles." The committee realizes that the more information it gives the floor, the less authority will be delegated to the agency. Although this is fine if the committee and floor are allies, it may be undesirable (for the committee) if the committee is closer to the agency than it is to the floor. Thus, Epstein & O'Halloran (1999:70) find that the presence of an ideologically compatible agency may induce a committee to transmit less information to its parent body. (This holds even if getting information is free; hence, the finding does not turn on a collective action problem.)

These findings reveal that specialized attention to legislative institutions, on the one hand, and executive structures, on the other, can blind us to important interactions across organizational boundaries: "comittee decision making, and legislative organization more generally, should not be studied in a vacuum; they exist in the shadow of delegation to the executive, and the committee's anticipations about the anticipated delegation regime will influence committee members' actions earlier on" (Epstein & O'Halloran 1999:71).

Volden (2000) raises two questions about the Epstein & O'Halloran model and crafts his own model in response. First, he points out that although their model is supposed to be a theory of the major institutions that make national policy, in fact it does not match the federal institutions very well. For example, the President cannot veto bills passed by Congress. (Hence, in some ways, the Epstein & O'Halloran model better represents a unicameral parliamentary system than one with separation of powers.) Second, Volden notes that although the model focuses on essentially new agencies, most major legislation involves bureaus that already exist and so enjoy some status quo level of discretion. [We would add that although their theory focuses on new agencies, with a clean delegation slate, most of their data (Appendix B) pertain to preexisting agencies that already have some discretion.]

Volden thus modifies the Epstein & O'Halloran model in several ways: The President has a veto, and agencies may have some preexisting level of discretion. (He also omits an integral part of their model, the legislative committee and its signaling to the floor.) These changes yield results that differ in some ways from those of Epstein & O'Halloran. For example, suppose the bureau chief's ideal point is in between the President's and the FM's. Under some conditions, the legislature will want to reduce the agency's discretion, but the President opposes this move. If he has a veto, he may be able to block the change; without a veto, he could not.[13] Moreover, limiting the agency's discretion is possible only when the bureau chief's preferences are extreme relative to those of both the legislature and the President, and even in this case, such limitations are more likely when the political leaders' preferences are similar. Volden (2000:12) remarks about this last result, "This finding of a more-unified government as the most-likely condition for the limitation of discretion stands in sharp contrast to earlier work that suggested that such limitations are more likely to arise under divided government."

DELEGATION IN REPEATED CONTEXTS

In all of the preceding models and many of the verbal theories, the delegation problem was fundamentally one-shot. (In many cases, the game unfolded in stages, but the boss made only one delegation decision.) This is a sensible starting point for formal analysis, but in the real world, many delegation issues recur. Hence, it was a salutary development when scholars started to construct models of repeated delegation (Diermeier 1995).

[13]Epstein & O'Halloran (1999:59) justify the omission of presidential vetoes by arguing that although inclusion of a veto would lead to higher equilibrium levels of discretion, the model's comparative statics would be unchanged (1999:59).

Before we turn to specific models, a few overall remarks about repeated-game theory and delegation are in order. In general, repeated interaction yields the possibility of stick-and-carrot strategies of conditional cooperation. For delegation, this means that both the boss and the subordinate are more able to deter each other from cheating. For example, if the subordinate cheats (say by exploiting the discretion given to him), then the boss might retaliate by seizing control in the next period. Or if the boss cheats (say by grabbing credit), then the subordinate could retaliate by shirking in the next period.

Further, under certain parametric conditions, these stick-and-carrot strategies are individually rational and so form Nash equilibria. (Moreover, they could involve only credible punishment threats and so be subgame perfect.) Thus, repetition may reduce the harsh separation between what is individually rational and what is collectively optimal. To see how, consider the toughest delegation circumstance identified by our typology, when in the one-shot game both parties have dominant strategies to cheat on the benign arrangment of (delegate, work). Thus the Pareto-inferior outcome of (control, shirk) is supported by the rock-solid foundation of dominant strategies. It is, in short, the notorious Prisoner's Dilemma.

However, if the game is repeated, then the strategic repertoire expands greatly, which may permit cooperation to be stabilized. Suppose, for instance, that each side uses the role-appropriate definition of Tit for Tat. The subordinate will work hard in his first encounter with his boss. Thereafter, in any period $t > 1$, he will work hard if and only if in $t - 1$ the boss delegated. Similarly, if the boss plays Tit for Tat, then she would begin the relationship by delegating. Subsequently, she would delegate in period $t > 1$ if and only if the subordinate had worked hard in $t - 1$. As is well-known (e.g. Axelrod 1984), two Tit for Tat strategies form a Nash equilibrium in the Prisoner's Dilemma if and only if the future is sufficiently important for both players.[14] This implies that an efficient institutional arrangement can be strategically stable. (Obviously, when this deal can stand up in the most difficult delegation case, then it also works in less trying circumstances, e.g. when only one party has a one-shot dominant strategy of cheating.)

An important caveat: Although the "cooperative" outcome of (delegate, work) becomes individually rational once repetition is added to the picture, many other outcomes—including the bad one of (control, shirk)—are also equilibria. This fact, known in game theory as the folk theorem, implies that the good outcome is not guaranteed. Repeat play merely makes it a live option, in contrast to its dead-on-arrival status in the one-shot game.

The preceding was a "free" application of the theory of repeated games to delegation issues. We used standard results from the literature, which, though not specialized to the study of delegation, apply directly. The models we now examine are tailored more specifically for delegation problems.

---

[14]This holds whether or not the game is symmetric, which matters because the delegation game is obviously asymmetric—the players have different roles and action sets.

Delegation with Overlapping Generations

In the real world, people retire or die, so no one plays an infinitely (or even indefinitely) repeated game. Thus, the assumption of the standard repeated-game models that if a player reaches period t, the probability that he will reach period $t + 1$ is a fixed probability is unwarranted. What remains, then, of the implications of the standard models, of (for example) the idea that delegation and decentralized effort may be maintained by longterm reciprocity between principal and agent? To answer the general question, game theorists have constructed models of organizations populated by overlapping generations of finitely lived members. The idea is elegantly simple.

For example, suppose that each generation or cohort in an institution lives seven periods. A new generation enters every period. Everyone in a particular cohort enters and leaves the institution at the same time. Every generation has n members. Thus, in the steady state, the organization has $7n$ members. Suppose that in every period everyone has a choice of either providing a collective good, to be shared equally by all organization members, or not. Providing the collective good imposes a private cost of $c > 0$. The game is an N-person Prisoner's Dilemma. In the one-shot game, each person has a strictly dominant strategy of shirking, so the only Nash outcome is that everyone shirks, but the all-work outcome is Pareto-superior to the all-shirk outcome. Further, if there were only one cohort of (finitely lived) players, or if there were many but they did not overlap, then again individual rationality would single out the dismal outcome as the unique prediction.

Even if the generations overlap, nothing can be done about players in their last period. Because they are in End Game, they are certain to shirk. Thus, full cooperation is unattainable. Consider, however, the following idea. Since "old" members are going to shirk no matter what, the proposed semicooperative equilibrium will allow for that, without punishment. The young and middle-aged (those in their first five periods in the organization) are expected to provide collective goods, and anyone shirking in these cohorts is punished. The key is that the punishment is delivered not only by all "workers" who are in the organization when the violation occurs; newcomers also punish the deviant by shirking after they arrive. For example, someone who shirks in his fifth period in the organization is punished by being denied retirement pay from the young and middle-aged cohorts who normally would have worked in his sixth and seventh periods. Assuming that the standard payoff conditions are met—the one-period temptation of switching to shirking is outweighed by the subsequent loss of cooperation—it is individually rational to work in periods one through five and retire in periods six and seven.

Such arrangements can work only if certain temporal and demographic conditions hold. In particular, people must live long enough, and cohorts must overlap sufficiently, so that retirement benefits supplied by current workers are attractive enough to induce effort from the young (Cremer 1986). But when these conditions do hold, finitely lived agents (in indefinitely enduring communities) can be induced to cooperate much of the time. Thus, models of overlapping generations drive a wedge between the lifespan of people and the lifespan of their institutions, and so (in Cremer's words) reveal the significance—indeed, the necessity—of institutions in stabilizing good outcomes.

Diermeier (1995) puts this idea to work in the complex setting of a majority-rule legislature. The relations between the committee and the floor in the stage game are (by design) canonical, though for simplicity he does not explain how information is transmitted from committee to floor. Instead, if the committee specializes, then all legislators are automatically informed about the random shock's realization. (By finessing the complexities of signaling models, this conserves analytical resources for the repeated-game aspects of the theory.) There is a fixed set of "teams" whose members have identical preferences. People live for a known number of periods; after they die, they are replaced by someone from the same team.

Diermeier's main result is that, given the usual repeated-game provisos (the future must be sufficiently important, the payoff from reneging must not be too big, etc), there exists a benign Nash equilibrium wherein the committee specializes and the floor defers to the committee's bill. However, because the players have finite lifespans, the standard proviso about the future's importance goes beyond the usual requirement on discount factors. In addition, the institution's demography must have certain properties. For example, generational overlap cannot be too short, for this would preclude the required transfer of benefits across cohorts. (In the extreme, if the teams turned over completely in one period then floor-committee cooperation would collapse.) Further, random shocks to the demography—e.g. a sudden increase in new members from electorally insecure districts (Diermeier 1995:351)—could destabilize the delegation equilibrium. Thus, an overlapping-generations model of delegation generates new and interesting predictions.

More generally, models of repeat play show that the floor need not tie its own hands procedurally to induce the committee to specialize. A tacit understanding, upheld by strategies of conditional cooperation, can sustain the (delegate, work) outcome.

Delegation and the Search for Policies

In the standard formulation, policy uncertainty is represented by a random shock that perturbs programs. But this is only one type of relevant uncertainty that affects governmental policies in the real world. Often, all decision makers—principals and agents alike—are unsure which kind of program is preferable. Do charter schools outperform conventional public schools? Is missile system x better than system y?

To represent such problems, search-theoretic models, typically set in a repeated-game framework, seem a natural choice. Delegation occurs in these contexts because the boss lacks the time or expertise to carry out search, so the boss's basic choice is similar to that of the standard formulation. She can either delegate and later make a more informed choice—possibly biased by the subordinate's goals—or choose under ignorance.

Ting (1999:Ch. 3) has constructed a search-theoretic model of delegation. In his setup, decision makers are initially uncertain about the distributions of outcomes produced by different policies. By experimenting with various options in different periods, they can learn how these distributions compare. In decision theory, these are called multi-armed bandit problems. (The name evokes the image of people playing slot machines.) Multi-armed bandit models are usually cast as single-person optimization problems. Ting's setting is strategic; the boss can delegate search authority to more than one agent, and the agents' preferences may differ from each other and from the boss's.

Search-theoretic models lend themselves naturally to investigating issues that arise from the interactions of multiple agents searching in parallel. (In contrast, in the standard "outcomes = policies + shocks" model, the boss typically needs only one agent to observe the perturbation and then choose an appropriate policy.) Several of Ting's results pertain to these interactions.[15]

1. Suppose the boss delegates. Then simply adding agents to engage in parallel search does not ensure that there will be more experimentation. The reason is that some agents may free-ride on others' efforts. "[I]nformation is a public good, and rational bureaucrats may shirk by choosing conservative policies and letting others bear the risk of experimentation" (Ting 1999:63).
2. This informational free-riding is more likely if (holding beliefs constant) all agents who search are allies of the boss than if some of them are not allies. Thus, Ting's results show that when search matters, the ally principle need not hold in its unvarnished form.

CREDIBLE COMMITMENT AND DELEGATION

Thus far, the ally principle—that a boss prefers subordinates who resemble herself ideologically—has stood up well. Although we noted a few caveats, they only weakly challenge the principle. Formal theorizing seems to track informal thinking here. However, the study of delegation has uncovered an important class of situations in which it is optimal for a boss to violate the ally principle. These situations

[15]It is well established in the literature on bureaucracy that having multiple, information-providing agents is more reliable than having only one, when subordinates are fallible but nonstrategic (Landau 1969, Bendor 1985, Heimann 1997). Under these conditions, engineering-reliability theory tells us that redundant systems are more reliable than nonredundant ones. But entirely new problems appear when agents can behave strategically, by e.g. engaging in biased search driven by "mission orientations" (Bendor et al 1987) such as the Air Force's preference for planes over missiles.

are characterized by problems of credible commitment, often between a political leader and his constituents.

Recall the essence of the game in which the problem arises. In the first stage, a leader makes a promise, say by passing a law, to some or all of his constituents, e.g. to avoid expropriating wealth generated by investments (North & Weingast 1989). In the second stage, the constituents can take an action—for example, invest—based on their beliefs about the leader's promise. In the third stage, the leader moves again, for example by faithfully implementing the tax law or by acting outside the law. Everyone would be better off if the leader could commit to following through on his promise to obey the law. But in the game sketched above, it may be suboptimal for the leader to do so. Instead, if the citizens invest in stage two, then he will renege on his promise in stage three and expropriate their profits. Anticipating this doublecross, businessmen refuse to invest in stage two. (More generally, if the model allows for degrees of investment, then investment will be suboptimally low in that stage.)

In this game, constituents can be seen as the boss, and the political leader as the subordinate. Voters who recognize the commitment problem may choose to elect a leader who will avoid expropriation. As Persson & Tabellini (1994) suggest, the majority elects a policy maker who, after the investments are made, favors a lower tax rate than the majority does.

Related historical experience (North & Weingast 1989) bears out this analysis. Under the Stuart monarchy and until the Glorious Revolution in 1688, the British Crown raised money in ways that hurt investment. It reneged on loans, seized private assets, undermined the common law courts by creating its own set of courts to uphold the legality of its actions, and tried to rig parliamentary representation in its favor. Ultimately, private lenders became unwilling to make loans to the Crown at all. Following the Glorious Revolution, courts closely tied to the Crown were abolished, and all cases involving private property had to be tried by common law courts. Common law judges could now be removed only for violations of good behavior. A law requiring the regular meeting of Parliament was passed. Parliament's exclusive authority to raise new taxes was reestablished. Parliament gained the right to audit how the government spent its funds. Royal prerogative powers were limited.

In short order, the new King borrowed far more money and at far lower interest rates than had his predecessors. North & Weingast argue that the central reason is that the Crown, because of the institutional changes made during and after the Glorious Revolution, became credibly committed to honoring its financial obligations. It could no longer renege on these obligations because it had lost its authority to do so—such decisions were now Parliament's. And the diversity of interests in the legislature, as well as the strong presence of the commercially minded Whigs, made Parliament unlikely to renege on the government's debts.

The idea that a boss might delegate in order to make a policy credible has been especially prominent in the literature on central banks and monetary policy.

Delegation and Commitment Problems in Monetary Policy

To examine delegation of monetary policy, we must first briefly describe some of the effects of monetary policy. Although in the short run an increase in the money supply can increase employment and output, workers and firms who realize that demand for labor and for goods is higher may demand higher wages and higher prices, generating inflation. The problem may be even more severe. Firms and workers who anticipate an increase in the money supply may increase wages and prices, thereby reducing demand for goods and labor. Government may then want to stimulate the economy to avoid a recession and may therefore increase the money supply. The anticipated, and realized, increased money supply would then leave the economy with the same output and employment, but with higher prices. If, instead, firms and workers expected little increase in the money supply, they would not increase prices and wages, and the economy would enjoy the same level of output with lower prices.

In the following, we think of Congress or the Executive as the boss delegating monetary policy to a central bank. If the central bank has the same objectives as the boss, then the delegation has no real effects. The interesting question is, can the performance of the economy be improved by delegating to a central bank whose preferences differ from the boss's? The surprising answer is yes.

The credibility problem can be formulated in terms of the objective function of the boss, which is often called the social welfare function. Let social welfare directly decline with inflation (p) and decline with the gap between actual output, y, and an ideal output y^*. (Higher output may sometimes be undesirable, perhaps because it increases the trade deficit, reduces prospects for future growth, or increases inequality.) That is, let the social welfare function be

$$U = -(y - y^*)^2 - \theta p^2, \qquad 1.$$

where θ represents the weight on inflation.

Let output increase with the size of unanticipated inflation, which is the difference between actual inflation (p) and expected inflation (p_e).

$$y = p - p_e \qquad 2.$$

Substituting Equation 2 into Equation 1 gives

$$U = -(p - p_e - y^*)^2 - \theta p^2. \qquad 3.$$

Alternatively, we can view the objective as minimizing the social loss,

$$L = (p - p_e - y^*)^2 + \theta p^2. \qquad 4.$$

Suppose first that the boss could credibly commit to an inflation rate, p. From Equation 4 it is clear that the optimal choice is $p = 0$. Since the boss committed to $p = 0$, that is the inflation rate expected by firms, workers, and consumers (in short, by economic agents). So $p - p_e = 0$, and the social loss under commitment, L^c, is just

$$L^c = (y^*)^2.$$

Suppose next that the boss cannot commit. She instead takes expectations of inflation as given, minimizing Equation 4 given those expectations. The first-order condition for minimizing L is

$$\frac{\partial((p - p_e - y^*)^2 + \theta p^2)}{\partial p} = 0,$$

with the solution

$$p = \frac{p_e - y^*}{1 + \theta}.$$

If we assume that people have rational expectations, so that $p_e = p$, we find that the solution under discretion, called p^d, is

$$p^d = \frac{y^*}{\theta}. \qquad 5.$$

Substituting Equation 5 into Equation 4 yields

$$L^d = \frac{(y^*)^2(1 + \theta)}{\theta}.$$

Note that for all positive finite values of θ, $(y^*)^2 < \frac{(y^*)^2(1+\theta)}{\theta}$. Thus, if the boss aims to maximize social welfare but cannot commit to fixing inflation at zero, she will be tempted to stimulate the economy through inflation; firms, workers, and consumers will anticipate this inflation, and social welfare will be lower than it would be with commitment. [This idea was formulated by Barro & Gordon (1983) and Backus & Driffill (1985); Persson (1988) offers a more complete discussion.]

Three proposals have been offered to ameliorate the problem. All involve delegating decisions to a central banker but making his objective differ from the boss's. The first is to delegate control of monetary policy to a "conservative" central banker, one who strongly dislikes inflation, as indicated by a high value of θ (Rogoff 1985). Such reasoning played a role in President Carter's appointment of Paul Volcker as Chairman of the Federal Reserve Bank in 1979 (Greider 1987). The nomination of Volcker, described as "rigidly conservative, very right-wing, and not a team player," was applauded by business and banking leaders.

As we saw, however, no finite value of θ can attain the solution attainable under commitment. Other tools can do better. Consider setting an inflation target, p_b. [The seminal work on this topic is by Svensson (1997). For a discussion of the credibility of inflation targeting, see Cukierman (2000).] The central bank is somehow induced to minimize not Equation 4 but rather to minimize

$$(p - p_e - y^*)^2 + \theta(p - p_b)^2.$$

Assuming again that the boss cannot commit to policy, but that economic agents anticipate the central bank's actions when they forecast inflation, realized inflation will be

$$p^t = \frac{y^* + \theta p_b}{\theta}.$$

To induce an outcome with zero inflation, the boss should set p_b to satisfy

$$\frac{y^* + \theta p_b}{\theta} = 0,$$

obtaining

$$p_b = -\frac{y^*}{\theta}.$$

Realized inflation will be zero, and social loss the same as under commitment. So delegation combined with inflation targeting solves the commitment problem.

The third tool is for the boss to delegate and then to impose a fine on the central banker of f per unit of inflation. This is called an inflation contract. The central banker minimizes

$$L^r = (p - p_e - y^*)^2 + \theta p^2 - fp.$$

With rational expectations by economic agents, realized inflation is

$$p^r = \frac{2y^* + f}{2\theta}.$$

The value of f that would induce zero inflation is $f = -2y^*$. So an inflation contract, like an inflation target, can induce the central banker to choose the level of inflation that maximizes social welfare.

These results are reasonably robust. One important exception is that the model described above assumes that the boss fully knows the central banker's preferences. If there is uncertainty (say about θ), then gaining the benefits from delegation may require the boss to both set an inflation target (or use an inflation contract) and try to choose a central banker who dislikes inflation (Muscatelli 1999).

A serious criticism of these approaches is that they assume that at some level the boss can commit, whereas at others she cannot (McCallum 1995, Jensen 1997). Consider inflation targeting, where the boss assigns the central banker an inflation target, p_b, that enters into the banker's loss function. If a surprise oil shock hurts the economy, why wouldn't the boss who announced an inflation target surreptitiously change it, inducing the banker to increase inflation and thus output? Or why not surprise the public by appointing a central banker who cares little about inflation?

Summary Our discussion of central banking shows that the government may increase welfare by delegating authority to an official whose preferences differ from the government's. We also see that such benefits from "strategic delegation" can apply in many more situations.

These results are interesting mainly because they show that it can be optimal to ignore the ally principle, and they explain why and when this is so. After all, common sense supports the finding that it is often rational for an uninformed principal to delegate authority to an informed agent; it is rather obvious that tapping the agent's greater expertise can provide gains. (Further, when delegation is beneficial for this reason, then the ally principle is typically operative.) But the value of deliberately handing authority over to an agent whose goals differ markedly from one's own—more, that this preference difference is essential to delegation being useful—is much less intuitive. Hence, it is in such contexts that noncooperative game theory and the analysis of subgame perfection reveal their value.

The Difficulties of Credible Commitment

In the provocative opening of one of his papers on "the politics of structural choice," Moe (1989:267) asserts that "American public bureaucracy is not designed to be effective." This is an intriguing claim. To argue that an institution turns out to be inept is one thing; to maintain that it was not designed to be effective is quite another. Why would this happen?

In Moe's (informal) theory (Moe 1989, 1990a,b, 1991; Moe & Caldwell 1994; Moe & Wilson 1994), the central problems facing politicians creating a new agency in a democracy are political turnover and political uncertainty. The party in power today can give a new agency statutory authority, but in a democracy, power is ephemeral. Eventually the opponents will run things, and then they might gut the agency or turn it in an unpalatable direction. What to do?

Moe argues that the party currently in power (say, the Democrats) faces two distinct choices. On the one hand, the Democrats could heed the classical reasons for discretion and give the agency much leeway so that it can adapt to changes in its task environment. Doing that, however, simultaneously makes it possible for their opponents to redirect the agency. On the other hand, the Democrats could enmesh the agency in structural and procedural constraints. Doing so would confer a political advantage—these constraints would make it hard for new political superiors to influence the agency in unwanted ways—but it would simultaneously make the agency rigid and thus technically inefficient. Essentially, then, Moe is suggesting that the Democrats may prefer to have a somewhat inefficient, but still environmentally oriented, Environmental Protection Agency today *and tomorrow* over the bundle of an effective, environmentally oriented EPA today and an (effectively) gutted EPA tomorrow.

There is a puzzle, however: Nobody likes inefficient agencies. Thus, the Republicans could suggest the following deal: "Don't burden the agency today with constraints that degrade performance. Let it remain flexible. In return, we promise that when we come into power we won't gut the agency but will only moderate its environmental enthusiasm." Such a deal may well be mutually beneficial (under plausible assumptions politicians prefer "policy-smoothing" over a volatile path with the same average policy), but there is a hitch: The party in power must do its part in the present while the out-party is agreeing to deliver in the future. Will it? If the Democrats doubt the word of their opponents, then they may do the relatively safe thing, namely insulate and rigidify the agency. Hence, the Pareto-inferior outcome of ineffficent agencies arises precisely because future principals cannot make credible commitments today about how they will run agencies tomorrow. Consequently, Moe's theory can be seen as a pessimistic counterpoint to the studies of central banking. Whereas in those studies, quasi-independent agencies were the solution to problems of credible commitment, in Moe's account they reflect the inability of politicians to credibly commit to stable and efficient policy compromises.

This theory posits that the turnover of political principals is a central problem for the design of bureaucracies, but one could challenge this key premise and its presumed effects. So what if there will be turnover of principals? Today's governing party should rationally create an organization that is best suited to carry out the party's optimal policy; if the out-party takes over, it will do the same. Such is life in a competitive polity. And if the system at hand is a parliamentary one—particularly a parliamentary system with only two major parties, as in Britain—this point has merit (Moe & Caldwell 1994). In such systems, if a single party takes control of Parliament it will be in a position to sweep away the procedural and structural constraints imposed on agencies by previous governments. Thus, agencies in these systems cannot be insulated from the influence of future principals. And since by hypothesis this insulation comes at a price—inefficient rigidity—rational parties in power would not do it in (two-party) parliamentary democracies.

In contrast, in systems with separation of powers, it is unlikely that any one party will have the kind of commanding position enjoyed by (single-party) winners in parliamentary systems; American-type polities have too many veto points. Hence, Moe argues, if the Democrats enmesh the EPA today in constraining laws, tomorrow the Republicans may be unable to overturn this statutory status quo. (This was exactly what President Reagan and EPA head Gorsuch found out in the early 1980s.) Separation of power systems are designed to favor retaining the status quo, which tempts the incumbent party to surround an important agency with stabilizing (yet debilitating) constraints.

Although Moe's theory is plausible, his specific predictions depend on specific assumptions concerning the actors' expectations about future political trends. Moe argues that when the members of the governing coalition believe the future will become politically less favorable for their program, they will be inclined to constrain the agency, so that neither the agency nor future politicians can easily modify the program. Sometimes, however, ruling politicians believe that the tides of political fortunes are in their favor. In this case, they may give the agency discretion so that it can unilaterally adapt to new contingencies without having to engage in time-consuming negotiations with the future Congress and President. This modification, which hinges on the politicians' forecasts about political trends and on their degree of risk aversion, might allow Moe's theory to account for the fact that Congress has at times given agencies great legal discretion.

CONCLUSIONS

The study of delegation is flourishing in political science. It displays unusual degrees of coherence and cumulation. These two properties are related. Scholars working in this area have shown an admirable degree of self restraint; resisting the temptation to engage in ceaseless but undisciplined innovation, they have built on each other's work to an extent that is rare in the discipline.

This incremental research strategy has facilitated theoretical progress. It greatly enhances comparability across models, making it easier to figure out when new assumptions (e.g. superiors can monitor agents ex post) matter—that is, when they affect predicted outcomes. This cumulative work has helped us understand an important piece of conventional wisdom, the ally principle, that is central to the politics of delegation. Now we not only have rigorous models explaining why rational superiors would use the principle but we also better understand when they would not. Perhaps most striking here are the models that analyze problems of credible commitment, in which superiors deliberately delegate to subordinates who have different goals in order to demonstrate that they are serious about certain policies. Explicit theorizing, by generating surprising yet not implausible results, shows a clear "value added" here.

Of course, because all research strategies involve trade-offs, this cumulation and coherence has come at a price. In particular, although the subfield has benefited from using a common set of building blocks in the different models—even down to the quadratic utility functions, uniform noise, and additive policy-shock technology—it is time to stop relying on such a narrow set of assumptions and to start generalizing results. After all, where is it written that policy shocks are uniformly distributed, or preferences quadratic? The field is mature enough to work on theoretical sensitivity testing. What would happen, for example, if signaling models relied only on an assumption that superiors are risk-averse, rather than assuming a particular functional form? Would the qualitative pattern of results about, say, the ally principle stand up if we relaxed the assumption about uniformly distributed noise and instead assumed a much larger class of disturbances? These are not mere technical issues; they go to the heart of what we believe matters substantively. Typically, informal theorizing uses broad notions—e.g. decision makers are risk-averse—rather than specific postulates, such as quadratic preferences. Thus, if we wish to faithfully represent our informal hunches, we should work as much as possible with the broad notions. If we then discover that certain conjectures do not hold under the general premises, we will have learned something.

A second problem is that too little attention is paid to a central empirical issue: What real-world institution or process is being modeled by a particular formulation? We have no quarrel at all with a research strategy of starting with the simplest of models in the simplest of settings and then incrementally making the models more complex (and, one hopes, more realistic). Indeed, as we argued earlier, this incremental model-building strategy is highly desirable. Yet many modelers (present company included!) have been rather casual about the prima facie plausibility of their models.

A third common problem is that even when the real-world institutions are adequately represented in a model, the decisional context may not be. In particular, models often presume that principals are designing on a blank slate—that they delegate without an ongoing agency or an ongoing program in the background. Yet this background—e.g. whether an agency already exists and already has at least some de facto authority—probably matters. Changing an existing level of discretion is politically harder than giving discretion to an entirely new agency because, for example, multiple actors may have vetos over changes in an agency's status quo level of discretion (Volden 2000:2).

Finally, consider delegation in complex projects, e.g. the D-Day invasion. Given well-known cognitive constraints (Simon 1990), it was impossible for General Eisenhower to explicitly delegate all requisite authority to all the relevant field commanders. Instead, by virtue of the complexity and uncertainty of their tasks, those officers had a great deal of discretion "on the ground" that Eisenhower could not have anticipated. [See Ambrose (1994) for a fascinating description of the improvisation on the beaches; see Lindblom (1959) for a relevant theory.] Yet current models of delegation in political science blithely assume that the principal is perfectly rational, regardless of the complexity of the task facing her.

All of these issues stand as challenges to the ongoing study of delegation in political science. Given the strides that have been made in the past 15 years, we are confident that these challenges will be taken up and overcome.

LITERATURE CITED

Ambrose S. 1994. *D-Day, June 6, 1944: The Climactic Battle of World War II*. New York: Simon & Schuster

Aranson PH, Gellhorn E, Robinson GO. 1982. A theory of legislative delegation. *Cornell Law Rev.* 68:1–67

Arnold RD. 1987. Political control of administrative officials. *J. Law Econ. Org.* 3:279–86

Axelrod R. 1984. *The Evolution of Cooperation*. New York: Basic Books

Backus D, Driffill J. 1985. Rational expectations and policy credibility following a change in regime. *Rev. Econ. Stud.* 52:211–21

Baron D. 2000. Legislative organization with informational committees. *Am. J. Polit. Sci.* 44:485–505

Barro RJ, Gordon DB. 1983. Rules, discretion and reputation in a model of monetary policy. *J. Monetary Econ.* 12:101–21

Bawn K. 1995. Political control versus expertise: congressional choices about administrative procedures. *Am. Polit. Sci. Rev.* 9:62–73

Bawn K. 1997. Choosing strategies to control the bureaucracy: statutory constraints, oversight, and the committee system. *J. Law Econ. Org.* 13:101–26

Bendor J. 1985. *Parallel Systems: Redundancy in Government*. Berkeley: Univ. Calif. Press

Bendor J, Glazer A, Hammond TH, Meirowitz A. 2000. *Simple spatial models of delegation*. Unpubl. ms., Grad. School Bus., Stanford Univ., Stanford, Calif.

Bendor J, Taylor S, Van Gaalen R. 1987. Stacking the deck: bureaucratic missions and policy design. *Am. Polit. Sci. Rev.* 81:873–96

Calvert R, McCubbins M, Weingast BR. 1989. A theory of political control and agency discretion. *Am. J. Polit. Sci.* 33:588–611

Cremer J. 1986. Cooperation in ongoing organizations. *Q. J. Econ.* 101:33–49

Cukierman A. 2000. Establishing a reputation for dependability by means of inflation targets. *Econ. Gov.* 1:53–76

Diermeier D. 1995. Commitment, deference, and legislative institutions. *Am. Polit. Sci. Rev.* 89:344–55

Epstein D, O'Halloran S. 1999. *Delegating Powers: A Transaction Cost Politics Approach to Policy Making under Separate Powers.* Cambridge: Cambridge Univ. Press

Fiorina M. 1982. Legislative choice of regulatory forms: legal process or administrative process. *Pub. Choice* 39:33–66

Fiorina M. 1986. Legislative uncertainty, legislative control, and the delegation of legislative power. *J. Law Econ. Org.* 3:287–335

Gilligan TW, Krehbiel K. 1987. Collective decision-making and standing committees: an informational rationale for restrictive amendment procedures. *J. Law Econ. Org.* 3:287–335

Gilligan TW, Krehbiel K. 1989a. Asymmetric information and legislative rules with a heterogeneous committee. *Am. J. Polit. Sci.* 33:460–90

Gilligan TW, Krehbiel K. 1989b. Collective choice without procedural commitment. *Models of Strategic Choice in Politics*, ed. P Ordeshook, pp. 295–314. Ann Arbor: Univ. Mich. Press

Gilligan TW, Krehbiel K. 1990. The organization of informative committees by a rational legislature. *Am. J. Polit. Sci.* 34:531–64

Greider W. 1987. *Secrets of the Temple: How the Federal Reserve Runs the Country.* New York: Simon & Schuster

Hammond TH, Knott JH. 1996. Who controls the bureaucracy? Presidential power, congressional dominance, legal constraints, and bureaucratic autonomy in a model of multi-institutional policymaking. *J. Law Econ. Org.* 12:121–68

Hammond TH, Miller GJ. 1985. A social choice perspective on authority and expertise in bureaucracy. *Am. J. Polit. Sci.* 29:611–38

Heimann CFL. 1997. *Acceptable Risks: Politics, Policy, and Risky Technologies.* Ann Arbor: Univ. Mich. Press

Hill JS, Brazier JE. 1991. Constraining administrative decisions: a critical examination of the structure and process hypothesis. *J. Law Econ. Org.* 7:373–400

Horn MJ, Shepsle KA. 1989. Commentary on 'Administrative arrangements and the political control of agencies': administrative process and organizational form as legislative responses to agency costs. *Virg. Law Rev.* 75:499–508

Huber JD, Shipan CR. 1999. A comparative theory of statutory control of bureaucrats. Presented at Annu. Meet. Am. Polit. Sci. Assoc., 95th, Atlanta

Jensen H. 1997. Credibility of optimal monetary delegation. *Am. Econ. Rev.* 87:911–20

Krehbiel K. 1991. *Information and Legislative Organization.* Ann Arbor: Univ. Mich. Press

Krishna V, Morgan J. 2001. Asymmetric information and legislative rules: amendments. *Am. Polit. Sci. Rev.* In press

Landau M. 1969. Redundancy, rationality, and the problem of duplication and overlap. *Pub. Admin. Rev.* 29:346–58

Lindblom CE. 1959. The science of 'muddling through'. *Publ. Admin. Rev.* 19:79–88

Mashaw JL. 1994. Improving the environment of agency rulemaking: an essay on management, games, and accountability. *Law Contemp. Prob.* 57:185–257

McCallum BT. 1995. Two fallacies concerning central bank independence. *Am. Econ. Rev.* 85:207–11

McCubbins M, Noll RG, Weingast BR. 1987. Administrative procedures as instruments of political control. *J. Law Econ. Org.* 3:243–77

McCubbins M, Noll RG, Weingast BR. 1989. Structure and process, politics and policy: administrative arrangements and the political control of agencies. *Virg. Law Rev.* 75:431–82

Miller GJ. 1992. *Managerial Dilemmas: The Political Economy of Hierarchy.* Cambridge: Cambridge Univ. Press

Miller GJ, Hammond TH. 1994. Why politics is more fundamental than economics: incentive-compatible mechanisms are not credible. *Pub. Choice* 6:5–26

Moe TM. 1989. The politics of structural choice. *Can the Government Govern?* ed. J Chubb, P Peterson, pp. 267–329. Washington, DC: Brookings

Moe TM. 1990a. Political institutions: the neglected side of the story. *J. Law Econ. Org.* 6:213–54

Moe TM. 1990b. The politics of structural choice: toward a theory of public bureaucracy. *Organization Theory: From Chester Barnard to the Present and Beyond*, ed. O Williamson, pp. 116–53. New York: Oxford Univ. Press

Moe TM. 1991. Politics and the theory of organization. *J. Law Econ. Org.* 7:106–29

Moe TM, Caldwell M. 1994. The institutional foundations of democratic government: a comparison of presidential and parliamentary systems. *J. Inst. Theor. Econ.* 150:171–95

Moe TM, Wilson SA. 1994. Presidents and the politics of structure. *Law Contemp. Prob.* 57:1–44

Muscatelli VA. 1999. Inflation contracts and inflation targets under uncertainty: Why we might need conservative central bankers. *Economica* 66:241–54

North DC, Weingast BR. 1989. Constitutions and commitment: the evolution of institutions governing public choice in seventeenth-century England. *J. Econ. Hist.* 44:803–32

Persson T. 1988. Credibility of macroeconomic policy: an introduction and a broad survey. *Eur. Econ. Rev.* 32:519–32

Persson T, Tabellini G. 1994. Representative democracy and capital taxation. *J. Pub. Econ.* 55:53–70

Robinson GO. 1989. Commentary on 'Administrative arrangements and the political control of agencies': political uses of structure and process. *Virg. Law Rev.* 75:483–98

Rogoff K. 1985. The optimal degree of commitment to an intermediate monetary target. *Q. J. Econ.* 110:1169–90

Sen A. 1970. The impossibility of a Paretian liberal. *J. Polit. Econ.* 78:152–57

Shepsle K. 1979. Institutional arrangements and equilibrium in multidimensional voting models. *Am. J. Polit. Sci.* 23:27–59

Simon HA. 1990. Invariants of human behavior. *Annu. Rev. Psychol.* 41:1–19

Svensson LEO. 1997. Optimal inflation targets, 'conservative' central banks, and linear inflation contracts. *Am. Econ. Rev.* 87:98–114

Taylor S. 1984. *Making Bureaucracies Think: The Environmental Impact Statement Strategy of Administrative Reform.* Stanford, CA: Stanford Univ. Press

Ting M. 1999. *Essays on the positive theory of bureaucratic politics.* PhD thesis. Stanford Univ., Stanford, CA

Volden C. 2000. The political economy of restrictions on bureaucratic discretion. Unpubl. ms., School Politics & Econ., Claremont Grad. Univ., Claremont, CA

Annu. Rev. Polit. Sci. 2001. 4:271–93

TIME-SERIES–CROSS-SECTION DATA: What Have We Learned in the Past Few Years?

Nathaniel Beck
Department of Political Science, University of California, San Diego, La Jolla, California 92093-0521; e-mail: beck@ucsd.edu

Key Words robust standard errors, feasible generalized least squares, random coefficients, spatial econometrics, error correction

■ **Abstract** This article treats the analysis of "time-series–cross-section" (TSCS) data, which has become popular in the empirical analysis of comparative politics and international relations (IR). Such data consist of repeated observations on a series of fixed (nonsampled) units, where the units are of interest in themselves. An example of TSCS data is the post–World War II annual observations on the political economy of OECD nations. TSCS data are also becoming more common in IR studies that use the "dyad-year" design; such data are often complicated by a binary dependent variable (the presence or absence of dyadic conflict). Among the issues considered here are estimation and specification. I argue that treating TSCS issues as an estimation nuisance is old-fashioned; those wishing to pursue this approach should use ordinary least squares with panel correct standard errors rather than generalized least squares. A modern approach models dynamics via a lagged dependent variable or a single equation error correction model. Other modern issues involve the modeling of spatial impacts (geography) and heterogeneity. The binary dependent variable common in IR can be handled by treating the TSCS data as event history data.

1. INTRODUCTION

Time-series–cross-section (TSCS) data are commonly analyzed in political science and related disciplines. TSCS data are characterized by repeated observations (often annual) on the same fixed political units (usually states or countries). For convenience, I refer to units and countries interchangeably, and similarly refer to time period and years. Although I refer only to political science applications, there are also many purely economic uses of TSCS data, particularly in the study of economic growth (e.g. Grier & Tullock 1989).

Although there are myriad applications, the prototypical application is the study of political economy, and in particular the impact of political arrangements on economic performance in advanced industrial societies. Here I use an example drawn from Garrett (1998), who examines the political economy of government economic policy and performance in 14 OECD nations from 1966 to 1990. In particular, he is interested in whether labor organization and political partisanship affect economic policy and/or performance, and whether the impacts of those variables have changed over time (whether globalization has limited the impact of domestic political arrangements).

Other applications rely on more or fewer repeated observations. Although there is no strict lower limit to the number of repeated observations, there must be enough for some averaging operations to make sense. Thus, for example, our[1] simulations use a minimum of 15 repeated observations. There is no reason in principle that the observations need be annual, but they typically are. Although quarterly or monthly data would increase the number of repeated observations, such data are often not meaningful in the political economy context. There is no upper limit to the number of repeated observations we can study, and more repeated observations simply improve the performance of TSCS estimators.

Although the 14 units studied by Garrett is a typical number (for other studies, see Hall & Franzese 1998, Hicks & Kenworthy 1998, Iversen 1999, Radcliffe & Davis 2000), other researchers have studied the 50 American states (e.g. Fiorina 1994, Fording 1997, Smith 1997, Su et al 1993) or the 100 or so nations on which good data exist (e.g. Blanton 2000, Burkhart & Lewis-Beck 1994, Gasiorowski 2000, Poe et al 1999), or even the 654 parishes of Louisiana (Giles & Hertz 1994). The critical issue, as Section 2 shows, is that the units be fixed and not sampled, and that inference be conditional on the observed units.

TSCS data has also become of interest in international relations (IR). Many quantitative IR researchers use a "dyad-year" design (Maoz & Russett 1993), in which pairs of nations are observed annually for long periods of time (ranging from 40 to over 100 years). The dependent variable of interest in these studies is often the binary indicator of whether a dyad was in conflict in a given year. Binary dependent variables cause special problems. (Although binary dependent variables are most common in the study of international conflict, they also arise in studies of the diffusion of innovation, such as Berry & Berry 1990. The same logic holds for such studies.)

I discuss the characteristics of TSCS data in Section 2 and use that characterization to discuss estimation issues in Sections 3 and 4. Section 3 concerns old-fashioned estimation issues, which center on generalized least squares. Generalized least squares methods treat the interesting properties of TSCS data as nuisances that cause estimation difficulties. These methods have poor statistical performance. Section 4 provides the current solution to the old-fashioned estimation nuisance problem. Although the solution is also old-fashioned, it at least has good statistical properties.

[1]This paper reports work done jointly with Jonathan N Katz, and the use of "our" or "we" always denotes Katz and myself.

The next sections consider a more modern approach, which treats the interesting properties of TSCS data as something to be modeled. I begin with dynamics in Section 5. I then turn to the modeling of spatial or geographic factors (Section 6), followed by the modeling of heterogeneity (Section 7). Section 8 discusses the binary dependent variable case of interest in IR.

2. CHARACTERIZING TSCS DATA

TSCS uses the following notation (assuming a "rectangular" structure for notational convenience but with no loss of generality):

$$y_{i,t} = \mathbf{x}_{i,t}\beta + \epsilon_{i,t}; \quad i = 1, \ldots, N; \quad t = 1, \ldots, T, \qquad 1.$$

where $\mathbf{x}_{i,t}$ is a K vector of exogenous variables and observations are indexed by both unit (i) and time (t). Assume Ω to be the $NT \times NT$ covariance matrix of the errors with typical element $E(\epsilon_{i,t}\epsilon_{j,s})$. I assume, until Section 8, that the dependent variable, y, is continuous (at least in the sense of social science, where seven-point scales and the like are treated as continuous). Given the nature of typical TSCS data, I often refer to the units as countries and the time periods as years, but the discussion generalizes to any data set that is TSCS.

Equation 1 hides as much as it reveals. In particular, it does not distinguish "panel" data from TSCS data. Panel data are repeated cross-section data, but the units are sampled (usually they are survey respondents obtained in some random sampling scheme), and they are typically observed only a few times. TSCS units are fixed; there is no sampling scheme for the units, and any "resampling" experiments must keep the units fixed and only resample complete units (Freedman & Peters 1984). In panel data, the people observed are of no interest; all inferences of interest concern the underlying population that was sampled, rather than being conditional on the observed sample. TSCS data are exactly the opposite; all inferences of interest are conditional on the observed units. For TSCS data, we cannot even contemplate a thought experiment of resampling a new "Germany," although we can contemplate observing a new draw of German data for some year.

The difference between TSCS and panel data has both theoretical and practical consequences, which go hand in hand. Theoretically, all asymptotics for TSCS data are in T; the number of units is fixed and even an asymptotic argument must be based on the N observed units. We can, however, contemplate what might happen as $T \rightarrow \infty$, and methods can be theoretically justified based on their large-T behavior.

Panel data have the opposite characteristic. However many waves a panel has, that number is fixed by the design, and there can be no justification of methods by an appeal to asymptotics in T. There are, however, reasonable asymptotics in N, as sample sizes can be thought of as getting larger and larger.

Many common panel methods are justified by asymptotics in N. In particular, the currently popular "general estimating equation" approach of Liang & Zeger

(1986) is known to have good properties only as N becomes large. Thus, although it might be a very useful method for panel data, there is no reason to believe that the general estimating equation is a good approach for TSCS data.

The methods Katz and I propose require that T be large enough that averages over the T time periods for each unit make sense. We also use standard time-series methods to model the dynamics of TSCS data; this is possible only when T is not tiny. Panel data methods, conversely, are constructed to deal with small Ts; one would not attempt to use a lagged dependent variable when one has only three repeated observations per unit!

Thus, TSCS methods are justified by asymptotics in T and typically require a reasonably large T to be useful. Again, there is no hard and fast minimum T for TSCS methods to work, but one ought to be suspicious of TSCS methods used for, say, $T < 10$. On the other hand, TSCS methods do not require a large N, although a large N is typically not harmful. Thus, estimation on 14 OECD nations does not violate any assumption that justifies a (correct) TSCS method, but estimation on thousands of fixed units via TSCS methods is perfectly acceptable (though it might be numerically difficult). In contrast, panel methods are designed for and work well with very small Ts (three, or perhaps even two) but require a large N for the theoretical properties of the estimators to have any practical consequences. Panel estimators are also designed to avoid practical issues that arise from the large (and asymptotically infinitely large) N that characterizes panel data. Because much of the econometric literature conflates the analysis of panel data with the analysis of TSCS data, it is critical to keep in mind the distinction between the two types of data.

3. ESTIMATION ISSUES

Equation 1 can be estimated by ordinary least squares (OLS). OLS is optimal if the error process for Equation 1 meets the Gauss-Markov assumptions. Several of the Gauss-Markov assumptions are often suspect for TSCS data. An old fashioned approach is to treat these violations as a nuisance and correct for them using feasible generalized least squares (FGLS). I use the term old-fashioned because this perspective views violations of the Gauss-Markov assumptions as an estimation nuisance rather than something to be modeled. The modern perspective, at least in time series, is to regard these "violations" as interesting features to be modeled and not swept under the rug (Hendry & Mizon 1978). The situation for TSCS data differs from that for single time series in that the FGLS approach can do considerable harm with TSCS data; this is because it is possible to estimate some error properties of TSCS data that cannot be estimated with either a single time series or cross section. I therefore consider the old-fashioned methods primarily as a warning of what can go wrong and for historical reasons. (Lest I be accused of beating a dead horse, I note that the horse was quite alive only three or four years ago, and that I can claim some credit for helping to kill it!)

The Gauss-Markov assumption is that each of the $\epsilon_{i,t}$ is independent and identically distributed; that is,

$$E(\epsilon_{i,t}\epsilon_{j,s}) = \begin{cases} \sigma^2 \text{ if } i = j \text{ and } s = t \\ 0 \quad \text{otherwise.} \end{cases} \qquad 2.$$

It is well known that OLS will be inefficient, and its reported standard errors may be incorrect, if the error process does not look like Equation 2. In particular, the errors may show (*a*) panel heteroskedasticity, i.e. each country may have its own error variance (Equation 4); (*b*) contemporaneous correlation of the errors, i.e. the error for one country may be correlated with the errors for other countries in the same year (Equation 3); or (*c*) serially correlated errors, i.e. the errors for a given country are correlated with previous errors for that country (Equation 6). We would expect the errors from TSCS models to often "violate" the Gauss-Markov assumptions. If nations vary so that the error variance varies from nation to nation, we expect to observe panel heteroskedasticity; alternatively, we may observe panel heteroskedasticity because one or two units do not fit the basic specification well. Panel heteroskedasticity is one type of interunit heterogeneity. As we shall see in Section 7, there are many more interesting forms of unit heterogeneity to assess and model.

We will observe contemporaneously correlated errors if unobserved features of some countries are related to unobserved features in other countries. (Although we use the term errors, these are only errors of the observer, i.e. omitted variables.) Thus, if the Dutch and German economies are linked, then we would expect omitted variables for each country also to be linked.

Finally, since TSCS data consist of a group of time series, we would expect the data to show the usual features of time-series data, that is, temporally dependent observations. In the old-fashioned approach, these are modeled as serially correlated errors.

These are seen as nuisances in the old-fashioned approach. After discussing the old-fashioned approach, I return to the modeling of each of these interesting features of TSCS data. In this section and the next, however, I treat these problems as nuisances that cause problems in estimation. For expository purposes, I assume in this section and the next that observations are temporally independent, returning to that issue in Section 5. As we shall see, the modern approach to dynamics fits easily with our recommended estimation fix.

Feasible Generalized Least Squares

TSCS models with contemporaneously correlated and panel-heteroskedastic errors have Ω as an $NT \times NT$ matrix block diagonal matrix with an $N \times N$ matrix of contemporaneous covariances, Σ [having typical element $E(\epsilon_{i,t}\epsilon_{j,t})$], along the block diagonal. This follows from the assumption that the error process can be characterized by

$$E(\epsilon_{i,t}\epsilon_{j,s}) = \begin{cases} \sigma_i^2 & \text{if } i = j \text{ and } s = t \\ \sigma_{i,j} & \text{if } i \neq j \text{ and } s = t \\ 0 & \text{otherwise.} \end{cases} \qquad 3.$$

Note that the data provide T sets of residuals to estimate Σ. Thus, FGLS could be used to estimate Equation 1 with the panel heteroskedastic and contemporaneously correlated error matrix. Such a procedure first does OLS, uses the OLS residuals to estimate Σ, and uses the standard FGLS formulae to estimate model parameters and standard errors. This procedure was first described by Parks (1967) and was popularized by Kmenta (1986), so it is usually known as Parks or Parks-Kmenta.

Unlike many common FGLS applications, this procedure requires estimating an enormous number of parameters for the error covariances. Note that FGLS assumes that the parameters of Σ are known, not estimated. We have shown (Beck & Katz 1995) that the properties of the Parks estimator for typical TSCS Ts are very bad, and that, in particular, the estimated standard errors could be underestimating variability by from 50% to 200%, depending on T. The FGLS standard errors underestimate sampling variability because FGLS assumes that Σ is known, not estimated. Our conclusion is that the Parks-Kmenta estimator simply should not be used.

Table 1 shows why many researchers liked Parks-Kmenta; it gives the nice t-ratios that are so prized by journal editors. The Parks-Kmenta estimator of the basic Garrett model is in the third set of columns of the table. Note that with a T of 25, standard errors are anywhere between 50% and 100% smaller than corresponding OLS standard errors. Although this may make one's results easier to publish, the simple fact is that the Parks-Kmenta standard errors are wrong, and perhaps worse, they are wrong in the direction of being wildly optimistic.

Some researchers, noting this problem, avoided Parks-Kmenta but still used FGLS to correct for panel heteroskedasticity. In this model, all error covariances between different units are assumed to be zero, but each unit has its own error variance, σ_i^2. Panel heteroskedastic errors thus yield

$$E(\epsilon_{i,t}\epsilon_{j,s}) = \begin{cases} \sigma_i^2 \text{ if } i = j \text{ and } s = t \\ 0 \;\; \text{otherwise.} \end{cases} \qquad 4.$$

Panel heteroskedasticity differs from simple heteroskedasticity in that error variances are constant within a unit.

This model appears to avoid the craziness of Parks-Kmenta, since only N error parameters need be estimated (and N is typically not enormous for TSCS studies). The FGLS correction for panel studies proceeds, as usual, by a first round of OLS and a second round of weighted OLS, with weights being inversely proportional to the estimated σ_i for each unit (and these σ_i estimated in the obvious manner). This procedure can be called panel-weighted least squares (PWLS).

Although our simulations do not show that PWLS has horrible properties (at least for reasonable N and T), we do feel that it is very problematic. This

TABLE 1 Comparison of ordinary least squares (OLS) and feasible generalized least squares (FGLS) estimates of the Garrett model of economic growth in 14 advanced industrial democracies, 1966–1990[a]

	OLS/PCSE[b]			Panel. Het.[c]		Cont. Corr.[d]	
Variable	$\hat{\beta}$	**SE**	**PCSE**	$\hat{\beta}$	**SE**	$\hat{\beta}$	**SE**
GDP Lagged	0.13	0.05	0.07	0.10	0.05	0.08	0.05
OIL	−6.62	6.26	6.42	−5.92	5.79	−4.71	3.12
DEMAND	.064	0.11	0.16	0.60	0.10	0.72	0.07
LABOR	−0.13	0.62	0.56	−0.44	0.52	−0.03	0.29
LEFT	−0.68	0.42	0.31	−0.57	0.27	−0.65	0.13
LEFTxLABOR	0.23	0.16	0.12	0.23	0.14	0.23	0.06
PER6673	1.41	0.55	0.74	1.56	0.49	1.85	0.40
PER7479	0.04	0.56	0.77	0.29	0.49	0.52	0.40
PER8084	−0.54	0.58	0.80	−0.51	0.51	−0.18	0.42
PER8690	−0.14	0.55	0.76	−0.2	0.49	0.13	0.40
CONSTANT	2.39	1.36	1.36	2.90	1.19	1.84	0.79

[a]All models estimated with fixed effects.

[b]OLS with OLS standard errors and panel correct standard errors (PCSE).

[c]FGLS estimates correcting for panel heteroskedasticity.

[d]FGLS correcting for both contemporaneous correlation of the errors and panel heteroskedasticity (Parks-Kmenta).

is because the weights used in the procedure are simply how well the observations for a unit fit the original OLS regression plane. The second round of FGLS simply downweights the observations for a country if that country does not fit the OLS regression plane well. Thus, on the second round, fit will be good! In other, non-TSCS applications, the correction for heteroskedasticity is theoretical and does not simply downweight poorly fitting observations. The closest analog to PWLS in the cross-sectional world would be to run a cross-sectional regression and then weight each observation by the inverse of its residual. That would yield nice R^2's and t's, but it would be an odd procedure. We reanalyzed (Beck & Katz 1996) a PWLS study of Burkhart & Lewis-Beck (1994) that analyzed economic growth in more than 100 countries and found that three quarters of the weight in the second-round regression came from only 20 advanced industrial societies that fit the first-round regression well. PWLS does less harm in the Garrett example (the middle columns of Table 1), but it does seem wrong to use a procedure that weights observations by how well they fit a prior regression.

This is not to say that we should ignore heterogeneity across units; far from it. As Section 7 demonstrates, the modern approach is to model this heterogeneity directly, or at least to inquire whether all units are governed by the same regression equation. But given the choice between simply ignoring panel heteroskedasticity (and hence using OLS) or using PWLS, the former seems less mischievous. It is also easy, as we will see in the next section, to modify OLS to avoid incorrect standard errors in the presence of panel heteroskedasticity; this modification comes at almost no cost.

4. PANEL CORRECT STANDARD ERRORS

The results of the previous section are negative. Parks-Kmenta has very poor properties and the FGLS correction for panel heteroskedasticity is, in my view, inherently flawed. This does not mean, however, that OLS is a good estimator for TSCS data; the errors are likely, after all, to show both panel heteroskedasticity and contemporaneous correlation of the errors. Under these conditions, OLS is still consistent, though inefficient, and the OLS standard errors may be wrong. Although inefficiency may be an important issue, it is easy to at least compute panel correct standard errors (PCSEs), which correctly measure the sampling variability of the OLS estimates, $\hat{\beta}$.

The usual OLS formula for the standard errors may be misleading for TSCS data. The correct formula is given by the square roots of the diagonal terms of

$$\mathrm{Cov}(\hat{\beta}) = (\mathrm{X}'\mathrm{X})^{-1}\{\mathrm{X}'\Omega\mathrm{X}\}(\mathrm{X}'\mathrm{X})^{-1}. \qquad 5.$$

The OLS standard errors are produced by assuming that the Ω matrix is just a constant times an identity matrix; this assumption will often be incorrect for TSCS data.

Fortunately, it is easy, given the repeated time structure of TSCS data, to estimate Ω by $\hat{\Omega}$ and then use $\hat{\Omega}$ in place of Ω in Equation 5 to produce PCSEs. The PCSEs are simply the square roots of the diagonal terms of Equation 5, using $\hat{\Omega}$. Although the details are a bit complicated (see Beck & Katz 1995), the basic idea is quite simple. Ω is a block diagonal matrix, where each block is identical. We thus have T replications of the error that can be used to estimate this block; for large T, this estimate is quite good. Simulations reported by Beck & Katz (1995) indicate that PCSEs are very accurate (to within a few percent) for $T > 15$. This is true even when the errors meet the Gauss-Markov assumptions. Thus, there is no cost, and some potential gain, to using PCSEs in place of the usual OLS standard errors. They are, in addition, easy to compute and are implemented in standard software (such as Stata and LIMDEP). We therefore recommend that researchers who are worried about using OLS because of the complicated errors found in TSCS data use the OLS estimates of β combined with PCSEs. This approach, though still old-fashioned, works much better than the FGLS "fix" of the previous section.

The third column of Table 1 shows the PCSEs for the Garrett model. The reported PCSEs differ from their OLS counterparts by about one third. Thus, for example, the OLS standard errors understate our uncertainty about the critical political interaction term; with correct standard errors, we can clearly reject the null hypothesis that this interaction has no effect on economic growth. Since the

PCSEs are always as good as (and usually better than) their OLS counterparts, this leads to the correct inference that nations with powerful left parties and centralized bargaining grow faster than nations with only one of those attributes.

5. MODELS WITH TEMPORALLY DEPENDENT OBSERVATIONS

So far I have dealt only with cross-sectional issues. I now turn to problems caused by dynamics. Obviously TSCS data will often show dynamics. The old-fashioned treatment is to think of these dynamics as a nuisance, that is, to model them as serially correlated errors so that

$$\epsilon_{i,t} = \rho\epsilon_{i,t-1} + \nu_{i,t}, \qquad 6.$$

where the νs are independent and identically distributed. Models with such an error process must be estimated by FGLS (Prais-Winsten or the like).[2] This correction requires the estimation of only one serial correlation parameter, so it does not have bad statistical properties. But it is not consistent with modern time-series analysis.

Modern time-series analysts model the dynamics directly as part of the specification. The simplest form of this is the use of lagged dependent variables, but depending on the data, other forms, such as single equation error correction (Davidson et al 1978), may be tried. Whatever we can do for time series we can do for TSCS data. Because typical TSCS data are annual, it is often the case that a single lagged dependent variable is all that the data warrant; it is easy to test for more complicated dynamics via standard Lagrange multiplier tests described below.

Following the identical argument for time series, we can usually replace serially correlated error models with models involving a lagged dependent variable. This simplifies other estimation issues so long as the error process, conditional on the lagged dependent variable being in the specification, is temporally independent. It is easy to test for this independence via a standard Lagrange multiplier test.[3] The

[2]FGLS here consists of running OLS, then estimating the autoregressive parameter in a regression of the residuals on their lags, and then transforming the data by subtracting the estimated autoregressive parameter times the prior observation from the current observation. This is identical to the single time-series correction of serially correlated errors; see Beck & Katz (1996) for more details.

[3]This test regresses the OLS residuals on their lags, as well as all other independent variables, including the lagged dependent variable. The advantage of this test over others is that all estimation is done under the null hypothesis of no serial correlation of the errors, so all estimation can be done using OLS. A similar regression, but with higher-order lagged residuals, tests whether the data indicate the need for a more complex dynamic structure, involving higher order lags. Tests on the Garrett model indicate that the single lag of the dependent variable is adequate, and that there is no remaining serial correlation of the errors. As in the single time-series case, the use of a lagged dependent variable with temporally dependent errors makes OLS inconsistent. As in that case, this is seldom a problem in practice.

modeling of dynamics via a lagged dependent variable allows researchers to estimate their specification using the same methodology recommended in Section 4, OLS with PCSEs.

The Garrett data appear to be well modeled by stationary time-series methods, so no attempt was made to investigate error correction models of the growth of gross domestic product. But this need not have been the case. Had Garrett modeled the level of GDP, rather than its rate of growth, we might well have observed nonstationary data ("unit roots"). Issues of nonstationary data have been extensively studied for single time series; they are also analyzed for large-N panel studies. But we know little about nonstationary TSCS data. One solution that should work well is the TSCS variant of the single equation error correction model. As in the single time-series case, this models the change in a dependent variable of interest as a function of changes in the relevant independent variables and the amount by which the variables are out of equilibrium. We thus have

$$\Delta y_{i,t} = \Delta \mathbf{x}_{i,t}\beta + \rho(y_{i,t-1} - \mathbf{x}_{i,t-1}\gamma) + \epsilon_{i,t};$$
$$i = 1, \ldots, N; \quad t = 2, \ldots, T, \qquad 7.$$

which could then be estimated by OLS with PCSEs. Both Iversen (1999) and Franzese (2001) have used error correction models for studying OECD political economy with some success.

6. SPATIAL MODELING

The Parks FGLS method was designed to correct for OLS problems caused by relationships between the various units. Although the correction has bad properties, we would expect the observations of the various countries in a TSCS study to be interrelated. It is better, however, to try to model this relationship than to leave it as an unspecified nuisance. Such modeling is standard among economic geographers and spatial econometricians (Anselin 1988). These ideas are hard to implement in simple cross-sectional models, but they are easy to implement in TSCS models if we are willing to assume that spatial effects operate with a temporal lag.

The Parks approach simply allowed for an unspecified contemporaneous correlation of the errors that varied by unit but not by time. The inordinate number of parameters in this model is the cause of its terrible performance. Spatial econometricians, on the other hand, assume that there are a few parameters that describe the relationship among units. Geographers typically assume that units are related in proportion to their closeness. Although closeness is often defined in a purely geographic manner, there is no reason it cannot be defined by the degree of economic relationship between nations.

Spatial econometricians allow for two types of spatial dependence. The errors of nearby units may be correlated (spatial autocorrelation), with the degree of correlation inversely related to the closeness of the two units. Alternatively, a "spatial lag," that is, the weighted sum of the dependent variable of all other units, may be added to the specification. The weights in this sum are again proportional to the closeness of the units. If one has only cross-sectional data, spatial econometrics presents formidable technical challenges. But with TSCS data, one can assume that neighbors have an effect only with a temporal lag. Then, so long as the remaining errors are temporally independent, one can use spatial econometric methods quite easily.

Although it is easy to add spatially autocorrelated errors to the model using FGLS methods, it seems more natural to use spatial lags. Remember that the "errors" are errors of the observer, that is, omitted variables that the researcher either could not or did not choose to include in the model. Thus, if we assume that only the errors show autocorrelation, then we are assuming that only the unmeasured variables are spatially related and that there is no relationship between measured variables. This is, however, far from the ideal way to think about spatial independence, at least for models of open economies (Alt 1985, Franzese 2001, Garrett 1998).[4] We would expect that the economies of trading partners are linked, so that if the economies of a nation's trading partners are doing well, that nation's economy also should be doing well. If we assume that this spatial effect also operates with a temporal lag (so that it takes some time, say a year, for an improving German economy to be reflected in an improving Dutch economy), then we simply add to Equation 1 a term $S_{i,t-1}$, which is a weighted average of the lagged dependent variable for all units except unit i.

This average is a weighted average, with prespecified (not estimated!) weights. Geographers often use a weighting scheme in which abutting units are given a weight of one and all others are weighted zero. This scheme might make sense in some cases, and it is used in Berry & Berry's (1990) study of the adoption of state lotteries. But for political economy models, the right weighting is almost certainly the importance of trade between unit i and the other units; the German economy, lagged one year, will have a strong effect on the Dutch economy in proportion to the importance of Dutch-German trade in the Dutch economy (that is, as a proportion of Dutch GDP). Thus, for each nation and each year, a researcher must compute the weighted average of the economic performance of all trading partners, weighted by the importance of that trade.

Many researchers use a spatial lag of the dependent variable in their models without explicitly noting the geographic interconnection of their data. Thus, for example, the lagged spatial lag has already been included in the Garrett specification I have been estimating. His *DEMAND* variable is a trade weighted average (for each country) of the growth of GDP in all other OECD countries. Its inclusion in the model reflects two obvious ideas: (*a*) When the world's economy improves, nation *X*'s economy will probably improve, and (*b*) how much better nation *X* is

---

[4]I focus here on political economy models, but the same logic holds for models of the adoption of innovations by states, such as those of Berry & Berry (1990). In those models, it is the spatial lag of the innovations of other states that has an effect; states are more likely to adopt a lottery, for example, if geographically nearby states have done so.

doing reflects how much better other nations are doing, weighted by the importance of those others nations to X's economy. As the tables show, the performance of one's trading partners has an important impact on one's own economic performance. Omitting this variable will yield either inefficient or biased estimates of the impact of domestic variables on economic performance.

As long as the performance of one's partners operates with a temporal lag, it is easy to estimate a model that contains a spatial lag by OLS. One must ensure that the errors show no temporal correlation, but the lagged dependent variable will usually do so. Any remaining contemporaneous correlation of the errors, or panel heteroskedasticity, can be handled by the use of PCSEs. For this methodology to work, care must be taken that no independent variable is correlated with its own error term. Since the temporal lag of the spatial lag is clearly correlated with the temporal lag of all other unit error terms, it is critical that the temporally lagged dependent variable sop up all, or almost all, of the dynamics so there is no (or almost no) remaining temporal serial correlation of the errors. This is easy to test for by using the Lagrange multiplier test described in the previous section. Although my own experience indicates that the lagged dependent variable eliminates serial correlation of the errors, clearly this will not always be the case, and so a strict adherence to testing is required.

7. HETEROGENEITY

Equation 1 assumes that the countries are completely homogeneous, differing only in the levels of their explanatory variables. The FGLS approach was designed to guard against one type of heterogeneity, unequal unit error variances. A more modern approach would presume that heterogeneity is an interesting feature of TSCS data and attempt to model that heterogeneity. That approach would allow for heterogeneity in the parameters of interest, the β in Equation 1.

TSCS researchers never assume a completely homogeneous universe. Instead, they typically assert that some subset of countries is homogeneous and include those countries in the analysis, excluding all others. It would be interesting to allow for a more nuanced view of heterogeneity. Before discussing the modeling of heterogeneity, it is first relevant to discuss tests for homogeneity.

Assessing Heterogeneity via Cross Validation

The standard test for homogeneity is a normal F-test. We estimate the two models

$$H_0 : y_{i,t} = \mathbf{x}_{i,t}\beta + \epsilon_{i,t} \quad 8.$$

$$H_1 : y_{i,t} = \mathbf{x}_{i,t}\beta_i + \epsilon_{i,t} \quad 9.$$

and test the null hypotheses $H_0 : \beta_i = \beta$. This is done by the usual F-statistic, which compares the difference in sums of squares residuals from estimating Equations 8 and 9, divided by the appropriate number of degrees of freedom and then divided by the mean square error of Equation 9.

We might reject the null of pooling either because of slight variations in all the β_i or because one particular country is not well fit by Equation 8. We also might fail to notice an "outlying" country because the F-test averages variation over all units. Finally, we might reject the null of pooling when there is little parameter variation because of the large sample sizes common in TSCS data sets. In any event, great care must be taken in interpreting the result of the F-test.[5]

We can assess whether the F-test rejected homogeneity because one or two countries were outliers by using cross validation (Stone 1974). For the Garrett data, this procedure also assesses whether the small F-statistic resulted from averaging many homogeneous units with one outlying unit. The simplest form of cross validation is to leave out one observation, fit a regression with all the others, and "predict" the left-out observation. For all but very small data sets, this procedure is useless. But for TSCS data, it makes perfect sense, except that instead of leaving out one observation at a time, we leave out one unit at a time. We can then compare specifications by seeing how they perform in terms of mean absolute (or square) "prediction" error, or we can see if any units are predicted less well than the others. Table 2 demonstrates such an exercise.

In that table, we see that typical mean absolute forecast errors range from 1.2% to 2% (the unit is percent growth in GDP), except for Japan, which has a forecast error of 3.2%. Thus, Japan fits the basic specification much less well than any other OECD nation. A researcher might be well advised to drop the Japanese data from the Garrett specification.[6] Dropping Japan from the analysis increases the impact of the critical *LEFTxLABOR* interaction term by about 20%.

Fixed Effects Models

Having checked for unit heterogeneity, how do we proceed? The old-fashioned approach was to eliminate the estimation problems caused by the nuisance of heterogeneity. The modern approach is to model this heterogeneity. The simplest way of doing so is to assume that each unit has its own intercept, thus changing Equation 1 to

$$y_{i,t} = \mathbf{x}_{i,t}\beta + f_i + \epsilon_{i,t}, \qquad 10.$$

[5]A test for pooling in the Garrett model, taking fixed effects as given, yields an F-statistic of 1.29 with 130 and 196 degrees of freedom. This just misses being statistically significant at the conventional level ($P < 0.06$). But the statistic is very small and is only nearly significant because of the huge number of degrees of freedom in the numerator. Thus, given a choice between a fully pooled and a completely unpooled model, I would simply estimate the pooled model, with fixed effects, for these data. To pursue the issue further, one would do an F-test for pooling on interesting subsets of the coefficients.

[6]This makes sense particularly because the Japanese political economy differs in many ways from other OECD political economies. I would be less sanguine if a country such as the Netherlands had the worst forecast errors. It is important to make sure one is not achieving good fits simply by dropping units that fit poorly. But in this case, both cross validation and knowledge of the OECD nations leads me to argue that Japan should not be included in the analysis.

TABLE 2 Out of sample forecast errors (ordinary least squares) by country for Garrett model of economic growth in 14 advanced industrial democracies, 1966–1990[a]

Country	**Mean Absolute Error (%)**
United States	1.9
Canada	1.7
United Kingdom	1.7
Netherlands	1.6
Belgium	1.6
France	1.2
Germany	1.4
Austria	1.3
Italy	1.7
Finland	2.0
Sweden	1.2
Norway	1.5
Denmark	1.7
Japan	3.2

[a]No effects in model.

where f_i is a dummy variable marking unit i. Note that this model introduces very little heterogeneity. The effect of the independent variables does not vary by country; each country simply has its own intercept.

The panel literature contains great debates about how to model the effects, and in particular, whether we should treat them as fixed or random. That argument, however, is for panel data; for TSCS data, it is clear that fixed effects are appropriate (Hsaio 1986: 41–43). Hsaio shows that fixed effects are appropriate if one wants to make inferences to the observed units, whereas the random effects model (which assumes that the effects are drawn from some distribution) is appropriate if one thinks of the observed units as a sample from a larger population and if one wants to make inferences about the larger population. In TSCS data, the units (countries) are fixed and we are not interested in extending inference to a larger, hypothetical, population of similar countries. Furthermore, with a large T, fixed and random effects converge. As is well known (see e.g. Greene 1999: 568–70), fixed effects and random effects differ by $\frac{\sigma_\epsilon 2}{\sigma_\epsilon^2 + T\sigma_\alpha^2}$. As T gets large, this term goes to zero, so that the random-effects and fixed-effects estimators become identical.

It is easy to test whether the fixed effects are required via a simple F-test comparing the sums of squared errors from Equations 1 and 10. Obviously, fixed effects are not theoretical variables; to say that Germany grew faster because it was

Germany is hardly a satisfying explanation. But if we cannot otherwise explain unit variations in growth, and the *F*-test indicates we need fixed effects, then estimating Equation 1 without fixed effects means that we are estimating a misspecified model (Green et al 2001).[7]

We should note that the use of fixed effects comes with its own costs. Fixed effects are clearly collinear with any independent variables that are unchanging attributes of the units, so they force us to drop such unchanging variables from the specification. These variables (perhaps characteristics such as democracy) might be of interest. And although we can estimate Equation 10 with slowly changing independent variables, the fixed effects will soak up most of the explanatory power of those slowly changing variables. Thus, if a variable such as type of bargaining system changes over time, but slowly, the fixed effects will make it hard for such variables to appear either substantively or statistically significant (Beck & Katz 2001).

TSCS analysts should test to see whether fixed effects are needed in the specification. If not, then there is no problem. If an *F*-test indicates that fixed effects are required, then researchers should make sure they are not losing the explanatory power of slowly changing or stable variables of interest. (Sometimes we use stable variables of no substantive interest, and it is not harmful to eliminate these from the specification.) If variables of interest are being lost because of the inclusion of fixed effects, the researcher must weigh the gains from including fixed effects against their costs. If the gains, in terms of decreased sum of squared errors, are slight, albeit statistically significant, then it might be better to omit the fixed effects and suffer slight omitted-variable bias. Like most interesting issues, this is a matter of judgment, not slavish adherence to some 0.05 test level (see Beck & Katz 2001 for a fuller discussion).

The Random Coefficients Model

The random coefficients model (RCM) is an interesting compromise between assuming complete homogeneity and assuming complete heterogeneity. This model is the same as the Bayesian hierarchical model. Western (1998) provides a full discussion of this model in the context of TSCS data.

The RCM is a compromise between estimating the fully pooled Equation 1 and a fully unpooled estimate, that is, a separate OLS for each unit. There are not enough data for the latter (that is, separate OLS estimations will have huge standard errors), but the former requires the very strong assumption of complete pooling. The RCM uses the idea of "borrowing strength" (Gelman et al 1995). This Bayesian notion shrinks each of the individual unit OLS estimates back to the overall (pooled) estimate. RCMs simply generalize random effects from the intercept to all parameters of interest.

---

[7]The *F*-statistic on the null hypothesis that fixed effects are not needed in the Garrett specification is 4.88 with 13 and 326 degrees of freedom. We can therefore reject the null hypothesis that fixed effects are not needed in the specification with a *P* value of zero to many decimal places.

The RCM is

$$y_{i,t} = \mathbf{x}_{i,t}\beta_i + \mathbf{z}_{i,t}\gamma\epsilon_{i,t}, \tag{11.}$$

where the $\beta_i \sim N(\beta, \sigma_\beta^2)$ and the γ represent fixed coefficients. Note that if we allow only the intercept to be random, the RCM reduces to the usual random effects model. This is a complex model, but it can be estimated by either classical maximum likelihood (Pinheiro & Bates 2000) or Bayesian methods, typically with diffuse priors (Western 1998).[8]

The RCM can be made more useful, as Western showed (1998), by allowing the β_is to be functions of other unit variables, z_i. This step allows for modeling differential effects as a function of differing institutions. (The z_is are time invariant, so they only measure properties of units.) This is particularly important in comparative politics, where we might expect that the effect of some x on the dependent variable is contingent on structural features that vary from country to country. For example, the Garrett model asserts that the effect of having a left government is contingent on the type of labor bargaining in each country. We can then write:

$$\beta_i = \mathbf{z}_i\gamma + \beta + \alpha_i. \tag{12.}$$

Substituting Equation 12 into Equation 11, we see that this model is simply an interactive model with random coefficients on the linear terms only.

This model is difficult to estimate. In its most general form, with many random coefficients, it requires the estimation of a huge number of parameters in the variance covariance of the random terms. Researchers can ask less of the data by allowing as many as possible of the coefficients to be fixed. It also makes sense to assume, as Western does, that the random coefficients are independently distributed, so no covariance terms need be estimated. This simplifies the estimation problem dramatically.

The RCM is seldom used in TSCS applications. One reason is that the RCM estimates of the β will be similar to the OLS estimates, in that OLS is still consistent, albeit inefficient if the coefficients really are random. Given the large sample sizes of typical TSCS data, this inefficiency may not be important. The OLS standard errors will of course be wrong. But, as Western (1998) shows, the RCM is of greater interest if we care about the estimated unit coefficients, the β_is. These are of great interest in the study of comparative politics. In what countries does politics have the greatest, or least, impact on economic performance?

All RCMs work by estimating the individual OLS estimates of the β_i, estimated one country at a time, and then shrinking them back to the overall pooled estimate of β. The degree of shrinkage is proportional to both how homogeneous

[8]In econometrics, the RCM dates back to Swamy (1971), who proposed a two-step estimator. Madalla & Hu (1996) report the inferior performance of the two-step estimator. Katz and I also have unpublished simulations showing that the two-step estimator performs poorly, even for very simple models. A variety of technical reasons for this poor performance are detailed by Beck (2000).

the units appear to be and how confident we are in our unit-by-unit estimates. This confidence is determined by T. In panel data, with small T, the RCM (known in that context as the hierarchical model) has been of great use. The issue is much less clear for TSCS data, especially as T gets large. It is also the case that we will observe the least shrinkage (that is, the least "borrowing of strength") when we most need it (i.e. when the units are heterogeneous) and the greatest shrinkage when we least need it (i.e. when the units are relatively homogeneous).[9] Thus, although RCMs appear to be an interesting way of modeling heterogeneity, the verdict on their utility for comparative politics is not yet clear.

8. BINARY DEPENDENT VARIABLES

So far we have assumed a continuous dependent variable, but what if we have binary TSCS (BTSCS) data?[10] Such data are particularly common in IR, where the dependent variable is whether a pair of nations was involved in a dispute in a given year and the independent variables are characteristics of the dyad (such as how democratic each nation is, or the level of dyadic trade). IR BTSCS analysts typically use the dyad-year design, where the variables are observed on pairs of nations annually over a long period (Maoz & Russett 1993). Observations on pairs of nations can produce a large N (4000 or so in the largest studies); the T in these studies ranges from ~50 to 100. These data sets present interesting problems that were usually ignored until very recently. My own current efforts deal with some BTSCS issues using an old-fashioned "treat the nuisance" approach, but some recent work attempts to model the interesting features of BTSCS data (see Beck & Tucker 1997 for further discussion).

Binary-dependent-variable panel studies are of great interest in biostatistics and econometrics. Many medical trials involve observing a large number of subjects a few times, with each observation recording a binary dependent variable (e.g. whether the subject showed a particular symptom). Although these studies are interesting, their relevance to BTSCS data is unclear; all of them are justified by asymptotics in N, and all were designed to work for small Ts. To give but one example, it is hard to allow for fixed effects in binary panel data, but fixed effects are as good (or as bad!) in BTSCS data as in TSCS data. Other popular BTSCS panel

[9]See Madalla & Hu (1996) for a computation of the shrinkage as a function of sample size and heterogeneity. Using his formula, I find that the RCM would shrink the unit OLS coefficients by only about 25%, back to the overall pooled estimates for the Garrett model we have been using. We have already seen that the pooled estimates for this model are quite acceptable. Thus, the RCM results for the Garrett model I have been using are not very interesting, and I do not report them here. This is not to say that RCM estimates of the β_i might not be more interesting in other data sets, such as that used by Western (1998).

[10]We could complicate matters further by allowing the data to be polychotomous or censored, but I restrict myself to the simple binary dependent variable case. Little is known about the more complex cases.

approaches, such as Liang & Zeger's (1986) "general estimating equation," may possibly work with BTSCS data, but all that has been proved about this method is that it works well for panel data.

Until 1999 or so, most analysts working with BTSCS data used ordinary logit (all results hold for probit also). This approach ignores both temporal and spatial dependencies in the data, which leads to inefficient estimation and incorrect standard errors. A modern approach attempts to model these features of the data. (See Gleditsch & Ward 2000 for a discussion of spatial issues.)

Dynamics: An Old-Fashioned Fix

Although it may seem odd to admit that an article I published two years ago has an old-fashioned solution, the fix for dynamic issues recommended in Beck et al (1998) treats dynamic issues as a nuisance that impedes estimation. The best solution would obviously be to directly model the dynamics; unfortunately this is very difficult. But failing to deal with the dynamics, either by old-fashioned or modern methods, can cause serious problems.[11]

Our old-fashioned solution for BTSCS data in IR is to think of them as event history data. Thus, the conflict data sets really contain information on the length of time between conflicts. This approach works if conflict is rare, so that most dyads manifest a long period of peace followed by an interlude of conflict.[12]

The advantage of thinking of BTSCS data as event history data is that event historians always allow for the possibility that the observations are temporally linked. For an event historian, the probability that a dyad will be in conflict, given that it is currently at peace, is a function of the past history of the dyad and not simply a function of current conditions.

To be more specific, it is easy to view BTSCS dyad-year data as grouped duration data suitable for a grouped Cox (1972) proportional hazards semiparametric estimation. The discrete version of the grouped duration Cox model is a complementary log-log model with a series of time dummy variables added to the specification. It is hard to see much difference in practice between the complementary log-log specification and the more common logit or probit. We thus recommend that researchers with data similar to the IR dyad-year conflict data do logit or probit but add the temporal dummies to their specifications.

Table 3 compares a discrete grouped time logit analysis (from Beck et al 1998) with an ordinary logit analysis (from Oneal & Russett 1997). The major consequence of including the temporal variables is that the pacific effects of international trade disappear.

---

[11]The problems are most severe when the errors are correlated and the independent variables trend. We have presented (Beck & Katz 1997) simulation results showing that, in the presence of severe trending and autocorrelation, standard errors can be off by 50% or more.

[12]The event history approach also sensitizes us to many other features of IR BTSCS data [see Beck et al (1998) and Beck & Katz (2001) for other insights we can reach by thinking like event historians].

TABLE 3 Comparison of ordinary logit and grouped duration analyses ($N = 20{,}990$)

	Ordinary	Logit	Grouped Duration	Logit[a]
Variable	$\hat{\beta}$	**SE**	$\hat{\beta}$	**SE**
Democracy	−0.50	0.07	−0.55	0.08
Economic growth	−2.23	0.85	−1.15	0.92
Alliance	−0.82	0.08	−0.47	0.09
Contiguous	1.31	0.08	0.70	0.09
Capability ratio	−0.31	0.04	−0.30	0.04
Trade	−66.13	13.44	−12.67	10.50
Constant	−3.29	0.07	−0.94	0.09
Log likelihood	−3477.6		−2554.7	
Degrees of freedom	20983		20036[b]	

[a]34 temporal dummy variables in specification not shown.

[b]Three dummy variables and 916 observations dropped.

Dynamics: A Modern Approach

A modern approach would, as we saw in Section 5, explicitly model the dynamics. Although this has not been done, I can sketch a reasonable approach. It starts with the latent variable setup for a logit model:

$$\begin{aligned} y^*_{i,t} &= \mathbf{x}_{i,t}\beta + \rho y^*_{i,t-1} + \epsilon_{i,t} \\ y_{i,t} &= 1 \text{ if } y^*_{i,t} > 0 \\ y_{i,t} &= 0 \text{ if } y^*_{i,t} \leq 0. \end{aligned} \tag{13}$$

This model looks like the standard dynamic setup, with the underlying latent variable for conflict, the propensity to be in conflict, being a function of its lagged value. This model is difficult to estimate by standard methods, but is estimable using Markov Chain Monte Carlo methods (see Jackman 2000a,b for political science applications). This appears to be a promising approach for future research.

The explicit model in Equation 13 also helps us to think about alternative dynamic specification. Some have suggested using the realization of the lagged dependent variable, $y_{i,t-1}$, in place of the latent lag in Equation 13. Looking at the specification, we see this is equivalent to asserting that a current conflict increases the propensity for a future conflict, but a current pacific year decreases that future propensity. Such a model is very easy to estimate (simply add $y_{i,t-1}$ to the logit), but is it sensible to do this? If a dyad has a high propensity for conflict but fails to engage in conflict during a given year, does this increase or decrease the likelihood of future conflict? A more sensible model, which might be called "strain relief," replaces the lagged latent variable in Equation 13 with the strain in the dyad, i.e. the lagged difference between the propensity for conflict and whether a conflict actually occurred ($y^*_{i,t-1} - \gamma y_{i,t-1}$). This strain relief model is akin to the continuous dependent variable error correction model that is so appealing. This model can also be estimated by Markov Chain Monte Carlo methods. Although this has not yet been done, the approach is promising.

Heterogeneity

BTSCS researchers have recognized the issue of heterogeneity. Thus, many analysts (Maoz & Russett 1993) limit their analysis to the so-called politically relevant dyads (involving major powers or contiguous states), assuming that other dyads are unlikely to be in conflict. Assuming two types of homogeneous dyads, those never in conflict and those that are politically relevant, is of course a very strong assumption. Beck et al (2000) argued that a more flexible way to handle this type of heterogeneity is to allow for massive interactions in a neural network model. These massive interactions allow for an independent variable of interest, say democracy, to have almost no effect in most dyads but a large effect in a few "conflict prone" dyads. More work is required before we can be confident about the utility of this approach.

A much simpler approach has been suggested by Green et al (2001). They suggest simply adding fixed effects (basically a dyadic-specific dummy variable) to the logit. Although fixed effects cannot be used in panel models, they may perhaps be useful for BTSCS data. However, the use of fixed effects in the IR conflict data causes us to believe that dyads that are never in conflict can give us no information about the impact of variables such as democracy on conflict. Because 90% of dyads are never in conflict, and since these dyads are more likely to be democratic, this is a very serious problem. For this reason, fixed effects are almost never a good idea for BTSCS data (Beck & Katz 2001). This is not to say that modeling heterogeneity is not important; far from it. But at present we do not have a good method for modeling heterogeneity in BTSCS data.

9. CONCLUSION

Katz and I became interested in TSCS data in about 1993. TSCS models were becoming of great interest in political science because they appeared to allow students of comparative politics (broadly defined) to use powerful statistical methods that had been the province of students of American politics (typically studying voting behavior via large-N surveys). Most studies either ignored TSCS issues or treated those issues as a nuisance, using an FGLS estimation method. In the early 1990s, researchers were using some procedures that, to my mind, had poor statistical properties or seemed otherwise dangerous. One reason that TSCS data is of interest is that the richness of the data allows us to do many things; but many of those things should not be done.

By now, most political science articles appear to use our recommended methodology of OLS estimates of β coupled with PCSEs, with dynamics modeled via a lagged dependent variable. Of course this seems to me like a reasonable way to estimate the fully pooled TSCS model. My hope is that researchers will take the error correction dynamic model seriously, although in practice stationary models have appeared to perform adequately. The use of (single equation) error correction models does not require researchers to leave the simple OLS world. This is not to imply that error correction models are easy to estimate or that there are no issues in using them. But a full discussion of these issues would take this essay too far afield.

Now that estimation issues have been dealt with, interest should focus on specification. Presumably political scientists have a comparative advantage in specification, not estimation! One current area of research is modeling TSCS data with a binary dependent variable; this is a particularly hot topic in the study of international conflict. Although this can be thought of as an arena of high technique, the important issues have to do with specification—that is, do the BTSCS data look like event history data, or should they be modeled with a lagged latent variable in a dynamic probit setup? Two other pressing issues are the incorporation of spatial effects and the modeling of heterogeneity. The former seems straightforward, and many researchers might take pleasure in noting that they have been estimating spatial models all along. Heterogeneity appears to be a more difficult problem, although "high-tech" approaches such as Bayesian RCMs should not detract from the use of simpler ideas, such as cross validation. In the end, all these issues are primarily issues of specification, not (difficult) estimation. Thus, we can begin to return the modeling of phenomena in comparative politics and IR back to political scientists, rather than leaving it in the hands of econometricians or biometricians.

ACKNOWLEDGMENTS

This paper reports work done jointly with Jonathan N Katz, and the use of "our" or "we" denotes Katz and myself. Thanks to Geoffrey Garrett, John Oneal, and Bruce Russett for supplying the data used here, to Simon Jackman for helpful discussions, and to Chad Rector and Laurie Rice for comments on a previous draft.

LITERATURE CITED

Alt J. 1985. Political parties, world demand and unemployment: domestic and international sources of economic activity. *Am. Polit. Sci. Rev.* 79:1016–40

Anselin L. 1988. *Spatial Econometrics: Methods and Models*. Boston: Kluwer Acad. 284 pp.

Beck N. 2000. Issues in the analysis of time-series–cross-section data in the year 2000. In *Social Science Methodology in the New Millennium. Proc. Int. Conf. Logic Methodol., 5th, Cologne, Oct. 3–6*, ed. E de Leeuw. Cologne: Int. Sociol. Assoc.

Beck N, Katz JN. 1995. What to do (and not to do) with time-series cross-section data. *Am. Polit. Sci. Rev.* 89:634–47

Beck N, Katz JN. 1996. Nuisance vs. substance: specifying and estimating time-series–cross-section models. *Polit. Anal.* 6:1–36

Beck N, Katz JN. 1997. *The analysis of binary time-series–cross-section data and/or the democratic peace.* Presented at Annu. Meet. Soc. Polit. Methodol., July, Columbus, OH

Beck N, Katz JN. 2001. Throwing out the baby with the bathwater: a comment on Green, Kim and Yoon. *Int. Organ.* In press

Beck N, Katz JN, Tucker R. 1998. Taking time seriously: time-series–cross-section analysis with a binary dependent variable. *Am. J. Polit. Sci.* 42:1260–88

Beck N, King G, Zeng L. 2000. Improving quantitative studies of international conflict: a conjecture. *Am. Polit. Sci. Rev.* 94:21–36

Beck N, Tucker R. 1997. *Conflict in time and space.* Cent. Int. Aff. Work. Pap. 97–8, Harvard Univ., https://wwwc.cc. columbia.edu/sec/dlc/ciao/wps/tur01

Berry FS, Berry WD. 1990. State lottery adoptions as policy innovations: an event history analysis. *Am. Polit. Sci. Rev.* 84:395–415

Blanton SL. 2000. Promoting human rights and democracy in the developing world: US rhetoric versus US arms exports. *Am. J. Polit. Sci.* 44:123–31

Burkhart R, Lewis-Beck M. 1994. Comparative democracy: the economic development thesis. *Am. Polit. Sci. Rev.* 88:903–10

Cox DR. 1972. Regression models and life tables. *J. R. Stat. Soc. Ser. B* 34:187–220

Davidson J, Hendry D, Srba F, Yeo S. 1978. Econometric modelling of the aggregate time-series relationship between consumers' expenditures and income in the United Kingdom. *Econ. J.* 88:661–92

Fiorina M. 1994. Divided government in the American states—a byproduct of legislative professionalism. *Am. Polit. Sci. Rev.* 88:304–16

Fording R. 1997. The conditional effect of violence as a political tactic: mass insurgency, welfare generosity, and electoral context in the American states. *Am. J. Polit. Sci.* 41:1–29

Franzese RJ. 2001. *The Political Economy of Macroeconomic Policy in Developed Democracies.* New York: Cambridge Univ. Press. In press

Freedman D, Peters S. 1984. Bootstrapping a regression equation: some empirical results. *J. Am. Stat. Assoc.* 79:97–106

Garrett G. 1998. *Partisan Politics in the Global Economy.* New York: Cambridge Univ. Press. 208 pp.

Gasiorowski MJ. 2000. Democracy and macroeconomic performance in underdeveloped countries: an empirical analysis. *Comp. Polit. Stud.* 33:319–49

Gelman A, Carlin JB, Stern HS, Rubin DB. 1995. *Bayesian Data Analysis.* London: Chapman & Hall. 526 pp.

Giles M, Hertz K. 1994. Racial threat and partisan identification. *Am. Polit. Sci. Rev.* 88:317–26

Gleditsch KS, Ward MD. 2000. Peace and war in time and space: the role of democratization. *Int. Stud. Q.* 44:1–29

Green D, Kim SY, Yoon D. 2001. Dirty pool. *Int. Organ.* In press

Greene W. 1999. *Econometric Analysis.* Upper Saddle River, NJ: Prentice Hall. 1004 pp. 4th ed.

Grier K, Tullock G. 1989. An empirical analysis of cross-national growth, 1951–80. *J. Monetary Econ.* 24:259–76

Hall P, Franzese R. 1998. Mixed signals: central bank independence, coordinated wage bargaining, and European monetary union. *Int. Organ.* 52:505–35

Hendry D, Mizon M. 1978. Serial correlation as a convenient simplification, not a nuisance: a comment on a study of the demand for money by the Bank of England. *Econ. J.* 88:549–63

Hicks A, Kenworthy L. 1998. Cooperation and political economic performance in affluent democratic capitalism. *Am. J. Soc.* 103:1631–72

Hsaio C. 1986. *Analysis of Panel Data.* New York: Cambridge Univ. Press. 246 pp.

Iversen T. 1999. *Contested Economic Institutions: The Politics of Macroeconomics and Wage Bargaining in Advanced Democracies.* New York: Cambridge Univ. Press. 221 pp.

Jackman S. 2000a. Estimation and inference via Bayesian simulation: an introduction to Markov Chain Monte Carlo. *Am. J. Polit. Sci.* 44:375–404

Jackman S. 2000b. Estimation and inference are "missing data" problems: unifying social-science statistics via Bayesian simulation. *Polit. Anal.* 8:307–32

Kmenta J. 1986. *Elements of Econometrics.* New York: Macmillan. 655 pp. 2nd ed.

Liang K-Y, Zeger SL. 1986. Longitudinal data analysis using generalized linear models. *Biometrika* 73:13–22

Madalla GS, Hu H. 1996. The pooling problem. In *The Econometrics of Panel Data*, ed. L Mátyás, P Sevestre, pp. 307–22. Dordrecht: Kluwer Acad. 2nd ed.

Maoz Z, Russett BM. 1993. Normative and structural causes of democratic peace, 1946–1986. *Am. Polit. Sci. Rev.* 87:639–56

Oneal JR, Russett BM. 1997. The classical liberals were right: democracy, interdependence, and conflict, 1950–1985. *Int. Stud. Q.* 41:267–94

Parks R. 1967. Efficient estimation of a system of regression equations when disturbances are both serially and contemporaneously correlated. *J. Am. Stat. Assoc.* 62:500–9

Pinheiro JC, Bates DM. 2000. *Mixed Effects Models in S and S-Plus*. New York: Springer. 528 pp.

Poe SC, Tate CN, Keith LC. 1999. Repression of the human rights to personal integrity revisited: a global cross-national study covering the years 1976–1993. *Int. Stud. Q.* 43:291–313

Radcliffe B, Davis P. 2000. Labor organization and electoral participation in industrial democracies. *Am. J. Polit. Sci.* 44:132–41

Smith K. 1997. Explaining variation in state-level homicide rates: Does crime policy pay? *J. Polit.* 59:350–67

Stone M. 1974. Crossvalidatory choice and assessment of statistical prediction. *J. R. Stat. Soc. Ser. B* 36:111–33

Su T-T, Kamlet M, Mowery D. 1993. Modeling United States budgetary and fiscal policy outcomes—a disaggregated, systemwide perspective. *Am. J. Polit. Sci.* 37:213–45

Swamy PAVB. 1971. *Statistical Inference in Random Coefficient Models.* New York: Springer-Verlag. 209 pp.

Western B. 1998. Causal heterogeneity in comparative research: a Bayesian hierarchical modelling approach. *Am. J. Polit. Sci* 42:1233–59

Annu. Rev. Polit. Sci. 2001. 4:295–316

THE ORIGINS AND WAR PRONENESS OF INTERSTATE RIVALRIES

John Vasquez and Christopher S. Leskiw

Department of Political Science, Box 1817-B, Vanderbilt University, Nashville, Tennessee 37235; e-mail: John.A.Vasquez@Vanderbilt.edu; Christopher.S.Leskiw@Vanderbilt.edu

Key Words rivalry, war, territory, power politics, militarized disputes

■ **Abstract** The study of interstate rivalry, which has made major contributions to theory and research on war, is reviewed, and new research on the role of territory in the origin and war proneness of rivalries is presented. Recent research has shown that states that are rivals are much more likely to go to war than are other states, and that about half the wars fought since 1815 have involved states that are rivals. This review describes the origins of interstate rivalries in terms of whether they begin over territorial disputes, policy disputes, or disputes over the nature of a state's regime. It finds that states that dispute territory have a greater probability of becoming rivals than expected by chance, compared with states that dispute other issues. It also investigates the extent to which territorial disputes and the recurring of disputes, despite their content, are related to the onset of war.

INTRODUCTION: Literature Review

The study of interstate rivalry has provided a major conceptual breakthrough in the scientific study of international relations and produced important findings on the outbreak of war. This article seeks to review this contribution and to extend our knowledge of interstate rivalry by testing a territorial explanation of the origins and war proneness of rivalries.

Although the term rivalry can be found in the traditional lexicon of international relations and diplomatic history, it is only in the past decade that the study of interstate rivalries has been the focus of systematic and scientific investigation. The term is from the Latin *rivalis*, meaning "one using the same stream as another." From this comes the conventional dictionary definition of rival as "one who is in pursuit of the same object as another; one striving to reach or obtain something which another is attempting to obtain, and which only one can possess; a competitor" (*Webster's New Twentieth Century Dictionary Unabridged*, 2nd ed.). The scientific study of interstate rivalry has been promising both in terms of reconceptualizing how international politics is studied and in terms of research results. The earliest scientific studies, i.e. those that collected and analyzed data, used the concept of rivalry to set either the context or the domain of the hypothesis under investigation. These early studies, however, did not directly examine rivalries in their own right. Instead, rivalries were a means of identifying dyads that had a high propensity for militarized conflict.

Arguably, the first such endeavor that treated interstate rivalry as important was the study by Wayman (1983). Although primarily interested in testing the power transition hypothesis, Wayman used rivalries to identify and characterize dyads whose members perceived significant levels of threat from each other (see Wayman 1996). Wayman operationalized rivalries as those dyads that had at least two militarized interstate disputes with each other during a ten-year period. Likewise, Diehl (1985) sought to test the hypothesis that arms races are related to disputes' escalation to war by examining mutual military buildups between states that could be considered rivals. States were deemed rivals when they had a certain number of recurring disputes within a specified number of years. Other studies (e.g. Gochman & Maoz 1984) also began to identify rivalries as dyads that engage in a disproportionate share of the total number of militarized disputes.

Differences in operationalization led to different lists of rivalries (for a review, see Goertz & Diehl 1993). Wayman & Jones (1991) identified enduring rivals as having at least five reciprocated militarized disputes within 25 years. This definition is intended to identify what Wayman (1983:8) calls a pattern of "enduring disputation" in the hopes of explaining both why this "disputatiousness" occurs and what effect it has on bringing about war. Goertz & Diehl (1992) defined enduring rivalries as those dyads that engage in six or more disputes over a 20-year span (Goertz & Diehl 1992:44, Diehl & Goertz 2000). On the basis of this definition, they then created a threefold typology of rivalry—isolated conflict, proto-rivalry, and enduring rivalry (Goertz & Diehl 1992). Isolated conflict refers to a dyad that experiences one or two disputes, whereas a proto-rivalry refers to those that have more than two disputes but do not fulfill the criteria for an enduring rivalry.

Some researchers are highly skeptical of the dispute-threshold approach to defining rivalry, especially since it means that a rivalry cannot be identified ex ante, i.e. before the requisite number of disputes is reached. For them, a definition based on simply counting the number of militarized disputes is too atheoretical. Thus, Vasquez (1996) argues that an adequate concept of rivalry must be able to predict when two states will have recurring disputes and not make the number of disputes a defining condition. In this way, recurring disputes becomes the dependent variable and the concept of rivalry the independent variable. Vasquez (1996:532) defines rivalry as "a relationship characterized by extreme competition and psychological hostility, in which the issue positions of contenders are governed primarily by their attitude toward each other rather than by the stakes at hand." Drawing on his earlier work with Mansbach, rivalry begins when a state switches from using a cost-benefit calculus of the stakes at issue to using a negative-affect calculus to determine its issue position. When a state resorts to a negative-affect calculus, it is more concerned about who gets what than about the value of the stakes. In that situation, hostility toward a specific state, rather than the intrinsic value of the stakes, determines one's issue position. Such an "actor orientation" results from persistent disagreement and the reliance on "negative acts" (i.e. conflictive actions), which result in psychological hostility. Eventually, an actor orientation links the various issues under contention into one grand, overarching issue of "us versus them" (see Mansbach & Vasquez 1981:197–203, 240–54; Vasquez 1993:75–82). From this perspective, mostly rivals, not all states as realists argue, are apt to be concerned with relative gains (cf Grieco 1988). Although this conceptualization leaves unanswered how terms such as hostility or relative gains will be measured, it does predict that these factors will make disputes recur.

Bennett (1996, 1998) adopts an issues approach to determine when rivalries end. He rejects the approaches of Wayman (1983) and Goertz & Diehl (1992, 1995), all of whom simply terminate rivalries after a certain number of years (10 and 15, respectively) without a dispute. For Bennett, rivalries end when the governments involved explicitly settle the issue (or issues) that has driven the rivalry. By determining (through historical analysis) what specific issue has produced a rivalry and identifying when that issue has been settled, Bennett (1996) provides more precise termination points of rivalries. This not only adds to our substantive knowledge but also is important for duration studies of rivalries (e.g. Bennett 1998, Cioffi-Revilla 1998).

Even more skeptical of the dispute-threshold approach is Thompson (1995), who argues that rivalry must be based on a state's perception of who its principal enemy is. Besides Wayman & Jones (1991) and Goertz & Diehl (1992), Thompson (2000a) is the only scholar to produce a list of interstate rivals. His method is to delve deeply into the historical record to determine which states see each other as their principal rival for a given period. Both Thompson and Vasquez (1996) attempt to conceptualize rivalries in a manner that would make it possible to identify them ex ante, rather than ex post facto. Both are only partially successful, however, because they each see hostility or perceptions, respectively, as growing out of crises, although Vasquez (1993:75–82) sees early crises as producing a psychological threshold that insures dispute recurrence, and Thompson (2000a) believes that principal rivals can exist without militarized disputes ever occurring, even if this is atypical.

Thompson and Vasquez see rivals as states that, by definition, are competitive with one another and able to instill mutual fear and insecurity. Therefore, both believe that true rivals must be relatively equal, at least in status if not in capability. Diehl & Goertz (2000:147–48), however, prefer to treat this as an empirical question. To Vasquez (1996:533) and Thompson (1995:195–97), it makes little sense to have a single concept cover the dynamics of the Soviet-American or Anglo-German rivalry on the one hand and United States–Ecuadoran or Anglo-Turkish conflict on the other.

Theoretically, the study of rivalry has been important because it has led to a major breakthrough in how the dynamics of conflict is conceptualized. The typical way scholars quantitatively study interstate war and conflict is to analyze the characteristics of the international system [e.g. whether capability is concentrated or dispersed (Singer et al 1972)], the characteristics of states [e.g. their expected utility for conflict (Bueno de Mesquita 1981)], and the characteristics of individual disputes or crises [e.g. the presence of arms races (Wallace 1982)] to see whether these distinguish the cases that go to war from those that do not. Each of these approaches, although producing important insights and findings (see Vasquez 2000a), employs a cross-sectional design that ignores the history of relations between states. Goertz & Diehl (1993) were in the forefront of making this point (see also Diehl & Goertz 2000:1–8).

To analyze each dispute two states might have without looking at how its dynamics are related to preceding disputes is to assume that the underlying relationship between states is unimportant, a dubious proposition. As far back as Leng (1983), research was beginning to show that there is a pattern to recurring crises. Each subsequent dispute tends to exhibit an increase in the level of escalation (see also Brecher & Wilkenfeld 1997:826–27), which suggests that learning of some sort is taking place (see also Maoz & Mor 1996).

At about this time, the preferred level of analysis in the field of peace research was shifting from the international system to the dyadic level (the relations of two states). An examination of dyads implies that studying what states do to each other and how they interact is critical to understanding why they go to war (Kegley & Skinner 1976:308–11, Singer 1982:37–38, Bueno de Mesquita & Lalman 1988, Vasquez 1993:43–45). Bremer's (1992) analysis of the characteristics that make for dangerous dyads demonstrated the fruitfulness of such an approach. The finding that democratic states do not fight each other (see Russett 1993) consolidated the shift to dyadic analysis.

This intellectual shift provided a receptive environment for the study of interstate rivalries because they provided a way of classifying the innumerable dyads into a typology that purports to distinguish those that are most war prone. The shift also implies that the dynamics of relations are a key to understanding why rivals are different from other dyads.

Methodologically, the emphasis on interstate rivalries provides an important criticism of research designs that compares individual disputes. Such designs treat disputes as statistically independent and unrelated to each other, but the latent theory of the rivalry approach denies that this is always the case. Many disputes between the same states are not independent of each other; rather, they follow a dynamic that stems from the underlying relationship of the two states. Hence, the use of significance tests (which assume independent observations) is inappropriate in these instances.

This criticism is probably even more important today than when it was initially made, given the current popularity of the dyad-year as the unit of analysis. The dyad-year attempts to capture the conflict involvement of a pair of states for every year both states exist (see Bennett & Stam 2000). Technically, a dyad-year analysis compares each pair of states in the world (or a theoretical subset) in a given year to every other pair, including the same two states in a different year. This is often done for the 1816–1992 temporal domain and easily results in hundreds of thousands of cases (for all possible dyads, the *N* in this temporal domain is approximately 447,000, depending on data availability; for "politically relevant" dyads, the *N* is approximately 48,000). Typically, logit coefficients and a chi square are then calculated.

Two problems exist with this type of data analysis. First, such a large *N* is very sensitive to small differences between cases, which makes it easy to attain statistical significance. Therefore, the best one could say for such a design is that if there is any relationship among the variables, this design will find it (i.e. it is good at avoiding type II errors but bad at avoiding type I errors). Second, and more important, the large number of cases produced by this design does not constitute (as it assumes) a sample of several hundred thousand observations but rather a considerably smaller number divided into many tiny pieces.

In addition to recognizing the obvious point that the behavior of a dyad in one year is not typically independent of the behavior of the same dyad in the previous and following years, the rivalry approach identifies where the more subtle division errors lie. Some dyads (rivals) have many recurring disputes, but others have only a few. The rivalry approach argues that the former cases should not be comingled with the latter because in these cases disputes are linked, and what links them is important for understanding why war occurs.

The idea that disputes are connected by some internal logic has led researchers to try to model how disputes are related to each other. Hensel (1996, 1998) argues that the recurring disputes within rivalries follow an evolutionary model, with hostility increasing over time until war breaks out (see also Vasquez 1993:82–83, 155–57). Diehl & Goertz (2000:Ch. 7) argue that a punctuated equilibrium model might be more appropriate.

Others have attempted to model the duration of rivalries (Cioffi-Revilla 1998) and the impact of conflict resolution (Bercovitch & Diehl 1997) and territorial settlement on the termination of rivalries (Gibler 1997). Such questions naturally lend themselves to a return to history. Thompson (1999) has been at the forefront of bringing together historians and political scientists to study rivalries using a common framework. His compendium of the major "great power" rivalries will go far in ending the ahistorical nature of much of the analysis on the onset of war.

These theoretical insights and methodological criticisms appear persuasive, but it is fair to say that they have attracted attention only because they have proved valuable in conducting research and advancing knowledge by producing new findings. This is where the study of interstate rivalries has made its major contribution. Indeed, these findings have had such an impact that those who question the existence of rivalries, arguing that they are really a statistical artifact (see Gartzke & Simon 1999), have not received much of an audience. The main findings to come out of the rivalry approach are that (*a*) conflicts are not independent of each other across time, (*b*) a few dyads are responsible for a majority of disputes, and (*c*) enduring rivals are highly war prone.

Beginning with the seminal work of Goertz & Diehl (1992), research has found that among all the pairs of states that interacted and engaged in militarized disputes from 1816 through 1992, the ones considered rivals (*a*) have a much greater probability of going to war and (*b*) account for most of the wars that occurred during that period. In their most recent analysis, Diehl & Goertz (2000:61–63) find that enduring rivals have a 0.59 probability of having fought at least one war between 1816 and 1992, whereas the probability for proto-rivals is 0.32, and the probability for states with isolated conflict is 0.16. In addition, they find that 49% of the wars that occurred in this period involved enduring rivalries. Similarly, in his study of strategic rivalries, Thompson (2000b:14) finds that approximately three of every four wars fought in the post-1815 period were linked in some way to a strategic rivalry.

Wayman (1996) deepens our knowledge of how war and rivalry are related. Generally, major states have a higher probability of going to war than other states (Bremer 1980, 2000). Wayman (1996) finds that the probability of going to war is even higher when major states that are rivals face each other on opposing sides. This probability of war increases even further if major-major rivals experience a power transition or rapid change in capability (see Table 5, p. 311, for examples of major-major rivals).

These findings have immense implications for the study of war. They reinforce the notion that war stems from a series of steps that states take against one another (Vasquez 1993, Bremer & Cusack 1995). They also provide evidence that recurring disputes between the same parties increases the probability of war. From a research angle, these findings suggest that understanding the dynamics of interactions will lead to additional insights about how and why war breaks out. From a theoretical point of view, they suggest that learning and an examination of bargaining and strategy are of potential importance (see Maoz & Mor 2001).

In the search for the causes of war and the conditions of peace, studying rivalries encourages researchers to look at the factors that produce rivalries in the first place, the factors within rivals' relations that make disputes recur and eventually escalate to war, and the factors that permit some rivals to successfully manage their interactions to avoid war and even peacefully terminate their rivalry. A few case studies on the endings of rivalries have been recently conducted (see e.g. Larson 1999, Leng 2000).

CRITICISMS OF THE RIVALRY APPROACH

Like any other research program in international relations, the study of rivalry is not without its critics. The predominant criticisms can be grouped into three categories: selection bias, the problem of (in)dependent observations, and the origins of rivalries. Selection bias refers to the process by which the cases used for analysis are selected from the entire population of potential observations. As its name implies, selection bias occurs when a nonrandom method of culling cases from the population is employed. Making inferences from such a sample may be problematic because researchers do not ask themselves what factors produce the sample in the first place. It may be these factors rather than the variables in the model that are having the major impact on the dependent variable (Achen 1986, Morrow 1989, Bueno de Mesquita 1996:61–63). A number of scholars have recently explored this problem both empirically (Gartner & Siverson 1996, Huth 1996b, Reed 2000) and theoretically, especially as it relates to questions of strategic choice (Smith 1999).

Selection bias can arise from the unintended actions of the researcher or from purposive acts such as "selecting on the dependent variable," causing little or no variance in the dependent variable (see King et al 1994:Ch. 4, Beck et al 2000:23). The rivalry approach becomes prone to selection bias by establishing rules to include only those dyads that meet a standard of a certain number of military conflicts within a given temporal domain. One cannot investigate how nonmilitarized rivalries differ from militarized ones, since the former are excluded by definition (Thompson 1995, 2000a). Furthermore, if we rely on a dispute threshold, the beginning and ending dates for rivalries may be suspect, since nonmilitarized periods of a rivalry are not captured. Others may regard the starting and ending dates of a sample as arbitrary, although this criticism is easier to defend for ending dates, which may be for convenience, than for starting dates (such as 1816), which have more historical significance.

Although the criticism regarding selection biases and their potential effects on the dependent variable raises important points, it must be remembered that it presents a logical argument; it remains to be seen if such effects actually occur empirically. In this sense, criticisms of research designs or existing data based on possible selection effects are not unlike challenging an empirical result by raising the question of spuriousness. Just because a relationship may seem spurious does not mean that it is. Criticisms based on spuriousness (and selection bias) are most productive when they give rise to new research. Such criticisms should be treated as alternative hypotheses rather than logical points that summarily dismiss findings without empirical testing.

Likewise, the fact that there may be reasons why a given set of cases are in a sample does not mean that important things cannot be learned by studying that sample. By utilizing a threefold typology of all dyads with militarized disputes, Diehl & Goertz (2000) can analyze a given dyad as it progresses over a varying degree of militarization (isolated, proto-, and enduring rivalries). They find that once states are enduring rivals they are more likely to go to war. They cannot, however, using their sample, tell us why states that have militarized disputes have disputes in the first place, and whether there is something about the dispute onset process that makes certain dyads more prone to become enduring rivals and/or go to war. They and others who take the rivalry approach assume that, once there is a dispute, the dynamics of disputation or variables related to that dispute are the key factors leading to recurring disputes and to war. Critics who raise the selection effects argument are pointing out that this may not, in fact, be the case—that the key factors may lie in the process by which states came to dispute in the first place. In our view, such disagreements need to be resolved empirically and not simply by logical or theoretical argumentation.

A second type of criticism states that the rivalry approach falsely assumes that militarized disputes are causally related across time. Traditionally, statistical methods have been applied in research that assume independence of cases across time and space. That is, a dispute between State A and State B in time t was not caused by a dispute between A and B in time $t - 1$. In fact, the rivalry approach points out that one cannot assume independence of cases, but this is based on research that has shown how past disputes influence future disputes in terms of initiation and severity (Leng 1983, Anderson & McKeown 1987, Hensel 1996). In an intriguing study, Gartzke & Simon (1999:787) question this assumption and posit that the observed pattern of related disputes is actually a result of a stochastic process: "If we are to be confident that a series of events are linked causally, we must show that the events occur in a manner that is significantly different from a series of unrelated events." Such a series in which low-probability events occur in a seeming pattern is called a hot hand. For example, if one tossed an unbiased coin (probability of heads 0.50) 100 times, one would not be surprised to find a long streak of just heads. Gartzke & Simon conduct tests that illustrate their claim that enduring rivalries, defined by the thresholds of disputes described in previous sections, seem to be an "artifact of systemic chance" (1999:788). Diehl & Goertz (2000:167) respond to this "hot hand" criticism by stating that enduring rival dyads are not like unbiased coins. Some dyads have a higher baseline chance of militarized disputes, that is, the patterns of enduring rivalries are more akin to a biased (weighted) coin toss.

Nevertheless, if those who take a rivalry approach are correct in assuming that their observations are not independent, then they need to take account of the problems this nonindependence of cases can pose for statistical analysis (see Beck et al 1998). In particular, Beck & Tucker (1996) find that including a test for duration dependence using a sample of Bennett's (1996) data can produce different results. Bennett (1998) follows up this critique with a more systematic study that also shows the importance of testing for duration dependence (see also Bennett 1999). Basically, he finds the longer a rivalry exists, the less likely it is to continue to exist (see also Cioffi-Revilla 1998). More important, he advances our knowledge beyond his previous study in that he finds in the presence of this positive duration dependence that issue salience (whether the rivalry involves questions of homeland territory) makes a rivalry last longer, whereas a change in polity in one of the rivals makes a rivalry shorter.

Duration dependence is only one way in which observations might be related and illustrates only one problem it poses for statistical analysis. As Bennett (1998:1207) points out, it can also lead to incorrect standard error estimates, so clustering or dependence within a rivalry must be taken into account. Likewise, Signorino's (1999:281) analysis of the ways in which strategic interdependence might affect statistical analysis and how these might be dealt with has yet to be applied to rivalry studies. If any set of dyads is apt to be subject to strategic interdependence, rivalries are certainly among them. Signorino (1999) argues that standard logit analyses do not do well in treating strategic interdependence [see

Beck et al (2000) for additional criticisms on the use of logit models to analyze conflict].

A final criticism is that the empirical literature contains very little on the origins of rivalries. Other theories are relied on to explain why the initial dispute or series of disputes may become an enduring rivalry (Gartzke & Simon 1999). Are the initial years of a pre-enduring rivalry qualitatively different from conflict in other contexts? Rivalries, particularly enduring ones, it is maintained, can only be identified ex post. Although this may be true of some studies, it is not the case that there has been no theory and research on what produces rivalries. Vasquez (1993:135, 311) argues that rivalry, especially between neighbors, is a product of territorial disagreements [see Wayman (2000) for some evidence]. Thompson (1988, 1995) maintains that the most important rivalries for the history of the system are over global leadership, but that rivalries can occur between any two states over positional issues (where one is in the pecking order) or spatial (territorial) issues. Huth (1996a) finds that certain kinds of territorial issues are more apt to result in rivalries than other kinds of territorial issues.

The remainder of this article addresses the questions of the origins of interstate rivalry and the war proneness of rivals by presenting new research on the role territory plays in each.

THEORY AND RESEARCH DESIGN

In a study of wars of rivalry, Vasquez (1993) argues that territorial disagreements are more apt to produce rivalries than are other types of issues and that they are more likely to result in war than are other types of disputes. Territorial issues, however, only increase the probability of war; they are not sufficient conditions for war. In fact, many individual territorial disputes do not escalate to war; whether they do depends on how they are handled. Territorial disputes that are handled in a power-politics fashion have a greater probability of going to war, in part because among equals, power politics fails to resolve a territorial issue and encourages disputes to recur—i.e. it encourages rivalry. Because resorting to power politics also encourages the recurrence of disputes, states whose relations are dominated by nonterritorial issues could in principle become rivals if those relations are dominated by power politics. However, this should be less likely when territorial issues are not involved. According to this theory,

1. Dyads dominated by territorial disputes are more apt to become enduring rivals than those dominated by other types of disputes (Hypothesis 1).

The theoretical explanation also sees territorial disputes and the use of power politics as increasing the probability of war. This suggests that

2. Rivals dominated by territorial disputes have a greater probability of going to war than would be expected by chance (Hypothesis 2).

The utility of each of these hypotheses for adding to our knowledge of interstate rivalry is explored below after a brief outline of the research design.

By adopting the rivalry approach to studying war and peace, one departs from the traditional analyses in a number of ways. Aside from clear theoretical differences, the rivalry approach introduces new empirical advantages and challenges. Typically, the units of analysis in the conflict-processes literature are the dispute, the dyadic dispute, and the dyad-year. The dispute unit focuses on the characteristics of a given militarized interstate dispute (MID). The dyadic-dispute approach breaks down a given dispute into its components, pairing up states on either side of the conflict. The dyad-year captures the conflict involvement of a pair of states for every year both states exist. As discussed above, each of these units of analysis ignores the history of relations of the states.

Because we are most interested in relationships between states across time, we employ the dyad as the unit of analysis, with a focus on collecting data that essentially summarize the conflict history of a dyad. Each observation constitutes a longitudinal record of the MIDs that occur between the two states. Such a record might also count the number of MIDs a particular dyad has and the number of those MIDs that escalate to war. This dyad record lacks independence across observations within it (e.g. MIDs and wars may be related), but this is not a problem statistically because each dyad record is treated as a single observation. We then can examine what kinds of issues dominate this dyad, whether it has ever had a war, and whether other kinds of issues emerge just before a war or a series of recurring disputes.

For this test, we use Diehl & Goertz's (2000) threefold typology of isolated conflict, proto-rivalry, and enduring rivalry to determine when a dyad is an enduring rivalry. To determine whether a dyad is dominated by territorial disputes or some other kind of dispute, the revision type code in the MID is employed. This variable labels revisionist states in a MID as seeking a change in territory, in a state's foreign policy or regime, or in regard to some miscellaneous question (see Jones et al 1996:178). Using Diehl & Goertz's (2000:145–46) classification makes us susceptible to some of the criticisms of their data, namely that their identification of enduring rivals is ex post facto. Nevertheless, since we wish to show that territorial disputes increase the probability of states becoming rivals, we feel compelled to show that the enduring rivals that Diehl & Goertz (2000) identify will follow this pattern. It must also be pointed out that part of this criticism is undercut by our including in our sample any dyad that has a militarized dispute, regardless of whether it becomes a proto- or enduring rivalry.

Three different measures can be used to determine the dominance of territorial disputes in a given relationship. One measure is whether at least 25% of the MIDs in a dyad are over territorial questions. A second measure, which we call issue dom, can be used to determine what kinds of disputes dominate the relations of two states. Basically, if 50% of a dyad's MIDs are focused on one revision type (territory, policy, regime, or other), we consider this the issue that dominated their relations. If no one type reached 50%, then the mode is used. In cases of ties, a combination of types is used (e.g. territory and policy).

In this analysis, we are also interested in the early issues that led states to become rivals. We measure this "prior issue" variable by examining only the MIDs that occurred prior to reaching the threshold of an enduring rivalry; i.e. we examine only the MIDs that occurred during the proto-rivalry and isolated conflict stages of the relationship that eventually became an enduring rivalry. For example, the relationship between the United States and Soviet Union before World War II is considered a proto-rivalry. During this time, they contended predominantly over regime issues. From 1946 until 1986, the United States and the Soviet Union were enduring rivals (here they contended predominantly over policy issues). Therefore, we determine the pre-enduring dispute history of this dyad to concern regime issues. (For data on each of these measures, see Table 5, p. 311.) Although such data are ex post facto, this does not diminish their historical accuracy, nor should it affect the hypothesis testing, since the data on territorial as well as policy, regime, and miscellaneous disputes are created in the same manner. To determine whether a dyad ever had a war, we utilize the war data of the Correlates of War project (see Small & Singer 1982) and include all the war joiners it lists.

FINDINGS ON ORIGINS

Table 1 provides evidence to support Hypothesis 1, namely that a pair of states whose relations involve numerous territorial disputes is more apt to have recurring disputes and, hence, is likely to become an enduring rivalry. A comparison of the observed and expected columns shows that dyads with <25% territorial disputes would be predicted by chance to have 41.8 enduring rivalries but in fact have only 30. Conversely, those with >25% territorial disputes would be expected by chance to have 21.2 enduring rivalries but in fact have 33. More formally, the

TABLE 1 Cross-tabulation of rivalry type and >25% territorial MIDs, 1815–1992[a]

Rivalry type	Obs	Exp	Total	Base *P*	Cond *P*	Z	*P*
<25% Territory							
Isolated	615	583.4	880	0.755	0.796	2.65	<0.01
Proto	128	147.8	223	0.191	0.166	–1.77	0.038
Enduring	30	41.8	63	0.054	0.039	–1.845	0.032
>25% Territory							
Isolated	265	296.6	880	0.755	0.674	–3.73	<0.001
Proto	95	75.2	223	0.191	0.242	2.52	<0.01
Enduring	33	21.2	63	0.054	0.084	2.631	<0.01

[a]MID, militarized interstate dispute; Obs, observed; Exp, expected; Cond, conditional; *P*, probability; Z, Z test.

evidence presented shows that dyads with ≥ 25% of their MIDs devoted to territorial questions have a greater probability of becoming an enduring rivalry than those with < 25% of their MIDs focusing on territorial questions. The overall probability of a dyad becoming an enduring rivalry in this sample is 0.054 (the base probability), which can be used as a benchmark. The (conditional) probability of those with <25% territorial disputes becoming an enduring rivalry is less than the benchmark (0.039), producing a −2 score, whereas for those with more territorial disputes the probability is greater than the benchmark (0.084), producing a +2 score. These differences between the conditional and base probabilities are statistically significant, as indicated in the last two columns of Table 1. The significance level for this and all subsequent tests is based on a one-tailed test because the hypotheses specify the direction of the relationship (see Blalock 1960:122–24).

Table 2 goes to the heart of the question of the origins of rivalries. Here the dependent variable is rivalry type and the independent variable is the prior issue, i.e. a dyad's history of disputes prior to becoming an enduring rivalry. In Table 2, we are interested in the issues over which dyads fought before they were rivals. Although we do not contend that enduring rivalries are "born" rather than grown or evolved, the following analysis may shed some light on the hypothesis that enduring rivalries are qualitatively different from other dyads at their beginnings.

Table 2 analyzes the relationship between rivalry types and their issue origins while controlling for status. Minor-minor and major-major enduring rivals seem to

TABLE 2 Cross-tabulation of rivalry type and prior issue dominance of territory, controlling for status, 1815–1992[a]

Rivalry type	Obs[b]	Exp	Total	Base *P*	Cond *P*	Z	*P*
Minor-minor							
Isolated	35	34.9	83	0.697	0.70	0.046	0.480
Proto	8	10.9	28	0.218	0.160	−0.99	0.460
Enduring	7	4.2	10	0.084	0.14	1.427	0.070
Major-minor							
Isolated	24	24.1	144	0.778	0.774	−0.054	0.480
Proto	6	5.4	32	0.173	0.194	0.309	0.378
Enduring	1	1.5	9	0.049	0.032	−0.438	0.330
Major-major							
Isolated	1	2	19	0.404	0.20	−0.929	0.460
Proto	2	2.1	20	0.426	0.40	−0.118	0.452
Enduring	2	0.9	8	0.17	0.40	1.369	0.085

[a]Obs, observed; Exp, expected; Cond, conditional; *P*, probability; Z, Z test.

[b]The number of observations is reduced due to the fact that a number of dyads begin as enduring rivals and do not have a prior history of militarized interstate disputes, i.e. they are "left-censored." See Table 5 for these cases.

conform to the pattern stated in Hypothesis 1. Prior to becoming enduring rivals, both of these types of dyads have a history of disputes dominated by territorial issues. In minor-minor enduring rivalries, chance alone would predict the relationships of 4.2 dyads to be dominated by territorial disputes prior to their enduring rivalries. Instead, 7 of these dyads behave in this manner. Put another way, the (base) probability of a minor-minor dyad becoming an enduring rivalry is 0.084, but the (conditional) probability that a minor-minor dyad will become a rivalry if its early disputes concern territory is 0.14. This difference is statistically significant at the 0.07 level—below the 0.10 level, which although not as strict as the 0.05 level is acceptable given the small *N*. In addition, this finding is consistent with Wayman's (2000:230–31) review of the case evidence, in which he finds that the relations of most minor-minor rivals are dominated by territorial disputes.

The number of cases is even smaller for major-major enduring rivalries, but the findings are similar. The (base) probability of a major-major dyad becoming an enduring rivalry is 0.17, but the (conditional) probability of a major-major dyad whose early disputes concern territory becoming an enduring rivalry is 0.40, which is significant at the 0.085 level. This finding suggests that enduring rivalries between states equal in status may result from an early history of disputes over territorial issues. We might tentatively conclude that enduring rivalries have qualitatively different origins from other types. As can be seen from Table 2, having territorial disputes has no significant impact on dyads engaging in isolated conflict or becoming proto-rivals.

This relationship does not hold for the mixed dyads (major-minor), i.e. when states are unequal. Unequal states in territorial disputes are no more likely to become enduring rivals than would be expected by chance, as is demonstrated by comparing the observed and expected columns in Table 2. This finding supports Vasquez's (1993) contention that the concept of rivalry should be confined to states of relatively equal status. Although Table 2 presents evidence that states whose relations are dominated by territorial disputes are more apt to become rivals, this should not be taken to mean that all types of territorial issues are equally likely to give rise to militarized disputes or to rivalry. Huth (1996a) finds that certain kinds of territorial claims are more apt to have these effects. Examining only dyads that have territorial claims, he finds that territorial issues associated with ethnic questions (as opposed to strategic territory or economically valuable territory) are more likely to give rise to rivalry in the post-1950 period (see also Huth 1996b).

Further analysis of equal dyads also shows that such dyads that contend over territorial questions have the highest probability of becoming enduring rivals. Indeed, only a prior history of territorial disputes increases the likelihood of equal dyads becoming a rivalry. When equal states have a prior history of policy or regime disputes, they are pushed in the opposite direction, i.e. they are less likely to become an enduring rivalry, although the observed cases are usually close to what is randomly expected. The remaining question is: Do rivals that contend over territorial disputes also have a higher probability of going to war?

FINDINGS ON WAR PRONENESS

Like Diehl & Goertz (2000:61–64), we have found that the war proneness of a dyad increases along the continuum from isolated conflict to enduring rivalry. For example, dyads that have only isolated conflict have fewer wars than randomly expected; their conditional probability of war is 0.28, significantly lower than the overall base probability of 0.32. Conversely, enduring rivals have more wars than expected, with a conditional probability of war of 0.571, which is significantly higher than the base probability of war of 0.32.

When we examine the prior-issue variable to determine whether rivals whose early history focused on territorial disputes are more war prone than would be expected by chance, we find that the relationship is not statistically significant and that the difference is not even in the right direction (Table 3). Proto-rivalries and dyads that have isolated conflict with a prior history of territorial disputes do have more wars than would be expected, but enduring rivals do not (5 versus 5.6). Although these findings are not statistically significant, the unexpected direction of the findings implies two things. First, it suggests that dyads that are not rivals (but have territorial disputes) may have a greater probability of going to war than would be expected by chance. In other words, territorial disputes may produce war between states long before relations reach a rivalry stage. Second, although our measure of prior issue predicts fairly well whether a dyad contesting territory will become an enduring rivalry, it is less useful for predicting whether they will go to war. To more accurately predict the war proneness of rivals, one must look at the later MIDs and not just the early ones.

Table 4 does this by employing a variation on the issue dom measure, which looks at the entire history of a dyad's MIDs. (In this variation, "Issue Dom2" combines dyads dominated by territorial disputes with dyads dominated by both territorial and policy disputes.) Here, we find that for each of the categories, including enduring rivals, the direction of the relationship is as predicted by Hypothesis 2. Dyads with territorial disputes have more wars than are expected by chance. The base probability of war goes up from isolated conflict to proto-rivalry to enduring rivalry (.28, .408, and .571), as does the conditional probability of war for dyads

TABLE 3 Cross-tabulation of prior issue dominance of territory and occurrence of war, controlling for rivalry type, 1815–1992[a]

Rivalry type	Obs[b]	Exp	Total	Base *P*	Cond *P*	Z	*P*
Isolated	28	23.4	96	0.39	0.467	1.22	0.112
Proto	10	8.6	42	0.538	0.625	0.698	0.245
Enduring	5	5.6	15	0.556	0.500	−0.356	0.359

[a]Obs, observed; Exp, expected; Cond, conditional; *P*, probability; Z, Z test.

[b]The number of observations is reduced due to the fact that a number of dyads begin as enduring rivals and do not have a prior history of militarized interstate disputes, i.e. they are "left-censored." See Table 5 for these cases.

TABLE 4 Cross-tabulation of issue dominance (2) of territory and occurrence of war, controlling for rivalry type, 1815–1992[a]

Rivalry type	Obs[b]	Exp	Total	Base *P*	Cond *P*	Z	*P*
Isolated	121	71.6	246	0.28	0.473	6.87	<0.001
Proto	34	23.3	91	0.408	0.596	2.88	<0.01
Enduring	15	12.6	36	0.571	0.682	1.05	0.147

[a]Obs, observed; Exp, expected; Cond, conditional; *P*, probability; Z, Z test.

[b]The number of observations is reduced due to the fact that a number of dyads begin as enduring rivals and do not have a prior history of militarized interstate disputes, i.e. they are "left-censored." See Table 5 for these cases.

dominated by territorial questions (.473, .596, and .682). The difference between the base and conditional probabilities is significant at or below the 0.01 level for isolated conflict and proto-rivalries, but not for enduring rivalries, where it only reaches a *p* value of 0.14. These findings, although not consistent with Hypothesis 2, underscore the war proneness of territorial disputes—they can produce war in the absence of rivalry.

The findings in Table 4 imply that dyads that contend in territorial disputes have a greater probability of going to war than is expected by chance, regardless of whether dyads are enduring rivals. At the same time, the findings imply that rivals have a greater probability of going to war than do other dyads, even if they are contending over nonterritorial questions.

Tables 3 and 4 suggest not so much that Hypothesis 2 is technically false but that it is incomplete. They imply the need to reformulate the hypothesis. The implicit model in Hypotheses 1 and 2 (Figure 1) of territorial disputes leading to rivalry, and territory being the main factor making rivals war prone, is too simple. The findings are more consistent with a model in which territorial disputes are directly related to the onset of war (by increasing its probability) and directly related to the emergence of rivalry. The reason rivals go to war may lie in territory, but it may also lie in other factors, such as the mere repetition of disputes or, more likely, resorting to power politics to handle repeated disputes [which is consistent with Vasquez (1993:86–87, 195–97)]. This reasoning gives rise to Hypothesis 3, also depicted in Figure 1:

3. The reason rivals have a greater probability of going to war than do other dyads is that they tend to consist of dyads that are dominated either by territorial disputes or by the use of power politics.

Table 5 may help clarify these relationships. It lists the issue origins of each enduring rivalry identified by Diehl & Goertz (2000) grouped by the status of actors. The minor-minor rivals are much more focused on territorial disputes than are the major-major rivals. About half of the minor-minor rivals focus on territory and about 60% have at least 25% of their MIDs over territory. The minor-minor dyads are more apt to conform to the model of Hypotheses 1 and 2, especially since

HYPOTHESES 1 & 2 MODEL

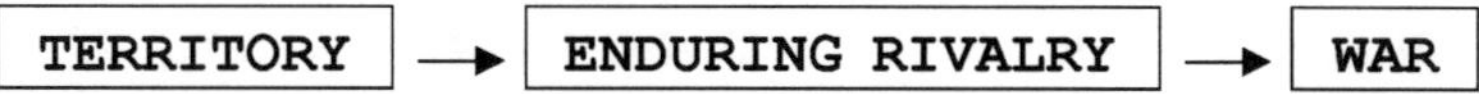

HYPOTHESIS 3 MODEL

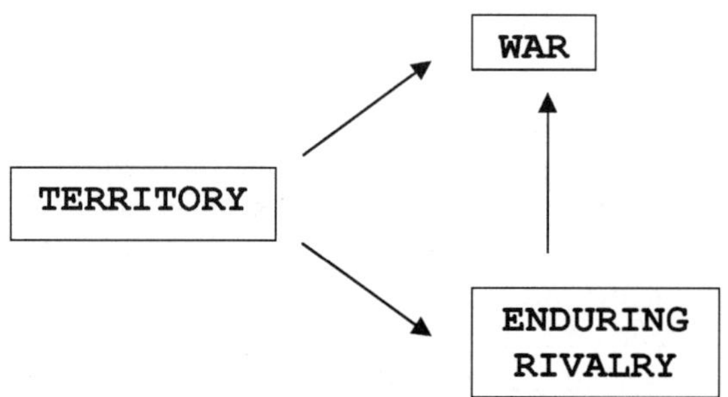

Figure 1 Alternate models of the relationship among territory, enduring rivalry, and war. The figure suggests that territorial disputes and rivalry provide two different routes to war. One route is directly from territorial disputes to war regardless of whether these reach the stage of enduring rivalry. The second route is from enduring rivalry to war, which can also include an indirect route of territorial dispute to enduring rivalry to war.

previous analyses reported herein have shown that the reason for this distribution is that territorial disputes are likely to recur and, thus, produce rivalries.

Conversely, the reason so many minor-minor rivals focus on policy disputes is not that these disputes recur (in fact they are less likely to recur than would be expected by chance), but simply that so many minor-minor dyads have policy disputes in the first place that a certain number are bound to end up in rivalry, even though this is not statistically significant.

This selection effect does not seem to be at work with major-major rivals, however. Here, we have few rivals focusing on territorial questions—at best 3 of 9, although 5 have at least 25% of their MIDs devoted to territorial questions. A number of these rivalries originated in policy disagreements. Because all these rivals go to war, it is likely that there is a separate path to war from the territorial path to war.

It is beyond the scope of this analysis to identify the other path, but the literature holds several suggestions. Rasler & Thompson (2000) argue that principal rivals are focused on two separate issues: spatial (territorial) and positional

TABLE 5 Enduring rivalries and key variables, 1816–1992[a]

Rivalry name	>25% terr.	Prior issue	Issue dom	# of mids	COW war
Minor-Minor Dyads					
US-Mexico	0		2	17	0
US-Spain	0	2	2	10	1
Honduras-Nicaragua	0		3	6	1
Ecuador-Peru	1	1	1	21	0
Chile-Argentina 1873–1909	1	1	1	10	0
Chile-Argentina 1952–84	1	1	1	17	0
Spain-Morocco	1	2	2	8	1
Yugoslavia-Bulgaria	1		2	8	1
Greece-Bulgaria	0		2	9	1
Greece-Turkey 1866–1925	1	5	1	17	1
Greece-Turkey 1958–89	1	1	1	14	1
Cyprus-Turkey	0		2	7	0
Congo-Zaire	0		2	7	0
Uganda-Kenya	1		2	6	0
Somalia-Ethiopia	1		1	16	1
Ethiopia-Sudan	0		2	8	0
Morocco-Algeria	1		2	6	0
Iran-Iraq	1	1	1	20	1
Iraq-Israel	1	1	2	6	1
Iraq-Kuwait	1		1	9	1
Egypt-Israel	1		1	36	1
Syria-Jordan	0		2	9	0
Syria-Israel	1		1	45	1
Jordan-Israel	1		1	13	1
Israel-Saudi Arabia	1		2	6	1
Saudi Arabia-Yemen	0	1	2	6	1
Afghanistan-Pakistan	1		1	11	0
N. Korea-S. Korea	0		3	20	1
S. Korea-Japan	0		2	15	0
India-Pakistan	1		1	40	1
Thailand-Cambodia	1		1	14	0
Thailand-Laos	0		1	13	0
Thailand-N.Vietnam	0		3	6	1
Major-Minor Dyads					
US-Cuba	0	2	2	15	0
US-Peru	0	1	2	6	0
US-UK	1		2	8	0
US-North Korea	0		3	18	1
US-Ecuador	0		2	8	0
UK-Brazil	1	2	1	6	0
UK-Turkey	0	2	2	10	1

(*Continued*)

TABLE 5 *(Continued)*

Rivalry name	>25% terr.	Prior issue	Issue dom	# of mids	COW wa
UK-Iraq	0	3	2	10	1
Belgium-Germany	1	2	2	8	1
France-Turkey	1	2	2	11	1
France-China	1		2	6	1
Italy-Yugoslavia	1		1	8	1
Italy-Ethiopia	1		1	6	1
Italy-Turkey	0	0	2	14	0
USSR-Norway	0		2	9	0
USSR-Iran	0		2	18	0
Russia-Turkey	0	2	2	12	0
China-S. Korea	0		5	9	1
China-India	1		1	22	1
Major-Major Dyads					
US-USSR	0	3	2	53	0
US-China	1	2	5	24	1
UK-Germany	1	2	2	7	0
UK-Russia	0	2	2	18	1
UK-USSR	0	2	2	17	0
France-Germany 1830–87	0		2	12	1
France-Germany 1911–45	1	2	2	9	1
Germany-Italy	0	1	2	7	0
USSR-China	1		1	50	1
USSR-Japan	0	1	2	43	1
China-Japan	1		2	34	1

[a]Value of 1 in the >25% Terr. column means that those dyads have 25% or more of their MIDs over territorial issues. The COW War variable equals 1 when the dyad has experienced at least one war as identified in the Correlates of War Project's War List. Prior issue values are as follows: 1 = dyad dominated by territory; 2 = policy; 3 = regime; 4 = other; 5 = dyad dominated by territory and policy equally.

(struggles over power and global leadership). They see major-state rivals as concerned primarily with the latter. Whether the policy origins of the major-major rivals listed in Table 5 turn out to be positional issues must await further research, but certainly the evidence here leaves that possibility open. Another possibility is that major-major states come to war primarily through multilateral wars rather than direct two-party wars (see Vasquez 1996). From this perspective, dyadic wars tend to be a result of states fighting over territory, whereas more complex multilateral wars involve linking issues as well as contagion effects. A third possibility is that major-major rivals have recurring disputes and go to war because they handle their nonterritorial disputes in a power-politics fashion (see Vasquez 1993:86–90, 157–58, 195–97). Preliminary research by Valeriano (2001) shows that major-major enduring rivals tend to resort to the power-politics practices of alliances and arms races significantly more frequently than other major-major dyads that have disputes.

It is noteworthy that few rivalries stem from regime disputes. Among the major states, there has been only the Soviet-American rivalry, which later became dominated by policy disputes. Among minor states, there are only three—Honduras-Nicaragua, North and South Korea, and Thailand–North Vietnam.

Besides helping to elucidate the statistical analyses presented in this review, Table 5 also provides the first listing of the issue origins of interstate enduring rivalries from 1816 through 1992, based on the coding of the MID data. We hope this list will spur more in-depth historical case studies.

CONCLUSION

The study of interstate rivalry has reintroduced the importance of the history of relations between states for understanding conflict and war. It has emphasized the idea that war is a process that emerges out of repeated disputes. Research on rivalry has shown that enduring rivals have a much greater probability of going to war than other states involved in militarized confrontations and that these rivals account for almost half the wars fought during the period 1816–1992.

This review has sought to identify the origins of interstate rivalry and to show how the issues that give rise to rivalry affect the war proneness of states. We find that states that contend over territorial issues are much more apt to become enduring rivals (Table 1). We also find that this tendency is most pronounced in equal dyads whose early disputes are over territorial questions (Table 2) and that it does not hold for unequal dyads. The origin of interstate rivalry, then, appears to lie in territorial disputes.

Like other studies, our analysis indicates that enduring rivals are much more apt to go to war than other pairs of states. We expected to find the reason for this in the war proneness of territorial disputes. We find that dyads with territorial disputes have a significantly higher probability of going to war than would be expected by chance—even if they do not reach the enduring rivalry stage. However, territorial disputes do not fully account for the war proneness of enduring rivalries (Tables 3 and 4). Enduring rivals without territorial disputes also go to war fairly frequently. This finding suggests that although territory may provide one path to war, there is another path for rivals whose disputes are nonterritorial.

An examination of rivals' issues of contention (Table 5) suggests that minor-minor rivals are most apt to take the territorial path to war. Major-major rivals may also follow this path, but a number of them follow another path whose origins lie in policy disputes. Whether there is something peculiar about these policy disputes that leads states to go to war, or whether war results because these disputes are handled in a power-politics fashion, is a question that awaits further research. Nevertheless, it is clear that the repetition of disputes, whether territorial or policy-related, is critical in making states go to war. Studying the dynamics of rivalry, therefore, is important to explain the onset of war.

ACKNOWLEDGMENTS

The research reported in this article has been supported by a grant from the National Science Foundation (SES 9818557). Our thanks to Bruce Bueno de Mesquita and Marie T Henehan for valuable comments. Since we have not always taken their suggestions, neither should be seen as necessarily agreeing with the analysis herein.

LITERATURE CITED

Achen CH. 1986. *The Statistical Analysis of Quasi-Experiments*. Berkeley: Univ. Calif. Press

Anderson PA, McKeown TJ. 1987. Changing aspirations, limited attention, and war. *World Polit.* 40:1–29

Beck N, Katz JN, Tucker R. 1998. Taking time seriously: time-series-cross-section analysis with a binary dependent variable. *Am. J. Polit. Sci.* 42:1260–88

Beck N, King G, Zeng L. 2000. Improving quantitative studies of international conflict: a conjecture. *Am. Polit. Sci. Rev.* 94:21–35

Beck N, Tucker R. 1996. *Conflict in space and time: time-series-cross-section analysis with a binary dependent variable*. Presented at Annu. Meet. Am. Polit. Sci. Assoc., San Francisco

Bennett SD. 1996. Security, bargaining, and the end of interstate rivalry. *Int. Stud. Q.* 40:157–83

Bennett SD. 1998. Integrating and testing models of rivalry. *Am. J. Polit. Sci.* 42:1200–32

Bennett SD. 1999. Parametric models, duration dependence and time-varying data revisited. *Am. J. Polit. Sci.* 43:256–70

Bennett SD, Stam AC. 2000. Research design and estimator choices in the analysis of interstate dyads: when decisions matter. *J. Confl. Resolut.* 44:653–85

Bercovitch J, Diehl PF. 1997. Conflict management of enduring rivalries: frequency, timing and short-term impact of mediation. *Int. Interact.* 22:299–320

Blalock HM. 1960. *Social Statistics*. New York: McGraw-Hill

Brecher M, Wilkenfeld J. 1997. *A Study of Crisis*. Ann Arbor: Univ. Mich. Press

Bremer SA. 1980. National capabilities and war proneness. In *The Correlates of War* Vol. II, ed. JD Singer, pp. 57–82. New York: Free

Bremer SA. 1992. Dangerous dyads: conditions affecting the likelihood of interstate war, 1816–1965. *J. Confl. Resolut.* 36:309–41

Bremer SA. 2000. Who fights whom, when, where, and why? In *What Do We Know about War*? See Vasquez 2000b, pp. 23–36

Bremer SA, Cusack TR, eds. 1995. *The Process of War*. Amsterdam: Gordon & Breach

Bueno de Mesquita B. 1981. *The War Trap*. New Haven, CT: Yale Univ. Press

Bueno de Mesquita B. 1996. The benefits of a social science approach to studying international affairs. In *Explaining International Relations Since 1945*, ed. N Woods, New York: Oxford Univ. Press

Bueno de Mesquita B, Lalman D. 1988. Empirical support for systemic and dyadic explanations of conflict. *World Polit.* 41:1–20

Cioffi-Revilla C. 1998. The political uncertainty of interstate rivalries: a punctuated equilibrium model. In *The Dynamics of Enduring Rivalries*, ed. PF Diehl, pp. 64–97. Urbana: Univ. Illinois Press

Diehl PF. 1985. Arms races to war: testing some empirical linkages. *Sociol. Q.* 26:331–49

Diehl PF, Goertz G. 2000. *War and Peace in International Rivalry*. Ann Arbor: Univ. Mich. Press

Gartner SS, Siverson RM. 1996. War expansion

and war outcomes. *J. Confl. Resolut.* 40:4–15

Gartzke E, Simon M. 1999. Hot hand: a critical analysis of enduring rivalries. *J. Polit.* 61:777–98

Gibler DM. 1997. Control the issues, control the conflict: the effects of alliances that settle territorial issues on interstate rivalries. *Int. Interact.* 22:341–68

Gochman CS, Maoz Z. 1984. Militarized interstate disputes, 1816–1976: procedures, patterns, and insights *J. Confl. Resolut.* 28:585–616

Goertz G, Diehl PF. 1992. The empirical importance of enduring rivalries. *Int. Interact.* 18:151–63

Goertz G, Diehl PF. 1993. Enduring rivalries: theoretical constructs and empirical patterns. *Int. Stud. Q.* 37:147–71

Goertz G, Diehl PF. 1995. Taking "enduring" out of enduring rivalry: the rivalry approach to war and peace. *Int. Interact.* 21:291–308

Grieco JM. 1988. Anarchy and the limits of international cooperation: a realist critique of the newest liberal institutionalism. *Int. Org.* 42:485–507

Hensel P. 1996. *The evolution of interstate rivalry.* PhD thesis. Univ. Illinois, Urbana-Champaign

Hensel P. 1998. Interstate rivalry and the study of militarized conflict. In *Conflict in World Politics: Advances in the Study of Crises, War and Peace*, ed. F Harvey, B Mor, pp. 162–204. London: Macmillan

Huth PK. 1996a. Enduring rivalries and territorial disputes, 1950–1990. *Confl. Manage. Peace Sci.* 15:7–41

Huth PK. 1996b. *Standing Your Ground: Territorial Disputes and International Conflict.* Ann Arbor: Univ. Mich. Press

Jones DM, Bremer SA, Singer JD. 1996. Militarized interstate disputes, 1816–1992: rationale, coding rules, and empirical patterns. *Confl. Manage. Peace Sci.* 15:163–213

Kegley CW, Skinner RJ. 1976. The case-for-analysis problem. In *In Search of Global Patterns*, ed. J Rosenau, pp. 303–18. New York: Free

King G, Keohane RO, Verba S. 1994. *Designing Social Inquiry: Scientific Inference in Qualitative Research.* Princeton, NJ: Princeton Univ. Press

Larson DW. 1999. The US-Soviet rivalry. In *Great Power Rivalries*, ed. WR Thompson, pp. 371–89. Columbia: Univ. South Carolina Press

Leng R. 1983. When will they ever learn? Coercive bargaining in recurrent crises. *J. Confl. Resolut.* 27:379–419

Leng R. 2000. *Bargaining and Learning in Recurring Crises: The Soviet-American, Egyptian-Israeli, and Indo-Pakistani Rivalries.* Ann Arbor: Univ. Mich. Press

Mansbach RW, Vasquez JA. 1981. *In Search of Theory: A New Paradigm for Global Politics.* New York: Columbia Univ. Press

Maoz Z, Mor B. 1996. Enduring rivalries: the early years. *Int. Polit. Sci. Rev.* 17:141–60

Maoz Z, Mor B. 2001. *International Hate Affairs: The Evolution of Enduring Rivalries.* Ann Arbor: Univ. Mich. Press. In press

Morrow JD. 1989. Capabilities, uncertainty, and resolve: a limited information model. *Am. J. Polit. Sci.* 33:941–72

Rasler K, Thompson WR. 2000. Explaining rivalry escalation to war: space, position, and contiguity in the major power subsystem. *Int. Stud. Q.* 44:503–30

Reed W. 2000. A unified statistical model of conflict onset and escalation. *Am. J. Polit. Sci.* 44:84–93

Russett B. 1993. *Grasping the Democratic Peace.* Princeton, NJ: Princeton Univ. Press

Signorino CS. 1999. Strategic interaction and the statistical analysis of international conflict. *Am. Polit. Sci. Rev.* 93:279–98

Singer JD. 1982. Confrontational behavior and escalation to war 1816–1980. A research plan. *J. Peace Res.* 19:37–48

Singer JD, Bremer SA, Stuckey J. 1972. Capability distribution, uncertainty, and major power war, 1820–1965. In *Peace, War, and Numbers*, ed. BM Russett, pp. 19–48. Beverly Hills, CA: Sage

Small M, Singer JD. 1982. *Resort to Arms: International and Civil Wars, 1816–1980*. Beverly Hills, CA: Sage

Smith A. 1999. Testing theories of strategic choice: the example of crisis escalation. *Am. J. Polit. Sci.* 43:1254–88

Thompson WR. 1988. *On Global War*. Columbia: Univ. South Carolina Press

Thompson WR. 1995. Principal rivalries. *J. Confl. Resolut.* 39:195–223

Thompson WR, ed. 1999. *Great Power Rivalries*. Columbia: Univ. South Carolina Press

Thompson WR. 2000a. *Identifying rivals and rivalries: caveat emptor and chacun a son gout*. Unpublished paper, Dep. Polit. Sci., Indiana Univ., Bloomington

Thompson WR. 2000b. *Whither strategic rivalries?* Unpubl. paper, Dep. Polit. Sci, Indiana Univ., Bloomington

Valeriano B. 2001. *Steps to rivalry: power politics and rivalry initiation*. Presented at Annu. Meet. Int. Stud. Assoc., Chicago

Vasquez J. 1993. *The War Puzzle*. Cambridge, UK: Cambridge Univ. Press.

Vasquez J. 1996. Distinguishing rivals that go to war from those that do not. *Int. Stud. Q.* 40:531–58

Vasquez J. 2000a. What do we know about war? See Vasquez 2000b, pp. 335–70

Vasquez J, ed. 2000b. *What Do We Know About War?* New York: Rowman & Littlefield

Wallace MD. 1982. Armaments and escalation: two competing hypotheses. *Int. Stud. Q.* 26:37–51

Wayman FW. 1983. *Power transitions, rivalries, and war, 1816–1970*. Unpubl. paper, Univ. Mich.

Wayman FW. 1996. Power shifts and the onset of war. In *Parity and War*, ed. J Kugler, D Lemke, pp. 145–62. Ann Arbor: Unpubl. paper, Univ. Mich.

Wayman FW. 2000. Rivalries: recurrent disputes and explaining war. See Vasquez 2000b, pp. 219–34

Wayman FW, Jones DM. 1991. *Evolution of conflict in rivalries*. Presented at Annu. Meet. Int. Stud. Assoc., Vancouver

Annu. Rev. Polit. Sci. 2001. 4:317–43

The Political Economy of International Monetary Relations

J. Lawrence Broz[1] and Jeffry A. Frieden[2]
[1]*Department of Politics, New York University, New York, New York 10003; e-mail: lawrence.broz@nyu.edu*
[2]*Department of Government, Harvard University, Cambridge, Massachusetts 02138; e-mail: jfrieden@harvard.edu*

Key Words exchange rates, currency policy, monetary policy, international capital mobility, monetary regimes

■ **Abstract** The structure of international monetary relations has gained increasing prominence over the past two decades. Both national exchange rate policy and the character of the international monetary system require explanation. At the national level, the choice of exchange rate regime and the desired level of the exchange rate involve distributionally relevant tradeoffs. Interest group and partisan pressures, the structure of political institutions, and the electoral incentives of politicians therefore influence exchange rate regime and level decisions. At the international level, the character of the international monetary system depends on strategic interaction among governments, driven by their national concerns and constrained by the international environment. A global or regional fixed-rate currency regime, in particular, requires at least coordination and often explicit cooperation among national governments.

INTRODUCTION

The study of international monetary relations was long the domain of economists and a few lonely political scientists. It was routinely argued that, unlike international trade, debt, or foreign investment, exchange rates and related external monetary policies were too technical, and too remote from the concerns of either the mass public or special interests, to warrant direct attention from political economists (Gowa 1988). This was never really accurate, as demonstrated historically by the turbulent politics of the gold standard and more recently by the attention paid to currency policy in small, open economies such as those of Northern Europe and the developing world. But the tedious predictability of currency values under the Bretton Woods system lulled most scholars into inattention (exceptions include Cooper 1968, Kindleberger 1970, Strange 1971, Cohen 1977, Odell 1982, and Gowa 1983).

The collapse of Bretton Woods increased the interest of political scientists in the issue, and in the 1980s, international monetary affairs took so prominent a place in domestic and international politics as to warrant widespread scholarly attention. The 50% real appreciation of the US dollar and the domestic and international firestorm of concern it prompted, dramatic currency collapses in many heavily indebted developing countries, and the controversial attempts to fix European exchange rates all drew researchers toward the topic.

Since 1990, international monetary relations have become extremely prominent in practice, and the study of their political economy has accordingly increased in importance. Exchange rate policies have been at the center of what are arguably the two most striking recent developments in the international economy: the creation of a single European currency and the waves of currency crises that swept through Asia, Latin America, and Russia between 1994 and 1999.

Although most research on the political economy of international monetary relations is relatively recent, it has already given rise to interesting and important theoretical approaches, analytical arguments, and empirical conclusions. We summarize this work without attempting to cover exhaustively a complex and rapidly growing literature. In this section, we outline the analytical problem, delineating the range of outcomes in need of explanation. The next section focuses on one set of things to be explained, the policy choices of national governments, surveying work on the domestic political economy of exchange rate choice. The third section looks at the second set of things to be explained, the rise and evolution of regional and global exchange rate institutions.

Two interrelated sets of international monetary phenomena require explanation. The first is national: the policy of particular governments towards their exchange rates. The second is global: the character of the international monetary system. These two interact in important ways. National policy choices, especially of large countries, have a powerful impact on the nature of the international monetary system. The United Kingdom and the United States were essentially the creators of the classical gold standard and the Bretton Woods monetary order, respectively, and their decisions to withdraw from these systems effectively ended them. By the same token, the global monetary regime exercises a powerful influence on national policy choice. A small country, such as Belgium or Costa Rica, is much more likely to fix its exchange rate—to gold before 1914, to the dollar or some other currency since 1945—when most of its neighbors have done so. The national and the international interact in complex ways, but for ease of analysis it is useful to look at separate dependent variables: the national policy choices of governments and the character of the international monetary system.

National Exchange Rate Policy

Each national government must decide whether to fix its currency—to the dollar, to another national currency, or to gold (in earlier periods)—or to allow it to float. If it chooses to let its currency float, it must decide whether it intends to let currency markets freely set the currency's value or whether it intends to target a particular range of exchange rates. If the latter, the government needs to determine the desired level of the currency's value—whether, generally speaking, it prefers the exchange rate to be "strong" (relatively appreciated) or "weak" (relatively depreciated). In specific instances, governments may be faced with more immediate choices, such as whether to defend or devalue a currency under attack. There are, roughly speaking, two kinds of national decisions to be made. One concerns the regime under which the currency is managed (fixed or floating, for example), and the other concerns the level of the currency (strong or weak).

These choices have significant economic and political implications, and there is no reigning economic argument as to the optimal national exchange rate policy. In this, international monetary policy differs from trade policy. There are powerful economic arguments for the welfare superiority of free trade, and free trade can usefully be considered a baseline from which national policies deviate, with the "distance" from free trade a measure worth explaining. In currency policy, there is no clear economic-efficiency argument for or against any particular level of the real exchange rate. A strong (appreciated) currency is one that is valuable relative to others; this gives national residents greater purchasing power. However, a strong currency also subjects national producers of tradable products (goods and services that enter into international trade) to more foreign competition, for the strong currency makes foreign products relatively cheaper. Although politicians certainly care about these effects—weighing the positive effects of increased mass incomes versus the negative effects of increased foreign competition—there is no purely economic reason to opt for one or the other. There is a reigning economic approach to currency unions (and, somewhat by extension, to fixed exchange rates), drawn from the literature on optimal currency areas. But this literature is by no means conclusive, so even here there are few purely economic factors that could explain national government policy.

This means that national exchange rate policy must be made with an eye toward its political implications, since the tradeoffs governments must weigh are largely among values given different importance by different sociopolitical actors. Governments must evaluate the relative importance of the purchasing power of consumers, the competitiveness of producers of tradable products, and the stability of nominal macroeconomic variables. Below we survey the political considerations that affect policy, but first we describe the international level of analysis in international monetary affairs.

International Monetary Systems

There are effectively two ideal types of international monetary regime, with actual systems tending toward one or the other. One is a fixed-rate system, in which national currencies are tied to each other at a publicly announced (often legally established) parity. Some fixed-rate systems involve a common link to a commodity such as gold or silver; others use a peg to a national currency such as the US dollar. The other ideal-typical monetary regime is is a free-floating system, in which national currency values vary according to market conditions and national macroeconomic policies. There are many potential gradations between these extremes.

In the past 150 years, the world has experienced three broadly defined international monetary orders. For about 50 years before World War I, and again in substantially modified form in the 1920s, most of the world's major nations were on the classical gold standard, a quintessential fixed-rate system. Under the gold standard, national governments announced a fixed gold value for their currencies and committed themselves to exchange gold for currency at this rate. From the late 1940s until the early 1970s, the capitalist world was organized into the Bretton Woods monetary order, a modified fixed-rate system. Under Bretton Woods, national currencies were fixed to the US dollar and the US dollar was fixed to gold. However, national governments could and did change their exchange rates in unusual circumstances, so that currencies were not as firmly fixed as under the classical gold standard. From 1973 until the present, and briefly in the 1930s, the reigning order has been one in which the largest countries had more or less freely floating national currencies with no nominal anchor, whereas smaller countries tended either to fix against one of the major currencies or to allow their currencies to float with varying degrees of government management.

Monetary regimes can be regional as well as global. Within the international free-for-all that has prevailed since 1973, a number of regional fixed-rate systems have emerged or been contemplated. Some have involved simply fixing the national currencies of relatively small countries to the currency of a larger nation; for instance, the CFA (African Financial Community) franc zone ties the currencies of 12 African countries to each other and to the French franc (and now to the euro). Several countries in Latin America and the Caribbean have similarly tied their currencies to the US dollar, and others are considering this link. Another type of regional fixed-rate system involves the linking of a number of regional currencies to one another, often as a step toward adoption of a common currency. This has been the case with European monetary integration, which began with a limited regional agreement, evolved into something like a Deutsche mark link, and eventually became a monetary union with a single currency and a common European central bank. Countries in the Eastern Caribbean and southern Africa have also developed monetary unions.

Our dependent variables, then, are (*a*) the national exchange rate policies of particular national governments, especially their choice of the level and regime of their currencies; and (*b*) the international monetary regime, especially the degree to which currencies are fixed against one another. To be sure, these two dependent variables are jointly determined. National policy choices depend on the character of the international monetary system, and the evolution of global monetary relations is powerfully affected by the decisions of the major trading and investing nations. By the same token, international monetary relations interact with other economic policies. Currency misalignments have often led to protectionist pressures and even trade wars, just as the evolution of trade relations affects exchange rate policy choices. Policies toward international financial and investment flows are similarly affected by, and affect, exchange rate movements. These complex interactive effects are important, but we do not know how to think about them in an integrated and systematic way. This essay focuses on the political economy of international monetary policy in and of itself, emphasizing potential answers to our two more narrowly defined explanatory questions.

Cognate literatures on the political economy of other important international economic policies are useful to the analysis of international monetary policy. Analyses of international trade and investment begin with a prior notion of the distributional interests at stake—factoral, sectoral, and firm-specific—derived either from theory or from empirical investigation. They then explore how these interests are aggregated and mediated by such sociopolitical institutions as labor unions and business associations, political parties, electoral systems, legislatures, and bureaucracies. Finally, they explore the interactions between these nationally derived policies and those of other countries, especially in contexts in which interstate strategic interaction is likely to be important, such as where national government policies depend on the responses of other governments. The emerging structure of analysis and explanation of international monetary and financial politics follows this pattern. In the next section, we summarize the domestic level of analysis, especially how interests and institutions interact in the formation of national policy.

THE DOMESTIC POLITICAL ECONOMY OF EXCHANGE RATE POLICY

National policy makers make decisions about the exchange rate regime and the desired level of the currency. The regime decision is whether to allow the currency to float freely or to fix it against some other currency. Pure floats and irrevocably fixed regimes are, of course, only two possible options. There are at least nine existing regimes on a continuum that runs from a full float to a currency union—an extreme kind of fixed-rate system (Frankel 1999). For all regimes between the two extremes of this continuum, policy makers also confront choices related to the level of the exchange rate. Level decisions involve policies that affect the price at which the national currency is valued in foreign currencies. The exchange rate may itself be a target for policy, with a definite rate being set or a clearly observable formula applied. Alternatively, the exchange rate may be actively managed in conjunction with other components of monetary policy. Some governments announce a band within the currency will be allowed to move, or they act (without public announcement) to restrict exchange rate movements to such a target band. Whatever the mechanism, level decisions fall along a second continuum that runs from a more depreciated to a more appreciated currency. Although regime and level decisions are interconnected, we treat them separately for heuristic purposes. We attempt to delineate the domestic political economy factors that influence governments' choices along the two continuums.

Like other areas of economic policy, exchange rate decisions involve tradeoffs between desired goals. An established economics literature examines the costs and benefits of alternative currency policies from the perspective of a benevolent social planner, which is a useful starting point for gauging the attractiveness of policies in terms of national welfare. However, the more recent political economy scholarship incorporates the role of interest-group and partisan pressures, political institutions, and the electoral incentives of politicians. One major theme is that currency policy has domestic distributional implications that shape the sociopolitical environment in which policy makers assess costs and benefits. A second theme is that domestic electoral, legislative, and bureaucratic institutions influence the incentives of politicians as they confront currency policy tradeoffs. We develop these themes below, emphasizing that the economic tradeoffs are politically and institutionally conditioned.

To Fix or to Float?

Our discussion of regime choice focuses on the extreme regimes—hard pegs and pure floats—because the analysis of intermediate cases flows from that of the extremes. The tradeoffs we describe apply to the intermediate choices—target zones, crawling pegs and bands, etc—albeit never as starkly as with the extremes (Frankel 1999). Economic treatments of regime choice come from two perspectives: (*a*) open economy macroeconomic approaches, including consideration of optimal currency area criteria; and (*b*) rational-expectations treatments of the credibility problem in monetary policy.

From the open economy perspective, the principal advantage of a fixed-rate regime is to lower the exchange rate risk and transaction costs that can impede international trade and investment (Mundell 1961, McKinnon 1962, Kenen 1969). Volatile exchange rates create uncertainty about international transactions, adding a risk premium to the costs of goods and assets traded across borders. Although it is possible to hedge against this risk in derivatives markets, hedging invariably involves costs, which increase with the duration of the transaction. And recent experience indicates that there is a great deal of unexplained volatility in currency markets, which makes hedging particularly difficult for small countries' currencies. By opting to stabilize the currency, a government can reduce or eliminate exchange rate risk and so encourage greater trade and investment—a desirable objective. Taking the next step to a currency union does away with the remaining transactions costs, providing an even stronger impetus toward economic integration.

Pegging, however, has costs. To gain the benefits of greater economic integration by fixing the exchange rate, governments must sacrifice their capacity to run an independent monetary policy. The "impossible trinity" principle explains that where capital is internationally mobile, a fixed rate and monetary independence are not simultaneously attainable (Mundell 1962, 1963). The principle says that a country must give up one of three goals: exchange rate stability, monetary independence, or financial market integration. When capital is mobile internationally, domestic interest rates cannot long differ from world interest rates, as capital flows induced by arbitrage opportunities quickly eliminate the differential. There is strong evidence in both developed economies (Marston 1995) and the developing world (Edwards 1999) that financial integration has progressed so far that capital mobility can be taken more or less as a given, which reduces the choice to sacrificing exchange rate stability versus giving up monetary independence.[1] A fixed exchange rate with international capital mobility renders monetary policy ineffective, meaning that there is no leeway to use monetary policy for purposes of demand management or balance-of-payments adjustment. This poses a tradeoff between two competing values: stability and flexibility. Achieving monetary stability can be a substantial benefit for countries that have endured high and highly variable inflation and other domestic monetary disturbances. But since achieving this stability means forgoing monetary flexibility, this can be a substantial cost for countries that face severe external shocks to which monetary policy might be the appropriate response.

Whereas the traditional case for stable exchange rates hinges on the benefits of integration, recent analyses tend to place more emphasis on credibility issues and the role of fixed regimes in stabilizing inflation expectations. With roots in the rational expectations literature, this work builds on the time inconsistency problem described by Kydland & Prescott (1977) and Barro & Gordon (1983). The problem arises when monetary policy is set with discretion and wages and prices are not fully flexible. Under these conditions, a policy maker may try to fool private agents by inflicting an inflationary surprise, in the hope of engineering a temporary boost in output. However, forward-looking private actors anticipate this incentive and take it into account when forming their ex ante inflationary expectations. These expectations thus introduce an inflationary bias into wage bargaining and price setting. Consequently, when the policy maker adopts surprise inflation, the equilibrium outcome is higher inflation but not higher output. The key to solving this time inconsistency problem is credibility. If the private sector believes that the preannounced policy is credible, then expected inflation is kept in check at no cost to output.

Pegging the exchange rate provides an automatic rule for the conduct of monetary policy that avoids the time inconsistency problem and enhances the credibility of the government's commitment to low inflation (Giavazzi & Pagano 1988, Canavan & Tommasi 1997). In a fixed regime, monetary policy must be subordinated to the requirements of maintaining the peg, effectively eliminating the discretion of the authorities. This privileges such domestic objectives as price stability over such external objectives as payments balance and competitiveness. Historically, a national commitment to a gold standard was the most important

[1]Intermediate regimes may allow countries to pursue both objectives to some degree (Edwards & Savastano 1999).

such external anchor. More recently, many countries have pegged to the currency of a large, low-inflation country (Mishkin 1999).

Although pegging is not the only way to commit policy to low inflation—central bank independence with price level or inflation targets may be an alternative—its transparency makes it a common commitment technology in contexts where the alternatives cannot easily be monitored by the public (Herrendorf 1999, Canavan & Tommasi 1997). When a government commits to a peg, it makes an easily verifiable promise. Either the government follows macroeconomic policies consistent with the peg, or it does not, in which case the peg collapses. There is in fact no technical reason why a peg cannot be maintained, even in the face of a large speculative attack (Obstfeld & Rogoff 1995). Therefore, devaluation is a public signal that the government has not lived up to its promise. The transparency of a peg enhances the credibility of the government's commitment to low inflation but comes at price, measured in terms of lost monetary policy flexibility. The tradeoff here is between credibility and flexibility.

Do countries that choose pegs experience increases in trade and credibility? Time-series studies of the relationship between exchange rate volatility and trade (or investment) typically find small, weak negative effects (Frankel 1995). However, much stronger effects are evident in cross-sectional evaluations. Countries that share a common currency (or have a long-term peg) trade more than three times as much as comparable countries that have separate currencies (Rose 2000). As for credibility, pegs tend to be favored commitment devices in countries seeking a quick resolution to chronic inflation (Vegh 1992). Systematic evidence from 136 countries over a 30-year period shows that pegging is indeed associated with lower inflation, but at the cost of more variable output than in flexible exchange rate regimes (Ghosh et al 1997).

Theory and evidence thus suggest that fixing the exchange rate to the currency of a low-inflation country (*a*) promotes international trade and investment and (*b*) disciplines monetary policy by providing an observable nominal anchor for the value of domestic money. The advantages of a floating exchange rate, on the other hand, reduce to the single, albeit crucial, property that it allows a government to have its own independent monetary policy. Under a full float, demand and supply for domestic currency against foreign currency are balanced in the market. There is no obligation or necessity for the central bank to intervene. Therefore, domestic monetary aggregates need not be affected by external flows, and a monetary policy can be pursued without regard to monetary policy in other countries. This independence is valuable because it provides flexibility to accommodate foreign and domestic shocks, including changes in the external terms of trade and interest rates. More generally, floating allows monetary policy to be set autonomously, as deemed appropriate in the domestic context (e.g. for stabilization purposes), and the exchange rate becomes a residual, following whatever path is consistent with the stabilization policy.

A related advantage of floating is that it allows the exchange rate to be used as a policy tool. This flexibility is valuable when real appreciation, caused by inertial inflation or rapid capital inflows, harms international competitiveness and threatens to generate a balance-of-payments crisis—a common syndrome in developing and transition economies that use a fixed exchange rate as a nominal anchor for credibility purposes (Edwards & Savastano 1999). When residual inflation generates an inflation differential between the pegging country and the anchor, it induces a real appreciation that, in the absence of compensating productivity gains, leads to balance-of-payments problems. A more flexible regime allows policy makers to adjust the nominal exchange rate to ensure the competitiveness of the tradable goods sector. However, the more flexible the regime, the smaller the credibility gains. The tradeoff between credibility and competitiveness is particularly relevant in countries where inflation has been a persistent problem (Frieden et al 2001).

Which regime is best for a particular country is partly a matter of the economic characteristics of the country. The literature on optimal currency areas points to several considerations, with openness, economic size, sensitivity to shocks, and labor mobility between regions heading the list. Broadly speaking, when a region is characterized by easy movement of labor, or is highly integrated with its neighbors such that they share common disturbances, the gains of fixed exchange rates are likely to outweigh the costs of giving up monetary independence (Frankel 1995). Countries that are particularly sensitive to external disturbances (e.g. volatility in the terms of trade) are generally better off floating, whereas countries concerned about domestic monetary shocks gain from pegging. Furthermore, when the shocks affecting a country and it neighbors are highly correlated, there is less need of monetary independence because a single policy response is appropriate for the whole region. Beyond this, there is little consensus on the welfare criteria for exchange rate regime choice (Frankel 1999). Given the diversity of economic conditions relevant to selecting the optimal regime, it is not surprising that empirical findings are typically weak or contradictory (Tavlas 1994, Edison & Melvin 1990).

A more fundamental weakness of the both the credibility and open economy approaches is their implicit assumption that policy makers select currency regimes to maximize aggregate social welfare. There is little reason to believe that currency policy is made any less politically than other economic policies. In the next section, we depart from the benevolent social planner assumption and survey work that endogenizes the political incentives and constraints that shape regime decisions.

Interest Groups and Regime Choice

What is optimal for a country as a whole may not be optimal for particular groups within a country. A policy of free trade, for example, creates both winners and losers even though it is widely regarded as welfare-enhancing for the nation. These distributional effects form the basis of "endogenous tariff theory," which accounts for deviations from free trade by delineating the groups that favor and oppose protection and the conditions under which they are most influential (Milner 1999). Currency regime choice, like the choice between free trade and protection, has domestic distributional consequences.

We begin by examining the strengths and weaknesses of pressure group or "demand-side" approaches to regime choice, which take the distributional consequences of exchange rate regime choice as part of the explanation of its causes. We then introduce "supply-side" considerations, such as the character of domestic political and monetary institutions and the incentives of self-seeking politicians that inhabit them. Although aspects of the link between interests, politics, and policies remain underdeveloped, this literature contains the building blocks of the political economy of regime choice.

Regime choice involves tradeoffs between goals, as discussed above. Arguments that stress the demand for regimes maintain that societal groups have different preferences in the stability-vs-flexibility tradeoff. Recall that one important advantage of fixed rates is that international trade and investment can be conducted with minimal risk of capital losses due to currency fluctuations. The tradeoff is that fixed rates require the subordination of domestic monetary policy to currency and balance-of-payments considerations. A preliminary framework identifies how social groups align on the stability-vs-flexibility tradeoff (Frieden 1991, Hefeker 1997). In its simplest manifestation, groups are arranged along a continuum that measures the extent to which they are involved in international or domestic economic activity. Groups heavily involved in foreign trade and investment (i.e. producers of exportables, foreign direct and portfolio investors, and international merchants) should favor exchange rate stability, since currency volatility is an everyday concern that makes their business riskier and more costly. By the same token, these actors are relatively insensitive to the loss of monetary autonomy, since they typically conduct business in several countries and can therefore respond to unfavorable domestic macroeconomic conditions by shifting business or assets abroad.

By contrast, groups whose economic activity is confined to the domestic economy benefit from a floating regime. The nontradables sector (e.g. services, construction, transport) and import-competing producers of tradable goods belong in this camp. Producers of nontradables are not required to deal in foreign exchange, since their activities are, by definition, domestic. Thus, they are free of the risks and costs of currency volatility. The nontradables sector is, however, highly sensitive to domestic macroeconomic conditions and therefore favors the national autonomy made possible by floating. The same logic holds for producers of import-competing traded goods, with the added proviso that currency volatility may reduce competition from imports by adding to the risks and costs of importing.

The strength of the pressure group approach is that it yields clear predictions on the regime preferences of social groups in a manner similar to endogenous tariff theory. It also provides the basis for refining predictions. For example, the degree to which an export industry is sensitive to currency volatility will depend on its ability to "pass through" the costs to consumers in the form of price changes. Typically, industries in which product differentiation and reputation are important have less pass-through than producers of standardized goods, in which competition is based primarily on price (Goldberg & Knetter 1997). This implies that producers of internationally traded specialized products will be more concerned to reduce currency volatility than producers of standardized manufactured goods or commodities, and thus more likely to favor fixed exchange rates.

Pressure group arguments, however, are very difficult to evaluate. One problem is that, unlike trade policy, exchange rate regime decisions are rarely subject to votes in legislatures and hardly ever figure prominently in nationwide electoral outcomes and campaigns. The most systematic work on pressure groups and regime choice looks back over a century to the gold standard controversy for suitable data. In the 1890s, the US Congress voted repeatedly on the choice between the gold and silver standards (Frieden 1997). Similarly, the 1896 US presidential election was a rare nationwide election in which the central issue was the exchange rate regime; William Jennings Byran ran on a platform of monetizing silver and floating the dollar against gold standard currencies (Eichengreen 1995). European monetary integration in the nineteenth century provides a few additional cases (Hefeker 1995). These analyses, controlling for other factors, find that pressure group influences are significantly related to vote outcomes.

The number of cases available for empirical analysis may be increasing, as exchange rates have again gained domestic political prominence in recent years. The renewed salience may be due to the revival of international capital mobility, since capital mobility heightens the "impossible trinity" problem (Frieden 1996). In Europe, the post-Maastricht period was characterized by increasing turmoil and polarization on currency union. In developing countries, regime choice is currently a source of heated policy and electoral debate, and countries are experimenting with a variety of regimes (Edwards & Savastano 1999). The considerable variation of currency regimes in Latin America can be exploited to investigate the influence of interest group pressures. In this context, the credibility-vs-competitiveness tradeoff is especially important because of problems controlling inflation in the region. Consistent with the interest group perspective, economies with larger manufacturing sectors are more prone to adopt either floating regimes or backward-looking crawling pegs,[2] both of which tend to deliver more competitive exchange rates (Frieden et al 2001). The influence of the manufacturing sector on the exchange regime is also found to be more important when trade is relatively open, because liberalized trade subjects manufacturers to greater foreign competition. These findings support the argument that the degree to which policy makers opt to sacrifice credibility to competitiveness is a function of the political influence of tradables producers.

The cross-sectional approach appears promising, even among developed countries, where the tradeoff between stability and flexibility is likely to dominate (Henning 1994, Frieden 2000). However, measuring group preferences and political influence is never easy, and data limitations leave analysts with crude proxies (e.g. a sector's share of gross domestic product as a measure of its influence). An alternative strategy is to take the distributional arguments to the individual level

[2]In a backward-looking crawling peg, the nominal exchange rate is adjusted mechanically according to past inflation differentials.

of analysis and make use of available public opinion data on regime preferences and voting behavior (Scheve 1999). Scheve finds that asset ownership and high skill endowments are positively related to individuals' expressed level of support for European monetary integration and to their voting behavior in nationwide elections. This connects individual preferences on monetary integration to voting, thus providing a direct test of the distributional implications of the open economy approach.

Despite these advances, it is unlikely that the interest group approach will spawn a literature as deep and rich as analogous work on trade policy. Pressure group activity on exchange rates is more limited than in trade affairs, owing to the macroeconomic nature of exchange rates and associated collective action constraints. Exchange rates have broad distributional effects, which reduce the incentives to lobby. For example, stable exchange rates benefit all industries in the export sector; in contrast, trade protection can be narrowly targeted to create rents for specific industries (Gowa 1988). Exchange rate policy is less excludable than trade policy, implying more free riding (Olson 1971). But just as work on trade has endogenized the free rider problem, so can analysis of currency policy. For example, highly concentrated industries should be more effective lobbyists for exchange rate policies, just as they are in trade policy (Trefler 1993). Although exchange rates may not evince as much lobbying as trade policy, lobbying is possible, even predictable across industries and countries. More attention to collective action considerations would help us develop the links between group preferences, lobbying, and government regime decisions.

Class-Based (Partisan) Approaches to Regime Choice

Inasmuch as exchange rates have broad distributional effects, it makes sense to analyze the politics of regime choice at a broad level of political aggregation. Class-based partisan approaches typify this strategy. Where political parties aggregate the monetary preferences of social classes, centrist and rightist parties are presumed to be more inflation averse than leftist parties (Hibbs 1977). Center-right parties are thus likely to support fixed regimes, since their business constituencies benefit from the credible commitment to low inflation that fixing brings (Simmons 1994, Oatley 1997). By the same token, center-right parties are expected to be enthusiastic about stable exchange rates because of the expansion of trade and investment made possible by fixing. Left-wing parties, by contrast, favor flexible regimes, since labor bears the brunt of adjusting the domestic economy to external conditions (Simmons 1994).

Tests of the partisan arguments have produced mixed and often perverse results. For example, countries with more left-wing representation in government had a *higher* probability of staying on the gold standard during the interwar period than those with less (Simmons 1994, Eichengreen 1992). The reason may be that leftist governments had more need for the credibility that a commitment to gold could bring. However, left-wing governments devalued more frequently, conditioned on a downturn in the business cycle (Simmons 1994). This effect is also evident in contemporary Europe; leftist parties supported stable exchange rates in the mid-1980s (Garrett 1995, Oatley 1997). More generally, the partisan composition of government had small, weak, and occasionally perverse effects on the stability of European currencies between 1972 and 1994 (Frieden 2000). Another study of OECD countries in the post–Bretton Woods period found no relationship between partisanship and regime choice (Bernhard & Leblang 1999).

Partisan influences on regime choice are thus not straightforward. Indeed, the literature contains a number of factors that condition parties' regime preferences and their political influence. Several of the most important mitigating factors include the degree of capital mobility (Goodman & Pauly 1993); linkage to other issue areas, such as trade, foreign, and agricultural policy (Giavazzi & Giovannini 1989, Frieden 2001); policy makers' beliefs and the role of ideas (Odell 1982, Collins & Giavazzi 1993, McNamara 1998); the centralization of wage bargaining institutions (Hall & Franzese 1998); and the independence of the central bank (Simmons 1994, Oatley 1997). Given the wide range of mitigating factors, it is not surprising that the ideology and influence of political parties vary tremendously among countries. Although this variation makes it difficult to construct generalizations, some of it may be due to analogous variation in electoral and legislative institutions.

Political Institutions and Regime Choice

Various combinations of electoral and legislative institutions can affect the electoral incentives of politicians in governing parties to adopt alternative exchange rate regimes (Bernhard & Leblang 1999). In countries where the stakes in elections are high, politicians might prefer floating exchange rates, so as to preserve the use of monetary policy as a tool for building support before elections (Clark & Hallerberg 2000). This is expected in majoritarian (single-member plurality) electoral systems, where a small swing in votes can lead to a large change in the distribution of legislative seats and to the ouster of the governing party. Electoral stakes are also a function of legislative institutions. In systems with weak, noninclusive committees, the costs of being in the minority are larger than in systems with strong, inclusive committees, since the opposition has little influence over policy. High electoral stakes imply that politicians in "majoritarian–low opposition influence" systems will want a flexible regime to preserve monetary independence, so as to use monetary policy to engineer favorable (if temporary) macroeconomic conditions before elections. In contrast, where elections are not as decisive—as in systems with proportional representation and strong, inclusive committees—fixed exchange rates impose lower electoral costs on politicians, implying that fixed regimes are more likely to be chosen.

A related argument concerns the timing of elections, which in some systems is determined endogenously by the government and in others is predetermined. When election timing is predetermined, governing parties are loath to surrender monetary policy flexibility by pegging, since monetary policy can be a valuable tool for winning elections. In contrast, when election timing is endogenous, there is less need to maintain monetary flexibility for electoral purposes; hence pegging is more likely (Bernhard & Leblang 1999). These arguments and the supporting evidence suggest that the structure of democratic institutions shapes the regime preferences of politicians and governing parties, so much so that it dominates the influence of partisanship on regime choice. This approach, however, seems to be restricted to developed countries, where democratic structures are well established and stable, and where partisanship typically has a class basis. In developing countries, it may be the extent of democracy rather than its specific form that matters.

Political regime type (democratic to authoritarian) is in fact highly correlated with exchange rate regime choice in developing countries (Leblang 1999, Broz 2000). Nondemocratic systems are significantly more likely to adopt a fixed regime for credibility purposes than are democratic countries. Why authoritarian governments prefer pegs as a means to lower inflation is a matter of debate. Autocratic governments may peg because they are more insulated from domestic audiences and thus bear lower political costs of adjusting the economy to the peg (Simmons 1994, Leblang 1999). That is, lower political costs ex post increase the likelihood that autocracies will choose a peg ex ante. A weakness of the argument is that pegging is an inefficient means of generating credibility, given the availability of alternatives, such as central bank independence (CBI), that do not require a loss of exchange rate policy flexibility and that appear effective at reducing inflation (see Alesina & Summers 1993, Debelle & Fischer 1994, as compared to Ghosh et al 1997, on the relative inefficiency of currency pegs). An authoritarian regime that is insulated enough to maintain a peg would surely be capable of adopting an independent central bank, which would seem likely to improve inflation performance at a lower cost.

A competing argument is that the transparency of a pegged regime makes it a preferred commitment technology in authoritarian systems (Broz 2000). When political decision making is not transparent, as in autocracies, governments must look to a commitment technology that is more transparent and constrained (pegged exchange rates) than the government itself. For autocratic governments, a highly visible commitment substitutes for the lack of openness in the political system to engender low inflation expectations. In the case of legal CBI—an opaque commitment—democratic institutions provide an alternate source of transparency. For democracies, an opaque commitment such as CBI is rendered transparent indirectly through active monitoring by the media, inflation hawks in society, and the political opposition—audiences with stakes in exposing the government's broken promises (Wittman 1989, Fearon 1994). Autocracies are thus more likely to adopt pegs than are democracies. In addition, the effectiveness of CBI in limiting inflation is conditioned on the level of political system transparency (Broz 2000). This suggests that the transparency of the monetary commitment and the transparency of the political system are substitutes. It also challenges the view that fixed regimes and CBI are complementary commitment mechanisms (Simmons 1994, Maxfield 1997).

Although there is no consensus on the role of politics in exchange rate regime choices, it is recognized that considerations of aggregate social welfare provide a partial explanation at best. Regime decisions involve tradeoffs with domestic distributional and electoral implications; thus, selecting an exchange rate regime is as much a political decision as an economic one.

To Appreciate or Depreciate?

If a nation's regime lies between a pure float and an irrevocable peg on the regime continuum, its policy makers face choices about the desired level of the exchange rate. Completely free floats are in fact rare, for most governments act to reduce currency volatility even when the exchange rate is not publicly fixed. By the same token, countries that opt for a pegged regime always have the choice of abandoning the peg (Calvo & Reinhart 2000). Thus, under most regimes, a government must decide whether it prefers a relatively appreciated or a relatively depreciated currency. A full analysis of the costs and benefits involved in choosing the level of the exchange rate depends on the model of exchange rate determination to which one subscribes (portfolio balance, overshooting, new classical, speculative bubble, etc). For simplicity, we consider the tradeoff between competitiveness and purchasing power as especially crucial to the calculations of national policy makers.

The value of the real exchange rate affects the demand for domestic traded goods in both local and foreign markets. In the case of a real appreciation, domestic goods become more expensive relative to foreign goods; exports fall and imports rise as a result of the change in competitiveness. Real depreciation has the opposite effects, improving competitiveness. Real exchange rate changes sometimes stem from deliberate policy actions (see above). These policies are known as expenditure-switching policies because they alter the allocation of spending between domestic and foreign goods (equivalently, between traded and nontraded goods). Although a weaker currency increases the competitiveness of the international sector, it also raises the prices of foreign goods and services to domestic consumers, thereby eroding national purchasing power. If a nation imports many vital items, such as oil, food, or capital goods, depreciation can reduce living standards and retard economic growth, as well as cause inflation.

Beyond considerations based on the tradeoff between competitiveness and purchasing power, there is little agreement on what the appropriate level of the exchange rate should be. A real depreciation, for example, can encourage exports and a switch from imports to domestic goods, thereby boosting aggregate output. However, depreciation can also be contractionary, owing to its negative impact on real money balances that follows from a higher price level. Suffice it to say that changes in real exchange rates unleash a series of changes in economic relations, some positive and some negative, and the net effect on overall national welfare is very hard to calculate.

Interest Groups and the Level of the Exchange Rate

Despite this ambiguity, it is clear that the level of the exchange rate always has distributive consequences domestically, implying a role for interest group politics. Exporting and import-competing industries lose and domestically oriented (nontradables) industries gain from currency appreciation (Frieden 1991). Domestic consumers also gain as the domestic currency price of imported goods falls, lowering the cost of living. Currency depreciations have the opposite effects, helping exporting and import-competing industries at the expense of domestic consumers and producers of nontraded goods and services.

Like regime decisions, the currency preferences and political capabilities of groups are conditioned by many factors. For example, the degree to which tradables producers are directly affected by changes in the exchange rate conditions their sensitivity to currency movements. If import-competing firms faced by an appreciation of the home currency are able to keep their prices high—typically because foreign producers do not in fact pass the expected price decline through to local consumers—they will be less concerned by such an appreciation (this is typically the case in markets for specialized, highly differentiated products, such as automobiles).

Generally speaking, tradables industries with high pass-through are more sensitive to the relative price effects of currency movements than those with low pass-through, since their prices respond more directly to changes in exchange rates. By extension, the level of the exchange rate is likely to be more politicized in developing countries than in developed countries, since the former tend to produce standardized goods and primary commodities, for which pass-through is high. The extent to which an industry relies on imported intermediate inputs will also determine whether it is harmed or helped by appreciation. An industry with heavy dependence on imported inputs relative to export revenue may actually see its profitability improve with appreciation (Campa & Goldberg 1997).

Within this complex range of possibilities, there are regularities that can be identified. These are related to points made above about regime preferences. For example, the argument that producers of simple tradables are relatively insensitive to currency volatility complements the argument that they are very sensitive to the level of the exchange rate. Such producers (of commodities and simple manufactures) will prefer a flexible regime and a tendency toward a depreciated currency. On the other hand, the argument that producers of complex and specialized tradables are very sensitive to currency volatility complements the argument that they are relatively insensitive to the level of the exchange rate. These producers will prefer a fixed regime. Capturing an industry's (or an entire nation's) sensitivity to exchange rate changes involves measuring the extent to which it sells products to foreign markets, uses foreign-made inputs, and, more indirectly, competes with foreign manufacturers on the basis of price (Frieden et al 2001).

In most instances, interest group activity on the level of the exchange rate is episodic and asymmetric. By episodic, we mean that it can take extraordinary conditions to move group members to organize on the issue. The 50% real appreciation of the dollar in the early and middle 1980s is a case where traded goods industries lobbied hard for policies to depreciate the dollar (Destler & Henning 1989, Frankel 1994). The rarity of such cases is partially understandable in collective action terms, as lobbying for depreciation is a public good for the entire traded goods sector. By asymmetric, we mean that lobbying from the "winners" of real appreciation (nontradables, consumers) does not usually arise to counteract pressure from the "losers." That is, the groups that enjoy income gains from appreciation do not seem to mobilize politically. Consumers, of course, face high costs of collective action, and the same constraint may apply to the nontradables sector (Henning 1994). But using the rule of thumb that advanced economies are divided roughly equally between tradables and nontradables, the barriers to collective action should be symmetric.

Why we do not observe symmetric lobbying (or non-lobbying) on the exchange rate is a puzzle. The reason might be that tradables producers have the advantage of prior organization, having paid the startup costs to influence trade policy. A related point is that traded goods industries have the option of lobbying for industry-specific trade policies when the currency appreciates. Note that currency policy and trade policy are close substitutes in terms of the compensation they provide: A 10% real depreciation is equivalent to a 10% import tax plus a 10% export subsidy (McKinnon & Fung 1993). Hence, the tradables sector can organize on an industry-by-industry basis to seek trade barriers or export subsidies, thus mitigating the free rider problem (Stallings 1993). In practice, policy makers do seem to address currency misalignments when demands for protection intensify (Destler & Henning 1989). For the nontradables sector, trade policies are not available, rendering lobbying for currency policies a sector-wide public good. An implication is that the bias in favor of tradables should diminish when free trade or international agreements restrict the ability of governments to use trade policy as a compensatory instrument. Take away trade policy and neither sector organizes. However, liberalizing trade might motivate previously organized traded goods industries to lobby on the exchange rate directly (Frieden et al 2001).

Political Institutions and the Level of the Exchange Rate

Direct interest group activity on the level of the exchange rate is muted, for the distributional effects are very broad based. Indeed, the cleavages implied by the competitiveness–vs–purchasing-power tradeoff map to interest groups only under an expansive definition of the concept (or, as above, when we introduce links to other policies). A class-based partisan approach is not much help, since the distributional effects of the real exchange rate on profits and wages cut across sector (tradables vs nontradables) and not factor (labor vs capital) lines. That is, a strong currency harms workers and capital employed in the traded goods sector and benefits factors engaged in the production of nontradables. There is thus little reason to believe that class-based political parties will find common ground on the preferred level of the exchange rate. More generally, the absence of class cleavages may distinguish currency level politics from currency regime politics.

Whatever the nature of interest group and partisan political pressures on the level of the exchange rate, elections and voting are likely to be of recurrent importance. A voluminous literature on "economic voting" provides robust support for the proposition that good macroeconomic conditions keep politicians in office whereas bad times cast them out (Lewis-Beck & Stegmaier 2000). The real exchange rate affects broad aggregates such as purchasing power, growth rates, and the price level—the stuff of national elections. Put another way, the macroeconomic effects of the real exchange rate may map closely to electoral processes, the broadest form of political aggregation.

Consumer/voters care about their purchasing power and inflation. Since voting is a low-cost activity, politicians are sure to be concerned with the electoral consequences of the exchange rate. Indeed, governments tend to maintain appreciated currencies before elections, delaying the necessary depreciation/devaluation until after the election (Klein & Marion 1997, Leblang 2000, Frieden et al 2001). An "exchange rate electoral cycle" gives a boost to voters' income in the run-up to an election and imposes costs on voters only after the government is in office. The delay results in a depreciation that is larger (more costly) than if it had occurred immediately, but newly elected governments appear to follow the rule of "devalue immediately and blame it on your predecessors" (Edwards 1994).

The role of electoral cycles in exchange rate policy helps explain some characteristics of the currency crises that have been common over the past 20 years. Although the causes of currency crises are controversial (Corsetti et al 1998), delaying a devaluation certainly makes the problem worse. Given the expected political unpopularity of a devaluation-induced reduction in national purchasing power, however, governments may face strong incentives to avoid devaluing even when the result is a more severe crisis than would otherwise be expected. In Mexico, for example, the attempt to delay a devaluation of the peso until after the 1994 election almost certainly led to a far more drastic collapse of the currency than would have been the case without the electorally driven delay. As it became clear that the government was manipulating the exchange rate for political purposes, investors sold off the peso in droves, for the government's exchange rate promises had lost all credibility. This run on the peso in turn called into question the credibility of other Latin American currency pegs, creating negative externalities for the region.

The electoral cycle is likely to be muted in countries where the central bank has sufficient insulation from political pressures or the government has a time horizon long enough to endogenize the higher costs of delayed action on the exchange rate. Where an independent central bank is in charge of exchange rate policy, the pursuit of price stability implies that politicians will be less able to manipulate the exchange rate for electoral purposes (Clark & Reichert 1998). Likewise, a government that expects to be in the majority across elections may have less incentive to exploit the short-term gains of real appreciation. The point is that political institutions condition the extent to which politicians have the capacity and/or the incentive to act on their short-run electoral goals, at the expense of macroeconomic stability and the competitiveness of their economies (Henning 1994).

The real exchange rate has international as well as domestic distributional consequences and thus plays an important role in international economic policy making.

Increasing the competitiveness of the domestically produced goods sector by depreciating the currency necessarily means reducing the competitiveness of foreign goods. The use of the exchange rate to gain a competitive advantage, of course, cannot work when other countries retaliate with similar depreciations, as happened during the Great Depression. This is but one of many instances in which the domestic impact of national currency policy depends on the character of interstate monetary relations. This implies a direct connection between national exchange rate policies and the state of the international monetary system, to which we now turn.

THE INTERNATIONAL POLITICAL ECONOMY OF EXCHANGE RATE POLICY

The above analysis of national policies has left aside the important question of how to explain the development of global or regional monetary systems. Perhaps more than any other economic area, national exchange rate policies depend on those of other nations.[3] This is certainly true with regard to the level of the nominal exchange rate, which is after all only meaningful in relationship to other countries' nominal exchange rates. Another basic limitation of national analyses is that they do not take into account the nature of the international monetary system. This is especially the case when countries are faced with the choice of a fixed or flexible regime for national currencies, since fixing is a fundamentally different enterprise in the context of a global fixed-rate system than in the context of generalized floating. In the former case, such as under the gold standard or Bretton Woods, choosing whether or not to fix was tantamount to choosing whether or not to participate in a worldwide monetary order. A similar consideration applies to broad regional fixed-rate arrangements, such as the various monetary integration schemes of the European Union after 1973, or the Latin and Scandinavian monetary unions before 1914. Conversely, when the world monetary system is one of floating currencies, a national choice to fix the exchange rate is principally available to small countries that want to lock their currencies into step with their principal trading and investment partner, as many small Caribbean countries have done with the United States for decades. Especially given the analytical and empirical importance of international fixed-rate systems, it is important to investigate the reasons for their origins and evolution.

Generally speaking, three interrelated factors affect the evolution of international monetary systems. The first are the sorts of national policy choices discussed above, especially in the principal members of the system. The second are

[3] We are reminded of the remark attributed—apocryphally, no doubt—to a provincial American policy maker, who angrily told European complainers, "You worry about your exchange rates, we'll worry about ours!"

global economic factors that may affect global monetary relations, such as trends in the international economy (growth, stagnation, crisis) and the state of international trade and payments. Third are purposive relations among states, including strategic interaction among governments, driven by their national concerns and constrained by the international environment.

In this section, we focus on this third set of factors, the interaction among states' international monetary policies. Such interaction can be thought of as involving coordination among national government policies and/or cooperation among them, which is more complex. By coordination, we mean interaction among governments whose principal challenge is for national policies to converge on a focal point, for which the mutual adjustment of policies is unnecessary—such as simply choosing to link national currencies to gold or to the dollar. This implies the existence of a Pareto-improving Nash equilibrium (often more than one), as is the case in a Battle of the Sexes game—countries benefit from choosing the same currency regime, although there may be disagreement over which one to choose. By cooperation, we mean interaction in which national policies must be adjusted consciously to support each other—such as joint intervention in currency markets to support mutually agreed-on exchange rates. This implies the existence of a Pareto-inferior Nash equilibrium, which can be improved on (i.e. to a Nash bargaining solution), as is the case in a Prisoners' Dilemma game—countries can work together to improve their collective and individual welfare. The two problems are not mutually exclusive, or even strikingly different; indeed, the resolution of one usually presupposes the resolution of the other. But for purposes of analysis it is helpful to separate the idea of a fixed-rate system as a focal point, for example, from the idea that its sustainability requires deliberately cooperative policies.

Coordination in International Monetary Relations

An international or regional fixed-rate regime, such as the gold standard or the European Monetary System, has important characteristics of a focal point around which national choices can be coordinated (Frieden 1993). As a focal point, a fixed-rate system can be self-reinforcing; the more countries that were on gold, or that tied their currencies to the Deutsche mark, the greater the incentive for other countries with significant commercial and financial ties to go down this path. Coordination here is particularly important as an ever larger monetarily integrated trading and investment area provides ever greater opportunities to other countries that might consider joining. This can be the case even if the motivations of countries differ. One might particularly appreciate the monetary stability of a fixed rate, another the reduction in currency volatility. It does not matter, so long as the attractions of the regime increase with its membership (Broz 1997).

Most fixed-rate regimes do appear to grow in this way. This was certainly the case of the pre-1914 gold standard, which owed its start to the centrality of gold-standard Britain to the nineteenth-century international economy and owed its eventual global reach to the gradual accession of other major industrial nations to the British-led system. The same kind of growth characterized the process of

European monetary integration, in which the Deutsche mark zone of Germany, Benelux, and Austria gradually attracted more and more European members. It should be noted, however, that just as the focal nature of a fixed-rate system can lead to a "virtuous circle" as more and more countries sign on, so too can the unraveling of the regime lead to a "vicious circle." The departure of any important commercial or financial centers from the system can dramatically reduce its centripetal pull, as was the case with the collapse of the gold standard in the 1930s. Britain's exit began a stampede that led virtually the entire rest of the world off gold within a couple of years. To some extent, then, the gold standard, Bretton Woods, and other such international and regional monetary regimes represent simple solutions to a coordination problem.

Cooperation in International Monetary Relations

International monetary relations may require more than simple convergence around a visible anchor and indeed may call for the resolution of more serious problems of cooperation. In other words, fixed-rate systems may only be stable when governments actively choose to cooperate with one another. A fixed-rate system may, in fact, give governments incentives to cheat, such as to devalue for competitive purposes while taking advantage of other countries' commitment to monetary and currency stability.[4] Such a system would not be stable should such free riding overcome attempts at coordination. By the same token, even a system as simple as the gold standard might have relied on explicit or implicit agreements among central gold currency countries to support each others' monetary authorities in times of difficulty. An enduring monetary system, in this view, thus requires explicit cooperation at least among its principal members.

The problem is a familiar one, in which there are international gains from cooperation but potential national costs. It is useful to identify explicitly both the welfare gain associated with international collaboration and the issues over which nations are likely to disagree. In the international monetary realm, the gains from a stable system of fixed rates are several. First, reduced currency volatility almost certainly increases the level of international trade and investment. Second, fixed rates tend to stabilize domestic monetary conditions, so that international monetary stability reinforces (and may even increase) domestic monetary stability. Third, predictable currency values can reduce international trade conflicts—for a rapid change in currency values, particularly the appreciation of one currency against others, often leads to an import surge, then protectionist pressures, and eventually commercial antagonism.

But, as discussed above, commitment to a fixed exchange rate has costs, and the form of the international monetary regime affects these costs. The principal

[4]The status of this problem is somewhat ambiguous. After all, a country that devalues is reducing its purchasing power. However, it is not difficult to imagine that governments are concerned about the competitiveness of their tradables producers, in the context of which a unilateral devaluation can be tantamount to cheating.

cost is that the government cannot use the exchange rate to affect the domestic economy; it must, so to speak, adjust the economy to fit the exchange rate. The most common source of international conflict in this regard has to do with the international distribution of adjustment costs. For example, under Bretton Woods and the European Monetary System, one country's currency served as the system's anchor or key currency. This forced other countries to adapt their monetary policies to the anchor country's and led to pressures from the other governments on the key-currency government to bring its policy more in line with conditions elsewhere. Under Bretton Woods, from the late 1960s until the system collapsed, European governments wanted the United States to implement more restrictive policies to bring down American inflation, while the US government refused. In the European Monetary System in the early 1990s, governments in the rest of the European Union wanted the Germans to implement less restrictive policies to combat the European recession, but the German central bank refused. This conflict between the attempts of the anchor country and others to shift the burden of adjustment has been a common theme of international and regional currency systems and the source of much acrimony. Generally speaking, closer countries come to agreement about the distribution of the costs of adjustment, the more likely they are to create and sustain a common fixed-rate regime (on closely related problems of international macroeconomic policy coordination, see Espinosa & Yip 1993).

Historical analyses tend to support the idea that the success or failure of intergovernmental cooperation has been crucial to the durability of fixed-rate international and regional monetary systems. Eichengreen's (1992) magisterial study of the interwar gold standard points explicitly to the centrality of international cooperation based on credible domestic political support. Such cooperative activities might include lending by the Bank of France to the Bank of England in the event of pressure on the pound sterling or the coordination of monetary policy measures in a time of international financial distress. Credible cooperation among the major powers before 1914 was the foundation stone of the classical gold standard, according to Eichengreen, and its absence explains the failure of the feeble interwar attempts to revive the gold standard.[5] Many regional monetary unions, too, seem to obey this logic. Where political and other factors have encouraged cooperative behavior to safeguard the common commitment to fixed exchange rates, the systems have endured, but in the absence of these cooperative motives, they have decayed (Cohen 2001).

This raises the question of what stimulates cooperation on exchange rate issues. Cooperation is stimulated within the specifics of international monetary relations by much the same factors as elsewhere in international politics (Willett 1999, Simmons 2000). One factor is a shared interest in currency stability. A major reason for the collapse of the Bretton Woods system was that American policy makers simply were much less concerned about the effects of exchange rate volatility than

[5]For the view that cooperation was not central to the gold standard, see Gallarotti (1995).

Europeans were. A second factor is linkage to other policies. The existence of cooperative ventures outside the monetary realm can stimulate currency cooperation. It is in fact doubtful that Economic Monetary Union (EMU) would have been possible had it not been part of a broader process of European integration (Garrett 2001, Martin 2001). A third, often related, factor is the institutionalized nature of interstate cooperation. Formal or informal mechanisms for governments to work out their monetary differences appear to be associated with greater cooperation. A fourth factor is numbers—the presence of a small group of large states willing and able to take the lead in monetary relations has been common to most successful fixed-rate orders, whether during the gold standard, Bretton Woods, or any number of regional systems. A final factor is environmental economic conditions. Most cooperative monetary arrangements have been sorely taxed by recurrent or protracted macroeconomic downturns.

It should be kept in mind that the relevant level of international monetary cooperation in many instances may be regional rather than global. There have been at least three distinctive global monetary regimes, whose emergence, evolution, and demise are all worth explaining. But there have been many more formal or informal regional monetary regimes, and they have had varying degrees of success, from the Latin Monetary Union of the nineteenth century to the East African Community of the 1960s and 1970s. Proposals for new regional currency arrangements have proliferated in recent years, with the successful establishment of EMU the most prominent example. Analysis of such international monetary ventures requires attention to the focal-point nature of fixed-rate systems, to the welfare gains such a system provides and the distributional effects it implies, and to the factors widely understood to affect interstate cooperation more generally.

Two of the most recent such regime-related topics, EMU in Europe and ongoing debates over dollarization in Latin America, illustrate the operation of these international factors. Dollarization appears to raise ideal-typical coordination issues, as national governments consider independent choices to adopt the US dollar. The United States has indeed explicitly ruled out any meaningful cooperation with dollarizing governments. The principal attraction for potential dollarizers is association with large and dynamic dollar-based capital and goods markets; and the more countries dollarize, the greater this attraction will be. On the other hand, although the course of EMU from 1973 to completion did have features of a focal point, especially in the operation of the European Monetary System as a Deutsche mark bloc, the more complex bargained resolution of the transition to EMU went far beyond this. This bargaining solution involved mutual, indeed unanimous, agreement on the structure of the new European Central Bank, the national macroeconomic policies necessary for membership in the monetary union, and a host of other considerations. These difficult bargains were unquestionably made much easier by the small number of central players (arguably only Germany and France), the highly institutionalized EU environment, and the complex network of policy linkages between EMU and other European initiatives.

CONCLUSIONS

Until recently, scholarly analysis of the political economy of national exchange rate policies and of international monetary relations lagged far behind their political and economic importance. Over the past decade, however, substantial progress has been made in understanding why governments pursue the currency policies they do, and why regional and international currency regimes emerge and evolve. Many of these advances build on preexisting work on the political economy of international trade and investment, but others come specifically from the study of international monetary politics.

At the domestic level, we now have a reasonably well-developed set of arguments about the economic interests at stake and about how political institutions affect currency policy choice. The theoretical and empirical status of these arguments remains undecided, but together they constitute an emerging body of scholarship with clear dependent and candidate explanatory variables. At the international level, the study of global and regional monetary regimes has incorporated developments in the analysis of international cooperation, using them to explain the ebb and flow of such systems over the past two centuries.

Future research on the political economy of international monetary relations has to confront several challenges. First, it needs to clarify and work toward resolution of the various theoretical and empirical ambiguities in existing scholarship. Second, it needs to work toward an integration of the international and domestic sources and effects of exchange rate policy, for the two are integrally interrelated. Third, in concert with research in other areas of political economy, it needs to incorporate the impact of such closely related issue areas as trade and financial policy on international monetary affairs. These are substantial challenges, but the past decade has seen impressive progress in the study of international monetary policy, and there is no reason to doubt that the coming decades will be just as fruitful.

ACKNOWLEDGMENTS

The authors acknowledge the helpful comments of Marc Busch, Benjamin J Cohen, Randall Henning, Lisa Martin, and Andrew Rose.

LITERATURE CITED

Alesina A, Summers LH. 1993. Central bank independence and macroeconomic performance: some comparative evidence. *J. Mon. Cred. Bank.* 25:151–62

Barro RJ, Gordon D. 1983. Rules, discretion, and reputation in a model of monetary policy. *J. Mon. Econ.* 12:101–22

Bernhard W, Leblang D. 1999. Democratic institutions and exchange-rate commitments. *Int. Organ.* 53:71–97

Broz JL. 1997. The domestic politics of international monetary order: the gold standard. In *Contested Social Orders and International Politics*, ed. D Skidmore, pp. 53–91. Nashville, TN: Vanderbilt Univ. Press

Broz JL. 2000. *Political system transparency and monetary commitment regimes*. Presented at Annu. Meet. Am. Polit. Sci. Assoc., Washington, DC

Calvo GA, Reinhart CM. 2000. *Fear of floating*. Natl. Bur. Econ. Res. Work. Pap. No. 7993

Campa J, Goldberg L. 1997. The evolving external orientation of manufacturing: a profile of four countries. *Fed. Reserv. Bank NY Econ. Pol. Rev.* 3:53–70

Canavan C, Tommasi M. 1997. On the credibility of alternative exchange rate regimes. *J. Dev. Econ.* 54:101–22

Clark WR, Hallerberg M. 2000. Mobile capital, domestic institutions, and electorally induced monetary and fiscal policy. *Am. Polit. Sci. Rev.* 94:323–46

Clark WR, Reichert U. 1998. International and domestic constraints on political business cycles in OECD economies. *Int. Organ.* 52:87–120

Cohen BJ. 1977. *Organizing the World's Money*. New York: Basic

Cohen BJ. 2001. Beyond EMU: the problem of sustainability. See Eichengreen & Frieden 2001, pp. 179–204

Collins S, Giavazzi F. 1993. Attitudes toward inflation and the viability of fixed exchange rates. In *A Retrospective on the Bretton Woods System*, ed. M Bordo, B Eichengreen, pp. 547–77. Chicago: Univ. Chicago Press

Cooper RN. 1968. *The Economics of Interdependence*. New York: McGraw-Hill

Corsetti G, Pesenti P, Roubini R. 1998. *What caused the Asian currency and financial crisis?* Parts I and II. Natl. Bur. Econ. Res. Work. Pap. Nos. 6833 and 6844

Debelle G, Fischer S. 1994. How independent should the central bank be? In *Goals, Guidelines, and Constraints Facing Monetary Policymakers*, ed. JC Fuhrer, pp. 195–221. Boston, MA: Fed. Reserv. Bank Boston

Destler IM, Henning CR. 1989. *Dollar Politics: Exchange Rate Policymaking in the United States*. Washington, DC: Inst. Int. Econ.

Edison H, Melvin M. 1990. The determinants and implications of the choice of an exchange rate system. In *Monetary Policy for a Volatile Global Economy*, ed. W Haraf, T Willett, pp. 1–50. Washington, DC: Am. Enterp. Inst.

Edwards S. 1994. The political economy of inflation and stabilization in developing countries. *Econ. Dev. Cult. Change* 42(2)

Edwards S. 1999. How effective are capital controls? *J. Econ. Perspect.* 13:65–84

Edwards S, Savastano M. 1999. *Exchange rates in emerging economies*. Natl. Bur. Econ. Res. Work. Pap. No. 7228

Eichengreen B. 1992. *Golden Fetters*. Oxford, UK: Oxford Univ. Press

Eichengreen B. 1995. The endogeneity of exchange rate regimes. In *Understanding Interdependence*, ed. P Kenen, pp. 3–33. Princeton, NJ: Princeton Univ. Press

Eichengreen B, Frieden J, eds. 2001. *The Political Economy of European Monetary Unification*. Boulder, CO: Westview. 2nd ed. In press

Espinosa M, Yip CK. 1993. International policy coordination: Can we have our cake and eat it too? *Fed. Reserv. Bank Atlanta Econ. Rev.* 78:1–12

Fearon JD. 1994. Domestic political audiences and the escalation of international disputes. *Am. Polit. Sci. Rev.* 88:577–92

Frankel JA. 1994. The making of exchange rate policy in the 1980s. In *American Economic Policy in the 1980s*, ed. M Feldstein, pp. 293–341. Chicago: Univ. Chicago Press

Frankel JA. 1995. Monetary regime choice for a semi-open economy. In *Capital Controls, Exchange Rates and Monetary Policy in the World Economy*, ed. S Edwards, pp. 35–69. Cambridge, UK: Cambridge Univ. Press

Frankel JA. 1999. No single currency regime is right for all countries or at all times. *Essays Int. Econ.* No. 215, Princeton Univ. Press

Frieden J. 1991. Invested interests: the politics of national economic policy in a world of global finance. *Int. Organ.* 45:425–51

Frieden J. 1993. The dynamics of international monetary systems: international and domestic factors in the rise, reign, and demise of the classical gold standard. In *Coping with Complexity in the International System*, ed. R Jervis, J Snyder. Boulder, CO: Westview

Frieden J. 1996. Economic integration and the politics of monetary policy in the United States. In *Internationalization and Domestic Politics*, ed. RO Keohane, HV Milner, pp. 108–36. Cambridge, UK: Cambridge Univ. Press

Frieden J. 1997. Monetary populism in nineteenth-century America: an open economy interpretation. *J. Econ. Hist.* 57:367–95

Frieden J. 2000. The political economy of European exchange rates: an empirical assessment. Unpubl. pap.

Frieden J. 2001. Making commitments: France and Italy in the European Monetary System, 1979–1985. See Eichengreen & Frieden 2001, pp. 23–48

Frieden J, Ghezzi P, Stein E. 2001. Politics and exchange rates: a cross-country approach to Latin America. In *The Currency Game: Exchange Rate Politics in Latin America*, ed. J Frieden, E Stein. Baltimore, MD: Johns Hopkins Univ. Press. In press

Gallarotti G. 1995. *The Anatomy of an International Monetary Regime: The Classical Gold Standard, 1880–1914*. New York: Oxford Univ. Press

Garrett G. 1995. Capital mobility, trade, and the domestic politics of economic policy. *Int. Organ.* 49:657–87

Garrett G. 2001. The politics of Maastricht. See Eichengreen & Frieden 2001, pp. 111–30

Ghosh A, Gulde AM, Ostry JA, Wolf HC. 1997. *Does the nominal exchange rate regime matter?* Natl. Bur. Econ. Res. Work. Pap. No. 5874

Giavazzi F, Giovannini A. 1989. *Limiting Exchange Rate Flexibility*. Cambridge, MA: MIT Press

Giavazzi F, Pagano M. 1988. The advantage of tying one's hands: EMS discipline and central bank credibility. *Eur. Econ. Rev.* 32:1055–75

Goldberg PK, Knetter MM. 1997. Goods prices and exchange rates: What have we learned? *J. Econ. Lit.* 35:1243–72

Goodman JB, Pauly LW. 1993. The obsolescence of capital controls? *World Polit.* 4:50–82

Gowa J. 1983. *Closing the Gold Window: Domestic Politics and the End of Bretton Woods*. Ithaca, NY: Cornell Univ. Press

Gowa J. 1998. Public goods and political institutions: trade and monetary policy processes in the United States. *Int. Organ.* 42:15–32

Hall PA, Franzese R. 1998. Mixed signals: central bank independence, coordinated wage-bargaining, and European Monetary Union. *Int. Organ.* 52:505–36

Hefeker C. 1995. Interest groups, coalitions and monetary integration in the nineteenth century. *J. Eur. Econ. Hist.* 24:489–536

Hefeker C. 1997. *Interest Groups and Monetary Integration*. Boulder, CO: Westview

Henning CR. 1994. *Currencies and Politics in the United States, Germany, and Japan*. Washington, DC: Inst. Int. Econ.

Herrendorf B. 1999. Transparency, reputation, and credibility under floating and pegged exchange rates. *J. Int. Econ.* 49:31–50

Hibbs D. 1977. Political parties and macroeconomic policy. *Am. Polit. Sci. Rev.* 71:1467–87

Kenen P. 1969. The theory of optimum currency areas. In *Monetary Problems in the International Economy*, ed. R Mundell, A Swoboda. Chicago: Univ. Chicago Press

Kindleberger C. 1970. *Power and Money: the Economics of International Politics and the Politics of International Economics*. New York: Basic Books

Klein M, Marion N. 1997. Explaining the duration of exchange-rate pegs. *J. Dev. Econ.* 54:387–404

Kydland FE, Prescott EC. 1977. Rules rather than discretion: the inconsistency of optimal plans. *J. Polit. Econ.* 85:473–92

Leblang D. 1999. Democratic political institutions and exchange rate commitments in the developing world. *Int. Stud. Q.* 43:599–620

Leblang D. 2000. *To devalue or defend: the political economy of exchange rate policy*. Presented at Annu. Meet. Am. Polit. Sci. Assoc., Washington, DC

Lewis-Beck MS, Stegmaier M. 2000. Economic determinants of electoral outcomes. *Annu. Rev. Polit. Sci.* 3:183–219

Marston RC. 1995. *International Financial Integration*. Cambridge, UK: Cambridge Univ. Press

Martin L. 2001. International and domestic institutions in the EMU process and beyond. See Eichengreen & Frieden 2001, pp. 131–55

Maxfield S. 1997. *Gatekeepers of Growth: The International Political Economy of Central Banking in Developing Countries*. Princeton, NJ: Princeton Univ. Press

McKinnon RI. 1962. Optimum currency areas. *Am. Econ. Rev.* 53:717–25

McKinnon RI, Fung KC. 1993. Floating exchange rates and the new interbloc protectionism. In *Protectionism and World Welfare*, ed. D Salvatore, pp. 221–44. Cambridge, UK: Cambridge Univ. Press

McNamara K. 1998. *The Currency of Ideas: Monetary Politics in the European Union*. Ithaca, NY: Cornell Univ. Press

Milner HV. 1999. The political economy of international trade. *Annu. Rev. Polit. Sci.* 2:91–114

Mishkin FS. 1999. *International experiences with different monetary policy regimes*. Natl. Bur. Econ. Res. Work. Pap. No. 7044

Mundell RA. 1961. A theory of optimum currency areas. *Am. Econ. Rev.* 51:657–64

Mundell R. 1962. *The appropriate use of monetary and fiscal policy under fixed exchange rates*. IMF Staff Pap. No. 9. Washington, DC: Int. Monet. Fund

Mundell R. 1963. Capital mobility and stabilization policy under fixed and flexible exchange rates. *Can. J. Econ. Polit. Sci.* 29:475–85

Oatley T. 1997. *Monetary Politics: Exchange Rate Cooperation in the European Union*. Ann Arbor: Univ. Mich. Press

Obstfeld M, Rogoff K. 1995. The mirage of fixed exchange rates. *J. Econ. Perspect.* 9:73–96

Odell JS. 1982. *U.S. International Monetary Policy: Markets, Power, and Ideas as Sources of Change*. Princeton, NJ: Princeton Univ. Press

Olson M. 1971. *The Logic of Collective Action*. Cambridge, MA: Harvard Univ. Press

Rose A. 2000. One money, one market: estimating the effect of common currencies on trade. *Econ. Pol.* 30:7–46

Scheve K. 1999. *European economic integration and electoral politics in France and Great Britain*. Presented at Annu. Meet. Am. Polit. Sci. Assoc., Atlanta, GA

Simmons B. 1994. *Who Adjusts?* Princeton, NJ: Princeton Univ. Press

Simmons B. 2000. International law and state behavior: commitment and compliance in international monetary affairs. *Am. Polit. Sci. Rev.* 94:819–35

Stallings DA. 1993. Increased protection in the 1980s: exchange rates and institutions. *Public Choice* 77:493–521

Strange S. 1971. *Sterling and British Policy: A Political Study of an International Currency in Decline*. London: Oxford Univ. Press

Tavlas G. 1994. The theory of monetary integration. *Open Econ. Rev.* 5:211–30

Trefler D. 1993. Trade liberalization and the theory of endogenous protection. *J. Polit. Econ.* 101:138–60

Vegh CA. 1992. *Stopping high inflation: an analytical overview*. IMF Staff Pap. 39. Washington, DC: Int. Monet. Fund

Willett TD. 1999. Developments in the political economy of policy coordination. *Open Econ. Rev.* 10:221–53

Wittman D. 1989. Why democracies produce efficient results. *J. Polit. Econ.* 97:1395–424

Annu. Rev. Polit. Sci. 2001. 4:345–69

BIOLOGY AND POLITICS: Linking Nature and Nurture

R.D. Masters
Department of Government, Dartmouth College, Hanover, New Hampshire 03755; e-mail: Roger.D.Masters@Dartmouth.edu

Key Words environmental toxins, learning disabilities, crime, public water supplies, political theory

■ **Abstract** Although millions of Americans take psychoactive medicines (e.g. Prozac and Ritalin), few social scientists believe biological theories and findings should be integrated with research on human behavior. Four topics illustrate current studies linking politics and the life sciences: (*a*) Developments in genetics and medicine indicate that governmental policies have greatly underrated the dangers posed by radiation and the social transformations that will result from DNA sequencing. (*b*) Research on brain structures and neurochemistry shows how toxic chemicals undermine normal emotions and behavior. Heavy metal burdens are higher in violent criminals, and exposure to these toxins is significantly correlated with rates of violence (controlling for socioeconomic, ethnic, and demographic factors). (*c*) An untested chemical used to treat water supplied to 140 million Americans significantly increases both odds of dangerous lead uptake and behavioral dysfunctions in children and adults. (*d*) The complexity of gene-environment interactions challenges accepted theories of gender, sociopolitical inequalities, ethnocentrism, and history. Such research in biopolitics can illuminate policy controversies in education, substance abuse, and crime.

INTRODUCTION

Rapid and profound changes in biology over the past 50 years have major implications for political science. Advances in the life sciences change not only technologies of reproduction, health care, and agriculture, but make possible terrifying new weapons. Even more important, biological sciences challenge widely accepted explanations of human sociopolitical behavior. Although philosophers from Plato and Aristotle to Locke and Rousseau assumed that an adequate political theory required an accurate understanding of "human nature," this foundation of our discipline must now be reconsidered in the light of such fields as genetics, cell biology, neuroscience, ecology, and evolutionary theory.

Among facets of human politics illuminated by biopolitics are the dynamics of face-to-face behavior among leaders and followers (Masters 1975, 1981;

Sullivan & Masters 1988; Masters et al 1991; Schubert & Masters 1994), effects of environment and genes on behavior (Bryce-Smith 1986, Gottschalk et al 1991), and the evolution of societies that led to the formation of states (Masters 1981, 1983a,b). Technologies from genetic engineering to biological weapons can transform both peace and war (Mangold & Goldberg 1999). Advances in brain imaging (such as PET, MRI, and CAT scans) make it possible convert mysteries of cognition and emotion into visible processes (Gazzaniga et al 1998).

The links between brain chemistry and behavior reveal problems that hinder research in social and political science if the life sciences are ignored. An estimated 11 million American children take Ritalin, and many others exhibit attention deficit disorder (ADD), attention deficit/hyperactivity disorder (ADHD), or other learning disabilities. Over 83 million Americans take Prozac, Zoloft, and other medications for depression or other psychological conditions, including seasonal affective disorder and sexual addiction (McGuire & Troisi 1998, Slater 2000). More directly related to politics, environmental toxins such as lead, cadmium, mercury, arsenic, or manganese can damage the brain and increase risks of criminal violence and other behavioral problems. These empirical observations are relevant to public policies in education, criminal justice, or health care, and indicate the need to reconsider theories of human social and political behavior. To do so, however, is impossible without a detailed knowledge of human biology.

THE SCOPE OF BIOPOLITICS

To assess the sociopolitical implications of contemporary biology, researchers in many disciplines are creating the discipline of biopolitics. The variety of issues included in this emerging field is evident from the following list of the panels at the Association for Politics and the Life Sciences' 2000 meeting: The Role of USAMIRIID in Defense Against Biological Warfare and Bioterrorism; Facing the Biological Weapons Threat; Fetal and Children's Health Issues; Environmental Security; Reproduction, Kinship, and Behavior; Challenges of Adaptation; Enlightenment and Hyper-Enlightenment Quests in the Sociobiology Debate; Strengthening the Biological Weapons Convention; Food Safety and the Right to Know; Biomedical Technology; Politics of Environmental Disasters; Comparative Reception of Sociobiology (3); Recent Developments in Gene Therapy; Use of Biological Weapons; Moral Issues in Medical Decision-Making; Darwinian Medicine; Population Growth and Population Density; Mechanisms and Processes of Leadership; Roots and Resolution of Conflict; Protecting the Planet in the Age of Globalization (2); Former Soviet Union's Biological Warfare Program; Public Policy for the End of Life; Government, Research, and Public Policy; Evolutionary Theory and the Social Sciences; Biology as Precedent; The Hype and Hope of Genetically Modified Food; Biodefense in an Age of Asymmetric Threats; Genetic Engineering and Cloning; Toxicology, Birth Defects, and Behavior; Religion, Bioethics, and Public Policy; Agricultural Warfare; Science, Morality and Public Policy; The

Ethics of Marketing Health Care; Complexity, Climate Change, and International Politics; Are We Saving Apes or Consuming Them?; Reciprocity, Altruism, and Social Responsibility; Biological Weapons: Threats and Responses; Comparative Nations Study of Making Arts Policy; Concepts of Nature and the Natural in Genetic Engineering; Ecology of Contemporary Politics; Culture and Evolution.

In contrast, the divisions listed in the call for papers for the 2001 convention of the American Political Science Association (PS 2000) include four in political theory, three in teaching and methods, five in comparative politics, six in international relations, nine on institutional domains of American politics (such as the presidency or state politics), three on specific components of the electorate (such as race), five on functional attributes (such as public opinion), six that are interdisciplinary (such as political economy), and two oriented to political action (New Political Science and Ecological and Transformational Politics). Of over 40 divisions, only one—Science, Technology, and Environmental Politics—might focus on work from a biological perspective, but rarely does actual work this area reflect the scope and importance of the issues addressed at the biopolitics convention.

Although biopolitics deals with a wide range of topics, the area rests on a common theoretical framework (neo-Darwinian evolutionary biology), whereas political science as a discipline lacks such a shared foundation. Moreover, many issues of enormous practical import that are addressed at the Association for Politics and the Life Sciences are rarely touched on at APSA conventions. Among these are the earlier onset of puberty and changes in sexual behavior, gene therapy, pollution, and biological warfare. The following review, though selective, suggests the promise of this research area.

GENETICS, RADIATION, AND HEALTH

The rough draft of the entire human genome was recently decoded. Humans vary genetically, and in matters of health, knowledge about these differences is sometimes a matter of life and death. When establishing public policies, it is now important to know whether genetic differences make a subset of the population especially sensitive to foods, toxins, or events that are safe for others.

Because there are many reasons why people vary in behavior, capabilities, and health, genetics cannot explain everything. But is it conceivable that genetic engineering will have no social and political effects? Can political scientists continue to ignore human genetics by relegating it to a narrow corner of health policy?

A congressional staff member with whom I discussed genetic research remarked that in 50 years or less, most Americans will probably have an individual "genome card" like one of today's credit cards. He expects that this information will be used as widely as we now use our social security numbers (which by law were to be rigorously private information rather than the national identification number they are becoming). If this prediction is fulfilled, won't some applicants for insurance coverage, elite jobs and universities, or other key positions be rejected for genetic reasons (and, in some cases, might such exclusions be desirable)?

Tradition has it that Lord Rutherford, the British Nobel prize–winning physicist, once said that all science is "either physics or stamp-collecting." Rutherford sometimes made mistakes, as when he dismissed as "rubbish" Leo Szilard's idea that a nuclear chain reaction could be used to make a terrifying weapon. (Fortunately, after this rebuff, Szilard came to the United States, told Einstein about his idea, and the rest is history.) From genetics to ecology, although contemporary biology is neither pure physics nor stamp-collecting, it surely is a science. Can the same be said of political science if it persists in erroneous opinions like Rutherford's rejection of Szilard's conception of nuclear fission?

Other issues posed by nuclear radiation illustrate the error of assuming that biology and politics are not related. Mutation rates and other health risks from radiation have long been interpreted primarily on the basis of contested studies of Japanese mortality rates following the explosions over Hiroshima and Nagasaki. A recent biography of Dr. Alice Stewart, who discovered that X-rays of pregnant women are associated with infant cancer, reveals how political pressures obscured her later finding that "the nuclear weapons industry is about twenty times more dangerous than worker safety standards admit" (Greene 1999:1). This account shows not only that the US government has exposed some of its employees to intolerable health risks but that administrators have blocked scientific discussion of the issue. In research on genetics, radiation, and toxicity, the distinction between political self-interest and objective science can easily disappear.

TOXINS AND BEHAVIOR

Toxins are environmental factors that influence behavior through biological mechanisms and pose serious political problems. The lasting effects of fetal alcohol syndrome and lead poisoning on normal brain development and behavior are well documented (Bryce-Smith 1983, 1986; Juberg 1997; Kessel & O'Connor 1997; Millstone 1997). In addition to the implications for regulatory policies and health care, such findings show that biological factors can be directly related to learning disabilities, violent crime, and many other dimensions of human behavior.

Traditionally, toxins have been viewed as sources of cancer and other diseases. Today, as advances in neuroscience reveal the role of neurotransmitters in behavior, it is becoming evident that the brain is an especially vulnerable target of toxic substances. Because heavy metals such as lead and manganese downregulate serotonin, dopamine, and other neurotransmitters essential to cognitive processing and the control of social interactions, neurotoxicity can influence behavior even when its effects are otherwise subclinical.

Consider the dangers of lead toxicity (Stapleton 1994, Abados & Llados 1997, Bower 1998, Lanphear 1998, Lanphear et al 1998). Although it has long been known that lead is harmful to physical health, precise studies of its effects on neurotransmitter function and behavior are relatively new (Rutter & Jones 1983, Hammond 1998, Rabin 1989, Cory-Slechta 1995, Tiffany-Castiglioni et al 1996). Among the probable negative consequences of lead uptake are fetal and early-childhood developmental deficits, premature birth, low cranial circumference, lower intelligence quotient, learning deficits, attention deficit disorder (ADD), hyperactivity (ADHD), and reduced impulse control (Bryce-Smith 1986, Mushak & Crocetti 1989, Needleman 1989, Needleman et al 1990, Needleman & Gatsonis 1991, Aschengau et al 1993, Rice 1994, Tuthill 1996, Mendelsohn et al 1998). In adults, lead neurotoxicity has been linked with higher rates of aggressive or criminal behavior in both correlational analyses (Schauss 1981, Pihl & Ervin 1990, Werbach n.d., Gottschalk et al 1991, Marlow et al 1991, Schrauzer et al 1992) and prospective studies (Denno 1994, Needleman et al 1996). Whereas acute exposure to lead also increases susceptibility to hypertension, heart disease, renal disease, or cancer, evidence of disease risk from chronic, low-level exposure is mixed, suggesting the importance of other risk cofactors (Staessen et al 1994, Castellino 1995, Shell 1995, Hu et al 1996). The behavioral effects of lead neurotoxicity may well be more important, especially for political science (Masters 1997, 1999; Masters et al 1998).

HYPERACTIVITY AND LEARNING DISABILITIES

An important topic touching on biopolitics and ignored by mainstream political science is the vastly increased incidence of hyperactivity, and use of Ritalin to treat it, among American children. Although the US Department of Education has estimated the incidence of "learning disabilities" at around 5% (Liebmann-Smith 2000), results of my own informal survey of Massachusetts high schools were substantially different and indicated the paucity of reliable data. Of 39 schools replying, only 22 provided data for the total number of students coded with learning disabilities. Pooling these schools (since school size is an important variable and sampling could well bias results), out of a total enrollment of 14,056 students, 1774 or 12.9% were coded as learning disabled.

Do official governmental estimates ignore important differences in the incidence of different learning disabilities and confuse treatment (the use of Ritalin to control ADD/ADHD) with diagnosis? According to one physician who makes this charge, 3–5% of all US schoolchildren, and more than 10 % of elementary school-age boys, currently take Ritalin or other drugs for hyperactive behavior, attention deficits, and impulsiveness (Walker 1998:5). If Dr. Walker's estimates are correct, the US Department of Education greatly underestimates special education needs by equating the proportion of children on Ritalin with the incidence of all learning disabilities.

Given the unreliability of such estimates and much of the available data, it is hard to judge who is correct. My own small survey (which relied on direct reports from schools) suggests both that the US Department of Education underestimates the overall problem of learning disabilities and that Dr. Walker's estimate needs to be considered with prudence. In the 28 Massachusetts High Schools whose replies included relevant data, 4.2% of enrolled students (1377 of 32,841) were classified with ADD or ADHD; of these, 540 children (39.2% of the ADD/ADHD children and 1.6% of total enrollment) received Ritalin from the school nurses. Whether representative or not, these statistics remind us that a substantial number of American children are receiving behavior-control medications from school nurses or other government employees and that a much larger proportion of children have serious learning disabilities of various kinds.

This example illustrates a defect in the theories of human behavior tacitly accepted by most political scientists. For decades, we have heard that biology poses the issue of genes versus environment, based on the distinction between innate influences and learning from the social environment. Hyperactivity and many other behavioral disorders challenge this dichotomy. Although some children may suffer from ADD or ADHD because of genetic traits, many others exhibit similar behavior resulting from exposure to toxins such as lead, manganese, carbon monoxide, or alcohol due to fetal alcohol syndrome (Walker 1998). An important source of behavioral and learning difficulties is very often a biological factor in the environment (Crocetti et al 1990, Mielke 1993, Lanphear et al 1998, Vivarette et al 1996), cutting across the customary nature/nurture dichotomy.

The explanation of hyperactivity depends in part on the biochemistry of the brain (Lippard & Berg 1994, Gazzaniga et al 1998, McGuire & Troisi 1998). A variety of neurotransmitters, receptors, reuptake inhibitors, and other molecules regulate the connections and firing of neurons. Motor behavior is partially controlled by the basal ganglia, where circuits excite or inhibit body movement, crudely comparable to an automobile's accelerator and brake. This system allows continuous changes in movement and force, as in walking or playing tennis. The mechanisms can be paradoxical, since in the inhibitory circuits, excitatory neurotransmitters can activate inhibition (like pushing on a brake pedal), and inhibitory chemicals can block inhibition (and hence function as an accelerator).

These complexities explain why the most frequent medication for hyperactive children is Ritalin (Windholz et al 1983), which is an excitatory chemical like amphetamine. How does an excitatory medication slow down hyperactive children? The answer seems to be that hyperactivity often arises from too little activity in the brain centers that normally inhibit behavior, so Ritalin activates the inhibition. But this raises the question of what causes the failure of inhibitory brain circuits.

Oddly enough, a clue comes from temporal and geographical differences in rates of learning disabilities. Why is there suddenly an epidemic of ADHD? If more Tom Sawyer–like children are merely "coming out of the closet," why are there age-related and geographic differences in today's rates of hyperactivity? The answers begin with toxic chemicals that reduce the activity of the key neurotransmitters (Needleman 1999). In one case, for example, carbon monoxide from a faulty heating system undermined blood transport of oxygen and thereby led to hyperactive behavior (Walker 1998:7–9).

Diet can also matter (Schoenthaler 1985), as is shown by the work of the Feingold Association of the United States (Hersey 1999) as well as by the Pfeiffer Treatment Center of Naperville, Illinois (a pioneer in the identification and treatment of abnormalities in brain chemistry). Whereas Ritalin and Prozac treat symptoms by masking the chemical causes, often with uncertain long-term effects, diet or detoxification frequently have surprising success with minimal side effects and lower expense.

Heavy metal absorption can also contribute to ADD/ADHD (Minder et al 1994, Needleman 1999). Although some studies do not find this association (e.g. Kahn et al 1995), Tuthill (1996) found that many ADHD children in one Massachusetts community had absorbed high levels of lead. In animal studies, moreover, impulsive responses are significantly increased by lead exposure (Brockel & Cory-Slechta 1998). Others have suggested similar effects of manganese.

Effects of toxins on neurotransmitters make this association plausible. Lead downregulates dopamine and glutamate, whereas manganese downregulates serotonin (Bryce-Smith 1983; Needleman & Gatsonis 1991, Needleman et al 1996). In addition, these heavy metals have effects related to calcium's crucial function as a neurotransmitter and cofactor in many brain systems.

Research in cognitive neuroscience shows how important such effects can be. For example, the inhibitory function of the basal ganglia relies in part on dopamine, which is downregulated by lead (e.g. Gazzaniga et al 1998:413–420). Calcium plays a key role in the hippocampus, essential to the basic learning process known as long-term potentiation (LTP) (Gazzaniga et al 1998:283–88). Not surprisingly, ADHD has been linked to deficits in dopamine function (Cook et al 1995).

Although some critics question the efficacy of lead removal (chelation), it has successfully been used to replace drug treatment for a subset of ADD/ADHD cases (Walker 1998). Toxicity could therefore account for a substantial portion of ADD/ADHD cases, especially since early lead exposure is so widespread and damaging to children (Aschengau et al 1993, Bellinger et al 1994, Mielke 1998, Levitt 1999). Alas, without further research using methods now usually ignored in the social sciences, no one knows how much of this problem (or others, such as childhood asthma) is due to pollution.

MOOD DISTURBANCES AND SUBSTANCE ABUSE

Hyperactivity and Ritalin use is one of many issues that can be illuminated through biopolitics. In addition to the millions of children treated chemically for ADD/ADHD, over 83 million Americans routinely take psychoactive medications such as Prozac. Why has this occurred, and what are its possible effects?

Just as lead can lower the function of dopamine, manganese can lower serotonin, which plays an important role in regulating moods and behavior (Fairhall & Neal 1943, McGuire & Troisi 1998). Where serotonin levels are low, feelings of depression and suicidal thoughts are frequent. In such cases, drugs called selective serotonin reuptake inhibitors (SSRIs), such as Prozac and Zoloft, prevent the neurotransmitter's breakdown and reduce symptoms of depression, seasonal affective disorder, or sexual addiction (Masters & McGuire 1994, Slater 2000).

In addition, serotonin is directly linked to leadership. Among both humans and nonhuman primates, after an individual achieves dominant status, serotonin levels rise over a period of several weeks. When dominance is lost, serotonin falls (Masters & McGuire 1994). Since low levels of serotonin are less pleasurable than higher levels, it is little wonder that power is said to be addictive.

Could reduced levels of serotonin produce feelings of inferiority that contribute to such behaviors as a selfish orientation to pleasure and lower political commitment? Such hypotheses are extremely difficult to test because the complex relationships between neurotransmitters and toxins also vary depending on personality and life history. Although it is usually difficult to measure biochemical influences on attitudes or mood, rates of behavior are somewhat easier to record. Abuse of alchohol and drugs, for example, has been associated with heavy metal burdens (Kivatkin & Stein 1995, Kuhar 1992, Slusher et al 1997, Masters & Coplan 1999b). Violent crime is probably a more important focus for biopolitical analysis at this time because of extensive data and persistent public concern.

TOXINS AND VIOLENT CRIME

In addition to generating depressive or acerbic moods, uptake of manganese and other toxins has been associated with aggressive behavior. Why should this be?

From a biological perspective, unwanted or unpleasant disease symptoms are often the product of evolutionary processes and in some cases have adaptive benefits. For example, the pallor associated with high fever is not a sign of iron deficiency needing treatment; this symptom results from the body's sequestering of iron during the fever, which slows bacterial proliferation (Nesse & Williams 1994). "Darwinian psychiatry" shows that many apparently dysfunctional mental states are consequences of evolved cognitive and emotional mechanisms (McGuire & Troisi 1998). When such a perspective is extended to behavioral neurotoxicity, it can explain otherwise puzzling aspects of violent behavior (Daly & Wilson 1988, Brennan et al 1995).

For nonhuman primates or earlier hominids, aggression among young males living in adverse environments need not have been maladaptive (Tiger 1969, Schubert & Masters 1994). Low levels of lead and manganese are widespread in the earth's soil and atmosphere (e.g. Shotyk et al 1998), and their uptake is facilitated by dietary deficits in calcium, zinc, iron, and other key minerals (Murphy et al 1991, Masters et al 1998). As Cosmides and Tooby have argued, male-male aggressive behavior may have been adaptive "in prehistoric times of food shortages and other harsh conditions" (Bower 1998:154). In addition to competition within groups, male aggressiveness can be adaptive in intergroup conflict over scarce resources (Manson & Wrangham 1991).

Today, however, when large segments of the population are exposed to chemicals that downregulate essential neurotransmitter function, industrial civilization has created a novel problem (Mielke 1992, 1994, 1998; Masters 1997; Masters et al 1998; Masters & Coplan 1999a). From a biological perspective, cognitive neuroscience and the behavioral effects of neurotoxins make it possible to discover environmental factors that have a remarkably strong effect on rates of violent behavior.

The harmful effects of lead and manganese on behavior have been noted above. This hypothesis can be tested by measuring individual differences in these and other toxins among violent criminals (Pihl & Ervin 1990, Denno 1994, Violence Research Foundation 1994). For example, in six studies comparing levels of heavy metals in violent offenders and nonviolent offenders in the same jails, either lead or manganese was significantly higher in violent offenders than in nonviolent offenders (Masters et al 1998: Table 1). Since the jail environments of the violent and nonviolent offenders in these studies were the same, the higher levels of heavy metals in the violent criminals can hardly be attributed to prison food or the soap in the showers. Emotional responses and inhibition of violence, which are regulated by neurotransmitters such as dopamine and seratonin, are deficient in behaviorally disturbed children as well as in adult criminals (Fisher & Blair 1998).

The hypothesis that heavy metal toxicity is one risk factor for violent crime can also be tested by correlating industrial pollution with geographic variations in crime rate (Land et al 1990, Masters et al 1998). The toxic release inventory of the US Environmental Protection Agency (EPA) provides geographic data, by county, of the release of lead and manganese. The United States has over 3000 counties, so the sample size is reasonably large. In different years, both lead and manganese pollution had statistically significant effects on crime rates (Figure 1). Moreover, if alcoholism rates are added to the analysis, there are (*a*) a significant two-way interaction between lead and manganese (i.e. counties with both toxins in the environment have higher crime rates than those with only one), (*b*) significant two-way interactions of either lead or manganese with alcoholism, and (*c*) a three-way interaction between alcoholism, lead, and manganese pollution.

To confirm that these effects are not spurious, multiple regression analysis and other multivariate calculations were computed. Controlling for social variables usually associated with crime (population size and density, socioeconomic status, income, etc), crime rates are higher where the population is exposed to the neurotoxins that destroy inhibitory neurotransmitter function. In short, heavy metal pollution is associated with crime, and alcohol aggravates these effects (Masters et al 1998).

Using historical data, the hypothesis can be further tested by studying how the US crime rate changed after the congressional ban on leaded gasoline. Since lead exposure during pregnancy and the infant's first year can damage developing brain structures, the most serious harm due to exhaust from leaded gasoline might have been the long-term effect on infants rather than its short-term effects on

TABLE 1 Correlations between gasoline sales and US violent crime rates lagged by increasing time intervals (1976–1997)

Year lag	Correlation	n
0	−0.906	26
1	−0.897	27
2	−0.88	28
3	−0.85	29
4	−0.79	30
5	−0.74	30
6	−0.675	30
7	−0.610	30
8	−0.542	30
9	−0.465	30
10	−0.369	30
11	−0.247	30
12	−0.111	30
13	0.050	30
	Average 0–13:−0.57	
14	0.236	30
15	0.431	30
16	0.618	30
17	0.778	30
	Average 14–17:0.516	
18	0.902	30
19	0.961	30
20	0.979	29
20	0.979	29
21	0.964	28
22	0.956	27
23	0.939	26
24	0.919	25
	Average 18–24:0.95	
25	0.910	24
26	0.900	23
27	0.885	22
28	0.882	21
29	0.878	20
30	0.874	19
31	0.859	18
32	0.856	17
33	0.868	16
34	0.878	15
	Average 25–34:0.879	
35	0.891	14
36	0.880	13
37	0.819	12
38	0.728	11
39	0.642	10
40	0.439	9
	Average 37–40 :0.702	

Source: FBI, Supplementary Homicide Reports, 1976–1979.

neurotransmitters such as dopamine in young adults. Whereas immediate loss of inhibition due to recent exposures to leaded gasoline exhaust would be measured by a correlation between each year's sales of leaded gasoline and simultaneous crime rates, effects of lead on infant brain development would be revealed by a correlation between sales of leaded gasoline and rates of violent crime, and especially homicides (which are more likely to result from a loss of self-control during a fight), committed about 17 years or more later. The relative importance of these two mechanisms can be compared by correlating leaded gasoline sales per year with the rates of homicides lagged zero to 24 years.

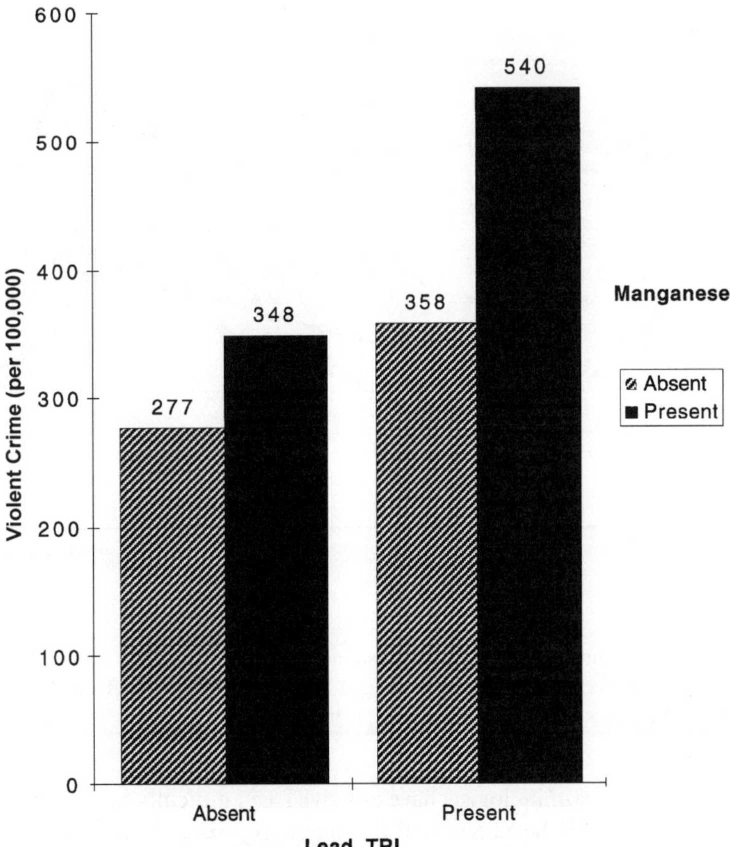

Figure 1 Lead and manganese pollution and rates of violent crime per 100,000 in 1991: 2899 US counties (from data in Masters et al 1998). Lead and manganese pollution: industrial releases in US Environmental Protection Agency's Toxic Release Inventory (TRI). If rates of death from alcoholism are dichotomized at national mean (43/10,000), significance in three-way ANOVA is as follows: manganese TRI: t ratio 11.32, $p < 0.0001$, $F1{,}2898 = 128.25$; lead TRI: t ratio 9.66, $p < 0.0001$, $F1{,}2898 = 93.22$; alcoholism: t ratio -11.99, $p < 0.0001$, $F12{,}2898 - 143.64$. Interactions: manganese and alcoholism: $p < 0.0001$; lead and alcoholism: $p < 0.0027$; lead and manganese: $p < 0.0001$; lead, manganese, and alcoholism: $p < 0.0169$.

Although leaded gasoline sales are not highly correlated with contemporaneous crime rates, effects are evident for criminals over age 16 who had been exposed to leaded gasoline fumes when they were infants (r between 0.70 and 0.95) (Table 1). Moreover, the parallel curves of murders by 14- to 17-year-olds and leaded gasoline sales during their gestation or infancy are striking (Figure 2). If these figures represent genuine effects, the drop in violent crime in the United States since

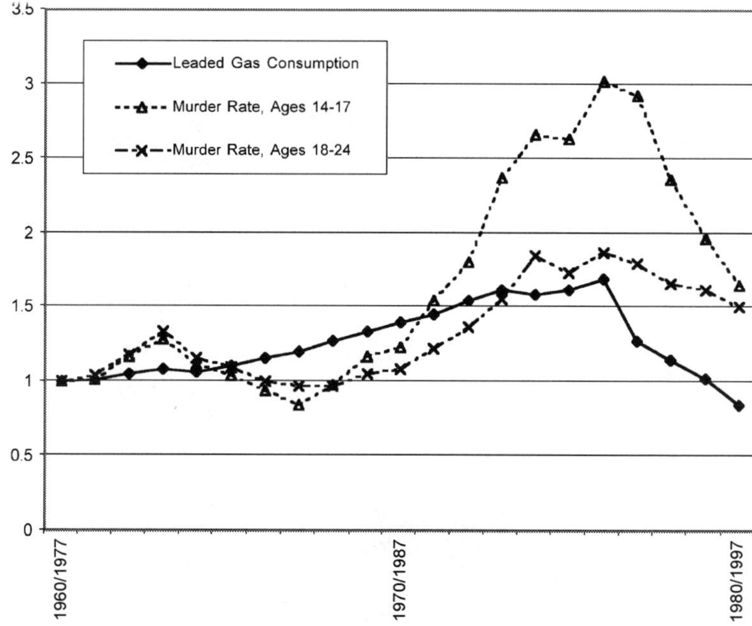

Figure 2 Annual sales of leaded gasoline (normalized to 1960 = 1) and contemporary rates of murders committed by those aged 14–17 and 18–24 in the United States from 1960 to 1997.

1991, which criminologists have otherwise had difficulty in explaining, might be due in part to reduced neonatal and infant exposure to particulate lead after the congressional ban on leaded gasoline (cf Pirkle et al 1994).

Of course, individual personality, which varies in all cultures, also plays a role in crime. Many violent offenders have the traits of what psychiatrists call primary psychopaths. Even if such traits are in part genetically transmitted, they can be exacerbated by the effects of toxins on brain chemistry (Chen et al 1994, Heath et al 1994, Patrick 1994). In biopolitics, different explanatory hypotheses can each explain part of the picture. As many areas in the biology of behavior show, it is necessary to abandon the assumption that nature and nurture are mutually exclusive.

WATER TREATMENT, TOXINS, AND BEHAVIOR

The potential of biopolitics to illuminate political controversy is illustrated by the practice of fluoridating water supplies to improve dental health. Although widely adopted in the United States since the 1950s, this policy remains controversial (Waldbott et al 1974; CDC 1986, 1992a,b; AWAA 1988). Despite the Surgeon

General's recent claim that "community water fluoridation remains one of the great achievements of public health in the twentieth century" (US Dep. HHS 2000: vii), numerous critics and citizens challenge this assessment. In November 2000, nine municipal referenda favored the initiation of fluoridation, while similar referenda were defeated in fourteen communities. To understand this long-lasting political controversy, interdisciplinary research is needed. The result, astonishingly, may be the discovery of the worst toxin since leaded gasoline. If confirmed, however, this time the poison is distributed by public water systems following a recommendation of the Surgeon General.

The history of the origins of water fluoridation is extremely confusing (Rymer 2000), and some recent EPA decisions concerning its safety have been questionable (Coplan & Masters 2000a,c). The principal puzzle in this history concerns the specific chemicals used for water fluoridation. Supporters of the practice speak of the benefits of "fluoridation" without reference to the fact that all tests of safety concern sodium fluoride (NaF), a chemical familiar from its widespread use in toothpaste but used in less than 10% of America's fluoridated water. Until recently, neither critics nor supporters seem to have been aware that over 90% of the Americans receiving fluoridated water (some 140 million in number) consume water treated with either fluosilicic acid (H_2SiF_6) or sodium silicofluoride (Na_2SiF_6).

Addition of these chemicals (jointly called silicofluorides) to water has not been adequately tested for safety, even though the National Library of Medicine (Toxnet 2000) lists the compounds themselves as "very toxic" (lethal dose 1 ounce or less) or "extremely toxic" (lethal dose 1 teaspoon or less). Although the silicofluorides are now used for over 90% of the water fluoridation in the United States, animal studies in the 1930s showed substantial differences in metabolism between sodium silicofluoride and sodium fluoride (Kick et al 1935). Other studies also suggest differences in fluoride metabolism from these chemicals (Zipkin et al 1956). Moreover, a German study revealed that the silicofluorides have effects on the permeability of red blood cells and acetylcholinesterase (Westendorf 1975), both of which would seem to be of direct relevance to toxicity. A study of primates shows that the levels of other enzymes are also changed by silicofluorides (Manocha et al 1975).

Despite some early studies showing differences between sodium fluoride and sodium silicofluoride (McClure & Mitchell 1931, McClure 1933, Kick et al 1935), the substitution of silicofluorides in public water treatment facilities has never been subjected to appropriate animal or human testing. Recently, the Assistant Administrator of the EPA admitted that his agency had no data on the toxicity of the silicofluorides (Fox 1999). Indeed, recent tests of the effects of fluoridation have continued to use sodium fluoride (e.g. Bucher 1991, Sprando et al 1997), despite the fact that it is used for only a small proportion of the fluoridated water in the United States (CDC 1992a).

The paucity of animal or human testing is particularly troubling because the chemical effects of silicofluoride use in water treatment are suspect for a number of reasons:

1. Total dissociation of the constituents in commercial-grade silicofluorides into nothing but fluoride ion and silicic acid is highly unlikely. Residue of fluorine-bearing silicon species are very likely to survive in water plant water (Westendorf 1975). Among these would probably be some amounts of fluorinated siloxanes, low-molecular-weight fluorinated polysilicic acid, and even some silicon tetrafluoride (SiF_4) (Hudleston & Bassett 1921, Rees & Hudleston 1936, Ryss & Slutskaya 1940, Crosby 1969, Ciavatta et al 1988, Busey et al 1998).
2. Traces of other toxins, including arsenic, heavy metals, and uranium and its radiodecay progeny, may also be present in commercial-grade silicofluorides. The latter can be traced to the uranium in the phosphate rock from which silicofluorides are produced as byproducts of phosphate fertilizer manufacture (Coplan & Masters 2000b).
3. The silicofluoride anion may also react with other chemicals in water-plant water, producing such species as aluminum fluoride and/or fluorinated aluminosilicates, as well as complexes with traces of heavy metals.
4. The levels of several enzymes were modified in squirrel monkeys exposed to fluosilicic acid at 1 ppm (Manocha et al 1975). Silicofluoride residues may in themselves facilitate membrane transport of heavy metals across cell membranes (Westendorf 1975), and if commercial grades of silicofluorides also bear radiodecay products of uranium, such as alpha-particle emitters radon and polonium, these too can enhance vascular permeability.
5. In any event, reassociation of silicofluoride dissociation products may occur during various food-processing steps that concentrate water, or when such dissociation products enter the gastric environment at its normal low pH. Thus, "nearly total" silicofluoride dissociation in the water plant would not guarantee total dissociation of ingested silicofluoride residues.

To assess the hypothesis of increased lead uptake where silicofluoride-treated water is in use, a Massachusetts survey of lead levels in 280,000 children (Bailey et al 1994) was reanalyzed. Controlling for other risk factors, we found significantly higher lead levels ($p < 0.001$) in the blood of children from silicofluoride-treated communities (Masters & Coplan 1999a). This finding has been confirmed in epidemiological analyses of about 150,000 children from New York towns of 15,000 to 75,000 population (Masters et al 2001) and almost 4000 children in the National Health and Nutrition Evaluation Survey (Masters et al 1999). In addition, multivariate analysis of these samples shows that silicofluorides enhance the uptake of lead from old houses or public water supplies, particularly among the poor and minorities, whose diets are insufficient in calcium and other essential minerals. Logistic regressions confirm that, controlling for other risk factors, the odds ratio of high blood lead is significantly increased where silicofluorides are used—and that these effects are more serious for minorities (e.g. Figure 3).

In the sample of over 30,000 criminals in 24 cities in a National Institute of Justice study, we found higher rates of alcoholism, substance abuse, and crime associated with silicofluoride usage (Masters & Coplan 1999a). Since Mannuzza (1989, 1998) and others have demonstrated a correlation between hyperactivity and criminal behavior, these associations probably indicate a pattern of weakened impulse control due to heavy metal uptake.

These findings are corroborated by analyzing county-level crime data from the entire United States for 1985 and 1991 (Figure 4). To check the analysis of

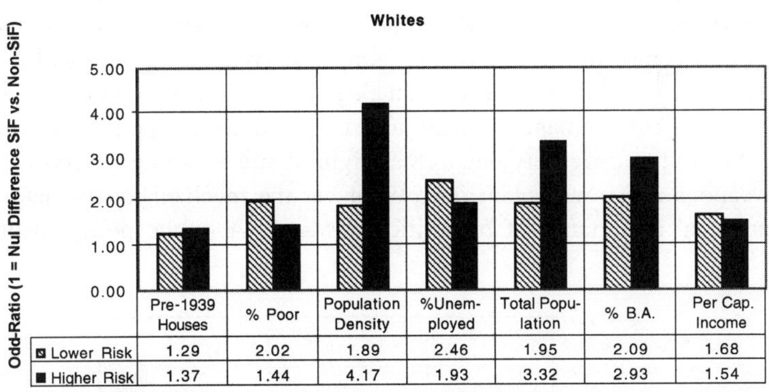

	Pre-1939 Houses	% Poor	Population Density	%Unem-ployed	Total Popu-lation	% B.A.	Per Cap. Income
Lower Risk	1.29	2.02	1.89	2.46	1.95	2.09	1.68
Higher Risk	1.37	1.44	4.17	1.93	3.32	2.93	1.54

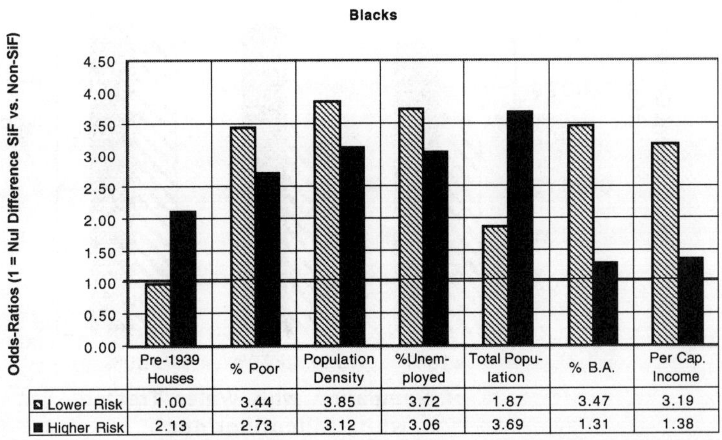

	Pre-1939 Houses	% Poor	Population Density	%Unem-ployed	Total Popu-lation	% B.A.	Per Cap. Income
Lower Risk	1.00	3.44	3.85	3.72	1.87	3.47	3.19
Higher Risk	2.13	2.73	3.12	3.06	3.69	1.31	1.38

Figure 3 Odds ratios for blood lead > 10 g/μdL in communities using versus not using silicofluorides, NY communities low/high for known risk factors for lead uptake (data from Masters et al 2001). Odds risk = 1.0: no difference in rates of high blood lead where silicofluorides are used in water.

variance, multiple regression models were computed using nine variables, including the percentage of the population receiving silicofluoride-treated water, to predict rates of violent crime for each year. Controlling for the eight other covariates (percentage unemployed, per capita income, per capita income of blacks, median grade of school completed, median percentage of college graduates, median age of housing, percentage rural, and percentage black), in both years, silicofluoride water treatment was significantly associated with higher crime rates ($p < 0.0001$). As in the studies of Massachusetts and New York, moreover, in each year the effects of industrial lead pollution were significantly exacerbated by the use of silicofluorides in water.

Although the precise biochemical mechanisms for these findings are not clear, a German study never cited in the United States (Westendorf 1975) showed that fluorides increase red blood cell permeability and silicofluorides change acetylcholinesterase function. Because comprehensive testing of silicofluoride-treated water has never been done, it is not clear whether other factors play a role, such as chemical contaminants, formation of intermediate compounds that increase lead uptake, or radioactivity due to the origin of silicofluorides in processing nuclear weapons and power-plant fuel. Whatever the mechanism, the data suggest the practical importance of biopolitical research. A public policy instituted in the

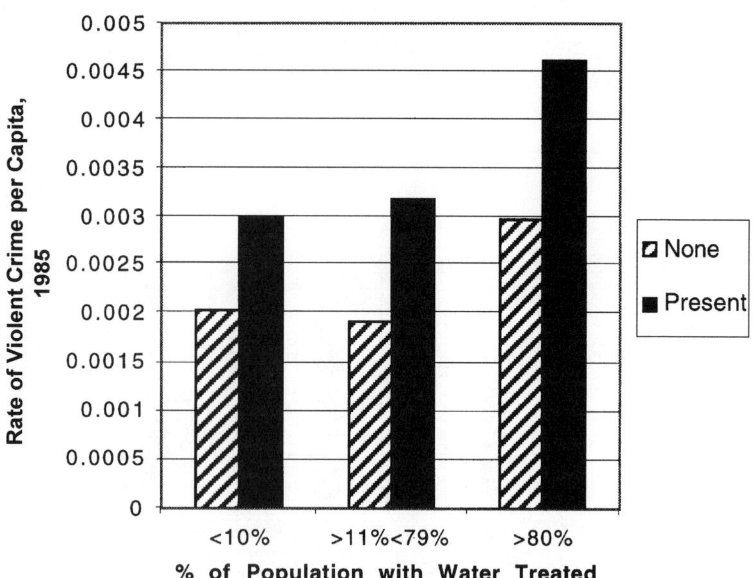

Figure 4 Silicofluoride water treatment and lead pollution as factors associated with violent crime rates, 1985 and 1991 (2870 US counties). Rates of violent crime, all US counties with data on percentage of population receiving water treated with silicofluorides (trichotomized as <10%, 11%–79%, >80%) and dichotomized for presence or absence of lead pollution (EPA Toxic Release Inventory).

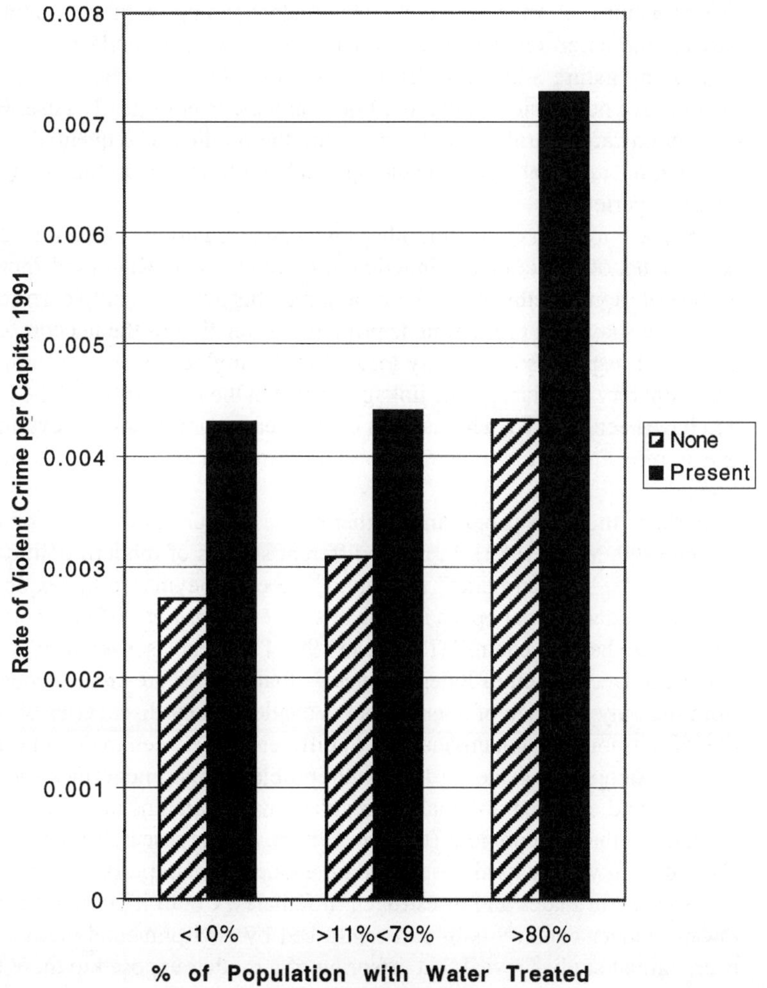

Figure 4 (*Continued*)

name of health should not expose 140 million Americans to an untested chemical that seems to be associated with negative health and behavioral effects.

BIOPOLITICS AND POLITICAL THEORY

Biopolitics goes beyond analyses of behavior and public policy to address issues in political theory (Masters 1977, 1989a,b, 1993). It is often remarked that the principles of the American regime are primarily derived from the writings of Locke. His theories of representative government derive from the principle that by nature, all men are equal. This understanding of human nature rests in part on the assertion that each human is born with a tabula rasa (that is, the brain is by nature a blank slate). It is now established, particularly by research in cognitive neuroscience, that the Lockean view is empirically false. From conception onward, learning and behavior are the product of sequential interactions between innate capabilities (including localized functions in the brain) and individual experience.

On the European continent, other intellectual traditions had influence comparable to that of Locke in the United States. For example, Kant used "pure reason" as the criterion for ethical standards of human behavior. Cognitive neuroscientists now have shown that reasoning is primarily a function of the neocortex, whereas emotional responses are mainly located in the limbic system. Unfortunately for contemporary Kantians, if the linkages between the neocortex and the limbic system have been severed, a human can neither learn nor remember anything. Unless one is referring to a computer, Kant's pure reason seems to be as mythical as Locke's tabula rasa.

Perhaps more disturbing than either of these issues is the question of gender (Tiger 1969, Watts 1983). In many different strands of modern political thought and practice, "human being" and "man" were synonyms. In the explosive challenge to feudalism that opens Rousseau's *Social Contract*, "Man is born free, and everywhere he is in chains" (Rousseau 1999:I, ii). The "self-evident" truth of the American Declaration of Independence—"that all men are created equal"—is far from the only instance of a usage that is challenged by discoveries of the crucial role of hormonal and neuroanatomical differences between males and females.

Two examples indicate the depth of the problem. First, endocrines—testosterone in males and estrogen in females—regulate many domains of behavior, of which sexuality is the most obvious (Masters 1983c). Recent research confirms that toxic chemicals in widely used pesticides are endocrine disruptors, lowering levels of testosterone in males and of estrogen in females. Could it be that the movement toward gender equality is in part reinforced by environmental pollution? Moreover, animal studies reveal that offspring of a mother exposed to these endocrine disruptors are highly likely to prefer same-gender sexual partners (Crews et al 2000). Is Vermont's highly controversial Civil Union law an unconscious response to changed behaviors influenced by environmental toxins?

Second, one of the physical differences that tend to arise between males and females concerns the structure of the brain (Gazzaniga et al 1998). The human cortex is divided into two hemispheres, with certain cognitive functions specialized primarily on one side and others distributed bilaterally. One crucial structure that makes normal thought and behavior possible is the corpus collossum, composed of fibers linking the two hemispheres. In populations studied to date, females tend to have a larger corpus collossum than males. Whether or not this justifies the traditional belief in feminine intuition, it surely reminds us that there are biological differences between the sexes that can unconsciously influence thought and behavior (Tiger 1969, Watts 1983).

In the United States and elsewhere, many overarching political issues in the coming century will depend on responses to such contradictions between the new biology and traditional concepts underlying our political systems (McGuire et al 1997). As the demise of Soviet communism revealed, a regime based on evidently false theoretical premises is particularly vulnerable to collapse. One wonders whether the new subfield of biopolitics will—or should—play a central role in the decades ahead.

CONCLUSIONS

The foregoing description of some research in biopolitics, though selective, points to several conclusions that challenge widespread beliefs and academic theories.

First, despite the press attention given to genetics, the area of behavioral biology in which the most astounding advances have occurred concerns the brain. Research in neuroanatomy, neurochemistry, cognitive neuroscience, and techniques of brain imaging confirms that apparently similar people differ in response to the same socioeconomic or political stimuli for reasons that may have little to do with conventional social or economic incentives.

Second, many types of behavior—including depression/anxiety, learning disabilities, and violence—can now be traced to brain chemistry or anatomy. The earlier onset of puberty, which has led to the explosion of teenage sexuality, is a global phenomenon caused by multiple factors in industrial society (Sprinkle 1999, 2001). Brain chemistry can be significantly influenced by genetics, toxins, or other biological factors.

It follows that the prevailing theories in the social sciences—including both neo-Marxism and Skinnerian behaviorism—are radically incomplete and often incorrect. In seeking causes of behavior, the long-standing dichotomy between genes and environment must be abandoned. Paradoxically, our explanations of human behavior and approaches to public policy resemble a sixteenth-century discussion of transatlantic voyages in terms of a "flat earth" model (an anachronism because Amerigo Vespucci used one of Toscanelli's globes as well as measurements of latitude as the basis of his realization that Columbus had found a "new" continent).

For those in biopolitics, it is too early to predict the precise outlines of future scientific approaches to the study of human political and social behavior. But given the ongoing revolution in the life sciences, it seems highly unlikely that it will be possible to maintain the rigid distinction between political science and biology over the coming century.

ACKNOWLEDGMENTS

My recent research has been made possible by support from the Earhart Foundation, the US Environmental Protection Agency, and the Rockefeller Center for the Social Sciences at Dartmouth College. Without Myron J Coplan, PE (Intellequity

Consulting), study of the behavioral and health effects of silicofluorides would never have occurred. My other research projects in biopolitics developed from collaboration with colleagues including the late John Lanzetta (Psychology, Dartmouth), Denis G Sullivan (Government, Dartmouth), Michael T McGuire (Neuroscience, University of California at Los Angeles), Lionel Tiger (Anthropology, Rutgers), and Siegfried Frey (Psychology, Duisburg, Germany). I am deeply grateful for their friendship and advice, without which this interdisciplinary research would have been impossible, and for the help of Suzanne Saxton as well as numerous Dartmouth students and research assistants

LITERATURE CITED

Abadin H, Llados F. 1997. *Draft Toxicological Profile on Lead*, pp. 202–3. Atlanta, GA: Agency for Toxic Subst. and Dis. Regist., Dep. Health Hum. Serv.

Aschengau A, Ziegler S, Cohen A. 1993. Quality of community drinking water and the occurrence of late adverse pregnancy outcomes. *Arch. Environ. Health* 48:105–13

AWWA (American Water Works Association). 1988. *Water Fluoridation Principles and Practices*, pp. 13–14. Denver, CO: Am. Water Works Assoc. 3rd ed.

Bailey AJ, Sargent JD, Goodman DC, Freeman J, Brown MJ. 1994. Poisoned landscapes: the epidemiology of environmental lead exposure in Massachusetts children 1990–1991. *Soc. Sci. Med.* 39:757–76

Bellinger D, Leviton A, Allred E. 1994. Pre- and postnatal lead exposure and behavior problems in school-aged children. *Environ. Res.* 66:12–30

Brennan PA, Mednick SA, Volavka J. 1995. Biomedical factors in crime. In *Crime*, ed. JQ Wilson, J Petersilia, pp. 65–90. San Francisco: ICS

Brockel BA, Cory-Slechta DA. 1998. Lead, attention, and impulsive behavior: changes in a fixed-ratio waiting-for-reward paradigm. *Pharmacol. Biochem. Behav.* 60:545–52

Bower B. 1998. Incriminating developments. *Sci. News* 154:153–55

Bryce-Smith D. 1983. Lead induced disorder of mentation in children. *Nutr. Health* 1:179–94

Bryce-Smith D. 1986. Environmental chemical influences on behavior and mentation. *Chem. Soc. Rev.* 15:93–123

Bucher JR. 1991. Results and conclusions of the national toxicology program's rodent carcinogenicity studies with sodium fluoride. *Int. J. Cancer* 487:733–37

Busey RH, Schwartz E, Mesmer RE. 1980. Fluosilicate equilibria in sodium chloride solutions from 0 to 60°C. *Inorg. Chem.* 19:578–61

Castellino N, Castellino P, Sannolo N. eds. 1995. *Inorganic Lead Exposure: Metabolism and Intoxication*. Boca Raton, FL: Lewis

CDC (Centers for Disease Control and Prevention). 1992a. *Fluoridation Census 1992*, 2 vols. Atlanta, GA: Cent. Dis. Control Prev.

CDC (Centers for Disease Control and Prevention). 1992b. Knowledge of the purpose of community water fluoridation—United States 1990. *Morb. Mortal. Wly. Rep.* 41:919, 925–27

CDC (Centers for Disease Control and Prevention). 1986. *Water Fluoridation: A Manual for Engineers and Technicians*, pp. 8, 21–22. Atlanta, GA: US Public Health Serv.

Chen C, Rainnie DG, Green RW, Tonegawa SJ. 1994. Abnormal fear response and aggressive behavior in mutant mice deficient for α-calcium calmodulin kinase II. *Science* 266:291–98

Ciavatta L, Iuliano M, Porto R. 1988. Fluorosilicate equilibria in acid solution. *Polyhedron* 7:1773–79

Cook EH Jr, Stein MA, Leventhal BL. 1995. Association of attention deficit disorder and the dopamine transporter gene. *Am. J. Hum. Genet.* 56:993–98

Coplan M, Masters R. 2000a. *Scientific misconduct at EPA*. Rep. to Kenneth Calvert, Chair of Subcommittee on Energy and the Environment, Committee on Science, US House of Representatives, Sep. 25

Coplan M, Masters R. 2000b. *Response to EPA staff unsupportable dismissal of evidence of adverse silicofluoride health effects*. Rep. to EPA, June 12

Coplan M, Masters R. 2000c. *Should silicofluoride be used to fluoridate municipal water?* Rep. to Kenneth Calvert, Chair of Subcommittee on Energy and the Environment, Committee on Science, US House of Representatives, Apr. 6

Cory-Slechta DA. 1995a Relationships between lead induced learning impairments and changes in dopaminergic, cholinergic, and glutamatergic neurotransmitter system functioning. *Annu. Rev. Pharmacol. Toxicol.* 35:391–95

Crews D, Willingham E, Skipper JC. 2000. Endocrine disrupters: present issues, future directions. *Q. Rev. Biol.* 75:243–60

Crocetti AF, Mushak P, Schwartz J. 1990. Determination of numbers of lead-exposed U.S. children by areas of the United States: integrated summary of a report to the U.S. Congress on childhood lead poisoning. *Environ. Health Persp.* 89:109–20

Crosby NT. 1969. Equilibria of fluorosilicate: solutions with special reference to the fluoridation of public water supplies. *J. Appl. Chem.* 19:100–2

Daly M, Wilson M. 1998. *Homicide*. Hawthorne, NY: Aldine de Gruyter

Denno DW. 1994. Gender, crime, and the criminal law defenses. *J. Crim. Law Criminol.* 85:80–180

Fairhall LT, Neal PA. 1943. *Industrial Manganese Poisoning*. Natl. Inst. Health Bull. No. 182. Washington, DC: US Gov. Print. Off.

Fisher L, Blair RJR. 1998. Cognitive impairment and its relationship to psychopathic tendencies in children with emotional and behavioral difficulties. *J. Abnorm. Child Psychol.* 26:11–19

Fox JC. 1999. Letter to Congressman Kenneth Calvert, Chair of Subcommittee on Energy and the Environment, Committee on Science, US House of Representatives, June 23

Gazzaniga M, Ivry RB, Mangun GR. 1998. *Cognitive Neuroscience*. New York: Norton

Gottschalk L, Rebello T, Buchsbaum MS, Tucker HG, Hodges HL. 1991. Abnormalities in trace elements as indicators of aberrant behavior. *Compr. Psychiatry* 342:229–37

Greene G. 1999. *The Woman Who Knew Too Much: Alice Stewart and the Secrets of Radiation*. Ann Arbor: Univ. Mich. Press

Hammond PB. 1998. Metabolism of lead. In *Lead Absorption in Children*, ed. JJ Chisholm, DM O'Hara pp. 11–20. Baltimore, MD: Urban & Schwartzenberg

Heath AC, Cloninger CR, Martin NG. 1994. Testing a model for the genetic structure of personality. *J. Pers. Soc. Psychol* 66:762–75

Hersey J. 1999. *Why Can't My Child Behave?* Alexandria, VA: Pear Tree

Hodgman CD. 1945. *Handbook of Chemistry and Physics*. Cleveland, OH: Chem. Rubber Publ. 31st ed.

Hu H, Aro A, Payton M, Korrick S, Sparrow D, et al. 1996. The relationship of bone and blood lead to hypertension. *JAMA* 275:1171–76

Hudleston LJ, Bassett H. 1921. Equilibria of hydrofluosilicic acid. *J. Chem. Soc.* 119:403–16

Juberg DR. 1997. *Lead and Human Health*. New York: Am. Counc. Sci. Health

Kahn CA, Kelly PC, Walker WO. 1995. Lead screening in children with attention deficit hyperactivity disorder and developmental delay *Clin. Pediatr.* 34:498–501

Kessel I, O'Connor JT. 1997. *Getting the Lead Out*. New York: Plenum Trade

Kick CH, Bethke RM, Edgington BH, Wilder OHM, Record PR, et al. 1935. Fluorine in animal nutrition. *Ohio Agric. Exp. Stn. Bull.* 558:1–77

Kivatkin EA, Stein EA. 1995 Fluctuations in nucleus accumbens dopamine during cocaine self-administration behavior. *Neuroscience* 64:599–617

Kuhar J. 1992. Molecular pharmacology of cocaine: a dopamine hypothesis and its implications. In *Cocaine: Scientific and Social Dimensions*, pp. 81–95. CIBA Found. Symp. 166. Chichester, UK: Wiley

Land KC, McCall PL, Cohen LE. 1990. Structural covariates of homicide rates: Are there any invariances across time and social space? *Am. J. Sociol.* 95:922–63

Lanphear BP. 1998. The paradox of lead poisoning prevention. *Science* 281:1617–18

Lanphear BP, Byrd RS, Auinger P, Schaffer SJ. 1998. Community characteristics associated with elevated blood lead levels in children. *Pediatrics* 101:264–71

Levitt M. 1999. Toxic metals, preconception, and early childhood development. *Soc. Sci. Inf.* 38:179–201

Liebmann-Smith J. 2000. Spotting trouble signs. *Your Child: Newsweek Spec. 2000 Ed.*, Fall-Winter:32

Lippard SJ, Berg JM. 1994. *Principles of Bioinorganic Chemistry*. Mill Valley, CA: Univ. Sci. Books

Mangold T, Goldberg J. 1999. *Plague Wars: The Terrifying Reality of Biological Warfare*. New York: St Martin's

Manocha SL, Warner H, Okowski ZL. 1975. Cytochemical response of kidney, liver and nervous system to fluoride ions in drinking water. *Histochem. J.* 7:343–55

Mannuzza S, Klein RG, Bressler A, Malloy P, LaPadula M. 1998. Adult psychiatric status of hyperactive boys grown up. *Am. J. Psychiatry* 155:493–98

Mannuzza S, Klein RG, Konig PH, Giampino TL. 1989. Hyperactive boys almost grown up. *Arch. Gen. Psychiatry* 46:1073–79

Manson JH, Wrangham RW. 1991. Intergroup aggression in chimpanzees and humans. *Curr. Anthropol.* 32:369–90

Marlow M, Schneider HG, Bliss LB. 1991. Hair: a mineral analysis in emotionally disturbed and violence prone children. *Biosoc. Med. Res.* 13:169–79

Masters RD. 1975. Political behavior as a biological phenomenon. *Soc. Sci. Inf.* XIV:7–63

Masters RD. 1977. Human nature, nature, and political theory. In *Human Nature in Politics*, ed. R Pennock, J Chapman, pp. 69–110. New York: Lieber-Atherton

Masters RD. 1981. Linking ethology and political science: photographs, political attention, and presidential elections. In *Biopolitics: Ethological and Physiological Approaches*, ed. MW Watts, pp. 61–80. San Francisco: Jossey-Bass

Masters RD. 1983a. The biological nature of the state. *World Polit.* 35:161–93

Masters RD. 1983b. Social biology and the welfare state. In *Comparative Social Research*, ed. RF Tomasson, 6:203–41. Greenwich, CT: JAI

Masters RD. 1983c. Explaining "male chauvinism" and "feminism": differences in male and female reproductive strategies. In *Biopolitics and Gender*, ed. MW Watts, pp. 165–210. New York: Haworth

Masters RD. 1989a. *The Nature of Politics*. New Haven: Yale Univ. Press

Masters RD. 1989b. Classical political philosophy and contemporary biology. In *Politikos*, ed. K Moors, I:1–44. Pittsburgh, PA: Duquesne Univ. Press

Masters RD. 1993. *Beyond Relativism: Science and Human Values*. Hanover, NH: Univ. New England Press

Masters RD. 1997. Environmental pollution and crime. *Vermont Law Rev.* 22:359–82

Masters RD. 1999. *Poisoning the well: neurotoxic metals, water treatment, and human behavior*. Plenary lecture at Assoc. Polit. and Life Sci., Atlanta, GA, Sep. 2

Masters RD, Coplan M. 1999a. Water treatment with silicofluorides and lead toxicity. *Int. J. Environ. Stud* 56:435–99

Masters RD, Coplan M. 1999b. A dynamic, multifactorial model of alcohol, drug abuse, and crime: linking neuroscience and behavior to toxicology. *Soc. Sci. Inf.* 38:591–624

Masters RD, Coplan MJ, Hone B, Dykes J. 1999. *Heavy metal toxicity, cognitive development, and behavior*. Poster session, Annu. Neurotoxicol. Conf., 17th, Little Rock, AR, Oct. 17–20

Masters RD, Coplan MJ, Hone BT, Dykes J. 2000. Association of silicofluoride treated water with elevated blood lead. *Neurotoxicology* 21:1091–1100

Masters RD, Frey S, Bente G. 1991. Dominance and attention: images of leaders in German, French, and American TV News. *Polity* 25:373–94

Masters RD, Hone BT, Doshi A. 1998. Environmental pollution, neurotoxicity, and criminal violence. In *Environmental Toxicology*, ed. J Rose, pp. 13–48. London: Gordon & Breach

Masters RD, McGuire MT, eds. 1994. *The Neurotransmitter Revolution*. Carbondale, IL: So. Ill. Univ. Press

McClure FJ. 1933. A review of fluorine and its physiological effects. *Physiol. Rev.* 13:277–99

McClure FJ, Mitchell HH. 1931. The effect of fluorine on the metabolism of albino rats and the composition of the bones. *J. Biol. Chem.* 90:297–320

McGuire MT, Troisi A. 1998. *Darwinian Psychiatry*. New York: Oxford Univ. Press

McGuire MT, Troisi A, Raleigh MJ, Masters RD. 1997. Ideology and physiological regulation. In *Ideology, Warfare, and Indoctrinability*, ed. F Salter, I Eibl-Eibesfeldt, pp. 263–76. Oxford, UK: Berghahn

Mendelsohn AL, Dreyer BP, Fierman AH, Rosen CM, Legano LA, et al. 1998. Low-level lead exposure and behavior in early childhood. *Pediatrics* 101:e10

Mielke HW. 1992. Lead dust-contaminated communities and minority health: a new paradigm. In *The National Minority Health Conference*, ed. BL Johnson, RC Williams, CM Harris. Princeton, NJ: Princeton Sci.

Mielke HW. 1993. Lead dust contaminated U.S.A. communities: comparison of Louisiana and Minnesota. *Appl. Geochem.* 2(Suppl.):257–61

Mielke HW. 1994. Lead in New Orleans soils: new images of an urban environment. *Environ. Geochem. Health* 16:123–28

Mielke H. 1998. Lead in the inner cities. *Am. Sci.* 87:62–73

Millstone E. 1997. *Lead and Public Health*. London: Taylor & Francis

Minder B, Das-Smaal EA, Brand EF, Orlebeke JM, Jacob F. 1994. Exposure to lead and specific attentional problems in schoolchildren. *J. Learn. Disabil.* 27:393–98

Murphy VA, Rosenberg JM, Smith QR, Rapoport SI. 1991. Elevation of brain manganese in calcium-deficient rats. *Neurotoxicology* 12:255–64

Mushak P, Crocetti AF. 1989. Determination of numbers of lead-exposed American children as a function of lead source: integrated summary of a report to the U.S. Congress on childhood lead poisoning. *Environ. Res.* 50:210–29

Needleman HL, ed. 1989. *Human Lead Exposure*. Boca Raton, FL: CRC

Needleman HL. 1999. *Environmental neurotoxins and attention deficit disorder*. Presented at Conf. Environ. Neurotoxins and Dev. Disabil., NY Acad. Med., New York, May 24–25

Needleman HL, Gatsonis B. 1991. Meta-analysis of 24 studies of learning disabilities due to lead poisoning. *JAMA* 265:673–78

Needleman HL, Riess JA, Tobin MJ, Biesecker GE, Greenhouse JB. 1996. Bone lead levels and delinquent behavior. *JAMA* 275:363–69

Needleman HL, Schell A, Bellinger D, Lenton A, Allred RN. 1990. The long-term effects of exposure to low doses of lead in childhood. *New Engl. J. Med.* 322:83–88

Nesse R, Williams GC. 1994. *Why We Get Sick*. New York: Random House

Patrick CJ. 1994. Emotion and psychopathology. *Psychophysiology* 31:319–30

Pihl RO, Ervin F. 1990. Lead and cadmium levels in violent criminals. *Psychol. Rep.* 66:839–44

Pirkle J, Brody DJ, Gunter EW, Kramer RA, Paschal DC, et al. 1994. The decline in blood lead levels in the United States. The National Health and Nutrition Examination Surveys. *JAMA* 272:284–291

Rabin R. 1989. Warnings unheeded: a history of child lead poisoning. *Am. J. Public Health* 79:668–74

Rees AG, Hudleston LL. 1936. The decomposition of fluosilicate ion in aqueous solution. *J. Chem. Soc.* 288:1334–38

Rice DC. 1994. Behavioral deficit (delayed matching sample) in monkeys exposed from birth to low levels of lead. *Toxicol. Appl. Pharmacol.* 75:337–45

Rutter M, Jones RR, eds. 1983. *Lead versus Health*. New York: Wiley

Rymer A. 2000. *The (political) science of fluoridating public water supplies*. Senior honors thesis, Dartmouth College, NH, 112 pp.

Ryss IG, Slutskaya MM. 1940. Kinetics of decomposition of fluorosilicate ions under the action of alkali. *J. Phys. Chem. USSR* 14:701–10 (in Russian)

Schauss AG. 1981. Comparative hair-mineral analysis results in a random selected behaviorally "normal" 21–59 year old population and violent criminal offenders. *Int. J. Biosoc. Res.* 1:21–41.

Schoenthaler SJ. 1985. Diet and delinquency. *J. Biosoc. Res.* 7:108–31

Schrauzer GN, Shrestha KP, Flores-Arce MF. 1992. Lithium in scalp hair of adults, students, and violent criminals. *Biol. Trace Element Res.* 34:161–76

Schubert G, Masters RD, eds. 1994. *Primate Politics*. Lanham, MD: Univ. Press Am.

Shell ER. 1995. An element of doubt. *Atl. Mon.* 276:24–28

Shotyk W, Weiss D, Appleby PG, Cheburkin AK, Gloor RTM, et al. 1998. History of atmospheric lead deposition since 12,370 (14)C yr BP from a peat bog, Jura Mountains, Switzerland. *Science* 281:1635–39

Slater L. 2000. How do you cure a sex addict? *NY Times Mag. Nov.* 19:96–102

Slusher BS, Tiffany CW, Olkowski JL, Jackson PF. 1997. Use of identical assay conditions for cocaine analog binding and dopamine uptake to identify potential cocaine antagonists. *Drug Alcohol Depend.* 48:43–51

Sprando RL, Collins TF, Black T, Olejnik N, Rone J. 1997. Testing the potential of sodium fluoride to affect spermatogenesis of rats. *Food Chem. Toxicol.* 35:881–90

Sprinkle RH. 1999. *Coming of age in the politics of adolescence*. Presented at Sem. Soc. Stud. Med., Mar. 17, Faculty of Medicine, McGill Univ., Montreal, Can.

Sprinkle RH. 2001. The missing politics and unsettled science of the trend toward earlier puberty. *Polit. Life Sci.* In press

Staessen JA, Bulpitt CJ, Fagard R, Lauwerys RR, Roels H, et al. 1994. Hypertension caused by low-level lead exposure: myth or fact? *Curr. Sci.* 1:87–97

Stapleton MS. 1994. *Lead is a Silent Hazard*. New York: Walker

Sullivan DG, Masters RD. 1988. "Happy warriors": Leaders' facial displays, viewers' emotions, and political support. *Am. J. Polit. Sci.* 32:345–68

Tiffany-Castiglioni E, Legare ME, Schneider LA, Hanneman WH, Zenger E, et al. 1996. Astroglia and lead neurotoxicity. In *The Role of Glia in Neurotoxicity*, ed. M Aschner, HK Kimelberg, pp. 175–200. Boca Raton, FL: CRC

Tiger L. 1969. *Men in Groups*. New York: Random House

Toxnet 2000. Hazardous Substance Database (HSDB) entries for FLUOSILICIC ACID (http://toxnet.nlm.nih.gov/cgibin/sis/search/f?./temp/~BAA2XaydE1:FULL) and SODIUM SILICOFLUORIDE (http://toxnet.nlm.nih.gov/cgi-bin/sis/search/f?./temp/~BAA-2XaydE.2:FULL). Nat. Library Med., Nat. Inst. Health, US Dep. Health Hum. Serv.

Tuthill RW. 1996. Hair lead levels related

to children's classroom attention-deficit behavior. *Arch. Environ. Health* 51:214–20

US Department of Health and Human Services. 2000. *Oral Health in America: A Report of the Surgeon General*. Rockville, MD: Natl. Inst. Health

Violence Research Foundation and Citizens for Health. 1994. *Brief of Amici Curiae, Ethyl Corp. v. Browner*, US Court of Appeals for District of Columbia Circuit, Case No. 94-1505

Viverette L, Mielke HW, Brisco M, Dixon A, Schaefer J, et al. 1996. Environmental health in minority and other underserved populations: benign methods for identifying lead hazards at day care centers of New Orleans. *Environ. Geochem. Health* 18:41–45

Waldbott GL, Burgstahler AW, McKinney HL. 1978. *Fluoridation: the Great Dilemma*. Lawrence, KS: Coronado

Walker S. 1998. *The Hyperactivity Hoax: How to Stop Drugging Your Child and Find Real Medical Help*. New York: St. Martin's

Watts M, ed. 1983. *Biopolitics and Gender*. New Haven, CT: Haworth

Werbach MR. n. d. Aggressive behavior. *Nutritional Influences on Mental Illness: A Sourcebook of Clinical Research*, pp. 6–15. Tarzana, CA: Third Line

Westendorf J. 1975. *Die Kinetik der Acetylcholinesterase-hummung und die Beeinflussung der Permeabilität von Erythrozxytenmembranen durch Fluorid und Fluorokomplex-Jonen*. Doctoral Diss., Hamburg, Univ. Hamburg Fachberich, Chemie

Windholz M, Budavari S, Blumettl RP, Otterbein ES, eds. 1983. *Merck Index*. Rahway, NJ: Merck. 10th ed.

Zipkin I, Likins RC, McClure FJ, Steer AC. 1956. Urinary fluoride levels associated with use of fluoridated water. *Public Health Rep.* 71:767–72

Annu. Rev. Polit. Sci. 2001. 4:371–90

WOMEN'S MOVEMENTS AT CENTURY'S END: Excavation and Advances in Political Science

Karen Beckwith
Department of Political Science, The College of Wooster, Wooster, Ohio 44691; e-mail: kbeckwith@acs.wooster.edu

Key Words social movement, political movement, feminist movement

■ **Abstract** Over the past two decades in the United States, research on women's movements has proliferated in women's studies, in sociology, and, to a much lesser extent, in political science. Focusing specifically on women's movements, this review considers current research within this emerging subfield of political science, particularly because political science and the subfield of women's movements research share a focus on the state and on comparative politics. This review assesses the contribution that scholarship of women's movements has made to empirical political science and to political movement theory. It concludes with a discussion of gender and political movements and suggests areas for future research.

INTRODUCTION

Research on women's movements has proliferated in women's studies, in history, in sociology, and, to a lesser extent, in political science during the past two decades in the United States, concurrent with an interdisciplinary flourishing of social movements research generally. Despite the contemporaneous development of these literatures, the extent to which each has been informed by the other has been limited. The potential for progress in both women's movements research and political movements scholarship is high, however, and the prospects of its realization are increasing. Focusing primarily on political science scholarship on women's movements, I review the recent literature and consider the advances within this emerging subfield. In doing so, I attempt to identify points of intersection—or missed opportunities for them—with the social movements literature. I conclude with a discussion of the relationship between the study of women in women's movements and the gendered analysis of political movements, suggesting areas for future development in both.

In examining women's movements scholarship, I distinguish three conceptually distinct research foci: (*a*) women's movements, (*b*) feminist movements, and (*c*) women in political movements.

By women's movements, I mean political movements characterized by "the primacy of women's gendered experiences, women's issues, and women's leadership and decision making. The relationship of women to these movements is direct and immediate; movement definition, issue articulation, and issue resolution are specific to women, developed and organized by them with reference to their gender identity" (Beckwith 1996:1038).

Feminist movements are political movements that are distinguished by "a gendered power analysis of women's subordination and [they] contest political, social, and other power arrangements of domination and subordination on the basis of gender" (Beckwith 2000a:437). Feminist movements, therefore, constitute a subset of women's movements.[1]

Women are active in political movements that are neither feminist nor primarily directed by women or by concerns with their issues. Research on women in political movements is a modest but increasingly important focus in political science (Alvarez 1990, Crawford et al 1993, Blee 1998, Kaplan et al 1999, Sekhon 1999).

In the United States, women's movements research has been concurrent with the development and experience of women's movements themselves. The first two decades of the twentieth century were marked by extensive, visible, and successful organizing by women's suffrage movements in North America, Australia, New Zealand, Great Britain, and several West European nations. Characteristics of many of these movements—their visibility, their primarily middle-class activist base, the extent of their written documentation (both by movements and by the states whose policies they challenged), and the fact that the life span of many of their activists extended into our own—shaped the research tradition that emerged from them.

Early research on the US women's movement (e.g. Flexner 1975, Gurko 1976, DuBois 1980, Kraditor 1981) was, in methodological terms, primarily qualitative, relying on archival data and, in some circumstances, interviews. Generally atheoretical, the early body of scholarship on the women's movement undertook the necessary excavation of the movement's history, identifying activists, revealing opponents, chronicling events, acknowledging intersections with other movements, and mapping the course of the movement's failures and ultimate success. Its research focus was on public events, on movement-state interaction, and on feminist issues (particularly suffrage). To the extent that activism in the women's suffrage

[1]Most of the political science research on women's movements has focused on feminist movements; indeed, the terminology used in the subfield conflates feminist movement and women's movements generally. For example, women's collective action that is not explicitly feminist is analyzed in the work of Maggard (1990) and Robnett (1997). In this article, most of the discussion concerns feminist movements, following the subfield, but also identifies new research that concerns nonfeminist women's movements, particularly in comparative perspective.

movement—the most visible of women's nineteenth- and twentieth-century mobilizations in the West—had been "hidden from history," this literature initiated the project, still unfinished, of establishing and legitimizing women's movements scholarship within political science.

The last three decades of the twentieth century have likewise been marked by extensive feminist movement organizing and women's movement activism in a wide variety of nations. The legitimizing tradition of the early movements scholarship in the United States continues to influence successive research on the women's movement. First, marked by descriptive narratives, relying primarily on qualitative methods, contemporary women's movements scholarship extends the methodology of the preceding literature even as this methodological continuity locates an emerging debate and a departure. Continued reliance on archival data underscores the nature of the project of revealing women's political activism within movements (e.g. McAdam 1992; Crawford et al 1993; Fonow 1998; Katzenstein 1998; Blee 1996, 1998; Shadmi 2000). The primary methodological advance is the use of field research and interviews that extend the excavation project (Alvarez 1990, 1994; Banaszak 1996; Beckwith 1996; Fonow 1998; Katzenstein 1987, 1998; Robnett 1997; Taylor 1999). Consistent with other scholarship on women and politics, as well as with social movements research in sociology, the emphasis on qualitative methodology is necessary for understanding both women's activism in movements and women's movements themselves. In short, the excavation project of knowing about women in movements is still necessary, and archival and field research, participant observation, and interviews provide its crucial evidential underpinnings.

The methodological departure, within political science and sociology, is the move to an explicitly quantitative social movements scholarship, based upon construction of large, publicly funded data sets to facilitate statistical analyses of protest events, political violence, macropolitical and economic variables, and other trend data (Costain 1987, 1992; Kriesi 1995; Tarrow 1989, 1992, 1996, 1998). This methodological shift rests uneasily, at least in part, with previous qualitative work and reflects the tensions evident in the broader category of women-and-politics scholarship, where methodological and epistemological disputes remain unresolved (Cohen et al 1997; Flammang 1997; Weinbaum 1997).[2] Given the hegemony of quantitative analysis within political science, the development of large statistical data sets that can be analyzed quantitatively may serve to validate the study of movements within the discipline while departing from the dominant and still necessary qualitative focus of women-and-movements scholarship.

---

[2]These disputes primarily concern the utility of "male" models of political science (especially behaviorism), analytical concepts based on male experience and the exclusion of women, quantitative methodology, statistical analysis, survey research, and a focus on women's "integration" (rather than on structural change) (Cohen et al 1997:11, Flammang 1997:3–34).

A second continuity with the early women's movements scholarship is the focus of contemporary research on feminist issues and events that involve interaction with the state and that are located in traditional "public" venues. Studies include the emergence of the contemporary US feminist movement (Freeman 1975; Klein 1984; Costain 1987, 1992; Ryan 1992; Echols 1997), feminist activism around abortion rights in the United States (Luker 1984, McDonagh 1996, O'Connor 1996, Staggenborg 1991), movement organizing and emergence (e.g. Katzenstein & Mueller 1987, Nelson & Chowdhury 1994, Basu 1995, Baldez 2000), women's suffrage movements (Banaszak 1996), the relationship between women's movements and political parties (Costain 1987, 1992; Freeman 1987; Hellman 1987a; Lovenduski & Norris 1993), women's electoral mobilization (Carroll 1992; Marshall 2000; Mueller 1987, 1988), and feminist public policy initiatives (Katzenstein & Mueller 1987, Nelson & Chowdhury 1994, Muszynski 1999, Banaszak 2000, Elman 2000) and their successes and failures (Beckwith 1987, Bashevkin 1998). The continuity of focus on the interaction of women's movements with the state fits clearly within the disciplinary purview of political science and its concerns with the state, with governance, and with citizen participation. Although political scientists, like sociologists, have contributed to the development of collective identity and feminist consciousness research (Fulenwider 1980; Jenson 1985, 1987; Klein 1987; Reingold 1998; Tolleson-Rinehart 1992; Conover & Sapiro 1993), they have located attitudinal, cultural, and discursive research firmly within the boundaries of women's movements and states.[3] The goodness of fit between the concerns of women's movements scholarship and those of political science in general is striking. Also remarkable, unfortunately, is the meager representation of women's movements scholarship in the major political science journals; such underrepresentation cannot be explained by a lack of agreement about the central focus of women's movements research and political science's disciplinary foci.[4]

[3]One particular potential contribution of women's movements scholarship is its increasingly comparative political scope. The wealth of comparative movements research, focusing on women's movements, should be redounding more heavily in political science, especially in comparative politics. For example, recent attention by political scientists to nationalist movements should be replete with references to the comparative movements literature generated by women's movements scholars; the absence of such citations is lamentable. For a critical discussion of comparative movements research and its silence on women's movements, see Beckwith (2000a:456–59).

[4]For example, between October 1989 and July 1997, *World Politics* published only two articles related to women and politics, one of which concerned women's movements (Waylen 1994). Between March 1992 and March 2000, the *American Political Science Review* published only nine articles (including review articles) related to women and politics. It is possible (although unlikely) that this paucity reflects a lack of submissions by women-and-politics scholars to these journals. My point is not to explain the underrepresentation of women and politics research in these journals but to identify the absence of such work where the discipline itself has substantive scholarly grounds for soliciting and publishing it.

More specifically, the primary focus of women's movements scholarship in political science has been on feminist movements and specific feminist issues, such as abortion and the Equal Rights Amendment in the United States. The study of women's movements, as the term is almost universally employed by scholars, has been primarily the study of feminist movements, which represent only a subset of women's movement activism, involvement, and impact. Political scientists concerned with women and political movements, relying on the foundational research of the 1980s, are extending the excavation project to research on nonfeminist women's movements and to women active in political movements not primarily concerned with women's issues per se. This literature is only now beginning to reach critical mass (e.g. Crawford et al 1993; Beckwith 1996; Blee 1996; Katzenstein 1987, 1998; Robnett 1997; Fonow 1998) [for a discussion of the difficulties with the term women's movements in comparative political research, see Beckwith (2000a)].

Third, contemporary scholarship on women's movements remains, with many exceptions, undertheorized and overly reliant on the foundational movement theories of sociology (specifically, political opportunity structure, resource mobilization, and cultural framing). To the extent that women's movements scholarship has been primarily concerned with finding out about women's movements, it has not undertaken a project of theory development for political movements [for exceptions, see discussion below; see also Katzenstein (1998), Robnett (1997), Rowbotham (1996); see also Banaszak et al (2000)]. Women's movements scholarship has continued the project of compiling information, identifying event sequences, explicating specific movements and campaigns, and locating women's activism in multiple movements (social movement spillover), relying on models developed largely without reference to scholarship on women's movements.

The continuities with the earliest women's movements scholarship—primarily qualitative, focused on state-movement relations, concerned with feminism, and undertheorized—are realities rather than necessary limitations of current research, which has been shaped by its history, and are the foundation for subsequent research.[5] The more recent women's movements scholarship, rather than refuting this tradition, builds on and extends it. Excavation of women's movements is the necessary preliminary to advancing a political movements theory that takes both women and women's movements into account.

[5]Critiques of early research in women and politics, for example, dismissive of such work on the grounds that it examined the wrong questions and used traditional "male" frameworks, theories, and methodologies, fail to recognize that this type of excavating work emerged during a historically contingent moment and has provided the foundation that has made more recent research possible. In critiquing and assessing women's movements scholarship, this review recognizes the limitations of the early scholarship but also acknowledges its contributions to subsequent work, only now positioned to undertake theoretical advances.

FRAMEWORKS AND THEORY: Contextualizing Women's Movements

Among political scientists, political opportunity structure has been the most influential and most frequently employed (partial) theory for the study of women's movements (Costain 1987, 1992; Katzenstein & Mueller 1987; Gelb 1989; Waylen 1994; Banaszak 1996; Bashevkin 1998; Sawyers & Meyer 1999). Tarrow (1998: 76–77) defines political opportunity as "consistent . . . dimensions of the political environment that provide incentives for collective action by affecting people's expectations for success or failure." Specific dimensions of political opportunity include increasing access to participation, realignment within the political system, emergence of influential allies, a fractured or fracturing political elite, and "a decline in the state's capacity or will to repress dissent" (Tarrow 1998:76; see also Tarrow 1989:34–35, Kitschelt 1986, Kriesi 1995, Rucht 1996:188–89). Because political opportunity structure applies to movement-state relations and is useful for mapping movement emergence, mobilization, and impacts, women's movements scholars adapted it to extend the project of laying down the parameters of knowledge about women's movements.

One of the earliest considerations of the applications of political opportunity models to women's movements was the edited collection *The Women's Movements of the United States and West Europe*. In her introductory essay, Katzenstein (1987:4) identified three major factors shaping political opportunities for feminist movements: (*a*) the availability of left parties as political movement allies, (*b*) the position of other organized interests within the state, the most important being organized labor, and (*c*) the nature of the state itself. Based on West European and US case studies, Katzenstein concluded that two combinations of these factors offered the greatest opportunities for feminist movement organizing and success. First, "centralized states with a strong labor movement" (Katzenstein 1987:6–7) and strong left parties (1987:15–16) facilitate feminist policy successes; yet, second, decentralized states also provide opportunities. A decentralized state, with a weak labor movement and no major dominating organized interests, and without a strong left-right party cleavage, presents a more open political field on which feminist movements can make policy advances, primarily noneconomic ones.[6] Unitary states with weak labor movements offer the fewest alliance opportunities and the fewest points of state access through political parties (Ruggie 1987).

Among the first concerns of women's movements scholars was an examination of alliances between parties and women's movements. In particular, the research on women's movements and parties attempted to establish the tradeoffs between autonomous and party-based strategies of feminist movements in their interactions

[6]Katzenstein (1987:16) writes that "the absence of a leftist or ideological party system appears to encourage the reevaluation of a particular array of policies and practices" and, in the United States, led to legislation concerning wife beating, sexual harassment, and rape, among other feminist concerns.

with the state. A substantial body of research, collectively comparative, underscores the importance of alliances between left parties and feminist movements, especially where feminist movements encourage the belief that female voters will make a difference in election outcomes (Costain 1987:206, 1992; Jenson 1985; Freeman 1987; Mueller 1987, 1988; Beckwith 2000b).[7] Although the earliest of this research relied on cases from North America and West Europe, more recent scholarship has confirmed this general pattern for women's movements and left parties in Latin American nations (Alvarez 1990, 1994; Sternback et al 1992; Jaquette 1994; Kampwirth 1996; Saint-Germain 1997; Baldez 2000). This pattern has also been confirmed, if negatively, by research on women's movements "in an epoch of restructuring" (Brenner 1996:18) and on "women's movements facing a reconfigured state" (Banaszak et al 2000), where the decline of trade unionism and electoral weaknesses of left parties have exposed feminist movements to state attack and have encouraged movement moderation (Costain 1992, Banaszak et al 2000) and the search for alternative alliances (Lovenduski & Randall 1993; Brenner 1996:30, 56).

A substantial literature has chronicled the emergence and trajectory of the US feminist movement in response to major social and economic changes in the second half of the twentieth century (e.g. Freeman 1975; Klein 1984, 1987; Ryan 1992; Ferree & Hess 1994; Ferree & Martin 1995). Political opportunity models have also elucidated government behavior and the strategic decisions of governing parties in responding to these same economic and societal transformations. Costain (1992) argues that changes in women's participation in the economy and other major socioeconomic changes, in the context of electoral uncertainty, led governments, particularly but not exclusively the Kennedy administration, to initiate policies and to offer symbolic gestures concerning women's rights, helping to evoke rather than responding to an organized feminist movement. As political opportunity structures began to change, Costain argues, it was the government that "invited women's rebellion" as much as it was organized women seizing the day. Women's increased access to participation, government concerns about political realignment, and competing interests among the political elite shaped governments' willingness to welcome and encourage women's activism, as well as shaping women's opportunities to organize in their own interests.

Political opportunity structures have also been employed by women's movements scholars to explain movement behavior under conditions of closing opportunities. "Women's rebellion" was invited but also discouraged, as Costain demonstrates in her analysis across presidential administrations. The Reagan administration and the defeat of the Equal Rights Amendment combined to shift the feminist agenda and the movement's strategy, in the absence of government allies, from a national focus to a more autonomous and local focus (Costain 1992:

[7]The case for left party alliances should not be overinterpreted. Left parties have often resisted feminist movement policy initiatives and have frequently responded as movement allies only symbolically (e.g. Beckwith 1985; Jenson 1985; Hellman 1987a,b).

120–21). Lovenduski & Randall (1993) also present evidence of feminist movement strategic adaptation to firmly closing opportunities in Britain during the Thatcher governments, leading similarly to an increased autonomy of the British feminist movement, weak alliances with a weakened trade union movement, and increasingly moderate policy initiatives.

Bashevkin (1998) explicitly examined feminist movements in Britain, Canada, and the United States under conditions of conservative governments, economic programs of austerity, and generally hard times. In these nations, feminist movements' strategic and policy successes were transformed or repealed as governments changed hands from one party to another, as new elites emerged, and as alliances weakened. As left-center or liberal parties were replaced in all three nations in the 1980s by center-right and rightwing parties, Bashevkin found, the ability of women's movements to sustain themselves and to advance (or protect) public policies varied across the three nations. In particular, a weakened or declining trade union movement represented, especially in Canada but also in the United States, a detrimental shift in reliable allies and weakened the ability of autonomous women's movements to defend policy advances made during previous governments or administrations. Women's movements were better sustained where court rulings or constitutional protections remained constant (or, in the Canadian case, were implemented), where social conservatism was not employed to justify policy changes, and where the movement had developed "a long history of successful lobbying, litigating, and fund-raising" (Bashevkin 1998:231) that a government could not easily dislodge (as in the US case). Alliances with less conservative parties, such as the US Democrats, British Labour, and the Canadian Liberals, following the long tenure of rightwing governments in each nation, did not serve women's movements as well as had been anticipated. In no case did the new governing liberal parties overturn the deconstruction of state welfare policies, if only because they "had a less stable and less fertile revenue base on which to rely" (Bashevkin 1998:238). Bashevkin concludes, "perhaps surviving was equivalent to political success in the dark days" (1998:245).

Bashevkin also assessed specific state configurations and evaluated their impact on movement successes. The relatively high internal discipline of British and Canadian governments in implementing policy changes under conservative party governance was matched by radical policy change in the United States, less highly disciplined but every bit as effective. Federalism offered varying protections from attacks on policies advanced by feminist movements. In the United States, government attacks on feminist policies were less successful in individual states than at the national level. In Canada, budget cutbacks in social policy funding led to the transfer of programs to the provinces and a weakening of public policies supported by the women's movement (Bashevkin 1998:223–24).

Banaszak (1996) similarly considers how federal states might be more easily played to achieve policy results and to evaluate specific alliances for their constraining or facilitating effects on the efforts of women's movements (see also Gelb 1989). This literature suggests that, at least for women's movements, what form the state takes—unitary, federal, or something else—may matter less than the configuration of power within the state at any given time. For example, federal states may both increase and delimit the political opportunities of women's movements, offering the US women's movement the advantage of moving across levels to initiate and defend public policies (e.g. Banaszak 1996, Bashevkin 1998) while diminishing the impact of the Canadian feminist movement in hard times. The experience of the British feminist movement under Thatcher, Bashevkin (1998) suggests, was shaped less by the unitary nature of the state than by the social conservative ideology that reframed public policy discussions (see also Lovenduski & Randall 1993) and by the weakness of previously powerful allies such as organized labor (Ruggie 1987, Gelb 1989, Lovenduski & Randall 1993, Bashevkin 1998).

Findings that emphasize the importance of left party and labor movement alliances over the type of state conflict with earlier research that identifies formal structures and power configurations as equally important in conditioning opportunities for the policy influence and success of women's movements. Katzenstein (1998) reiterates the importance of formal structures in shaping organized women's opportunities for achieving their ends. She demonstrates that, in two cases, the presence or absence of facilitating laws and legal norms predicts policy change for organized women. Focusing on organized women in the US military and the US Catholic Church, where exclusion of women from specific power positions is formally inscribed in law or doctrine, Katzenstein identifies activists in these male-predominant institutions as feminist, that is, women whose work "[challenges] at least *some aspect* of a system of institutional inequality based on gender" (Katzenstein 1998:21, emphasis in original). Each case constitutes an institutional venue where women are discriminated against on the basis of their gender, where the system of hierarchy and command is closed, where negative sanctions are difficult to resist, and whose internal repressive capacity is great (Katzenstein 1998:13). A major distinction between the two institutions is their location vis-à-vis the state: The US military constitutes part of the state, and the Catholic Church is separate from the state and protected against its interference. This distinction, Katzenstein argues, shapes feminist protest strategy within each institution.

Women in the military employ "moderate, interest-group, influence-seeking" political strategies (Katzenstein 1998:16), in large part because the military's location within the state makes it, at some points, susceptible to claims of equal opportunity and equal treatment encoded in national legislation (Katzenstein 1998:80). Such strategies, relying on bargaining, compromise, and moderate goals, succeed in employing state tools for achieving a group's ends (Katzenstein 1998:99).[8] As Katzenstein claims (1998:53), "[F]eminism in the military has depended on the support of either Congress or the courts." In the case of women in the US military, however, the capacity of the institution to identify dissenters and to punish

[8]Organized women were also successful in advancing their interests based on claims of "enhanced national security, military preparedness, military professionalism, [and] equality" (Katzenstein 1998:51).

protest is sufficiently high that radical protest is unrealistic. The Catholic Church, in contrast, is independent of state control and able to enforce its decisions and policies, unsusceptible to legal pressures, congressional legislation, or court directives. In the absence of legal footing from which to advance feminist interests, activist "women religious"[9] employed internal free spaces for autonomous organizing, developing a discursive politics that relied in part on the Church's articulated norms and practices. Discursive politics, or "meaning-making," is "the effort to reinterpret, reformulate, rethink, and rewrite the norms and practices of society and the state" (Katzenstein 1998:17), relying primarily but not exclusively on language to provide an alternative feminist vision. Women religious in the US Catholic Church employed a discursive politics rather than the interest-group politics of women in the US military.

As distinct as they are, both the US military and the Catholic Church structure the daily lives of their members and "assign value to what people do, [shaping] the very self-definitions people come to hold" (Katzenstein 1998:33). The components of political opportunity structure—capacity for repression, availability of (internal and external) allies, and a range of political environmental factors that cue activists for collective action (Tarrow 1998:76–77)—include not only legal parameters and formal institutions but also "constructed meanings" that result from the interaction of activists and their opponents (Tarrow 1998:107). As Katzenstein (1998:166) claims, "[i]t is not opportunities by themselves but their interactive relationship with norms, beliefs, and values that drives feminist protest within institutions."

Despite the strong influence of political opportunity structure on women's movements scholarship, even the earliest political science studies of women's movements took into account the impact of culture and values, or what is now more commonly referred to as cultural framing (see Snow & Benford 1992, 1988; Tarrow 1992, 1998:106–22; Gamson & Meyer 1996; McAdam et al 1996). Among political scientists, scholars of women's movements have been major contributors to the development of discourse, language, and culture as conceptual tools for understanding political movements, a contribution not well noted or recognized in the general literature on movements.

Two articles by Jenson (1985, 1987) exemplify the early focus on how language and cultural values shaped political movement opportunities. Jenson argues that political movement chances are bounded by the "universe of political discourse" (1985, 1987). The universe of political discourse "identifies those aspects of social relationships which are considered political . . . ultimately [inhibiting] or, conversely, [encouraging] the formation of new collective identities" (Jenson 1985:7–8) [regarding "mobilization of bias," see also Schattschneider (1997:30, 69)]. Constituted by and constitutive of collective identities, the universe of political discourse undertakes active "production of meaning" in a context where new actors must struggle to advance their interests and to "overcome the resistance of

[9]Katzenstein uses the term "women religious" synonymously with "nuns" and "sisters," all of whom are "vowed women in the church . . . , an elite class that is more faithful or 'religious' than nonvowed members of the church" (1998:177n2).

established political formations which act as guardians of the prevailing discourse" (Jenson 1985:9). Jenson employs the French feminist movement's campaigns concerning state reproductive policies as a case for demonstrating how discourse struggles eventually shifted the political opportunity structure for activist women in France.

Similarly, Hellman (1987a,b), in her work on Italian feminism, demonstrated that language and political meanings could foreclose opportunities for activist women seeking to advance interests not easily encompassed (or actively opposed) by the dominant political culture. She details how "workerist" culture, memory, and language was employed in Turin to preclude feminist influence in local party politics and city policies. Hypothesizing that feminist movement opportunities were shaped by "long-standing traditions and by the specific political environment of the Left" (1987b:112), Hellman links the Turinese workerist culture—"defensive," factory-centered, and "[viewing] all of society as organized against them and all struggle as consisting essentially of holding their ground in the factories, defending their jobs and place in production" (1987b:113)—with the stifling of feminist movement development in Turin (see also Hellman 1987a).

I also address issues of identity and language in a study of women active in supporting mining strikes, where women located in a movement that is neither feminist nor a women's movement articulate and transform their political standing as a means of asserting their participation, autonomy, and leadership. I define political standing as "an explicitly articulated rationale of actors' position and presence in a movement that asserts a status of legitimacy in making claims and demands as primary actors within the movement" (Beckwith 1996:1040). An interactive concept, political standing "is an assertion by movement actors to both internal and external reference groups of their legitimate presence and involvement in a movement" (Beckwith 1996:1040). It is also a necessary preliminary to full movement activism and leadership. Insofar as women advance their interests in groups and movements that are not exclusively female or feminist, the particular situation of organized women often requires language-based, culture-based, discursive struggles as a necessary prelude to full movement participation. This argument, and others involving political discourse claims, suggests that women's movements are uniquely positioned to contribute to theory building in cultural framing.[10]

As Bashevkin argues, "language shifts are crucial to political change" (1998: 242). One importance of framing and discourse is the extent to which they serve to create and to shape political opportunities, including structural political opportunity factors. As Tarrow (1996:43–45, 1998:200–1) reminds us, political structures are not immutable but operate with greater or lesser impact according to prevailing state strategies, relations with (other) institutions, and interactions with a variety of groups and movements over time. Political structures, including state structures,

---

[10]Tarrow writes that "if a sign of a movement's vitality is its capacity to 'spin off' new 'master frames' . . . , the American women's movement was a shining success" (1998:172). Tarrow describes the US feminist movement as being heavily reliant on "the conventional, the discursive, and the symbolic" (1998:173).

offer openings for movements, shut down movement activities, and favor some movement organizations while repressing others. At the same time, structures can be shifted in response to who the actors are, the frames they interactively exploit, and the language and symbols they employ to cast the context in which collective action takes place. Costain suggests this when she comments that a "new tolerance of a greater political role for women can itself be viewed as creating the preconditions for further growth in the women's movement" (1992:77). As multiple scholars of women's movements demonstrate, the success of women's movements depends on how cultural framing, collective identity, and political discourse transformed the political opportunity structure for activist women and feminists, across a wide range of states.

CONCLUSION: Gendering Movement Theory in Political Science?

Although my discussion of women's movements has mostly concerned women's movements in the United States (and other liberal representative political systems), it is nonetheless the case that in political science, women's movements and feminist movements have been the focus of an established and growing body of comparative political research. This scholarship has extended the excavation project of detailing and analyzing women's movement activism in Latin America, Africa, Central and East Europe, and Asia (Jaquette 1994, Waylen 1994, Basu 1995, Rai & Lievesley 1996, Bystydzienski & Sekhon 1999, Baldez 2000). Much of this work is explicitly comparative, or comparatively analyzed in the context of edited volumes, and has helped to develop a series of constructs and questions concerning women's political movement involvement and activism, constituting political science's specific contribution to the study of political movements (see Beckwith 2000a).

The careful description, explication, and analysis of women's movement activism evidenced in this literature reveals that scholars have risen to the "challenge of specifying the conditions under which activism assumes particular forms and leads to particular results," recognizing and demonstrating that "what holds for one social movement [does not apply] equally well to others" (Katzenstein 1998:39, 36; see also Tarrow 1992:185). In this regard, careful elucidation and excavation of women's movements continues to be important, positioning the study of women and movements for major theoretical advances. Among many possible, I identify three arenas in which the study of women and movements might advance political movement theory: (*a*) contentious politics (McAdam et al 1996, 2001); (*b*) political loss; and (*c*) gender and movement.

Contention and Women

Women's movements offer an excellent location from which to begin to map contentious politics. Activist women across many nations have engaged in collective action, in various forms of contention, to advance women in public office; to influence elected officials; to militate for workplace changes; to institute autonomous community institutions to address local problems; to disrupt state activities; and to pressure states for policy changes. The range of locations in which activist women have mobilized, even as they constitute a continuum of feminist movement, indicates the extent to which women's movements are excellent cases for integrating citizen challenges to states and societies. Activist women's and feminists' presence within government (Stetson & Mazur 1995, Davis 1997, Hartmann 1998), within political parties (e.g. Lovenduski & Norris 1993), within interest groups (e.g. Costain 1992, Ferree & Martin 1995, Flammang 1997:253–71), and within autonomous and/or separatist groups, which are themselves part of a larger, identifiable women's movement (Echols 1997, Barakso 1998, Marshall 2000, Swers 2000), suggests that conventional distinctions between governments, parties, interest groups, and movements are less useful than a continuum of activist locations/targets that unifies them.

Movements and Loss

Women's movements research will benefit from, and will make a major contribution to, the larger social movement literature, to the extent that it begins to take movement outcomes seriously. Major research advances would result from a focus on (*a*) political loss and the identification of factors that shape losses for women's movements (specifically); (*b*) the consequences of political failure for subsequent mobilization (or demobilization); (*c*) how understandings of success and failure are shaped by framing and discourse, and with what consequences; and (*d*) the dimensions along which a movement's success or failure might be manifested. Research on women's community activism, often tied to political movements, frequently valorizes local political struggle as empowering women, particularly women of color and working-class women (Sen 1997, Weinbaum 1997), without evaluating the relationship between the articulated goals of the activists and the eventual outcome of the collective action. Other research suggests a disjunction between activist women's contributions to movement success and women's success in self-empowerment (Maggard 1990) or in advancing women's interests. Specific research on women's activism and movement loss suggests that the daily context of struggle and the construction of defeat influence future mobilizing possibilities, regardless of whether movement goals were actually achieved (Beckwith 2000c). This modest body of research offers possibilities of further development and eventual contributions to theory.

Gender and Movements

Perhaps most important, the study of women's movements in political science can contribute to the understanding of how political movements, collective action frames, and political opportunity structures are gendered. As Taylor reminds us, social movements research reveals the pervasiveness of gender hierarchy such that "even in movements that purport to be gender-inclusive, the mobilization, leadership patterns, strategies, ideologies, and even the outcomes of social movements are gendered" (1999:8–9). To that end, Taylor has called for a "systematic theory of gender and social movements" (1999:9). At the very least, a gendered analysis of political movements will further inform and enrich existing theories.

Taylor recommends a focus "on the way that shifts in gender *differentiation* and gender *stratification* contribute to the formation and mobilization of collective identities" (1999:14). Given the contribution of women's movements scholars to understanding the impact of political discourse and cultural framing on female movement activists, it may be useful to think of movement frames that are, first, gender frames and, second, gendered frames, which may shape collective identities and collective action possibilities. By gender frame, I mean cognitive understandings distinguished by a content of difference between women and men and between masculinities and femininities that has political relevance and resonance and that is movement specific. Gender frames could be evidenced in framing contests involving a political movement, its opponents, and the mass media, or in movement discourse relying on military- or sports-based language. Gender frames could also be evidenced in explicit collective action. A gender frame might shape collective action by limiting leadership roles and public speaking to male activists, by developing tactics that involve all-women sit-ins or all women on the front lines of a demonstration, by state responses that list no women in injunctions against collective action, by differentiating separate movement tasks for women and for men, and by excluding female activists from control over outcome decisions. Gender frames actively employ gendered values, symbols, beliefs, and language in the context of concerted collective action (Beckwith 2001).

By gendered frames, I mean extant political movement frames, not evidently gendered in content or intentional practice, that nonetheless have different relevances for women and for men. A rights-based frame, for example, that relies on understandings of equality under the law and equal opportunities may carry unintended gender-specific policy consequences (see Katzenstein 1998:96). Both gendered and gender frames are actively constructed, consciously or inadvertently, in the contexts of collective identity construction, mobilization, collective action, and interaction with opponents, states, and others. Both gender and gendered frames are dynamic and are constituted by and constitutive of a movement's collective action experience. By investing how gender is framed in political movements, we will be able to "advance our understanding of gender change by making explicit the role of social movements both in affirming and challenging the gender order" (Taylor 1999:26).

A major advance for scholarship on women and political movements, and for movements generally, is how gender intersects with political opportunity structures. Several movements scholars have argued that political opportunity structures, including state structures, are dynamic and susceptible to influence and transformation by movement action (Banaszak 1996, Gamson & Meyer 1996, Tarrow 1998). How are political opportunities gendered? Are political opportunity structures responsive to collective action or to specific collective actors, e.g. women? In any specific context, are opportunity structures gendered against activist women? Conversely, are they gendered in ways that offer advantages to women's or feminist movements? What gender frames, if any, can facilitate the success of women's movements?

A tentative response to some of these questions emerges from comparative work on movements in Germany (Rucht 2000). In his study of German women's, labor, environmental, peace, and antinuclear movements, Rucht found that although the movements have traits in common, overlap considerably ("e.g. women's groups in labor, peace and environmental movements"), and are frequently in alliance, the German government's response to them varied considerably (Rucht 2000:14). In part, state response can be explained by movement tactics: Women's movements rarely employ disruptive protest tactics.[11] From 1974 to 1990, women's issues constituted a small percentage of all protest issues (1.9%) and involved few protesters (0.6%) (Rucht 2000:15). Women's movement issues were advanced through confrontational but nonviolent (and increasingly nonconfrontational) means across the two decades (Rucht 2000:17), compared with other movements' issues. Finally, even in presumably the same political opportunity structure, women's movements were more likely to target the national state than were other movements (although local government was also a target). The state, according to Rucht, was the women's movement's preferred target; political parties, employers, firms, and other interest groups were unlikely targets of women's movement protest. These findings are suggestive of the possibility of a gendered political opportunity structure. Although it is not Rucht's purpose in this chapter, he nonetheless concludes that "the German state has become more permeable [by] those movements whose demands are . . . negotiable and suited for compromise [and, like women's movements,] engaged in more or less continuous interactions with the state" (2000:18).

Earlier research on women's movements (Hellman 1987a,b; Jenson 1987, 1985) similarly suggests that political opportunities for movements are gendered. States (and parties) respond more favorably—or at least differently—to other movements than to women's movements in the same political opportunity context in the same time period. Again, the concern in women's movements scholarship with the universe of political discourse, discourse politics, and political standing, and with their contributions to cultural framing, suggest both that political opportunity structure may be gendered and that cultural tools and strategies can actively recast the gendered frame of political opportunity. The articulation of how political opportunities are gendered and careful attention to specifying conditions and

[11]Rucht relies on data from the Prodat project that he directs. Protest data "are derived from a systematic sample (all weekend protests plus five workday protests in each fourth week) of two nationwide 'quality newspapers,' the *Süddeutsche Zeitung* and the *Frankfurter Rundschau*. The relative weight of the protest activities of the five movements in different time periods can be seen from the number of protests and participants of each movement" (Rucht 2000:7).

relationships in women's and other movements may increase the possibilities of developing a theory of gender and political movements.

At century's end, scholarship on women's movements has completed significant excavation. Political scientists are now poised to advance a gendered analysis of political movements, and political science as a discipline should prepare to receive it.

ACKNOWLEDGMENTS

My thinking on these issues has developed across the course of multiple discussions with colleagues in political science. Three particularly instrumental venues have included the Roundtable on "The Concept of Gender: Research Implications for Political Science," at the 1997 American Political Science Association meetings; the Women and Politics Research Section's 1998 Seminar for Advanced Graduate Students on "Frontiers of Women and Politics Research"; and the meetings of the "Women's Movements Facing the Reconfigured State" research group (1997–1999). I am grateful to the participants of all these meetings, who are far too numerous to identify individually. I would be remiss, however, not to express my gratitude to Lee Ann Banaszak, Alexandra Dobrowolski, Donatella della Porta, Jane Jenson, Mary Fainsod Katzenstein, Joni Lovenduski, David Meyer, Dieter Rucht, Sidney Tarrow, and Celia Valiente.

LITERATURE CITED

Alvarez S. 1990. *Engendering Democracy in Brazil: Women's Movements in Transition Politics*. Princeton, NJ: Princeton Univ. Press

Alvarez S. 1994. The (trans)formation of feminism(s) and gender politics in democratizing Brazil. See Jaquette 1994, pp. 13–63

Baldez L. 2000. *Why Women Protest: Right-wing and Left-wing Women's Movements in Chile*. Unpublished manuscript

Banaszak LA. 1996. *Why Movements Succeed or Fail*. Princeton, NJ: Princeton Univ. Press

Banaszak LA. 2000. The women's movement policy successes and the constraints of state reconfiguration: abortion and equal pay in differing eras. See Banaszak et al 2000

Banaszak LA, Beckwith K, Rucht D, eds. 2000. *Women's Movements Facing the Reconfigured State*. Unpublished collection

Barakso M. 1998. *Strategy change in social movement organizations*. PhD thesis. MIT, Cambridge, MA

Bashevkin S. 1998. *Women on the Defensive: Living Through Conservative Times*. Chicago: Univ. Chicago Press

Basu A, ed. 1995. *The Challenge of Local Feminisms: Women's Movements in Global Perspective*. Boulder, CO: Westview

Beckwith K. 1985. Feminism and leftist politics in Italy: the case of UDI-PCI relations. *W. Eur. Polit.* 8(4):19–37

Beckwith K. 1987. Response to feminism in the Italian Parliament: divorce, abortion, and sexual violence legislation. See Katzenstein & Mueller 1987, pp. 153–71

Beckwith K. 1996. Lancashire women against pit closures: women's standing in a men's movement. *Signs* 21(4):1034–68

Beckwith K. 2000a. Beyond compare? Women's movements in comparative perspective. *Eur. J. Polit. Res.* 37:431–68

Beckwith K. 2000b. The gendering ways of states: Women's representation and state transformations in Britain, Italy, and the United States. See Banaszak et al 2000

Beckwith K. 2000c. *Mobilization after loss? Women's organizing and political learning.* Presented at Annu. Midwest Polit. Sci. Assoc. Meet., Chicago, Apr. 27–30

Beckwith K. 2001. Gender frames and collective action: configurations of masculinity in the Pittston Coal strike. *Polit. Soc.* In press

Blee KM. 1996. Becoming a racist: women in contemporary Ku Klux Klan and Neo-Nazi groups. *Gender Soc.* 10:680–702

Blee KM, ed. 1998. *No Middle Ground: Women and Radical Protest.* New York: New York Univ. Press

Brenner J. 1996. The best of times, the worst of times: feminism in the United States. See Threlfall 1996, pp. 7–72

Bystydzienski JM, ed. 1992. *Women Transforming Politics: Worldwide Strategies for Empowerment.* Bloomington: Indiana Univ. Press

Bystydzienski JM, Sekhon J, eds. 1999. *Democratization and Women's Grassroots Movements.* Bloomington: Indiana Univ. Press

Carroll SJ. 1992. Women state legislators, Women's organizations, and the representation of women's culture in the United States. See Bystydzienski 1992, pp. 24–40

Cohen CJ, Jones KB, Tronto JC, eds. 1997. *Women Transforming Politics.* New York: NY Univ. Press

Conover PJ, Sapiro V. 1993. Gender, feminist consciousness, and war. *Am. J. Polit. Sci.* 37:1079–99

Costain AN. 1987. Strategy and tactics of the women's movement in the United States: the role of political parties. See Katzenstein & Mueller 1987, pp. 196–214

Costain AN. 1992. *Inviting Women's Rebellion: A Political Process Interpretation of the Women's Movement.* Baltimore, MD: Johns Hopkins Univ. Press

Crawford VL, Rouse JA, Woods B, eds. 1993. *Women in the Civil Rights Movements: Trailblazers and Torchbearers, 1941–1965.* Bloomington: Indiana Univ. Press

Davis RH. 1997. *Women and Power in Parliamentary Democracies: Cabinet Appointments in Western Europe, 1968–1992.* Lincoln: Univ. Nebraska Press

DuBois E. 1980. *Feminism and Suffrage: The Emergence of an Independent Women's Movement in America, 1848–1869.* Ithaca, NY: Cornell Univ. Press

Echols A. 1997. Nothing distant about it: women's liberation and sixties radicalism. See Cohen et al 1997, pp. 456–76

Elman RA. 2000. Refuge in reconstructed states: shelter movements in the United States, Britain and Sweden. See Banaszak et al 2000

Ferree MM, Hess BB. 1994. *Controversy and Coalition: The New Feminist Movement Across Three Decades of Change.* New York: Twayne. Rev. ed.

Ferree MM, Martin PY, eds. 1995. *Feminist Organizations: Harvest of the New Women's Movement.* Philadelphia: Temple Univ. Press

Flammang J. 1997. *Women's Political Voice: How Women Are Transforming the Practice and Study of Politics.* Philadelphia: Temple Univ. Press

Flexner E. 1975. *Century of Struggle: The Woman's Rights Movement in the United States. Cambridge*, MA: Harvard Univ. Press. Rev. ed.

Fonow MM. 1998. Protest engendered: the participation of women steelworkers in the Wheeling-Pittsburgh steel strike of 1985. *Gender Soc.* 12(6):710–28

Freeman J. 1975. *The Politics of Women's Liberation.* New York: McKay

Freeman J. 1987. Whom you know versus whom you represent: feminist influence in the Democratic and Republican parties. See Katzenstein & Mueller 1987, pp. 215–44

Fulenwider CK. 1980. *Feminism in American*

Politics: A Study of Ideological Influence. New York: Praeger

Gamson WA, Meyer DS. 1996. Framing political opportunity. See McAdam et al 1996, pp. 275–90

Gelb J. 1989. *Feminism and Politics: A Comparative Perspective*. Berkeley: Univ. Calif. Press

Gurko M. 1976. *The Ladies of Seneca Falls: The Birth of the Woman's Rights Movement*. New York: Schocken Books

Hartmann SM. 1998. *The Other Feminists: Activists in the Liberal Establishment*. New Haven, CT: Yale Univ. Press

Hellman JA. 1987a. *Journeys Among Women*. New York: Oxford

Hellman JA. 1987b. Women's struggle in a workers' city: feminist movements in Turin. See Katzenstein & Mueller 1987, pp. 111–31

Jaquette JS, ed. 1994. *The Women's Movement in Latin America: Participation and Democracy*. Boulder, CO: Westview. 2nd ed.

Jenson J. 1985. Struggling for identity: the women's movement and the state in Western Europe. In *Women and Politics in Western Europe*, ed. S Bashevkin, pp. 5–18. London: Cass

Jenson J. 1987. Changing discourse, changing agendas: political rights and reproductive policies in France. See Katzenstein & Mueller 1987, pp. 64–88

Kaplan C, Alarcón N, Moallem M, eds. 1999. *Between Woman and Nation: Nationalisms, Transnational Feminisms, and the State*. Durham, NC: Duke Univ. Press

Kampwirth K. 1996. Confronting adversity with experience: the emergence of feminism in Nicaragua. *Soc. Polit.* 3(2/3):136–58

Katzenstein MF. 1987. Comparing the feminist movements of the United States and Western Europe: an overview. See Katzenstein & Mueller 1987, pp. 3–20

Katzenstein MF. 1998. *Faithful and Fearless: Moving Feminist Protest Inside the Church and the Military*. Princeton, NJ: Princeton Univ. Press

Katzenstein MF, Mueller CM, eds. 1987. *The Women's Movements of the United States and Western Europe*. Philadelphia: Temple Univ. Press

Kitschelt H. 1986. Political opportunity structures and political protest: anti-nuclear movements in four democracies. *Br. J. Polit. Sci.* 16:57–85

Klein E. 1984. *Gender Politics: From Consciousness to Mass Politics*. Cambridge, MA: Harvard Univ. Press

Klein E. 1987. The diffusion of consciousness in the United States and Western Europe. See Katzenstein & Mueller 1987, pp. 23–43

Kraditor AS. 1981. *The Ideas of the Women's Suffrage Movement: 1890–1920*. New York: Norton

Kriesi H. 1995. The political opportunity structure of new social movements: its impact on their mobilization. In *The Politics of Social Protest*, ed. JC Jenkins, B Klandermans, pp. 167–98. Minneapolis: Univ. Minn. Press

Lovenduski J, Norris P, eds. 1993. *Gender and Party Politics*. London: Sage

Lovenduski J, Randall V. 1993. *Contemporary Feminist Politics: Women and Power in Britain*. Oxford, UK: Oxford Univ. Press

Luker K. 1984. *Abortion and the Politics of Motherhood*. Berkeley: Univ. Calif. Press

Maggard SW. 1990. Gender contested: women's participation in the Brookside Coal strike. See West & Blumberg 1990, pp. 75–98

Marshall A. 2000. *Organizing across the divide: feminist activism, everyday life, and the election of women to public office*. Presented at Annu. Meet. Midwest Polit. Sci. Assoc., Chicago, Apr. 27–30

McAdam D. 1992. Gender as a mediator of the activist experience: the case of Freedom Summer. *Am. J. Sociol.* 97:1211–40

McAdam D, McCarthy JD, Zald MN, eds. 1996. *Comparative Perspectives on Social Movements: Political Opportunities, Mobilizing Structures, and Cultural Framings*. Cambridge, UK: Cambridge Univ. Press

McAdam D, Tarrow S, Tilly C. 1996. To map contentious politics. *Mobilization* 1(1):17–34

McAdam D, Tarrow S, Tilly C. 2001. *Dynamics of Contention*. Cambridge, UK: Cambridge Univ. Press

McDonagh EL. 1996. *Breaking the Abortion Deadlock: From Choice to Consent*. New York: Oxford Univ. Press

Meyer DS, Whittier N. 1994. Social movement spillover. *Soc. Probl.* 41:277–98

Morris A, Mueller CM, eds. 1992. *Frontiers in Social Movement Theory*. New Haven, CT: Yale Univ. Press

Mueller CM. 1987. Collective consciousness, identity transformation, and the rise of women in public office in the United States. See Katzenstein & Mueller 1987, pp. 89–108

Mueller CM, ed. 1988. *The Politics of the Gender Gap: The Social Construction of Political Influence*. Newbury Park, CA: Sage

Muszynski A. 1999. Sexual assault and the Canadian case: participatory democracy struggles within a liberal democracy. See Bystydzienski & Sekhon 1999, pp. 305–27

Nelson BJ, Chowdhury N, eds. 1994. *Women and Politics Worldwide*. New Haven, CT: Yale Univ. Press

O'Connor K. 1996. *No Neutral Ground? Abortion Politics in an Age of Absolutes*. Boulder, CO: Westview

Rai SM, Lievesley G, eds. 1996. *Women and the State: International Perspectives*. London: Taylor & Francis

Reingold B. 1998. Exploring the determinants of feminist consciousness in the United States. *Women Polit.* 19(3):19–48

Robnett B. 1997. *How Long? How Long? African-American Women in the Struggle for Civil Rights*. New York: Oxford Univ. Press

Rowbotham S. 1996. Mapping the Women's movement. See Threlfall 1996, pp. 1–16

Rucht D. 1996. The impact of national contexts on social movement structures: a cross-movement and cross-national analysis. See McAdam et al 1996, pp. 185–204

Rucht D. 2000. Interactions between social movements and states in comparative perspective. See Banaszak et al 2000

Ruggie M. 1987. Workers' movements and women's interests: the impact of labor-state relations in Britain and Sweden. See Katzenstein & Mueller 1987, pp. 247–66

Ryan B. 1992. *Feminism and the Women's Movement: Dynamics of Change in Social Movement Ideology and Activism*. New York: Routledge

Saint-Germain MA. 1997. Mujeres' 94: democratic transition and the women's movement in El Salvador. *Women Polit.* 18(2):75–99

Sawyers TM, Meyer DS. 1999. Missed opportunities: social movement abeyance and public policy. *Soc. Probl.* 46(2):187–206

Schattschneider EE. 1975. *The Semisovereign People*. Hinsdale, IL: Dryden

Sekhon J. 1999. Grassroots social action and empowerment in India: the case of Action India women's Program. See Bystydzienski & Sekhon 1999, pp. 25–48

Sen R. 1997. Winning action for gender equity: a plan for organizing communities of color. See Cohen et al 1997, pp. 302–23

Shadmi E. 2000. Between resistance and compliance, feminism and nationalism: women in black in Israel. *Women Stud. Int. Forum* 23(1):23–34

Snow DA, Benford RD. 1988. Ideology, frame resonance, and participant mobilization. In *From Structure to Action: Social Movement Participation Across Cultures*, ed. H Kriesi, S Tarrow, pp. 197–217. Greenwich, CT: JAI

Snow DA, Benford RD. 1992. Master frames and cycles of protest. See Morris & Mueller 1992, pp. 133–55

Staggenborg S. 1991. *The Pro-Choice Movement*. New York: Oxford Univ. Press

Sternback NS, Navarro-Aranguren M, Chuckryk P, Alvarez SE. 1992. Feminisms in Latin America: from Bogotá to San Bernardo. *Signs* 17(2):393–434

Stetson DMcB, Mazur A, eds. 1995. *Comparative State Feminism*. Thousand Oaks, CA: Sage

Swers M. 2000. *Show horses versus work horses: working behind the scenes for women's issues*. Presented at Annu. Meet. Midwest Polit. Sci. Assoc., Chicago, Apr. 27–30

Tarrow S. 1989. *Struggle, Politics, and Reform: Collective Action, Social Movements, and Cycles of Protest*. Ithaca, NY: Cornell Cent. Int. Stud.

Tarrow S. 1992. Mentalities, political cultures, and collective action frames: constructing meanings through action. See Morris & Mueller 1992, pp. 174–202

Tarrow S. 1996. States and opportunities: the political structuring of social movements. See McAdam et al 1996, pp. 41–61

Tarrow S. 1998. *Power in Movement: Social Movements and Contentious Politics*. Cambridge, UK: Cambridge Univ. Press

Taylor V. 1999. Gender and social movements: gender processes in Women's self-help movements. *Gender Soc.* 13(1):8–33

Tolleson-Rinehart S. 1992. *Gender Consciousness and Politics*. New York: Routledge

Threlfall M, ed. 1996. *Mapping the Women's Movement: Feminist Politics and Social Transformation in the North*. London: Verso

Waylen G. 1994. Women and democratisation: conceptualising gender relations in transition politics. *World Polit.* 46(3):327–54

Weinbaum E. 1997. Transforming democracy: rural women and labor resistance. See Cohen et al 1997, pp. 324–29

West G, Blumberg RL, eds. 1990. *Women and Social Protest*. Oxford, UK: Oxford Univ. Press

Annu. Rev. Polit. Sci. 2001. 4:391–416

TAKING STOCK: The Constructivist Research Program in International Relations and Comparative Politics

Martha Finnemore[1] and Kathryn Sikkink[2]

[1]*Political Science Department, Funger Hall 625, George Washington University, Washington, D.C. 20052; e-mail: finnemor@gwu.edu*

[2]*Department of Political Science, University of Minnesota, 267 19th Avenue S., Minneapolis, Minnesota 55455; e-mail: ksikkink@polisci.umn.edu*

Key Words constructivism, ideas, identity, norms, culture, beliefs

■ **Abstract** Constructivism is an approach to social analysis that deals with the role of human consciousness in social life. It asserts that human interaction is shaped primarily by ideational factors, not simply material ones; that the most important ideational factors are widely shared or "intersubjective" beliefs, which are not reducible to individuals; and that these shared beliefs construct the interests of purposive actors. In international relations, research in a constructivist mode has exploded over the past decade, creating new and potentially fruitful connections with long-standing interest in these issues in comparative politics. In this essay, we evaluate the empirical research program of constructivism in these two fields. We first lay out the basic tenets of constructivism and examine their implications for research methodology, concluding that constructivism's distinctiveness lies in its theoretical arguments, not in its empirical research strategies. The bulk of the essay explores specific constructivist literatures and debates in international relations and comparative politics.

INTRODUCTION

In his 1988 presidential address to the International Studies Association, Robert Keohane noted the rise of a new approach to international politics and put forward a challenge: Success or failure of the new approach would depend on its ability to inspire and support a vigorous program of empirical research (Keohane 1988).[1] Thirteen years later, we believe that this challenge has been easily met. Constructivist empirical research is thriving in the study of international affairs and has been applied in virtually every issue of interest to scholars. Indeed, ten

[1]Keohane referred to this new approach as a "reflective" approach; since that time, the standard name has become "constructivism."

years after Keohane's challenge, he, Katzenstein, and Krasner acknowledged that constructivism and rationalism provide the major points of contestation shaping the field in years to come (Katzenstein et al 1999).

In this essay, we take stock of the constructivist research program. Several excellent works have now been written that survey the range of constructivist theoretical arguments (Adler 1997, Price & Reus-Smit 1998, Ruggie 1998, Wendt 1999). However, the empirical research program, on which the "success" of this theorizing depended in the eyes of many, has received much less systematic treatment. Since it was unclear to Keohane and others how scholars working in a constructivist vein would or could carry out empirical research, how did they solve these problems? What kinds of research have emerged? What have been the foci of this research, what have been its strengths and weaknesses, and where is it going?

To address these questions, we survey constructivist empirical research with several purposes in mind. We begin with a brief discussion of the core features of constructivist theorizing that have informed this research. In the second section, we take up the question of whether there is a "constructivist methodology" for empirical research. One of the concerns about early constructivist writings was that they provided little guidance for developing concepts and methods of empirical analysis. Scholars have now responded to these problems in various ways, and we survey the results of their work. We conclude that constructivist analysis is compatible with many research methods currently used in social science and political science. Constructivism's distinctiveness lies in its theoretical arguments, not in its empirical research strategies.

The next section reviews constructivist empirical research in international relations (IR). We organize this review around major research questions that have motivated constructivists and note trends in IR empirical research that build bridges to comparative politics by inviting, and even requiring, comparative politics research to substantiate claims. Comparativists have long been interested in questions of culture, ideas, and identity, but few comparative authors identify themselves as constructivists. Using the core features of constructivism as our criteria, we identify and discuss a range of works in comparative politics that could be called constructivist. We conclude by exploring the ways in which constructivism, which arose in the IR field, opens new connections between IR and comparative politics.

CORE FEATURES OF CONSTRUCTIVISM

"Constructivism is about human consciousness and its role in international life" (Ruggie 1998:856). Constructivists focus on the role of ideas, norms, knowledge, culture, and argument in politics, stressing in particular the role of collectively held or "intersubjective" ideas and understandings on social life. Specifically, constructivism is an approach to social analysis that asserts the following: (*a*) human interaction is shaped primarily by ideational factors, not simply material ones; (*b*) the most important ideational factors are widely shared or "intersubjective" beliefs, which are not reducible to individuals; and (*c*) these shared beliefs construct the interests and identities of purposive actors (Adler 1997, Price & Reus-Smit 1998, Ruggie 1998, Wendt 1999). Constructivism focuses on what Searle (1995) has called "social facts"—things like money, sovereignty, and rights, which have no material reality but exist only because people collectively believe they exist and act accordingly. Understanding how social facts change and the ways these influence politics is the major concern of constructivist analysis. Constructivism's main analytical competitors have thus been approaches of two kinds: (*a*) materialist theories, which see political behavior as determined by the physical world alone, and (*b*) individualist theories, which treat collective understandings as simply epiphenomena of individual action and deny that they have causal power or ontological status. All constructivist analyses use an ideational ontology and holism in some way.

Constructivism is a differnt kind of theory from realism, liberalism, or marxism and operates at a different level of abstraction. Constructivism is not a substantive theory of politics. It is a social theory that makes claims about the nature of social life and social change. Constructivism does not, however, make any particular claims about the content of social structures or the nature of agents at work in social life. Consequently it does not, by itself, produce specific predictions about political outcomes that one could test in social science research. Constructivism in this sense is similar to rational choice. Like rational choice, it offers a framework for thinking about the nature of social life and social interaction, but makes no claims about their specific content. In a rational choice analysis, agents act rationally to maximize utilities, but the substantive specification of actors and utilities lies outside the analysis; it must be provided before analysis can begin. In a constructivist analysis, agents and structures are mutually constituted in ways that explain why the political world is so and not otherwise, but the substantive specification of agents and structures must come from some other source. Neither constructivism nor rational choice provides substantive explanations or predictions of political behavior until coupled with a more specific understanding of who the relevant actors are, what they want, and what the content of social structures might be.

Rational choice has been used extensively in the service of materialist and individualist theories such as neorealism and neoliberalism, in which the relevant actors are states who want material security and/or wealth. The substantive predictions of these theories are not predictions of rational choice, however, but of the political arguments that inform it. Constructivist frameworks have been joined to a variety of substantive specifications with diverse results (reviewed below). The particular findings of these efforts are not the substance of constructivism, however, nor are predictions that flow from these findings the predictions of constructivism any more than Waltzian realism is the prediction or singular result of rational choice. They are the findings and predictions of scholars, which flow from their chosen substantive starting point for constructivist analysis.

LOGIC AND METHODS OF INQUIRY

Constructivism's core assumptions have shaped its empirical research program in several important ways. They have shaped the kinds of questions constructivists tend to ask by opening up for inquiry issues that other approaches had failed to engage. Since, by ontological assumption, constructivists understand that actors are shaped by the social milieu in which they live, one obvious research question for them is: How does this shaping happen and with what results? Unlike proponents of materialist and utilitarian theories, constructivists cannot take identities and interests for granted, and understanding the processes by which they originate and change has been a big part of the constructivist research program. To frame research designs on these questions, scholars have supplemented constructivism's minimalist social-theoretic claims with a variety of more specific, often more substantive, theories about the mutual constitution process and the behavior that results from it. Constructivists have explored Foucauldian analyses of the power of discourse to understand these processes (Ferguson 1990; Keeley 1990; Price 1995, 1997). They have explored theories of agency and culture (Bukovansky 2001), Goffman-type analyses about self-presentation in public life (Barnett 1998), Karl Deutsch's notions about security communities (Adler & Barnett 1998), theories about organizational behavior (Finnemore 1996a,b; Barnett & Finnemore 1999), social movement theory (Smith et al 1997, Keck & Sikkink 1998), Habermasian theory about communicative action (Risse 2000, Checkel 2001), and mediation theory (Ratner 2000), to name a few.

Their focus on these process questions, on how identities and interests are created, has led many constructivists to think more broadly about the nature of causality and explanation than some of their rationalist or utilitarian colleagues. Constructivists are skeptical about claims to all-encompassing truth [what Price & Reus-Smit (1998) call "Big-T" claims] and instead produce and evaluate "small-t" contingent claims. Such partial and contingent claims may still constitute causal explanation, albeit in a somewhat different sense than realists or liberals understand causality. For constructivists, understanding how things are put together and how they occur is not mere description. Understanding the constitution of things is essential in explaining how they behave and what causes political outcomes. Just as understanding how the double-helix DNA molecule is constituted materially enables understandings of genetics and disease, so, too, an understanding of how sovereignty, human rights, laws of war, or bureaucracies are constituted socially allows us to hypothesize about their effects in world politics. Constitution in this sense is causal, since how things are put together makes possible, or even probable, certain kinds of political behavior and effects (Wendt 1998, Barnett & Finnemore 1999). Because they are permissive and probabilistic, however, such explanations are necessarily contingent and partial—they are small-t truth claims. However, the fact that constitutive explanations have causal properties means that the distinction between constitutive explanations and other forms of explanation may not be sharp in practice, particularly in empirical work.

Constructivism's core assumptions have also shaped the methods by which constructivists go about answering their questions. Constructivists need methods that can capture the intersubjective meanings at the core of their approach. Constructivists recognize that all research involves interpretation, and thus there is no neutral stance from which they can gather objective knowledge about the world (Price & Reus-Smit 1998), but they differ about how this interpretation should be done and what kinds of explanation it yields. The clearest division is between what Price & Reus-Smit term modern and postmodern variants of constructivism. Postmodernist constructivists reject efforts to find a point from which to assess the validity of analytical and ethical knowledge claims. This stance makes it possible to deconstruct and critique the knowledge claims of others but makes it difficult to construct and evaluate new knowledge claims. For modern constructivists, on the other hand, acceptance that the world is always interpreted does not imply that all interpretations or explanations are equal; some types of explanation and evidence are more persuasive or logically and empirically plausible than others.

Modern constructivists may therefore be tackling different kinds of questions with broader notions of what constitutes causality than their rationalist or utilitarian colleagues, but practical investigation of these questions often leads them to similar methodological tasks. Like other social scientists, they must gather evidence, assess it, and arbitrate among explanations. Relevant and reliable evidence comes from many of the same sources widely used in other types of social analysis. Many of the world polity theorists in sociology, for example, use quantitative methods to describe overall characteristics of normative or cultural structures and plot change in these over time. Strang (1991), Boli (1987), and Ramirez et al (1997) have done this to track changes in the global distribution of sovereignty, citizenship rights, and women's rights. These analyses can provide correlative evidence about the timing and patterns of normative change but are less suited to understanding how and why change happens. To accomplish this, constructivists have used a variety of tools to capture intersubjective meanings, including discourse analysis, process tracing, genealogy, structured focused comparisons, interviews, participant observation, and content analysis.

In assessing this evidence and arbitrating among interpretations, constructivists use similiar criteria, as other researchers. They judge an interpretation of evidence by comparing it with alternative explanations. They search for evidence that would confirm alternatives and disconfirm the explanation being assessed. They ask if an explanation is supported by multiple streams of data (Putnam 1993). For example, they examine whether speech acts are consistent with other kinds of behavior in a case under investigation; whether qualitative findings are supported by or at least consistent with relevant statistical data; and whether actors explain and justify actions in similar ways in different settings (e.g. in private versus in public). Depending on the type of research, modern constructivists might also ask if the research can be duplicated. Good research need not be completely replicable (as participant-observer research may not be), but replication can enhance the plausibility of an interpretation.

There is no single constructivist method or research design. Constructivism opens up a set of issues, and scholars choose the research tools and methods best suited to their particular question. In some cases, quantitative methods yield particular insight. In other cases, qualitative and interpretative methods are more appropriate. Many research projects have used a combination of these methods to illuminate different parts of a larger puzzle. In this sense, designing constructivist research is not fundamentally different from designing other kinds of research. Constructivists, like any other researchers, use the full array of available tools.

ISSUES MOTIVATING RESEARCH IN INTERNATIONAL RELATIONS

Unlike utilitarian (or rationalist) researchers, constructivists are not elaborating competing theories and engaging in wars among various "isms" (realism versus liberalism, for example). Rather, the modern constructivist research program seems to be developing in ways analogous to comparative politics. It focuses on issues, not on competing constructivist theories, and it aims at contingent generalizations. Surveying the empirical research, we see constructivists clustering around several prominent problems, engaging each other in debates about how to approach them and about what drives events in these areas, much as comparativists do. Our review of this research is organized around these issues.

Global Norms versus Local Effects

In a discipline that denied the independent causal effect of norms, rules, and social structures of meaning generally, the first task for constructivist empirical research in IR was obviously to establish that norms (and other social structures) matter. Much of the earlist constructivist work focused on this task. Katzenstein's edited volume, *The Culture of National Security*, was a conscious attempt to make this case to the most skeptical of audiences—the realists in security studies. Essays on weapons taboos, on military culture, on humanitarianism, and on identity politics all demonstrated how social structures of different kinds reshape actors' interests, self-understandings, and behavior (Katzenstein 1996a). Constructivists working on other political issues produced well-documented empirical studies showing the effectiveness of norms, which could not be easily reduced to interests of powerful states, in such diverse areas as foreign aid, opposition to slavery, piracy, trafficking in women, science policy, development, racism, and laws of war (Nadelman 1990; Finnemore 1993, 1996a; Crawford 1993; Lumsdaine 1993; Klotz 1995; Price 1995, 1997). The sociological institutionalists and world polity theorists, whose work began to be read in IR at this time, offered a similar causal focus. It showed how "world culture" reconfigured state policies, particularly the policies of developing states, in many different policy arenas (Meyer & Hannan 1979, Bergesen 1980, Thomas et al 1987, Finnemore 1996b, Meyer et al 1997). All of these studies demonstrated that norms, culture, and other social structures have causal force and that these structures are not simple reflections of hegemonic state interests.

In an intellectual discourse where the causal status of social structures was widely questioned, simply establishing that these things matter was an important showing for constructivist scholars. However, this research, which focused on causality in only one direction—norms and social understandings influencing agents—was quickly questioned. Scholars were quick to notice that norms and social understandings often had different influences on different agents, and explaining these differences was soon identified as a crucial constructivist research task. Checkel's essays in the *European Journal of International Relations* (1997) and *World Politics* (1998) were prominent and early examples of this critique. Not only do different states react differently to the same international norms, he argued, but the mechanisms by which norms are internalized within states differ as well. Without understanding how these domestic processes worked, we could not understand the political effects of these global social structures. By bringing investigation of global norms back into domestic politics, Checkel and others have created an important point of intersection between international relations and comparative politics.

Following Checkel's critique, a variety of studies have investigated how international norms influence different actors (usually states) differently. A study of ten countries' reactions to international human rights norms showed how regime type, civil war, and the presence of domestic human rights organizations affect the degree to which states will comply with international human rights norms (Risse et al 1999). The authors proposed a generalized model of the process by which this happens. Checkel's own research (2001) on variations in compliance with European norms by Ukraine and Germany follows a similar pattern. Gurowitz (1999), in a study of the impact of refugee norms, argued that states with insecure international identities, such as Japan, respond more to international norms than countries with secure international identities, such as Germany.

The blind spots and biases of these two groups of constructivist researchers are predictable and complementary. One group is trying to show that global social structures exist and have powerful effects. These scholars tend to emphasize adherence with international norms or rules and downplay variations in compliance. The danger in this view comes when scholars forget that there is local variation in reaction to these norms and begin to treat international norms as a global "oobleck" that covers the planet and homogenizes us all (Seuss 1970). Similarly, these scholars sometimes overlook the fact that international norms have to come from somewhere and may not identify feedback effects from local agents onto global structures (Kaufman & Pape 1999). World polity and world culture research in sociology often look dangerously biased in these ways to political scientists. The other group of scholars is interested precisely in these local variations in norm effects and tends to obscure or take for granted the other group's finding of the strong overall impact of ideational phenomena. The danger here is that scholars can become so concerned with detailing the variations in local reaction that they lose sight of large overall shifts in the global normative fabric. Disagreements between these groups flow from their different vantage points. They are not, as far as we can tell, disagreeing that social construction is going on and that it has large overall effects, nor even disagreeing about how it might happen.

Ideas and Power

In their efforts to establish independent causal force for norms and ideas, many constructivist studies have emphasized the ways in which ideas and norms run counter to or undermine conventional conceptions of strong state interests. Human rights norms, the preference of the weak, have been shown to triumph over strong actors and strong states; environmental norms prevail over powerful corporate business preferences (Wapner 1996, Keck & Sikkink 1998, Risse et al 1999). However, another strand of constructivist scholarship has been much more skeptical about this autonomy of ideas from power. Work of "critical" constructivism has intellectual roots in critical social theory, including such figures as Anthony Giddens, Jurgen Habermas, and Michel Foucault. Although it shares the core features of constructivism identified above, critical constructivism adds a belief that constructions of reality reflect, enact, and reify relations of power. Critical constructivists believe that certain powerful groups play a privileged role in the process of social construction. The task of the critical scholar is both to unmask these ideational structures of domination and to facilitate the imagining of alternative worlds. Critical constructivists thus see a weaker autonomous role for ideas than do other constructivists because ideas are viewed as more tightly linked to relations of material power (Weldes et al 1999, Price & Reus-Smit 1998).

Critical constructivists are increasingly engaged in rich empirical work. Their purpose is not to build or test new causal theory but to denaturalize dominant constructions, in part by revealing their connection to existing power relations. Weldes' work on the Cuban missile crisis, for example, argues that the crisis was a social construction forged by US officials in the process of reasserting its identity as a leader of the free world (Weldes 1996). Doty (1996) shows how the powerful western countries constructed civilizing discourses about the southern countries in order to justify violent counterinsurgency policies and economic exploitation. Weber (1999) uses gendered and sexual metaphors to explain the US obsession with relatively small perceived threats in the Caribbean and Central America, which she sees as strategies for recovering phallic power, lost in its encounter with Cuba.

An important contribution of critical IR theory has been to remind IR theorists that many of the categories we treat as natural are in fact products of past social construction processes, processes in which power is often deeply implicated.

Identity and State Action

One of the main contributions of constructivism is the notion that state identity fundamentally shapes state preferences and actions. Wendt (1992, 1994) and

Katzenstein (1996a,b) helped put identity issues at the center of much constructivist theorizing. Constructivists agree that state identities were constructed within the social environment of international and domestic politics. They disagree, however, on the definitions of identity and the weight of international versus domestic environments in shaping state identities. Wendt's systemic constructivism places more emphasis on the impact of the international environment. For the authors in Katzenstein's edited volume (1996a), identity was mainly a domestic attribute arising from national ideologies of collective distinctiveness and purpose that in turn shaped states' perceptions of interest and thus state policy (Barnett 1996, Berger 1996, Risse-Kappen 1996).

The ongoing difficulty in identity research is that there is still no clear, agreed-on definition of what we mean (and do not mean) by identity, how researchers can plausibly establish what state identities are, or what range of prominent identities may exist in international politics at any particular historical moment. Identity has become a catch-all term, helping to explain richly a wide variety of actions, but it does not yet permit us to suggest that states with particular types of identities will act in particular ways (Kowert & Legro 1996). As long as identity remains unspecified, it will produce very particularistic explanations for state action and provide little hope of contingent generalizations about identity and world politics.

Wendt (1999) has moved modern constructivism along in addressing this problem. Wendt argues that identities are rooted in an actor's self-understandings (and are thus subjective) but also depend on whether that identity is recognized by other actors, which gives them an intersubjective quality. Thus, identities are constituted by the interaction of these internal and external ideas. This suggests that the number of possible identities is not infinite and the concept not idiosyncratic, since identity formation is always limited by the array of possible identities in the international system at any historical moment.

Wendt suggests that two kinds of identities are particularly important for international affairs: type identities and role identities. Type identities are social categories of states that share some characteristics, such as regime types or forms of state. States may have multiple type identities—a democratic state, a capitalist state, an Islamic state, a European state. International social structure is important here, because at any one time, certain type identities have more or less international legitimacy. For example, monarchical states are less legitimate today, and democratic and capitalist states are increasingly so. Role identities are the product of dyadic relationships among countries. States may be friends, rivals, or enemies. Role identities are uniquely social—they exist only in relation to others. Knowing about a state's perception of its identity (both type and role) should help us to understand how the state will act.

Much more work, both theoretical and empirical, is needed to clarify what are the range of possible type identities at any particular historical moment, how internal and external factors interact to produce actors with particular identities, and how, in turn, such identities affect state action. Work in comparative politics on ethnic identities may be useful for IR constructivist scholars working on identity.

Most comparative scholars working on identity see it as socially constructed but argue that actors may strategically construct their identities from a more limited menu of type identities that are appropriate at a given historical moment (Laitin 1998, Fearon & Laitin 2000). This menu also is socially constructed, and thus there are significant changes from one historical period to another. Yet, in each period, it is likely that this menu of possible type identities is limited.

Mechanisms and Processes of Social Construction

Another big research problem being tackled by constructivists is the identification of mechanisms and processes by which social construction occurs. Once it was established that norms and social structures matter, a next obvious step was to investigate how, exactly, they came to matter and how they came to exist at all. Work on this set of problems has highlighted a variety of possible mechanisms.

NORM ENTREPRENEURS

One broad swathe of research has focused on the purposive efforts of individuals and groups to change social understandings. People who dislike existing norms and rules in politics often band together and try to change them. A number of scholars have sought to understand how these groups operate and the conditions that might contribute to their success. These cases present attractive research puzzles because activists working for change often have few levers of conventional power relative to those controlling existing structures (often the state or corporations); to the extent that activists succeed, these situations are not easily explained by dominant utilitarian approaches, and they open space for constructivist alternatives.

Wapner (1996) shows that much of the important work of environmental activists happened outside of the arena of the state, where IR scholars traditionally focus. He provides extensive evidence of the transformative effects of civic interactions between private actors with transnational characteristics—in his case, multinational corporations and transnational activist groups. Much of what is important in world environmental politics, he argues, happens "beyond the state." Transnational civil society frames issues, helps set agendas, and mobilizes publics. States, in many instances, are only reacting to political changes fomented in an increasingly transnational civil society.

A complementary line of research has explored activism with particular emphasis on activists' work within, not beyond, states. Klotz (1995) and Thomas (2001) both emphasize the ways in which activists work with and within the bureaucracies of important states to achieve and consolidate new norms and social understandings. Klotz (1995) explores how antiapartheid activists steered the US and Commonwealth foreign policies in new directions, resulting in a very different normative climate for the apartheid regime in South Africa. Thomas (2001) similarly investigates the ways in which Helsinki movement activists were able to work through western governmental structures to press their human rights cases during the Cold War.

Once the importance of these nonstate actors was established, the next step for these researchers was to unpack the tools they used in their social construction work. Keck & Sikkink (1998) and Risse et al (1999) analyzed the techniques used by activist groups, including strategic use of information, symbolic politics, leverage politics and accountability politics, issue framing, and shaming. Risse et al (1999) propose a five-stage model of how human rights violators become compliers.

INTERNATIONAL ORGANIZATIONS AND LAW

Other constructivists have focused on the role of international organizations in disseminating new international norms and models of political organization. Finnemore (1993, 1996a,b) outlines the ways that international organizations "teach" states new norms of behavior. Similarly, Adler (1998) shows how the Organization for Security and Cooperation in Europe (OSCE) uses its legitimacy and perceived impartiality to carry out "seminar diplomacy" among its members—teaching them new values and new models of behavior. The mechanisms for social construction elaborated here draw heavily on Max Weber's work and on organization theory in sociology. Organizations are effective agents of social construction in part because the rational-legal authority they embody is widely viewed as legitimate and good. Further, the perceptions that these organizations are merely technical (not political) and that the social models they push are chosen because they are efficient and effective add to the power of these norms (Boli & Thomas 1998, Barnett & Finnemore 1999).

Other scholars have emphasized additional features of organizations that makes the effective engines of social construction. Ratner's (2000) study of the OSCE's High Commissioner for Minorities shows that his organizational role places the High Commissioner (HC) in a unique position to construct new international norms and rules. States often appeal to the HC for policy guidance, and he uses his position creatively to mediate conflicts by constructing new rules and new understandings of the existing rules or law acceptable to disputing parties. His legitimacy in his role, and the organization's authority in these matters, contributes to compliance with these new rules.

EPISTEMIC COMMUNITIES

Interest in the political effects of experts and specialized knowledge has existed in IR for decades. It coalesced into a research program on "epistemic communities" in the late 1980s and early 1990s (Haas 1992). Some of this work focused on knowledge effects in ways that were compatible with utilitarian approaches—knowledge as a road map or focal point that helped utility-maximizing actors achieve their ends more effectively (Goldstein & Keohane 1993). This is what Hasenclever et al (1997) call weak cognitivism and is similar to some of the "ideas" research in comparative politics, discussed below. But another group of epistemic communities researchers uses a broader understanding of knowledge and has contributed greatly to constructivist theorizing as well as the research program. Groups with specialized knowledge often have a common set of norms and world views; many scholars would argue that technical knowledge is never value neutral and always comes with an array of shared normative understandings that make it meaningful, therefore powerful, in social life. As they deploy their knowledge, these epistemic communities often disseminate new norms and understandings along with technical expertise. Consequently, they can act as powerful mechanisms of social construction. Adler's work (1992) on the ways in which arms control strategists in the United States learned game theory from the Rand Corporation in the Kennedy years and "taught" it and the entire deterrence framework to their Russian counterparts, making mutually assured destruction (MAD) seem rational, is one powerful example of social construction by such a group.

Expertise often resides inside formal organizations, so the two mechanisms can become intertwined in interesting ways. Adler's (1998) work on the "seminar diplomacy" of OSCE personnel explores aspects of this relationship, as does Finnemore's work (1993, 1996a) and Haas' earlier work on the Mediterranean clean-up endeavor (1989). Lawyers have been shown to do extensive social construction again, often in conjunction with international institutions that consolidate and formalize the new social facts lawyers create. Burley & Mattli's (1993) analysis of the efforts of community lawyers to empower the then-new European Court of Justice illustrates the ways in which professional groups can translate their own shared understandings into formalized organizations and legal structures. Ratner's work (2000), discussed above, shares similar features.

SPEECH, ARGUMENT, AND PERSUASION

Other constructivists, following Habermas, have explored the role of argument as a mechanism of social construction. IR scholars have tended to treat speech either as "cheap talk," to be ignored, or as bargaining, to be folded into strategic interaction. However, speech can also persuade; it can change people's minds about what goals are valuable and about the roles they play (or should play) in social life. When speech has these effects, it is doing important social construction work, creating new understandings and new social facts that reconfigure politics. In one of the pioneering works of the field, Kratochwil (1989) examined the role of legal reasoning in persuasion and other social construction processes. More recently, German scholars have explored possibilities for Habermasian "communicative action" to change minds and world views (Risse 2000). Crawford follows a slightly different tack. She calls attention to the roles of both cognition and emotion in making arguments persuasive and shows how these are intertwined in deterrence, peace building, and other political projects (Crawford 1993, 2000).

STRUCTURAL CONFIGURATION

Most of the foregoing mechanisms for social construction explore the agentic side of this mutual constitution process; they identify new ways in which agents construct new social facts or new kinds of agents that might do the constructing. Bukovansky (2001) explores the structural side of this process in more detail and emphasizes the ways in which contradictions and complementarities in social structure create opportunities for agents. Using insights from sociologist Margaret Archer's work, she shows how an international political culture (the European Enlightenment) created a pattern of contradictions and complementarities that allowed some kinds of political legitimacy claims to succeed and not others. Reus-Smit (1999) has similarly explored the ways in which the structure of different "fundamental institutions" in international society shape the kinds of politics that are possible.

This list of mechanisms is not exhaustive. Constructivist researchers are identifying more mechanisms of social construction all the time. Further, these mechanisms often interact or even presuppose each other. For example, Habermasian persuasion presupposes a degree of affect (empathy) among participants. International organizations are almost always staffed by people with specialized knowledge who are involved in epistemic communities, creating interactions between bureaucracies and knowledge bases. Contradictions and complementarities cannot create new social structures by themselves; agents must react to these structures, using whatever means are at their disposal, to effect change. We suspect that an exploration of these interactive effects will be important in future constructive empirical research.

A Bias Toward Progressive Norms?

One consistent complaint about constructivist research has been its research focus on norms most of us would consider "good," such as human rights, protecting the environment, and promoting democracy. Constructivists have been quick to point out that there is no necessary reason for this orientation. To some extent, it is an artifact of the dominant approaches with which constructivism engaged in its early years. Neorealist and neoliberal theories that flowed from economic approaches to social analysis tended to understand interests consistently as self-interest; other-regarding behavior was an anomaly to be explained. Consequently, social construction projects that were not obviously self-interested (e.g. promoting human rights for people far away or saving whales and dolphins) were difficult for dominant theories to explain and opened space for a constructivist alternative.

The bias toward "nice" norms has persisted, however, even after constructivism established itself as a legitimate analytic approach in IR. Constructivists in IR have tended not to investigate the construction of xenophobic and violent nationalisms, for example, and the focus on social structures most of us admire has continued. Research has begun, however, on negative effects of these well-intentioned social construction projects. For example, authors in a Carnegie-funded project on democratization efforts in the former Soviet Union (Mendelson & Glenn 2000) show how efforts to transform social facts in the former Soviet Union actually imperil human rights by empowering activists but then not protecting them, and make societies more corrupt by creating new conflicts between international normative demands and local social contexts. Similarly, Barnett & Finnemore (1999) have begun researching the "pathologies" of international organizations, which often act as agents of social construction, and show how they can become captives of their own rules and procedures in ways that make them repressive, ineffective, or even counterproductive.

CONSTRUCTIVIST ANALYSIS IN COMPARATIVE POLITICS

For a number of reasons, it is difficult to relate debates in comparative politics to the constructivist debates in IR. First, comparativists rarely use the term constructivism to refer to their own work, and when they do, they often mean something different from constructivism in IR (Fearon & Laitin 2000). Comparativists have tended to eschew the paradigm battle of the "isms" that has dominated IR, focusing instead on mid-level theoretical propositions for specific issue areas. Research in comparative politics tends to be driven by efforts to explain puzzles or questions rather than by the need to test a particular theoretical model. Scholars of comparative politics do not feel as compelled to maintain a consistent theoretical identity or to ensure that their work furthers a particular "ism" in the paradigm trench wars, and it is not at all unusual for a comparative scholar to work on different problems using different theoretical approaches (see, for example, the work of O'Donnell or Laitin). Second, the ideational concerns of the two subfields are on different levels of analysis. Cultural or ideological approaches were never absent from comparative politics, as they were absent from IR in the 1970s and 1980s, but these approaches focused on cultural and ideological forces in a particular country or region. Comparativists are often suspicious of, or less attentive to, arguments about the influence of international ideational and normative factors on domestic politics. Thus, they may resist the basic tenet of constructivism in IR that international-level ideational structures exercise a powerful force in the world creating similar global effects in many countries. Finally, comparativists have not had the same debates over method as IR scholars. Although comparativists have strived for conceptual clarity, refined comparative methods for case selection, and developed diverse and rigorous field research methods, many never embraced a strongly positivist model of social science. Many rely extensively on fieldwork and interpretive methods, which sit uneasily with the stricter positivist dictates of nonconstructivist IR.

The recent heated debate in comparative politics has been framed not as rationalism vs constructivism, as in IR, but as rational choice vs area studies. Sometimes the rational choice vs area studies division parallels the rationalism vs constructivism debate in IR, but often it does not. Issues of culture, language, and ideology have been present in some rational choice approaches to comparative politics (Laitin 1986, 1998), whereas many area studies scholars stress economic factors more than ideological or cultural ones. Other aspects of comparative politics scholarship display similar eclecticism. Two prominent "constructivist" critiques of comparative method were not written by comparative politics scholars at all but by a political theorist (McIntyre 1972) and an economist (Hirschman 1970). Other classic constructivist works that sometimes appear on comparative syllabi are likewise not by comparativists (Said 1979, Geertz 1980, Escobar 1984, Shapiro 1988).

When we look for constructivists in comparative politics, we find instead more eclectic scholars who at times make compelling arguments about discourses, language, ideas, culture, or knowledge relevant to specific thematic areas. Most of the comparative scholars who work on these issues are what Hasenclever et al (1997) would call weak cognitivists—although they focus on the independent role of ideas and knowledge, they often see their theories as complementing rather than supplanting interest-based theories. Below, we briefly explore four areas of comparative politics where such weak cognitivist arguments have been prevalent: the ideas literature, especially its treatment of the role of ideas in economic policy making; the political culture literature; the debates over the rise and role of social movements; and the literature on identities, especially national and ethnic identities.

Ideas and Political Change

Perhaps the most developed of these cognitivist literatures has been the ideas literature, used especially in the subfield of comparative political economy to explain the influence of economic ideas on economic policy making (Hall 1989, 1993, 1997; Sikkink 1991; Jacobson 1995; Blyth 1997; Berman 1998, 2001; McNamara 1998). The ideas literature echoes the first central tenet of constructivism on the importance of ideas and asks three main questions (Berman 2001, Sikkink 1991): (*a*) How do new ideas emerge and rise to prominence? (*b*) How do ideas become institutionalized and take on a life of their own? (*c*) How, why, and when do ideas matter in any particular circumstance? In answering the first question, this literature explicitly contests the common explanation in comparative politics that new ideas are imposed by those with political, military, or economic power. It stresses instead processes of learning in situations characterized by complexity, failure, anomaly, and new information. Heclo sums up the essence of such an approach: "Governments not only power. . .they also puzzle" (1974:305).

Learning approaches understand humans as engaged in reasoning and processing new information from the environment in an attempt to make sense of their world. The units of analysis in such work may be the individual, the community of individuals sharing common ideas, or the institutions in which ideas become embodied. The ideas literature is interested in the processes by which ideas initially held by a small number of individuals (such as a small school of economists) become widely held (intersubjective). Some of the ideas literature also stresses the third central tenet of constructivism: The interests of actors are constructed by these shared ideas rather than given by nature (Hall 1989, Sikkink 1991).

Comparative authors writing about ideas are in dialogue with IR literatures, but they tend to cite the "weak cognitivist" literature in IR, such as Goldstein & Keohane (1993) or Haas's (1992) work on epistemic communities, rather than the constructivist writers discussed above. The comparative literature on ideas has more in common with this IR literature; both emphasize the role of ideas in facilitating action in situations of complexity or providing focal points around which political coalitions can form (Goldstein & Keohane 1993). When they explain why some ideas win out over others, these literatures tend to emphasize neither the constitutive power of ideas nor an idea's intrinsic force, but rather its ability to clarify uncertainty or reconcile the interests of elites (Jacobson 1995). As a consequence, the ideas literature has been criticized by scholars who argue that it does not offer an alternative to the dominant rationalist perspective, but only ad hoc modifications of it (Blyth 1997, Laffey & Weldes 1997).

Authors who use an ideas approach have pointed out that new ideas often emerge in response to dramatic policy shocks, failures, or crises, where past policies have failed to resolve problems, leading to a search for new conceptions on which to base new policies (Odell 1982, Kowert & Legro 1996). This relationship between crisis and failure and the adoption of new ideas has been found in a number of different countries and time periods. The two types of crisis or failure most often mentioned are major depressions and war. But a failure argument alone is insufficient. Failure may explain why old ideas lose influence, but they do not explain the content of new models that are adopted. McNamara (1998) explains the adoption of monetary policies in the European Union based on three factors: policy failure, policy paradigm innovation, and policy emulation. In thinking about why people adopt new ideas, a useful supplement to the simple notions of failure or success is Hall's (1989) notion of persuasiveness. What makes an idea persuasive is the way the idea relates to the economic and political problems of the day. Both success and failure are interpreted in terms of what are perceived as the most pressing problems facing a country at a particular time.

Another explanation for the influence of new ideas focuses on a Kuhnian argument about the accumulation of anomalies—i.e. outcomes that do not fit the expectations induced by the existing paradigm. Rather than dramatic failure or crises, the anomaly argument suggests that it is the accumulation of small discrepancies that cannot be explained with the old model that eventually leads to the adoption of new ideas (Hall 1993, Sikkink 1997).

Comparativists have also pointed out that the strength and continuity of new ideas often depends on the degree to which they become embodied in institutions, and an important part of the ideas literature explores how ideas become institutionalized and what difference it makes. The ideas that are successfully implemented and consolidated are those that have been instilled within an institutional home, where a team of like-minded people transform their individual ideas into institutional purpose (Adler 1987, Hall 1997, Berman 1998, McNamara 1998, Sikkink 1991). Many of these institutions are state institutions, but institutions outside the state, including universities, labor unions, and political parties (Berman 1998), have also played important roles in the transmission and continuity of policy ideas. Differences in how new ideas fit existing institutions can help explain divergent policy responses (Skocpol & Weir 1985, Hall 1993). Finally, in order to be internalized, new ideas need not only to be institutionalized, but also to fit or be congruent with historically formed ideologies or the structure of political discourse of a nation (Hall 1989). This line of argument has obvious complementarities with the work of IR constructivists on the role of organizations in social construction.

A related literature in comparative politics in the "learning" literature, which has focused in particular on political learning and redemocratization. This literature draws more explicity on the social psychological studies to argue that learning and the internalization of new attitudes and behavior are an important source of political change. Like the ideas literature, it argues that crisis or trauma, such as those caused by intense repression, can lead actors to reject their previous attitudes supporting authoritarianism and develop attitudes supporting democracy. The mechanisms that lead to learning include interaction (with domestic and international actors), comparison (with prior national experiences and with other countries' experiences), reflection (including internal debates and self-criticism), and personnel change (Bermeo 1992, McCoy 2000).

Political Culture

The concept of political culture has been a staple of the comparative politics literature since the 1960s (Turner 1995). One of the two main variants of modernization theory offered a strong cultural account of underdevelopment, arguing that many less developed countries lacked the elements of political culture required for democracy to flourish (Lipset 1967, Silvert 1967, Wiarda 1982). It stressed (without using the words) that culture constructed the individual and that cultural elements created the possibility (or the impossibility) for particular types of political institutions to flourish or even survive (compare Thomas et al 1987 for a theoretically similar argument in an explicitly constructivist mode). This version of modernization theory was criticized, both for ethnocentrism and for its inability to explain the diversity of development paths followed by the West and the less developed world. It further implied that individuals are virtual prisoners of their culture. This powerful critique of an all-encompassing cultural account of development may have had the side effect of discrediting strong cultural accounts in comparative politics.

Some would claim that the political culture theorists in comparative politics are doing something quite different from constructivists in IR, but this literature clearly fits the two core tenets of constructivism better than the ideas literature. Here culture is seen as the primary explanation for change, it is clearly intersubjective, and it has real constitutive force. Wildavsky (1989), for example, argues that "culture constitutes one's political self." IR scholars, in their enthusiasm for concepts of culture and socialization, could find a cautionary tale in the political culture literature—both the controversies it generated and the difficulties it encountered with definitions, operationalization, and research design.

More recent arguments about political culture in comparative politics include work by Inglehart (1988, 1990, 1997), Laitin (1998), and Putnam (1993). All offer powerful arguments about the importance of political culture, but in each case, culture is ultimately an intervening variable rather than the primary explanation. Inglehart (1990) argued that a particular stage of development in advanced industrial countries leads to a "culture shift" to a set of "post-materialist" values, which in turn explains key aspects of politics. More recently (Inglehart 1997), he has updated and expanded this argument, using data from the World Values Surveys, to claim that industrialization and economic development throughout the world are leading to cultural change and political change. To Inglehart, values play the crucial intervening variable role but are not constitutive.

The recent political culture arguments do not stress the intrinsic power of particular cultural beliefs to explain their influence and wide acceptance. Inglehart (1997) argues that certain cultural characteristics survive and spread because they serve functional purposes in particular settings. Post-materialist values would not appear in poor contries because they would undermine development (Inglehart 1997; also see Berman 2001). Anderson's (1990) critique of Inglehart, using data from peasants in Costa Rica and Nicaragua, argues that culture has more of an independent effect, claiming that post-materialist values are present in societies that have not attained high levels of development. Putnam sees social capital, and a particular culture of trust, as the result of centuries of association (1993). Once again, the independent variable is association—people joining groups—which leads to social capital and a culture of trust, which in turn contributes to making democracy work and to economic development.

Social Movement Theory

Another subfield of comparative politics that has developed a debate about what we could call constructivism is social movement theory. The debate in social movement theory between the resources mobilization school, political opportunity structures approaches, and the new social movement perspective reflected some aspects of the debate between rational choice and constructivist approaches to comparative politics. Resource mobilization theories, originally dominant in the United States, stressed strategy, organization, rationality, expectation, and interests. Political opportunity structure approaches explored social movements operating within a structure of constraints and opportunities that made their survival and success more or less likely. The new social movement approach, dominant in Europe and Latin America, emphasized that collective identities were as essential for understanding the emergence and actions of social movements (Escobar & Alvarez 1992). This debate was summed up as "strategy vs. identity" (Cohen 1985) and came to be understood as a debate over whether social movement actors were mainly driven by a need to express their identity or mainly driven by more strategic concerns of where and when they could win.

For a few years, the social movement literature was characterized by a clash of paradigms, as proponents of resource mobilization, political opportunity structure, or new social movements approaches struggled for dominance. But like other debates in comparative politics, the clarity of this debate (strategy versus identity) did not last long, and the modern social movement scholar tends to be theoretically eclectic. Identity proponents recognized that they may have prematurely celebrated new identities while tending to neglect the constraints that movements faced (Escobar & Alvarez 1992). Strategy proponents realized that they were often puzzled by the emergence of a wide range of new identity-based movements. Many scholars argued for theoretical synthesis and cross-pollination, and such efforts are well under way. European, US, and Latin American scholars are currently integrating propositions from various models to determine not which model is superior, but rather which concepts are useful for understanding particular aspects and stages of social movements (Escobar & Alvarez 1992, Starn 1992, McAdam et al 1996, Klandermans 1997).

Whereas IR theorists talk of norms, social movement theorists tend to talk of collective or shared beliefs. Social movement theorists have long been preoccupied with the process of meaning creation, and in the 1990s, "the social construction of meaning [became] a central part of social movement theory" (Klandermans 1997). Movements help to create and recreate meanings through "framing" or "the conscious strategic efforts by groups of people to fashion shared understandings of the world and of themselves that legitimate and motivate collective action" (McAdam et al 1996:6) Social movements turn new ideas into frames that define the issues at stake and the appropriate strategies for action. Framing occurs not only through what movements say but also through what they do—through their choices of tactics and the connections between their actions and their rhetoric (McAdam et al 1996). Movements then use these frames to attempt the "mobilization of consensus," that is, communication intended to persuade others to take their side (Klandermans 1997). Because of the proliferation of transnational social movements, this is one area where there has been some fruitful theoretical exchange between IR scholars and comparativists [Tarrow 2001 (Chapter 1 of this volume), Smith et al 1997].

Identity and Ethnicity

Anderson's *Imagined Communities* (1983) is a premier example of constructivist theorizing by a comparativist. Anderson argues that all communities larger than primordial villages are imagined, and thus are to be distinguished "not by their falsity or genuineness, but by the style in which they are imagined." For Anderson, the rise of national identity is closely linked to the expansion of capitalism, the rise of printing, and the use of vernacular languages, but once the community is imagined, it takes on a powerful life of its own.

Others, working in the related area of the ethnic identities, also point to the constructed and imagined nature of ethnic identity. But once again, this literature takes a different slant from the debates in IR between rationalists and constructivists. Indeed, the main debate over identity in comparative politics is not whether identity matters (this is the IR debate) but whether identity is inherited like skin color (primordialism) or is, in Laitin's (1998) words, constructed like an art object. In this schema, Geertz, whom most IR theorists would consider a constructivist, is sometimes classified as a primordialist, because he assumes that culture and symbols are powerful and unchanging influences on life. Laitin, who is identified with rational choice theory, calls himself a constructivist because he argues that identities are socially constructed. These scholars argue that it is fully consistent to believe that identities are socially constructed but that actors may make rational choices about how to construct their identities.

In *Politics, Language, and Thought: The Somali Experience* (1977), Laitin underscored the power of language to construct political identities and action. A change in the official language led Somalis to change the ways they thought and acted politically. In *Hegemony and Culture* (1986), however, Laitin argued that religious change among the Yoruba, contrary to what Weber or Geertz might lead us to expect, did not lead to adjustments in social and political behavior. Laitin claimed that both religion and tribe were potential identities that could be the basis for collective action, and he explored the conditions under which a particular cultural divide in a society is seen as deeper or more important for collective action than another. He joined together an interpretive account of culture, a rational actor approach, and a "neo-positivist" method aimed at providing both contextual understanding and the possibility for falsification. *Identity in Formation: The Russian Speaking Populations in the Near Abroad* (Laitin 1998) continues this project of uniting constructivism with rational choice. According to Laitin (1998:12), "construction and choice, rather than blood and inheritance, is now the standard line about identities." This blurs the distinctions used in IR, where the distinction is construction versus choice, not construction and choice versus blood and inheritance. For comparativists in this tradition, if identities are constructed, this implies that actors have choices about identities and might use rational calculations in constructing their identities. Identities, in this view, have a dual nature: They appear natural to members of groups even as individuals engage in projects of identity construction (Laitin 1998). This literature argues that actors construct or choose these identities from a menu of existing choices. The menu is historically and culturally constructed, but individuals choose rationally from the items that are on the menu at any given point.

POSSIBILITIES FOR FRUITFUL CROSS-FERTILIZATION

Although there has not yet been extensive contact between comparativistis and IR scholars, there are a number of avenues for promising cross-fertilization. Comparativists have long pursued building mid-level theory similar to what Price & Reus-Smit (1998) call small-t theoretical generalizations. Since these generalizations are now increasingly the object of much modern constructivist theorizing, there may be less mismatch between the macro theorizing in IR and mid-level theory in comparative politics.

Second, the processes of globalization have made even the most passionate country specialists aware of the increasing influence of international factors, both material and ideational, on domestic politics around the globe. Comparativists are becoming increasingly attentive to the interpenetration of international affairs and domestic politics (Putnam 1988, Whitehead 1996). For example, social movement theorists now realize that they need to be attentive not only to domestic social movements but also to transnational social movements and to the linkages between domestic and transnational movements. Social movement theorists are increasingly aware that social movements operate in both a domestic and an international environment; they speak of "multi-layered" opportunity structure including a "supranational" layer, or a "multi-level polity," or highlight how international pressures influence domestic opportunity structures (McAdams et al 1996, Klandermans 1997, Tarrow 2001). One area for future fruitful exchange between ideational scholars of comparative politics and IR is to conceptualize theories of how domestic and transnational political opportunity structures might interact with one other in a continuous manner and what characteristic patterns would result.

At the same time, IR scholars with comparative training have made compelling arguments that a better understanding of domestic political and ideational structures is a necessary precondition to furthering constructivist theorizing about when and why international norms and cultures influence specific domestic settings (Risse-Kappen 1995; Katzenstein 1996a,b; Checkel 1997, 1998). To further this agenda, they will increasingly engage in comparative politics research and in dialogues with comparative scholars.

LITERATURE CITED

Adler E. 1987. *The Power of Ideology: The Quest for Technological Autonomy in Argentina and Brazil.* Berkeley: Univ. Calif. Press

Adler E. 1992. The emergence of cooperation: national epistemic communities and the international evolution of the idea of nuclear arms control. *Int. Org.* 46:101–45

Adler E. 1997. Seizing the middle ground: constructivism in world politics. *Eur. J. Int. Relat.* 3:319–63

Adler E. 1998. Seeds of peaceful change: the OSCE's security community–building model. In *Security Communities*, ed. E Adler, M Barnett, pp. 119–59. New York: Cambridge Univ. Press

Adler E, Barnett M. 1998. *Security Communities*. Cambridge, UK: Cambridge Univ. Press

Anderson B. 1983. *Imagined Communities: Reflections on the Origins and Spread of Nationalism.* London: Verso

Anderson L. 1990. Post-materialism from a peasant perspective: political motivation in Costa Rica and Nicaragua. *Comp. Polit.* 23:80–113

Barnett MN. 1996. Identity and alliances in the Middle East. See Katzenstein 1996a, pp. 400–47

Barnett MN. 1998. *Dialogues in Arab Politics*. New York: Columbia Univ. Press

Barnett MN, Finnemore M. 1999. The politics, power, and pathologies of international organizations. *Int. Org.* 53:699–732

Berger TU. 1996. Norms, identity and national security in Germany and Japan. See Katzenstein 1996a, pp. 317–56

Bergesen A, ed. 1980. *Studies of the Modern World-System* New York: Academic

Berman S. 1998. *The Social Democratic Moment: Ideas and Politics in the Making of Interwar Europe*. Cambridge, UK: Harvard Univ. Press

Berman S. 2001. Ideas, norms and culture in political analysis. *Comp. Polit.* In press

Bermeo N. 1992. Democracy and the lessons of dictatorship. *Comp. Polit.* 24:273–91

Blyth M. 1997. Any more bright ideas? *Comp. Polit.* 29:229–50

Boli J. 1987. Human rights or state expansion? Cross-national definitions of constitutional rights, 1870–1970. In *Institutional Structure: Constituting State, Society and the Individual*, ed. G Thomas, JW Meyer, FO Ramirez, J Boli, pp. 133–49. Newbury Park, CA: Sage

Boli J, Thomas GM, eds. 1998. *Constructing World Culture: International Nongovernmental Organizations Since 1875.* Stanford: Stanford Univ. Press

Bukovansky M. 2001. *Ideas and Power Politics: The American and French Revolutions in International Political Culture*. Princeton, NJ: Princeton Univ. Press

Burley AM, Mattli W. 1993. Europe before the court: a political theory of legal integration. *Int. Org.* 47:41–76

Checkel JT. 1997. International norms and domestic politics: bridging the rationalist-constructivist divide. *Eur. J. Int. Relat.* 3:473–95

Checkel JT. 1998. The constructivist turn in international relations theory. *World Polit.* 50:324–48

Checkel JT. 2001. Why comply? Social learning and European identity change. *Int. Org.* forthcoming

Cohen J. 1985. Strategy or identity: new theoretical paradigms and contemporary social movements. *Soc. Res.* 52:663–716

Crawford N. 1993. Decolonization as an international norm: the evolution of practices, arguments, and beliefs. In *Emerging Norms of Justified Intervention*, ed. L Reed, C Kaysen, pp. 37–61. Cambridge, MA: Am. Acad. Arts Sci.

Crawford N. 2000. The passion of world politics. *Int. Sec.* 24:116–56

Doty RL. 1996. *Imperial Encounters.* Minneapolis: Univ. Minn. Press

Escobar A. 1984. Discourse and power in development: Michel Foucault and the relevance of his work to the Third World. *Alternatives* 10:377–400

Escobar A, Alvarez S, eds. 1992. *The Making of Social Movements in Latin America: Identity, Strategy, and Democracy.* Boulder, CO: Westview

Fearon J, Laitin D. 2000. Violence and the social construction of ethnic identity. *Int. Org.* 54:845–77

Ferguson J. 1990. *The Anti-Politics Machine: Development, Depolitization, and Bureaucratic Power in Lesotho.* New York: Cambridge Univ. Press

Finnemore M. 1993. International organizations as teachers of norms: the United Nations educational, scientific, and cultural organization and science policy. *Int. Org.* 47:565–97

Finnemore M. 1996a. *National Interests in International Society.* Ithaca, NY: Cornell Univ. Press

Finnemore M. 1996b. Norms, culture, and world politics: insights from sociology's institutionalism. *Int. Org.* 50:325–47

Geertz C. 1980. *Negara: The Theater-State in 19th Century Bali.* Princeton, NJ: Princeton Univ. Press

Goldstein J, Keohane RO, eds. 1993. *Ideas and Foreign Policy: Beliefs, Institutions and Political Change.* Ithaca, NY: Cornell Univ. Press

Gurowitz A. 1999. Mobilizing international noms: domestic actors, immigrants, and the Japanese state. *World Polit.* 51:413–45

Haas P. 1989. Do regimes matter? Epistemic communities and Mediterranean pollution control. *Int. Org.* 43:377–405

Haas P, ed. 1992. Knowledge, power, and international policy coordination. *Int. Org.* 46 (spec. issue)

Hall PA. 1989. Conclusion: the politics of Keynesian ideas. In *The Political Power of Economic Ideas*, ed. P Hall, pp. 351–91. Princeton, NJ: Princeton Univ. Press

Hall PA. 1993. Policy paradigms, social learning, and the state. *Com. Polit.* 25:275–96

Hall PA. 1997. The role of interests, institutions, and ideas in the comparative political economy of the industrialized nations. In *Comparative Politics: Rationality, Culture, and Structure*, ed. M Lichbach, A Zuckerman, pp. 174–207 New York: Cambridge Univ. Press

Hasenclever A, Mayer P, Rittberger V. 1997. *Theories of International Regimes.* Cambridge, UK: Cambridge Univ. Press

Heclo H. 1974. *Modern Social Policies in Britain and Sweden.* New Haven, CT: Yale Univ. Press

Hirschman AO. 1970. The search for paradigms as a hindrance to understanding. *World Polit.* 22:329–43

Inglehart R. 1988. The renaissance of political culture. *Am. Polit. Sci. Rev.* 82:1203–30

Inglehart R. 1990. *Culture Shift in Advanced Industrial Society.* Princeton, NJ: Princeton Univ. Press

Inglehart R. 1997. *Modernization and Postmodernization: Cultural, Economic, and Political Change in 43 Societies.* Princeton, NJ: Princeton Univ. Press

Jacobson JK. 1995. Much ado about ideas: the cognitive factor in economic policy. *World Polit.* 47:283–310

Katzenstein PJ, ed. 1996a. *The Culture of National Security Norms and Identity in World Politics.* New York: Columbia Univ. Press

Katzenstein PJ. 1996b. *Cultural Norms and National Security Police and Military in Postwar Japan.* Ithaca, NY: Cornell Univ. Press

Katzenstein PJ, Keohane RO, Krasner SD, eds. 1999. *Exploration and Contestation in the Study of World Politics.* Cambridge, MA: MIT Press

Kaufmann C, Pape R. 1999. Explaining costly international moral action: Britain's sixty-year campaign against the Atlantic slave trade. *Int. Org.* 53:631–68

Keck M, Sikkink K. 1998. *Activists Beyond*

Borders: Advocacy Networks in International Politics. Ithaca, NY: Cornell Univ. Press

Keeley J. 1990. Toward a Foucauldian analysis of international regimes. *Int. Org.* 44:83–105

Keohane RO. 1988. International institutions: two approaches. *Int. Stud. Q.* 32:379–96

Klandermans B. 1997. *The Social Psychology of Protest*. Oxford, UK: Blackwell

Klotz A. 1995. *Norms in International Relations: The Struggle against Apartheid*. Ithaca, NY: Cornell Univ. Press

Kowert P, Legro J. 1996. Norms, identity, and their limits: a theoretical reprise. See Katzenstein 1996a, pp. 451–97

Kratochwil F. 1989. *Rules, Norms, and Decisions: On the Conditions of Practical and Legal Reasoning in International Relations and Domestic Affairs*. Cambridge, UK: Cambridge Univ. Press

Laffey M, Weldes J. 1997. Beyond belief: ideas and symbolic technologies in the study of international relations. *Eur. J. Int. Relat.* 3:193–237

Latin D. 1977. *Politics, Language and Thought: The Somali Experience*. Chicago: Univ. Chicago Press

Laitin D. 1986. *Hegemony and Culture: Politics and Religious Change among the Yoruba*. Chicago: Chicago Univ. Press

Laitin D. 1998. *Identity in Formation: The Russian Speaking Populations of the Near Abroad*. Ithaca, NY: Cornell Univ. Press

Lipset S. 1967. Values, education, and entrepreneurship. In *Elites in Latin America*, ed. S Lipset, A Solari, pp. 3–60. New York: Oxford Univ. Press

Lumsdaine D. 1993. *Moral Vision: The Foreign Aid Regime 1949–1989*. Princeton, NJ: Princeton Univ. Press

McAdam D, McCarthy JD, Zald MN, eds. 1996. *Comparative Perspectives on Social Movements: Political Opportunities, Mobilizing Structures, and Cultural Framings*. New York: Cambridge Univ. Press

McCoy J, ed. 2000. *Political Learning and Redemocratization in Latin America: Do Politicians Learn from Political Crises?* Miami, FL: North-South Ctr.

McIntyre A. 1972. Is a science of comparative politics possible? In *Philosophy, Politics, and Society*, ed. P Laslett, WG Runciman, Q Skinner, pp. 8–26. Oxford, UK: Blackwell

McNamara K. 1998. *The Currency of Ideas: Monetary Politics in the European Union*. Ithaca, NY: Cornell Univ. Press

Mendelson S, Glenn J. 2000. Democracy assistance and NGO strategies in post-communist societies. Work. Pap. No. 8, Carnegie Endowment for International Peace, Feb. 2000

Meyer JW, Boli J, Thomas GM. 1987. Ontology and rationalization in the Western cultural account. In *Institutional Structure: Constituting State, Society, and the Individual*, ed. G Thomas, JW Meyer, FO Ramirez, J Boli, pp. 12–37. Newbury Park, CA: Sage

Meyer JW, Boli J, Thomas GM, Ramirez FO. 1997. World society and the nation state. *Amer. J. Sociol.* 103:144–81

Meyer JW, Hannan MT, eds. 1979. *National Development and the World-System: Educational, Economic and Political Change, 1950–1970*. Chicago: Univ. Chicago Press

Meyer JW, Ramirez FO, Soysal Y. 1992. World expansion of mass education, 1870–1980. *Soc. Ed.* 65:128–49

Nadelman E. 1990. Global prohibition regimes: the evolution of norms in international society. *Int. Org.* 40:479–526

Odell J. 1982. *U.S. International Monetary Policy: Markets, Power, and Ideas as Sources of Change*. Princeton, NJ: Princeton Univ. Press

Price R. 1995. A genealogy of the chemical weapons taboo. *Int. Org.* 49:73–104

Price R. 1997. *The Chemical Weapons Taboo*. Ithaca, NY: Cornell Univ. Press

Price R, Reus-Smit C. 1998. Dangerous liaisons? Critical international relations theory and constructivism. *Eur. J. Int. Relat.* 4:259–94

Putnam R. 1988. Diplomacy and domestic politics: the logic of two-level games. *Int. Org.* 42:427–60

Putnam R. 1993. *Making Democracy Work:*

Civil Traditions in Modern Italy. Princeton, NJ: Princeton Univ. Press

Ramirez FO, Soysal Y, Shanahan S. 1997. The changing logic of political citizenship: crossnational acquisition of women's suffrage rights, 1890–1990. *Am. Sociol. Rev.* 62:735–45

Ratner SR. 2000. Does international law matter in preventing ethnic conflict? *J. Int. Law Polit.* 32:591–698

Reus-Smit C. 1999. *The Moral Purpose of the State: Culture, Social Identity, and Institutional Rationality in International Relations*. Princeton, NJ: Princeton Univ. Press

Risse T. 2000. "Let's argue!": Communicative action in world politics. *Int. Org.* 54:1–40

Risse T, Ropp S, Sikkink K, eds. 1999. *The Power of Human Rights: International Norms and Domestic Change*. Cambridge, UK: Cambridge Univ. Press

Risse-Kappen T, ed. 1995. *Bringing Transnational Relations Back In: Non-State Actors, Domestic Structures, and International Institutions*. New York: Cambridge Univ. Press

Risse-Kappen T. 1996. Collective identity in a democratic community: the case of NATO. See Katzenstein 1996a, pp. 357–99

Ruggie JG. 1998. What makes the world hang together? Neo-utilitarianism and the social constructivist challenge. *Int. Org.* 52:855–87

Said E. 1979. *Orientalism*. New York: Vintage

Searle J. 1995. *The Construction of Social Reality*. New York: Free

Seuss D. 1970. *Bartholomew and the Oobleck*. New York: Random House

Shapiro MJ. 1988. *The Politics of Representation*. Madison: Univ. Wisc. Press

Sikkink K. 1991. *Ideas and Institutions: Developmentalism in Brazil and Argentina*. Ithaca, NY: Cornell Univ. Press

Sikkink K. 1997. Development ideas in Latin America: paradigm shift and and the Economic Commission for Latin America. In *International Development and the Social Sciences: Essays on the History and Politics of Knowledge*, ed. F Cooper, R Packard, pp. 228–56. Berkeley: Univ. Calif. Press

Silvert K. 1967. The politics of social and economic change in Latin America. *Sociol. Rev. Mon.* 11:47–58

Skocpol T, Weir M. 1985. State structures and the possibilities for Keynesian responses to the depression in Sweden, Britain, and the United States. In *Bringing the State Back In*, ed. P Evans, D Rueschemeyer, T Skocpol, pp. 107–63. Cambridge, UK: Cambridge Univ. Press

Smith J, Chatfield C, Pagnucco R, eds. 1997. *Transnational Social Movements and Global Politics*. Syracuse, NY: Syracuse Univ. Press

Starn O. 1992. "I dreamed of foxes and hawks": reflections on peasant protest, new social movements, and the Rondas Campesinas of Northern Peru. See Escobar & Alvarez 1992, pp. 89–111

Strang D. 1991. Anomaly and commonplace in European political expansion: realist and institutionalist accounts. *Int. Org.* 45:143–62

Tarrow S. 2001. Transnational politics: contention and institutions in international politics. *Annu. Rev. Polit. Sci.* 4:1–20

Thomas D. 2001. *The Helsinki Effect: International Norms, Human Rights, and the Demise of Communism*. Princeton, NJ: Princeton Univ. Press

Thomas GM, Meyer JW, Ramirez FO, Boli J, eds. 1987. *Institutional Structure: Constituting State, Society and the Individual*. Newbury Park, CA: Sage

Turner FC. 1995. Reassessing political culture. In *Latin America in Comparative Perspective*, ed. PH Smith, pp. 195–224. Boulder, CO: Westview

Wapner P. 1996. *Environmental Activism and World Civic Culture*. Albany: State Univ. NY Press

Weber C. 1999. *Faking It: U. S. Hegemony in a "Post-Phallic" Era*. Minneapolis: Univ. Minn. Press

Weldes J. 1996. *Constructing National Interests: The United States and the Cuban Missile Crisis*. Minneapolis: Univ. Minn. Press

Weldes J, Laffey M, Gusterson H, eds. 1999. *Cultures of Insecurity: States, Communities, and the Production of Danger*. Minneapolis: Univ. Minn. Press

Wendt A. 1987. The agent-structure problem in international relations theory. *Int. Org.* 41:335–70

Wendt A. 1992. Anarchy is what states make of it. *Int. Org.* 46:391–425

Wendt A. 1994. Collective identity formation and the international state. *Am. Polit. Sci. Rev.* 88:384–96

Wendt A. 1998. Constitution and causation in international relations. *Rev. Int. Stud.* 24:101–17

Wendt A. 1999. *Social Theory of International Relations*. Cambridge, UK: Cambridge Univ. Press

Whitehead L. 1996. Three international dimensions of democratization. In *The International Dimensions of Democratization: Europe and the Americas*, ed. L Whitehead, pp. 3–25. Oxford, UK: Oxford Univ. Press

Wiarda H. 1982. Social change, political development and the Latin American tradition. In *Politics and Social Change in Latin America: The Distinct Tradition*, ed. H Wiarda, pp. 3–25. Amherst, MA: Univ. Massachusetts Press. 2nd ed.

Wildavsky A. 1989. Choosing preferences by constructing institutions: a cultural theory of preference formation. In *Political Culture and Public Opinion*, ed. AA Berger, pp. 21–46 New Brunswick, NJ: Transaction

Annu. Rev. Polit. Sci. 2001. 4:417–38

VIACRATIC AMERICA: *Plessy* on Foot v. *Brown* on Wheels

Douglas W. Rae
School of Management and Department of Political Science, Yale University, New Haven, Connecticut 06520; e-mail: douglas.rae@yale.edu

Key Words race, technology, segregation, urban, suburban, social history

■ **Abstract** The United States has undergone a profound spatial reorganization over the course of the twentieth century, and it influences the working of democratic and judicial institutions profoundly. The critical feature is differential access to transportation and place, and the major instrument is of course the automobile. Other technologies—the AC electric grid most fundamental among them—have allowed a finer and finer sorting of the population into relatively homogeneous income strata. The failure of *Brown v. Board of Education* (1954) is a leading example of this phenomenon. The trivialization of local politics—when resources are separated from needs in a region—is another.

INTRODUCTION

If we ask what were the most consequential public decisions undertaken at the last turning of a century in America, *Plessy v. Ferguson* (1896) seems a strong candidate, confirming as it did the separate-but-equal scheme of racial apartheid forged by slavery, challenged briefly by reconstruction, and affirmed by reconstruction's dramatic failure. *Plessy* set the target for mid-twentieth-century civil rights activism, in the courts if not the streets. It was, after all, the vital legitimation of race-driven governance against which so much effort would be expended by the National Association for the Advancement of Colored People (NAACP) from its 1909 founding through its apparent success in *Brown v. Board of Education* (1954). Here is Friedman's (1973) telling of that story, still infused by measured optimism about the efficacy of the landmark decision:

> After 1940, the changing attitude of the Supreme Court toward black litigants became very marked. At first, the constitutional war on racism achieved only incremental results. In a series of cases, the Supreme Court declared this or that situation or practice (segregated law schools, for example) unconstitutional; but it did not want to reach the ultimate issue: whether segregation under the fig leaf of "separate but equal" doctrine had

> any warrant in law at all. The NAACP pushed and pulled; the Court was a reluctant bridegroom. Its decisions were clearly compromises: the blacks won, most of the time, in each particular case; on the other hand, the larger issue was avoided. . . . The Court came closer to the heart of segregation in *Shelley v. Kraemer* (1948). This struck down, as unenforceable, land covenants that forbade sale or rental of property to blacks. But the climax of the long struggle for equality was "black Monday," in 1954, when the Court handed down the case of *Brown v. Board of Education*. This was surely the most momentous of all Supreme Court decisions. . . . The *Brown* case ordered an end to segregated schools. To be sure, even today most blacks, North and South, go to schools which are totally black, or almost so. Nonetheless *Brown* had an enormous impact, not least of all on the schools. It sounded the death knell of *Plessy v. Ferguson*, though at first only by indirection. Later cases made the Supreme Court's meaning abundantly clear. No form of segregation was permissible.

At the twenty-first century's dawning, the very limited efficacy of *Brown* and its companion cases is clear. The difference between segregation de jure and segregation de facto owes its strategic centrality to another set of innovations dating from the same era as *Plessy*. At that time, the United States was organized primarily around what now seem relatively limited powers of movement (*Plessy* was, after all, about railroad seating). One could move with speed between fixed points such as rail stations, but one then entered a world of shoe leather, trolleys, and slow travel within local society. This combination of good long-distance transportation over a fixed-path grid of terminals and weak local transport over variable paths to specific destinations tended to strengthen and center local communities—and to narrow the difference between de jure and de facto outcomes in matters of segregation.

By the time *Brown* reached its conclusion half a century later, the country was organized around rapid movement. By rail or air, even by highway, one moved quickly across long distances. And, critically, within the local context of everyday life, one now moved rapidly over a variable-path grid between home and office, work and school, cultural event and shopping mall. In matters ranging from education to property rights, from risk of criminal assault to opportunities for employment, the kinetics of daily life had become overwhelmingly important to the real structure of national governance. The resulting "viacratic" regime offers highly developed spatial mobility on a selective basis, creating a politico-economic order in which access to place becomes a decisive instrument for the creation and perpetuation of advantage.

Although the evolution of viacratic regimes is national in scope, its realization is repeated in localized regions across the continent. I thus speak of the generic viacratic regime as a national template and of particular regional cases as its applications. There are important differences among regions, but the general American case is powerfully viacratic. This means it offers disproportionate leverage to people and institutions with the power to choose among places, and as a result, powerful sorting and homogenizing tendencies with respect to race and class. Such a regime did not exist at the time of *Plessy* and was approaching maturity by the time of *Brown*.[1] It may not be too much to suggest that the segregating powers of *Plessy* before the rise and maturation of viacratic life are inferior to those of *Brown* after its arrival. It is now, at century's end, a mature system demanding the attention of scholars and citizens who would seek to promote—even merely to understand at the level of practice—the possibilities of a democratic society.

The change came with remarkable swiftness, starting in the same era as the *Plessy* decision. In 1893, Karl Benz demonstrated his first four-wheel auto (he had begun with three-wheelers), and Henry Ford demonstrated his prototype for a cheap, gasoline-fueled, internal combustion engine. In 1899, William McKinley became the first US President to ride in an automobile, a Stanley Steamer. The Olds Company initiated mass production of cars by rolling out 400 copies of the same vehicle in 1901. By 1913, when the maturation of Ford's rolling assembly process had made the Model T accessible to middle-income buyers, the basis for a new regime of national governance was launched. In 1909, Ford charged $950 for each of the 12,292 Model Ts sold; by 1916, the company had captured world-historic economies of scale in mass manufacturing. The firm dropped its price to $390 and sold a remarkable 577,036 copies of the same design that year (Hounshell 1984:224).The critical efficiency was achieved in labor hours per car, which fell from 1260 in 1912 to 533 in 1915 (and to 228 by 1923). Instead of building cars standing in place, Ford began to build them as they rolled (or were carried mechanically) from work station to work station in an assembly line. The stupendous economies in assembly cost yielded lower retail prices and a vast increase in unit sales. The yearly totals shot up from about 14,000 Model Ts in 1909–1910 to 785,000 of them in 1916–1917 (see especially Biggs 1996).

This in turn provided an incentive for the rapid expansion of oil drilling and refining, created a national constituency for the Highway Act of 1921, and kick-started scores of car-related industries ranging from rubber manufacturing to automotive glass production. It also led, in time, to the formation of perhaps the most powerful of American labor unions, the United Auto Workers. By the middle decades of the twentieth century, capital's great lever of change was no longer the railroads but the automobile industry and its innumerable paved tentacles across the landscape (Paxton 1946). These are details in a larger movement, known to everyone yet ignored by most of us in the reading of political change, which I sketch in this paper. The automobile is its star, but a host of other innovations in energy technology—alternating current electricity, broadcasting, telephone, telegraph—comprise its supporting cast. The transformation depends on an inegalitarian income distribution and a succession of federal policies on housing that accentuate the resulting inequalities of access to movement and place. The joint impact of these changes

[1]As is so often true, the seeds of a new order were sown earlier, in the form of streetcar suburbs, and were germinating at the time of *Plessy* (see Warner 1978, Stilgoe 1988, Fishman 1987).

is a regime of governance as different in its practical operation from the original American republic as the former was from, say, the monarchy of George III.

SOME ENABLING CONDITIONS OF VIACRATIC LIFE: A Short History of American Horsepower[2]

We begin with the year 1850, just after Marx had composed the first version of his evocative story of an urbanized working class organized around the satanic power of steam-driven factories—concentrated by the rigid technology in places where coal and steel could be joined to human muscle. Rail and ship brought materials to Manchester, Pittsburgh, Philadelphia, St. Louis, New Haven; the weakness and costliness of local transport kept plants close to the points at which ships and trains unloaded their cargoes, and housing for workers clustered closely around the plants. Beyond the direct muscle power of human beings—at something less than 0.1 horsepower (HP) per head—the total available energy in the US economy totaled roughly 8,495,000 HP in 1850 (*Historical Statistics*[3] 1975). Most of this power—5,960,000 HP or 70%—came from the direct force of work animals, mainly horses. Factories and mines, powered by steam and water mills, accounted for another 1,210,000 units (or 14% of the total.) The famed EI duPont munitions plant on Brandywine Creek in Delaware generated a total of just 500 HP when its water turbines reached full power in 1843—less than, say, a top-class drag racer today (Nye 1998:47). Railroads, powered by wood- and coal-fired steam, added 586,000 HP; sailing ships added 400,000 HP and steamships added 325,000 HP. The power available was stupendous by the standards of all previous centuries, with roughly one third horsepower available for every person in the country, although the totals were very modest in comparison to what would come over the next century.

Two other generalizations about the composition of this "power structure" can be carried away from these data:

1. A very high fraction of the total available force was produced by stationary (mines, factories) or slow-moving (work animals) sources. These immobile sources constitute 84.4% of the grand total.
2. All of the faster-paced power plants—aboard rail and steamship—were designed for fixed-path movement. By "fixed path" I mean that a train or

[2]One horsepower, for those who care, is the capacity to lift 550 pounds one foot in one second—no small accomplishment when repeated for hours and days! Put another way, 1 HP is the power to do 33,000 foot-pounds of work per minute. The unit of measure was thought up by steam engineer Thomas Watt, who sought to express the work powers of brewery horses as a means of comparing the powers of steam engines (see Petroski 1997:120).

[3]All other data prior to 1980 are from the same source. Data thereafter are from the parallel series in *US Statistical Abstracts*. To avoid double counting, the data count only "prime movers," i.e. the machines that first generate any given stream of power. Detailed horsepower estimates are available only through 1992.

ship would carry people and goods only along predetermined routes, with infrequent stops, typically between one urban node and another, and could not be expected to alter course in light of individual destinations. Both of these features would change sharply over the succeeding century.

By 1890—the day before yesterday as *Plessy* was being heard—a good deal had changed. Total available power had expanded to 44,086,000 HP, fivefold more than in 1850 in raw force, nearly double on a per capita basis.[4] Of this power, just over 57% came from immobile sources, leaving 47% to vehicular transport.[5] The economy of horsepower had thus grown in total and had become more mobile. But the growth in mobility was concentrated on fixed path modes of transport, since the major gainers in vehicular energy were the railroads (16,980,000 HP) and steamships (1,124,000 HP). The rate of growth here is remarkable: For every horsepower of rail service available in 1850, 29 HP were available 40 years later. This is a period in which the deployment of vehicular transport is strong across fixed paths and weak across variable paths, with large industrial concentrations arising at strategic points in the fixed-path grid defined by rail and steamship terminals. Increasing reliance on steam energy further tended to concentrate activity in small central zones of industrial activity. Figure 1, from the later date of 1934, shows one such concentration in New Haven, Connecticut.

These modes of powered movement—most of all rail—were vital in producing national markets and in providing a seedbed for the emergence of integrated joint stock corporations, such as Standard Oil, US Steel, the Pennsylvania Railroad, Armour packing, and McCormick reaper, that were capable of exercising market power on continental scale (see especially Chandler 1977). The horsepower generated by factories and mines expanded 600% between 1850 and 1890. The immense economic power of such production in turn led to an upward spiral of demand and generally declining real prices (prices stated in hours or days of ordinary labor, e.g. the hours of wage pay corresponding to the price of a loaf of bread or a cotton shirt), which in turn spurred further development of the transport system. The rail network had long since spanned the continent (the so-called Golden Spike had been pounded into the Utah desert by 1869), and total first-track mileage had increased from 9021 in 1850 to 166,703 in 1890 (*Historical Statistics* 1971, updated by *Historical Abstracts of the United States* each year since).[6] America was becoming a kinetic giant, if still a somewhat muscle-bound one better suited to the clumsy moves of rail than to the nimble moves of automobile and electric current.

Since 1890, the most fundamental change is the explosive growth of total horsepower, as is indicated by Table 1. In the early years of the twentieth century,

---

[4]Total US population had expanded from 23.2 million in 1850 (of whom 2.3 million were enslaved) to 62.9 million in 1890.

[5]The immobile power sources were as follows: work animals (15,970,000 HP), factories (6,308,000 HP), mines (1,445,000 HP), farm machinery (1,452,000 HP), and windmills (80,000).

[6]"First track" means that where two tracks run parallel, only one is counted in the mileage figure.

Figure 1 Fairchild Aerial Survey of New Haven harbor and rail, 1934. Note the convergence of heavy rail (running from lower left to upper right) meeting a switching yard (center) and linking to ocean shipping at the piers (upper right). The photo also shows the dense concentration of housing, mainly of the working class, concentrated near these facilities. Major manufacturers, such as New Haven Clock, Armstrong Tire and Rubber, and Sargent Hardware, provided the incentive for workers to live in this central location.

horsepower grew as if utterly without limit or constraint. Between *Plessy*'s decade and *Brown*'s decade, total horsepower would expand nearly 108:1, from 44,086,000 to 4,754,038,000 HP—almost certainly the greatest run of energy expansion in the history of any society, industrial or otherwise (the full century following 1890 produced a 790:1 change). On a per capita basis, the run from 44 million to 4.7 billion is diminished to a 44-to-1 upturn as population grew from about 62 million to nearly 151 million. But the expansion thus defined is dramatic indeed: The average (not to say typical) individual American in 1950 commanded about 30 HP,[7] whereas she or he had commanded a little less than 1 HP in 1890. This monumental rate of kinetic growth, continuing into the last years of the century at a diminished yet considerable rate, transformed the country.

A second line of development is equally important. Power was increasingly devoted to motion, and the fastest rate of conversion toward vehicular horsepower

[7] 30 HP corresponds exactly to the capacity of the smallest passenger car then on the market, namely the Volkswagen Beetle.

TABLE 1 Total horsepower in the US economy

Year	Total horsepower × 1000
1990	34,958,000
1980	28,922,000
1970	20,408,000
1960	11,007,889
1950	4,754,038
1940	2,773,316
1930	1,663,944
1920	453,450
1910	138,810
1900	63,952
1890	44,086
1880	26,314
1870	16,931
1860	13,763
1850	8,495

occurred in the *Plessy* to *Brown* decades. In 1850, 85% of all horsepower was stationary. Well under half of all horsepower was devoted to motion in 1890 (41.7% in Table 2). By 1950, more than 19 of every 20 units of horsepower were vehicular (95.9%, a level that has remained roughly static ever since). Given the 100-fold increase in the total, these are remarkable, even staggering, developments. The use of mechanical force for static production—for manufacturing in urban centers—had passed from overwhelming dominance to relative marginality in a society that put most of its horsepower behind the task of moving people and things rapidly and conveniently across space.

A third important line of change occurred within the vehicular stream of horsepower. The automobile developed from the risky idea of the 1890s into a dominant, institution-forming, regime-bending phenomenon by the 1950s. Its expansion has continued throughout the twentieth century and into the new millennium. Having accounted for nothing in 1890, the automotive family—mostly the car, with bus, truck, motorcycle, and taxi along for the ride—now commands 99% of all the horsepower devoted to vehicles. It is of course true that a Boeing 747 puts out plenty of horsepower, as does a Union Pacific diesel engine, but there just are not many of them compared with cars. In 1993, the United States registered 146.3 million passenger cars, along with nearly 50 million other motor vehicles. The cars logged 1624 billion miles, with trucks running up 656.6 billion miles in addition

TABLE 2 Changes in vehicular and automotive percentages of total horsepower

Year	Total horsepower × 1000	Vehicular as % of total HP	Automotive HP as % of vehicular HP
1990	34,958,000	95.6	99.0
1980	28,922,000	95.6	98.9
1970	20,408,000	96.0	98.7
1960	11,007,889	95.2	99.0
1950	4,754,038	95.9	96.6
1940	2,773,316	94.5	95.8
1930	1,663,944	93.1	92.1
1920	453,450	81.1	76.4
1910	138,810	57.1	31.1
1900	63,952	41.5	0.4
1890	44,086	41.7	0.0
1880	26,314	36.7	0.0
1870	16,931	31.9	0.0
1860	13,763	23.7	0.0
1850	8,495	15.4	0.0

(*US Statistical Abstracts* 1996:Tables 1340 and 1341). Table 3 displays the corresponding development history in tabular form. The fuel required for all this coming and going reached 140.1 billion gallons by 1994 and had long since become a primary issue of US geopolitical strategy (*US Statistical Abstracts* 1996:Table 1019). Notice, once again, that the years between *Plessy* and *Brown* are a time of revolutionary change with immense increases in both good roads and automotive vehicles—with a generally declining rate of growth from a very high base in years since the 1950s. (Other features of note include the decline of auto sales during the Depression years and the expansion of highways in the late 1970s as the interstate system approached completion.) The result is an all-but-irreversible commitment to being a society dominated by the power of movement.

The political significance of the automobile lies most obviously in its being the centerpiece of a vast industrial complex entailing steel, glass, cement, rubber, oil extraction and refining, electronic control systems, and auto parts production, to name only the most important categories. The corporations that finance and govern these activities are among the most powerful organizations in the national economy. In 1995, for instance, the three top corporations in the United States (judging by sales volume) were General Motors, Ford Motor, and Exxon. Mobil, Chrysler, and Texaco were close by, ranking 8, 9, and 12. These paragons of the variable

TABLE 3 Historical trends in paved roads and motor vehicle registration

Year	Miles of paved roads × 1000	% Increase over previous datum	Motor vehicle registrations × 1000	% Increase over previous datum
1910	204	NA	468	NA
1920	369	80.9	9,239	1874.1
1930	694	88.1	26,749	189.5
1940	1,367	97	32,453	21.3
1950	1,939	41.8	49,161	51.5
1960	2,557	31.9	73,868	50.3
1970	2,949	15.3	108,407	46.8
1980	3,857	30.8	155,796	43.7
1990	3,880	0.6	188,798	21.2
1993	3,905	0.6	194,063	2.8

path are vital to any national political coalition, and their union counterparts—the teamsters and the UAW most visibly—cannot be ignored in any consequential debate on national policy (Kay 1997, Lewis 1997).

Still more important is the fact that cars and other motor vehicles provide high-speed, variable-path transportation to every habitable nook and cranny of the 3.5 million square miles of land that constitute the United States. Except for arid wasteland, some mountains, and the most remote corners of our park system, you can go anywhere you like[8] in a private automobile so long as you can afford the operating cost.[9] This is a revolutionary fact, unparalleled in any previous era and unmatched in scale by any other national system. Running on nearly 4 million miles of paved roads, automobile travel offers those who can afford it an utterly unprecedented form of power—the power to substitute elective movement for loyalty and submission, to exclude one's threatening inferiors from the habitus of personal and family life (see e.g. Sennett 1970; for a more polemical treatment of the same questions, see Kunstler 1993), to thwart the will of any merely local political majority, and to create polities in which the vital material stakes are mooted by the absence of those who would seek redistribution. These are among the powers of a viacratic regime.

Another technological development—alternating current electricity—has functioned as a powerful complement to the automobile. The dominant energy source of nineteenth-century life, steam generated by burning coal, was a centralizing

[8]A key exception: Gated communities, where streets are privately owned and regulated on the same legal basis as the interior of a residential property, are on the rise (see e.g. McKenzie 1994).

[9]Average operating costs, taking account of depreciation and insurance, run about $0.45 per mile (see *US Statistical Abstracts* 1996:Table 1015).

technology. The cost-effective shipment of bulk coal could be accomplished only by rail, ship, or canal barge, i.e. on fixed-path systems to central nodes, usually located in major cities. The closer the steam-generating boilers were to those nodes, the lower the transport costs of the coal, and the more competitively the engines would function. Moreover, once power was generated by steam turbines, the cost of transmission to other points was very high. In a typical manufacturing plant, belts and pulleys would transmit steam power across the shop floor to innumerable work stations, at some real loss due to friction. Economical transmission of kinetic force from steam across longer distances—miles, say—was out of the question. This meant that central places were in a vital way privileged in the energy economy.

Enter electricity, particularly electricity transmitted as alternating current (AC). The key advantage here is spatial flexibility: You can send electricity over long distances, with a fine-grained branching network comparable to roads and streets, so as to deliver energy fairly efficiently across vast spaces. This fact, coupled with the automotive revolution, meant that housing could be located at great distances from cities without the occupants suffering a disadvantage in the use of energy for appliances, lighting, and the like. It also meant that manufacturing and commercial development were freed of all tethers to central place in matters of energy delivery, permitting developers to follow the logic of interstate access to its green-field conclusion in one region of the country after another.

Finally, the emergence of electric and electronic communications—telegraph, telephone, radio, television—accomplished a further enabling step for the development of viacratic America. Although the telegraph had been an early companion to the railway, the telephone took hold between 1878 (when the first US telephone exchange began to be established in New Haven) and World War I, spreading outward from eastern cities, forming a national and eventually worldwide grid of instantaneous real-time "narrow-casting." It was now possible to be "plugged in" no matter where you lived, although there was some cost advantage to central place. Radio broadcasting, begun commercially by Pittsburgh's KDKA, was a phenomenon of the 1920s and reached universality in the United States just after World War II. Television, first commercialized in the late 1940s, burst into general use by the early 1960s and has exerted hypnotic control over most members of each generation born since. With the arrival of cable and satellite transmission of broadcast signals, even the most remote location is a full participant in the resulting consumer economy of information and entertainment. According to 1993 statistics, an average US household consisting of 2.65 people commanded 2.1 television sets and 5.6 radio receivers (top of the world table), and 1.6 telephones (surpassed only by Denmark and Switzerland).[10]

The impact of all these developments together is to remove from our lives the most ancient of our challenges, which is to live in communities we have not

[10]See *US Statistical Abstracts* 1996:Table 1342. Telephone data are for 1994, others for 1993.

chosen for ourselves, and, within those communities, outcomes we do not like. Communities have become elective. In the evocative language of community offered by Ehrenhalt (1995:23):

> To worship choice and community together is to misunderstand what community is all about. Community means not subjecting every action in life to the burden of choice, but rather accepting the familiar and reaping the psychological benefits of having one less calculation to make in the course of the day. It is about being Ernie Banks and playing for the Chicago Cubs for twenty years; or being one of John Fary's customers and sticking with his tavern at Thirty-sixth and South Damen year in and year out. It is being with the Lennox Corporation and knowing that Marhalltown, Iowa, will always be your home.

This difference, to a considerable extent, accounts for the widely reported decline of social capital and civic engagement in American life over the final decades of the twentieth century. To the degree that civic engagement is rooted in places—in neighborhoods, in clubs, in meeting halls—we have allowed ourselves to choose our way out of their burdens and their rewards alike (see especially Putnam 2000, Skocpol 1999).

ON THE DIFFERENCE BETWEEN TECHNOLOGICAL DETERMINISM AND TECHNOLOGICAL ENABLEMENT

The point is not that these technologies cause or determine the shift toward a viacratic regime. It is, rather, that they enable and allow firms, governments, and consumers to make previously unavailable choices that lead toward viacracy. There are two relevant zones of indeterminacy.

First, an element of choice precedes the creation, elaboration, and implementation of any technology. Once the internal combustion engine exists, it is not inevitable that the United States should eventually have 200 million registered motor vehicles. It is, of course, true that within a capitalist framework, decisions that resist or ignore innovation leading to competitive advantage are suicidal—both for firms and for communities. Car-free cities would, for instance, have done poorly in attracting residents at any time after about 1910. Thus, it is not a feasible option for one American state to resist automotive development while the rest of the country adopts it, unless relative impoverishment is acceptable to its electorate (Oregon and Vermont are the closest we'll come to exceptions, and that is not very close).

Second, even a fully deployed technology does not literally determine the organization of society. It enables, it entices (with help from entrepreneurs), it sometimes entraps, but it does not determine. We have chosen, in our millions, one trip or crankshaft at a time, to transform the nation in which we live. Neither technology nor the devil made us do it, we did it to and for ourselves—to and for one another.

The disappearance of urban trolley lines beginning in the 1930s provides an instructive instance. Start with two facts: (*a*) By the 1920s, General Motors had set its sights on the conversion of trolley lines to bus routes, and (*b*) beginning in the 1890s, trolleys had been converted to electric power, and had thus come under the aegis of major utility trusts controlled by Samuel Insull, General Motors, and Morgan banking (Goddard 1994:128ff). In the early New Deal, Franklin Roosevelt and the Congress focused attention on trusts and monopolies, and one result was the Wheeler-Rayburn Act of 1935. One of the act's effects was to compel electric utilities to divest themselves of subsidiaries that failed to produce electricity. This turned out to mean the (increasingly unprofitable) trolley lines, which were dumped on the market in large numbers at depressed prices. General Motors, acting through a holding company titled National City Lines, bought up one trolley line after another and replaced its services with buses as promptly as possible. This increased its hold on the diminishing public transport market and put it in a position to promote the more profitable alternative of automobile transport later on. Consumers above the economy's belt-line responded as desired, adopting the nation's "freedom machine" and leaving public transport mostly to those who could afford nothing else. Is this technological determinacy at work? Surely not in any simple way, but by creating an opening that people were eager to exploit, technology enabled revolutionary change. Once we figure capital into the equation and reckon that the government will not be immune to its blandishments, the technology seems an absolutely central element of history. We fell in love with cars, but not without having been placed in the way of temptation.[11]

Another important story illustrates the same relationship of partial determination. I have in mind the very widespread and quite sudden adoption of zoning ordinances, beginning with the first such statute, in New York in 1916.[12] With the pivotal law case on zoning's constitutionality—*Euclid v Ambler*—settled in 1926, zoning swept across urban and suburban America in a few short years and changed our ways of building cities quite radically. Prior to zoning, mixed-use development was standard practice in most places, placing housing and retailing, office and commerce in close, generally unplanned juxtaposition. Most high-density urban neighborhoods hosted innumerable small retail establishments (as late as the1920s, New Haven hosted no fewer than 500 stores selling food goods,

[11]Scully (1994:222) wrote amusingly of this development: "The automobile was, and remains, the agent of chaos, the breaker of the city.... Whatever other factors have been involved in the disintegration of community, it is still the automobile—and how much we all love it—which has done the job."

[12]Here I refer to land-use zoning, which turns out to be heavy in racial implications, as distinct from explicit racial zoning. Such zoning ordinances were adopted by many cities in the years right after *Plessy*, including Baltimore, Richmond, Atlanta, St. Louis, Indianapolis, and Dallas. All these were struck down in 1917 by *Buchanan v Warley*.

almost all of them very small).[13] Zoning's principal objective was to separate "incompatible" land uses, thus to homogenize space: retail here, residential there, manufacturing somewhere else. This could never have occurred before the rise of automobiles, because the slowness of variable-path transport made intermingling of land uses all but imperative on efficiency grounds (one does not walk to the big-box retail center). With the rise of cars, it became possible for influential strata in society to embrace the notion of homogeneous land use. Soon enough the same mechanism would become a weapon for enforcing homogeneous class occupancy of those same spaces. But invention alone is not enough. It was critical to the emergence of tendentious zoning across the land that someone like Richard Ely should have the goals suggested by this passage (Randle 1989:43):

> Richard T. Ely held firmly in 1924 to his turn-of-the-century beliefs in the "fundamental and inescapable fact that the ideals of political democracy and equality of economic opportunity are empty of meaning except for fairly homogenous people. . . . Exclusion must be practiced.

Here, as so often, technology opens a window but does not throw us through it without our choosing to leap.

MONEY DIFFERENCES

In a broadly egalitarian economy, none of the changes in technology we have been considering would have led to the viacratic regime we now confront. It is hardly necessary to document the extensive income disparities that mark the US economy at this time; the "American way" has come to symbolize the use of relatively harsh market inequalities as a spur to economic growth and as a hedge against inflation. Indeed, we have become a nation in which the Federal Reserve can be counted on to tighten credit immediately upon hearing that official unemployment rates are dangerously below 5%. In simplest terms, the American economy has become increasingly tough on the poor since about 1973 and has been almost embarrassingly hospitable to the procreation of serious wealth since the early 1980s. The corresponding growth in the national product has been well appreciated by middle-income Americans, many of whom have drifted into what were once upper-middle-class patterns of consumption and investment. And, at least for the moment, the tightness of labor markets at the end of Clinton's second term has provided unusual opportunity for the country's working class. Nevertheless, two generalizations remain uncontroversial:

1. The United States is and will continue to be an unabashedly capitalist system, with a distribution of wealth and income decidedly inegalitarian by the standards of advanced systems worldwide.

---

[13]Count from the 1927 New Haven Bell Yellow Pages.

2. That same economy distributes its advantages and disadvantages in ways that fully reflect a history of racial and ethnic discrimination, even as many members of disadvantaged groups move into higher income strata and begin to accumulate wealth.

Allow me to briefly review this pair.

The general shape of the income curve has been more or less constant in recent decades, with a detectable drift toward increasing inequality. The Gini index, measuring overall inequality in household incomes, drifted up from ~0.39 to ~0.43 in the past 25 years, with stagnant incomes toward the bottom and considerable growth at the very top of the scale (US Department of Commerce 1991). Table 4, giving income data for households, sums up the pattern. If we tease out the per-household income ratio between the top 5% and bottom 20%, the time series goes like this: 16.1:1 in 1970, 15.7:1 in 1980, and 19.0:1 in 1990. For present purposes, the point is that the resources required to participate in our transportation system, and to purchase or rent real estate in desired places, will be largely beyond the bottom fifth of the country and will exact tough trade-offs for the next fifth. The system is quite affordable for the higher groups. Given the pressure of world markets on lower-skilled labor, the rising importance of technical and managerial know-how, and the general decline of union leverage over wage outcomes, it is fair to surmise that these differences will not decline in coming years (Freeman 1993; for a more general roundup, see Thurow 1966).

These patterns bear upon (and cut through) all major population groups. Groups are unequally served by the overall distribution (and their internal distributions of income show broadly similar patterns of inequality.) Table 5 distributes each race/ethnic-origin grouping by internal quintiles of income for the group's households. It shows that whites, blacks, and households of Hispanic origin have similar income distributions, disregarding very different mean values, each of which has grown somewhat less egalitarian over the period considered. All three groups have seen more dollars flow to the top 5%, and dollars flowing to the bottom 20% have declined somewhat more among black and Hispanic households than among whites.

Turn now to the other side of our question. How unequally are different groups, each taken as a whole, treated by the income stream? The answers, all too familiar, are given in the 1993 data on households summed up in Table 6 (*US Statistical*

TABLE 4 Percent of total income by quintile, all groups (whites, blacks, and hispanics).

Year	Lowest 5th	Second 5th	Third 5th	Fourth 5th	Top 5th	Top 5%
1990	3.9	9.6	15.9	24	46.6	18.6
1980	4.2	10.2	16.8	24.8	44.1	16.5
1970	4.1	10.8	17.4	24.5	43.3	16.6

TABLE 5 Percent of group total income by quintiles

Year and group	Lowest 5th	Second 5th	Third 5th	Fourth 5th	Top 5th	Top 5%
1990 Whites	4.2	10	16	23.9	46	18.3
1980 Whites	4.4	10.5	17	24.6	43.5	16.3
1970 Whites	4.2	11.1	17.4	24.3	42.9	16.5
1990 Blacks	3.1	7.8	15	25.2	48.9	18.3
1980 Blacks	3.7	8.7	15.3	25.2	47.1	16.9
1970 Blacks	3.7	9.3	16.3	25.2	45.5	16.4
1990 Hispanics	4	9.5	15.9	24.3	46.3	17.9
1980 Hispanics	4.3	10.1	16.4	24.8	44.5	16.5
1972 Hispanics	5.3	11.2	17.2	24	42.3	16.2

Abstracts 1996:Table 714). Blacks and households of Hispanic origin are piled up in disproportionate numbers at the bottom, as are female-header households across all ethnicities.

These money differences relate to viacratic practices in two main ways. Recall that a viacratic regime is a society offering highly developed spatial mobility on a selective basis, creating a politicoeconomic order in which differential access to place becomes a decisive instrument for the creation and perpetuation of advantage. First, inequalities of income and wealth substantially determine the way a viacratic regime offers spatial mobility on a differential basis. If the minimum entry fee for automobile ownership is arbitrarily imagined to be $4000, and if we assume that the cheapest possible food, clothing, child care, and shelter command

TABLE 6 Percent total income by quintile within selected groups

Year and group	Lowest 5th	Second 5th	Third 5th	Fourth 5th	Top 5th	Top 5%
Whites	17.7	19.7	20.4	21	21.4	5.4
Blacks	36.8	22.6	18	13.3	9.3	1.7
Hispanics	27.9	25.6	21.4	15.1	10	1.8
Married couple families	7.3	16.1	20.9	25.8	30	7.8
Female-headed households	45.4	24.9	15.4	9.6	4.8	1

Source: U.S. Statistical Abstracts, 1996, Table 714.

the first $4000 of a household's income, then what chance does a poor household have of meeting that entry price? Take the mean of the bottom fifth, with a total 1990 income of $4004 (US Department of Commerce, 1991:Table B-3)[14]—you see the point. Now consider the mean of the next fifth, with a 1990 household income of $10,169. Take away $4000 for the essentials, leaving $6169. Is it realistic to suppose that $4000 of this discretionary budget—nearly 65% of it—can be devoted to transportation? Leaving that question aside, envision the time-price of access to the automobile as it varies across income strata. Suppose a year has 200 work/income-generating days in it. In the top fifth, entry-level access to the transportation system will cost perhaps 5 to 15 days' income before taxes. In the bottom fifth, it will run as high as perhaps 130 to 180 days, again before taxes. We see the effect everywhere: different rates of access to rapid, variable-path movement, achieved at widely varied opportunity costs to the households in question. For example, we might compare the passenger car fleets of central-city New Haven and suburban Bethany. New Haven's 1999 population of 122,193 is served by 39,741 cars (0.32 cars per capita); Bethany's 4456 people rely on 3554 cars (0.80 per capita). To be sure, cars are essential to suburban life and slightly less so for city dwellers, but the difference is stark indeed. Much the same comparison will be observed with respect to housing costs, with a hierarchy of increasing values allowing differential opportunities as we move through the class structure of a region. Returning to our Connecticut example, Bethany's median residential sale for 1999 was $170,000, whereas New Haven's was $83,000. Bethany recorded just 17 sales below $50,000, New Haven over 500 such sales in 1999. These strategic goods (cars, houses) are of course different from other commodities, all of which have price systems, in that the very terms on which one lives are set by place in a viacratic setting.

The second link between viacracy and money differences relates to the consequences of differential access to place. Such access is an instrument for the creation and perpetuation of advantage. The chain of connections to jobs, investment opportunities, credit, credibility, and many other valuable but hard-to-measure things is linked to place in a viacratic system. The most obvious instance of this—known to economists as the "spatial mismatch" between skills and geographically accessible employment opportunities—directly limits the income potential of people whose lack of mobility limits them to central-city locations (Holzer 1992, Ihlanfedt 1994). Although it is possible to argue about the specifics, it is difficult to deny the general role of income-determined differences in spatial mobility, which lead circularly to further differences of income, tending to precipitate further differences of mobility, and so on.

[14]From US Department of Commerce 1991:Table B-3. In-kind transfers—e.g. food stamps, housing vouchers—may supplement this astonishingly low figure, but not enough to change its implication for the present purpose.

THE SPATIAL INCOME STRUCTURE OF URBAN REGIONS: The Freedom Mart Illustrated

The intuitive idea of viacratic life is that an urban region, typically centering on a once-dominant core city, offers a hierarchy of communities, arrayed by cost and reliance on automotive transport from top to bottom. As one goes up the scale, costs increase, incomes mount, zoning regulations grow more restrictive, criminal risk to property and person is believed to decline, educational opportunity is perceived to improve, access to workplace networks improves, the mix of haves to have-nots grows richer, and the practical underwriting of individual and household rights grows more secure. Communities near the top are homogeneous in income for one reason; those near the bottom are homogeneous in income for another. Blacks, notably lower-income blacks, are confined to lower-ranking places. In the Old South, unlike the rest of the United States, very-low-income blacks are dispersed across regions, reflecting a history of agricultural settlement. In most northern cities, low-income blacks are concentrated in relatively small areas near aging industrial plants in well-worn private housing and project-based HUD (US Department of Housing and Urban Development) properties. At the same time, the jobs providing educational, social, and regulatory services to lower-ranking communities are by and large concentrated in higher-ranking communities, creating a considerable social distance between provider and client (Hall 1999). People, households, and organizations with high degrees of mobility exert considerable leverage in communities they join but could leave; others, lacking such mobility, enjoy far less leverage. The critical power to bargain or to improve one's environment is, at every turn, the differential access to strategically privileged space. At some basic level, real estate becomes the master commodity through which virtually every other value is bought and sold—from personal security to educational opportunity, from the security of property rights to the social capital that supports family life, from access to better jobs to participation in mainstream culture.

Let us take St. Louis and its region as an example. The city of St. Louis grew through annexation between 1856 and 1876 from 4.5 square miles to 61 square miles (Jackson 1985). Thereafter, its boundary has remained static, while independent suburban communities have flourished around it. The central city has declined sharply in the years since *Brown*, with its population falling from 856,796 in 1950 to 396,685 in 1990 and an estimated 339,316 in 1998. If we draw an 80-mile radius around downtown St. Louis, we sweep through 457 municipalities, which form a regional hierarchy, spread across 17,655 square miles. A simple median income array runs from about $60,000 down to about $10,000 in the 1990 census, with some distant rural places joining some central locations at the bottom, and with affluence concentrated in a band of second- and third-ring suburbs, such as Clayton, Meramec, Queeny, Spencer Creek, and Harvester in Missouri. Across the great river in Illinois are similarly affluent places such as Pin Oak, Blair, Maxwell, and Moro. Lesser places enumerated in the 1990 census, such as Country Life Estates, show medians in six figures ($150,001). Other census places run close behind, as for instance Westwood, Missouri at $139,331 and Ladue, Missouri at $107,583.

But focus on the narrower question, "Where do (and don't) the low-income blacks live?" Figure 2 shows two subsets of the region's 457 municipalities. One subset consists of 358 municipalities that have in common a total lack of resident low-income blacks. In a combined total of 333,180 households (914,901 individuals), these communities share a grand total of 7820 black persons and 1188 such households, of which exactly none had an income below $10,000 in the 1990 census data. These are indicated in outline, with (what else) white interiors. It is not as if these places are without any of the poor: They share a total of 45,119 households below the $10,000 mark. It is, rather, that 44,812 of these are white households, and the remaining 307 identify themselves as neither white nor black.

The other subset in Figure 2 consists of 20 communities that together share 95% of the low-income blacks in the entire region, shown in black (see also Table 7). All except one (Centralia, Illinois) are clustered closely around St. Louis itself. St. Louis is comprised of nearly 16% low-income black households, and two of its satellites greatly exceed that proportion. East St. Louis and Stites, Illinois are each well over 40% low-income black. Of the region's 45,342 black households with incomes under $10,000, all but 2243 are concentrated in these 20 places, constituting about 2% of the region's land and just over one third of the total households. It is little wonder that Jackson reports a St. Louis school administrator in the 1970s claiming that suburbanites had "erected a wall of separation which towers above the city limits and constitutes a barrier as effective as did those of ancient Jericho or that of the Potsdamer Platz in Berlin" (1985:141–42).

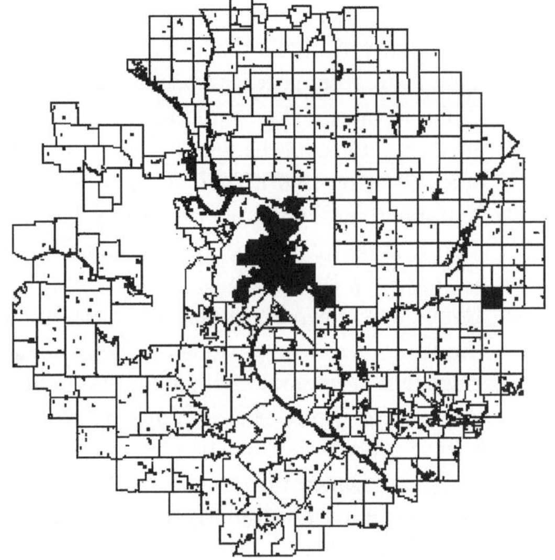

Figure 2 St. Louis region, showing municipalities with zero low-income black households (outlined in black; n = 358) and 20 municipalities that share 95% of the regional total (shaded black).

TABLE 7 Twenty St. Louis–region municipalities accounting for 95% of the region's low-income black households, 1990 Census

Name	Population	Households	Household median income	Black households under $10,000	% of all households that are low income & black
Stites IL	1,201	416	10,638	180	43.27
East St. Louis IL	40,944	13,009	12,627	5,471	42.06
Venice IL	8,587	3,251	15,949	737	22.67
Canteen IL	15,217	5,205	16,119	891	17.12
St. Louis MO	396,685	164,404	19,458	25,791	15.69
Centreville IL	32,262	10,602	22,687	1,429	13.48
Normandy MO	42,514	15,606	25,117	2,013	12.90
Alton IL	32,905	12,963	22,948	993	7.66
Hadley MO	38,732	15,514	26,240	945	6.09
St. Ferdinand MO	48,240	18,362	28,658	1,058	5.76
Airport MO	33,815	13,332	26,339	693	5.20
Ferguson MO	43,899	16,985	29,500	706	4.16
Centralia IL	16,825	6,822	21,814	190	2.79
Creve Coeur MO	55,579	23,946	39,208	663	2.77
St. Clair IL	27,086	10,482	34,442	209	1.99
Midland MO	39,445	15,765	29,077	299	1.90
Bonhomme MO	37,998	14,963	41,895	196	1.31
Jefferson MO	33,770	14,111	40,807	175	1.24
Spanish Lake MO	60,867	22,049	41,423	258	1.17
Belleville IL	42,705	17,786	26,668	202	1.14
20-Town subtotals	1,049,276	415,573		43,099	10.37
Rest of region	1,908,999	699,664		2,243	0.32

If integration of schools, or other facilities, is to occur within municipalities and not between them, then it is in sum and substance not going to occur.

VIACRATIC SEGREGATION: *Brown* on Wheels versus *Plessy* on Foot

Massey & Denton (1993) recognize the significance of changing spatial structures in their powerful work, *American Apartheid* (see also Massey & Denton 1988a,b, 1989; Massey et al 1987):

> At the close of the Civil War, American cities were just beginning to throw off the trappings of their pre-industrial past. Patterns of urban social and spatial organization still reflected the needs of commerce, trade, and small-scale manufacturing.... People got around by walking, so there was little geographic differentiation between places of work and residence. Land use was not highly specialized, real estate prices were low, and socially distinctive residential areas had not yet emerged. In the absence of structural steel, electricity, and efficient mechanical systems, building densities were low and urban populations were distributed uniformly. Such a spatial structure is not conducive to high levels of segregation by class, race, or ethnicity. (Massey & Denton 1993:42)

Massey & Denton provide quantitative data on segregation within cities, using the index of dissimilarity, which reads zero when populations are evenly mixed and 100 when fully segregated. Calculating within the municipality of St. Louis (leaving aside the smaller communities mentioned above) on the basis of wards, their data show the trend shown in Table 8.

The same forces are doubtless at work in these figures, but on a smaller canvas. The larger canvas considered here simply confirms and extends the conclusion reached by Massey & Denton. Their data extend and systematize the in-city pattern to places as diverse as Boston, Chicago, Cincinnati, Cleveland, Indianapolis, Milwaukee, New York, Philadelphia, San Francisco, Wilmington, Augusta, Baltimore, Charleston, Jacksonville, Mobile, Nashville, and New Orleans.

TABLE 8 Index of dissimilarity for St. Louis, Missouri (Massey & Denton 1993)

Year	Comparison	Degree of dissimilarity
1860	Free blacks vs whites	39.1
1910	Blacks vs native whites	54.3
1940	Whites vs nonwhites	92.6

Visit the Annual Reviews home page at www.AnnualReviews.org

LITERATURE CITED

Biggs L. 1996. *The Rational Factory: Architecture, Technology, and Work in America's Age of Mass Production.* Baltimore, MD: Johns Hopkins Univ. Press

Chandler AD. 1977. *The Visible Hand: The Managerial Revolution in American Business.* Cambridge, MA: Belknap

Ehrenhalt A. 1995. *The Lost City: Discovering the Forgotten Virtues of Community in the Chicago of the 1950's.* New York: Basic Books

Fishman R. 1987. *Bourgeois Utopias: The Rise and Fall of Suburbia.* New York: Basic Books

Freeman R. 1993. How much has deunionization contributed to the rise of male earnings inequality? In *Uneven Tides: Rising Inequality in America,* ed. SG Danziger, D Peter, pp. 133–63. New York: Russell Sage Fdn.

Friedman LM. 1973. *A History of American Law,* pp. 671–72. New York: Simon & Schuster

Goddard SB. 1994. *Getting There: The Epic Struggle between Roads and Rail in the American Century.* New York: Basic Books

Hall PD. 1999. Vital signs: organizational population trends and civic engagement in New Haven, Connecticut, 1850–1998. In *Civic Engagement in American Democracy,* ed. T Skocpol, M Fiorina, pp. 211–48. Washington, DC: Brookings Inst.

Historical Statistics of the United States. 1971. Washington, DC: Gov. Print. Off.

Holzer HJ. 1992. The spatial mismatch hypothesis: What has the evidence shown? *Urban Stud.* 28:105–22

Hounshell DA. 1984. *From the American System to Mass Production, 1800–1932.* Baltimore, MD: Johns Hopkins Univ. Press

Ihlanfedt K. 1994. Spatial mismatch between jobs and residential location within urban areas. *Cityscape* 1:219–44

Kay JH. 1997. *Asphalt Nation: How the Automobile Took over America and How We Can Take it Back.* New York: Crown

Kunstler JH. 1993. *The Geography of Nowhere: The Rise and Decline of America's Man-Made Landscape.* New York: Simon & Schuster. 303 pp.

Lewis T. 1997. *Divided Highways: Building the Interstate Highways, Transforming American Life.* New York: Viking Books

Massey DS, Condran GA, Denton NA. 1987. The effects of residential segregation on black social and economic well-being. *Soc. Forces* 66:29–56

Massey DS, Denton NA. 1988a. The dimensions of residential segregation. 67:281–315

Massey DS, Denton NA. 1988b. Suburbanization and segregation in U.S. metropolitan areas. *Am. J. Sociol.* 94:592–626

Massey DS, Denton NA. 1989. Hypersegregation on U.S. metropolitan areas: black and Hispanic segregation along five dimensions. 26:373–91

Massey DS, Denton NA. 1993. *American Apartheid: Segregation and the Making of the Underclass.* Cambridge, MA: Harvard Univ. Press

McKenzie E. 1994. *Privatopia: Homeowner Associations and the Rise of Residential Private Government.* New Haven, CT: Yale Univ. Press

Nye DE. 1998. *Consuming Power: A Social History of American Energies.* Cambridge, Mass: MIT Press

Paxson FL. 1946. The highway movement, 1916–1935. *Am. Hist. Rev.* 5:236–53

Petroski P. 1997. *Remaking the World.* New York: Knopf

Putnam R. 2000. *Bowling Alone: The Collapse and Revival of American Community.* New York: Simon & Schuster

Randle WM. 1989. Professors, reformers, bureaucrats, and cronies: the players in Euclid v.

Ambler. In *Zoning and the American Dream*, ed. CMK Haar, Jerold S, pp. 31–69. Chicago: Am. Planning Assoc.

Scully V. 1994. The architecture of community. In *The New Urbanism*, ed. P Katz, pp. 221–30. New York: McGraw Hill

Sennett R. 1970. *The Uses of Disorder: Personal Identity and City Life*. New York: Norton. 198 pp.

Skocpol T. 1999. How Americans became civic. In *Civil Engagement in American Democracy*, ed. T Skocpol, MP Fiorina, pp. 27–80. Washington, DC: Brookings Inst. Press

Stilgoe JR. 1988. *Borderland: Origin of the American Suburb, 1820–1939*. New Haven, CT: Yale Univ. Press

Thurow LC. 1966. *The Future of Capitalism: How Today's Economic Forces Shape Tomorrow's World*. New York: Morrow

1996. *US Statistical Abstracts*. Washington, DC: Gov. Print. Off.

US Department of Commerce. 1991. *Money Income of Households, Families, and Persons in The United States: 1991*. Washington, DC: Gov. Print. Off.

Warner SBJ. 1978. *Streetcar Suburbs: The Process of Growth in Boston, 1870–1900*. Cambridge, MA: Harvard Univ. Press. 208 pp.

Subject Index

J